THEGREENGUIDE
Dordogne
Berry Limousin

Château de Beynac-et-Cazenac, Périgord Noir / © Hervé Lenain / hemis.fr

THEGREENGUIDE **DORDOGNE BERRY LIMOUSIN**

Editorial Director	Cynthia Clayton Ochterbeck
Contributing Writer	Terry Marsh
Production Manager	Natasha George
Cartography	John Dear
Photo Editor	Sean Sachon
Interior Design	Chris Bell
Layout	Anna Gatt, Natasha George
Cover Design	Chris Bell, Christelle Le Déan
Cover Layout	Michelin Travel Partner, Natasha George

Contact Us
Michelin Travel and Lifestyle North America
One Parkway South
Greenville, SC 29615
USA
travel.lifestyle@us.michelin.com
www.michelintravel.com

Michelin Travel Partner
Hannay House
39 Clarendon Road
Watford, Herts WD17 1JA
UK
☎01923 205240
travelpubsales@uk.michelin.com
www.ViaMichelin.com

Special Sales
For information regarding bulk sales,
customized editions and premium sales,
please contact us at:
travel.lifestyle@us.michelin.com
www.michelintravel.com

HOW TO USE THIS GUIDE

PLANNING YOUR TRIP

The blue-tabbed PLANNING YOUR TRIP section at the front of the guide gives you **ideas for your trip** and **practical information** to help you organize it. You'll find tours, practical information, a host of outdoor activities, a calendar of events, information on shopping, sightseeing, kids' activities and more.

INTRODUCTION

The orange-tabbed INTRODUCTION section explores Dordogne Berry Limousin's **Nature** and geology. The **History** section spans from prehistoric man to the modern day. The **Art and Culture** section covers architecture, art, literature and music, while the **Region Today** delves into the modern region.

DISCOVERING

The green-tabbed DISCOVERING section features Principal Sights by region, featuring the most interesting local **Sights**, **Walking Tours**, nearby **Excursions**, and detailed **Driving Tours**. Admission prices shown are normally for a single adult.

ADDRESSES

We've selected the best hotels, restaurants, cafés, shops, nightlife and entertainment to fit all budgets. See the Legend on the cover flap for an explanation of the price categories. See the back of the guide for an index of where to find hotels and restaurants.

Sidebars

Throughout the guide you will find blue, orange and green-coloured text boxes with lively anecdotes, detailed history and background information.

😊 A Bit of Advice 😊

Green advice boxes found in this guide contain practical tips and handy information relevant to your visit or to a sight in the Discovering section.

STAR RATINGS★★★

Michelin has given star ratings for more than 100 years. If you're pressed for time, we recommend you visit the ★★★, or ★★ sights first:

★★★	**Highly recommended**
★★	**Recommended**
★	**Interesting**

MAPS

- 🗺 Country map
- 🗺 Principal Sights map
- 🗺 Region maps
- 🗺 Maps for major cities and villages
- 🗺 Local tour maps

All maps in this guide are oriented north, unless otherwise indicated by a directional arrow. The term "Local Map" refers to a map within the chapter or Tourism Region. A complete list of the maps found in the guide appears at the back of this book.

PLANNING YOUR TRIP

INTRODUCTION TO DORDOGNE BERRY LIMOUSIN

DISCOVERING DORDOGNE BERRY LIMOUSIN

CONTENTS

Welcome to Dordogne Berry Limousin

The Dordogne, Berry, and Limousin regions include some of the most- and the least-visited areas in France. The Dordogne and the Quercy, with their characteristic castles, caves and river valleys, are well known. The unspoilt, verdant countryside and plateaux of the Berry and Limousin are much less familiar.

Jardins de Marqueyssac, Périgord Noir

©Clichesdumonde/Fotolia.com

DORDOGNE

The modern Dordogne coincides roughly with the old province of the Périgord, which is divided unofficially into four colours. The Périgord Noir (Black Perigord) owes its name to its high density of trees; the Périgord Blanc (White Perigord) is so named for its outcrops of chalky limestone; the Périgord Vert (Green Perigord) is thus known for the verdant countryside of the north; and the Périgord Pourpre (Purple Perigord) is a reference to its vineyards.

The area has been occupied since prehistoric times, and some of the earliest artistic expressions known to man are still visible within rock shelters and caves along the Vézère valley. Before the Roman occupation, which left its mark most notably in the capital city, Périgueux, the Périgord was inhabited by the Pétrocores. Following incursions by the Vandals, Visigoths, Franks, Moors and Vikings, the area finally came under the control of the English in 1152. Later, during the Hundred Years War (1337–1453), the area was much disputed, and this rich history gave rise to a series of picturesque fortresses of which many still overlook the Dordogne River.

BERRY

The province of Berry is one of the oldest agricultural regions of France. It corresponds approximately with the modern *départements* of Cher and Indre and is located between the Paris Basin and the Massif Central, but its definition is more linked to its shared heritage than its geography.

The region consists of a low-lying plateau that rises in the northeast to the famous wine-producing Sancerre Hills and gives way in the west to the Brenne nature park. Berry is a relatively quiet region that has always had a resolutely French identity. During the Hundred Years' War, the capital of the Berry–Bourges, an important town since Gallo-Roman times–was the seat of the French king. The region has also produced some extremely colourful characters, such as the patron of the arts Jean de Berry; the eminent trader, Jacques Coeur; and the eccentric 19C-writer George Sand.

Vineyard in autumn outside Sancerre

© Hervé Lenain / hemis.fr

Etang des Oussines, Parc naturel régional de Millevaches-en-Limousin

© Christian Guy / hemis.fr

LIMOUSIN

The unspoilt countryside of the Limousin has it all: medieval villages, hills, gorges, verdant meadows, and moorlands ideal for breeding horses. In fact, the Anglo-Arab horse originated at Pompadour.

Today, the Parc Natural Périgord-Limousin is a vast preserved area ideal for outdoor activities.

The Limousin region on the western slopes of the Massif Central is comprised of three *départements*: Creuse, Haute-Vienne and Corrèze. The Creuse borders the Berry in the north; the Haute-Vienne is adjacent to the Poitou-Charentes and the Aquitaine in the west and southwest respectively, while the Corrèze borders the Midi-Pyrenees to the south and the Auvergne to the west. Inhabited by a Gallic tribe known as the Lemovices, from which the area took its name, the region became part of Roman Aquitania following the conquest of Gaul. After the Romans, the Franks eventually gained control before the area came under the suzerainty of the English crown in 1152. Like its neighbours, the Limousin was the scene of fierce fighting during the Hundred Years War, before it was eventually taken back under French sovereignty.

QUERCY

Quercy stretches from the Massif Central in the east to the plains of Aquitaine in the west and from the Limousin in the north to the Midi-Pyrénées in the south. Although it is no longer an administrative entity, the area has a strong historical unity and in the Middle Ages Quercy belonged to the province of Guyenne or Aquitaine. Today, Quercy comprises all of the Lot and part of Tarn et Garonne *départements*.

It was first occupied by the Cadurques, or Cadurci, a Celtic tribe. From the mid-1C BCE it was part of Roman Gaul until it succumbed to the Barbarian invasions of the 5C.

Part of the Duchy of Aquitaine in the Middle Ages, the region was heavily involved in the Hundred Years War. Later, the region was again ravaged by warfare as it was heavily involved in the Wars of Religion and also the French Revolution.

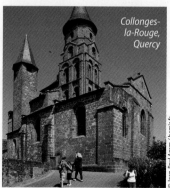

Collonges-la-Rouge, Quercy

© Jean-Paul Azam / hemis.fr

Although the region is lesser known to tourists than its neighbour the Dordogne, tourism is increasing in the area, with more than 1 million visitors per year visiting the enchanting village of Rocamadour atop its rocky cliff, and 400 000 exploring the extensive cave systems, which offer spectacular geological wonders.

Cingle de Trémolat,
Dordogne valley, Périgord Pourpre
© Julian Elliott / agefotostock

When and Where to Go

WHEN TO GO

This inland region is open to oceanic influences from the Atlantic. The climate on the whole is mild, winter frosts are limited, spring comes early and is warm and the summertime is hot. Rainfall is evenly distributed throughout the year. In the Berry, however, several microclimates make for small, distinct weather systems within the region. For example, the Champagne Berrichonne, with its vast fields of grain crops, is often dry and gets very hot in the summer, while the humidity keeps things cooler in the Boischaut, the Brenne wetlands and the high forests of the Motte d'Humbligny. The climate in the Limousin is also variable, in particular with regard to altitude. The prevailing southwest winds blow hard against the foothills of the Massif Central mountain range, provoking significant rainfall (1 200–1 700mm/47–67in per year) – although summer droughts are not unusual. Winter on the high plateaux (Millevaches, Gentioux, Monédières, Combraille) is long and harsh, with low temperatures and chill, stiff winds. Elsewhere in the region, winters are milder, with less rain, but crops are often damaged by freezing temperatures in the spring and autumn.

The Dordogne is more clement on the whole. While the climate is nearly Mediterranean, there is enough water to keep the landscape green and crops prosperous throughout the summer. A blanket of flowers soon covers the countryside, as the region quickly warms to the new season.

The **summer** holidays bring many tourists to enjoy the delights of the beautiful natural settings, towns and monuments, and the many festivals and activities organised for visitors. During summer in the Dordogne, rain can sometimes fall in torrential storms, in the wake of a hot wind blowing steadily from the west. In the **winter**, snow is infrequent; the springtime heralds frosty nights and foggy mornings.

Autumn is quieter and a lovely time to appreciate the flowering heather, the browns and golds of the changing leaves, the colourful markets with an abundance of harvest produce or the delights of wild mushrooms served with game from the forest.

WHERE TO GO

DORDOGNE

Weekends away – Bergerac, the capital of Périgord Pourpre, has its own airport. Wine is the main interest here and a visit to the Maison des Vins is a must. Don't forget about Cyrano – his statue is in the main square!

One week – There are enough castles and bastide towns in the Périgord to keep the visitor busy for at least a week! The town of Sarlat, the impressive fortresses of Beynac and Castelnaud that face each other across the Dordogne River, the unusual bastide of Domme and the gardens of Marqueyssac are just some of the splendours of the valley. A trip down the river on a *gabarre* or canoe is a good way to see many of the most prominent castles at once.

Second week – The prehistoric paintings and sculptures at Lascaux and Les Eyzies are world famous. To best appreciate them, the International Prehistory visitor centre, or the National Museum of Prehistory, both located in Les Eyzies, are good starting points.

QUERCY

Weekends away – Cahors is the capital of the Lot and can easily be reached from Toulouse. The famous black wine of Cahors can be sampled here, and the impressive medieval towers of the Pont de Valentré should be not be missed.

One week – The Lot valley in either direction is fascinating and provides much interest. To the east, the hilltop village of St-Cirq-Lapopie is a splendid sight (best visited in the early morning or evening to avoid the crowds) while to the west, where the vineyards are located, the meanders of the River Lot lead to the fascinating small towns of Luzech and Puy l'Évêque.

Second week – The Parc Naturel des Causses du Quercy is well worth spending some time exploring. This dry moorland contains many surprises and the town of Martel on the Causse de Martel is no exception. On the Causse de Gramat, the Gouffre de Padirac and the spectacular site of Rocamadour invite further exploration. South of Lot the Causse de Limogne is another arid area, and while there are few settlements here, there are dolmens, megaliths and white truffle oaks.

LIMOUSIN

Weekends away – Limoges is the capital of the Limousin region and is famous for its porcelain, which you'll find in virtually every shop. A visit to the round kiln of the Four de Cassoux, just outside the city centre, is fascinating.

One week – The capital city itself has enough to interest the visitor for a few days, and other sights are within easy reach: the commemorative site of Oradour-sur-Glane, the village destroyed by the Nazis in WW2; the Église Abbatiale de Solignac; and the Parc Zoologique at the Parc Reynou are some examples.

Second week – The Limousin is best explored in sections, perhaps starting with the Upper Dordogne valley in the south, being sure to visit the "most beautiful villages" of Beaulieu-sur-Dordogne and Collonges-la-Rouge, followed by the adjacent Upper Corrèze and Vézère valleys. In the north, the Marche and Upper Creuse have fewer sights, but don't miss the Basse Marche.

BERRY

Weekends away – Bourges, currently the capital of the Berry, and once briefly the capital of France, can be reached from Paris (Orly) in 2½ hours. This gem of a city has a splendid cathedral, half-timbered houses and the well-appointed 15C residence of Jacques Cœur.

One week – Much of the Berry can be visited from Bourges. The wine region of the Sancerrois to the north of the city is of interest to wine lovers. Slightly to the west lies the Sologne and Aubigny-sur-Nère.

Second week – The area to the west of Bourges includes the old town of Issoudun, which has associations with Richard the Lionheart, and further west, the Château de Valençay is reminiscent of the castles of the Loire valley.

THEMED TOURS

Travel itineraries on specific themes have been mapped out to help you to discover the regional architecture and the traditions that make up the cultural heritage of the region. As you drive through this region, you are likely to see signs posted for the routes listed below: feel free to go to the nearest tourist office for more information, or just follow along!

PREHISTORY, HISTORY
Prehistoric Périgord-Quercy

Below is a list of the main prehistoric caves of the Périgord and Quercy areas mentioned in this guide; they all contain paintings or engravings: **Bara-Bahau** (Périgord), **Bernifal** (Périgord), **Combarelles** (Périgord), **Cougnac** (Quercy), **Font-de-Gaume** (Périgord), **Lascaux II** (a facsimile in the Périgord), **Le Pech-Merle** (Quercy), and **Rouffignac** (Périgord).

HISTORIC ROUTES

Routes historiques are local itineraries following an architectural and historical theme. The ***route historique Jacques-Cœur***, for example, takes in an abbey, ten private châteaux and six towns to present the life and times of the 15C merchant.

The signposts are accompanied by an explanatory booklet, available from local tourist offices. www.routes-historiques.com.

TRADITIONS AND CULTURAL HERITAGE

These thematic routes have been created by regional associations; contact the local tourist offices for details and maps.

Dordogne

- **Sentiers Romans en Quercy Blanc**
  Romanesque churches in the Quercy Blanc area.
  ☎05 65 21 84 39.

- **Route des Métiers d'Art en Périgord**
  The itinerary includes 66 workshops of traditional craftsmen (clock makers, stringed instrument makers, book binders, gilders, stone cutters, brass workers, glass blowers, potters, cutlers, leather workers and more).
  ☎05 53 31 56 23.
  www.cm-perigueux.fr.

- **Route des Metiers d'Art dans le Lot**
  Discover the exceptional workshops of 29 traditional craftsmen (potters, cabinet makers, sculptors, glass workers).
  ☎05 65 35 13 55.
  www.tourisme-lot.com.

- **Vallée de la Dordogne**
  Eight short itineraries from Souillac across the Périgord Noir and Quercy areas.
  www.dordogne-perigord-tourisme.fr.

- **Route des Vins**
  Discovering local wines in the Bergerac area.
  www.pays-de-bergerac.com/english/wine.

- **Route de la Noix**
  In the Corrèze, Lot and Dordogne, four major itineraries corresponding to the types of walnuts grown in the area.
  www.noixduperigord.com.

Berry

- **Chemin des Lavoirs dans le Cher**
  Fifteen waterside wash-houses to discover in the Germigny valley, maintained by the Association nos Villages en Berry.

- **Ronde des Champs d'Amour**
  The Champagne Berrichonne region around Issoudun invites you to discover the lover's village of Saint Valentin.

- **Route des Vignobles du Cœur de France**
  A tour of the vineyards of the Berry region, Quincy, Reuilly, Menetou-Salon, Sancerre, Coteaux du Giennois and Châteaumeillant, producing fine AOC wines.
  www.vins-centre-loire.com.

- **Route de la Porcelaine**
  Factories, museums, workshops and shops devoted to porcelain between Vierzon and St-Amand-Montrond.

- **Vallée des Peintres**
  In the footsteps of Guillaumin, Monet and other artists along the Creuse valley from Argenton to Glénic.

Limousin

- **Circuit du Châtaignier**
  A day trip in chestnut country, where hoop-wood strips for barrel making are still crafted in the traditional way; May–Nov.
  ☎05 55 78 49 92.

- **Parcs et Jardins du Limousin**
  The tour includes over 30 parks and gardens selected by the association Découverte du Patrimoine Paysager et Botanique.

COOKERY COURSES

If your favourite recreation takes place with pots and pans for equipment, why not spend 2 or 3 days in a French kitchen for a holiday? In the Dordogne, the season for preparing foie gras generally runs from October to mid-December and from mid-January to April. A number of farmhouse-inns offer sessions which include lessons on preparing foie gras, preserved duck, stuffed goose neck and other delights, along with board and lodging. In most cases, you are required to buy your own duck or goose, but by the end of your stay you'll have delicious souvenirs to take home.

For information, contact:

◆ **Loisirs-Accueil Corrèze**
Quai Aristide Briand,
19000 Tulle. ℘05 55 29 98 70.

◆ **Loisirs-Accueil Dordogne**
25 rue du Président-Wilson,
BP 2063, 24002 Périgueux.
℘05 53 35 50 24, or 05 53 35 50 30.

◆ **Loisirs-Accueil Lot**
Place François-Mitterrand,
46000 Cahors. ℘05 65 53 20 90.
www.reservation-lot.com.

Beyond mere learning, two family-run operations specialising in goose and duck respectively, take the visitor right into the heart of local matters. Excellent cooking and facilities and a warm welcome await you at:

◆ **Ferme du Fort de la Rhonie**
Coustaty Family, Boyer,
24220 Meyrals.
℘05 53 29 29 07.

◆ **La Maurinie**
Alard Family, 24330 Eyliac.
℘05 53 07 57 18.

Sessions open when enough participants have enrolled. You are also welcome to stay and eat as a regular guest, without cooking, and just enjoy the food, the company, and farm life.

EQUESTRIAN TOURS
Horse-drawn caravans
Savour the countryside at a gentle pace aboard a horse-drawn caravan. At 4kph/2.5mph, you will have ample time to look around the back roads and lanes you are travelling. This nomadic life can last for 2–7 days, according to the itinerary.

Équitation et Roulottes du Périgord
La Métairie du Roc, 24560 Faux.
℘/Fax 05 53 24 32 57.
http://metairieduroc.free.fr.
Les Roulottes du Quercy
46700 Sérignac. ℘05 65 31 96 44.
Château d'Aynac (Castel SARL)
Château d'Aynac, 46120 Aynac.
℘05 65 11 08 00.
www.castel-aynac.fr.

Horse-drawn carriage rides
These last 1hr, half a day or 1 day (with picnic).
Calèche de Dordogne
Ferme de Charmonteil, 24350 Lisle.
℘05 53 03 58 35.
Les Attelages du Haut Repaire
Haut Repaire, 24390 Coubjours.
℘05 53 50 32 79.
Le Périgord en Calèche
Le Bourg, 24550 Mazeyrolles.
℘05 53 29 98 99.

Donkey-trekking
If you plan a long walking tour, a donkey is a useful companion for carrying your luggage (up to 40kg/88lb), and children usually feel motivated by its presence.
The **Fédération Nationale Ânes et Randonnées (FNAR)**, 16 route de Canlers, 62310 Ruisseauville,
℘06 33 97 91 54, www.ane-et-rando.com, will provide general information. You can rent a donkey for a day or a week with or without a guide from:
Arcâne
La Ferme du Clédou, Ravary,
24250 Cenac.
℘05 53 59 63 79 or 06 07 75 90 84.
www.arc-ane.com.
Brahmâne
Cazillac, 82110 Cazes-Mondenard.
℘05 63 95 84 61.

PORCELAIN
&See the Introduction.
Limoges is synonymous with fine china, which you can find in any number of shops, including factory outlets (*vente directe d'usines*) just outside of town. You'll see many workshops (*manufactures*) and showrooms (*magasins*) on the road between Vierzon and Bourges. The larger outlets often have interesting museums, video presentations and demonstrations.
Limoges is also a historical and contemporary centre for the production of enamelware (*émaux*). Look for shops around Place Wilson in town, or stop at one of the many workshops in the area.

Porcelaine à pâte dure

True porcelain (hard-paste) or china: Resonates when tapped, translucent, made from ground feldspathic rock and kaolin clay.

Porcelaine tendre

Artificial porcelain (soft-paste): Softer than true porcelain, this material can be cut with a file, whereas true porcelain cannot. Dirt accumulated on an unglazed base can only be removed with difficulty; on true porcelain it comes off easily.

Porcelaine phosphatique

Bone china: This translucent ware, neither hard-paste, *Porcelaine hybride*, nor soft-paste porcelain, contains kaolin, petuntse and bone ash.

Faience fine

White earthenware, opaque porcelain or creamware: A generic term for a fine, hard, durable earthenware.

Grès or Grès céramique

Stoneware: Glassy in appearance, or semi-vitreous, with a fine texture, stoneware is always hard and is always fired in a high-temperature kiln; the non-porous clay does not require a glaze.

Terre Cuite

Terracotta, redware: This clay is fired at a low temperature to a rather soft and porous body ranging in colour from pinkish-buff to brick-reds and reddish browns. As a rule it is covered with a soft lead glaze.

RAIL-BIKING

Pedal away along disused railtracks aboard specially adapted rail trucks:

Les Cyclo-draisines d'Aubigny
Route de Clémont,
18700 Aubigny-sur-Nère,
℘02 48 81 50 07 (weekdays),
℘02 48 58 35 81 (weekends and holidays).

Vélo-rail de Bussière
Plan d'eau des Ribières, 87230 Bussière-Galant, ℘05 55 78 86 12,
http://espace-hermeline.com;

departures at 11am, 3pm and 5.30pm: Apr–Jun and Sept school and public holidays and weekends; Jul–Aug daily. €25 (2hr 30min maximum).

RIVER CRUISING

Houseboats

For a weekend or a week, enjoy the pleasant pace of life as you cruise the River Lot, where new sections of locks have been opened for pleasure craft. No licence is required; the captain must simply be an adult, and go through a brief course given on board before departure. The rental agent explains, in particular, the methods for going through a lock and for docking, which is about all you need to know to operate these holiday barges.

Babou Marine
Port St-Mary, 46000 Cahors.
℘05 65 30 08 99.
www.baboulene-jean.fr.

Le Boat
℘04 68 94 42 80.
www.leboat.fr and ℘0844 334 8761; www.leboat.co.uk.

Lot Navigation Nicols
Route du Puy-St-Bonnet, 49300 Cholet. ℘02 41 56 46 56.
www.nicols.com.

Maps and guides are available from:

Éditions Grafocarte-Navicarte
125 rue Jean-Jacques-Rousseau, BP 40, 92132 Issy-les-Moulineaux Cedex. ℘01 49 93 22 53.

Éditions du Plaisancier
43 porte du Grand-Lyon, 01700 Neyron. ℘04 72 01 58 68.

Boat trips

For a shorter trip, and without the responsibility of the helm, take a cruise on the Lac de Vassivière, or the Lac de Val at Bort-les-Orgues, or enjoy a ride in a traditional *gabarre* on the Dordogne from Chalvignac, Spontour, Pont du Chambon, Barrage du Chastang, La Roque-Gageac, Vezac-Beynac or Bergerac.

Canoeing on the River Lot

© S. Sauvignier / Michelin

Gabarres de Beynac

24250 St-Martial-de-Nabirat.
℘05 53 28 51 15.
www.gabarre-beynac.com.
Apr–Oct, 10am–12.30pm and
2–6pm. €8. Departures every
30min in season.

Gabarres Norbert

La Roque-Gageac.
℘05 53 29 40 44. www.norbert.fr.
Apr–Oct: 1hr trips with commentary.
Departures every hr (Oct pm only).
€9.

TOURIST TRAINS

In the **Limousin**, different routes
are travelled by vintage 1930s trains,
with a steam engine leading the way.
Visit the Haute Vallée de la Vienne
(Limoges–Eymoutiers–Limoges);
the Millevaches Plateau (Limoges–
Meymac–Limoges); the Vienne Gorges
(Eymoutiers–Châteauneuf-Bujaleuf–
Eymoutiers) or the Realm of Ventadour
(Meymac–Ussel–Meymac).
🚹 Contact local tourist offices, ℘05 55
34 46 87 (Limoges) or 05 55 69 27 81
(Eymoutiers) or **Vienne Vézère
Vapeur**, www.trainvapeur.com. In
the **Dordogne**, **Autorail Espérance**
offers a guided tour and a taste of
regional cooking, travelling from
Sarlat to Bergerac in 1hr (reservation
required: ℘05 53 59 55 39).
The **Chemin de Fer Touristique
du Haut-Quercy "Le Truffadou"** runs
full steam ahead between Martel and
St-Denis-près-Martel along the top of
80m cliffs overlooking the Dordogne

valley; ℘05 65 37 35 81.
www.trainduhautquercy.info.

TAKE TO THE SKIES

Several options are available for a
bird's-eye view of **Périgord**:
hot-air balloon, light aircraft, glider,
microlight…

Montgolfière du Périgord

Clos St-Donat, 24250 La Roque
Gageac.℘05 53 28 18 58. www.
montgolfiere-du-perigord.com.
Preparation and flight (1hr or 2hr
30min) daily morning and late
afternoon spring and autumn, the
rest of the year once per day pm;
prices start at 190€.

The Aéroclub de Brive

Aéroport de Brive-Souillac Vallée
de la Dordogne
℘05 55 86 88 37. Open daily
9am–noon, 2–6pm; excl. Mon am.
Offers introductory flights aboard
a plane or a glider.

The Aéroclub du Quercy

Aérodrome de Cahors-Labenque,
46230 Cieurac. ℘05 65 21 05 96.
Offers flights over the area.

The Aéroclub du Sarladais

Aérodrome de Sarlat-Domme,
24250 Domme. ℘09 62 10 09 18.
Tours on a plane or microlight.

**The Association Rocamadour
Aérostat**

Town hall. ℘05 65 33 62 74.
Year-round 45min flights over
Rocamadour. Reservation
required. €150 per person.

What to See and Do

OUTDOOR FUN
WATER SPORTS

This inland region is awash with man-made lakes, many of which are well equipped for swimming and boating. The rivers and streams are inviting, too. The region's leading water sports centre is the **Lac de Vassivière** (*970ha/2 397 acres*), which offers beaches suitable for youngsters as well as opportunities for sailing and windsurfing. (*see Lac de VASSIVIÈRE*).

For general information on water-skiing, contact the **Fédération Française de Ski Nautique et de Wakeboard**, 9–11 rue du Borrégo, 75020 Paris; ℘01 53 20 19 19; www.ffsnw.fr. The village of Trémolat, on the Dordogne, also has an international water sports centre (℘05 53 22 81 18).

CANOEING AND KAYAKING

Canoeing is a popular family pastime on the peaceful waters of the region. In fact, on some weekends in Dordogne, there seem to be more people on the water than on the road! **Kayaking** is practised on the lakes and, for more experienced paddlers, rapid sections of the rivers. For beginners, the Dordogne, Vézère and Lot rivers are not only ideally calm, but also offer splendid views. The Corrèze, Elle, Auvézère, Céou and the upper parts of the Dronne, Isle and Célé rivers are more of a challenge. In all cases, be sure to wear the buoyant life jacket the rental agent is obliged to provide.

For general information contact:
- **Fédération Française de Canoë-kayak**
  87 quai de la Marne, BP 58, 94344 Joinville-le-Pont. ℘01 45 11 08 50. www.ffck.org.

- **Ligue Régionale du Centre de Canoë-kayak**
  5, avenue de Florence, 37000 Tours. ℘02 47 63 13 98. www.canoe-regioncentre.org.
- **Comité Régionale Canoë-kayak du Limousin**
  https://limousincanoe.wordpress.com.
- **Comité Régional de Canoë-kayak d'Aquitaine**
  Route de Hon, 40380 Gamarde-les-Bain. ℘05 58 98 50 06.
- **Comité Régional de Canoë-kayak de Midi-Pyrénées**
  Allées du Duc-de-Ventadour, 31810 Venerque. ℘05 61 08 74 40.

Or, try the **Comité Départemental de Canoë-kayak** of the following *départements*:
- **Corrèze**
  232 Route du Champ des Bruyères, 19130 Voutezac. ℘06 81 86 16 64. www.canoe-kayak-correze.com.
- **Creuse**
  La Chassagne, 23320 Gartempe. ℘05 55 81 30 22.
- **Dordogne**
  Moulin de Sainte Claire, 24000 Périgueux. www.perigueuxcanoe.org.
- **Haute-Vienne**
  1 bis rue de la Caraque, 87700 Aixe-sur-Vienne. ℘05 55 70 35 62.
- **Lot**
  314 route de Laroque, 46000 Cahors. ℘05 65 30 15 37.

Whether or not you are experienced, you can hire a boat and sometimes a guide at most canoeing/kayaking centres. A pick-up point downstream carries boaters and boats back to the base. Mountain bikes are sometimes available at the same sites.

FISHING

The rivers, lakes and streams are a joy for those who love to fish. A *Carte de Pêche* (fishing permit) is required. You may purchased one for a day or for the year in sports clubs and some local businesses; contact a tourist information centre for more information. Be aware of local regulations; crayfish are protected in most areas, and you should know which fish are in season. Frogs are a speciality of the Brenne wetlands. For further details, contact the **Conseil Supérieur de la Pêche,** Immeuble "Le Péricentre", 16 avenue Louison-Bobet, 94132 Fontenay-sous-Bois Cedex, ℘ 01 45 14 36 00, or the **Fédération Départementale de Pêche** of the following départements:

- **Cher**
  103 rue de Mazières, 18000 Bourges. ℘02 48 66 68 90. www.federationpeche.fr/18.
- **Corrèze**
  Place Abbé-Tournet, 19000 Tulle. ℘05 55 26 11 55. www.federationpeche.fr/19.
- **Creuse**
  60 avenue Louis-Laroche, 23000 Guéret. ℘05 55 52 24 70. www.federationpeche.fr/23.
- **Dordogne**
  Jacques Laguerre, 16 rue des Prés, 24000 Périgueux. ℘05 53 06 84 20. www.federationpeche.fr/24.
- **Haute-Vienne**
  31 rue Jules-Noël, 87000 Limoges. ℘05 55 06 34 77. www.federation-peche87.com.
- **Indre**
  17–19 rue des Etats-Unis, 36000 Châteauroux. ℘02 54 34 59 69. www.peche-indre.com.
- **Lot**
  133 Quai Albert Cappus, 46000 Cahors.℘05 65 35 50 22. www.pechelot.com.

WALKING

There is an extensive network of well-marked footpaths in France, which make walking a breeze. Several Grande Randonnée (GR) trails, recognisable by the red and white horizontal marks on trees, rocks and in towns on walls, signposts etc, go through the region. Petite Randonnée (PR) paths are blazed with yellow for a full circuit and green for a junction path. Tourist information centres

generally carry the Topo-Guides for their areas, or you can order them from the **Fédération Française de la Randonnée Pédestre**, ℘01 44 89 93 90; www.ffrandonnee.fr. Some English-language editions are available as well as an annual guide (*Rando Guide*), which includes ideas for overnight itineraries and places to stay as well as information on the difficulty and accessibility of trails.

Local tourist organisations also provide maps of itineraries. In Sarlat the tourist office publishes *Promenades et Randonnées en Périgord Noir*, a series of 27 walks that you can buy as a collection, individually or by group of five.

The **Comité Départemental du Tourisme du Lot** publishes *Promenades et Randonnées Pays du Cahors et du Sud du Lot*, which contains 27 walking and cycling routes.

USEFUL ADDRESSES

- **Comité Régional de la Randonnée Pédestre en Aquitaine**
  Maison Régionale des Sports, 119 Boulevard du Président Wilson 33200 Bordeaux. ℘05 57 88 26 43. http://aquitaine.ffrandonnee.fr.
- **Comité Régional de la Randonnée Pédestre en Midi-Pyrénées**
  Maison des Sports, 190 rue Isatis, BP 81908, 31319 Labège Cedex. ℘05 62 24 18 77. www.randonnees-midi-pyrenees.com.
- **Comité Régional de la Randonnée Pédestre Centre**
  Maison des Sports, 89/22 allée des Platanes, 36000 Châteauroux. ℘02 54 35 55 63. http://centre.ffrandonnee.fr.

Information is also available from the **Comité départemental de la randonnée pédestre** of the following *départements*:

- **Cher**
  Maison des Sports–Esplanade de l'aéroport, 4 rue Didier-Daurat,

LAKES AND PONDS	Dép.	Acreage	Swimming	Water sports	Fishing
Argentat (Lac de Feyt)	19	198	🏊	–	🎣
Aubazine (Plan d'eau du Coiroux)	19	59	🏊	–	Cat. 1
Bessais (Étang de Goule)	18	334	🏊	⛵	🎣
Bort-les-Orgues (Lac de Val)	19	3459	🏊	⛵	Cat. 2
Bourges (Lac du Val d'Auron)	18	203	–	⛵	Cat. 2
Bujaleuf	87	198	🏊	⛵	🎣
Carsac-de-Gurson (Lac de Gurson)	24	27	🏊	–	🎣
Compreignac (Lac de St-Pardoux)	87	815	🏊	⛵	Cat. 2
Egletons (Lac du Deiro)	19	32	🏊	–	Cat. 1
Éguzon (Lac de Chambon)	36	741	🏊	⛵	🎣
Gimel (Étang de Ruffaud)	19	49	🏊	-	🎣
Guéret (Étang de Courtille)	23	30	🏊	⛵	🎣
Lissac-sur-Couze (Lac du Causse)	19	222	🏊	⛵	Cat. 2
Luzech (Base de Caix)	46	371	🏊	–	🎣
Marcillac (Barrage de la Valette)	19	568	🏊	⛵	Cat. 2
Meymac (Lac de Sechemailles)	19	104	🏊	⛵	Cat. 2
Mézières (Étang de Bellebouche)	36	247	🏊	⛵	🎣
Neuvic (Lac de Triousoune)	19	1013	🏊	⛵	🎣
Seilhac (Lac de Burnazel)	19	79	🏊	–	🎣
Sénaillac-Latronquière (Lac du Tolerme)	46	17	🏊	⛵	Cat. 1
Sidiailles (Lac de)	18	222	🏊	⛵	🎣
St-Estèphe (Étang de)	24	74	🏊	⛵	🎣
Trémolat (Barrage de Mauzac)	24	247	🏊	⛵	🎣
Treignac (Lac de Bariousses)	19	247	🏊	–	Cat. 2
Vassivière (Lac de)	23	2471	🏊	⛵	Cat. 2
Viam (Lac de)	19	467	🏊	–	Cat. 2
Videix (Plan d'eau de Lavaud)	87	99	🏊	⛵	Cat. 2
Vigeois (Lac de Pontcharral)	19	35	🏊	–	–

Dép means **département**: 18 Cher; 19 Corrèze; 23 Creuse; 24 Dordogne; 36 Indre; 46 Lot; 87 Haute-Vienne. *Lac* means **lake**. *Étang* means **pond** or **small lake**. *Barrage* means **dam**. *Plan d'eau* means a **flat body of water**.
Category 1: Fish from the Salmonidae family (trout), usually the upper portion of major rivers. **Category 2**: Cyprinidae (carp, barbels, tench, bream, chub, dace, shiners).

Guidelines for Walkers

Choosing the right equipment for a walking expedition is essential: flexible shoes with non-slip soles, a rain jacket or poncho, an extra sweater, sun protection (hat, glasses, lotion), drinking water (1–2l per person), high-energy snacks (chocolate, cereal bars, banana), and a first aid kit. You'll need a map (and a compass if you plan to leave the main trails). Plan your itinerary well, keeping in mind that while the average walking speed for an adult is 4kph/2.5mph, you will need time to eat and rest, and children will not keep up the same pace. Leave your itinerary with someone before setting out.

Respect for nature is a cardinal rule and includes the following precautions: don't smoke or light fires in the forest, which are particularly susceptible in the dry summer months; always take your rubbish with you; leave wild flowers as they are; walk around, not through, farmers' fields; close gates behind you.

If you are caught in an electrical storm, avoid high ground, and do not move along a ridge top; do not seek shelter under overhanging rocks, isolated trees in otherwise open areas, at the entrances to caves or other openings in the rocks, or in the proximity of metal fences or gates. Do not use a metallic survival blanket. If possible, position yourself at least 15m from the highest point around you (rock or tree); crouch with your knees up and without touching the rock face with your hands or any exposed part of your body. A car is a good refuge as its rubber tyres earth it and provide protection for those inside.

18000 Bourges. &02 48 67 05 38. http://cher.ffrandonnee.fr.

- **Corrèze**
  16/18 avenue Victor Hugo, 19000 Tulle. &05 55 27 89 40. http://correze.ffrandonnee.fr.

- **Dordogne**
  Conseil Général de la Dordogne Pleine Nature, Animation Randonnées, 2, rue Paul Louis Courier, 24019 Périgueux Cedex. &05 53 51 70 30. www.rando24.com.

- **Haute-Vienne**
  35 rue Jean-Louis Paguenaud, 87100 Limoges. &08 99 23 59 29. www.randonnee-hautevienne.com.

- **Indre**
  Maison des Sports, 89 22 allée des Platanes, 36000 Châteauroux. &02 54 35 55 63. http://indre.ffrandonnee.fr.

- **Lot**
  Espace Clément Marot, 46000 Cahors. &05 65 23 06 28. http://www.ffrandonnee.fr.

CYCLING

For general information, write or call the **Fédération Française de Cyclotourisme** (12 rue Louis-Bertrand, 94207 Ivry-sur-Seine Cedex, &01 56 20 88 88; www.ffct.org). Off-road enthusiasts, contact the **Fédération Française de Cyclisme** (Vélodrome National de Saint-Quentin-En-Yvelines, 1 rue Laurent Fignon, CS 40 100, 78 069 Montigny le Bretonneux, &08 11 04 05 55; www.ffc.fr) and request the *Guide des Centres VTT*.

OTHER USEFUL ADDRESSES

- **Ligue Régionale de Cyclotourisme du Limousin**
  6 rue Léon-Tolstoï, 87100 Limoges. &05 55 38 26 11.

- **Ligue Régionale de Cyclotourisme de Midi-Pyrénées**
  7 rue André-Citroën, 31130 Balma. &05 61 99 86 46.

You can also contact the **Comité Départemental de Cyclotourisme** of the following *départements*:

◆ **Corrèze**
45 quai Aristide-Briand,
19000 Tulle. ✆05 55 20 71 46.

◆ **Creuse**
2 rue Hubert-Gaudriot, 23000
Guéret. ✆05 55 52 12 82.
www.tourisme-creuse.com.

◆ **Dordogne**
Hubert Prévost, 46 rue Kléber,
24000 Périgueux. ✆05 53 53 73 33.

◆ **Haute-Vienne**
5 rue Dupuytren, 87270 Fouzeix.
✆05 55 39 37 88.

◆ **Lot**
Milan, 46120 Leyme.
✆09 52 29 46 00.

Local tourist offices have a list of cycle
hire firms, which include SNCF train
stations in St-Amand-de-Montrond,
Uzerche, Bergerac, Le Bugue, Cahors,
Gourdon, Gramat, Rocamadour-
Padirac, Sarlat and Souillac. Maps and
suggested itineraries are provided.

HORSE RIDING

There are numerous itineraries
suitable for horse riding through
forested areas, across the *causses* and
along the main river valleys.
The **Comité National de Tourisme
Équestre** (41600 Lamotte Beuvron,
✆02 54 94 46 80, www.tourisme-
equestre.fr) is a useful source of
information if you want to plan
a riding holiday. It publishes the
brochure *Cheval Nature, l'Officiel du
Tourisme Équestre*, where you will
find the addresses of riding centres
(*Centres de Tourisme Equestre*) region–
by–region, and practical tips on
holidays for kids, insurance and more.

OTHER USEFUL ADDRESSES

◆ **Association Régionale de
Tourisme Équestre d'Aquitaine**
Hippodrome du Bouscat, BP 95,
33492 Le Bouscat Cedex.

◆ **Association Régionale de
Tourisme Équestre de Midi-
Pyrénées**
Jean Bergraser, 31 chemin des
Canalets, 31400 Toulouse.
✆05 61 14 04 58.

◆ **Association Régionale
de Tourisme Équestre
du Val de Loire-Centre**
ARTE Val de Loire-Centre,
34 rue de Villebrême, BP 50,
41914 Blois Cedex 9.
✆02 54 42 95 60. (Tue–Thu,
1.30–5.30pm).

Information on conditions and
opportunities is available from the
area **Comité Départemental de
Tourisme Équestre**:

◆ **Cher**
61, ave de Pré le Roi, 18230
St Doulchard. ✆02 48 24 04 38.

◆ **Corrèze**
Mante, 19700 St Clément.
✆06 11 41 35 39. www.tourisme-
equestre-correze.com.

◆ **Creuse**
La Motte, 23600 Leyrat
✆05 55 65 18 31.

◆ **Dordogne**
Du Pays de Beaumontois,
24440 Beaumont du Périgord.
✆05 53 22 50 99.
www.cdte24.ffe.com.
The map *Sentiers et Relais
Équestres du Périgord* is available
at the Comité Départemental de
Tourisme, 25 rue Président Wilson,
24000 Périgueux. ✆05 53 31 45 45.

◆ **Haute-Vienne**
14 rue Bos du Moulin,
87920 Condat sur Vienne.
✆05 55 31 07 60.

◆ **Indre**
Laleuf, 36250 Saint-Maur.
✆02 54 27 19 69.

◆ **Lot**
Association Départementale
de Tourisme Equestre du Lot.
✆05 65 35 80 82.
www.cheval-lot.com.

The map *Carte Départementale
de la Randonnée*, showing GR
footpaths and riding tracks,
is available at the Comité
Départemental de Tourisme,
quai Cavaignac, BP7,
46001 Cahors Cedex 9.
✆05 65 35 07 09.

EXPLORING CAVES

The Dordogne's limestone relief is pitted with caves and caverns.
Further information is available from:

- **Fédération Française de Spéléologie**
  23 rue Delandine, 69002 Lyon.
  ℘04 72 56 09 63.
  www.ffspeleo.fr.
- **Comité Spéléologique Régional d'Aquitaine**
  Centre Nelson Paillou, 12 rue Garrigou Lagrange, 64075 Pau Cedex. www.club.quomodo.com.
- **Comité Spéléologie Régional de Midi-Pyrénées**
  7 rue André-Citroën, 31130 Balma.
  ℘05 34 30 77 45.
  http://comite-speleo-midipy.com.
- **Comité Départemental de Spéléologie de la Dordogne**
  46 rue Kléber, 24000 Périgueux.
  ℘06 43 38 82 40.
- **Comité Départemental de Spéléologie du Lot**
  Mairie, 46240 La Bastide Murat.
  ℘05 65 31 11 50. www.cds46.fr.

GOLF

The Michelin map *Golf, les parcours français* (French golf courses) will help you locate golf courses in the region covered by this guide.

🖥 For further information, contact:
Fédération Française de Golf
68 rue Anatole-France,
92300 Levallois-Perret Cedex.
℘01 41 49 77 00. www.ffgolf.org.
Enquire at the tourist office for precise details on the dates of events.

ACTIVITIES FOR KIDS

This area of France has plenty to offer children, from boat trips on traditional *gabarres* to visits of caves, castles, museums and sights of special interest. In this guide, places that are particularly good for a family outing are indicated with a KIDS symbol (👫). Some attractions offer discounts for children.
Dordogne:

- Le Bugue, Village of Bornat and Aquarium 👫*p108*.

- Castelnaud, Museum of Warfare of the Middle Ages 👫*p107*.
- Les Eyzies, Prehistoric Park *p113*.

Berry:

- Aubigny-sur-Nère, Witchcraft Museum 👫*p400*.
- Nancay, Planetarium and Ciel Ouvert 👫*p401*.

Limousin:

- Eymoutiers, Ant City 👫*p301*.
- Guéret, Parc Animalier 👫*p363*.
- Ydes, Insects of the World exhibition 👫*p340*.

Quercy:

- Martel, Reptiland and Chemin de Fer Touristique du Haut Quercy "Le Truffadou" 👫*p224 and p227*.
- Rocamadour, Féerie du Rail and Fôret des Singes and Parc Animalier de Gramat 👫*p219*.

The towns and areas labelled **Villes et Pays d'Art et d'Histoire** by the Ministry of Culture offer activities for 6- to 12-year-olds. More information is available from local tourist offices and from www.vpah.culture.fr.

SHOPPING
MARKETS

Local products make great souvenirs, but remember that foie gras and truffles are expensive, even here at the source! Dordogne is also famous for its red fruit and nut liqueurs (especially in Villamblard and Brive), pork and duck preserves and wines from Cahors and Bergerac. The wines of Sancerre in Berry deserve their fine reputation. Many of the specialities can be purchased directly from the producer – look out for signs along the roadside (*dégustation – vente* for wines, *produits de la ferme* for preserves).
Fresh food and plants may not be carried home. It is acceptable to carry tinned products or preserves. Almost every village holds a weekly market all year round. Main markets in the region are held in Périgueux (Wed, Sat), Brive-la-Gaillard (Tue, Thu, Sat), Sarlat (Wed, Sat) and Brantôme (Fri).

Books and Films

BOOKS

Eleanor Of Aquitaine

Eleanor of Aquitaine, queen of France and England, a 12C divorcée, patroness of poets, source of inspiration for chivalry and courtly love, ruler of a kingdom that spanned from Scotland to the Pyrenees, mother of ten children (including Richard the Lionheart), lived her 82 years as few women in history before or since. Her fascinating life story is a good introduction to regional history:

Eleanor of Aquitaine: By the Wrath of God, Queen of England – Alison Weir, UK, Vintage 2008.

Eleanor of Aquitaine and the Four Kings – Amy Kelly, Cambridge MA, Harvard University Press, 1974.

George Sand

George Sand was a prolific novelist and correspondent, and many of her works have been translated. Her rustic tales of country life are suitable for younger readers, too, especially *The Story of My Life and Tales of a Grandmother.*

Infamous Woman: the Life of George Sand – Joseph Barry, 1977.

The Double Life of George Sand, Woman and Writer – Renée Winegarten, 1978.

Alain Fournier

Alain Fournier was the pen name of Henri-Alban Fournier. His only completed novel has been published in English as *Le Grand Meaulnes*, or "The Lost Domain".

Josephine Baker

Josephine Baker's life of scantily clad artistry, wartime heroism, social idealism, bankruptcy and triumph returns makes for good reading.

Jazz Cleopatra: Josephine Baker in Her Time – Phyllis Rose, NY, Doubleday, 1989.

Josephine – Josephine Baker and Jo Bouillon (Translated by Mariana Fitzpatrick), NY, Harper & Row, 1977.

Gastronomy

To whet your appetite:

The Wine Regions of France – Michelin APA Publications, 2010.

An in-depth guide for touring the wine regions of France.

At Home in France – Ann Barry, NY, Ballantine, 1996.

An American journalist explores happiness in Carennac.

FILMS

Many films are shot every year in the picturesque Périgord, especially in Sarlat. These include Jacques Tati's first film *Jour de Fête*, 1998's *Ever After: A Cinderella Story* starring Drew Barrymore and 2001's *The Musketeer*.

Jacquou le Croquant, 2007

Jacquou, a 19C rebel peasant boy, seeks revenge for the death of his parents from the evil Count of Nansac. The story, based on a novel by Eugène Leroy, evokes the perennial struggle between the peasantry and the ruling classes.

Timeline, 2003

This film is set in the Dordogne during the Hundred Years War and recounts how a group of archaeology students, led by actor Paul Walker, are zapped back through a wormhole to the 14C to rescue their time-travelling professor, played by Billy Connolly.

Le Souffle, 2003

A rather dark film set in the Limousin, dispelling the myth that rural life in France is always a bucolic paradise, by following a day in the life of a boy invited to join the men of the village for a feast.

Le Boucher, 1969

Claude Chabrol's film features his wife, actress Stéphane Audran, as the schoolmistress who begins an affair with the vllage butcher against the background of an outbreak of serial killings.

Calendar of Events

Festivities abound for Bastille Day, France's national day (14 July) and 15 August, also a public holiday. **Christmas markets** are held in December in many villages. Some of the largest in the region are: Brive, Aubusson, Guéret, Limoges, Bourges, Sarlat and Périgueux.

FESTIVALS
JANUARY–FEBRUARY
Limoges

Danse Emoi. Dance festival. ☎05 55 45 94 00.

APRIL
Bourges

Printemps de Bourges. International festival of popular contemporary music and songs. ☎02 48 27 28 29. www.printemps-bourges.com.

MAY–JUNE
Nohant

Festival de Nohant. ☎02 54 48 46 40. www.festivalnohant.com.

Solignac

Rencontres photographiques. Photography festival. ☎05 55 32 30 78.

MID-JUNE–MID-SEPTEMBER
Bellac

Festival National de Bellac. Jean Giraudoux theatre and music festival. ☎05 55 60 87 61. www.theatre-du-cloitre.fr.

Bourges

Un Été à Bourges. Classical music and jazz in various venues. ☎02 48 24 93 32.

Brantôme

Les Soirées Abbatiales. Concerts and cinema. ☎05 53 05 80 63. www.perigord-dronne-belle.fr.

JULY
Argenton-sur-Creuse

Mercuria. European folklore festival. ☎06 74 09 35 17. www.festivalmercuria.fr.

Cahors

Blues festival. ☎06 45 71 75 50. www.cahorsbluesfestival.com.

Gourdon

Chamber music festival (end July). ☎05 65 27 52 50.

La Châtre

Rencontres Internationales Frédéric-Chopin. Piano festival (third week of July). ☎02 54 48 46 40.

Montignac

Danses et Musiques du Monde (end of July). ☎05 53 51 86 88. www.festivaldemontignac.assoo.org.

Noirlac

Les Traversées-Rencontres de Noirlac. International music festival (second week of July). ☎02 48 96 17 16.

Souillac

Jazz festival. ☎05 65 37 04 93. www.souillacenjazz.fr.

JULY–AUGUST
Aubusson

Musique au Cœur de la Tapisserie. Organ and chamber music concerts. ☎05 55 66 32 12. www.orgue-aubusson.net.

Biron, Bergerac, Cadouin, Monpazier, Abbaye de St-Avit-Sénier

L'Été Musical en Bergerac. ☎05 53 74 30 94.

Bourges

Très Riches Heures de l'Orgue en Berry. Organ festival. ☎02 48 20 57 66. www.grandorguebourges.org.

Brive-la-Gaillarde

Festival de la Vézère. Various cultural events in selected venues. ☎05 55 23 25 09. www.festival-vezere.com.

Castelnau-Montratier, Lauzert, Montcuq

Festival de Musique du Quercy Blanc (early Aug). ☎05 65 22 90 73.

La Borne

Rencontre Internationale de la céramique. International ceramics festival (mid-July–early Aug). ☎02 48 26 96 21. www.ceramiclaborne.org.

Limoges and its region
Festival 1001 Notes en Limousin.
℘09 81 60 60 99.
www.festival1001notes.com.

Sarlat
Festival des Jeux de Théâtre
(mid-July to early Aug).
℘05 53 31 10 83.
www.festival-theatre-sarlat.com.

St-Céré
Festival Lyrique de Saint-Céré et du Haut Quercy (late July to mid-Aug).
℘05 34 50 40 10.
www.festival-saint-cere.com.

Tourtoirac, Badefols d'Ans, Hautefort
Festival du Pays d'Ans (mid-July to early Aug). Classical music, jazz, theatre. ℘05 53 51 13 63.

AUGUST
Audrix, Le Bugue, Les Eyzies, St-Cyprien
Musique en Périgord.
℘05 53 30 36 09.
www.musiqueenperigord.fr.

Belaye
Cello festival (early Aug).
℘05 65 22 40 57.
http://violoncelle-belaye.voila.net.

Bonaguil-Fumel
Theatre festival. ℘05 53 71 17 17.

Brive-la-Gaillarde
Orchestrades universelles.
Festival of youth orchestras
(mid-Aug). ℘04 78 35 87 14.

Périgueux
Mimos. International mime festival
(1st week Aug). ℘05 53 53 18 71.
www.mimos.fr.

Périgueux
MNOP. New Orleans music festival.
℘06 61 97 22 72.
www.mnop-festival.com.

St-Léon-de-Vézère, Montignac and St-Amand-de-Coly
Festival musical du Périgord Noir.
℘05 53 51 95 17.

SEPTEMBER–OCTOBER
Brantôme, Chancelade, Périgueux
Sinfonia en Périgord. Baroque music festival (late Aug to early Sept). ℘05 53 08 69 81.
www.sinfonia-en-perigord.com.

Tulle
Festival Les Nuits de Nacre.
Accordion festival (mid-Sept).
℘05 55 20 28 54.
www.accordeon.org.

OCTOBER–NOVEMBER
Châteauroux
Lisztomanias. International Franz Liszt festival. ℘02 54 34 10 74.
www.lisztomanias.fr.

Sarlat
Festival du Film de Sarlat.
℘05 53 31 04 39. www.
festivaldufilmdesarlat.com.

TRADITIONAL FESTIVALS, FAIRS AND MARKETS
JANUARY
Epiphany fairs are held in early January in Brive and Périgueux.
Sarlat
International truffle festival (mid-Jan). ℘05 55 31 45 45.
Sorges
Truffle festival. ℘05 53 46 71 43.

EASTER WEEKEND
Reuilly
Wine and gourmet food fair. ℘02 54 49 24 94. www.ot-reuilly.fr.

Son et Lumière

Sound and light shows are a great way to spend a summer night and give new perspectives on the monuments they highlight. Theme vary from living history plays to costumed pageantry and creative combinations of lighting effects and music that bring out details of architecture. Check with the local tourist office for details; in some cases you may need to bring your own blanket and chairs; in others, visitors stand and walk around the site. These shows are held in July and August, and generally start at nightfall, which may mean after 10pm.

APRIL
Aubazine
 Goat fair. ☎05 55 24 08 80.

MAY
Beaulieu-sur-Dordogne
 Strawberry fair (2nd or 3rd
 Sunday of the month).
 ☎05 55 91 09 94.
Turenne
 Goat and horse fair (early May).
 ☎05 55 24 12 95.
Vergt
 Strawberry fair. ☎05 53 03 45 10.

MAY–JUNE
Argentat
 International de canoë-kayak rally
 (mid-June). ☎05 55 28 86 45.
Domme
 Fête de la Saint-Clair.
 Folklore festival and concerts
 (1st weekend of June).
 ☎05 53 28 61 00.
Lignières
 Donkey and mule fair (Whit
 Sunday). ☎02 48 60 20 14.
Rocamadour
 Cheese fair (Whit Sunday–
 Pentecost). ☎05 65 33 22 00.
 www.rocamadour.com.
Sarlat
 Fête de la Ringueta. Traditional
 games (even-numbered years).
 ☎05 53 31 45 45.
 www.sarlat-tourisme.com.

JULY
Aubigny-sur-Nère
 Franco-Scottish Festival.
 Historical tableaux, parades,
 folk dancing and music
 ☎02 48 81 50 07.
Aubusson
 Cheese and wine fair.
Martel
 Wool fair (late July).
 ☎05 65 37 43 44.
Périgord
 Fête de la Félibrée. Folklore
 festival hosted by a different
 town in the Périgord every
 year. First Sun in July.
 ☎05 53 35 50 24.

JULY–AUGUST
Salignac-Eyvigues
 Fête des Vieux Métiers. Festival of
 old-fashioned trades (3 weekends
 in July and Aug). ☎05 53 28 81 93.

AUGUST
Argentat
 International ceramics fair
 ☎05 55 28 16 05.
Arnac-Pompadour
 Annual horse festival (mid-Aug).
 ☎05 55 73 71 00.
 www.pompadour.net.
Bué-en-Sancerre
 Foire au Sorciers. Village fair and
 folk festival (1st Sun of the month).
 ☎02 48 78 52 52.
Chambon-sur-Voueize
 International de Pétanque.
 International boules competition
 ☎05 55 82 15 89.
Duravel
 Wine and produce fair.
 ☎ 05 65 24 65 50.
Gourdon
 Medieval pageant in the old town.
 ☎05 65 27 52 50.

SEPTEMBER
Brive-la-Gaillarde
 Bird fair.
 ☎05 55 24 08 80.
Issoudun
 Foire du Rout et de la Curiosité.
 "A-bit-of-everything" fair: second-
 hand market, entertainment,
 tasting of local specialities (1st Sun
 of the month). ☎02 54 21 74 02.
Rocamadour
 Annual pilgrimage (2nd week of
 Sept). ☎05 65 33 22 00.

OCTOBER
Limoges
 Frairie des Petits Ventres (3rd Friday
 of the month). Regional festival
 for food and wine lovers.
 ☎ 05 55 34 46 87.

NOVEMBER
Brive-la-Gaillarde
 Book fair (first weekend).
 ☎ 05 55 24 08 80.

Know Before You Go

USEFUL WEBSITES

www.franceguide.com

The French Government Tourist Office/ Maison de la France site is packed with practical information and tips for those travelling to France. The homepage has a number of links to more specific guidance.

www.france-travel-guide.net

A practical and developing website for the traveller, written by a Francophile travel writer. Includes essential information, as well as a wide range of regional and local content.

www.f-t-s.co.uk

The French Travel Service specialises in organising holidays in France using the rail network. Let FTS organise your resorts and hotels anywhere in France.

www.holidayfrance.org.uk

The Association of British Travel Organisers in France has created this tidy site, which covers just about everything.

www.visiteurope.com

The European Travel Commission provides useful information on travelling to and around 27 European countries, and includes links to some commercial booking services (ie vehicle hire), rail schedules, weather reports and more.

www.ambafrance-us.org and **www.ambafrance-uk.org**

The French Embassies in the USA and the UK have a website providing basic information (geography, demographics, history), a news digest and business-related information. It offers special pages for children and pages devoted to culture, language study and travel, as well as links to other selected French sites (regions, cities, ministries).

TOURIST OFFICES

The best on-site source of information is the local tourist office, but you can also contact them in advance to receive brochures and maps.
The addresses and telephone numbers of tourist offices in the larger towns are listed after the ⛵ symbol, in the *Discovering Dordogne Berry Limousin* section of the guide. The following addresses are for local tourist offices of the *départements* and *régions* covered in this guide.

REGIONAL

Four regional tourist offices are concerned with the area covered by this guide; address inquiries to the **Comité Régional de Tourisme** (CRT):

- **Aquitaine**
  Cité Mondiale, 23 parvis des Chartrons, 33074 Bordeaux Cedex.
  ℘05 56 01 70 00.
  www.tourisme-aquitaine.fr.

- **Limousin**
  30 cours Gay Lussac, 87000 Limoges Cedex. ℘05 55 11 05 80.
  www.tourismelimousin.com.

- **Midi-Pyrénées**
  15 rue Rivals - CS 78543, 31685 Toulouse Cedex 6.
  ℘05 61 13 55 55.
  www.tourisme-midi-pyrenees.com.

- **Centre-Val de Loire**
  37 avenue de Paris, 45000 Orléans.
  ℘02 38 79 95 28.
  www.visaloire.com.

DEPARTMENTS

For each *département* within the region, address inquiries to the **Comité Départemental du Tourisme (CDT)**, unless otherwise stated:

- **Dordogne-Périgord**
  25 rue Wilson,
  BP 40032, 24002 Périgueux.
  ℘05 53 35 50 24.
  www.dordogne-perigord-tourisme.fr.

- **Cher**
  Carré des créateurs,
  11, rue Maurice Roy, CS 40314,
  18023 Bourges.
  ℘02 48 48 00 10.
  www.berryprovince.com.

- **Haute-Vienne**
  17 Bis Bl Georges Périn, 87000
  Limoges. ℘05 55 79 04 04.
  www.tourisme-hautevienne.com.

- **Corrèze**
  Maison du Tourisme, 45, quai
  Aristide Briand, 19000 Tulle.
  ℘05 55 29 98 78.
  www.tourismecorreze.com.

- **Indre**
  1 place Eugène Rolland,
  36003 Châteauroux Cedex.
  ℘02 54 07 36 36.
  www.berryprovince.com.

- **Creuse**
  43 place Bonnyaud,
  23000 Guéret.
  ℘05 55 51 05 20.
  www.tourisme-creuse.com.

- **Lot**
  CS90007 – 46001 Cahors cedex 9.
  ℘05 65 35 07 09.
  www.tourisme-lot.com.

- **Tarn-et-Garonne**
  Hôtel du Département, 100 Bd
  Hubert Gouze BP 534 - 82005
  Montauban. ℘05 63 21 79 65.
  www.tourisme82.com.

REGIONAL CENTRES

These regional promotion centres
provide a wide range of information
including special events, mapped-out
tours of the area and places to stay.

- **Maison Aquitaine**
  21 rue des Pyramides, 75001 Paris.
  ℘01 55 35 31 42.
  http://maison.aquitaine.fr.

- **Maison du Limousin**
  30 rue Caumartin, 75009 Paris.
  ℘01 40 07 04 67.

VILLES ET PAYS D'ART ET D'HISTOIRE

Nine towns and areas, labelled
Villes et Pays d'Art et d'Histoire
by the Ministry of Culture, are
mentioned in this guide (*Bourges,
Cahors, Figeac, Limoges, Pays Monts
et Barrages, Pays de la Vézère et de
l'Ardoise, Périgueux, Sarlat, and Vallée
de la Dordogne*).
They are particularly active in
promoting their architectural and
cultural heritage and offer guided
tours by highly qualified guides as
well as activities for 6–12-year-olds.
🗓 More information is available
from tourist offices and www.vpah.
culture.fr.

FRENCH TOURIST OFFICES ABROAD

🗓 For information, brochures, maps
and assistance in planning a trip to
France, travellers should apply to the
official French Tourist Office or Maison
de France in their own country:

- **Australia – New Zealand**
  Sydney – Level 13, 25 Bligh St,
  Sydney, New South Wales 2000.
  ℘(02) 9231 5244.
  http://au.rendezvousenfrance.com

- **Canada**
  http://ca.rendezvousenfrance.com
  Montreal – 1800 Avenue McGill
  College, Suite 1010, Montreal H3A
  3J6. ℘(514) 288-2026.
  Toronto – 30 St Patrick's Street,
  Suite 700, Toronto, Ontario M5T
  3A3. ℘(416) 593 6427.

- **South Africa**
  3rd floor, Village Walk, Office
  Tower, cnr Maude and Rivonia,
  Sandton. ℘(011) 523 8292.
  http://int.rendezvousenfrance.com

- **United Kingdom**
  Lincoln House, 300 High
  Holborn, London WC1V 7JH.
  ☎09068 244 123.
  http://uk.rendezvousenfrance.com

- **United States**
  http://us.rendezvousenfrance.com
  New York – 825 Third Avenue,
  29th floor (entrance on 50th
  Street), New York, NY 10022.
  ☎1 (514) 288 1904.
  Chicago – Consulate General
  of France, 205 North Michigan
  Avenue, Suite 3770, Chicago,
  IL 60601 ☎1 (312) 327 0290.
  Los Angeles – 9454 Wilshire
  Boulevard, Suite 210, Los Angeles,
  CA 90212 ☎1 (310) 271 6665.

Request further information from:
France on Call ☎(410) 286-8310.

INTERNATIONAL VISITORS
EMBASSIES AND CONSULATES

Embassies provide diplomatic help to
their citizens abroad, while consulates
are a local base in Paris and in
other large cities for adminstrative
formalities. See www.mfe.org for a
full list of consulates.

- **Australia Embassy**
  4 rue Jean-Rey, 75015 Paris.
  ☎01 40 59 33 00.
  www.france.embassy.gov.au.

- **Canada Embassy**
  35 avenue Montaigne, 75008 Paris.
  ☎01 44 43 29 00.
  www.amb-canada.fr.

- **Eire Embassy**
  4 rue Rude, 75116 Paris.
  ☎01 44 17 67 50. Fax: 01 44 17
  67 50. www.embassyofireland.fr.

- **New Zealand Embassy**
  7 ter rue Léonard-de-Vinci,
  75116 Paris. ☎01 45 01 43 44.
  www.nzembassy.com.

- **South Africa Embassy**
  59 quai d'Orsay,
  75343 Paris Cedex 07.
  ☎01 53 59 23 23.
  www.afriquesud.net.

- **UK Embassy**
  35 rue du Faubourg St-Honoré,
  75383 Paris. ☎01 44 51 31 00.
  www.ukinfrance.fco.gov.uk/en
  UK Consulate
  18bis rue d'Anjou, 75008 Paris.
  ☎01 44 51 31 00

- **USA Embassy**
  2 avenue Gabriel, 75382 Paris.
  ☎01 43 12 22 22. www.amb-usa.fr
  USA Consulate
  2 rue St-Florentin, 75001 Paris.
  ☎01 43 12 22 22.

ENTRY REQUIREMENTS
Passport

Nationals of countries within the
European Union entering France need
only a national identity card (or in
the case of the British, a passport).
Nationals of other countries must
have a valid national passport.
Visa – No **entry visa** is required for
Canadian, US or Australian citizens
travelling as tourists and staying less
than 90 days, except for students
planning to study in France. If in doubt,
apply to your local French consulate.
General passport information is
available by phone to US citizens toll-
free from the **Federal Information
Center,** ☎800-688-9889. US passport
application forms can be downloaded
from http://travel.state.gov.

CUSTOMS REGULATIONS

In Britain, go to the Customs Office
(UK) website at www.hmrc.gov.
uk for information on allowances,
travel safety tips, and to consult and
download documents and guides.
There are no limits on the amount
of duty and/or tax paid alcohol and
tobacco that you can bring back into
the UK as long as they are for your
own use or gifts and are transported

Sancerre wine with local cheese

© S. Sauvignier / Michelin

by you. If you are bringing in alcohol or tobacco goods and UK Customs have reason to suspect they may be for a commercial purpose, an officer may ask you questions and make checks.

Australians will find customs information at www.customs.gov.au; for **New Zealanders** Advice for Travellers is at www.customs.govt.nz.

HEALTH

First aid, medical advice and chemists' night service rota are available from chemists/drugstores *(pharmacies)* identified by the green cross sign.
It is advisable to take out comprehensive travel insurance cover, as tourists receiving medical treatment in French hospitals or clinics have to pay for it themselves.
Nationals of non-EU countries should check with their insurance companies about policy limitations. Remember to keep all receipts.
British and Irish citizens, if not already in possession of an EHIC (European Health Insurance Card), should apply for one before travelling. The card entitles UK residents to reduced-cost medical treatment. Apply at UK post offices, call ☎0845 606 2030, or visit www. ehic.org.uk. Details of the healthcare available in France and how to claim reimbursement are published in the leaflet Health Advice for Travellers, available from post offices.

All prescription drugs taken into France should be clearly labelled; it is recommended to carry a copy of prescriptions.
Americans and Canadians can contact the International Association for Medical Assistance to Travellers: ☎for the USA (716) 754-4883 or for Canada (416) 652-0137 or (519) 836-0102; www.iamat.org.

ACCESSIBILITY

The sights described in this guide most easily accessible to people of reduced mobility are indicated in the admission times and charges by the symbol ᵫ.
On French TGV and Corail trains there are wheelchair spaces in 1st-class carriages available to holders of 2nd-class tickets. On Eurostar and Thalys special rates are available for accompanying adults. All airports are equipped to receive physically disabled passengers. Disabled drivers may use the EU blue card for parking entitlements.
Information about accessibility is available from French disability organizations such as Association des Paralysés de France (17 bd Auguste Blanqui, 75013 Paris. ☎01 40 78 69 00; www.apf.asso.fr), who also maintain a nationwide network of branches throughout the country.
The guide Michelin Camping France indicates campsites with facilities suitable for the physically disabled.
The **French railways** (SNCF) (www.voyages-sncf.com), **Air France** (www.airfrance.fr) and major ski resorts, through **Handi-Ski** (found at www.esf.net), offer facilities for the disabled. The French federation for **Handisport** has a website at www.handisport.org.

Getting There and Getting Around

BY AIR

Choose between scheduled flights on Air France or commercial and package-tour flights with rail or coach link-ups or fly-drive schemes. Within France, air travel generally compares unfavourably with rail, for both price and time, especially when you consider transport to and from airports, and check-in times.
The following airlines operate flights from the UK to the Dordogne and Limousin areas, as well as to neighbouring regions in southwest France, but conditions change frequently, so check the websites:

- **Ryanair** www.ryanair.com;
- **easyJet** www.easyjet.com;
- **Flybe** www.flybe.com;
- **Jet2.com** www.jet2.com.

It is very easy to arrange air travel to one of Paris' two airports (Roissy-Charles-de-Gaulle to the north, and Orly to the south). Contact airline companies and travel agents for details of package tour flights with a rail link-up or fly-drive schemes.
You can get from CDG airport into the centre of Paris by using the Roissybus, Airport Shuttle, or by using a taxi, which is much more convenient, but hugely more expensive.
There is an extra charge (posted in the taxi) for baggage; the extra charge for airport pick-up is on the meter; drivers are usually given a tip of 10–15%.
The **main international airport** is Bordeaux, supported by regional airports at Limoges, Brive-la-Gaillarde and Bergerac.
You can fly directly to **Limoges** from the UK or from Paris. 𝒫05 55 43 30 30, www.aeroportlimoges.com. Details of the other main airports in the region are:

- ◆ **Aéroport de Périgueux-Bassillac**
  9km/5.6mi E of Périgueux.
  24330 Bassillac.
  𝒫05 53 04 68 92.

- ◆ **Aéroport de Bergerac-Dordogne Périgord**
  5km/3mi SE of Bergerac.
  Route d'Agen, 24100 Bergerac.
  𝒫05 53 22 25 25.

- ◆ **Aéroport de Brive-Vallée de la Dordogne**
  Aéroport, 19600 Nespouls.
  𝒫05 55 22 40 00. www.aeroport-brive-vallee-dordogne.com.

- ◆ **Aéroport de Bourges**
  SW of Bourges. Route Issoudun, 18000 Bourges.
  𝒫02 48 50 74 77.

BY SEA

There are competing **cross-Channel passenger and car** ferry services from the United Kingdom and Ireland. To choose the most suitable route between your port of arrival and your destination use the Michelin Tourist and Motoring Atlas France, Michelin Map 911 (which gives travel times and mileages) or Michelin maps from the 1:200 000 series.

- ◆ **Brittany Ferries** 𝒫0871 244 0744 (UK); 0825 828 828 (France). www.brittanyferries.com. Services from Portsmouth, Poole and Plymouth.

- ◆ **Condor Ferries** 𝒫01202 207216, www.condorferries.co.uk. Services from Weymouth, Poole and Portsmouth.

- ◆ **DFDS Seaways** now incorporate Norfolk Line and have taken over some LD Lines routes. They operate routes between Dover and Calais, Dover-Dunkerque Portsmouth-Le Havre and Newhaven-Dieppe. 𝒫(UK) 0871

574 7235 and 0800 917 1201;
www.dfdsseaways.co.uk.

+ **LD Lines** Services from
Portsmouth and Newhaven are
now operated by DFDS Seaways.

+ **MyFerryLink** *0844 2482 100.*
www.myferrylink.com. Services
between Dover and Calais.

+ **Norfolk Line** Norfolk Line is now
part of DFDS Seaways.

+ **P&O Ferries** *08716 642 121*
(UK), or 0825 120 156 (France),
www.poferries.com. Service,
between Dover and Calais.

BY TRAIN

Eurotunnel operates a 35-minute
rail trip for passengers with a car
through the Channel Tunnel between
Folkestone and Calais. *08705 35
35 35 (in the UK) or 08 10 63 03 04
(in France); www.eurotunnel.com.*
Eurostar runs from London
(St Pancras) to Paris (Gare du Nord)
in 2hr 15 (up to 20 times daily),
reducing in 2016 to just 2hr.
Bookings and information
08705 186 186 (£3 credit card
booking fee applies) in the UK,
www.eurostar.com. **Citizens of
non-European Economic Area**
countries will need to complete
a landing card before arriving at
Eurostar check-in. These can be found
at dedicated desks in front of the
check-in area and from Eurostar staff.
Once you have filled in the card please
hand it to UK immigration staff.
Eurostar passengers can connect to
the high-speed TGV train at Paris.
The TGV, speeding at up to 297km/h
(185mph), travels from Paris to
Bordeaux.
For **French railways** (SNCF)
reservations and information visit
www.voyages-sncf.com. Regional
trains, called TER, and SNCF buses
link the whole region in an efficient
network.

France Rail Pass and Eurail Pass are
travel passes that may be purchased
by residents of countries outside
the European Union. Contact: www.
voyages-sncf.com. If you are a
European resident, you can buy an
individual country pass, if you are not
a resident of the country where you
plan to use it.
At the SNCF (French railways) site,
www.sncf.fr, you can book ahead, pay
with a credit card, and receive your
ticket in the mail at home.
There are numerous **discounts**
available, 25–50 percent below the
regular rate. These include discounts
for using senior cards and youth cards,
group rates and seasonal promotions.
You can procure special passes and
ID cards in all SNCF stations and
boutiques; bring an ID photo. The
SNCF also operates a **travel service**
for accommodation, car rentals and
holiday packages. Remember to
validate *(composter)* tickets using the
orange automatic date-stamping
machines at the platform entrance.
Failure to do so may result in a fine.
SNCF also operates a **telephone
information, reservation and
prepayment service in English**
from 7am to 10pm (French time)
08 36 35 35 39.

RAIL TRAVEL FOR THE DISABLED

Details of services available to
welcome and accompany disabled
travellers at French railway (SNCF)
stations can be found at
www.accessibilite.sncf.com.
Or telephone *0890 640 650.*

BY COACH/BUS

www.eurolines.com has information
about travelling by coach in Europe.
From the UK call *0871 81 81 81;*
within France *0892 89 9091.*

BY CAR
PLANNING YOUR ROUTE

The area covered in this guide is easily
reached by main motorways and
national routes. **Michelin map 726**

indicates the main itineraries as well as alternate routes for avoiding heavy traffic during busy holiday periods and gives estimated travel times. **Michelin map 723** is a detailed atlas of French motorways, indicating tolls, rest areas and services along the route; it includes a table for calculating distances and times. The latest Michelin route-planning service is available on the Internet at **www.ViaMichelin.com**. Travellers can calculate a precise route for free using such options as shortest route, route avoiding toll roads, Michelin-recommended route and tourist information (hotels, restaurants, attractions).

The roads are very busy during the holiday period (particularly weekends in July and August) so to avoid traffic congestion it is advisable to follow the recommended secondary routes (signposted as *Bison Futé – itinéraires bis*). The motorway network includes rest areas (*aires de repos*) and petrol stations (*stations-service*), usually inlcuding restaurant and shopping complexes, about every 40km/25mi.

DOCUMENTS

Driving licence

Travellers from other European Union countries and North America can drive in France with a valid national or home-state **driving licence**. An **international driving licence** is useful because the information on it appears in nine languages (keep in mind that traffic officers are empowered to fine motorists). A permit is available (US$10) from the **National Automobile Club**, 1151 East Hillsdale Blvd, Foster City, CA 94404 *℘*650 294 7000 (toll free in the US: 1 800 622 2136) or www. nationalautoclub.com; or contact your local branch of the **American Automobile Association**.

Registration papers

For the vehicle, it is necessary to have the registration papers (logbook) and an approved nationality plate.

INSURANCE

Certain motoring organisations (AAA, AA, RAC and the Caravan Club) offer accident insurance and breakdown service schemes for members. Check with your current insurance company in regard to coverage while abroad.

ROAD REGULATIONS

The minimum driving age is 18. Traffic drives on the right. All passengers must wear **seat belts**. Children under the age of 10 must ride in the back seat. Headlights must be switched on in poor visibility and at night; dipped headlights should be used at all times outside built-up areas. Use sidelights only when the vehicle is stationary.

In the case of a **breakdown**, a red warning triangle or hazard warning lights are obligatory, as are reflective safety jackets, one for each passenger, and carried within the car. it is now compulsory to carry an in-car breathalyser kit, too; you can be fined if you do not. UK right-hand drive cars must use headlight adaptors.

In the absence of stop signs at intersections, cars must **give way to the right**. Traffic on main roads outside built-up areas (priority indicated by a yellow diamond sign) and on roundabouts has right of way. Vehicles must stop when the lights turn red at road junctions and may filter to the right only when indicated by an amber arrow. The regulations on **drinking and driving** (limited to 0.50g/l) and **speeding** are strictly enforced – usually by an on-the-spot fine and/or confiscation of the vehicle.

Speed limits

Although liable to modification, these are as follows:

◆ **Toll motorways** (*autoroutes*) 130kph/80mph (110kph/68mph when raining);

◆ **Dual carriageways** and **motorways** without tolls 110kph/68mph (100kph/62mph when raining);

◆ **Other roads** 90kph/56mph (80kph/50mph when raining) and in towns 50kph/31mph;

♦ **Outside lane** on motorways during daylight, on level ground and with good visibility – minimum speed limit of 80kph/50mph.

Parking regulations

In built-up areas there are zones where parking is either restricted or subject to a fee; tickets should be obtained from the ticket machines (*horodateurs* – small change necessary) and displayed inside the windscreen on the driver's side; failure to do so may result in a fine, or towing away and impoundment. In some towns you may find blue parking zones (*zone bleue*) marked by a blue line on the pavement or road and a blue signpost with a "P" and a small sqare underneath. In this case a cardboard disc (ask for a *disque de stationnement*, available from supermarkets and petrol stations) must be displayed with times indicated on it.

Tolls

In France, most motorway sections are subject to a toll (*péage*). You can pay in cash or with a credit card (Visa, Mastercard).

PETROL/GASOLINE

French service stations dispense:
♦ *sans plomb 98* (super unleaded 98)
♦ *sans plomb 95* (super unleaded 95)
♦ *diesel/gazole* (diesel)
♦ *GPL* (LPG).

Petrol is considerably more expensive in France than in the USA, but less expensive than in the UK. Prices are listed on signboards on the motorways; it is usually less expensive to fill up after leaving the motorway at one of the large hypermarkets outside of town. If you run out of petrol on the motorway, pull over onto the hard shoulder and call 112 or walk to the nearest emergency phone.

CAR RENTAL

There are car rental agencies at airports, railway stations and in all large towns throughout France. Most European cars have manual

RENTAL CARS – CENTRAL RESERVATION IN FRANCE	
Avis:	℘08 21 23 07 60 www.avis.com
Europcar:	℘08 25 358 358 www.europcar.com
Budget France:	℘08 25 00 35 64 www.budget.fr
Hertz France:	℘01 39 38 38 38 www.hertz.fr
SIXT-Eurorent:	℘08 20 00 74 98 www.e-sixt.com
National-CITER:	℘08 25 16 12 20 www.citer.fr
Ada:	℘08 25 16 91 69 www.ada.fr

transmission; automatic cars are available only if an advance reservation is made. Drivers must be over 21; between ages 21–25, drivers are required to pay an extra daily fee; some companies allow drivers under 23 only if the reservation has been made through a travel agent. Rental agencies have offices all over France; to find the one near where you want to rent, consult these websites:
♦ **Avis** www.avis.fr
♦ **Budget France** www.budget.fr
♦ **Europcar** www.europcar.fr
♦ **Hertz France** www.hertz.fr
♦ **National-CITER** www.citer.fr
♦ **SIXT-Eurorent** www.e-sixt.com

In France, you can call the numbers in the chart below.

MOTORHOME RENTAL
Worldwide Motorhome Rentals
Offers fully equipped camper vans for rent. ℘1 888 519 8969 (*US toll-free*). www.mhrww.com.

Auto Europe
Wide range of recreational vehicles. ℘1 888 223 5555 (*US toll-free*) or ℘1 207 842 2000 *within North America. Elsewhere:* ℘(00) 800 115 6218. www.autoeurope.com.

Where to Stay and Eat

WHERE TO STAY

We feature hotels throughout this guide. For a wide selection of places to stay, also use the **Michelin Guide France**, with its famously reliable star-rating system and hundreds of establishments all over France. The **Michelin Charming Places to Stay** guide contains a selection of 1 000 hotels and guesthouses at reasonable prices. If you prefer self-catering, then there are over one-third of a million properties to rent in France.

SELECTION

The legend on the cover flap explains the symbols and abbreviations used in this guide. We have reported the prices (double occupancy) and conditions as we observed them, but of course changes in management and other factors may mean that you will find some discrepancies. Please feel free to keep us informed of any major differences you might encounter.

BOOKING

Be sure to book ahead to ensure that you get the accommodation you want, not only in the tourist season, but year round, as many towns fill up during trade fairs, arts festivals etc. Some places require an advance deposit or a reconfirmation. Reconfirming is especially important if you plan to arrive after 6pm.

For further assistance, **Loisirs Accueil** is a booking service that has offices in some French *départements* – contact the local tourist offices for further information, or for Internet booking log on to: www.loisirsaccueilfrance. com or www.resinfrance.fr.

Logis et Auberges de France is a guide to good-value, family-run hotels available from the French Tourist Office, as are lists of other kinds of accommodation such as hotels, prestigious accommodations, bed-and-breakfasts etc.

Relais et Châteaux provides information on booking in luxury hotels and gourmet restaurants: 15 rue Galvani, 75017 Paris, ✆082 582 5180 (within France), ✆0800 2000 00 02 (from the UK), ✆1 800 735 2478 (from the US), or go to: www.relaischateaux.com.

ECONOMY CHAIN HOTELS

If you need a place to stop en route, these can be useful, as they are inexpensive and generally located near the main road.

While breakfast is available, there may not be a restaurant; rooms are small and simple, with a television and bathroom.

Rather than sort through hotels yourself, you can go to websites that cover several chains, from modest to luxurious. These sites allow you to select your hotel based on geographical location, price and level of comfort, and to book online.

www.viamichelin.com covers hotels in France, including famous selections from the Michelin Guide as well as lower-priced chains.

www.activehotels.com covers a wide range of hotels, and offers customer reviews.

- ◆ **Akena** ✆01 69 84 85 17; www.hotels-akena.com
- ◆ **B&B** ✆01 72 36 51 06; www.hotel-bb.com
- ◆ **Mister Bed** ✆01 46 14 38 00. You book through a bigger website such as http://en.venere.com
- ◆ **Best Hôtel** ✆03 28 27 46 69; www.besthotel.fr
- ◆ **Campanile**, **Kyriad**, **Bleu Marine**, **Première Classe**, **Louvre** ✆01 64 62 46 46; www.envergure.fr
- ◆ **www.ichotelsgroup.com** (Holiday Inn)
- ◆ **www.choicehotels.com** (Comfort)
- ◆ **www.bestwestern.fr** (Best Western)
- ◆ **www.etaphotel.com** (Étap Hotels)
- ◆ **www.ibishotel.com** (Ibis Hotels)

RURAL ACCOMMODATION

The **Maison des Gîtes de France** is an information service on self-catering accommodation in France.

Gîtes usually take the form of a cottage or apartment where visitors can make themselves at home. Bed and breakfast accommodation (*chambres d'hôtes*) consists of a room and breakfast at a reasonable price in an inhabitant's house.

For a list of Chambres d'Hôtes contact the **Gîtes de France** office at 56 rue St-Lazare, 75009 Paris, ℘01 49 70 75 75, or their representative in the UK, **Brittany Ferries** (℘see *Getting There and Getting Around*).

The Internet site, www.gites-de-france.com, has a good English version. From the site, you can order catalogues for different regions illustrated with photographs of the properties, as well as specialised catalogues (bed and breakfasts, chalets in ski areas, farm stays etc).

You can also contact the local tourist offices, which may have lists of available properties and local bed and breakfasts.

You can also refer to www.bed-breakfast-france.com, which has a good selection of country guest house accommodation throughout the region.

The **Fédération Française des Stations Vertes de Vacances**, 6 rue Ranfer-de-Bretenières, 21000 Dijon Cedex, ℘03 80 54 10 50, www.stationsvertes.com, is able to provide details of accommodation, leisure facilities and natural attractions in rural locations selected for their tranquillity.

The **Centre Permanent d'Initiation à l'Environnement** (CPIE, environment awareness centre), 35 rue Hersent-Luzarche, 36290 Azay-le-Ferron, ℘02 54 39 23 43, www.cpiebrenne.org, offers 76 beds (including six for disabled travellers) to those who wish to explore the Parc Naturel Régional de la Brenne. Entertainment for adults and children is organised at weekends. Equipment used for observation is available on location. There are various activities centred on nature and astronomy.

HOLIDAYS ON THE FARM

The guide *Bienvenue à la Ferme* is published by and available from the Assemblée Permanente des Chambres d'Agriculture, Service "Agriculture et Tourisme", 9 avenue Georges-V, 75008 Paris, ℘01 53 57 10 10, www.bienvenue-a-la-ferme.com. It includes the addresses of farmers providing guest facilities who have signed a charter drawn up by the Chambers of Agriculture. *Bienvenue à la Ferme* farms, vetted for quality and meeting official standards, can be identified by the yellow flower on a green square which serves as their logo.

WALKERS

Walkers can consult the guide *Gîtes d'Étapes et Refuges* by A and S Mouraret, which can be ordered from www.gites-refuges.com.

This guide, which lists 4 000 places to stay, also contains much information to help with planning itineraries and is intended for those who enjoy walking, cycling, climbing, skiing and canoeing-kayaking holidays. The site also includes a good list of institutional contacts.

HOSTELS, CAMPING

To obtain an International Youth Hostel Federation card (there is no age requirement, and there is a senior card available too), you should contact the IYHF in your own country for information and membership applications (US ℘001 301 495 1240; England ℘01707 324170; Scotland ℘01786 891400; Canada ℘001 613 2377 884, Toll free 1 800 663 5777; Australia ℘61 2 9283 7195).

There is a new booking service on the Internet (www.iyhf.org), which you may use to reserve rooms as far as six months in advance. The main youth hostel association (*Auberges de Jeunesse*) in France is the **Ligue Française pour les Auberges de** la Jeunesse (67 rue Vergniaud, 75013 Paris, ℘01 44 16 78 78; www.auberges-de-jeunesse.com). There are numerous officially graded **camp sites** with varying standards of facilities throughout the region. The **Michelin Camping France** guide lists a selection of camp sites. The area is very popular with campers in the summer months, so it is wise to reserve in advance. An International Camping Carnet for Caravans is useful but not compulsory; it can be obtained from motoring organisations or the Camping and Caravanning Club (www.campingandcaravanningclub. co.uk) or The Caravan Club (www. caravanclub.co.uk).

WHERE TO EAT

We feature hotels throughout this guide offering restaurant service. Restaurants usually serve lunch between noon and 2pm and the evening meal between 7.30 and 10pm. It is not always easy to find something in between those two meal times except a sandwich or pastry in a bakery or *snack* (fast food counters in tourist areas).

Eating out

Restaurants are found in all towns and cities. Food ranges from regional cooking to *nouvelle* and *haute cuisine* – expect to pay anything from 12€ upwards for a main course, depending on the type of food on offer. Many restaurants offer good value-for-money set menus at lunchtimes.

Truffles

© S. Sauvignier / Michelin

Vegetarians may find it a challenge to find places that cater exclusively for their needs.

Cafés generally only serve coffee and other beverages; **brasseries** offer inexpensive, classic French dishes; **relais routiers** offer straightforward, hearty food and are mainly frequented by lorry drivers. These can be found on A roads (www.relais-routiers.com); **auberges** and **tables d'hôtes** are usually found in the countryside and can be a good option to both eat and stay. Regional produce is served. The addresses are often well-kept secrets, so enquire with the local tourist information centre.

L'assiette de pays is a simple menu option of a reasonably priced single course, prepared from local produce and accompanied by a drink. Participating restaurants display a sticker in their window.

Fait maison: in 2014 the French government made it a requirement for all food establishments to identify those of its dishes that are truly home-made rather than industrially prepared, off-site.

In French restaurants and cafés, a service charge is included, so **tipping** is not necessary, but French people often leave the small change from their bill on their table, or about 5% . Among places in the Périgord-Quercy region that have been awarded the special distinction of **site remarquable du goût** (first-class gourmet shopping sites) are Brive-la-Gaillarde (fairs and markets), Sarlat (foie gras and poultry market), Martel-en-Quercy (walnut oil) and Monbazillac (sweet white wine). www.sitesremarquablesdugout.com.

Michelin Guide

For an extended selection, see the **Michelin Guide France**, with its famously reliable star-rating system and hundreds of establishments throughout the country.

Useful Words and Phrases

Sights

	Translation
Abbaye	Abbey
Beffroi	Belfry
Chapelle	Chapel
Château	Castle
Cimetière	Cemetery
Cloître	Cloister
Cour	Courtyard
Couvent	Convent
Écluse	Lock (Canal)
Église	Church
Fontaine	Fountain
Halle	Covered market
Jardin	Garden
Mairie	Town hall
Maison	House
Marché	Market
Monastère	Monastery
Moulin	Mill
Musée	Museum
Parc	Park
Place	Square
Pont	Bridge
Port	Port/harbour
Porte	Gate/gateway
Quai	Quay
Remparts	Ramparts
Rue	Street
Statue	Statue
Tour	Tower

Natural sites

	Translation
Abîme	Chasm
Aven	Swallow-hole
Barrage	Dam
Belvédère	Viewpoint
Cascade	Waterfall
Col	Pass
Corniche	Ledge
Côte	Coast, hillside
Forêt	Forest
Grotte	Cave
Lac	Lake
Plage	Beach
Rivière	River
Ruisseau	Stream
Signal	Beacon
Source	Spring
Vallée	Valley

On The Road

	Translation
Autoroute	Motorway/highway
Droite	Right
Essence	Petrol/gas
Est	East
Feu Tricolore	Traffic Lights
Garage	Garage (for repairs)
Gauche	Left
Horodateur	Parking meter
Nord	North
Ouest	West
Parking	Car park
Passage clouté	Zebra crossing
Péage	Toll
Permis de conduire	Driving licence
Pneu	Tyre
Sabot	Wheel clamp
Station essence	Petrol/gas station
Sud	South

Time

	Translation
Aujourd'hui	Today
Demain	Tomorrow
Hier	Yesterday
Hiver	Winter
Printemps	Spring
Été	Summer
Automne	Autumn/fall
Semaine	Week
Lundi	Monday
Mardi	Tuesday
Mercredi	Wednesday
Jeudi	Thursday
Vendredi	Friday
Samedi	Saturday
Dimanche	Sunday

Numbers

	Translation
0	Zéro
1	Un (m)/Une (f)
2	Deux
3	Trois
4	Quatre
5	Cinq
6	Six
7	Sept
8	Huit
9	Neuf
10	Dix
11	Onze
12	Douze
13	Treize

14	Quatorze
15	Quinze
16	Seize
17	Dix-sept
18	Dix-huit
19	Dix-neuf
20	Vingt
30	Trente
40	Quarante
50	Cinquante
60	Soixante
70	Soixante-dix
80	Quatre-vingt
90	Quatre-vingt-dix
100	Cent
1000	Mille

Shopping

	Translation
Banque	Bank
Boucherie	Butcher's
Boulangerie	Baker's
Cachets pour la gorge	Cough sweets
Entrée	Entrance
Épicerie	Grocer's
Fermé	Closed
Grand	Big
Librairie	Newsagent, Bookshop
Magasin	Shop
Ouvert	Open
Petit	Small
Pharmacie	Chemist's/Drugstore
Poissonnerie	Fishmonger's
Poste	Post Office
Pousser	Push
Sirop pour la toux	Cough mixture
Sortie	Exit
Timbres	Stamps
Tirer	Pull

Food and drink

	Translation
Agneau	Lamb
Assiette	Plate
Beurre	Butter
Bière	Beer
Bœuf	Beef
Couteau	Knife
Cuillère	Spoon
Déjeuner	Lunch
Dessert	Dessert
Dîner	Dinner
Eau minérale	Mineral water
Fourchette	Fork
Fromage	Cheese
Fruits	Fruit
Glace	Ice cream
Glaçons	Ice cubes
Jambon	Ham
Jus d'orange	Orange juice
Légumes	Vegetables
Pain	Bread
Petit-déjeuner	Breakfast
Poisson	Fish
Porc	Pork
Poulet	Chicken
Restaurant	Restaurant
Salade	Lettuce salad
Salade composée	Mixed salad
Sel	Salt
Sucre	Sugar
Verre	Glass
Viande	Meat
Vin rouge	Red wine
Vin blanc	White wine
Yaourt	Yoghurt

Menu reader

	Translation
Ballottine	Boned, stuffed leg of poultry
Bien cuit/à point/ saignant/cru	well-done/medium/ rare/ raw
Bréjaude	Pork and vegetable stew
Cabécou	Quercy goat's cheese
Canard	Duck
Cèpes	King bolete mushrooms (Boletus edulis)
Chabrol	Broth with wine
Champignons des bois	Wild mushrooms
Châtaignes	Chestnuts
Clafoutis	Cherry flan
Confit	Duck or goose preserved in its own fat
Crottin	Small, round goat's cheese
Dinde	Turkey
Écrevisse	Crayfish
Enchaud or anchaud	Pork confit
En conserve	Preserved
Farcidures	Potato dumplings
Foie de veau	Calf's liver
Foie gras	Fattened duck or goose liver
Fraise	Strawberry
Jambon galantine	Cold cuts in jelly
Gâteau au noix	Walnut cake
Gibier	Game

Girole	Chanterelle mushroom (*cantharellus cibarius*)
Langue de bœuf	Beef tongue
Lapin	Rabbit
Lièvre	Hare
Magret	Duck/goose filet
Marcassin	Young wild boar
Noix	Walnut
Œufs au vin	Eggs in wine sauce
Oie	Goose
Petit salé	Salt pork
Picard	Potato pâté
Pommes de terre	Potatoes
Potée	Boiled vegetables and meat in broth
Poulet en barbouille	Chicken in thick wine sauce
Pounti	Pork and prune loaf, served sliced
Pruneaux	Prunes
Rillettes	Shredded, salted meat pâté cooked in fat
Rognons	Kidneys
Sanciaux	Honey pancakes
Tourain blanchi	Garlic soup
Tourte	Savoury pie of pre-served duck, foie gras, potato and mushroom
Truffe	Truffle
Truffiat	Potatoes in pastry crust
Truite	Trout

Personal documents and travel

	Translation
Aéroport	Airport
Billet de train/d'avion	Train/plane ticket
Carte de crédit	Credit card
Douane	Customs
Gare	Railway station
Navette	Shuttle
Passeport	Passport
Portefeuille	Wallet
Valise	Suitcase
Voie	Platform

Clothing

	Translation
Coat	Manteau
Jumper/sweater	Pull
Raincoat	Imperméable
Shirt	Chemise
Shoes	Chaussures
Socks	Chaussettes
Stockings	Bas
Suit	Costume
Tights	Collant
Trousers	Pantalon

Commonly used words

	Translation
Au revoir	Goodbye
Bonjour	Hello/good morning
Comment	How
Excusez-moi	Excuse me
Merci	Thank you
Oui/non	Yes/no
Pardon/je suis désolé	I'm sorry
Pourquoi	Why
Quand	When
S'il vous plaît	Please

USEFUL PHRASES

Parlez-vouz anglais?
Do you speak English?

Je ne comprends pas
I don't understand

Parlez lentement
Talk slowly

Où est...?
Where is...?

À quelle heure part...?
When does the... leave?

À quelle heure arrive...?
When does the... arrive?

À quelle heure ouvre le musée?
When does the museum open?

À quelle heure sert-on le petit déjeuner?
When is breakfast served?

Ça coûte combien?
What does it cost?

Où se trouve la station essence la plus proche?
Where is the nearest petrol station?

Où puis-je échanger des chèques de voyage?
Where can I change traveller's cheques?

Est-ce qu'il y a un distributeur automatique près d'ici?
Is there an ATM nearby?

Où sont les toilettes?
Where are the toilets?

Acceptez-vous les cartes de crédit?
Do you accept credit cards?

Basic Information

BUSINESS HOURS

In provincial France, banks and post offices generally close on Mondays and between 12pm and 2pm. Post Offices are open from 9am to 12pm and 2pm to 5pm. If a holiday falls on a Tuesday or Thursday then the nearest Monday or Friday will be taken as well.

SHOPPING HOURS

Most of the larger shops are open Mondays to Saturdays from 9am to 7pm. Smaller, individual shops close from 12pm to 2pm. Food shops – grocers, wine merchants and bakeries – are generally open from 7am to 7pm or 7.30pm; some open on Sunday mornings. Many food shops close between noon and 2pm or 3pm and on Mondays.

INTERNET AND TELEPHONES

Internet access is widely available. E-mails are the cheapest way to communicate overseas. Many post offices and some tourist offices have public Internet terminals and cybercafés are quite widespread. For an updated list of cybercafés, go to www.world66.com/netcafeguide. In major cities, France Télécom has Internet kiosks on the street. Better hotels have business centres where you can access computers, and often hotel rooms have Wifi access.

European Emergency Call: ☎ **112**
French websites, especially those for tourists or offering commercial services, are often multilingual: just click on the little British or American flag on the home page.

EMERGENCY NUMBERS	
Police (Gendarme): ☎ 17	
Fire (Pompiers): ☎ 18	
Ambulance (SAMU): ☎ 15	

Most public phones in France use prepaid phone cards (*télécartes*) rather than coins. Some telephone booths accept credit cards (Visa, Mastercard/Eurocard). *Télécartes* (50 or 120 units) can be bought in post offices, branches of France Télécom, *bureaux de tabac* (cafés that sell cigarettes) and newsagents for national and international calls. You can receive calls at phone boxes with the blue bell sign; the phone won't ring, so watch the message screen.

NATIONAL CALLS

French numbers have ten digits; around Paris these begin with 01; 02 in NW France; 03 in NE France; 04 in SE France and Corsica; 05 in SW France.

INTERNATIONAL DIALLING CODES	
Australia	(00+) **61**
Eire	(00+) **353**
United Kingdom	(00+) **44**
Canada	(00+) **1**
New Zealand	(00+) **64**
United States	(00+) **1**

INTERNATIONAL CALLS

To call France from abroad, dial the country code (33) + nine-digit number (omit the initial 0). When calling abroad from France, dial 00, then dial the country code and area code.

International information (US/Canada): ☎ 00 33 12 11
International operator:
☎ 00 33 12 + country code
Local directory assistance: ☎ 12
Toll-free numbers:
In France these begin with 0800.

MOBILE/CELL PHONES

While in France, all visitors from other European countries should be able to use their mobile phone as normal. Visitors from other countries need to ensure before departure that their phone and service contract are compatible with the European system

(GSM). The three main mobile phone operators in France are SFR, Orange and Bouygues.

Orange www.orange.fr
Bouygues www.bouyguestelecom.fr
SFR www.sfr.fr

A number of service providers now offer the facility to use home-country units rather than paying roaming charges, but make a daily charge for this. If you plan to make regular use of a mobile phone while abroad, this is worth considering.

ELECTRICITY

The electric current is 220 volts. Circular two-pin plugs are the rule. Adapters and converters (for hairdryers, for example) should be bought before you leave home; they are on sale in most airports. If you have a rechargeable device (video camera, portable computer, battery recharger), read the instructions carefully or contact the manufacturer or shop. Sometimes these items only require a plug adapter, in other cases you must use a voltage converter as well.

DISCOUNTS

Significant discounts are available for senior citizens, students, youths under age 25, teachers and groups; for public transport, museums, monuments and for some leisure activities such as films (at certain times of day). Bring student or senior cards with you, as well as passport-size photos for discount travel cards.

The **International Student Travel Conference** (www.istc.org), global administrator of the International Student and Teacher Identity Cards, is an association of student travel organizations around the world. ISTC members collectively negotiate benefits with airlines, governments, and providers of other goods and services for the student and teacher community, both in their own countries and around the world. The non-profit association sells international ID cards for students,

youths under age 25 and teachers (who may get discounts on museum entry for example). The ISTC is also active in a network of international education and work exchange programmes. The coorporate headquarters address is Keizersgracht 174–176, 1016 DW Amsterdam, The Netherlands ℘31 20 421 28 00.

See Getting There: By Train for other discounts on transport. The coupon booklet *Pass Périg'Or* gives discounts on sights, hotels, restaurants and activities in the Dordogne. It is valid for 1 year and is free; you can obtain one at the *Comité Départemental de Tourisme* in the Dordogne or in most tourist information centres in the area.

POST/MAIL

Main post offices open Mondays to Fridays, 8am to 7pm, Saturdays, 8am to noon. Smaller branch post offices often close at lunchtime between noon and 2pm and in the afternoon at 4pm. Stamps are also available from newsagents and tobacconists. *Poste Restante* (general delivery) mail should be addressed as follows: Name, *Poste Restante*, *Poste Centrale*, post code of the *département* followed by town name, France. *The Michelin Guide France gives local postcodes*.

France	Letter	(20g) €0.66
UK	Letter	(20g) €0.83
North America	Letter	(20g) €0.98
Australia	Letter	(20g) €0.98
New Zealand	Letter	(20g) €0.98

MONEY
CURRENCY

There are no restrictions on the amount of currency visitors can take into France. However, visitors carrying a lot of cash are advised to complete a currency declaration form on arrival because there are restrictions on currency export.

The European currency unit, the **euro**, went into circulation as of 1 January

2002, and since 17 February 2002, euros are the only currency accepted as a means of payment. Notes in francs will be accepted by the Banque de France until 2012; coins in francs were accepted until 2005.

BANKS

For opening hours see Business Hours, above.

A passport is required as identification when cashing traveller's cheques in banks. Commission charges vary and hotels usually charge more than banks for cashing cheques.

One of the most economical ways to use your money in France is by using **ATM machines** to get cash directly from your bank account (with a debit card) or to use your credit card to get a cash advance. Be sure to remember your PIN number. You will always need it to use cash dispensers and to pay with your card in shops, restaurants and other venues. Code pads are numeric; use a telephone pad to translate a letter code into numbers. PIN numbers have four digits in France; enquire with the issuing company or bank if the code you usually use is longer.

Visa is the most widely accepted credit card, followed by Mastercard; other cards, credit and debit (Diners Club, Plus, Cirrus etc) are also accepted in some cash machines. American Express is more often accepted in premium establishments. Most places post signs indicating which card they accept; if you don't see such a sign and want to pay with a card, ask before ordering or making a selection. Cards are widely accepted in shops, hypermarkets, hotels and restaurants, at tollbooths and in petrol stations.

American Express 📞 01 47 77 70 00	
VISA 📞 0800 90 11 79	
MasterCard/Eurocard 📞 0800 901 387	
Diners Club 📞 0820820536	

A minimum charge is often required (between 7€ and 15€1).

Before you leave home, check with the bank that issued your card for emergency replacement procedures. Carry your card number and emergency phone numbers separate from your wallet and handbag; leave a copy of this information with someone you can easily reach.

If your card is lost or stolen while you are in France, call one of the 24-hour hotlines listed here:

You must report any loss or theft of credit cards or traveller's cheques to the local police who will issue you with a certificate (useful proof to show the issuing company).

PRICES

As a rule, the cost of staying in a hotel and eating in restaurants is significantly lower in the French regions than in Paris. Nevertheless, reserve a hotel room well in advance and take advantage of the choice of restaurants to make the most of your money.

Restaurants usually charge for meals in two ways: a *menu*, that is a fixed price menu with two or three courses, sometimes a small pitcher of wine, all for a stated price, or *à la carte*, the more expensive way, with each course ordered separately.

Cafés have very different prices, depending on where they are located. The price of a drink or a coffee is cheaper if you stand at the counter (*comptoir*) than if you sit down (*salle*) and sometimes it is even more expensive if you sit outdoors (*terrasse*).

PUBLIC HOLIDAYS

See the chart here for days when public services, museums and other monuments may be closed or may vary their hours of admission.

National museums and art galleries are closed on Tuesdays, and offer free admission the first Sunday of every month. Municipal museums

1 January	New Year's Day (*Jour de l'An*)
March/April	Easter Day and Easter Monday (*Pâques*)
1 May	May Day (*Fête du Travail*)
8 May	VE Day (*Fête de la Libération*)
Thurs 40 days after Easter	Ascension Day (*Ascension*)
7th Sun–Mon after Easter	Whit Sunday and Monday (*Pentecôte*)
14 July	France's National Day (*Fête de la Bastille*)
15 August	Assumption (*Assomption*)
1 November	All Saint's Day (*Toussaint*)
11 November	Armistice Day (*Fête de la Victoire*)
25 December	Christmas Day (*Noël*)

WHEN IT IS NOON IN FRANCE, IT IS	
11am	in London
7pm	in Perth
11am	in Dublin
9pm	in Sydney
6am	in New York
11pm	in Auckland
3am	in Los Angeles

are generally closed on Mondays. In addition to the usual school holidays at Christmas and in the spring and summer, there are long mid-term breaks (10 days to a fortnight) in February and November.

SMOKING

France has joined several other European countries and has banned smoking in all public places including in bars, cafés and restaurants. Many privately owned hotels no longer accept smokers. Ironically this has created a problem for non-smokers who want to sit outside on a terrace to enjoy the open air, where smoking is not prohibited.

TIME

France is 1hr ahead of Greenwich Mean Time (GMT). The country switches to daylight-saving time from the last Sunday in March to the last Sunday in October. The 24-hour clock is generally used.

VAT

There is a Value Added Tax in France (*TVA*) ranging from 5.5% to 19.6% on almost every purchase. VAT is included in the price displayed for the product. However, non-European visitors who spend more than €175 (figure subject to change) in any one participating store can get the VAT amount refunded. Usually you fill out a form at the store, showing your passport. Upon leaving the country, you submit all forms to customs for approval (they may want to see the goods, so if possible don't pack them in checked-in luggage).

The refund is usually paid directly into your bank or credit card account, or it can be sent by post. Big department stores that cater to tourists provide special services to help you; be sure to mention that you plan to seek a refund before you pay for goods (no refund is possible for tax on services). If you are visiting two or more countries within the European Union, you submit the forms only on departure from the last EU country. The refund is worthwhile for visitors who would like to buy clothing, furniture or other fairly expensive items, but remember, the minimum amount must be spent in a single shop (though not necessarily on the same day).

Turenne, Quercy
© Christian Guy / hemis.fr

The Region Today

The area's economy has long depended on its agricultural activities, as the scarcity of mineral wealth and raw materials prevented the development of major industrial centres. More recently, investment in a wider range of sectors, including high-tech industries and tourism, and the development of high-quality culinary and craft products have expanded the region's economic potential. The communication infrastructure has also improved, making the countryside less isolated. And of course, the region's trademark products continue to fly the region's flag, in particular Limoges porcelain, foie gras and truffles.

LIFESTYLE

There is a great emphasis on good food and wine, especially in the Dordogne and Quercy where the French paradox of long life and a rich diet is very apparent. Life begins earlier in the day than in the UK and the two-hour lunch break beginning at 12 noon is still common in rural areas. People may start the day earlier, but they also retire earlier in the evening – most small towns and villages become quiet after 9 or 10pm, with the notable exception of long summer evenings. There is a general sense of taking one's time, as in the expression *le quart d'heure périgourdin* (arriving somewhere fifteen minutes late).

ECONOMY
AGRICULTURE

Berry

Agriculture has long been the mainstay of the Berry economy, although improvements to the road network have enabled industrial development. Mechanisation and the use of fertilisers reaped rewards in **Champagne Berrichonne**, which has become France's second-largest grain-producing region. However, there are few processing plants to handle the harvest, and this impedes growth. In the Indre *département*, another handicap is the ageing of the farming population.

Limousin

As elsewhere, small farms have decreased in number over the years, to be replaced by larger, more modern operations. In the north, fields are planted with grain crops, whereas southern areas specialise in orchards, mostly apple.

Périgord-Quercy

Alongside the Lot-et-Garonne, the Dordogne *département* is the number one producer of **strawberries** in France, with almost 20 000t harvested annually. The protective plastic coverings visible in spring protect the young plants from bad weather and enable them to flower and grow in a controlled environment. The fruit ripens under these sheets before it is picked and packed off to the large markets of the Paris region and the north of France, where the Périgord strawberry is particularly appreciated. Although in decline, **walnuts** are another local speciality harvested in large quantity (5 000–7 000t per year). Several varieties are produced locally: Marbot walnuts ripen early and are often sold fresh; Grandjean are produced around Sarlat and Gourdon, accounting for most of the green walnuts; Corne is a small nut of good quality; while Franquette has increased in popularity in recent years. In 2002, these four varieties were awarded Appellation d'Origine Contrôlée (AOC) *Noix du Périgord* status.

Conditions in the Périgord and the Quercy, and southwest France as a whole, are favourable to the growing of **tobacco**, a hardy plant imported from America in the 16C and initially used for medicinal purposes (☞ *see BERGERAC: Musée du Tabac*).

The traditional dark tobacco that long gave French cigarettes their strong, distinctive flavour and aroma now grows side-by-side with lighter varieties such as Virginia tobacco, which have increased in popularity. Nowadays, there are around 3 000 planters in the region, mostly in family-run operations. The Dordogne is France's leading tobacco-producing *département* with 1 300 growers producing 15% of the country's crop. Perhaps the most evocative of all the region's products, however, is the rare and secretive fungus known as the **truffle**, which grows underground, at the base of a tree, where it is sniffed out by specially trained pigs or dogs. Exchanged at market for fabulous sums which seem incongruous with their lumpy, dusty appearance, these subterranean "black diamonds" are not as plentiful as in the past and are threatened by imports from countries such as Italy, Poland and China. Whereas a century ago hundreds of tonnes would have been harvested every year, today this figure has dwindled to around 4t. To encourage production, oak trees continue to be planted in areas where conditions favour growth of these *diamants noirs*.

STOCK-RAISING

Each region has developed its stock-raising in line with the natural fertility of its soil, with rich pastureland given over to the grazing of cattle, and more arid plateaux set aside for the rearing of sheep.

SHEEP

In bygone days sheep-rearing was the only way of earning a living when a lack of money and materials were major obstacles on the plains of the Berry.
The Berry breed is declining in numbers and is being replaced by the Charmois and the English Southdown. Much prized for their meat, they are now reared in sheepfolds and no longer roam the open pastureland. Goat herds are also increasing, particularly as a result of the rise in popularity of goat's cheese. The *causses* continue to play an important role in sheep-rearing: the plateau sheep or Gramat species is known as the spectacled breed, due to its white fleece and black rings around the eyes. These hardy, prolific animals bear fine wool,

Limousin cow
© S. Sauvignier / Michelin

but are especially prized for their meat, which contains very little fat.

LIMOUSIN CATTLE

Limousin beef-cattle, with their short withers (ridge between the shoulder blades) and distinctive russet hides, were already widely known in the 17C and 18C. Improved by culling and better feeding, the breed now produces some of the finest meat in the world. To supply market demands, Limousin farmers have turned to the production of young calves for white veal.
Natural features have transformed the Limousin into a leading area for the production and export of both the breed and its meat. Indigenous meadowland has been complemented by specially sown pastures where grass grows more profusely.

CRAFTS AND INDUSTRIES

The presence of metallic oxides, useful in the production of enamelware, resulted in the establishment of an **enamelling industry** in Limoges.
After three centuries of decline, the last 50 years have seen the re-establishment of Limoges' reputation, which is now as high as it was in the days of such master-enamellers as the Nardon Pénicauds, the Limosins and the Nouailhers.
The discovery of important deposits of kaolin near St-Yrieix at the end of the 18C was the catalyst for the development of the **china industry**. The first factories were scattered around the southern part of the Haute-Vienne, otherwise

the large amounts of wood needed for the kilns would have been liable to the payment of a toll upon entering the city of Limoges. By the end of the 19C, due to improvements in the production process, porcelain had become a major industry in the city. Another traditional manufacturing activity is centred around Aubusson, which is famous for its **tapestries**.

The **leather** industry and its many ancillary sectors developed thanks to abundant water supplies, tanning resins from the forests and hides obtained from large-scale stock-raising. In the early 19C, some 50 tanneries were established in the region. Today, shoes are made at Limoges and St-Amand-Montrond, and St-Junien is famous for its gloves. While this industry seems to be past its heyday, the forest holds promise for the development of the **paper industry**, which is on the upswing.

The area around Limoges has seen a steady increase in new **high-tech** businesses as a result of the development of national institutes (industrial ceramics, engineering, biotechnology, optical and microwave communication etc) and leading industries such as Ariane Espace and Airbus Industrie. Many smaller businesses have started up and experienced considerable international growth.

Prospection of the old Limousin granite massifs led to the discovery of the first uranium deposit near Crouzille in 1948, which became the largest processing centre in Western Europe. These mines are now closed. The very last **gold** mine of its kind in France, in Bourneix, closed in 2002; the economic environment had become unfavourable and viable reserves were exhausted.

FOLKLORE AND TRADITIONS

The regions of the Berry, Limousin and Dordogne are home to age-old rural civilisations. Traditional costumes and time-honoured crafts have been preserved in all three areas and are actively on display and promoted in the many local festivals (*see Calendar of Events*). Legends, superstitions and folk tales have continued to flourish alongside religious events in which the lives and legends of saints play an important role. In addition, alchemists, sorcerers and werewolves, and creatures such as toads, owls and wolves, to name but a few, have long fuelled the imagination of the region's inhabitants.

Local accents trace the boundaries of the different regions as clearly as a line drawn on a map. Regional patois (provincial dialects) are seldom heard nowadays, although interest in preserving the traditions of the *langue d'Oc* (Occitan language) is reviving.

LANTERNS OF THE DEAD

The earliest known reference to **lanterns of the dead** is found in a 12C text, *De Miraculis*, by Pierre le Vénérable, abbot of Cluny. The legend recounts how a young novice from the Abbaye de Charlieu (Loire) received a visit from his uncle Achard, the monastery's former prior, who had been dead for some years. The apparition led the youth to the cemetery, where wrapped in concentric circles of glowing light, a group of holy persons had gathered. "In the middle of the cemetery, a stone edifice rose up; on the top, there was a small compartment for holding a lamp which, nightly and in honour of the faithful resting there, lights this sacred place. Steps lead to a platform where two or three people can stand or sit down."

Lantern of the Dead, Feletin

© R. Corbel / Michelin

This definition is similar to one given in a study written in 1882 by a local abbot and scholar. Mostly built between the 11C and the 13C, in cemeteries near Romanesque churches, many of the lanterns were later destroyed, moved or converted to other uses.

These structures, dubbed lanterns of the dead in the 19C, seem to be the expression of ancient ideals. Their form, with a height equal to six or eight times their diameter, complies with ancient Roman canon. The vertical design is symbolic of prestige, but also denotes security, and indeed no reference to mourning or suffering seems apparent in the decoration or the exultant skyward movement. People have long believed that the spirits of those who have passed away seek out the light which death has extinguished for them. Although the early Christian church condemned the practice of lighting candles on tombs, the symbol of the eternal flame soon came to be totally assimilated.

THE LIMOUSIN OSTENSIONS

Every seven years the **Haute-Vienne** and **Creuse** *départements* honour their saints: St Martial, the apostle of the Limousin; St Valérie; the Good St Eligius, founder of the monastery at Solignac; St Stephen of Muret; hermits who lived in the forests of the Limousin and Marche; and St Junien, St Victurnien and St Leonard, founders of monasteries scattered in the region's valleys.

The *ostensions*, or solemn exhibitions of relics to the faithful, date back to the 10C. One of the earliest of these festivals was held at Limoges when a terrible epidemic of ergotism, also known as St Anthony's fire, was raging. To combat the malady, the relics of St Martial were brought out. A visitation – whether in the form of a plague or an illustrious personage – became an occasion for holding these ceremonies, which were later repeated at regular intervals.

Each town has a traditional ceremony of its own, hosting religious festivals also based on local folklore. The blessing of the banner, which is solemnly hoisted to the belfry pinnacle, marks the opening of the *ostension*. Once the festival has been opened on the Sunday after Easter, the relics are presented to the faithful for veneration in their shrines or reliquaries which, in some cases, are masterpieces of the gold and silversmith's art. Colourful processions pass through bunting and flower-decked streets in towns and villages, accompanied by fanfares, drums and banners, and escorted by guards of honour, representatives of different craft guilds, and other groups in rich finery. Neighbouring parishes often participate in these events; for example, 50 parishes come together in Le Dorat for the closing ceremonies. The next ceremony will be held in 2016.

THE FÉLIBRÉE

In July every year a different town in the Périgord hosts the Félibrée, a meeting of a society of poets and writers set up in the late 19C with the aim of preserving the **Occitan language**. The windows and doors of the chosen town are decorated with thousands of multicoloured paper flowers, and trees and shrubs are illuminated to form triumphal arches. The people of the Périgord flock from all corners of the *département* decked out in traditional costume: lace headdresses, embroidered shawls and long skirts for the women, and wide-brimmed black felt hats, full white shirts and waistcoats for the men.

The queen of the Félibrée, surrounded by a member of the Félibrige society committee and the guardians of local traditions, receives the keys of the town and makes a speech in the local dialect. The assembled gathering files off in procession to Mass, accompanied by the sound of hurdy-gurdies, before sitting down to a sumptuous feast. Traditionally, the meal begins with *le tourain*, a garlic soup typical of the southwest, which is served in dishes made especially for the occasion bearing the year and the name of the host town. When the soup bowls are nearly empty, *chabrol* is called for; this means pouring red wine into the rest of the soup and drinking it directly from the bowl.

History

PREHISTORY IN THE DORDOGNE

The Quarternary era is relatively young, since it began only about two million years ago. Nevertheless, it is during this short period that human evolution has taken place. There is no definitive evidence of life having existed on Earth in the Pre-Cambrian Age; reptiles, fish and tail-less amphibians appeared in the course of the Primary Era, mammals and birds during the Secondary Era. Primates, the most ancient ancestors of mankind, appeared at the end of the Tertiary Era and were followed in the Quarternary Era by ever more advanced species.

The slow pace of human progress during the Palaeolithic Age is quite extraordinary: it took people nearly two million years to learn to polish stone. Yet, the few thousand years that followed were witness to the development of brilliant civilisations in the Middle and Far East which culminated in the construction of the pyramids in Egypt. A few centuries later bronze was discovered, followed, in approximately 900BCE, by the discovery of iron.

RESEARCHERS

The study of prehistory is a science essentially French in origin which began in the early 19C. Until that time only the occasional reference by a Greek or Latin author, a study by the Italian scholar Mercati (1541–93) in the 16C and a paper by Jussieu, published in 1723, gave any hint of the existence of ancient civilisations. In spite of the scepticism of most learned men – led by Cuvier (1769–1832) – researchers pursued their investigations in the Périgord, Lozère and the Somme valley. **Boucher de Perthes'** (1788–1868) discoveries at St-Acheul and Abbeville were the catalyst for an important series of studies, but it was **Paul Tournal** who in 1831 first used the term **prehistory** to describe the evidence of ancient human culture that was emerging at the time from certain caves in France. Among the pioneers who laid modern archaeology's foundations are:

Édouard Lartet (1801–71), who undertook many excavations in the Vézère valley and established a preliminary classification for the various eras of prehistory; **Gabriel de Mortillet** (1821–98), who undertook and completed the classification, adding the names Chellean, Mousterian, Aurignacian, Solutrean and Magdalenian to correspond with the places where the most prolific or most characteristic deposits were found: **Chelles** in the Seine-et-Marne, **Le Moustier** in the Dordogne, **Aurignac** in the Haute-Garonne, **Solutré** in the Saône-et-Loire and **La Madeleine** in the Dordogne.

Excavations can only be performed by specialists with knowledge of the geological stratigraphy, the physics and chemistry of rock formations, the nature and form of stones and gravels, and the ability to analyse fossilised wood, coal and bone fragments.

In rock shelters and the entrances to caves, prehistorians have discovered hearths (accumulations of charcoal and kitchen debris), tools, weapons, stone and bone furnishings and bone fragments. These vestiges are collected in layers; during excavations each of these different layers is uncovered and the civilisation or period is reconstructed.

PREHISTORY IN THE PÉRIGORD

The Périgord has been inhabited since Palaeolithic times. The names **Tayacian** (Les Eyzies-de-Tayac), **Micoquean** (La Micoque), **Mousterian** (Le Moustier), **Perigordian** and **Magdalenian** (La Madeleine) are evidence of the importance of these prehistoric sites. Nearly 200 deposits have been discovered, of which more than half are in the **Vézère valley** near Les Eyzies-de-Tayac.

THE PALAEOLITHIC AGE

Our most distant ancestors (some three million years ago) were the early hominids (ie the family of man) of East Africa, who, unlike their instinctive predecessors, were rational thinkers. They evolved into *Homo habilis*, followed by *Homo erectus*, characterised by his upright walking (Java man or *Pithecan-*

thropus erectus, discovered by E Dubois in 1891, with a cranial capacity midway between that of the most highly developed ape and the least developed man), and Peking man or *Sinanthropus* (identified by D Black in 1927), who made rough-hewn tools, tools for chopping from split pebbles and heavy bifaced implements.

Neanderthal man appeared c 150 000 years ago. In 1856, in the Düssel valley (also known as the Neander valley, east of Düsseldorf, Germany) portions of a human skeleton were discovered with the following characteristics: a cranial capacity of approximately $1500cm^3/91.5in^3$, an elongated cranium (dolichocephalus), a sharply receding forehead, prominently developed jawbones and a small stature (1.60m/5ft 3in). Skeletons with similar characteristics were found in France at La Chapelle-aux-Saints (Corrèze) in 1908, at **Le Moustier** (Dordogne) in 1909, at **La Ferrassie** (Dordogne) in 1909 and 1911 and at **Le Régourdou** (Dordogne) in 1957. The Neanderthal group mysteriously disappeared 35 000 years ago; at the same time, the first burial sites started to appear.

Homo sapiens began flourishing in France about 40 000 years ago. Their essential characteristics – perfect upright stance, raised forehead, slightly projecting eyebrows – showed them to be highly developed and comparable to people today (*sapiens* means intelligent). Several races have been traced as belonging to this same family. Cro-Magnon individuals must have been quite similar in appearance to the present *Homo sapiens*.

Cro-Magnon man (named after skeletons found in the rock shelters of Cro-Magnon in the **Dordogne** and **Solutré** in the Saône-et-Loire) was tall – about 1.80m/5ft 11in – with long, robust limbs denoting considerable muscular strength; the skull was dolichocephalic in shape. These people lived in the Upper Palaeolithic to the Neolithic Ages.

Chancelade man (from a skeleton discovered in 1889 at **Chancelade**, near Périgueux) appeared in the Magdalenian Period; these people had a large cranium of dolichocephalic form, a long, wide face, pronounced cheekbones and a height of not more than 1.55m/5ft 1in.

CULTURE AND ART IN THE PALAEOLITHIC AGE

The oldest skeletons belonging to Neanderthals, found in the **Périgord** and the **Quercy**, date from the Mousterian Culture (Middle Palaeolithic).

Later, during the Ice Age, tribes are thought to have come from Eastern Europe and settled in the **Vézère** and **Beune** valleys. Bordering these valleys were cliffs and slopes pitted with caves and shelters offering many natural advantages that flat landscapes were unable to provide: protection from the cold, nearby springs and rivers abundant in fish, and narrow ravines used for intercepting game as it passed through. There were, however, several dwelling huts found in the **Isle valley**, upstream from Périgueux.

The Palaeolithic Age (*palaeos* means ancient, *lithos* means stones) covers the period in which people knew only how to chip flints. An intermediate age, the Mesolithic (*mesos* means middle), separates it from the Neolithic Age (*neos* means new), when they learnt to polish stone. The first group were predators (hunting, fishing and gathering), whereas the last group were farmers and breeders. Skill in flint-knapping evolved very slowly and, therefore, the Palaeolithic Age is subdivided into three periods: the Lower, Middle and Upper.

LOWER PALAEOLITHIC

This began about two million years ago. People living in this period in the Périgord knew how to use fire and hunted big game. The earth suffered three successive ice ages known as the Günz, the Mindel and the Riss (after the tributary valleys of the Danube where they were studied). Between each ice age, France and Britain had a tropical climate.

Flint-knapping began with a cut made by striking two stones violently one against the other, or by striking one against a rock which served as an anvil.

MIDDLE PALAEOLITHIC

This began about 150 000 years ago. Neanderthal society brought with it better-finished and more specialised tools. Mousterian industry used both bifaced implements and flakes. New methods enabled triangular points to be produced, also scrapers, probably used for working skins, and flints adapted to take a wooden handle and serve as hunting clubs (bear skulls pierced by such weapons have been found).

During the Mousterian Culture some cave entrances were used as dwellings; others were used as burial places. More sophisticated weapons were developed and used to hunt big game, and animal skins provided protection from the cold.

UPPER PALAEOLITHIC

This began about 35 000 years ago. Cro-Magnon and Chancelade individuals replaced Neanderthals. During this period the production of tools was constantly improving and living conditions were made easier as new hunting methods were perfected, resulting in more leisure time and, therefore, artistic expression.

Perigordian and Aurignacian cultures

These two cultures, following the Mousterian and Levalloisian cultures and preceding the Solutrean Culture, were contemporary but parallel.

Venus of Laussel
© World Illustrated / Photoshot

The **Aurignacian** stone industry produced large blades, stone flake tools, burins (a sort of chisel) and points made from antlers (early ones have a split base). Cave decoration, applied to blocks of limestone (**La Ferrassie** near Le Bugue) and in caves, featured engraved, painted or partially carved animals or female figures.

At the end of the Perigordian Culture, Gravettians made burins and points; these people decorated their shelter walls (**Le Poisson**, Laussel), and carved Venus figurines (small female statues with exaggerated curves evoking fertility). Burial places contained ornaments and jewellery, such as shells and bead necklaces. The first examples of wall decoration appear as hands placed flat against the rock and outlined in black or red; examples of these can be found at **Le Pech-Merle**, for example. By the end of this period, people had truly discovered their artistic nature, as the sculptures at the Abri du Poisson (fish shelter) and the engravings and paintings found at **Font-de-Gaume** and **Lascaux** show. The **Grève** cave with its engraved bison in turned profile dates from between the late Perigordian and early Solutrean periods.

Solutrean Culture

This period, very well represented in the Dordogne, is distinguished by exquisite low-relief sculptures carved out of limestone slabs, such as the **Devil's Oven**, found near Bourdeilles and now exhibited in the National Museum of Prehistory at Les Eyzies.

The stone-cutting industry also underwent a brilliant period during the Solutrean Culture. Flint blades, following a method of splitting under pressure, became much slimmer, forming blades in the shape of laurel or willow leaves. Shouldered points were used as weapons after being fitted with wooden shafts. It was during this period that needles with eyes appeared.

Magdalenian Culture

Bone and ivory craftsmanship reached its peak during this time. The existence of herds of reindeer, which is accounted for by the very cold climate that occurred at the end of the Würm Glacial Period, encouraged carvers to work with bone and antler, producing perforated, sometimes engraved batons, which were used as armatures for points and harpoon heads; projectile tips used as spears; and decorated flattened points. This is also the period when cave wall art, depicting essentially animal subjects, reached its peak. To protect themselves from the cold, people of the Magdalenian culture lived in the shelter of overhanging rocks or at the mouths of caves; inside, these caves were underground sanctuaries, at times quite some distance from the cave entrance. They decorated the shelter and sanctuary walls (as at the **Cap-Blanc** shelter) with low-relief carving, engraving and painting. Due to the juxtaposition or superimposition of the figures drawn and inevitable deterioration, the study of these paintings is not easy. Only a few Magdalenian caves are open to the public due to the difficulty in preserving the art.

After **Lascaux**, numerous cave-sanctuaries appeared during the Middle and Upper Magdalenian periods. Portable art, manifested through smaller objects, is another form of expression developed in the shelters. Animals are represented in increasingly realistic details in terms of their anatomy and movements and in the rendering of their physical aspects: coat, tail, eyes, ears, hoofs, antlers and tusks.

Nonetheless, the style is more ornamental. The perspective of the animals in profile, non-existent in the beginning, was pursued and even distorted during Lascaux's last period. New graphic techniques appeared: stencilling, areas left intentionally without colour, polychrome techniques and others. Towards the end of the Magdalenian culture, art became more schematic and human figures made their appearance. Animal art then disappeared from France and Spain, as the herds of reindeer migrated northwards in search of lichen, which was disappearing in the region at the end of the Würm Glacial Period.

GAULS AND ROMANS

BCE

The Périgord is inhabited by the **Petrocorii** and the Quercy by the **Caduici**.

6–5C The **Bituriges Cubi** people settle in the Berry.

59–51 Conquest of Gaul by **Caesar**. The last Gaulish resistance to Caesar is at **Uxellodunum**, which historians believe to be in the Quercy.

16 **Emperor Augustus** creates the province of Aquitaine. The capital of the land of the Petrocorii is **Vesunna** (Périgueux) and of that of the Caduici, **Divona Cadurcorum** (Cahors).

AD

1–3C **Pax Romana**. For three centuries towns develop and several public buildings are built. In the countryside around the towns new crops are introduced by the Romans: walnut, chestnut and cherry trees and, above all, vineyards.

late 3C The Berry and the Limousin are incorporated into primitive **Aquitaine**; Bourges is its capital.

235–284 **Alemanni and Franks** invade the region. In 276, several towns are razed. Vesunna defends itself behind fortifications hastily built from the stones taken from Roman public buildings.

313 **Edict of Milan**. Emperor Constantine grants Christians the freedom of worship.

476 End of the Roman Empire.

MEROVINGIANS AND CAROLINGIANS

486–507 **Clovis**, king of the Franks, conquers Gaul and Aquitaine.

8C The Quercy and Périgord become counties under the kingdom of Aquitaine.

800 **Charlemagne** is crowned Emperor of the West in Rome.

Charles V and du Guesclin

in 1253

at the start of the Hundred Years War

after the treaty of Brétigny (1360)

after Charles V and du Guesclin's reconquests (1380)

9C The Dordogne and Isle valleys and Périgueux are laid waste by **Vikings**.

10C **The four baronies** of the Périgord – Mareuil, Bourdeilles, Beynac and Biron – are formed as well as the overlordships of Ans, Auberoche, Gurson etc. The county of Périgord passes to the house of Talleyrand. Powerful families rule the Quercy.

c 950 Beginning of the **pilgrimage** to St James' shrine in Santiago de Compostela, Spain.

12C Many **influential abbeys** are founded in the region (Noirlac, Chancelade, Cadouin, Rocama-dour etc). Construction of the cathedral in Bourges begins.

WARS BETWEEN ENGLAND AND FRANCE

1152 **Eleanor of Aquitaine** marries **Henry Plantagenet**, bringing as her dowry all of southwest France. In 1154 Henry Plantagenet becomes King Henry II.

1190 The Quercy is ceded to the English with the exception of the abbeys of Figeac and Souillac.

1191 **Richard the Lionheart** dies at Châlus.

early 13C Albigensian Crusade. Simon de Montfort raids the Quercy and Périgord.

1234 **Louis IX** buys the Berry from the Count of Champagne.

1259 By the **Treaty of Paris**, St Louis cedes the Périgord and the Quercy to the English. The treaty puts an end to the constant fighting and enables the people of the region to live in peace until the Hundred Years War.

1273 Construction is started on the cathedral in Limoges.

1307 Philip IV of France condemns the order of the **Knights Templar**.

1324 **Bourges Cathedral** is consecrated.

1337 French king **Philip VI** declares the English-held Duchy of Guyenne confiscated, effectively marking the start of the **Hundred Years War**.

1340 **Edward III** of England proclaims himself king of France.

1346 Edward III defeats the French at the **Battle of Crécy**.

1355–1370 Edward the Black Prince begins his campaign, ravaging the Berry and Limousin. Edward defeats and captures **King Jean II** (Battle of Poitiers, 1356).

1360 The **Treaty of Brétigny** cedes Aquitaine to the English as part of the ransom for Jean II's liberty.

1369 The Quercy and Périgord are won back by the king of France (Charles V). **Du Guesclin**, constable of France, is active in the liberation of the Périgord.

During the period that follows, the lords of the north of Périgord owe allegiance to the king of France, while the lords of the south of Périgord serve the English, although some swap sides in unabashed support of their own interests.

1415   **Henry V** defeats the French at Azincourt (**Agincourt**).

1420   Henry V of England is recog-nised as king of France under the **Treaty of Troyes**. France is divided into three parts con-trolled by Henry V (Normandy, Guyenne, Paris area); **Philip the Good**, duke of Burgundy (other parts of the area in and around Paris, Burgundy); and the Dauphin (Central France and the Languedoc).

1444   **Truce of Tours** (Charles VII and Henry V); the English retain Maine, the Bordelais region, parts of Artois and Picardy and most of Normandy.

1449   The French begin a campaign in Guyenne, but the people of the region are hostile to the French from years of loyalty to the English crown; Bergerac falls in 1450, Bordeaux in 1451.

1453   Defeat of **John Talbot**, earl of Shrewsbury, at the **Battle of Castillon**, which marks the end of the Hundred Years War.

1463   University of Bourges founded.

2nd half of 15C–early 16C
Towns and castles are rebuilt during this period of peace.

1558   **England loses Calais** to the French.

WARS OF RELIGION

1562   **Massacre of Protestants** at Cahors.

1572   **St Bartholomew's Day** massacre (20 000 Huguenots die).

1570–90   War is declared; Bergerac and Ste-Foy-la-Grande are **Huguenot** bastions whereas

Hidden Agenda?

Eleanor's eagerness to go to the Crusades may have been coloured by the fact that her uncle Raymond of Poitiers was already in the Holy Land. Some chroniclers maintain that they had an affair and this led to her estrangement from Louis.

Périgueux and Cahors support the **Catholic League. Vivans**, the Huguenot leader, scours the Périgord; Périgueux falls in 1575 and Domme in 1588.

1580   Cahors is taken by Henri de Navarre (Henri IV).

1589   **Henri IV** accedes to the throne, converts to Catholicism in 1593 and is crowned in 1594.
Under Henri IV, the County of Périgord becomes part of the royal domain.

1594–95   Croquant peasant revolt.

1598   **Edict of Nantes** grants Huguenots freedom of worship and places of refuge.

1607   Viscounty of Limoges comes under the French crown.

1610   Henri IV is assassinated; **Louis XIII**'s reign begins.

1637   Croquants' revolt against Louis XIII's government and Richelieu's taxes.

1643–1715   Louis XIV's reign.

1685   Revocation of the Edict of Nantes. Huguenots flee France.

18C TO 20C

1743–57   Tourny, administrator of the Treasury of Bordeaux, instigates a number of town planning projects in the southwest (Allées de Tourny in Périgueux).

1763   **Peace of Paris** ends the French and Indian War (1754–63), marking the end of France's colonial empire in America.

1768   Kaolin is discovered in St-Yrieix-la-Perche.

1789	**Storming of the Bastille** and the beginning of the French Revolution.
1790	Creation of the Dordogne *département*.
1792	Proclamation of the **French Republic** after the Battle of Valmy.
1812–14	Périgord is a Bonapartist fief; several of Napoleon's generals and marshals (Murat, Fournier-Sarlovèze, Daumesnil) are natives of the region.
1868	**Phylloxera** destroys the vineyards of Cahors and Bergerac, causing a rural exodus. Discovery of Cro-Magnon cave skeletons.
20C	Marked by a continued rural exodus, the area essentially thrives on agriculture and tourism.
1914–18	**World War I**.
1940	Discovery of Lascaux Cave.
1942–44	The French Resistance movement intensifies in the Limousin during **World War II**.
1944	Massacres at Tulle and Oradour-sur-Glane.
1960–69	André Malraux restores Sarlat, among other historical areas, and opens the first **Maison de la Culture** in Bourges, as Minister of Culture.
1964	Limousin *région* is created.
1977	Le Printemps de Bourges music festival holds its first concerts.
1979	Fifteen prehistoric sites in the Vézère Valley are registered as World Heritage with UNESCO.
1989	The **Parc Naturel Régional de la Brenne** is established.
1994	**Channel Tunnel** links England and France's rail networks.
1999–2002	The **euro** replaces the franc.
2005	The European Constitution is rejected in referendum of the French electorate.
2007–2011	The global financial crisis contributes to a decline in economic activity.
2010	The **International Prehistory Centre** in Les Eyzies opens.
2012	**François Hollande** is elected President.
2013	The **A 89 autoroute** from Bordeaux to Lyon, also called the *Transeuropéenne*, is completed.

KEY HISTORICAL FIGURES

Over the centuries, three key figures have left an indelible mark on the region, sparking the imagination and bringing to life the history of this part of France.

ELEANOR OF AQUITAINE

In 1122, a daughter was born to William X, duke of Aquitaine and count of Poitiers, who was to become heiress to one of the largest domains in France (more extensive than the king's). In 1137, Eleanor wed **Louis VII**, who succeeded his father to the throne just one month later. The young queen of France was beautiful and influential, though some historians have criticised her juvenile frivolity. Eleanor accompanied her husband on the Second Crusade, where her capricious enthusiasm fired Louis' jealousy, and the marriage was annulled in 1152, shortly after their return to France. Thanks to feudal customs, she regained possession of Aquitaine, and two months later married Henry Plantagenet, count of Anjou and duke of Normandy. When her second husband became king of England (1154) as **Henry II**, England, Normandy and the west of France were united under one crown. In addition to her two daughters from her first marriage, Eleanor bore eight more children, including **Richard the Lionheart**, John Lackland, Eleanor (who married the king of Castille) and Joan (who married the king of Sicily and later the count of Toulouse). No wonder she is known as the grandmother of Europe! Eleanor was both a political and cultural force to be reckoned with. She turned the court at Poitiers into a centre of courtly life and manners, celebrated by the troubadours; she also promoted the

Wedding of Eleanor of Aquitaine and Louis VII in 1137

historical legends of Brittany, romantic songs in the Celtic tradition. She supported her sons in a failed revolt against their father; afterwards, Henry had her guarded under close watch in England until his death. Released at last, she became an invaluable advisor to her son Richard, keeping the kingdom intact and administering it during his long absences. She was 80 years old when she set off across the Pyrenees to fetch her granddaughter Blanche of Castille for marriage to the son of the French king, hoping thus to cement peace between the Plantagenets and the Capetians. Her influence was felt even after her death: following the loss of Normandy (1204), her ancestral lands, and not the old Norman territories, remained loyal to England. She died in 1204 in the monastery at Fontevrault where she had retired. The nuns of Fontevrault described this exceptional queen as "beautiful and just, imposing and modest, humble and elegant".

JEAN DE BERRY

In the 14C, when its population was about 350 000, the Berry was plunged into the turmoil of the Hundred Years War following the Black Prince's raids. The region had strategic importance as a potential base for the conquest of Poitou and Aquitaine. King **John the Good** elevated the Berry and Auvergne to the rank of duchies, and granted them to his third son; thus, in 1360, Jean de Berry came into control of at least one-third of the territory of France.

After a period of captivity in England, the young duke was in urgent need of funds. He taxed his lands heavily for the defence of the kingdom and spent lavishly on the arts. His military career was marked by a triumphant march on Limoges, which brought the local bourgeoisie and clergy into the Valois camp, but also led to terrible English reprisals. Pursuing his campaign with **Du Guesclin** and the duke of Anjou, he took control of Poitou in 1373.

Meanwhile, his brother, by then King Charles V, passed away, and his nephew, the young **Charles VI**, took the throne. As a member of the regency council from 1380–88, Berry shared royal powers while Charles was too young to rule. He thus gained control of the Languedoc. In conflict with the royal family, Berry also struggled against the peasants' revolt (1381–84), a consequence of his oppressive fiscal policies and opulent lifestyle. The king, although beset by fits of insanity, announced his determination to rule alone, but soon earned the surname Charles the Mad. Still bent on power, and always ready to take advantage, Berry handled negotiations between the conflicting factions of John the Fearless, duke of Burgundy, and his own brother Louis, duke of Orléans, and even promised the English to deliver the province of Guyenne (1412). The end result was the siege of Bourges by royal troops. Berry capitulated and died four years later at the age of 76. Throughout his life, he showered his fortune on the arts and artists, building palaces and fine residences in his cities, so much so that at his death there was not enough in the coffers to pay for his funeral. History has recognised his importance as a supporter of the arts, and the treasures he commissioned remain as his monument: paintings, tapestries, jewellery and illuminated manuscripts, including the world-famous *Très Riches Heures du Duc de Berry*.

JACQUES CŒUR

Born the son of a furrier in Bourges, Cœur's life is exemplary of the spirit of enterprise and the rise of the merchant classes in the period of prosperity that followed the Hundred Years War. His generation was perhaps the first in Europe to aspire to honours, noble rank, wealth and property, without having been born into the aristocracy. If he may be said to have represented the rise of the merchant class, his downfall signifies how difficult it was for such social changes to take root.

Jacques Cœur before Charles VII from a copy of 15C miniature, Chroniques de Monstrelet

©World Illustrated/Photoshot

Gifted with an uncanny flair for business opportunities, Cœur gained the confidence of Charles VII, and became his argentier, managing the royal funds like a modern-day investment tycoon. His power and fortune grew simultaneously as he became a member of the king's council, the tax collector for the Languedoc and the inspector general of the salt tax. He diversified his affairs, stocking all kinds of merchandise from around the world – cloth, spices, jewels, armour, wheat and salt – in his vast stores in Tours. He had a large staff of salesmen, shipowners (he himself owned seven ships) and negotiators, as well as 40 manor houses and a beautiful palace in Bourges, one of the finest examples of lay Gothic architecture in Europe. Cœur set up individual companies for each branch of trade and sought political support from all quarters. His prosperity was held up by a delicately spun web of bills of exchange, credit and fiscal receipts issued by the king. A creditor for many of France's aristocrats and the king himself, Cœur was the object of intense jealousy.

His rocketing career plummeted on 31 July 1451, when he was arrested on trumped-up charges of poisoning Agnès Sorel, the king's mistress. His enemies came forth with more accusations: currency fraud, trading arms with the infidels, returning a Christian slave to a Muslim master, running ships with slave crews, and abuse of power. Found guilty on all counts except the poisoning, he was banished, ordered to relinquish all of his goods and property and pay an impossibly high fine for his release.

Meanwhile, French troops, paid with the confiscated funds, won the final battle of the Hundred Years War. Cœur, the financial adventurer and proto-bourgeois, escaped and fled to Italy before setting out on a Papal naval expedition against the Turks. He is believed to have died on the Aegean island of Chios in 1456. The following year, in an attempt to make amends for his father's treatment of Cœur, King Louis XI returned his unsold property to Cœur's sons and revived some of his old companies.

Art and Architecture

ARCHITECTURE

The Vézère Valley, the prehistoric sites of Les Eyzies and the caves of the Quercy contain some of the finest known examples of prehistoric art (see HISTORY), the earliest manifestations of art in France. Since that time, art and architecture have evolved in close connection with the region's turbulent history. The significant periods of construction took place in periods of peace: the Pax Romana, the 12C (many monasteries date from this century) and the period spanning the end of the 14C to the 16C. During times of war – the Hundred Years War, the Wars of Religion – the main concern of the local population was its protection, hence the fortification of towns, castles and churches and the building of new towns called *bastides*.

GALLO-ROMAN ARCHITECTURE

Only a few buildings constructed by the Romans have withstood the test of time, although vestiges of the Gaulish period do still survive.

Excavations undertaken at **Drevant**, near St-Amand-Montrond, have established that a large Gallo-Roman centre developed on the site of a small Gaulish market town; a theatre, baths and a vast walled area which may have been a Gallo-Roman forum or temple have been uncovered here.

In **Limoges**, an amphitheatre was built on the outskirts of the town; it was razed to the ground in the 16C and its ruins are now under the Jardin d'Orsay.

In Périgueux, traces have been discovered of the ancient **Vesunna**, capital of the Petrocorii. The finds include the Vesunna tower, the temple of the goddess *Vésone*, the arena and the perimeter wall. The Puy d'Issolud near Vayrac is believed to be the site of the **Uxello-**

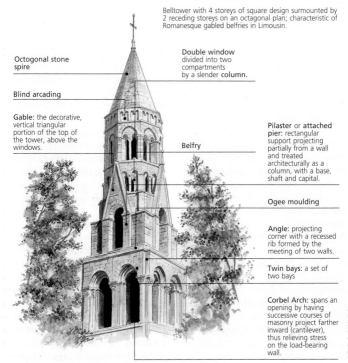

ST-LÉONARD-DE-NOBLAT – Church belltower (12C)

Belltower with 4 storeys of square design surmounted by 2 receding storeys on an octagonal plan; characteristic of Romanesque gabled belfries in Limousin.

Octogonal stone spire

Blind arcading

Gable: the decorative, vertical triangular portion of the top of the tower, above the windows.

Belfry

Double window divided into two compartments by a slender column.

Pilaster or attached pier: rectangular support projecting partially from a wall and treated architecturally as a column, with a base, shaft and capital.

Ogee moulding

Angle: projecting corner with a recessed rib formed by the meeting of two walls.

Twin bays: a set of two bays

Corbel Arch: spans an opening by having successive courses of masonry project farther inward (cantilever), thus relieving stress on the load-bearing wall.

© R. Corbel / Michelin

BEAULIEU-SUR-DORDOGNE – East end (chevet) of St-Pierre (early 12C)

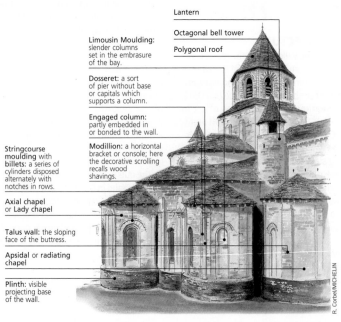

Lantern

Octagonal bell tower

Polygonal roof

Limousin Moulding: slender columns set in the embrasure of the bay.

Dosseret: a sort of pier without base or capitals which supports a column.

Engaged column: partly embedded in or bonded to the wall.

Stringcourse moulding with billets: a series of cylinders disposed alternately with notches in rows.

Modillion: a horizontal bracket or console; here the decorative scrolling recalls wood shavings.

Axial chapel or Lady chapel

Talus wall: the sloping face of the buttress.

Apsidal or radiating chapel

Plinth: visible projecting base of the wall.

R. Corbel/MICHELIN

dunum encampment – this was the last bastion of the Gauls in their resistance against the all-conquering Caesar. At Luzech, traces of the Imperial encampment which commanded a bend in the River Lot have been unearthed; the ruins of the Murcens oppidum have also been discovered near the Vers valley.

ROMANESQUE ART AND RELIGIOUS ARCHITECTURE

In the Berry

Though characteristics of the Poitou School are widely represented across the region, most Romanesque churches in the Berry have a precise plan with certain features peculiar to the area: the chancel generally consists of two bays flanked by aisles which communicate with the choir through arches resting on columns adorned with historiated capitals; the apse is semicircular; the transept has a dome on squinches above the crossing and barrel vaulting above the arms; the nave is wider than the transept crossing and communicates with the arms of the transept by narrow passages known as **Berrichon** passages.

The abbey churches are based on the Benedictine design, for the Order of St-Benedict spread throughout Berry and built abbeys at **Fontgombault**, **Chezal-Benoît** and at **Châteaumeillant**, where the church of St-Genès has an unusual arrangement of the chevet with six parallel apsidal chapels.

Noirlac was created by the Cistercians, **Plaimpied** and **Puy-Ferrand** by the Augustinian Canons Regular. One church in the Bourges diocese is designed quite differently: the basilica of **Neuvy-St-Sépulcre** was built in the form of a rotunda and was inspired by the Church of the Holy Sepulchre in Jerusalem.

The Limousin School

The Limousin School combines many of the characteristics of its neighbours: the Auvergne School, whose chief feature is the semi-barrel vaulting of the aisles or the galleries above the nave (**Beaulieu-sur-Dordogne**); the Poitou School, whose influence can be seen in the collegiate church of **St-Pierre in Le Dorat** – a blind nave with broken-barrel vaulting and aisles with groined

CARSAC-AILLAC – Vaulting in Saint-Caprais (12-16C)

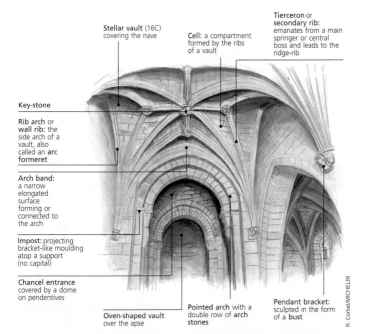

Stellar vault (16C) covering the nave

Cell: a compartment formed by the ribs of a vault

Tierceron or **secondary rib:** emanates from a main springer or central boss and leads to the ridge-rib

Key-stone

Rib arch or **wall rib:** the side arch of a vault, also called an **arc formeret**

Arch band: a narrow elongated surface forming or connected to the arch

Impost: projecting bracket-like moulding atop a support (no capital)

Chancel entrance covered by a dome on pendentives

Oven-shaped vault over the apse

Pointed arch with a double row of **arch stones**

Pendant bracket: sculpted in the form of a **bust**

R. Corbel/MICHELIN

vaulting; and the Périgord School – the domes on the church at **Solignac**.

Nevertheless, certain elements can be considered as purely Limousin. Firstly, the use of granite, which is found throughout the region and whose colour, while usually grey, sometimes verges on a golden tone.

Secondly, in the peculiar design of some belfries: the octagonal spire which crowns them is joined to the square tiers that form the base of the tower by one or two octagonal storeys; and the gables that stand on the upper square tiers are not only ornamental but play a part in the overall construction, since they divide and balance the weight of the upper octagonal tiers. The best examples of this style are the **belfries** at **St-Léonard**, **Collonges**, **Uzerche** and **Brantôme** (in the Périgord).

The belfry at **St-Junien** was probably planned to follow this pattern as the beginning of a steeply sloping gable can be seen above the second square tier.

Lastly, the façades present a more or less uniform style: massive belfry-porches adorned with blind arcades of various sizes and forms (**Le Dorat**, St-Junien); doorways with recessed elongated arcades on either side (St-Junien); a first storey flanked by bell turrets which are pierced at Le Dorat and encircled by a corbelled gallery at St-Junien; and doorways with twin doors framed by recessed covings, which in some cases are scalloped, showing the influence of Islamic art (Mozarabic style).

In the Dordogne

The plain, almost severe appearance of the area's many Romanesque churches was enhanced by the use of fine golden sandstone. The exteriors are startling for the extreme simplicity of their decoration: the doorways without tympana were embellished with recessed orders and carved with rounded mouldings and festoons in a saw-tooth pattern. Inside, the churches are equally plain, with apsidal chapels opening off the chancel, which is usually flat. Only a few churches were built with side aisles; as a general rule the nave stands alone.

The originality of the **Périgord Romanesque** style is in its vaulting and domes.

Some specialists believe that this shows eastern influence, others that it is a French invention.

The **dome** offers several advantages over cradle vaulting, which requires the use of powerful buttresses. The dome on pendentives allows the support of the weight of the vault to be divided between the side walls and the transverse arches of the nave. Often set over the transept crossing, domes also vault the nave when they follow one after another in a series (such as at **St-Étienne-de-la-Cité**, **Périgueux**).

The nave is thus divided into several square bays vaulted with a dome on pendentives.

The pendentives serve as a transition from a square base to the circular dome. The cathedral of **St-Front in Périgueux** (*see illustration: PÉRIGUEUX*) is unique, with its five domes erected above a Greek-cross plan. However, some of the region's numerous Romanesque churches illustrate different designs: as an example, in **St-Privat-des-Prés** and **Cadouin** the naves have aisles with rounded and pointed barrel-vaulting. Some façades are adorned with rows of arcades; this reflects the influence of the Saintonge and Angoumois regions. The neighbouring **Quercy** has a slightly different Romanesque style, characterised by richer sculptural embellishment (influence of the Moissac and Langue-doc schools). Inspired by Byzantine art, illuminations and antiquity, some of the carved doorways and tympana in this region are stunning: **Cahors**, **Carennac**, **Martel** and **Collonges-La-Rouge**, on the border with the Limousin.

Decorative arts

The **Abbaye de St-Martial**, **in Limoges**, with its many dependent priories, was the principal centre in the Limousin for the development of enamel-, gold- and silverwork. From the 10C onwards, the monks here produced shrines, episcopal rings and statues in gold and silver. The skill of the Limousin gold- and silversmiths and their proven technique paved the way for the subsequent development of **enamelwork**.

Using methods practised from the 6C onwards by Byzantine enamellers, the Limousin workshops at first undertook *cloisonné* ware, in which the colours are kept apart by thin outline plates. But in the 12C they turned entirely to *champlevé* enamelware, in which a thick sheet of copper is hollowed out in certain areas and the cavities are filled in with enamel.

Towards the end of the Romanesque period, colours became more subtle and often the cavities were filled with two or even four colours, placed one on top of the other. The folds of garments were rendered by the use of a highlight

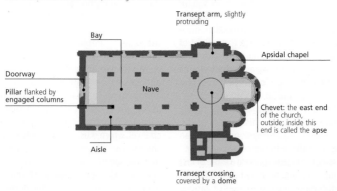

CADOUIN – Ground plan of the abbey church (1119-1154)

This ground plan is characteristic of the Aquitaine school of ecclesiastical architecture with aisles flanking the nave and chancel on both sides, forming a Latin cross with short arms.

Transept arm, slightly protruding

Bay

Apsidal chapel

Doorway

Pillar flanked by engaged columns

Nave

Chevet: the east end of the church, outside; inside this end is called the apse

Aisle

Transept crossing, covered by a dome

© R. Corbel / Michelin

– white, light blue or yellow – around areas of dark blue and green.

Most of the work was inspired by the art of illuminators, by manuscripts, ivories and Byzantine and Oriental silks. From the beginning of the 12C, small enamelled figures were represented on a background of smooth gilded copper. From 1170 onwards this background was chiselled with decorative foliage motifs, featuring fauna intermingled with religious symbols. The compositions, although often naïve, show a very strong artistic sense. Of the many objects produced in this way, the most remarkable are the reliquary shrines of **Ambazac**, **Gimel** and **Bellac**. The municipal museums of **Limoges** and **Guéret** contain rich collections of enamelwork.

GOTHIC ART AND ARCHITECTURE

Religious architecture

The essential elements of Gothic art – quadripartite vaulting based on diagonal ribs and the systematic use of the pointed arch – underwent various regional modifications. Diagonal ribs revolutionised construction and architects became masters of the thrust and balance of a building. Through the use of pointed arches, piers and flying buttresses, they freed the inner space so that a church could be lofty and light, illuminated by stained-glass windows.

The Berry

The most important Gothic building in the region, recognised worldwide as an architectural masterpiece inscribed on UNESCO's World Heritage list, is **Bourges Cathedral**. It bears no resemblance to any of the other great cathedrals of France; its high nave covered with sexpartite vaulting, its double side aisles which extend round the chancel and the absence of a transept make it unique.

The Limousin

The simultaneous influences of the Languedoc School (southern Gothic) and the schools of northern France were in play in the region. The passion for building in the 13C and 14C is illustrated in the **Cathedral of St-Étienne** and the churches of **St-Pierre-du-Queyroix** and **St-Michel-des-Lions at Limoges**, in the nave of the church of **St-Martin at Brive**, the collegiate church at **St-Yrieix**, and the belfry-porch of **Tulle Cathedral**.

The Dordogne

Saint Sacerdos Cathedral in Sarlat is an example of the influence of both southern and northern Gothic styles: the nave has wide side aisles and soaring flying buttresses typical of the north, whereas the side chapel shows southern influence. Another commonly found aspect of the Languedoc School is the nave's shape, almost as wide as it is high, with side chapels but no aisles (**Gourdon**, **Martel**, **Montpezat-du-Quercy** and **St-Cirq-Lapopie**).

In the Berry, Limousin and Dordogne, many **monasteries** were built during this period, although few have emerged intact from the ravages of time. In **Cadouin** and **Cahors**, there are still cloisters built in the Flamboyant style, and in **Périgueux** the cloisters were built between the 12C and the 16C.

During the 13C–14C, **fortified churches** were built in the region in response to unrest, in particular during the Hundred Years War. The sanctuaries provided villagers with a safe place of refuge from marauders and the churches and abbeys were like fortified castles in appearance, with crenellations, watch-paths and sometimes even protective moats.

Sculpture and painting
The Berry

Art in stained glass reached its climax in Bourges with the completion in the 13C of a remarkable series of windows. Around the middle of the 14C, under the guidance of Duke Jean de Berry, the Berry developed into a great intellectual and artistic centre. As an example, the stained-glass window known as the *Grand Housteau* in the cathedral at Bourges was a gift from the duke.

The duke assembled excellent artists but most of the masterpieces created in the studios and workshops in Bourges have unfortunately disappeared: only a few fragments of Berry's tomb remain in the cathedral crypt (originally placed in the **Sainte-Chapelle in Bourges**, since demolished). The greater part of the statuary, however, dates from this period and has survived. At **Issoudun**, in the chapel of the former **Hôtel-Dieu**, there is a fine carved Tree of Jesse.

The Limousin

In **Limoges**, two tombs executed in the purest 14C style can still be seen in the ambulatory around the chancel in the cathedral of St-Étienne; the village of **Reygade** in the Corrèze possesses an Entombment dating from the 15C which resembles the one at Carennac; and the church at **Eymoutiers** is ornamented with interesting 15C stained glass.

Limousin enamelwork, which flourished in the Romanesque period, was transformed in the 15C with the appearance of painted enamels produced under the direction of such master-craftsmen as Monvaerni and Nardon Pénicaud.

The Dordogne

From the second half of the 13C until the 15C, several remarkable works were produced: the tomb of St Stephen at **Aubazine**, a magnificent shrine carved in limestone in the second half of the 13C; the Entombment (15C) at **Carennac**; the tomb of the Cardaillacs at **Espagnac-Ste-Eulalie**; and the recumbent figures of Cardinal Pierre des Prés and his nephew Jean in the church at **Montpezat-du-Quercy**.

Frescoes, mural paintings produced with water-based paint on fresh plaster (which allows the colours to sink in), were used to decorate many chapels and churches. The west dome of **Cahors Cathedral** is entirely covered with 14C frescoes. Naïve 14C and 15C polychrome statuary and certain frescoes give a good idea of how peasants and nobility dressed at the time. In **Rocamadour**, the interiors of chapels are painted, with further embellishment on the façades.

CIVIL AND MILITARY ARCHITECTURE

A few Gothic residences remain in the region, the most noteworthy example of which is the **Palais Jacques Cœur** in **Bourges**, one of the finest Gothic palaces in Europe. Built on the vestiges of a Gallo-Roman wall, the building is a combination of massive, forbidding towers and a lively, sculpted façade. Inside, the architecture seems to hint at the approaching Renaissance in its graceful lines and fanciful motifs.

BASTIDES

These new, fortified towns (in the *Oc* language: *bastidas*) appeared in the 13C; their fortified aspect was further developed during the course of the following century.

Foundation

The principal founders of *bastides* were Alphonse de Poitiers (1249–71), count of Toulouse and brother to St Louis, and, from 1272 on, seneschal lords under Philip the Bold, Philip the Fair and King Edward I of England, who also held the title of duke of Aquitaine.

Development

Their construction satisfied economic, military and political needs, with founders taking advantage of the growth of the population and encouraging people to settle on their land, in turn rationalising its use and cultivation. In return, inhabitants were granted a charter, guaranteed protection, exempted from military service and given the right to inherit. The bailiff represented the king, dispensed justice and collected taxes, whereas the consuls, elected by the people, administered the town; towns flourished under this system. After the Albigensian Crusade, when the count of Toulouse, Raymond VII, built about 40 *bastides*, and with the outbreak of hostilities between the French and the English over the Périgord, Quercy and the Agenais, the political and military advantages of the *bastides* were confirmed. Alphonse de Poitiers built **Eymet**, **Catillonès** and **Villeréal** along the River Dropt as well as **Villefranche-du-Périgord** and **Ste-Foy-la-Grande**. The king of England responded with the construction of **Beaumont, Molières, Lalinde** and **Monpazier**, while in 1281 Philip the Bold founded **Domme**.

All of the *bastides*, French and English, were built to the same plan – a square or rectangle – and yet they differed because of the terrain, the type of site, the potential for population growth and their defensive plan. Occasionally, the *bastide* was built around a pre-existing building such as a fortified church (as at Beaumont) or a castle.

The design of Monpazier is most characteristic: it is built according to a quadrilateral plan with straight streets crossed at right angles by alleys known as **carreyrous**; narrow spaces, **andrones**, stand between the houses and serve as fire breaks, drains or even latrines. In the centre of town, the main square is surrounded by covered arcades or **couverts** (also known as **cornières**). The covered market, or **halle**, also stands in this square. The church and the cemetery stand nearby, and the outer walls are punctuated with towers and gateways. The best-preserved *bastides* are today found in **Monpazier, Domme** and **Eymet**.

THE BERRY AND LIMOUSIN

The fortresses of **Turenne, Merle, Ventadour, Châlus, Montbrun** and **Chalusset** all existed in the Limousin in the 13C. The ruins of **Crozant** overlooking the valley of the Creuse evoke what was once the powerful stronghold of the counts of Marche.

Numerous castles were built in the Berry during the Middle Ages: on Henry II's accession to the throne of England in 1154, the English controlled Aquitaine, threatening neighbouring Berry. Local lords therefore improved the fortification of their castles to resist the enemy. The **Château de Culan**, taken by Philip Augustus in 1188, was rebuilt in the 13C but retained its severity of appearance emphasised by its three round towers topped by a wooden hoarding. **Ainay-le-Vieil** is protected by its perimeter wall with nine towers, while Meillant still possesses its seven feudal towers.

THE DORDOGNE

There are few traces left of the civil architecture of the Romanesque period. The feudal fortresses erected in the 10C and 11C were greatly altered in later centuries and can scarcely be said to have withstood the warfare and destruction of the times. The only remaining buildings of this period are the square keeps – the last refuge of the defensive system. **Castelnau-Bretenoux** in the Quercy, with its strongly fortified keep, is a good example of feudal construction built on a hilltop site.

In the Périgord, parts of the castles of **Biron** and **Beynac, Bourdeilles, Commarque** and **Castelnaud** date back to the Romanesque period. Many of the castles in the Périgord and Quercy were constructed during the Gothic period, as is visible in their architectural detail; examples of these are at **Bourdeilles, Beynac-et-Cazenac, Castelnaud** and **Castelnau-Bretenoux**. **Bonaguil** is unique in that although it was built at the end of the 15C and in the early part of the 16C, it has all the features of a medieval fortress.

A considerable boom in **town** building occurred after the Hundred Years War with Sarlat, Périgueux, Bergerac, Cahors, Figeac, Gourdon and Martel all benefiting from this. The façades of townhouses were decorated with large pointed arches on the ground floor, where small shops were set up, while flattened arches or rose windows adorned the upper floors, with turrets crowning the roof. Among the finest examples of this period, note the Hôtel de la Raymondie in **Martel**, the Hôtel de la Monnaie in **Figeac**, the Hôtel Plamon in **Sarlat** and the famous Pont Valentré in **Cahors**.

THE RENAISSANCE

At the beginning of the 16C the artistic movement in France was revitalised by the influence of Italy. François I and the aristocracy were moved by the desire to copy Italian architecture and sculpture,

Architecture of the bastides

DOMME – Porte des Tours (late 13C)

In the 13C, the new towns known as bastides, often fortified, became common in Périgord and Quercy. This was the most important defensive gateway in the ramparts of Domme.

Crown of the tower, raised and fitted with loop-holes in the 14C

Two **circular towers**

Gable-wall

Curtain wall: an enclosing wall between two towers or bastions

Bartizan: a small overhanging turret with lookout holes and defensive loops

Balistraria: a cruciform loophole through which a crossbow could be fired.

Fortified gate: protected by two portcullis and a deadfall

Bossage: projecting, rough-finished stone; until the 15C, used only in military architecture

Arrow-loop

Moat (filled in)

© R. Corbel / Michelin

MONPAZIER – Central square in the bastide (late 13C and 14C)

The most typical and best preserved of the Périgord bastides, it is designed around a central rectangular area, bordered by a covered market on the southern side.

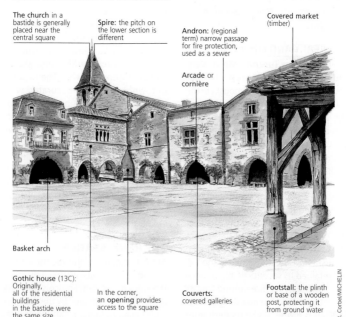

The church in a bastide is generally placed near the central square

Spire: the pitch on the lower section is different

Andron: (regional term) narrow passage for fire protection, used as a sewer

Covered market (timber)

Arcade or **cornière**

Basket arch

Gothic house (13C): Originally, all of the residential buildings in the bastide were the same size

In the corner, an **opening** provides access to the square

Couverts: covered galleries

Footstall: the plinth or base of a wooden post, protecting it from ground water

R. Corbel/MICHELIN

introducing new styles by using Italian artists. In the space of a century, hundreds of châteaux were built or restored as financial resources boomed with the end of the Hundred Years War.

Other factors encouraging this artistic movement in the region included improved returns on farm estates (thanks to the development of share-cropping), increased freedom of trade, the mining of iron ore, low labour costs and the advent of ready credit.

ARCHITECTURE
The Berry

At least half of the châteaux in the Berry were rebuilt in the years between 1430 and 1550, and most of the urban centres were transformed. Yet it took a long time for the Italian influence to be felt in the Berry where Gothic art was so strongly implanted. Generally, the Italian styles were interpreted, rather than copied. In **Bourges**, which was ravaged by fire in 1487, the most notable examples of Renaissance architecture are the Hôtel Lallemant, the Hôtel Cujas and the Hôtel des Échevins. In the countryside, **defensive castles** became more comfortable residences, as was the case with Ainay-le-Vieil, Meillant, La Verrerie and Villegongis.

The Limousin

In Limoges, the Renaissance influence can be seen on the St John's doorway (Portail St-Jean) – the monumental entrance to the cathedral. In Tulle, the Maison de Loyac is a manor house dating from the 16C. Châteaux that were built or transformed in what is considered a transitional style include those at **Rochechouart**, **Coussac-Bonneval**, **Pompadour** and **Sédières**.

The Dordogne

The new style flourished in **Montal** and **Puyguilhem**, which are similar in appearance to the châteaux of the Loire Valley. Most of the other 16C châteaux incorporate significant defensive features besides the windows, dormers, chimneys and other purely Renaissance elements; this is particularly evi-

Public building and civil engineering

FIGEAC – Hôtel de la monnaie (late 13C)

Probably a market place for money-changers, the "Oustal de lo Monédo" is representative of the urban architecture of Haut Quercy built during the Gothic period.

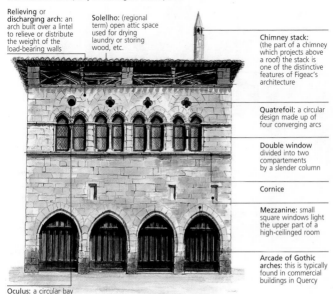

Relieving or **discharging arch:** an arch built over a lintel to relieve or distribute the weight of the load-bearing walls

Solellho: (regional term) open attic space used for drying laundry or storing wood, etc.

Chimney stack: (the part of a chimney which projects above a roof) the stack is one of the distinctive features of Figeac's architecture

Quatrefoil: a circular design made up of four converging arcs

Double window divided into two compartments by a slender column

Cornice

Mezzanine: small square windows light the upper part of a high-ceilinged room

Arcade of Gothic arches: this is typically found in commercial buildings in Quercy

© R. Corbel / Michelin

Oculus: a circular bay

Military and Civil Architecture

Château de MONTBRUN (12C and 15C)

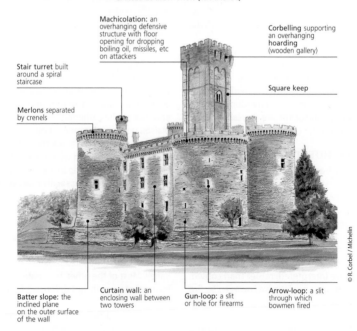

Machicolation: an overhanging defensive structure with floor opening for dropping boiling oil, missiles, etc on attackers

Corbelling supporting an overhanging **hoarding** (wooden gallery)

Stair turret built around a spiral staircase

Square keep

Merlons separated by crenels

Batter slope: the inclined plane on the outer surface of the wall

Curtain wall: an enclosing wall between two towers

Gun-loop: a slit or hole for firearms

Arrow-loop: a slit through which bowmen fired

© R. Corbel / Michelin

Château de MEILLANT – Western side (early 14C)

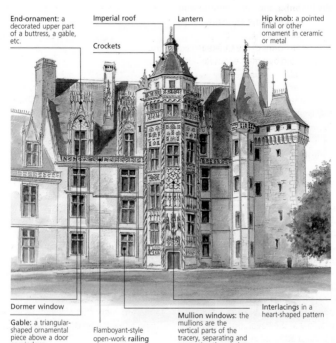

End-ornament: a decorated upper part of a buttress, a gable, etc.

Imperial roof

Lantern

Hip knob: a pointed finial or other ornament in ceramic or metal

Crockets

Dormer window

Gable: a triangular-shaped ornamental piece above a door or window

Flamboyant-style open-work railing

Mullion windows: the mullions are the vertical parts of the tracery, separating and supporting the window

Interlacings in a heart-shaped pattern

© R. Corbel / Michelin

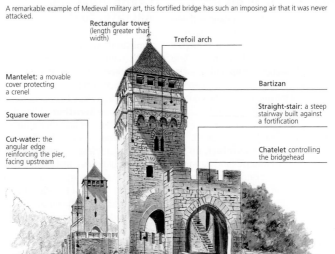

CAHORS – Pont Valentré (14C)

A remarkable example of Medieval military art, this fortified bridge has such an imposing air that it was never attacked.

Rectangular tower (length greater than width)

Trefoil arch

Mantelet: a movable cover protecting a crenel

Bartizan

Square tower

Straight-stair: a steep stairway built against a fortification

Cut-water: the angular edge reinforcing the pier, facing upstream

Chatelet controlling the bridgehead

Arch

Abutment: end support of mansonry that relieves the thrust of the arches

Crenelation

Deck

R. Corbel/MICHELIN

dent in **Monbazillac**. In **Cénevières, Bourdeilles, Lanquais, Les Bories** and **Rouffignac** (church), buildings were partially transformed; the **Château de Biron** is graced by a marvellous Renaissance chapel.

Civil architecture was also influenced by the Italian style, as witnessed in the Maison de Roaldès in **Cahors**, the Maison Cayla (or Maison des Consuls) in **Périgueux**, the Hôtel de Maleville in **Sarlat**, and **Brive**'s Hôtel Labenche.

SCULPTURE AND OTHER ARTS
The Berry and the Limousin

In the **Marche, tapestry-making** developed rapidly. Throughout the 16C the **Bourganeuf, Aubusson** and **Felletin** workshops profited from the growing demand for tapestries and hangings as part of contemporary furnishings; the latter two producing *verdures* (greeneries, in which plants and fantastic animals appeared against a background of foliage) as late as the Revolution. Sculpture can be best admired in the cathedral in

Limoges, where the magnificent rood screen, erected between 1533 and 1535, and the tomb of Jean de Langeac, are considered outstanding works of art.

Following the exceptional developments of the 12C to 14C, Limousin enamelwork found new favour in the 15C–16C through the Pénicaud, Nouailher and Limosin families. Léonard Limosin reached new artistic heights through the use of innovative techniques.

In **Bourges**, Lescuyer revided the art of making stained-glass windows.

The Dordogne

The inner court of the **Château de Montal** is an outstanding example of the Italian style, with its busts in high relief – superb works of art that are both realistic and refined. Inside, the remarkable staircase rivals those of the Loire valley châteaux. In the chapel at **Biron**, recumbent figures of the Gontaut-Biron family are decorated with figures influenced by the Italian Quattrocento (15C).

FROM THE 17C TO THE 20C

By copying the styles of Paris and Versailles, art lost all its regional character in the 17C. In the Berry, **François le Vau** – brother of the architect who designed the Louvre, Vaux and Versailles – planned the Château de Lignières in the style of the *Grand Siècle*: the frontons are supported by pilasters and the main buildings are reflected in sheets of water, with French-style gardens beyond.

The **Château de Hautefort**, on the border of the Limousin and Périgord, is a very good example of Classical architecture in its planning and unity of design; although it was ravaged by fire in 1968, it has since been completely restored. The **Château de Rastignac** in La Bachellerie (late 18C) is a scale model of the White House and one of the most interesting buildings of the period. It is not known whether the architect, a friend of Thomas Jefferson, influenced the architectural choices of the soon-to-be American president, at the time an ambassador in Paris, or vice versa.

In architecture, the 19C was largely devoted to the restoration and renovation of old buildings. Painting and tapestry, however, saw the introduction of numerous innovations. **Auguste Renoir** and **Suzanne Valadon** both heralded from the Limousin, although both left the province at a young age. Corot, on the other hand, was born in Paris and came to the region often to paint. His student, **Berthe Morisot**, a native of Bourges, was influenced by Renoir and Manet. **Claude Monet** painted 30 versions of the ruins at Crozant in 1889. **Ingres** and **Bourdelle**, both from Montauban, are considered the most eminent representatives of the Quercy from this period.

The art of tapestry-making was revived in the 20C thanks to the new ideas and techniques introduced by **Lurçat**, **Dufy**, **Marc Saint-Saëns**, **Gromaire** and the Association of Tapestry Cartoon Painters. Modern art is now displayed in many regional and municipal museums as well as at the Centre National d'Art et du Paysage at the Lac de Vassivière.

TRADITIONAL RURAL ARCHITECTURE

THE BERRY

Limestone, sandstone and cob (clay and straw) are the traditional building materials of the Berry countryside, yet distinctive differences in style exist between each area. For example, in the **Champagne Berrichonne**, large farm buildings are set around a courtyard. The low roof is covered in flat, brown tiles (or slate closer to the Loire); inside, where a big communal room is heated by a stone chimney, the floor is also tiled. The farms of the **Pays Fort** are more modest, with walls made from cob. Thatched roofs have gradually been replaced with tiles, with the extension of the eaves protecting the walls from wet weather. Around **Sancerre**, farms have a long façade of white limestone crowned with a roof punctuated with dormer windows; the living area is often flanked by a barn or stable. Other types of houses are found near the **Sologne** region and in **La Brenne**. Some features, however, are shared by all; these include ceramic finials, weathercocks or other ornaments placed on the ridge of the roof or at the apex of a gable, and plain interior furnishings.

THE LIMOUSIN

Most of the houses in the Limousin countryside date from the 19C and are made of local granite. In the area known as the **Montagne**, the low-built dwellings are attached to the barn and stable. Double-sloped roofs of thatch have been mostly replaced by slate. Many houses have lean-to additions next to the garden or orchard. In the past each farm had its own well or spring.

In the **Xaintrie**, barn dwellings are often built into a hillside. In the south of the area, half-timbering appears, along with upper storeys in the form of wooden terraces protected by overhanging *lauze* roofs. The granite houses of the **Haute-Marche** are usually built with a door and a small window on the ground floor, two small windows on the floor above, and an attic used for storing grain on top.

In the **Bas-Pays Corrézien**, the ground floor is used for storage, whereas the dwelling rooms are located above. The sandstone houses are covered with a four-sided sloping roof; an outer stairway links the two storeys by way of a landing; and the cellar entrance is at the bottom of the steps.

Higher up on the **plateau**, box-shaped buildings in blue or ochre granite have small windows and round-tiled roofs. Hay is stored above the animals in stables, and many farms have a special room for drying chestnuts or a dovecote. Farms are served by their own well.

THE DORDOGNE

The most typical kind of house found in the **Périgord Noir** is a sturdy, block-like construction in golden limestone, topped with a steeply pitched roof covered with flat, brown tiles or *lauzes*. The *lauzes* are neither slate nor layered schist tiles, but small limestone slabs. Set horizontally, their weight is such (500kg per m²/about 102lb per sq ft) that they require a strong, steeply pitched timberwork roof to distribute the weight. They are not fastened to the roof, but are cut in such a way that each *lauze* supports the one above. These beautiful roofs can last 500 years or more as long as the wooden beams below.

In the **Périgord Blanc**, low houses in grey or white limestone are lit through windows topped with bull's-eyes (*œils-de-bœuf*). The flat roof covered with Roman-style terracotta tiles reflects the more southern style.

In the forested area known as the **Double**, houses were traditionally built of cob and half-timbering.

In the vineyards of **Bergerac**, the houses of wine-growers are organised around the activities of winemaking; generally they form a U-shape or else have two adjoining courtyards. Tumbledown cottages in the surrounding vineyards are used as dwellings for labourers etc.

The houses of the **Quercy** are built in blocks of white limestone mortared in lime. The lower level (*cave*) is partly below ground; it was here that the stable, shed and storerooms were traditionally located. The floor above was reserved for the living quarters; the two levels are connected by an outside staircase above a terrace protected by a porch supported by columns.

Dovecotes

The region is dotted with numerous dovecotes. Some are no more than small towers attached to the main building; others stand alone, either resting on a porch or supported by columns. Before the Revolution, the right to keep pigeons was generally reserved for large landowners, although the Quercy and Périgord (where the right could be purchased for a fee) were exceptions. Dovecotes were built mainly for collecting pigeon droppings – their value is evident in the fact that when a property was divided up after a death, they were shared out between heirs in the same way as the livestock. Not only did they make excellent manure, but they were also prized by bakers (for the aroma it gave their bread) and by pharmacists as a relief for goitre – the swelling of the thyroid gland – among other conditions. The appearance of chemical fertilisers after 1850 led to a decline in production. The oldest types of free-standing dovecotes were arcaded (so-called hanging dovecotes), built on small columns to protect them from damp. The stubby capitals (*capels*) created overhangs to deter would-be predators from climbing up the columns.

Drystone Huts

These small constructions are dotted around the region, and can be found either standing in isolation in a field or, more rarely, grouped together. They are built entirely of dry stones and crowned with conical roofs of stones supported by joggles. They are known as *gariottes*, *caselles* or *bories*, but it is not known precisely what their function used to be, nor exactly when they were built.

Food and Drink

CUISINE
THE BERRY

The **cuisine** of the Berry is plain and simple and makes full use of farm produce. While vegetable, salt pork and bread dough combine to produce the typical regional stew known as *mique*, the true Berry speciality is *poulet en barbouille*. To make this dish, chicken is flambéed with brandy, cut into pieces and cooked with a blended sauce of blood and cream, an egg yolk and chopped liver. Dishes featuring a wine or cream sauce appear frequently on the tables of the Berry.

Also look out for traditional staples such as pumpkin pâté, *truffiat* (potatoes covered in pastry), stuffed rabbit, eggs in wine, ox-tongue au gratin, kidneys, calf's liver, game and fish, often garnished with fresh mushrooms. For dessert, try specialities such as plum flan, *sanciaux* (honey fritters) and *millats* (stewed black cherries).

THE LIMOUSIN

The hearty **cuisine** of the Limousin is typified by the traditional dish known as *bréjaude*, a pork rind and cabbage soup garnished with rye bread.

Paté with foie gras and truffle base

© Jean-Daniel Sudres / hemis.fr

Patés made from truffles or wrapped in pastry and garnished with a mixed veal and pork stuffing (especially the pâté de foie gras from Brive-la-Gaillarde), are deservedly famous.

Although the region is most renowned for its excellent beef, other delicious local dishes includes *lièvre en chabessal*, a dish made from hare stuffed with fresh pork and ham, and seasoned with salt, pepper, spices and condiments. Cabbage is a traditional Limousin ingredient and is served with partridge, in heart-warming *potées* (country stews) or braised with chestnuts. For a long time, chestnuts (*châtaignes*) were a staple of the farmer's diet, and can still be found garnishing turkey, goose, black pudding, veal and pork stew, or served as a purée with venison. Perhaps the dish most closely associated with the Limousin is *clafoutis*, a creamy flan with cherries.

THE PÉRIGORD AND QUERCY

Cuisine in the Dordogne (which the French invariably refer to as the Périgord when speaking of gastronomy) is one of France's culinary jewels. For centuries, the region has been synonymous with delicacies such as truffles, foie gras and confits. Sit down to a traditional meal here and you may never want to eat any other way again: perhaps start with *tourain blanchi* – a white soup made from garlic, goose fat and eggs, sometimes with sorrel or tomato added; next comes the foie gras or *pâté de foie* (a general term for liver pâté); the third course might perhaps be a delicious omelette made with *cèpes* (wild mushrooms) or delicately sliced truffles. For the main course, enjoy *confit de canard aux pommes sarladaises* (duck preserved in its own fat, fried until brown, with potatoes fried in goose fat and garlic and garnished with mushrooms). A refreshing salad drizzled in a light walnut oil dressing might be topped with a hot *cabécou* toast or followed by the cheese platter. To round things off, why not indulge in a slice of walnut cake or plum pie?

The **truffle** *(truffe)* is the elegant name of a knobby, black fungus which weighs about 100g/3.5oz, and imbues all it touches with its unique aroma. A truffle must be fresh or very carefully preserved; their rarity – as they cannot be cultivated – and price make them a gourmet luxury. The delicate black specks of grated truffles can be found in foie gras, pâté, poultry dishes, *ballotines* (boned, stuffed legs of poultry) and *galantines* (cold cuts). Truffles are also sliced thinly into salads, omelettes. and pasta. A truffle wrapped and cooked whole over an open fire – *à la cendre* – is a supreme extravagance.

FOIE GRAS

Foie gras is certainly the pride of the Périgord. You may visit farms where this tradition is demonstrated.

Overfeeding occurs naturally to prepare the birds for migration, which is why only some species of birds, namely goose and duck, can produce *foie gras*. The birds are first nourished with grains and alfalfa, which help expand the digestive system. After three months in the open air, the birds are placed in individual cages for 15–18 days. Progressively overfed, they are given ground meal then whole corn with a funnel-like feeding device known as the *gaveuse*. A duck thus absorbs 10–15kg/22–33lb, a goose up to 20kg/44lb of corn, tripling or even quadrupling the weight of its liver to achieve an ideal weight: 450-500g/1lb for a duck; 800–900g/2lb for a goose. Foie gras can be preserved with excellent results, and is labelled according to content; read the label or menu carefully to know what you are getting. A protected geographical indication *(IPG)* has been developed to help consumers identify the product's origin: look for *IPG Sud-Ouest* when buying.

Foie gras entier is sliced from a whole liver and represents the noblest form of the product; *mi-cuit* livers must be kept refrigerated and eaten fresh.

A **bloc de foie gras**, on the other hand, is reconstituted from bits of liver that have been emulsified with water. Other forms of foie gras are *parfait* (75% liver), *mousse, pâté, médaillon* and *galantine* (50% liver). Tinned foie gras should be served chilled (allow 50g/2oz per person) and cut with a sharp knife.

Raw foie gras can also be pan-fried and caramelized for a delicious hot starter. Sweet touches such as onion or fig confit make a nice garnish. It is important not to spread foie gras, but rather to top your bread with thick bites of it to enjoy its smooth texture. Enjoy a glass of cool, sweet Monbazillac wine with your foie gras.

CONFITS

Confits are the traditional base of the region's cuisine. Confit was first used as a method of preserving various parts of the goose or duck before the advent of the freezer. Now regarded as a gourmet dish, it is still prepared using traditional methods, although duck has largely replaced goose. The pieces of duck are cooked in their own fat for three hours and then preserved in large earthenware pots *(tupins)*.

This procedure is also used to preserve turkey and pork (pork confit is called *enchaud*). Goose grease is used instead of butter in local cooking, for example in *pommes de terre sarladaises*.

STUFFINGS AND SAUCES

Stuffings and sauces, often comprising foie gras and truffles, are used frequently to garnish poultry, game, suckling pigs and in a favourite regional dish – *cou d'oie farci* – stuffed goose neck.

The most commonly used sauces are the *rouilleuse*, which is used to give colour and to accompany poultry fricassee, and *sauce Périgueux*, a Madeira sauce made from a base of chicken stock, to which fresh truffles are added.

WINE
APPELLATIONS

French wines are classified according to a system that provides a rough guide to price and quality, although there is plenty of room for overlapping, especially where small growers are concerned. The lowest category is simply labelled **vin de table**. Such wines may have been elaborated using any variety of grape from any country in the EU (although this must be stated on the label). While generally to be avoided in shops and restaurants, you may buy satisfactory table wine from a local producer or cooperative (bring your own container). Next comes the **vin de Pays**, which bears a label identifying the place of origin and possibly the grape variety (if not a blend) and the year. The category following is the **VDQS**, *Vin Délimité de Qualité Supérieure*, which also shows place of origin and may show variety and year. The superiority comes from the fact that the grape varieties are approved and the district of production clearly defined; in addition, these wines pass a yearly taste test to confirm their quality.

The top 20% of French wines are labelled **Appellation d'Origine Contrôlée** (abbreviated as AOC or simply AC). These wines come from designated vineyards, use approved grape varieties and are vinified in a manner specific to each one. The system is controlled by the Institut National des Appellations d'Origine, and it is a serious business indeed. The AOC label is a reward for years of continuous merit and lobbying. Similar systems are now being used for other produce.

THE REGIONS

The renown and popularity of **wines** from the region date way back to the Middle Ages. **Cahors** wine was transported by barges (*gabares*) to Bordeaux and from there by ship to the capitals of Europe. A deep-red colour, with a robust flavour to match, Cahors accompanies hearty foods including game, roast meats and strong-flavoured cheese. The bouquet only achieves subtlety and loses its rather harsh presence on the tongue after ageing for two to three years in the cask and another dozen in the bottle.

The vineyards of **Bergerac**, largely planted with Sauvignon grapes, produce reds as well as whites. Among the latter, **Monbazillac** holds pride of place. Golden and smooth, and with a heady aroma, this syrupy wine is served as an aperitif, with foie gras or with dessert. Like other sweet, highly alcoholic wines (notably Sauternes), Monbazillac depends on the effects of the noble mould (*Botrytis cinerea*), a highly beneficent mould which forms on the skins of the ripening grapes, bringing about a concentration of sugar and flavour and a vast improvement in the quality of the resulting wine, without imparting any trace of this on the palate. The process has been employed since the Renaissance. The grapes are harvested in several batches as they reach the desired state. Monbazillac develops its full flavour after two to three years and will keep for up to 30 years.

Dry white wines such as **Montravel** and Bergerac, vigorous and fruity, go well with seafood and fish; sweeter wines like **Côtes de Bergerac**, **Côtes de Montravel**, **Rosette** and **Saussignac** are good as aperitif wines or with white meats.

Red Bergerac wines are firm, with a fruity bouquet, and can be enjoyed soon after bottling. **Pécharmant** is fuller-bodied, more complex, and must be left to mature before its charms can be fully appreciated.

Wines from the Berry are generally clean and crisp and of good quality. Sancerre is a well-known appellation known more readily for its white wines, although reds and rosés are also produced here. Many small growers are scattered around outlying villages, with some of the best wines produced in **Bué**, **Chavignol**, **Ménétréol** and **Fontenay** – the expressive characteristics of these wines are best enjoyed young. A good companion for local dishes and cheeses is **Ménétou-Salon**, a quality wine produced in limited quantities, which is hard to come across elsewhere. Grown in the same chalky soil as Sancerre, many find it to be fuller and more rounded than its well-known neighbour.

Sancerre

The wines of Sancerre are commonly classified as Eastern Loire valley wines. The upper reaches of the Loire are mostly planted with the Sauvignon Blanc grape, which produces two of the finest wines in France: **Sancerre** and **Pouilly-Fumé**. These wines are produced within 8km/5mi of each other, on different sides of the river, and yet their taste is, to the connoisseur, leagues apart. Mostly white wines are produced; the term *fumé* is in reference to the smoky bloom that forms on the skin of the fruit rather than to the resulting flavour. Sancerre is reputed for its full, round finish, whereas Pouilly-Fumé is considered a more complex, flowery wine.

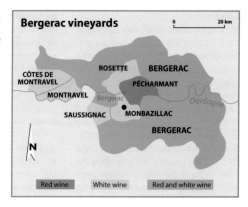

In addition to these famous labels, some of the other wines in the region are delightful discoveries for the traveller. Certain wines, produced in small quantity and difficult to find outside the region, make for a memorable and unique experience. It is worth a visit to the wine-growers of Bué, Chavignol, Ménétréol and Fontenay to savour the regional fare.

Mostly white, but also some rosé and red AOC wines are produced in the villages of **Ménétou-Salon**, **Quincy** and **Reuilly**. Reds and rosés are drawn from Sauvignon Blanc, Pinot Noir, Pinot Gris and Meunier grapes.

Sancerre is a beautiful wine town, surrounded by hillside vineyards that sweep away from the town like striped skirts on a lovely lady. The signposted wine route meanders around back roads and through the village of Chavignol, famous for its Crottin de Chavignol goat's milk cheese. The Sancerrois is not a very big region, but visitors will have plenty of temptation to stop and sample local wines and cheeses and to enjoy a slower pace of life.

Bergerac

Another leading wine-producing centre in the region covered in this guide is Bergerac, which has 12 different types of AOC wines. There is a well-marked wine route around the vineyards (*information at the Maison des Vins, Cloître de Récollets, in Bergerac*). The varieties grown are Cabernet Franc, Cabernet Sauvignon, Merlot, Cot, Semillon and Sauvignon Blanc. Bergerac, Côtes de Bergerac and Pécharmant are strong red wines; the rosés are less enticing, and the white wines are sweet (*moël-leux*) or if dry, bottled under a separate AOC, **Bergerac Sec.**

Ambrosial **Monbazillac** white wines, very sweet, are often served with foie gras. The flavour is similar to Sauternes, and the wine keeps for about four years, although a good year may age better. Rosette is a less sweet white wine produced in small quantity and not found elsewhere; enjoy it as an apéritif wine. Montravel vineyards are found in the Dordogne, but also on the far edge of Bordeaux territory. The white wines (from dry to sweet) are bottled as Montravel; reds are sold as Bergerac.

♦ **Maison des Vins de Bergerac**
  1 rue des Récollets, 24100 Bergerac.
  ☏ 05 53 63 57 55.
  www.vins-bergerac.fr.
  Wine tasting, tour of selected vineyards and cellars.

♦ **Cave Coopérative de Monbazillac**
  Route de Mont-de-Marsan, 24240 Monbazillac.
  ☏ 05 53 63 65 00.
  www.chateau-monbazillac.com.
  Wine tasting.

Cahors

The deep-red wines of Cahors are made from Malbec, Merlot and Jurançon grapes, grown in ruddy soil scattered with limestone pebbles. Start a tour of the regional vineyard right at the famous Pont de Valentré across the River Lot. From here you can go to Pradines and Douelle, where wine was once loaded onto flat-bottomed boats for transportation. The wine road is a beautiful route through the countryside and along the river; many of the vineyards have been producing wine for centuries. During the Roman occupation, the Emperor Dolmitian ordered the vines to be uprooted as punishment for an uprising, thus temporarily (for 200 years) halting production, which is now back in full swing. The AOC label was awarded to regional wines in 1971.

To earn the name **Cahors**, the hearty red wines must have at least 70% Malbec, and at most 20% Merlot and Tannot; the remaining 10% is Jurançon. While they are known for their dark colour bordering on black, and their robust and tannic flavour, Cahors wines are evolving to suit modern tastes and now more subtle vintages are coming to light. Labelled vieux (old), these have aged three years or more in a wooden cask.

You may obtain a booklet listing winegrowers' addresses from local tourist offices or the Union Interprofessionnelle du Vin de Cahors: ✆05 65 23 22 24 or www.vindecahors.fr.

Locally made Coteaux de Quercy, red and rosé wines from the Lot Valley are *vins de pays*.

♦ **Les Vignerons du Quercy – Cave Coopérative**
Quercy, 82270 Montpezat-de-Quercy. ✆05 63 02 00 60.
www.montpezat-de-quercy.com.
Wine tasting and sales.
Guided tours for groups by appointment.

Nature

LAND DIVISION

The *région* (there are 22 in France) is the largest administrative division in the country, followed by the *département* (96, excluding overseas territories), which is subdivided into *communes* run by an elected mayor. In total, there are 36 394 mayoral districts in France.

Berry (formerly Berri) is the name historically and popularly applied to the area south of the Paris basin, comprising the *départements* of Cher and Indre in the Centre *région*. This old county, later a duchy, came under the crown in the 13C.

Limousin is the name of an administrative *région* comprising three *départements*: Corrèze, Creuse and Haute-Vienne. For a long time an Anglo-Norman fief, it was united to the French throne by Henry IV, and later administered by appointed Intendants.

Dordogne is a *département*, which is part of the larger *région* of Aquitaine.

The French *départements* were created in 1790 and were generally given the name of the main river within the territory, hence the Dordogne, named after the two rivers (the Dore and the Dogne) which combine to form this famous waterway. Before that time, the same area was known as **Périgord** (named after the Petrocorii who occupied the area at the time of the Gauls), a free county dating back to the 11C, which fell into the possession of the Albret family. Henry IV, its last feudal lord, brought it under the authority of the French crown. Many French people still use the old appellation to refer to this popular holiday destination, especially when describing its culinary delights.

LAND FORMATION
PRIMARY ERA

This began about 600 million years ago. It was towards the end of this era that an upheaval of the Earth's crust took place. This upheaval or folding movement, known as the Hercynian fold, the V-shaped appearance of which is shown by dotted lines on the map, resulted in the emergence of a number of high mountains – notably the Massif Central, formed by crystalline rocks which were slowly worn down by erosion.

SECONDARY ERA

This began about 260 million years ago. Towards the middle of this era, there was a slow folding of the Hercynian base, resulting in the flooding of the area by the sea. Sedimentary deposits, mainly calcareous, accumulated on the edge of the Massif Central, forming the Quercy *causses* (limestone plateaux) during the Jurassic Period and then beds of Cretaceous limestone in the Périgord region. Similar formations are found in Champagne Berrichonne, Boischaut and Sancerre.

TERTIARY ERA

This began about 65 million years ago. During this period siderolithic deposits (clay and gravel, rich in iron) originating from the Massif Central covered some parts of the Quercy, such as the Bouriane region, whereas clay-rich sands accumulated to the west of Périgord, creating the heathlands of the Brenne, Sologne, Double and Landais regions, with their numerous lakes.

QUATERNARY ERA

This began about two million years ago. It was during this period that human evolution gathered pace. By this time, the effects of erosion had given the region its present-day appearance. Rivers, taking their source in the Massif Central, created the Vézère, Dordogne and Lot valleys.

THE COUNTRYSIDE TODAY

Regions totally different in character lie side by side in the area between the Berry and the plains of the Agenais. This region of contrasting countrysides is one of great natural beauty: the wide horizons of the Berry succeeded by the green mountain country of the Limousin; the limestone plateaux of the Quercy stretching out in stark silhouette; and the wooded plateaux of the Périgord divided by picturesque valleys and bountiful orchards. The area has many visible traces of its earliest settlers and is rich in prehistoric sites. Charming churches, the imposing religious sanctuaries of the Limousin and the hundreds of fortresses, castles, manors and mansions in a variety of architectural styles all bear witness to the region's rich historical past. In addition, the region is renowned for its delicious traditional cuisine and excellent local wines, offering the perfect accompaniment to your voyage of discovery.

DORDOGNE
PÉRIGORD VERT

The Green Périgord, located between the Nontronnais and Excideuil, comprises fragments of the old massif, small basins scoured out of the soft Lias marl, and the occasional table of limestone. Its landscape of woodlands, well-tended farms and patches of bright sunflowers echoes the neighbouring Limousin. The handful of towns scattered across this lush borderland act as centres for light industry and the marketing of locally produced farm products.

Contrasting colours are provided by pastures grazed by dairy cattle and calves (for veal), especially around **Ribérac**, and fields of cereal crops. Numerous agricultural markets are held in local towns.

PÉRIGORD BLANC

The White Périgord takes its name from the frequent outcrops of chalky limestone that illuminate this open landscape. The countryside of hills and slopes around Périgueux consists of meadows interspersed with coppices of oak and chestnut. This region is drained by the River Beauronne and River Vern, whose valleys are covered with pasture and arable land; the extensive **Vallée de l'Isle** is dotted with small industrial towns, its alluvial soil used as pasture, or for growing maize (corn), tobacco and walnuts. South of Périgueux, around **Vergt** and **Rouffignac**, the iron-rich siderolithic

© M. Janvier / Michelin

Chestnut tree

deposits covering the limestone have proven to be ideal for the cultivation of strawberries, which are exported to all parts of France.

To the northeast of the town, Central Périgord meets the **Périgord Causse**. This block of Jurassic limestone, scored by the **Isle, Auvézère and Loue valleys**, is characterised by its sparse vegetation, although its stunted oak trees harbour the famed, yet elusive truffle. The **Double** lying to the west, between the River Dronne and the River Isle, is an area of forests where tall oak and chestnut trees predominate; the clay soil here favours the formation of ponds. The **Landais**, to the south of the Isle, is a less rugged region abundant in fruit orchards. The maritime pine is more common here than the chestnut; meadows are also more abundant than to the north of the river.

PÉRIGORD POURPRE

The Purple Périgord around **Bergerac** is divided into several areas, all of which share a mild climate favourable to the cultivation of crops more commonly associated with more southerly parts of the country. The Dordogne valley, which is particularly wide here, is divided into plots of land where tobacco, maize (corn), sunflowers and cereals all flourish in the rich alluvial deposits.

Timber production predominates to the west of Bergerac, in an area whose slopes are covered with the vineyards of Bergerac and **Monbazillac**.

The town of Bergerac itself is an important centre for the tobacco and wine industries.

PÉRIGORD NOIR

Dissected by the Vézère and Dordogne valleys, the Black Périgord owes its name to the high density of trees growing in the sandy soil covering the limestone areas, and to the predominance of the holm oak, with its dark, dense foliage, particularly in the area around **Sarlat**. The alluvial soil of the valleys, whose river courses are lined with screens of poplar or willow, supports a variety of crops, including wheat, maize (corn), tobacco and walnuts. The bustling and colourful local markets all sell excellent nuts, mushrooms, truffles and foie gras. Springs, chasms and prehistoric caves and shelters with sculpted or painted walls offer further attractions for visitors to this area. Along the River Dordogne the landscape is gentle and harmonious, as can be seen from the viewpoints at Domme, and the castles of Beynac and Castelnaud. The former capital of Périgord Noir, **Sarlat-la-Canéda**, with its *lauze* roofs and medieval atmosphere, is a lively tourist centre and popular holiday base.

Vast stretches of gently undulating molassic hillside, with the occasional limestone outcrop and terrace, extend beyond the wine-producing slopes of Monbazillac. Small farms interspersed with woodlands are planted with cereal crops, vineyards (AOC Bergerac) and plum trees. To the east, in an area of transition with the Bouriane region in the Quercy, the dense **Forêt de Bessède**, a forest which continues to flourish on the millstone or siderolithic sands, has hardly been disturbed by the foundation of bastides and abbeys during the Middle Ages.

QUERCY

Quercy corresponds to a region that stretches from the Massif Central to the plains of Aquitaine and was occupied by the **Cadurques** who made **Cahors** their capital. The region has a strong historical unity: in the Middle Ages Quercy belonged to the province of **Guyenne**; under the Ancien Régime two regions were recognised – the Haut-Quercy, centred on Cahors and seat of the main administrative departments, and the Bas-Quercy, governed from **Montauban**. During the Revolution they were reunited as part of the Lot *département*. However, in 1808 **Napoleon** separated them once more, creating the *département* of Tarn-et-Garonne, which covers most of the Bas-Quercy, and parts of Rouergue, Gascony and Languedoc.

THE CAUSSES

This dry land, dissected by dry valleys known locally as *combes*, forms a protected area known as the **Parc Naturel Regional des Causses du Quercy**. Flocks of sheep graze on the sparse grass of the pastures, which are subdivided by drystone dikes. Stunted oaks and maples are the only trees growing here. The more fertile valleys are a mix of pasture, vineyards and other crops.

The **Causse de Martel** is a vast, arid, stone-covered plain, dissected by a relatively fertile zone. The numerous drystone walls here were built by shepherds as they cleared stones from the ground to allow sheep to graze and marked out boundaries. The area takes its name from the nearby agricultural town of Martel.

The **Causse de Gramat**, an extensive limestone plateau at an average altitude of 350m/1 150ft is home to a number of sites of natural interest (*see Gouffre de PADIRAC*) and unusual landscapes: to the north lie the **Ouysse** and **Alzou** canyons (the spectacular village of **Rocamadour** clings to the cliff face); to the south the much longer **Célé Canyon**. Between the narrow gashes of the Alzou and the Célé lies the waterless **Braunhie**, an arid region riddled with caves and ravines. Like many of their neighbours, the local towns of Gramat and Labastide-Murat have suffered from serious depopulation in recent decades.

The low-lying plateau of the **Causse de Carjac** is hemmed in by the banks of the River Célé and River Lot, the banks of which are particularly fertile.

The **Causse de Limogne**, with its drier climate, takes on a very different appearance. Bordered by the Lot valley, the plateau is dotted with dolmens and megaliths, which appear amid clusters of white truffle oak, juniper bushes and fields of lavender. Dotted around this landscape are unusual shepherds' shelters built of flat stone with strange conical roofs, known as *garriottes*, *cazelles*, or *bories* (*see SARLAT: Cabanes de Breuil*). There are few big towns in this area, although Limogne-en-Quercy and Lalbenque remain busy centres for the **truffle trade**.

THE VALLEYS

Cutting a wide swath through limestone, the region's rivers have carved out their valleys, shaping meanders which

Flock of sheep in the Causse de Gramat, Quercy

© Christophe Boisvieux / hemis.fr

Lot Valley

© S. Sauvignier / Michelin

enlarge as the valley broadens, to the point that they become ever-widening loops (*cingles*) in the course of rivers. The valleys of the **Dordogne**, **Célé** and **Lot** have been inhabited since prehistoric times. During the Roman era, settlers lived in fortified *oppidums*; castles and châteaux bear witness to the role of these valleys in the region's later history. Today, they are richly covered with crops, vineyards and orchards. The main centres of population in this area today are **Souillac** (Dordogne valley), **Figeac** (Célé) and **Cahors** (Lot).

HAUT-QUERCY

The major part of the Haut-Quercy comprises limestone plateaux or *causses* with an average altitude of 300m/1 000ft. The fertile areas of the **Limargue** and **Terrefort** extend across flat basins and vast plains; the soils of the area favour the production of a variety of crops including greengage plums and strawberries (*between Carennac and St-Céré*), grapes, walnuts and tobacco. The eastern part of the Haut-Quercy includes the **Châtaigneraie**, an area with a cold, damp climate and poor soil. This plateau, at an altitude of 700m/2 300ft, tilts eastwards and is cut by deep gorges. The widely cultivated chestnut tree has given the area its name; cereal crops are grown on lowering hilltops, while cattle are raised on small farms. The **Bouriane** is blanketed in heath, coppices and woods, and bears more

resemblance to the Périgord than the Quercy. In this area, timber, chestnuts and walnuts are harvested, maritime pines are tapped for resin and livestock is raised and sold. The capital of this area is the bustling town of **Gourdon.**

QUERCY BLANC

Southwest of the Lot valley and the town of Cahors, the Jurassic limestone disappears under tertiary limestone to create unusual landscapes known as *planhès* – vast undulating areas of white which have given the region its name (White Quercy). These plateaux are cut into narrow ridges *(serres)* by the rivers. The crests of the *serres* are levelled off into plains which are covered with pastures used for grazing sheep, oak forest and, occasionally, fertile fields of crops. Between the *serres*, the valleys are fertile corridors, spreading between the sandstone as they get closer to the Garonne. Pastures lined with poplars produce abundant crops of fruit, cereals and tobacco, in addition to wine from local vineyards. The lively market towns of **Montcuq**, **Lauzerte**, **Castelnau-Montratier** and **Montpezat-de-Quercy** are all situated on rocky hilltops known as *peuchs*.

LIMOUSIN

This vast region of crystalline rocks forms the western bastion of the Massif Central. The area takes its name from the Lemovices, the large tribe which occupied the country at the time of the Gauls. The individuality of the region is emphasised by its wet winter climate and verdant countryside. The Limousin has been aptly described by Jérôme and Jean Tharaud in their novel *La Maîtresse Servante*:

"Before us unrolled a green and ever-changing countryside, silent and impenetrable, cut by thick hedges, filled with dark shadows and watered by running brooks. No rivers, only streams; no lakes, only pools; no ravines, only valleys."

LA MONTAGNE

This vast series of plateaux, at altitudes no higher than 977m/3 205ft, has been levelled by erosion. The "mountain" is the source of many rivers and streams that filter across the rest of the region. The weather on these highlands is rugged, the rains heavy, the winds strong and snow has been known to lie on the ground for four months at a time. Farms are few and far between and stony wastes and moors are more common than ploughed land, particularly on the Plateau de Millevaches (&see MEYMAC) and in the Massif des Monédières (&see TREIGNAC). As you pass through this eerily quiet landscape, your eyes are drawn to a landscape of meadows, moors and woodlands of beech and pine, dotted with the ever-present sight of grazing sheep.

THE PLATEAUX OF HAUT-LIMOUSIN

The plateaux to the northwest are undulating in appearance – the **Monts d'Ambazac** and the **Monts de Blond** – with alternating escarpments and deeply incised valleys. The *bocage* is a patchwork of woods and fields. Trees thrive in this wet climate, with oak and beech on the uplands and chestnut trees at lower levels. Quickset hedges surround fields and meadows.

The pastures enriched by manure and artificial fertilisers make good cattle-grazing country. Farther north, the drier, less-wooded **Marche** area is a marshland between the Massif Central and the Pays de la Loire. The **Haute-Marche**, drained by the Creuse, is an area of stock-rearing, whereas arable farming is more prevalent in the **Basse-Marche**, particularly around Bellac.

To the west, the **Confolentais** is the name given to the green and forested foothills of the Massif Central, which are dissected by the River Vienne.

THE PLATEAUX OF BAS-LIMOUSIN

This area, where the influence of Périgord and Quercy is evident, is characterised by its wonderful quality of light, milder climate and fertile basins.

The **Xaintrie** is an area dotted with woods of pine and silver birch – this granite plateau is deeply incised by the Dordogne, the Maronne and numerous smaller rivers.

The depression of the **Bassin de Brive** straddles the Lower Limousin and the northernmost part of the Périgord. The Nontronnais is also partly in the Limousin and takes on a similar appearance, with its grassy fields, chestnut trees, heather, gorse and isolated farmhouses.

BASSIN DE BRIVE

The depression of the Brive Basin is a sunken zone between the crystalline escarpments of the **Uzerche Plateau** and the limestone ridges of the **Causses du Quercy**. It is an area of sandstone and schist, drained by the River Vézère

Beech

© M. Janvier / Michelin

and River Corrèze. In its green valleys demarcated by screens of poplar, the gentle south-facing slopes are given over to orchards. Today, Brive is an important centre for the fruit and vegetable canning industries.

South of Brive, the **Causse Corrèzien** is covered with large farms devoted to the rearing of geese and sheep, and truffle-oak plantations.

BERRY

This province is one of the oldest agricultural regions in France, with a unity that is the result of its shared heritage rather than of its geography. The geological position of the Berry lies at the contact point between the Paris Basin and the Massif Central.

The area consists of a vast low-lying plateau, rising in the northeast to the Sancerre Hills (highest point: the Motte de Humbligny at an altitude of 434m/1 424ft), tilting westwards in a series of steps towards the Brenne depression. To the south, the countryside is more undulating with numerous isolated hills and escarpments. The River Cher and River Indre are part of the Loire drainage system, whereas the Creuse is a tributary of the Vienne.

NORTHERN BERRY

The **Pays Fort** and **Sancerrois** are transitional areas bordering the Pays de la Loire. The former, characterised by its marl and clayey soils, slopes towards the Sologne, whereas the vine-covered, chalky slopes of the Sancerrois rise above the river banks. This once-forested landscape has been remodelled as *bocage* (wooded farmland). The Forêt d'Allogny, the last remaining area of primitive forest cover, overlooks the vast orchards of St-Martin-d'Auxigny.

The **Northern Boischaut**, meanwhile, is an area of rich pasture.

The **Southern Berry – Champagne Berrichonne** – is a region of plateaus and limestone soil extending between the Loire to the east and the Indre to the west, and is covered in the main by scattered woods and forests. Manure and rich fertilisers have transformed this light, sandy soil into excellent farmland. In addition to grain crops, sheep and Normandy dairy cows are bred indoors and fed on beetroot pulp; bee-keeping is also an important economic activity around Châteauroux.

Away to the east, the **Val de Germigny** is a long depression, formerly marshland, which runs along the foot of the escarpments crowned by the Bois de Meillant. The pastures here are grazed by Charolais cattle.

BOISCHAUT

This district lies between the Cher and the Creuse, its clay soils overlapping the neighbouring Marche province. This is an area of small farms where the emphasis is on livestock rearing, in particular the Charolais breed, and sheep.

The countryside, crisscrossed with many rivers, farms and gardens, is still much the same as when described by the novelist George Sand (*see NOHANT*).

BRENNE

This vast sand and clay depression, characterised by its abundant marshes, is predominantly covered with heather, pine trees and broom. Once the exclusive haven of hunters and fishers, the Brenne is now a nature park, popular with visitors interested in observing its exceptional flora and fauna (*see La BRENNE*).

FLORA AND FAUNA
WATER

The region has a dense network of rivers and streams. In the Limousin, the rivers tumble through picturesque valleys, whereas in the Berry they tend to flow more peacefully. With a few exceptions near urban areas, the waters are pure and clean, harbouring myriad species of fish. The region is home to numerous ponds and wetlands, manmade lakes, as well as abundant flora and fauna.

La Brenne

This nature park is part of the region's commitment to the preservation of wetlands and their ecosystems, and to the development of green tourism.

The hundreds of ponds and the diversity of habitats make it an ideal refuge for many species, including a host of migrating birds. (🔊 See La BRENNE for details and illustrations of local wildlife.)

Wetlands
These ecosystems, characterised by the presence of slow-moving water or saturated soil, are vitally important in maintaining the region's ecological balance. The protection of these often fragile areas has led to a better understanding of their morphology.

Wet meadows
The outer ring of the pond system, these meadows of variable size are often rich with wild flowers in springtime. The flora is diverse and in La Brenne includes as many as 50 species: marsh violets, gentian, wild orchids and more.

Swamps
The waterlogged banks of the region's ponds are invaded by willows which develop into groves extending from the water's edge to firmer ground. Trees provide nesting for green-winged teal; the branches dipping in the water protect paddling ducks; while the grey heron and the black-crowned night-heron gather beneath them. The muddy banks are teeming with molluscs which attract waders such as black-tailed godwits, curlews, crested lapwings and snipe. Partially submerged plant life includes perennial herbs, quillwort, clovers and ferns.

Marshes
Plant life in the mineral-rich soil is dominated by grasses in many forms, including sedge, reeds, cattails and bulrushes. Impenetrable and considered undesirable for fish hatcheries, these grassy areas are essential to the survival of certain rare species. Waders such as bitterns and other members of the heron family build their nests in these protected zones alongside marsh harriers, millerbirds, swamp sparrows, reed-buntings etc.

Ponds
Floating plants make good nests for crested grebes. Many species of duck are also found here – such as mallard, pintails and shoveler (with their wide, spatula-shaped bills). Osprey choose the region's ponds to rest during their annual migrations, while terns are a regular sight gliding over the water. European pond turtles are shy creatures, living off water lilies and sunbathing by the reeds. Insects are everywhere, with as many as 600 to 1 000 species identified. Snakes, frogs, toads, newts and some rare mammals have also been spotted, including a remarkable sighting of the European mink, at the Etang Ricot (*Réserve Naturelle de Chérine*).

The abundant **lakes and rivers** of the Limousin are popular with fishing enthusiasts: the **Creuse** is a favourite for trout; the **Gartempe** is popular for carp; the river's oxygen-rich rivers are the domain of trout, grayling and salmon. In still waters, look out for freshwater fish (carp, barbel, tench, bream, chub and dace). Several species of fish, in particular pike and perch, can grow to a considerable size.

MOORS AND FORESTS
Moorland and peatland
The **Brenne** is poor in pastureland and has been gradually abandoned by its rural population; as a result, the few tilled fields have mostly given way to idle, uncultivated land. The humid ground is covered with besom heather, a tall bushy plant with greenish-white flowers. On drier ground, gorse, Scotch broom and bracken grow beneath a few isolated trees. The skies here are populated with birds such as marsh harrier and buzzard, while the undergrowth provides a natural habitat for hare, boar, deer and badger.

In the Limousin, the high plateaux with their vast granite depressions (**Mille-vaches**, **Gentioux**) have highly acidic soil where sphagnum moss flourishes; consequently, parts of the countryside have developed into peat bogs. Near Meymac, the **Tourbière du Longéroux** harbours the source of the Vézère.

Peat is made by the slow decomposition of organic materials (especially sphagnum) in cold, acidic water and in a process that takes centuries. In **Longéroux**, where the average thickness of the peat is 2m/6.5ft, the analysis of fossilised pollen shows that the deposits began forming 8 000 years ago. The bog's inhabitants include lizards, snakes, toads, frogs, newts and the birds that prey on them, as well as the elusive otter, whose presence can often only be deduced by its spoor.

The granite hills around the site are drier, and are covered with common heather, fuzzy broom and scattered bilberry bushes. Over the decades, however, indigenous deciduous trees such as birch and ash have been disappearing as a result of unchecked development.

FORESTS

In the 19C, state-owned forests began operating a coppice-with-standards system, whereby selected stems are retained, as standards, at each felling to form an unevenly aged canopy which is then harvested selectively. The forest is managed so that part of the growth is natural and part of seedling origin, together forming a composite forest. The Indre *département*, one of the first to use this method, has become a leading producer of oakwood for panelling. The **Forêt de Châteauroux** (5260ha/13000 acres) and the **Forêt de Bommiers** (4 470 ha/11 000 acres) are remarkable examples of successful forestry. The dark, low-acidic soil has produced a seedling forest of English oak growing alongside plantations of hornbeam and ash, with ferns growing low to the ground. Boar, deer, martens, skunks, squirrels and wild cats wander the reserve, where the bird population includes wood pigeons and woodpeckers.

To the north, the acidic, wet soil of the Boischaut is home to birch (*Forêt de Gâtine*); oak and beech are found in the Marche; while pubescent oaks grow on the limestone plateaux in the southwest of the Indre *département*. On the highest plateaux of the Limousin, conifers have multiplied, with spruce, larch and pine replacing meadows of heather and fields of grain crops. To the south, and on the borders of the Périgord, deciduous hardwood forests prevail on the sunny slopes, and chestnut trees, which are native to the region, are cultivated for their nuts.

At certain times of the year, the region's woods become the haunt of mushroom-hunters searching for varieties including king bolete (*Boletus edulis*), bay bolete (*Boletus badius*), chanterelle (*Cantharellus cibarius*) and yellow morel (*Morchella esculenta*). If you are unsure about any mushrooms you have picked, by all means take them to the local *pharmacie* to have them identified before bringing them home.

FIELDS AND BOCAGE

The **Champagne Berrichonne**, an open land of large, ploughed fields that attracts numerous birds, is the most northerly area covered in this guide. South of this area, the **Boischaut-Sud** and parts of **La Brenne** are completely different, with a more secretive feel. The *bocage* landscape here is one of hedges and hedgerows, groves of trees, small plots of land and protected pastures. This maze of vegetation is further marked by *chemins creux* – tunnel-like pathways laid out between high banks topped with vegetation. These deep-sided lanes, many now overgrown and too narrow for tractors, prevented erosion; prickly bushes held climbing vines tight together to keep the animals safely enclosed; trees provided wood for cooking and making tools; and the leaves of elm trees could be used as fodder (ⓒsee ST-AMAND-MONTROND).

CAVES AND CHASMS IN THE DORDOGNE

Although dispersed throughout the region, the arid *causse* slices through the otherwise luxuriant landscape of the Périgord. In the Quercy, the limestone plateaux roll away to the horizon, stony, grey and deserted. The dryness of the soil is due to the calcareous nature of the rock which absorbs rain like a sponge.

Water infiltration

Rainwater containing carbonic acid dissolves the carbonate of lime found in the limestone. Depressions form, known as **cloups**, which are usually circular in shape and small in size. When the *cloups* increase in size, they form large, closed depressions known as **sotches**. Where rainwater infiltrates the countless fissures in the plateau more deeply, the hollowing out and dissolution of the calcareous layer produces wells or natural chasms which are called **igues**.

Underground rivers and resurgent springs

Infiltrating water eventually reaches the impermeable layers (marl) of the earth, developing into rivers, which sometimes flow for miles. The waters merge into more powerful streams, widening their beds and tumbling over falls. In zones where the impermeable marl comes close to the surface of a hillside, the water bubbles up to the surface, sometimes with great force, in the form of a **resurgent spring**.

The circulation of water underground through chasms and galleries follows an unpredictable course, for the cracks in the rock continually affect the underground drainage. There are many dry river beds underground where waters have sought out deeper domains.

When water flows slowly, as at Padirac, small lakes are formed by natural dams called **gours**. The walls holding back the waters are built up by the deposit of lime carbonate. Dissolution of limestone continues above the water level, with blocks of stone falling from the roof, resulting in the creation of domes. As the dome pushes upwards and its roof grows thin, it may cave in, opening the chasm to the surface above. The Gouffre de Padirac was thus formed, with the top of its dome just a few feet beneath the surface.

Cave formations

As it circulates underground, water deposits the lime it carries, building up concretions of fantastic shapes which seem to defy the laws of gravity. The

Spruce

© M. Janvier / Michelin

seeping waters deposit calcite (carbonate of lime) to form a series of stalactites, stalagmites, pendants, pyramids, draperies and eccentrics.

Stalactites are formed on the roof by water dripping down. The concretion builds up slowly as drops deposit calcite on the surface.

Stalagmites are a sort of mirror image, rising up from the deposits of dripping water from the ceiling above, eventually meeting the stalactite to form a **pillar**. Such concretions form very slowly: the rate of growth in temperate climates is about 1cm/0.5in every 100 years.

Eccentrics are very delicate protuberances, formed by crystallisation, which seldom exceed 20cm/8in in length. They emerge at odd angles, as slender spikes or in the shape of translucent fans.

Modern exploration

The caves and chasms of the Dordogne were initially inhabited by animals and then by people, who abandoned these natural shelters c 10 000 years ago.

At the end of the 19C, the methodical and scientific exploration of the underground world led to the discovery of a number of caves and their subsequent conversion into tourist attractions.

Yet, despite significant research, many mysteries remain beneath the Earth's surface.

DISCOVERING DORDOGNE
BERRY LIMOUSIN

Château de Castelnaud
© Arnaud Chicurel / hemis.fr

SARLAT AND PÉRIGORD NOIR

This beautiful region, the heart of which lies between the Rivers Vézère and Dordogne, is called the Black Périgord due to the dark colour of its forests, which consist mainly of oaks, chestnut and sea pines. This is the most visited part of the Perigord, with Sarlat at its centre – full of ancient villages to wander, stunning cave systems to explore and castles to admire.

Highlights

1 Walking amid **Sarlat**'s impeccably restored stone buildings (p91)

2 Panorama of the Dordogne from **Château de Beynac** (p105)

3 A nighttime visit to medieval **Château de Castelnaud** (p107)

4 **Lascaux**, one of Europe's finest prehistoric sights (p119)

5 Exploring Domme's unusually shaped **bastide** (p130)

The Périgord Noir

The Périgord Noir is the most popular of the four Périgords, with an amazing variety and number of sites.

Among the most picturesque are the medieval fortresses that stand on the rocky outcrops above the Dordogne River. Whether admired from the river or across the valley from the Marqueyssac gardens, across layers of morning fog or in the crisp evening light, their golden forms are always breathtaking.

View down a street in Domme

© Denis Badet / Fotolia.com

Sarlat-la-Canéda, with its concentration of historic buildings and medieval atmosphere, is the lively centre of the Périgord noir.

The Vézère river is synonymous with prehistory, and this is where you'll find the Lascaux cave facsimile, along with a great number of other prehistoric sites. The Pôle International de la Préhistoire has developed various ways to help you make the most of them, not least of which is the National Museum of Prehistory in Les Eyzies, the world capital of prehistory. The region's substrata conceals a labyrinth of caves, and in addition to prehistoric art, concretions can also be admired, thanks to the high level of calcium carbonate in the bedrock; the majestic caves of Proumeyssac and Le Grand Roc are just two examples.

The south of the area is bastide country, (see p129) beginning with the endearing perched village of Domme. Beautiful bastides such as Monpazier and abbeys such as Cadouin are among other well-kept medieval villages here.

To the north, rolling hills replace the craggy cliffs of the Vézère Valley. Hautefort Castle is the northernmost site of the area, attracting visitors by organizing cultural events in its romantic setting.

The Périgord Noir is the gastronomic highlight of the region, well-known for the high quality of its produce. It is especially known for such exceptional fare as foie gras, truffles and wild mushrooms, duck and goose in every imaginable form, soft fruit and its derived beverages, walnuts and walnut oil.

Saturday markets at Sarlat are a classic, extending through the whole town; but if you'd like to avoid the crowds, you may enjoy any number of markets, including increasingly popular night markets, in villages all over the region.

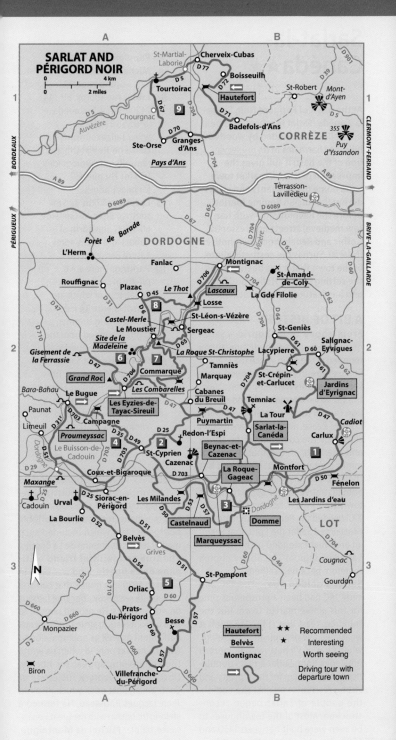

SARLAT AND PÉRIGORD NOIR

0 ————— 4 km
0 ————— 2 miles

BORDEAUX

PÉRIGUEUX

CLERMONT-FERRAND

BRIVE-LA-GAILLARDE

St-Martial-Laborie
Cherveix-Cubas
Tourtoirac
Boisseuilh
St-Robert
Mont-d'Ayen
Hautefort
9
Chourgnac
Auvézère
Granges-d'Ans
Badefols-d'Ans
CORRÈZE
355
Puy d'Yssandon
Ste-Orse
Pays d'Ans
Terrasson-Lavilledieu

A 89

Forêt de Barade

DORDOGNE

L'Herm
Fanlac
Montignac
St-Amand-de-Coly
Rouffignac
Plazac
Le Thot
Lascaux
La Gde Filolie
8
Losse
Castel-Merle
St-Léon-s-Vézère
Le Moustier
Sergeac
St-Geniès
Site de la Madeleine
La Roque St-Christophe
Lacypierre
Salignac-Eyvigues
Gisement de la Ferrassie
6
7
Tamniès
St-Crépin-et-Carlucet
Jardins d'Eyrignac
Grand Roc
Commarque
Marquay
Temniac
Bara-Bahau
Le Bugue
Les Combarelles
Cabanes du Breuil
La Tour
Les Eyzies-de-Tayac-Sireuil
Paunat
Campagne
Puymartin
Sarlat-la-Canéda
Carlux
Cadiot
Limeuil
Proumeyssac
4
D 25
Redon-l'Espi
1
Le Buisson-de-Cadouin
2
St-Cyprien
Beynac-et-Cazenac
Montfort
Cazenac
Coux-et-Bigaroque
La Roque-Gageac
Fénelon
D 703
Maxange
Les Jardins d'eau
Cadouin
Urval
Siorac-en-Périgord
Les Milandes
3
Dordogne
Domme
LOT
La Bourlie
Castelnaud
Belvès
Grives
Marqueyssac
Cougnac
N
St-Pompont
Gourdon
Orliac
5
Prats-du-Périgord
Besse
Monpazier
Biron
Villefranche-du-Périgord

Hautefort   ✶✶   Recommended
Belvès   ✶   Interesting
Montignac   Worth seeing
⇨   Driving tour with
                 departure town

89

Sarlat-la-Canéda★★

and Le Salardais

At the heart of Périgord Noir, Sarlat-la-Canéda (Sarlat for short) was built in a hollow surrounded by wooded hills. Its charm lies in its preservation of the past; it still gives the impression of a small market town – the home of merchants and clerks during the Ancien Régime (period before the Revolution) – with narrow medieval streets and restored Gothic and Renaissance townhouses (*hôtels*). Such is the aesthetic allure of the town that it has been used as the setting for two Hollywood films and has featured in many others.

A BIT OF HISTORY

From abbey to bishopric – Sarlat grew up around a Benedictine abbey founded in the 8C in which the relics of St Sacerdos, bishop of Limoges, were kept. The abbots were all-powerful until the 13C when internal strife and corruption caused their downfall. In 1299 the Book of Peace, an act of emancipation signed by the community, the abbey and the king, stated that the abbot might continue in his role of lord but that the consuls should be given all administrative power concerning the town itself. In 1317, however, Pope John XXII divided the Périgueux diocese and proclaimed Sarlat the Episcopal See of an area that extended far beyond the Sarladais region. The abbey church therefore became a cathedral.

Sarlat's golden age – The 13C and early 14C had been a prosperous time for this active market town, but the Hundred Years War (1337-1453) left it weakened and depopulated. Therefore, when Charles VII bestowed numerous privileges upon Sarlat and its population to thank them for their loyalty and strong resistance against the English, the people of Sarlat began reconstruction. Most of the townhouses to be seen were built between 1450 and 1500. This has created an architec-

▶ **Population:** 10 279.
🕭 **Michelin Map:** 329: I-6; and page 92.
🛈 **Info:** 3 rue Tourny, BP 144, 24200 Sarlat-la-Canéda. ℘05 53 31 45 46. www.sarlat-tourisme. com. The Tourist Office rents iPhone audioguides (€5 for 2hr plus €2 for headphones).
◐ **Location:** 52km/32.5mi south of Brive-la-Gaillarde, 60km/37.5mi north of Cahors and 74km/46mi east of Bergerac.
🅿 **Parking:** There are a plenty of car parks in Sarlat, four of which are free of charge (🕭 *see town plan*). In summer, traffic is banned from the town's historic quarter.
👁 **Don't Miss:** Old Sarlat; Place du Marché aux Trois Oies; Hôtel Plamon; Hôtel de Maleville; Maison de la Boétie; Saturday and Wednesday markets.

tural unity which is appreciated by the townspeople and tourists alike. The magistrates, clerks, bishops, canons and merchants formed a comfortable bourgeois class which included such men of letters as Étienne de La Boétie.

The true and faithful friend – Étienne de La Boétie, who was born in Sarlat in 1530 in a house that can still be seen (🕭 *see below*), became famous on many counts. He proved himself to be a brilliant magistrate in the Bordeaux Parliament as well as an impassioned writer – he was only 18 when he wrote the compelling appeal for liberty, *Discourse on Voluntary Subjection or Contr'un* (against one), which inspired Jean-Jacques Rousseau. He formed a lifelong friendship with the great Renaissance scholar **Michel de Montaigne**. Montaigne was at La Boétie's bedside when the young man died in 1563; with his friend in mind, Montaigne wrote his famous *Essay on Friendship* in which he formulated the excellent sentiment: "If I am urged to explain why I loved him, I feel I can only reply: because he was himself and I am myself."

🐾 WALKING TOUR

VIEUX SARLAT★★★

Sarlat's old district was cut in two in the 19C by the Traverse (rue de la République). The townhouses are quite unique: built with quality ashlar-work in a fine golden-hued limestone, with interior courtyards; the roofing, made of heavy limestone slabs (*lauzes*), necessitated a steeply pitched framework so that the enormous weight (500kg per m² – about 102lb per sq ft) could be supported on thick walls. Over the years new floors were added: a medieval ground floor, a High Gothic or Renaissance upper floor and Classical roof cresting and lantern turrets.

This architectural unit escaped modern building developments and was chosen in 1962 as one of the new experimental national restoration projects, the goal of which was to preserve the old quarters of France's towns and cities. The project, which began in 1964, has allowed the charm of this small medieval town to be recreated.

▶ Start from place du Peyrou.

Cathédrale St-Sacerdos

St Sacerdos church was built here in the 12C. In 1504, Bishop Armand de Gontaut-Biron had the church razed in order to build a cathedral.

However, when the bishop left Sarlat in 1519, the construction work ceased for more than a century and was completed during the 16C and 17C.

Inside, the most striking features are the elevation and harmonious proportions of the nave, which has ogive vaulting, and of the chancel surrounded by an ambulatory.

Ancien Évêché

To the right of St Sacerdos cathedral is the former bishopric. Its façade★ has windows in the Gothic style on the first floor, Renaissance on the second floor and an Italian Renaissance loggia above, added by the Italian bishop Nicolo Goddi, friend of Catherine de' Medici. *The tourist office is on the ground floor.*

Maison de la Boétie★

This house, built in 1525, is the birthplace of Étienne de La Boétie.

A large arch on the ground floor used to shelter a small shop; the two upper floors of Italian Renaissance style have large mullioned windows, framed by pilasters carved with medallions and lozenges.

Place de la Liberté at night

©Tibor Bognár/agefotostock

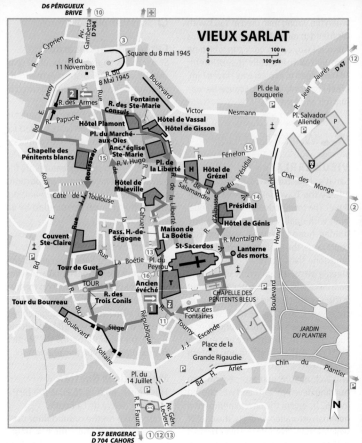

VIEUX SARLAT

WHERE TO STAY		WHERE TO EAT	
Cordeliers (Chambre d'hôte Les)......	③	Bistrot de l'Octroi (Le)............	⑩
Etape des Peupliers (Chambre d'hôte L')............	①	Chez le Gaulois............	⑪
Maison des Peyrat (Hôtel La)............	②	Jardins d'Harmonie (Les)............	⑬
Mas de Castel (Hôtel)............	⑫	Présidial (Le)............	⑭
Montaigne (Hôtel)............	⑬	Rossignol............	⑮
Récollets (Hôtel des)............	⑮	Rapière (La)............	⑯

On the left of the house is **passage Henri-de-Ségogne**, between Hôtel de Maleville and La Boétie's House. The alleyway leads visitors through an arch, a passageway and a covered passageway.

Picturesque half-timbered buildings have been restored and, in summer, craft shops do a brisk business.

Hôtel de Maleville★

This edifice is also known as the Hôtel de Vienne after the man who built it, Jean de Vienne. Born of humble parents in Sarlat in 1557, he successfully climbed the social ladder to become financial secretary under Henri IV.

Later, the townhouse was bought by the Maleville family; a member of this same family, Jacques de Maleville (⊙ see

DOMME), helped write the French *Code Civil*, the general rules of law.

Three existing houses were combined in the mid-16C to form an imposing mansion. In front of the tall, narrow central pavilion, like a majestic tower, is a terrace under which opens the arched main doorway surmounted by medallions depicting Henri IV and Marie de Medici. The right wing, overlooking place de la Liberté, has a late Renaissance gable.

▶ Take the covered passage to the left of the entrance, then take rue du Minage opposite, follow rue de la République and turn right onto rue des Consuls.

Rue des Consuls
The townhouses in this street are beautiful examples of Sarlat architecture from the 14C–17C.

▶ On the right after the bend.

Hôtel Plamon★
As identified by the shield on the pediment above the doorway, this townhouse belonged to the Selves de Plamon family, members of the cloth merchants' guild. Because it is made up of a group of buildings built in different periods, it is a particularly interesting illustration of the evolution of the different architectural styles used in Sarlat construction.

Left of the townhouse is the very narrow Plamon Tower with windows which get smaller the higher up they are; this architectural ruse makes the tower seem much taller than it is.

On the corner of the street is a rounded overhanging balcony supported by a squinch. Go into the courtyard to admire the elegant 17C wooden **staircase★**.

Fontaine Ste-Marie
Opposite the Hôtel de Plamon, the fountain splashes in a cool grotto.

Place du Marché aux Oies★
Appropriately called Goose Square, this was the traditional area of the Saturday morning market where live geese were sold.

The square is an elegant architectural collection of turrets, pinnacles and corner staircases.

Hôtel de Vassal
Located on a corner of place des Oies, this 15C townhouse consists of two buildings at right angles flanked by twin corbelled turrets. Beside it, the **Hôtel de Gisson** (16C) is made of two buildings joined by a hexagonal staircase tower with a remarkable pointed roof.

Place de la Liberté
Many pavement cafés liven up Sarlat's main square. The 17C **town hall** stands on the east side and the disused **Église Ste-Marie,** now converted into a covered market, on the north side. You can get a good **view★** from the belltower.

▶ Leave place de la Liberté and walk along rue de la Salamandre.

Hôtel de Grézel
Built at the end of the 15C, the townhouse straight ahead has a half-timbered façade with a tower and a lovely Flamboyant Gothic ogee-arched doorway. Continue onto rue Présidial, then rue Landry (as far as no 7), until you can see the 17C tower of the **Présidial**, former seat of royal magistrates (now a restaurant).

▶ Retrace your steps and turn left onto rue d'Albusse.

At the corner of the dead end (where the old post house can be seen) stands the **Hôtel de Génis**, a massive, plain 15C building with an overhanging upper storey supported by seven stone corbels.

▶ Follow rue Sylvain Cavaillez and enter the garden.

Lanterne des Morts
Built at the end of the 12C, this mysterious cylindrical tower is the tallest of its kind in Europe. Topped with a cone and split into tiers by four bands, it contains two rooms. The room on the ground floor has domed vaulting held up by

six pointed arches; the other room is in the cone part of the tower, which was inaccessible.

A number of hypotheses have been put forward concerning the lantern's function: was it a tower built in honour of the visit of St Bernard in 1147; a lantern of the dead; or a funerary chapel?

▷ Go down the stairs and walk around the Chapelle des Pénitents Bleus (12C). Go into cour des Chanoines then cour des Fontaines. Rue Munz and rue Tourny lead back to place du Peyrou.

☙ WEST SIDE TOUR★

This part of town, on the opposite side of rue de la République (the so-called Traverse), is quieter, a place of steep and winding lanes, off the main tourist track, and offer another image of Sarlat.

▷ Walk along rue de la République and turn left onto rue J-J-Rousseau.

Chapelle des Pénitents Blancs

Used by the Order of Pénitents Blancs, the chapel (1626) was part of the religious establishment of the Pères Récollets.

Rue Jean-Jacques Rousseau

This is the main street in this part of town, and many attractive old houses grace it. At no 9, on the corner of Côte de Toulouse, there is an admirable 18C façade (Hôtel Monméja); at the intersection with rue de la Boétie, you can see the bartizan which marks the site of **St Clare's Convent**, a vast 17C building once occupied by the Poor Clares, that today provides low-rent housing.

▷ Continue along rue du Siège then turn left onto rue Rousset.

Tour de Guet

Overlapping the buildings, the watchtower is crowned by 15C machicolations and flanked by a corbelled turret.

▷ Turn right onto rue du Cordil.

Rue des Trois-Conils (des Trois Lapins)

This street bends sharply left around the foot of a house flanked by a tower, which once belonged to relations of the La Boétie family.

Tour du Bourreau

The Executioner's Tower, which was part of the ramparts, was built in 1580.

▷ Walk along rue du Siège leading back to rue de la République.

EXCURSIONS
Jardins de Haute Terre

7km/4mi W along the D 25 and C 6 in Saint-André-d'Allas. ◔*Open year-round upon reservation and May–Aug 4–7pm.* ⊚ *€10 (children 12+ €5).* ℘*06 84 39 57 36. http://jardinsdehauteterre.free.fr.*
At nearly 300m elevation, this 4-ha/10-acre cultural and patrimonial garden includes a chestnut, hornbeam and pine grove and features wild orchids, heather, rock rose, daisy beds and more. Enjoy a sweeping **view★** over the landscape and nearby sights.

Réserve Zoologique de Calviac★

10km/6.2mi SE along the D 704 and D 704A. ◔*Open daily: Jul–Aug 9.30am–8pm; Apr–Jun and Sept 10am–7pm; Oct noon–6pm; 1–11 Nov and Christmas holidays 1.30–5pm; Feb–Mar 1.30–6pm.* ◔*Closed rest of year.* ⊚*€9 (3–12 years old €6), €1 discount for visitors on bikes.* ℘*05 53 28 84 08. www.reserve-calviac.org.*
At this original 3-ha/7.4-acre wildlife reserve you'll discover some of the world's most endangered species, many of which are absent from traditional zoos, such as the maned wolf, the tapir and the European mink. An ingenious system even allows you to get inside some of the animals' living areas, including those of the barn owl, lemur, wallaby and bald ibis.

Marquay

11.5km/7mi NW along D 47 and D 6.
This sought-after holiday resort surrounded by important Paleolithic sites has an unusual 12C church.

Tamniès

15km/9.3mi NW along D 47 and D 6.
The 12C village church and former priory overlook the Beune Valley. There is a lake with leisure facilities nearby.

🚗 DRIVING TOURS

② THE DORDOGNE TO THE BEAUNE★

60km/37.3mi round-trip – half a day. See route 2 on region map page 89.

After Beynac this route follows the Dordogne valley to St-Cyprien. From here it takes the backroads past sleepy hamlets through the unspoilt Périgord Noir.

▶ Drive SW out of Sarlat along the D 57; turn right onto the D 703 shortly after Vézac.

Beynac-et-Cazenac★★

See BEYNAC-ET-CAZENAC.
Continue on the D 703 to St-Cyprien then turn right as you leave the village.

Cazenac

This hamlet possesses a 15C Gothic church with a lovely view of the valley.

▶ Turn back and rejoin the D 703.

St-Cyprien

St-Cyprien clings to the side of a hill near the north bank of the Dordogne in a setting of hills and woodlands characteristic of the Périgord Noir. It is dominated by the massive outline of its **church**, the old houses of the village clustered close around. The large church was built in the 12C and restored in the Gothic period; the belfry keep is Romanesque. Inside, the enormous main body of the church has pointed vaulting. A wealth of 17C furnishings include altarpieces, a pulpit,

stalls, an organ loft and a wrought-iron balustrade. Close to the village are the carefully restored ruins of the **Château de Fages**.

▶ Drive NE along the D 25.

Chapelle de Redon-l'Espi

This remote Romanesque chapel is flanked by the ruins of a small monastery, destroyed during the Wars of Religion. The Virgin Mary is said to have appeared to a young shepherdess in the 19C, giving rise to a pilgrimage that still takes place in September.

▶ Rejoin D 25 (right); left on D 47 beyond Allas; right 1.5km/0.9mi on.

Cabanes du Breuil★

🕒🚹 *Open daily: Apr–Oct 10am–7pm; 1–mid-Nov 2–5pm; mid-Nov–Mar weekend and public holidays 2–5pm.* €6. 📞06 80 72 38 59. www.cabanes-du-breuil.com.
The hamlet of Breuil has the richest collection of drystone buildings known as *caselles* (or *gariottes*) in Périgord. There are five huts, forming an architectural grouping unique in the region.

▶ Turn back and turn left onto the D 47 towards Sarlat; turn left again 3km/1.9mi farther on.

Château de Puymartin★

Open daily: Apr–Jun and Sept 10.30–11.30pm, 2–6pm; 1–15 Jul 10am–noon, 2–6.30pm; 15 Jul–late Aug 10am–6.30pm; Oct–mid-Nov 2–5.30pm. €9. 📞05 53 59 29 97. www.chateau-de-puymartin.com.
Constructed in the 15C and 16C, considerably remodelled in the 19C, the castle consists of several buildings linked to towers, and protected by a curtain wall. The **interior decoration★** is impressive: period furnishings, Aubusson tapestries, painted beams and paintings.

▶ The D 47 takes you back to Sarlat.

ADDRESSES

🛏 STAY

⌂ Chambre d'hôte L'Étape des Peupliers – *25 ter r. de Cahors. ☎05 53 59 03 53. 5 rooms.* Just next to the historic district of Sarlat, enjoy simple, perfectly clean rooms. These open onto the hidden back garden, where you may also enjoy a splash in the swimming pool.

⌂⌂ Hôtel des Récollets – *4 r. Jean-Jacques-Rousseau. ☎05 53 31 36 00. www.hotel-recollets-sarlat.com. 18 rooms.* This unique hotel is in a former convent (17C). The rooms are not large, but they are quiet and all have been renovated with contemporary furniture, original beams and stone walls. Enjoy breakfast in a vaulted room or on the patio.

⌂⌂ Mas de Castel – *3km/1.8mi S of Sarlat via the D 704 and C 1. ☎05 53 59 02 59. www.hotel-lemasdecastel.com. 13 rooms.* An attractive hotel occupying an old farm in a peaceful rural setting. Pastel tones and rustic furniture in the bedrooms, some of which are on garden level. Swimming pool.

⌂⌂ La Maison des Peyrat – *Lac de la Plane (0.6 mi E of the town centre). ☎05 53 59 00 32. www.maisondespeyrat.com. 10 rooms.* Secluded in the hills of Sarlat, this gorgeous house, full of character, surrounded by walnut trees and pastures, offers light, airy rooms, refined breakfast and dinner upon reservation. Swimming pool.

⌂⌂ Montaigne – *Pl. Pasteur, Sarlat la Canéda. ☎05 53 31 93 88. www.hotel montaigne.fr. 28 rooms.* 150m from the cobbled medieval centre of Sarlat and housed in a beautiful historical building, the hotel offers comfortable and well-equipped rooms with free wi-fi Internet access.

⌂⌂ Chambre d'hôte Les Cordeliers – *51 r. des Cordeliers. ☎05 53 31 94 66. www. hotelsarlat.com. 6 rooms.* Located at the gateway to the historic centre, this pretty bourgeois house with royal blue shutters offers spacious rooms with large, sprung beds. The traditional breakfast is served in the living room which looks out onto a tree-lined square.

🍽 EAT

⌂ Chez le Gaulois – *9 r. Tourny. ☎05 53 59 50 64.* This convivial "ham cellar"-themed restaurant offers a selection of regional products. Copious cold meat platters with cheese and salad served on chopping boards. Delicious handmade ice cream.

⌂ La Rapière – *Pl. du Peyrou. ☎05 53 59 03 13.* One of Sarlat's classic restaurants, where locals come to enjoy flavoursome regional cuisine, such as chicken breast in a verjus sauce, goose Parmentier with bolete mushrooms, and roasted preserved duck. Pleasant service.

⌂⌂ La Petite Borie – *4 r. de Tourny. ☎05 53 31 23 69.* This pretty little spot offers refined regional cuisine for very reasonable prices. Large platters, homemade foie gras and wine bought directly from the winemaker.

⌂⌂ Le Bistrot de l'Octroi – *111 av. de selves (600m N of town centre). ☎05 53 30 83 40. www.lebistrodeloctroi.fr.* Enjoy fine local and regional cuisine and a warm welcome in this 1830s building. Choose from upstairs, downstairs or the outdoor terrace.

⌂⌂ Les Jardins d'Harmonie – *Pl. André Malraux. ☎05 53 31 06 69. www.lesjardins dharmonie.com. Closed Mon–Tue.* Very attractive little restaurant set in the old cobbled part of town, spilling out onto the streets beneath its awnings. Try one of their speciality salads, steaks or foie gras. They also have a tearoom.

⌂⌂ Rossignol – *15 r. Fénelon. ☎05 53 31 02 30. Closed Thu.* A simple, central, family-run restaurant, with one rustic-style dining room. Copious and unpretentious local cuisine, including fish.

⌂⌂🍽 Le Présidial – *6 r. Landry. ☎05 53 28 92 47.* Formerly the royal court of justice, this beautiful 17C building features a vast garden in the heart of historic Sarlat, making it an ideal setting for a romantic dinner. Good, classic cuisine and refined service.

Le Périgord Noir★★

With its castles perched along the cliff sides of the Dordogne valley, this area is the true the essence of the Périgord. The countryside is sprinkled with golden stone houses – often topped with *lauzes* – little Romanesque churches, duck farms and forests that are carpeted with *bolete* mushrooms in autumn. The river meanders among fields lined with poplars in a valley guarded by an army of fortified castles.

EXPLORING THE REGION

A **cycle path** along a former railway track leads from Sarlat to **Cazoulès** (*25km/15.5mi to the east*). This easy trail is ideal for a day with the family and a picnic along the Dordogne. In St Roma, you can take the path that leads to **Groléjac** (*12km/7.4mi to the south*), where the lake is equipped for leisure activities.

🚗 DRIVING TOURS

1 ROUND-TRIP FROM SARLAT★★
75km/47mi. Allow one day.
See route 1 on region map page 89.

The houses, castles, châteaux, manor houses and churches along this route have walls of golden-coloured local limestone and steeply pitched roofs covered with *lauzes*, or small flat tiles, in a warm brown hue. These architectural elements, combined with the rolling, wooded countryside, make a harmonious picture.

▶ Leave Sarlat travelling SE along the D 704 towards Gourdon. As you leave town, turn right to La Canéda.

Carsac-Aillac
The modest but delightful church of Carsac, in lovely golden stone, is set in countryside near the Dordogne. The porch has five recessed arches resting

- **Population:** 80 000.
- **Michelin Map:** 329 GHIJ6-7.
- **Info:** www.perigordnoir.com.
- **Location:** The Périgord Noir is within the triangle formed by the Dordogne valley (to the south), the Vézère valley (to the west) and the D 820 (to the east). Sarlat and Souillac are its gateways.
- **Don't miss:** Tasting foie gras; the view over the Cingle de Montfort; Josephine Baker's Milande castle.
- **Kids:** Playgrounds and climbing walls at Jardins de Marqueyssac.
- **Timing:** Besides the Vézère and Dordogne valleys, allow a full day for the centre of the Périgord Noir.

on small columns. The massive Romanesque belltower and the apse are roofed with *lauzes*. The nave and the lower aisles had stellar vaulting decorated with elegant discs or bosses added to them in the 16C.

▶ Leave Carsac travelling S along the D 704 to St-Rome and follow the signposts to the Jardins d'Eau.

Jardins d'Eau★
St-Rome. Open May–15 Oct, 9am–8pm. Guided tour on request at 10am and 4pm. €6. 05 53 28 91 96. www.jardinsdeau.com.
This 3ha/7.50-acre water garden is laid out along the riverside. The reception area is surrounded by a pond covered with exotic waterlilies; it is home to a colony of frogs and five different kinds of dragonflies. The great white waterlily pond, spanned by a Japanese bridge, evokes one of Monet's paintings, whereas the five varieties of iris bring Van Gogh to mind. The largest lotus flowers (2m high with leaves 70cm in diameter) grow near the fountain, next to six varieties of white lilies. Take the

footbridge wending its way above the lotus pond to admire the waterlilies floating on the tiered ponds among smaller water plants. You can buy plants in the nursery.

▶ Rejoin the D 704, cross the River Dordogne and turn left onto the D 50.

Château de Fénelon★

⏱Open: Jul–Aug 10.30am–6.30pm; Apr–Jun and Sept 10.30am–12.30pm, 2.30–6.30pm; Oct 2–7pm; ⏱Closed Nov–Mar; Tue am (except Jul–Aug), and Sat. Self-guided tours. ⬤€9. ✆05 53 29 81 45. www.chateau-fenelon.fr.

François de Salignac de Lamothe-Fénelon, later to become the duke of Burgundy's mentor and author of Télémaque, was born here on 6 August 1651 and spent his early childhood within these walls. His family had been feudal lords since the 14C and remained so until 1780. Built near Ste-Mondane village, on a hill overlooking the Dordogne and the Bouriane Forest, the 14C castle underwent substantial alterations in the 17C. Its triply fortified walls give it the appearance of being a very powerful fortress. The residential buildings and towers are still covered with *lauze* slate roofs. A beautiful **staircase** gives access to the main courtyard. From the terrace, there is a fine view of undulating countryside. Inside, the bedroom where Fénelon was born, the Louis XVI and Empire rooms,

the kitchen hollowed out of the rock and a collection of medieval military miscellany are all open to visitors.

▶ Follow D 50 to St-Julien-de-Lampon; cross to the north bank via the D 61.

The crossing of the Dordogne is guarded by the **Château de Rouffillac**; its attractive outline can be seen rising out of the green oak trees.

Carlux

Overlooking the valley from its commanding position, the village still has some old houses and a small covered market. Two towers and an imposing curtain wall are all that remains of the large castle, which once belonged to the viscounty of Turenne.

From the castle terrace, there is a lovely **view** of the valley and the cliffs, which were used as the castle foundations.

▶ Take the road behind the castle and follow the signposts for Jardins de Cadiot.

Jardins de Cadiot★

⏱Open May–mid-Oct, 10am–7pm. ⬤€7. ✆05 53 29 81 05. www.lesjardinsdecadiot.com.

This private 2ha/5-acre garden is surrounded by an oak wood. The tour starts with a vegetable garden and continues

Château de Fénelon

Allée des Charmes,
Jardins d'Eyrignac

© Eric Sander / Jardins d'Eyrignac

through ten areas of different colours: peony garden, hornbeam maze, rose garden containing 500 species of rose, poetry garden, English garden and French garden; each has its own charm.

▶ Continue along the D 61 towards Salignac and turn left onto the D 47 3km/1.9mi farther on. Turn right in Ste-Nathalène and drive towards Proissans.

Moulin de la Tour

♿⊙*Open Mon–Fri (and Sat pm Apr–Sept) 9.30am–noon and 2–6.30pm. ⊙Closed 1 Jan, 1 Nov, 25 Dec and Sun. ⊛€5. ℘05 53 59 22 08. www.moulindelatour.com.*
The 16C watermill, driven by the flow of the River Enea, continues the manufacture of walnut and hazelnut oils. There used to be many grain mills in Périgord, which were also adaptable for the production of walnut oil during the winter. The mill's mechanism is 150 years old.

▶ Return to Ste-Nathalène. Shortly before reaching the village, turn left towards the hamlet of La Tour.

Les Jardins du Manoir Eyrignac★★

♿⊙*Jan–Mar 10.30am–12.30pm and 2.30pm to dusk; Apr 10am–7pm; May–Sept 9.30am–7pm; Oct 10am–dusk; Nov–Dec 10.30am–12.30pm and 2.30pm–dusk. Guided tour. ⊛€9.50 (during winter), €12.50 Mar–Nov. ℘05 53 28 99 71. www.eyrignac.com.*
Laid out in the 18C by the Marquis de la Calprenède, these gardens were remodelled many times during the 19C and finally given their present aspect in the 1960s by Gilles Sermadiras de Pouzols de Lile. Five gardeners work full time to look after the 4ha/10-acre gardens. The result is a happy compromise between the French-style garden and Tuscan topiary art, rich in evergreens which make for year-round delight. The grassy paths are bordered with yew, creating little green chambers; there are apple trees in quincuncial arrangements (four trees in the corners and a fifth in the middle); cypress groves, urns, pools and dainty pavilions ornament the grounds of the 17C mansion, built in pale Sarlat stone. The latest addition to this enchanting place is the **Jardin blanc** (white garden); alleyways lined with white roses lead to five ornamental pools representing the five senses against a background of white rambling roses. See the website for events and children's activities.

▶ Rejoin the D 61 and turn left.

Salignac-Eyvigues

The market square, the façade of the 13C convent (Couvent des Croisiers) and the neighbouring streets, in particular rue Sainte-Croix, are a charming sight, just a few yards away from the entrance to the castle.

Château

☞ *Closed for restoration.*

There is a good overall view from the D 60, east of the village, of this medieval fortress which still belongs to the family of the archbishop of Cambrai, François de Salignac de la Mothe-Fénelon.

The castle, which was built between the 12C and 17C, is encircled by ramparts. Mullioned windows lighten the façade of the main building, which is flanked by round and square towers. The whole building is enhanced by the warm colour of the stone and the lovely stone-slab (*lauzes*) roofs.

▷ Drive W along the D 60 (Sarlat) and turn left as you leave the village.

Carlucet

The church of Carlucet has an unusual 17C cemetery. Some of the tombs have been set in carved recesses in the curtain wall.

▷ Drive SW out of Carlucet along a small winding road.

St-Crépin-et-Carlucet

The charming **Château de Lacypierre** (&♿☞*open Easter to 1 Nov, guided tour;* ⊙€6; ✆05 53 29 39 28), was built at the end of the 16C on the spot where a fortified building had once stood. The square main building is entirely roofed in *lauzes* and framed by turrets.

▷ Continue N along the D 60 to Salignac and turn left onto the D 61 2km/1.2mi farther on.

St-Geniès★

This is one good example of the Périgord Noir's many beautiful villages with its golden limestone houses covered in *lauzes*, the ruins of a Romanesque keep and the 15C castle next to the church. Located at the top of a mound behind the post office, the **Chapelle du Cheylard**, a small Gothic chapel, is decorated with lovely 14C **frescoes★** depicting the life of Christ and lives of popular saints.

▷ Leave St-Geniès travelling S along the D 64 towards the D 704 and follow signs for Sarlat. Turn left at Les Presses.

Temniac

The chapel of Notre-Dame, set on a hill overlooking Sarlat, offers a good **view★** of that town. Once a pilgrimage centre, this 12C structure has Romanesque Périgord School characteristics: a nave vaulted with two domes and a pentagonal chancel.

Near the chapel stands the curtain wall of a castle, once a commandery of the Knights Templar before it became the residence of the bishops of Sarlat.

▷ The D 57 leads back to Sarlat.

③ DORDOGNE IN THE PÉRIGORD★★★

♿*See LE PÉRIGORD NOIR.*
Round-trip from Sarlat – 70km/44mi. Allow half a day. See route 3 on region map page 89.

▷ Drive S out of Sarlat on D 704. At Carsac-Aillac, take the D 703 right.

Site de Montfort★

Occupying an advantageous site on the River Dordogne, Montfort has given its name to one of Périgord's most famous meanders.

Cingle de Montfort★

From the cliff road (*D 703 – car park*), there is a splendid **view★** of this meander in the river, known in French as the Cingle de Montfort, encircling the Tursac peninsula and its walnut tree plantations; the château clings to its promontory.

Château de Montfort★

The castle stands in a grandiose **setting★**, which aroused the envy of those who wished to rule Périgord; its history consisted of a long series of sieges and battles. Seized by Simon de Montfort in 1214 and razed to the ground, it was rebuilt and then later destroyed three times – during the Hundred Years War (1337–1453), under Louis XI (1461–83), and again by order of Henri IV (1562–1610). The renovation work carried out in the 19C gives it the whimsical look of a stage setting for light opera.

▶ Drive NW along the D 703 then turn right onto the D 46. Cross the Dordogne then turn right onto the D 50.

Domme★★
♿ See DOMME.

▶ Continue on the D 50.

Cénac
The only remaining evidence of the large priory built in Cénac in the 11C is the small **Romanesque church** which stands outside the village. Even the church did not escape the Wars of Religion, and only the east end escaped the depredations of the Protestants serving under Captain Vivans in 1589.
Go into the churchyard to get an overall view of the east end with its fine stone roof and its column buttresses topped with foliated capitals. Inside, in the chancel and the apse, there is a series of interesting historiated capitals.

▶ Continue along the D 50 to St-Cybranet then follow the D 57 towards Sarlat and turn left before the bridge.

Château de Castelnaud★★
♿ See Château de CASTELNAUD.

▶ Rejoin D 57 (left) then D 53, which follows the south bank of the Dordogne.

Château de Fayrac
The castle is tucked amid the greenery on the south bank of the Dordogne opposite Beynac-et-Cazenac. A double curtain wall surrounds the interior courtyard, which is reached by two drawbridges.

▶ Continue along the D 53.

Josephine Baker, c1932

©Keystone Archives H/age fotostock

Josephine Baker

An early symbol of the vitality of artistic expression in the American black community, Josephine Baker was also an honoured hero of WW2, winning the Croix de Guerre for her work as a member of the Free French forces and the Resistance. She began her theatrical career in her early teens, earning a place as a chorus girl in the revue *Shuffle Along*, which brought her to New York City. Still a young woman, she stirred sensation in Paris with her *danse sauvage*, playing on colonial fantasies and high-octane sexuality, while learning much about the world, her art and herself. She got star billing for her performance at the Folies-Bergère, clad in the famous banana skirt. Baker became a French citizen in 1937. When war broke out, she used her special position as an entertainer to carry secret messages and to spirit friends out of France to safety. She retired at age 50 but, short of funds and determined to continue building her dream and her family at Les Milandes, she returned to the stage within a few years, and worked tirelessly until the day of her death.

Château des Milandes★

🕒 *Apr–May 10am–6.30pm; Jun–10 Jul and Sept 10am–7pm; 11 Jul–Aug 9.30am–7.30pm; Sept 10am–7pm; Oct 10am–6.15pm.* ✆€9.50. ☎05 53 59 31 21. www.milandes.com.

Built in 1489 by François de Caumont, the estate remained the property of this family until the Revolution and was eventually purchased by American singer Josephine Baker, or *La Perle Noire* as she was known in her Paris cabaret heyday in the 1920s and 1930s. It was here that she sought to create a world village, gathering together and adopting children of different races, religions and nationalities, and bringing them up to promote mutual understanding.

Josephine Baker adapted the interior decoration to her own taste as visitors can gather from walking through various rooms devoted to the different periods of the singer's life.

An unrelated addition to the tourist attraction, falconry demonstrations are staged in the gardens surrounding the château. Visitors may also stroll through the park beyond.

▶ Rejoin the D 53 then turn right onto the D 50 and right again 4.5km/2.8mi farther to Allas-les-Mines. Cross the Dordogne and turn right onto the D 703 which follows the north bank.

Beynac-et-Cazenac★★

👉 *See BEYNAC-ET-CAZENAC.*
Continue along the D 703; turn left past the railway line onto the D 49 towards Sarlat then right onto the D 57.

▲▲ Jardins de Marqueyssac★★

👉 *See JARDINS DE MARQUEYSSAC.*

▶ Rejoin the D 703 (on the left).

Note, on your left, the **Château de la Malartrie**, a castle built in the 20C, greatly influenced by the 15C style.

La Roque-Gageac★★

👉 *See La ROQUE-GAGEAC.*

▶ Drive 2km/1.2mi on the D 703 and turn left onto the D 46 back to Sarlat.

ADDRESSES

🛏 STAY

🍴 **Camping La Bouquerie** – 24590 St-Geniès, 1.5km/0.9mi NW on D 704 route de Montignac, off a road to the right. ☎05 53 28 98 22. www.labouquerie.com. Mid–Apr to mid–Sept. ♿. Reservations encouraged. 197 pitches. This well-maintained campsite is spread out around a group of old buildings. Facilities are constantly improving, and more swimming pools are being added. Shady pitches and mobile home rental.

🍴 **Chambre d'hôte La Noyeraie** – 24590 Paulin. ☎05 53 29 25 09. www.pleinefage.com. Closed for Christmas. 🅿 🚭 5 rooms. This popular bed and breakfast is a stone barn conversion surrounded by a 40ha/98-acre garden. The large terrace and swimming pool offer a splendid view of the walnut orchard. The *auberge* serves farm produce including duck products.

🍴🍴 **Chambre d'hôte les Veyssières** – Les Veyssières, 24370 Prats-de-Carlux. ☎05 53 29 81 53. www.lesveyssieres.com. 🅿 🚭. 5 rooms. From the country road you'll notice the 18C dovecote. This working farm includes four pretty, spacious attic rooms and another that opens onto the orchard. Excellent regional cuisine.

🍴🍴 **Chambre d'hôte La Chèvrefeuille** – Pechboutier (D 48). 24220 St-Cyprien. ☎05 53 59 47 97. www.lechevrefeuille.com. Closed Nov–Mar. 🅿 🚭. 5 rooms. In sunny countryside full of walnut trees, this 18C farm includes a 13C bread oven. All the rooms open onto the exterior and a private space. Swimming pool and well-kept lawn.

🍴🍴 **Chambre d'hôte Les Filolies** – Les Filolies, 24200 St-Andréd'Allas. ☎05 53 30 31 84. www.lesfilolies.com. Closed 14 Nov–14 Feb. 🅿 🚭. 5 rooms. In the converted barn and stables of a former post house, each room includes wi-fi and opens onto the garden with its flowers and pretty swimming pool. Slightly small but comfortable. Breakfast includes regional products served in a rustic dining room.

😋😋 **Chambre d'hôte La Roseraie** – *Caudon, 24200 Vitrac.* ☎*05 53 59 26 48.* *www.chambres-la-roseraie.com. Closed Nov–Feb.* 🅿 🏊. *3 rooms.* On a road that leads to the shady riverbanks of the Dordogne, this house overlooks the valley and its cliffs. The pleasant garden includes red roses and a swimming pool. Breakfast is served on the terrace in warm weather.

😋😋 **Chambre d'hôte La Clos-Vallis** – *Chemin de Peyriniac, 24200 Sarlat (3.5km/2.17mi from the centre on D 47).* ☎*05 53 28 95 64. www.leclosvallis.com.* 🅿 🏊. *4 rooms.* The buildings of this lovingly restored farm are arranged around a Périgord-style courtyard. The simple, light and relaxing rooms are located in the former barn. Discreet, warm service.

😋 **Gîte de la Mouynarie** – *Route de Tamniès, 24590 St-Geniès.* ☎*05 53 59 68 85. www.lamouynarie.com.* 🅿 🏊. Enjoy the peace and quiet of this former Périgord-style farm, surrounded by 4ha/10acres of forest and prairies. The stone stables have been converted into three independent accommodations offering charm and comfort. The lovely swimming pool is surrounded by greenery.

😋😋 **Chambre d'hôte Les Granges Hautes** – *Le Poujol, 24590 St-Crépin-et-Carlucet.* ☎*05 53 29 35 60. www.les-granges-hautes.fr. Closed 13 Nov–Mar 7.* ♿🅿. *5 rooms.* An exceedingly charming stone house. Its non-smoking rooms are elegantly decorated and the two outbuildings have been converted into *gîtes.* The pretty garden includes a saltwater pool. Meals can be served on request.

😋😋 **Chambre d'hôte L'Ombière** – *Montfort, 24200 Vitrac.* ☎*05 53 28 11 38. www.lombriere.com.* 🅿 🏊. *4 rooms.* Perched on a little hillock facing the Montfort castle, this charming 18C estate offers comfortable upstairs rooms that give views over the surrounding natural environment. The living room includes a traditional fireplace; the garden overlooks the Dordogne. Serving Italian dishes made from local ingredients.

😋😋 **Chambre d'hôte Les Charmes de Carlucet** – *Carlucet, 24590 St-Crépin-et-Carlucet.* ☎*05 53 31 22 60 and 06 72 47 58 08. www.carlucet.com. Closed Dec–Feb.* ♿ 🅿. *4 rooms.* Luxury and special attention await you in the tranquillity of this superb Périgord-style property. The spacious

upstairs rooms are warmly decorated. There is also an independent *gîte* with terrace and private swimming pool in the dovecote. Discreet service.

😋 **Hôtel du Relais du Touron** – *Route de Sarlat on D 704, 24200 Carsac-Aillac.* ☎*05 53 28 16 70. www.lerelaisdu touron.com. Closed 11 Nov–31 May.* ♿🅿. *18 rooms.* In a wooded garden, this pretty Périgord-style house and its outbuilding gives you the choice between simple, rustic rooms or more recent rooms decorated in a Moorish style. A nice covered terrace and veranda across from the piscine. Regional cuisine.

😋😋😋 **Chambre d'hôte La Désirade** – *D 704, route de Gourdon, 24200 Carsac-Aillac.* ☎*05 53 29 52 47. www.ladesirade-dordogne.com.* 🅿 🏊. *3 rooms.* In the heart of a magnificent French-style garden with swimming pool, this large Périgord-style estate includes three finely decorated rooms including one suite. Upstairs, the dining room is original with its cobblestone floor and wrought-iron table. Very well-kept and friendly.

🍽/EAT

😋😋 **Ferme-Auberge La Garrigue-Haute** – *La Garrigue Haute, 24370 Prats-de-Carlux.* ☎*05 53 29 80 08. www. lagarriguehaute.fr. Closed 1 Nov–Easter. Evening meal only on Sun.* 🅿. *7 rooms.* In the countryside of Sarlat, this functioning farm offers simple but pleasant rooms and/or dining. Of course, farm products are on the menu: rillettes, foie gras, duck breast, preserved duck and a fabulous walnut cake. Make sure to reserve, as this is a well-known address!

😋😋 **Restaurant du Château** – *46590 St-Geniès.* ☎*05 53 28 36 77. www. restaurantduchateau.com.* 🅿. *Closed Tue and Wed except Jul and Aug. 3 rooms.* With a wine cellar occupying the 13C foundations, a large ceremonial room and a labyrinth of tavern-style rooms, the St-Geniès castle will transport you to medieval times. Périgord-style cuisine with an Italian touch, such as napoleon of aubergines and speck bread, or chopped duck with a parmesan and rocket salad.

😋😋 **The Black Duck** – *24590 St-Crépin-et-Carlucet.* ☎*05 53 28 80 51. Closed Mon.* 🅿. Don't look for the menu – there isn't one! Have a seat in this charming *auberge* with its wooden beams and vast fireplace and let yourself be carried away by the flavours of local products. You'll be glad you made the effort.

🍴🍴 **Ferme-auberge Montalieu-Haut** – *Montalieu-Haut. 24250 St-Cybranet. ℘05 53 28 31 74. www.montalieuhaut.com. Closed Nov–May and Mon in Jul–Aug.* 🅿🍽. *3 rooms.* Enjoy a pleasant meal in a countryside setting, with regional specialities prepared from farm produce. Bed-and-breakfast rooms and four gîtes offer a splendid view of the valley. Swimming pool, walking trails, and a short botanic circuit where you may find wild orchids.

🍴🍴 **La Ferme de Maraval** – *D 46, 24250 Cénac-et-St-Julien. ℘05 53 30 26 95. www.perigord.com/fermedemaraval. Closed Tue and Sat noon (Jul–Aug); for other days request information.* 🦽🅿. This former barn has been skilfully converted. The dining room is lovely with its wooden beams, stone walls and collection of farm equipment. Regional cuisine.

🍴🍴 **L'Auberge du Port d'Enveaux** – *Au port d'Enveaux, 24220 St-Vincent-de-Cosse. ℘05 53 28 55 18. http://ferme-du-portdenveaux.com. Closed Nov–Mar.* 🦽🅿🍽. This old auberge has become a restaurant, one that maintains its taste for local cuisine. The dining room is nice, but when it's sunny outside, you'll be tempted by a meal on the terrace with a lawn going down to the river.

🍴🍴 **Plaisance** – *Le Port, 46200 Vitrac. ℘05 53 31 39 39. www.hotelplaisance.com.* 🅿. *Closed Fri noon and mid-Nov–end Feb. 48 rooms.* Three generations run this family business, which offers a generous regional cuisine. All the fixed menus include the traditional soup. Refined table decoration and service. In the warm months, enjoy the lovely terrace shaded by old lime trees.

SHOPPING

Market – *℘04 68 21 01 33 (tourist information centre). 24220 St-Cyprien.* A colourful, lively market on Sun morning and a traditional market Thu and Fri morning all year round and Tue morning from May onwards. In Jul and Aug, gourmet food markets, wine fairs, bric-a-brac and more.

Domaine de Béquinol – *Béquignolles, 24370 Carlux. ℘05 53 29 73 41. www.bequignol.fr. Every day except Sat and Sun 9am–12pm and 1–5pm. Closed from end of Aug to beginning of Sep, 25 Dec–1 Jan and holidays.* Confectionary: *Arlequines de Carlux* (chocolate-covered walnuts dusted with cocoa), walnut bites, *Nogaillous du Périgord* (chocolate-covered walnuts) and *Noir et noix* (chocolate bar with walnut paste and caramel). Alcoholic beverages: *Béquinoix* (walnut-flavoured aperitif) and old prune brandy. You can find these treats in the main Périgord and Quercy stores and in the Ecomusée de la Noix in Castelnaud.

Foie Gras Crouzel – *Le Temple, 24590 Salignac-Eyvigues. ℘05 53 28 80 83. www.crouzel.com. Open daily except Sun 8am–noon (opens Sat 8.30am) and 2–6.30pm. Closed on public holidays.* Local products selected for their quality, culinary expertise in the most authentic tradition, passed down from generation to generation: this is the secret of the Crouzel family foie gras. A warm welcome.

LEISURE

👥 **A Canoë Raid** – *Campeyral, 24170 Siorac-en-Périgord. ℘05 53 31 64 11. www.a-canoe-raid.com. Easter–Oct 9am–7pm.* 🎟€15. Canoë Raid offers circuits in canoes or kayaks along the Dordogne and Vézère, for a day or several days, from its two centres: Siorac ou Cénac/Domme.

Canoë-Détente – *24220 St-Vincent-de-Cosse. ℘05 53 29 52 15. http://ferme-du-portdenveaux.com. 9am–7pm depending on the water level.* Treat yourself to a tranquil river circuit aboard a canoe for 1–4 people. This service brings you to the departure point, provides you with a canoe, life jacket and paddles, and allows you to drift down the Dordogne at your own pace.

👥 **Airparc** – *Au port d'Enveaux, 24220 St-Vincent-de-Cosse. ℘05 53 29 18 43. www.airparc-perigord.com. 10am–6pm. Closed Nov–Mar.* 🎟€20 (Children €8–12). Monkey bridges and zip-lines crossing the Dordogne. Three different circuits according to age and night activities upon reservation. Night camping under transparent tents available.

Beynac and Cazenac★★

The Château de Beynac stands on a remarkable site★★ crowning a rugged rockface. From this strategic position, it overlooks the beautiful Dordogne Valley as it winds its way between hills and castles.

CHÂTEAU★★

Climb to the top of the village.
🕐*Open Jun–Sept, 10am–6.30pm; Jan–Feb and Dec, noon to dusk; Mar–May, 10am–6pm; Oct–Nov, 10am to dusk.*
⊕€8. ℘*05 53 29 50 40.*
www.beynac-en-perigord.com.

A formidable stronghold – In medieval times, Beynac, Biron, Bourdeilles and Mareuil were the four baronies of Périgord. The castle was captured by Richard the Lionheart and used as a base by the sinister **Mercadier**, whose bands of men pillaged the countryside. In 1214, Simon de Montfort seized the castle and demolished it. The castle was later rebuilt, as we see it today, by a lord of Beynac. During the Hundred Years War, the Dordogne marked the frontier between the English and the French, and there were constant skirmishes between Beynac and Castelnaud (ⓒsee Ch. de CASTELNAUD). The castle is in the form of an irregular quadrilateral with a bastion on the south side. The austere crenellated keep dates

▶ **Population:** 547.
🖐 **Michelin Map:** 329: H-6.
🛈 **Info:** La Balme 24220 Beynac-et-Cazenac. ℘05 53 29 43 08. www.perigordnoir.com/en. Free guided tour (1hr) of Beynac, Thu 10.30am.
▶ **Location:** 64km/40mi SE of Périgueux and 12km/7.5mi SW of Sarlat.
🅿 **Parking:** Several paid car parks, including one near the château. Free parking for camper vans near the Parc Archéologique.
👁 **Don't Miss:** The view from the castle or a lazy boat trip on the Dordogne.
🕐 **Timing:** 1hr 20min with a visit to the château.

from the 13C. A double curtain wall protected the castle from attack from the plateau; on all the other sides there is a sheer drop of 150m to the Dordogne. The main building, dating from the 13C and 14C, is extended by the 15C seigneurial manor house to which a bartizan was added in the 16C.

The castle was abandoned from 1798 until 1961. The present owner has launched a vast renovation programme

Château de Beynac above the Dordogne River

© Sylvaine Poitau / Apa Publications

Beynac and Michelin

Marius Rossillon (1867–1946), alias O'Galop, who was the first to draw the Michelin man, lived in Beynac. The castle of Beynac has been the set of such films as Andy Tennant's *Ever After: A Cinderella Story* and Luc Besson's *The Messenger: The Story of Joan of Arc*.

due to last a century. The kitchens, the drawbridge, the guard-room and the keep have already been restored. Visitors enter the dark 13C guard-room and proceed to the next floor where the 14C kitchen and its two fireplaces can be admired. Above the kitchen is the great Hall of State; note the carvings decorating the fireplace from Italy. The oratory is adorned with Gothic frescoes. The grand 17C staircase leads to a drawing room furnished in Louis XIII style; note the paintings on wood decorating the ceiling. One last staircase leads to the watch-path and the south bastion, which overlook the Dordogne: there is a wonderful **panorama★★** of the valley. On the way down, visitors go through the 13C kitchen and across the drawbridge before leaving via the barbican.

VILLAGE★
Rue Tibal Lo Garrel★

This steeply sloping footpath leads from the bottom of the village, through rows of houses dating from the 15C to the 17C, to the castle. All along the climb the architectural decor exudes elegance and the prosperity of Renaissance Beynac. There are gabled doorways, façades decorated with coats of arms or discs, ornate dormer windows and small, beautifully laid out squares.
A *calvaire* (wayside cross) stands on the cliff edge, at the end of rue Tibal Lo Garrel. A **panorama★★** as wide as the one from the castle watch-path can be seen from this point.

Parc Archéologique

La Tour du Couvant (at the foot of the Château). ○*Open Jul to mid-Sep, daily except Sat, 10am–7pm.* ⊜€6. ℘05 53 29 51 28.
This includes about ten reconstitutions based on the discoveries of archaeological research, especially living quarters from the end of the Neolithic period, a fortified gateway and a Gallic potter's oven.

ADDRESSES

🛏 STAY / ♈EAT

⊜⊜**Le Relais des Cinq Châteaux** – *24220 Vézac (2km/1.2mi S of Beynac on D 57).* ℘05 53 30 30 72. www.relaisdes5 chateaux.com. ⚒🅿. *14 rooms.* The terrace of this prestigious estate looks out over the countryside and three fortified castles. The veranda restaurant allows you to enjoy this view as you savour regional cuisine. Comfortable rooms, including three luxury suites, and a pool.

SHOPPING

Markets – Every morning from mid-Jun–mid Sep in place de la Balme.

LEISURE

Gabarres de Beynac – *24250 St-Martial-de-Nabirat* . ℘05 53 28 51 15. www.gabarre-beynac.com. *May–Sept, 10am–6pm, boats leave every 30min; Apr and Oct, 11am–5pm, boats leave every hr. Departures from the car park (1hr).* €8. Boat trips along the Dordogne on traditional flat-bottomed *gabarre* boats.

Aux Canoës Roquegeoffre du Port d'Enveaux – *Enveaux rive droite, 24220 St-Vincent-de-Cosse.* ℘05 53 29 54 20. www.canoe-roquegeoffre.com. ○ *Daily 9am–7pm.* €15 (children under 18, €12). This leisure centre along the Dordogne offers river circuits in a canoe or kayac. Fishing boats are also available. Reserve the day before.

Hot-air balloon flights – *24220 Beynac (1.5km/0.9mi towards St- Cyprien).* ℘06 83 26 47 66. www. perigord-dordogne-mongolfieres.com. €200 (children under 12, €110). Breathtaking flights.

Château de Castelnaud★★

The impressive ruins of the Château de Castelnaud stand on a wonderful site★★ commanding the valleys of the Céou and the Dordogne. Just opposite stands the Château de Beynac (see BEYNAC-ET-CAZENAC), Castelnaud's implacable rival throughout the Middle Ages.

CASTLE

In 1214, Simon de Montfort (c 1165–1218, father of the English statesman and soldier) took possession of the castle, whose occupants had taken the side of the Cathars. In 1259, St Louis ceded the castle to the king of England who held it for several years.

During the Hundred Years' War the castle constantly changed hands between the French and the English. When at last peace was declared the castle was in a terrible condition.

During the whole of the second half of the 15C the castle was under reconstruction. Only the keep and curtain wall have kept their 13C appearance. In the 16C further changes were made and the artillery tower added. In 1969 a major restoration program enabled most of the buildings to be rebuilt. Castelnaud is a typical example of a medieval fortress with its powerful machicolated keep, curtain wall, living quarters and inner bailey. Nonetheless, certain parts of the castle – artillery tower, loopholes – which were added in later years reflect the evolution of weapons in siege warfare. Reconstructed hoarding, later replaced by machicolations, and audio-visual presentations offer an insight into siege warfare tactics in the Middle Ages; a model in one of the small rooms illustrates the siege of Castelnaud in 1442, when Charles VII attempted to finally expel the English from France.

A great variety of weapons and objects connected with warfare are on display: 15C and 16C guns in the artillery tower;

- **Michelin Map:** Michelin map 329: H-7.
- **Info:** Le Bourg –24250 Daglan. ℘05 53 31 30 00. www.castelnaud.com.
- **Location:** 69km/43mi SE of Périgueux and 13km/8mi SW of Sarlat.
- **Museum:** Open Jul–Aug, 9am–8pm; Apr–Jun and Sept, 10am–7pm; Feb–Mar and Oct to mid-Nov, 10am–6pm; mid-Nov–Jan, 2–5pm (Christmas holidays, 10am–5pm). €9.
- **Kids:** Musée de la Guerre au Moyen Âge.
- **Don't Miss:** The view from the terrace.

bows, crossbows in the lower part of the keep; catapult, battering ram and trebuchet in the siege-warfare room; 15C–17C swords in the sword room. One room on the ground floor contains a wide choice of comic strips and books about the Medieval period. From the ward the view extends southwards over the Céou valley. From the east end of the terrace there is an exceptional **panorama★★** of one of the most lovely views of the Dordogne valley.

In July and August, you may also visit the castle at night (Mon–Fri from 8.15pm). A new play, based on historical figures, is performed every year in the torch-lit rooms.

WALNUT MUSEUM
Écomusée de la Noix du Périgord – *Ferme de Vielcroze, 24250 Castelnaud.* ℘05 53 59 69 63. *http://ecomuseede lanoix.voila.net. Open Apr–mid-Nov, 10am–7pm.* €5. A restored farm is home to this museum, which explains the cultivation and uses of this precious local product. On-site shop and a scenic path through the huge walnut grove surrounding the museum.

Le Bugue

the Vézère to the Dordogne

This busy agricultural centre is situated at the gateway of the Périgord Noir, on the north bank of the Vézère, near its confluence with the Dordogne. A wide variety of leisure and cultural activities are available in and around the town, including museums, caves, castles and so on.

A BIT OF HISTORY

Le Bugue, located on the banks of the Vézère, has been inhabited since pre-historic times. A Benedictine monastery was founded here in the 10C, but the settlement didn't enjoy prosperity until the mid-12C when Périgord came under English control. The French and English crowns often disputed the town. One of Le Bugue's famous sons is the chemist and physician **Jean Rey** (1583–1645) who discovered the Law of the Conservation of Mass over a century before Lavoisier confirmed the hypothesis in 1789.

MARKET TOWN

This charming little market town with winding streets and traditional Périgordian houses is a convenient base for the many attractions of the area.

🧒 Aquarium du Périgord Noir★

Rue de la République. ♿🕐*Daily: Feb–Mar and Oct–Nov 2–6pm (Sun, 10am–6pm); Apr–May and Sept 10am–6pm; Jun 10am–7pm; Jul–Aug 10am–10pm.* 🎟€12.50 (children aged 4–16, €9). 🕿05 53 07 10 74. www.aquariumperigordnoir.com.

This aquarium has been designed to make visitors feel as if they were moving below the surface of the river. The open-topped aquariums have natural lighting and open onto large windows. They contain freshwater fish, crustaceans and invertebrates from various parts of Europe. Of particularly impressive dimensions are the gleaming catfish,

> **Population:** 2 818.
> **Michelin Map:** 329: G-6.
> **Info:** Rue Jardin Public,- 24260 Le Bugue. 🕿05 53 07 20 48.
> **Location:** 47km/29.4mi E of Bergerac.
> **Kids:** The Aquarium du Périgord Noir and Village du Bournat.
> **Don't Miss:** Be sure to visit one of the region's caves; La Bugue's Tuesday market is a must.
> **Timing:** Allow a full day to explore the Vézère and Dordogne valleys.

originating from the centre and east of the continent (some of the larger specimens are over 1.5m/5ft long), white and silver grass carp and sturgeons. There is a separate display on the breeding cycle of the salmon. Fish feeding by the touch pools with the biologists (*see website*).

Maison de la Vie Sauvage- Musée de Paléontologie

9 rue de la République. Open daily Jul–Aug & Sept 10am–1pm, 3–7pm; Apr–Jun Tue & Sat 10am–noon, 3–6pm. Rest of year telephone for times. 🎟€5 (child €3.50). 06 64 73 90 15.

🧒 **Vie Sauvage** *This section focuses on European birds, their habits and habitats, and includes a collection of stuffed and mounted specimens.*

Have you ever wondered about feathers, beaks and birdsong? This exhibition also explains techniques for flying, hunting and fishing, as well as migratory routes and their many dangers.

In the **Musée de Paléontologie** a collection of over 3 000 items are grouped together in families: ammonites, trilobites etc..

▶ Follow the rue de la République SW from town centre and take first right, Allée Souriau.

Gouffre de Proumeyssac

© Patrick Escudero / hemis.fr

👤👥 Parc le Bournat★★

♿ 🕐Mar–Sept 10am–6pm (Jul–Aug 7pm). ⊜€14 (children aged 4–12, €10). ✆05 53 08 41 99. www.lebournat.fr.

A reconstruction of a regional village-farm at the turn of the last century, complete with school, chapel, town hall, wash-house, wine cellar and more. In each of the buildings, figures stage the joys and chores of the past: harvest supper, a wedding celebration, washer-women at work. Bakers, smithies and other craftsmen perpetuate their traditional tradecraft, also highlighted by the collection of farm tools and machinery.

CAVES

Caverne de Bara-Bahau

1km/0.6mi W of Le Bugue via D 703
🕐Jul–Aug 9.30am–7pm; Feb–Jun 10am–12pm and 2–5.30pm (Sep-Dec until 5pm). 🚶Guided tours (35min). ⊜€8. ✆05 53 07 44 58. www.grotte-bara-bahau.com.

The cave, which is about 100m long, ends in a chamber blocked by a rock fall. Drawings can be made out on the roof of the chamber (Early and Middle Magdalenian Culture). Discovered in 1951 by the Casterets, they depict horses, aurochs, bison, bears and deer.

Gouffre de Proumeyssac★★

3km/2mi S via the D 31E. 🕐Feb and Nov–Dec 2–5pm; Apr–Jun and 1–15 Sept 9.30am–6pm; Mar and mid-Sept–Oct 9.30am–noon, 2–5.30pm; Jul–Aug 9am–7pm. 🚶Guided tours (45min). ⊜€10. Descent via lift by reservation: €19. ✆05 53 07 27 47 (free reservation ✆05 53 07 85 85). www.perigord.com/proumeyssac.

A tunnel drilled into a hill overlooking the Vézère leads to a platform built half-way up the chasm, from where visitors view this underground dome. Water seeps through abundantly, decorating the cave and especially the bases of the walls with fine yellow and white concretions, including numerous stalactites, draperies, stalagmites, eccentrics and triangular crystallisations. A sound and light show brings the scene to life. A short film explains the formation of the cave and a second sound and light show takes place after the descent into the depths of the chasm.

Until 1952, the tiny basket suspended in mid-air was the only way of getting into the chasm. The 52m descent in complete darkness at the mercy of the temperamental mule working the winch must have been an unforgettable experience for the four tourists allowed down each time with their guide! This primitive lift is available once more (apply in advance). Outside, a landscaped area dotted with explanatory panels offers visitors an insight into the geological features of the site. In summer, concerts and shows are organised inside the chasm. A woodland trail (30min there and back) leads to a spot overlooking the Vézère which offers a fine panorama of the river.

🚗 DRIVING TOUR

④ VÉZÈRE TO THE DORDOGNE

80km/50mi round-trip. Allow 1 day.
See route 4 on region map page 89.

▶ Drive SE out of Le Bugue along the D 703.

Campagne

At the opening of a small valley stands a small Romanesque church preceded by a belfry. The **castle** of the lords of Campagne, built in the 15C, was restored in the 19C.

The towers with crenellations and machicolations which flank the living quarters and the neo-Gothic elements give the castle the appearance of an English manor house. The last Marquis de Campagne gave the castle to the state in 1970.

▶ Continue E along the D 35.

St-Cyprien

♿See ST-CYPRIEN.

▶ Leave St-Cyprien travelling SW along the D 703E. The road skirts the north bank of the Dordogne. Turn left onto the D 703.

Siorac-en-Périgord

This small village, sought after for its riverside beach, has a restored 17C cas-tle, home of the Comte de Vivans, and a small Romanesque church.

▶ Return to the D 703E and continue to follow the River Dordogne.

Coux-et-Bigaroque

This village consists of two formerly independent parishes. Note the carved doorway of the Romanesque church of Coux and the picturesque streets of Bigaroque.

▶ Continue your journey along the Dordogne via the D 51 then turn left onto the D 51E to Le Buisson-de-Cadouin. Turn left beyond the railway line then left again and drive on for another 1.5km/0.9mi.

Les Grottes de Maxange★

Mesteguiral. ⏰*Open Jul–Aug, 9am–7pm; Apr–Jun and Sept, 10am–12pm, 2–6pm; Oct–Nov, 10am–12pm, 2–5pm.* ✆€8.50. ☏05 53 23 42 80. *www.lesgrottesdemaxange.com.*

These caves, discovered in a quarry in 2000, consist of galleries dug out of the limestone by the sea when it withdrew; they were later obstructed by alluvial deposits which have been cleared away. The different deposit strata can be seen in the lower gallery, whereas the upper gallery contains a great variety of concretions in fascinating shapes and colours, including stalactites, stalag-mites and eccentrics.

Coux-et-Bigaroque

© Patrick Escudero / hemis.fr

Belvès★

Perched on a limestone promontory on the site of a Gallo-Roman *castrum*, Belvès enjoys a marvellous position overlooking the Nauze valley. The surrounding rolling countryside is renowned for its wild mushrooms and chestnuts.

▸ WALKING TOUR

TOWN

Plaques identify the town's major monuments (a town plan is available at the tourist office).

The 11C belltower and 15C covered market (*halle*) with stone and wooden supports stand on **place d'Armes**, at the centre of the village. A complex of nine underground rooms situated in the medieval moat, beneath place d'Armes, gives an insight into the daily life of the families who lived in the **troglodyte dwellings** (◷ *open mid-Jun to mid-Sep;* ▸ *guided tours (45min) at noon, 3.45pm, 6pm; mid-Sep to mid-Jun, tours at 11am and 3.30pm;* €*5.50;* ✆*05 53 29 10 20*) between the 12C and 18C.

Take the covered passage to the right of the Archbishop's House, which leads to **rue Rubigan**. This attractive street leads to the Tour de l'Auditeur (auditor's tower), the former *castrum* keep. The Maison des Consuls (tourist office), is located along rue des Eiffols. Follow the street to the western edge of town, where you can admire the Gothic church of Notre-Dame-de-Montcuq (13C–15C), which used to be a Benedictine priory. Walk towards place Croix des Frères: the castle is on your right and a 14C octagonal keep, all that remains of a former convent, on your left.

Near the Place d'Armes on rue J Manchotte is the **Musée Organistrum et Vielles à Roues du Périgord Noir** (*no. 14;* ◷*open by prior arrangement;* ◌*no charge;* ✆*05 53 29 10 93*), which houses a small collection of reconstructed lutes, hurdy-gurdies and other medieval instruments.

- ▸ **Population:** 1 500.
- ◷ **Michelin Map:** 329: H-7.
- ◉ **Location:** 65km/40.5mi S. of Périgueux. Approach from the SW along the D 53 (the Monpazier road) for a charming view of the town with its old turreted houses, belltowers and leafy garden terraces.
- ▸ **Guided Tours:** In season, guided tours of Belvès take place daily (except Sun) in Jul and Aug at 6pm. **Tours of local area:** Guided tours by car on Tue and Thu (full day) in Jul and Aug.

🚗 DRIVING TOUR

5 CHESTNUT AND MUSHROOM COUNTRY

76km/47mi round-trip. Allow half a day. See route 5 on region map page 89.

◉ Drive S out of Belvès along the D 710; turn left onto the D 54 after 1km/0.6mi, then right 2km/1.2mi farther on. The road runs through fields and woodland dotted with charming small villages.

Orliac

This tiny village, buried in the hollow of a valley occupied by a pine forest, boasts a fortified church in which the nave served as a protective keep; the Renaissance doorway provides the only decorative touch.

Prats-du-Périgord

The Romanesque **Église St-Maurice★**, fortified in the 15C, has an unusual appearance, with its nave framed by a tall apse and a graceful belfry wall.

◉ Leave Prats to the south along the D 60.

Villefranche-du-Périgord

This bastide was founded in 1261 by **Alphonse de Poitiers**. An enormous

Belvès, decorated for a celebration

© Patrick Escudero / hemis.fr

covered market, with its heavy stone pillars, and part of the covered arcades are still standing. A chestnut market takes place here on Saturdays from late September to November.

Maison du Châtaignier, Marrons et Champignons

○*Phone for opening hours.* ⊛€2. ℘*05 53 29 98 37.*
This ecological museum is devoted to mushrooms and chestnuts. 🏃The 1km/0.6mi nature trail (*allow 30min*) is particularly popular. A chestnut market is held here every Saturday morning during the harvest season.

▷ Drive NE along the D 57.

Église de Besse

This church is famous for its carved **doorway★** in the west front, dating most probably from the 11C. Such features are rare in the architecture of the Périgord region, and this particular example is exceptional. The sculptures on the archivolt depict the Redemption, including images of Adam and Eve before and after the Original Sin, St Michael slaying the dragon and Isaiah being purified by a glowing coal.

▷ Continue NE along the D 57.

St-Pompont

This old village includes a good number of houses typical of the Périgord region with attractive dormer windows surmounted with shell ornamentation

and framed with spiral scrolls. Cross the small bridge by the town hall to reach the **fortified doorway★**, all that remains of a fortress built here by the English in the 15C.

Beyond the church, you will see the ruins of a castle dating from the same period. Farther east, on the road to Daglan, stands **Notre-Dame-de-Bedeau**, a chapel dating from the 13C and 17C and a gathering place for hunters at the start of the hunting season.

▷ Drive NW on the D 51 to Siorac, then turn left on the D 25 and left further on towards Urval.

Urval

Urval is nestled in a little valley in the dense **Bessède** forest. In case of an invasion, the fortified 11–12C church would shelter the inhabitants in two rooms above the nave and choir.
You'll notice a 15C bread oven at the apse. The bread was sold to the villagers to the benefit of the Lord of Urval, who owned the oven. Also note the pretty mill and water reservoir built on the Peyrat stream on the way out of Belvès.

Château de la Bourlie

○*Open Contact for all visitor information.* ℘*06 07 10 00 56.* *www.chateaudelabourlie.com.*
The 5ha/12.3-acre park, mainly landscaped in the 18C, boasts charming topiary and a scented rose garden.

▷ Take the D 52 back to Belvès.

ADDRESSES

STAY

◎◎ **Chambre d'hôte La Grande Marque** – 24220 Marnac. 9km/5.4mi NE of Belvès on the D 703 and to the right. ℘05 53 31 61 63. ⌷. 5 rooms. The view from this 17C hill-top house will take your breath away. Three recently re-decorated rooms under the eaves.

℉ EAT

◎◎ **Auberge de la Nauze** – Fongouffier, 24170 Sagelat. 1km/0.6mi N of Belvès on the D 53. ℘05 53 28 44 81. Closed 20–29 Jun, 29 Nov–14 Dec, Mon eve (exc Jul & Aug), Tue eve and Sat lunchtime Sept–Jun. This typical regional house stands above the picturesque town of Belvès. Large bay windows and warm colours brighten the dining room.

◎◎ **Ferme-auberge Les Tilleuls** – On the way out of the village, 24220 Marnac. ℘05 53 30 30 26. www.fermeles tilleuls.com. Closed 3 weeks in Mar, Sun night and Mon. &◘⌷. Open for mid-day and evening meals year-round. About 80% of products served here are grown or raised on the farm. Sales of duck products to take away with you.

SHOPPING

Markets in Belvès – Traditional market on Sat morning. Local growers' market Wed 7pm in Jul–Aug. Walnut market Wed morning Oct–Dec.

Markets in Villefranche-du-Périgord – 23km/13.8mi S of Belvès on the D 660. Traditional market on Sat morning, featuring chestnuts in Oct–Dec. Mid-Jul–late Aug, local growers' market Tue 7pm. Cèpe market weekdays from 4pm and Sun all day (depending on the growing conditions).

Les Eyzies-de-Tayac-Sireuil★★

the Beune and Vézère

The village of Les Eyzies occupies a grandiose setting on steep cliffs crowned with evergreen oaks and junipers at the confluence of the River Vézère and River Beune. The poplar-lined River Vézère winds between meadows and farmland, sometimes narrowing to flow between sheer, vertical walls of rock 50–80m high. Shelters cut out of the limestone base served as dwelling places for prehistoric people; caves located higher up on the cliff face were used as sanctuaries. The discovery within the last 100 years of many such dwellings within a limited radius of Les Eyzies has earned the town the title "European Capital of Prehistory."

A BIT OF HISTORY

The capital of prehistory – During the second Ice Age prehistoric people aban-

▶ **Population:** 846.
◔ **Michelin Map:** 329: H-6.
⊡ **Info:** Pl. de la Mairie, 24620 Les Eyzies-de-Tayac. ℘05 53 06 97 05. www.tourisme-vezere.com.
◐ **Location:** 45km/28mi SE of Périgueux and 21km/13mi W of Sarlat.
⚹⚹ **Kids:** Roc de Cazelle; Préhisto Parc.
◑ **Timing:** Allow a day for the archaeological sites in the Beune and Vézère valleys.
⚀ **Don't Miss:** Musée National de la Préhistoire; Grotte du Grand Roc; Grotte de Font-de-Gaume.

doned the northern plains and headed for the warmer areas of the south. The lower Vézère attracted the migrants because of its easily accessible natural caves and overhanging rocks, which could be hollowed out into shelters without much difficulty. People used these cave dwellings for tens of thousands of years and left in them traces of their daily tasks such as bones, ashes from their fires, tools, weapons, utensils and ornaments.

As their civilisation evolved, so did animal species: after elephants and cave bears came bison, aurochs, mammoths and, later still, musk-oxen, reindeer, ibex, stags and horses.

An archaeologists' paradise

Methodical study of the deposits in the Les Eyzies region has considerably increased our knowledge of prehistory. The Dordogne *département* has greatly contributed to the study of prehistory with more than 200 deposits discovered there, of which more than half are in the lower Vézère valley. Following these discoveries, two great periods of the Paleolithic Age were defined and named – Mousterian and Magdalenian.

SIGHTS
Musée National de la Préhistoire★★★

&.♿🚶Guided tours ⏱Open Jul–Aug, daily, 9.30am–6.30pm; Jun and Sep (daily except Tue), 9.30am–6pm; Oct–May (daily except Tue), 9.30am–12.30pm and 2–5.30pm. ✑€6, no charge 1st Sun of the month. ℘05 53 06 45 45. www.musee-prehistoire-eyzies.fr.

The museum is located in a modern building near the old castle of the barons of Beynac. The 13C fortress, restored in the 16C, clings to the cliff beneath a rocky outcrop overlooking the village. There is a good **view** of Les Eyzies and the valleys of Vézère and Beune from the terrace.

The vast museum collection illustrates the evolution of flint-cutting from around 2.5 million years BC and the successive civilisations through displays of tools dating from the major Paleolithic periods; anthropology and funerary rituals are also covered.

The impressive collection of modern man's first works of art includes a low-relief carving known as the **Devil's Furnace** (around 20 000 BCE). Other carved stone blocks (36 000–26 000 BCE) depict animals and various symbols. The latest

technology is used to bring prehistory to life through various media.

Pôle International de la Préhistoire (PIP)

35 avenue de la Forge. ⏱Open Jan–Apr and Oct–Dec daily except Saturday 9.30am–5.30pm; May–Sept daily 9.30am–6.30pm. ⏱Closed 1 Jan, 1May and 25 Dec. ✑No charge. &.🅿 ℘05 53 06 06 97. www.pole-prehistoire.com.

This orientation centre with its modern design in concrete and glass opened in July 2010. You'll pass over the Beune river on the walkway to the centre, which includes a prehistory discovery area with 3D model of the area, library with computer area, educational area with archaeological dig reconstruction and prehistoric science workshop, and temporary exhibition space. Film projections, souvenir shop and cafeteria.

Grotte de Font-de-Gaume★

Park next to the road to St-Cyprien opposite a cliff-spur. You'll climb a steep path up 400m to the cave entrance. 🚶Guided tours. Reservation several months in advance is advised in high season. 30 tickets are also sold each morning; it is advised to arrive before opening hours to obtain yours if you have not reserved.

⏱🚶Open mid-May–mid-Sept (45min), 9.30am–5.30pm; 16 Sept to 14 May, daily except Sat 9.30am–12.30pm and 2–5.30pm. ⏱Closed Sat, 1 Jan, 1 May, 1 and 11 Nov, 25 Dec. ✑€8. ℘05 53 06 86 00. http://eyzies. monuments-nationaux.fr.

This is the last prehistoric cave showing polychrome paintings open to the public in the world. The cave runs back in the form of a passage 120m long. All the drawings of horses, bison, mammoths, reindeer and other deer indicate great artistic skill and, after Lascaux, form the finest group of polychrome paintings in France. The frieze of bison, painted in brown on a white calcite background, is remarkable.

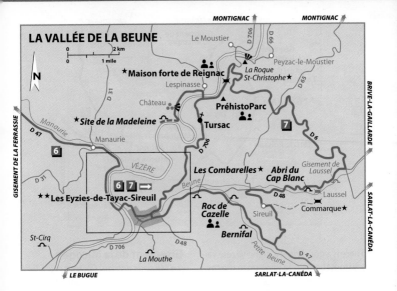

LA VALLÉE DE LA BEUNE

Abri Pataud *(Pataud shelter)*

⊙ *Open every day Apr–Oct.* 📷 €5.
📞 *05 53 05 65 65.*

A museum on site shows objects and bones discovered during excavation work; note in particular two large stratigraphic sections and 14 archaeological layers where bones, flints and the fireplace remains can be seen in place.

Abri de Cro-Magnon
(Cro-Magnon shelter)

This cave was discovered in 1868 and it revealed, in addition to flints and carved bones of the Aurignacian and Gravettian Cultures, five adult skeletons which were studied by Paul Broca, surgeon, anthropologist and founder the School of Anthropology in France. The discoveries made in this cave were of prime importance for prehistoric studies, since they were the first remains of *Homo sapiens* to be found. A commemorative plaque is all that is left of the site today.

Église de Tayac

⊙ *Open Jul–Aug 2–7pm.* 📞 *05 53 06 97 15.*
The warm, gold-coloured stone enhances this 12C fortified church. Two towers roofed with *lauzes* frame the main body of the church.
The doorway is intriguing; the first scalloped arch gives it an Eastern air

whereas the two outermost columns, with Corinthian capitals of white marble, show Gallo-Roman influence.

🚗 DRIVING TOURS

6 PREHISTORIC VÉZÈRE
24km/14.9mi trip. Allow 4hr. See route 6 on region map p89 and local map p123.

▶ Take the D 47 towards Périgueux. The first four sites are off this road.

Abri du Poisson

(Fish shelter) ⊙ *Open every Tue at 11.30am; bookings and tickets at entrance to Font-de-Gaume cave.*
📷 €8. 📞 *05 53 06 45 66. www.eyzies. monuments-nationaux.fr.*
This carving of a 1m-long fish on the roof of a small hollow represents a species of salmon which was very common in the Vézère until quite recently. It dates from the Gravettian Period (about 23000 years BCE), and is one of the oldest cave sculptures yet discovered.

Grotte du Grand Roc ★★

(Grand Roc Cave) 🕐 *Multiple opening hours; check website for current details.*
📷 €8–€10. 📞 *05 53 06 92 70.*
www.semitour.com.

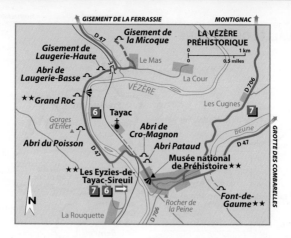

There is a good **view★** of the Vézère valley from the stairs leading up to the cave (discovered in 1924) and the platform at its mouth. The length (40m) of tunnel displays an extraordinary variety of stalactites, stalagmites and eccentrics resembling coral formations, as well as a wonderful variety of pendants and crystals.

Abri Préhistorique de Laugerie Basse

(Lower Laugerie deposit) &○*Multiple opening hours; check website for current details.* ✆*€7–€10 (combined ticket for cave and shelters).* ✆*05 53 06 92 70. www.semitour.com.*

Prehistoric bones, stone tools and other artefacts were discovered in this deposit, downstream from the Upper Laugerie deposit. They are in various museums and private collections, but an exhibition centre here contains reproductions of the best of them.

Gisement de Laugerie Haute

(Upper Laugerie deposit) ○*Open every Tue at 10am, or on request.* ✆*€7.*

Scientific excavations going on for over a century in a picturesque spot at the foot of high cliffs have revealed examples of the work and art of prehistoric people at different stages of civilisation.

Note the drip stones or channels cut into the rock in the Middle Ages to prevent water running along the walls and entering the dwellings.

Gisement de la Micoque

(La Micoque deposit) ○*Open every Tue at 2.30pm, or on request.* ✆*05 53 06 45 66 or at the Grotte de Font-de-Gaume.* ✆*€7.* ✆*05 53 06 86 00.*

This deposit revealed many items belonging to periods known as the Tayacian, Micoquian and Mousterian ages. Some of the finds are exhibited at Les Eyzies National Museum of Prehistory.

Gisement de la Ferrassie

○*Every Thu at 2.30pm, or on request.* ✆*€7.* ✆*05 53 06 86 00 or at the Grotte de Font-de-Gaume* ✆*05 53 06 86 00.*

The three shelters of this site, discovered in 1896, are called "le Petit", "le Grand" and "la Grotte". Eight Neanderthal skeletons from the Mousterian Period about 50 000 years ago, including a foetus, two newborns, three children and two adults, were found in the "Petit" shelter. The man appears to have been handicapped, demonstrating that he was taken care of. His teeth were worn on their interior, like those of some Inuits, indicating the chewing of animal skins. The "Grand" shelter reveals rough primitive art on stone blocks representing cups, simplified animals and female sexual organs.

7 ALONG THE BEUNE AND VÉZÈRE RIVERS

50km/31mi round-trip. Allow 1 day.
See route 7 on region map page 89 and local maps pages 115 and 116.

▷ Drive E out of Les Eyzies along D 47.

Grotte des Combarelles★

&.●▬*Open daily except Sat,
9.30am–5.30pm (mid-Sept–mid-May,
9.30am–12.30pm and 2.30–5.30pm).
🕐Closed 1 Jan, 1 May, 1 and 11 Nov and
25 Dec. ◎€7.50. 🖉05 53 06 45 66 or
the Grotte de Font-de-Gaume 🖉05 53
06 86 00.

A winding passage 250m long shows
many markings on its walls for the last
120m of its length, some of which are
superimposed upon one another. The
drawings include nearly 700 representations of animals (horses, bison, bears,
reindeer and mammoths can be seen
at rest or in full gallop) and human
caricatures. The cave, discovered in
1901, demonstrated the importance of
Magdalenian art at a time when some
scholars were still sceptical about the
worth of prehistoric studies.

▷ Continue along the D 47
towards Sarlat.

♟♙ Grottes du Roc de Cazelle

&.🕐Open Feb–Apr and Oct–Nov
10am–6pm; May–Jun and Sept
10am–7pm; Jul–Aug 10am–8pm;
Dec–Jan 11am–5pm (Christmas holidays
10am–5pm). ◎€8. Children 5–13 years
of age €4. 🖉05 53 59 46 09.
www.rocdecazelle.com.

These caves offer an insight into our
ancestors' lives from the Paleolithic
Period to the mid-20C. A marked path
leads visitors past scenes of prehistoric
daily life to the monolithic dwelling
occupied until 1966 by a farming couple.

Grotte de Bernifal

●▬*Guided tour (1hr) by prior arrangement. ◎€5. 🖉06 74 96 30 43.
Cave paintings and delicate carvings
from the Middle Magdalenian period
(16 000–13 000 BCE) are spread over
about 100m. They include mammoths,
horses, human figures, a bear and
shapes suggesting dwellings.

▷ Continue along D 47, which follows
the River Petite Beune and turn left

Grotte de Combarelles

© ARCO / Lenz G / age fotostock

2km/1.2mi further on. Beyond Sireuil,
drive N to join the D 48 on the right.

Abri du Cap-Blanc

(Cap-Blanc shelter) ●▬*Open daily
except Sat: mid-May to mid-Sept
9.30am–5.30pm; mid-Sept to mid-May,
9.30am–12.30pm and 2–5.30pm.
🕐Closed 1 Jan, 1 May, 1 and 11 Nov
and 25 Dec. ◎€7.50. 🖉05 53 59 60 30
or the Grotte de Font-de-Gaume.
🖉05 53 06 86 00.

Excavation of a small Magdalenian
deposit in 1909 led to the discovery of
carvings★ in high relief on the walls of
the rock shelter. Two bison and in particular a frieze of horses were carved
to take full advantage of the relief and
contour of the rock itself.

▷ Drive on along the D 48 for 1.5km/
0.9mi and turn left onto the D 6 to
Moustier.

You are leaving the Beune valley. The
plants in this area grow more stunted
as you leave the river. You'll get a view
of the Vézère Valley from Bel-Air.

▷ 9km/5.6mi further along, turn left
on the D 706 towards Eyzies-de-Tayac-
Sireuil.

♟♙ Maison Forte de Reignac

Self-guided visit. 🕐Open daily Mar
and Oct–mid-Nov; Apr 10am–6pm;
May–Jun and Sept 10am–7pm; Jul–Aug
10am–8pm. ◎€8 (children aged 5–13,

€4). ℘05 53 50 69 54.
www.maison-forte-reignac.com.
This fortified mansion is integrated into the cliff wall, its 14C façade a rock shelter. Windows were added in the 16C. After more than 50 years of archaeological digs to uncover Solutrean and Middle Magdalenian artefacts, it is now open to the public. Visit the fully furnished rooms on three levels and then stairs leading to a natural terrace overlooking the Vézère river. The site has a "cabinet of curiosities" and includes an exhibition room on the theme of the Inquisition, the death penalty and torture.

▷ Continue along the D 706.

⁂ Préhisto Parc

&🕐*Open daily mid-Feb–mid-Nov 10am–6pm (Jul–Aug 9.30am–7.30pm).* ⊜€7 *(child €4).* ℘05 53 50 73 19.
In a small cliff-lined valley, carpeted with undergrowth, a discovery trail reveals

some 20 reconstituted scenes of Neanderthal and Cro-Magnon daily life.

▷ Continue along the D 706 for 500m then turn right onto a minor road which soon crosses the River Vézère. Turn left in Lespinasse.

Site de la Madeleine
&*See SITE DE LA MADELEINE.*

▷ Turn back then right onto the D 706.

Tursac
The **church** is dominated by a huge, forbidding belltower. There is a series of domes, characteristic of the Romanesque Périgord style, covering the church. The road once more scales the cliff, giving good views of Tursac village and the Vézère Valley.

▷ The D 706 leads back to Les Eyzies.

Château de Commarque★★

The impressive remains of Commarque Castle stand on the south bank of the River Beune. Commarque was built as a stronghold in the 12C and 14C and for a long time it belonged to the Beynac family. In 1968, Hubert de Commarque, a descendant of the original owners, commenced a long-term restoration project.

& **Michelin Map:** Michelin local map 329: H-6.
▷ **Location:** 9km/5.5mi E of Les Eyzies and 14km/9mi W of Sarlat. From the castle keep, there is a fine view of the valley and of the elegant 15C-16C Château de Laussel perched on a cliff across the river.
🅿 **Parking:** Situated 600m from the château.

VISIT
🕐*Open Apr and Oct 10.30am–6pm; May–Jun and Sept 10am–7pm; Jul–Aug 10am–8pm.* ⊜€7.50. ℘05 53 59 00 25.
www.commarque.com.
The tour of the fortified village begins with the well-preserved chapel; next come four mansions once occupied by noblemen. The Maison à Contreforts (buttressed house) illustrates the successive building periods: a troglodytic base,

a 10C–11C wall, a 15C fireplace and 16C murals. Along a narrow street, separate entrances indicate that each household was independent.
The double keep comprises the 14C great hall covered with a five-rib vault: the carved pendant brackets are well preserved and the keystone represents a helmet bearing the arms of Pons de Beynac.

Grotte de Lascaux★★

Lascaux ranks among the finest prehistoric sites of Europe by dint of the number and quality of its paintings. It is closed to the public, but its facsimile is the most popular site in the Périgord.

A BIT OF HISTORY

Discovery of the cave – The cave was discovered on 12 September 1940 by four young boys looking for their dog, which had fallen down a hole. They found an extraordinary fresco of polychrome paintings on the walls of the gallery they were in.

In 1949 the cave was officially opened to the public. Unfortunately, in spite of all the precautions taken, carbon dioxide and humidity resulted in two damaging effects: the green effect (the growth of moss and algae) and the white effect (less visible but much more serious as it leads to a build-up of deposits of white calcite).

In 1963, in order to preserve such a treasure, it was decided to close the cave to the public. Ten years later, a project was put forward to build a replica; Lascaux II was opened in 1983.

♿ **Michelin Map:** 329: I-5.
🛈 **Info:** Pl. Bertran-de-Born, 24290 Montignac. ✆05 53 51 82 60. www.lascaux-dordogne.com.
▶ **Location:** 2km/1.2mi south of Montignac, and 26km/16mi north of Sarlat.
🕐 **Timing:** Allow 2hr for Lascaux II, and half a day for all the sights.

As early as 1966, the National Geographic Institute (*Institut Géographique National – IGN*) had undertaken a precise photographic survey of Lascaux. This survey enabled a shell to be constructed in reinforced concrete. Once the cave walls were reproduced, the painter Monique Peytral copied the cave paintings using slides and the results from numerous surveys she had made. She used the same methods and materials (pigments, tools etc) as the cave artists.

THE CAVE

The cave, carved out of Périgord Noir limestone, is a relatively small cavity, 250m long. It is made up of four galleries, the walls of which are covered with

Lascaux II

more than 1 500 representations, either engraved or painted. These works were created from around 17 000 BCE, during the Magdalenian Culture, a period when the climate was relatively mild. At that time the cave was open to the outside air. Some time after the cave artists had decorated the cave, the entrance collapsed and a flow of clay tightly closed it off.

The airtight entrance and the impermeable ceiling are the reasons for the lack of concretions and the perfect preservation of the paintings fixed and authenticated by a thin layer of natural calcite. The simplified scene of a wounded bison and a falling man offers one of the rare representations of a human figure. This collection of paintings is truly unique in the history of prehistoric art, in regard to the state of preservation, the number of works created over a long time-span, and the precision of execution.

A wide range of fauna is depicted on the cave walls, mainly animals hunted during the early Magdalenian Period: auroch, horse, reindeer, bison, ibex, bears and woolly rhinoceros appear side by side or superimposed, forming extraordinary compositions.

The Lascaux style – There is a definite Lascaux style: lively animals with small, elongated heads, swollen stomachs and short legs, and fur illustrated by dabs of coloured pigment. The horns, antlers and hoofs are often drawn in three-quarter view, at times even full face, while the animal itself is drawn in profile; this procedure is known as the turned profile. In addition, the artists used the wall contours to give relief to the subject matter. The most impressive feature is the conveyed movement, where the animals seem to leap around visitors.

LASCAUX II★★

Phone or check website for opening hours. Tickets are sold in the village of Montignac under the arcades next to the tourist office. They go on sale at 9am and are sold until 2 000 have been issued (this allocation can sell out very quickly). €9. ℘05 53 05 65 65. www.semitour.com.

Located adjacent to the original cave, the facsimile reconstitutes two galleries from the upper part of the cave; the Bulls' Hall and the Axial Gallery, which contain the majority of the cave paintings at Lascaux. Antechambers retrace the cave's history and present items discovered in the cave's archaeological strata; an explanation of the dating methods used; and displays on flint and bone knapping.

In the **Bulls' Hall** (La Rotonde), the paintings are on the calcite-covered upper part of the wall and the vaulting, so that the animals seem to be running along the natural rim as if along the horizon line. The second animal, the only imaginary animal figure painted at Lascaux, has been nicknamed the unicorn because of the odd-looking horns above a bear-like muzzle, on a body not unlike that of a rhinoceros. Look out for black bulls, red bison, small horses and deer.

The **Axial Gallery** (Le Diverticule Axial) contains a vault and walls covered with horses, cows, ibexes, bison and a large deer. A charming frieze of long-haired ponies, a great black bull and a large red pony, seeming to sniff at a branch, bear witness to a developed style of art.

♟♙ Régourdou

500m from Lascaux. Leave your car in the Lascaux car park. ⚐🐾🕐Open Jul–Aug, guided tour (1hr), 10am–7pm; Sept–Nov and Feb–Jun, 11am–6pm. Closed Dec–Jan.€7. ℘05 53 51 81 23. www.regourdou.fr.

This prehistoric site is older than Lascaux as it dates goes back to the time of Neanderthal man. This species was discovered in 1954. A great deal of objects and bones were discovered here, including a skeleton, Régourdou Man (70 000 BCE), now displayed in the Périgord Museum in Périgueux.

A **museum** presents various elements found on the site and elsewhere, which help to illustrate the evolution of man from the Stone Age to the Iron Age.

Site de la Madeleine

As you walk along the Vézère, you'll admire the vastness of the valley and the high cliffs, reminders of the river level in ancient times. Then suddenly, in a little clearing, you'll notice something like… doors and windows in the cliffside. This is the surprising troglodytic village of La Madeleine.

A BIT OF HISTORY

La Madeleine owes its name to a chapel. In the 15C this chapel was enlarged and a ribbed vault was added; it was then dedicated to Saint Mary of Magdala or Mary Magdalene. The site would then lend its name to a prehistoric period, the last part of the Paleolithic Era.

SITE DE LA MADELEINE★

Open daily mid-Feb–mid-Mar, 11am–5pm; mid-Mar–Jun and Sept–Oct 10am–6pm; Jul–Aug 9.30am–8pm. €6. 05 53 46 36 88. www.la-madeleine-perigord.com. The location of the site of La Madeleine (*access from Les Eyzies via Tursac and the bridge to L'Espinasse*) stands out very clearly, from the point where the wooded plateau meets the Vézère's allu-

- ⚲ **Michelin Map:** 329 H-6.
- ▷ **Location:** 8.5km/5.2mi NE of Les Eyzies-de-Tayac-Sireuil.
- 🅿 **Parking:** Large shady car park.
- 🕓 **Timing:** 45min to visit the village.

vial plain below. The terrain is formed by the river's narrowest and most distinctly shaped meander. On the rock above stand the remains of a medieval castle. Located midway up the cliff, this village was probably occupied from the end of the 10C (Viking invasions) to the 20C. The village consists of some 20 dwellings, capable of accommodating about 100 people, carved out of the rock near a spring and protected by a narrow fortified entrance.

At the foot of the cliff lies the **prehistoric deposit** which established the characteristics of the Magdalenian Culture. This culture predominated during the last 60 centuries of the Upper Paleolithic Age (15 000–9 000 BCE). The richness and quality of the items discovered here in 1863 is remarkable. The majority of the objects are exhibited in the museums at Les Eyzies and St-Germain-en-Laye.

Site de la Madeleine

© Hervé Lenain / hemis.fr

Jardins de Marqueyssac★★

On the tip of a rocky outcrop overlooking the Dordogne valley, the hanging gardens of Marqueyssac offer a landscape that varies according to the light, shifting as the seasons pass and taking on nuances as the hours go by. A storm that revives the scent of the box hedges, a morning mist that settles over the topiaries, the summer sun that flickers through the leaves of the green oaks… each moment has its own enchantment.

VISIT

👫🕐 *Daily Jul–Aug 9am–8pm; Apr–Jun and Sept 10am–7pm; Feb, Mar, Oct–mid-Nov 10am–6pm; mid-Nov–Jan 2–5pm.* ✆€8 (10-17 years old: €4). 📞05 53 31 36 36. www.marqueyssac.com.

The 22ha/54-acre park of Marqueyssac includes a serpentine garden where the paths are bordered by box hedges both hand-trimmed and left to their natural shape. At the entrance, the outbuildings are a reminder of the farming past of the estate. The manor house is a residence dating from the end of the 18C where you may visit some of the rooms. The ceremonial terrace that stretches before it offers the only geometric arrangement reflecting the symmetry of the building. On the **Bastion Terrace★★**, box hedges carefully trimmed in varied ornamental topiary shapes bring interest to the landscape, while cypress trees provide structure. Choose from **three footpaths** leading to the overlook; if you change your mind, you can cross over on one of the interconnecting paths. In the wooded area under the green oaks, the boxwood grows more freely. Some of the plants are arched into tunnels. Along the way, you'll notice signposts providing information on the fauna, flora and history of the garden. Thus you can learn as you stroll, stopping here and there to admire the views. Your children can play in the various playgrounds while

♿ **Michelin Map:** Michelin Local Map 329 I-6.
▶ **Location:** In the south of the Périgord Noir, between Beynac-et-Cazenac and La Roque-Gageac.
🅿 **Parking:** Large, shady car park at the entrance.
👫 **Kids:** A family-oriented site, with paths accessible to prams marked out. Two playgrounds for smaller children, while the older ones may learn climbing in-season. **Curieux de nature** (activity workshops) Jul & Aug.
🕐 **Timing:** Allow at least 1hr (three circuits offer various length and difficulties). In summer, visit in the coolness of the morning. You may be brought back from the edge of the park in an electric vehicle.
👁 **Don't Miss:** The spectacular view over the entire garden from the Bastion Terrace viewpoint.

you meditate under the foliage. The viewpoint, landscaped by Julien de Cerval, includes a footbridge that spans a 130m drop. From here, the **view★★** over the neighbouring villages and castles is stunning: La Roque-Gageac, Castelnaud, Fayrac, Beynac and the meanders of the Dordogne River brought to life in the summertime by a ballet of canoes and *gabarres*.

Before you leave, if you're curious, stop by the nature pavilion next to the aviary; there you'll see a collection of dioramas created in 1848 and 1864. In the summertime, you'll see the boxwood turner near the entrance. Boxwood is hard, compact and devoid of veins, and takes on a lovely golden colour when polished. This craftsman will enjoy describing his art to you.

Montignac
Terrasson and the Vézère

The old town of Montignac consisted of a group of houses around a tower, a last reminder of the fortress that once belonged to the counts of Périgord. In only a few years, this pleasant hamlet has become a busy tourist centre, thanks to the nearby Lascaux cave. The small town spreads out either side of the River Vézère: on the west bank lies the "feudal village" with its network of narrow medieval lanes; on the east bank lies the "suburb", once a trade centre and river port.

A BIT OF HISTORY

Man's presence here can be traced back to the Paleolithic era. The site was later occupied by the Romans. The fortress, built in the early part of the Middle Ages, turned Montignac into a stronghold. Taken and dismantled several times during successive wars, the castle was finally destroyed in 1825.

OLD TOWN

Start at the tourist office (east bank), housed in the former St John's Hospital dating from the 14C (note the gallery). Église St-Georges, an extension of the hospital chapel, now houses temporary exhibitions. Follow **rue de la Pègerie★** opposite: it is lined with medieval houses, including a fine 13C timber-framed house at the end of the street. Continue towards the river and admire, on the opposite bank, the houses built on piles and their wooden galleries. Walk to the old stone bridge and cross the river to Pautauberge square, where there is a bust of Eugène Le Roy, the novelist native to the Périgord who spent the last years of his life in Montignac. Exit the square opposite the 17C Hôtel de Bouillac; turn left then right onto rue des Jardins, offering a fine **view★**. Continue along rue de la Tour which skirts the 11C castle and walk down towards the church. Note the fine house with its wooden gallery on the left. Return to the old bridge along the quays.

▶ **Population:** 2 860.
⚲ **Michelin Map:** 329: H-5.
▯ **Info:** Pl. Bertran de Born. ℘05 53 51 82 60. www.tourisme-vezere.com.
◖ **Location:** On the banks of the Vézère, just 2km/1.2mi from the Lascaux caves and 25km/15km NW of Sarlat.
▲▪ **Kids:** La Roque St-Christophe.
◕ **Timing:** Allow a full day to explore the Vézère valley. Montignac holds a walnut and cherry market on Wednesdays in October and November.
◉ **Don't Miss:** St-Amand-de-Coly's fortified church.

EXCURSIONS
La Grande Filolie
5km/3mi E on D 704.
⊶ *Closed to the public.*
Set in the hollow of a small valley, this charming castle dating from the 14C and 15C consists of a group of overlapping buildings and towers linked together. This building, part-castle, part-farm, is built in golden-coloured limestone and covered with a superb roof of *lauzes*.

Fanlac
7km/4.3mi west.
This charming village was chosen by Eugène Le Roy as the setting of his most famous novel, *Jacquou le Croquant*. The nearby **Forêt Barade** is ideal for gentle strolls of a couple of hours.

St-Amand-de-Coly★
Tucked away in the fold of a small valley off the Vézère Valley is St-Amand-de-Coly, its old *lauze*-roofed houses clustering round the impressive abbey church, where concerts take place during the Festival du Périgord.
The **church★★** of fine yellow limestone is perhaps the most amazing of all Périgord's fortified churches. The Augustinian abbey it once belonged to saw its spiritual activity reduced during

the Hundred Years' War: consequently, it was transformed into a fortress. The elaborate defence system was designed to keep enemies at a distance, but also to drive them away should any forays be made into the church. The Huguenots occupying the church in 1575 were able to hold out for six days against 20 000 soldiers of the Périgord seneschal, who had powerful artillery back-up.

The **tower keep** gives an impression of tremendous strength. It is indented by the enormous pointed arch of the doorway, which supports a defence room intended to prevent anyone approaching. The harmony of the apsidal chapels is a contrast to the severity of the high walls of the nave and transept. A watch-path runs around the building beneath the *lauze*-covered roof. Its purity of line and simplicity of **decoration**, typical of Augustinian architecture, contribute to the beauty of the lofty space inside. The concern for protection also affected the interior design; remains of the defence system include a narrow passage enclosing the chancel, small look-out posts in the pillars of the crossing and the loopholes in the base of the dome.

The **Point Accueil-Information** opposite the church presents an audio-visual show on the abbey and its history. It is also the starting point of guided tours and a "Topo-guide" detailing eight local rambles is on sale. ○ *Guided tours leave from here. For information, call* ℘ *05 53 51 04 56 or 05 53 51 47 85 (town hall).*

Jardins de l'Imaginaire★

In Terrassson-la-Villedieu, 17km/11mi NE of Montignac. *guided tour (1hr) every 30 min.* ○ *Daily Jul–Aug, 10am–6pm; Apr–Jun and Sept–Oct, 10–11.30am and 2–5.30pm (5pm in Sept).* ○ *Closed Tue exc Jul–Aug.* ॐ€7.50. ℘ *05 53 50 86 82. www.jardins-imaginaire.com/en.*

6 ha/15 acres of terraced gardens overlook Terrasson and the Vézère valley. This contemporary creation by Kathryn Gustafson won the international competition held in 1992. The guided tour transports visitors to the realm of fantasy through a forest alive with elves

and imps, a water garden, a rose garden featuring 2 000 rose bushes, an arbour, an iris garden and a greenhouse covered with plants; this last is the work of the architect Ian Ritchie and houses temporary exhibitions.

🚗 DRIVING TOUR

⑧ VALLÉE DE LA VÉZÈRE★

55km/34mi round-trip. Allow 1 day. See route 8 on region map page 89.

From Montignac to Les Eyzies the road closely follows the course of the river, which is lined with magnificent poplars. This is the most attractive part of the valley.

▷ Drive SW out of Montignac along the D 706 towards Les Eyzies.

Le Thot, Espace Cro-Magnon★

○ *Open daily Jul–Aug 10am–7pm; Apr–Jun 10am–6pm; Sept–Oct 10am–12.30pm and 2–6pm; Nov–Dec 10am–12.30pm and 2–5.30pm.* ○ *Closed Mon and 3 Jan–31 Jan, 25 Dec.* ॐ€8 (child €5). ℘ *05 53 05 65 65. www.semitour.com.*

Using multimedia, the museum gives a large overview of the expression of prehistoric people through painting, sculpture, graffiti and the like; prehistoric cultures are placed in the historical context of civilisation, its evolution and driving forces. A second part of the Lascaux facsimile, **la Nef**, is on display. The **park** is home to a number of species which inhabited the area in prehistoric times, such as aurochs and Przewalski's horses. Extinct species, the mammoth and the woolly rhinoceros, are represented by animatronics.

▷ Continue along the D 706.

Château et Jardins de Losse★

Open May–Sept, guided tour (45min) of the grand logis, 12am–6pm. ○ *Closed Sat except public holidays.* ॐ€9. ℘ *05 53 50 80 08. www.chateaudelosse.com.*

Château de Losse

© Château et Jardins de Losse

This elegant 16C building set amid terraced gardens is perched high on a rock above the right bank of the River Vézère. A terrace adorned with a balustrade and supported by a fine basket-handled arch stretches before the main building, which is flanked by a round tower at one corner. A fixed bridge, which has replaced the original drawbridge, gives access to the main courtyard past a fortified gatehouse.

A walk along the ramparts offers a good overall view of the fortifications; from the **Tour Sainte-Marguerite**, now a dovecote (*video presentation of period costumes*), an alleyway lined with boxwood hedging leads to the **Tour de l'Éperon** housing a bath and resting room. Look down on the **Jardin Bas**: a restored garden planted with lavender, santalina and rosemary bushes, separated by a small canal. Nearby is an **outbuilding** presenting a film describing the castle and stone-slab roofing methods. Farther on are the **Jardins en Terrasse** inspired by 17C bowers.

Splendid furnishings and in particular **tapestries** make for fine decoration. Note the fresh colours of the Flemish tapestry, illustrating the traditional preparation for a tournament, and the Florentine tapestry depicting the Return of the Courtesan; both are 17C.

▷ Drive onto Thonac then turn right onto the D 45.

Plazac

The Romanesque church, in the centre of a churchyard planted with cypress trees, stands on a hillock overlooking the village. The 12C belfry-keep is roofed with *lauzes* and embellished with blind arcades resting on Lombard bands.

▷ Drive S along the D 6.

Le Moustier

This village, at the foot of a hill, contains a famous prehistoric shelter (**Abri du Moustier préhistorique** – ○*one visit per week by prior arrangement with the Grotte de Font-de-Gaume;* ℘*05 53 06 86 00.* ○*Closed 1 Jan, 1 May, 1 and 11 Nov and 25 Dec.* ⊚€*3.* ℘*05 53 06 86 00. www.monuments-nationaux.fr*). The prehistoric finds made here include the skeleton of a Neanderthal man and a large number of flint implements. The corresponding culture in the Middle Paleolithic was named "Mousterian" after the finds.

▷ From the village, drive towards Chabans passing Côte de Jor, which affords a panoramic view of the Vézère and St-Léon-sur-Vézère.

Château de Chabans

⟐ *Closed to the public.*
An avenue lined with old trees leads to this imposing castle still protected by defensive walls. The round tower dates from the 15C whereas the remainder of

the edifice was rebuilt in the 16C and 17C. The castle was tastefully restored at the end of the 20C.

▶ Return to Le Moustier. Cross the Vézère then turn left onto the D 66.

La Roque St-Christophe★

🕐☕Guided tours (1hr) Jan 10am–5pm; Feb–Mar and Oct–early Nov 10am–6pm; early Nov– early Jan, 10am–5.30pm; Jul–Aug 10am–8pm. €8 (child: €4.50). ℘05 53 50 70 45. www.roque-st-christophe.com.

👥 This long and majestic cliff rises vertically (80m) above the Vézère valley over a distance of more than 900m/0.5mi. It is like a huge hive with some 100 caves hollowed out of the rock on five levels. Excavations along its foot have shown that the cliff dwellings were inhabited from the Upper Paleolithic Age onwards.

In the 10C the cliff terraces served as the foundation for a fortress which was used against the Vikings and during the Hundred Years War (accommodating up to 1 500 people), and then subsequently destroyed during the Wars of Religion at the end of 16C. The drainage channels and water tanks, the fireplaces, the stairways and passages hollowed out of the rock all show that St Christopher's Rock was the site of continued, lively human activity. A house leaning against the cliff was reconstructed according to methods used in the 10C and 13C; in the **Cuisine de l'An Mil** (the AD 1000 kitchen) are displayed replicas of archaeological finds. On the **Grande Terrasse**, visitors can see a reconstruction of a medieval building site and a scale model of the whole site. From this terrace, admire the **view★** of the green Vézère valley.

▶ Continue along the D 66.

Peyzac-le-Moustier

The **Musée du Moustier** illustrates the evolution of living beings as well as technical progress from the first creatures going back to some 600 million years to the Gallo-Romans.

The park contains the sculpture of a dinosaur (11m long and 5m high) and several megaliths. 🕐Open by prior arrangement. €3. ℘05 53 06 86 00 (out of season).

▶ Leave Peyzac S and join the D 65.

St-Léon-sur-Vézère★

👣 See ST-LÉON-SUR-VÉZÈRE.

▶ Return to Peyzac, follow the D 65.

Sergeac

This village is pleasantly situated beside the Vézère at a spot where tall cliffs follow the line of the valley.

After passing the delicately carved 15C cross at its entrance, you'll admire the old houses roofed with *lauzes* and a turreted manor house, the remains of a commandery, which once belonged to the Knights Templar. The restored Romanesque **church** still retains a fortified appearance with loopholes, machicolations and a belltower.

Castel-Merle

This site, which is well-known to specialists, was closed to the public for many years. Some of the finds – bones, flints, headdresses – are exhibited in the museums of Les Eyzies, Périgueux and St-Germain-en-Laye (west of Paris).

Near the site, a small local **museum** exhibits a number of interesting artefacts from the Mousterian Age to the Gallo-Roman era. 🕐☕Guided tours (1hr), Jul–Aug 10am–7pm except Sat and by prior arrangement in advance; Apr–Jun and Sept (closed Sat) 10am–7pm (Sun 2–7pm). 🕐Closed Oct–Mar. ℘05 53 50 79 70.

Several shelters (*abris*) can be visited, one of which contains wall sculptures (bison, horses) from the Magdalenian Age. In the Souquette shelter a section of strata is shown with levels from the Aurignacian Age to the modern era.

▶ Return to Montignac on the D 65.

ADDRESSES

STAY

⊖ **Le Clos du Moulin** – *24120 Terrasson-Lavilledieu.* ℘*05 53 51 68 95. www.gite-dordogne.net. 14 chalets.* ⤢ This small holiday village in a verdant setting at the river's edge is very comfortable and well maintained. Heated swimming pool and on-site restaurant service.

⊖ **Camping Le Moulin du Bleufond** – *Av. Aristide-Briand, Montignac, 0.5km/ 0.3mi S on D 65 route de Sergeac, near the Vézère river.* ℘*05 53 51 83 95. www.bleufond.com. 83 pitches.* Built around a 17C mill, this campsite is in the heart of the Périgord Noir and the Vézère valley. Large heated swimming pool and paddling pool, spa, sauna and a terrace along the river.

⊖ **Hotel Le P'tit Monde** – *52 and 54 r. du IV Septembre, Montignac.* ℘*05 53 51 32 76 or 06 15 72 42 25. www.hotellepetit monde.com. 14 rooms.* Functional hotel at the entrance of the village; comfort in the rooms is kept to a bare minimum. Spa and sauna are available free of charge.

⊖⊖ **Chambre d'hôte La Licorne** – *Le Bourg, 24290 Valojoulx.* ℘*05 53 50 77 77. www.licorne-lascaux.com.* ▣ ⤢ *5 rooms. Meals served Mon, Tue, Thurs and Sat evenings.* At the centre of the village, facing the church, this authentic 17C and 18C Périgord-style house has well-decorated rooms. Stone walls and wooden beams provide character. Medicinal plant garden.

⊖⊖ **Hotel du Parc** – *Le Bourg, on D 706, 24290 Thonac.* ℘*05 53 50 70 20. www.hotel-du-parc.net.* ▣. This pretty stone hotel is located just next to its restaurant. The rooms are of a modest size and the decoration is a bit retro. The better ones are on the ground floor opening directly onto the lawn across from the Vézère river.

⊖⊖⊖ **Château de la Fleunie** – *24570 Condat-sur-Vézère. 11km/6.2mi NW of St-Amand via the D 62, D 704 and a secondary road.* ℘*05 53 51 32 74. www. lafleunie.com. 33 rooms.* A great place to relax. The 12C and 15C château with four round towers sits in the middle of a 100ha/247-acre park. The rooms in the castle have old-fashioned furnishings; those in the annex are more modern.

⊖⊖⊖ **Hostellerie La Commanderie** – *24570 Condat-sur-Vézère. 11km/6.6mi NW of St-Amand on the D 62 and D 704.* ℘*05 53 51 26 49. www.hotel-lacommanderie.com. 7 rooms.* In the heart of the village, this charming house was once a waystation on the road to Compostela. The pretty rooms under the vaulted ceilings of the upper floor are king-size. Quiet garden.

⚲/EAT

⊖ **Aux Saveurs des Jardins** – *Pl. Foirail, 24120 Terrasson-Lavilledieu.* ℘*05 53 50 30 91.* Located at the entrance to the Jardins de l'Imaginaire, this restaurant offers a pretty view over the old town. You can have your meal in a picnic basket to take away. Regional cuisine topped with edible flowers: original, pretty and delicious.

⊖ **Les Pilotis** – *6 r. Laffite, Montignac.* ℘*05 53 50 88 15.* This friendly, classic family-style restaurant owes its success to its simple, tasty and affordable cuisine. Regional dishes, generous salads, pizzas and more can be enjoyed on the terrace overlooking the Vézère.

⊖⊖ **Le Bareil** – *Le Bareil, 24290 La Chapelle-Aubareil.* ℘*05 53 50 74 28.* ⤢ Here, the adjective "gargantuan" is not used in vain: one after another, delicious dishes arrive on the table, from soup to *digestif*, passing through duck gizzard salad and cheeses with jams. Enjoy all this in a festive atmosphere.

⊖⊖⊖ **L'Imaginaire** – *Pl. du Foirail, 24120 Terrasson-Lavilledieu.* ℘*05 53 51 37 27. www.l-imaginaire.fr. Closed last week Feb–first week Mar, 11–31 Nov, Sun eve, Mon and Tue lunchtime from Sep to Apr, and Mon lunchtime from May–Aug.* A former 17C hospice is the setting for this elegant restaurant with a charming vaulted room.

⊖⊖⊖ **Le Moulin de Mitou** – *24290 Auriac-du-Périgord.* ℘*05 53 50 37 53. www. hotel-lemoulindemitou.com. 17 rooms.* The restaurant of this 3-star hotel is run by former Michelin-starred chef Serge Bégué.

La Roque-Gageac★★

The village of La Roque-Gageac, huddled against a cliff which drops vertically to the River Dordogne, occupies a wonderful site★★ – one of the finest in this part of the valley, in which Domme, Castelnaud and Beynac-et-Cazenac are all within a few miles of each other. At the top of the cliff there are clear traces to remind visitors of the tragic day in 1957 when a huge block of rock came away from the cliff face, killing three inhabitants.

THE VILLAGE

Attractive little streets run tightly along the rocky bluff. One of them, leading off to the right of the Carrier Hotel, climbs through luxuriant plant life to reach a kind of oasis backing onto the cliff face. It has taken Gérard Dorin 30 years to develop his exotic garden: the micro-climate favours the growth of Mediterranean vegetation (here, olive, lemon and banana trees thrive along with 20 varieties of palm trees).

Walk back down the street towards the troglodytic fort opposite. On your way,

La Roque-Gageac
© Patrick Escudero / hemis.fr

> ▶ **Population:** 432.
> ⚅ **Michelin Map:** 329: I-7.
> 🗊 **Info:** Bourg, 24250 La Roque Gageac. ℘05 53 29 17 01. www.sarlat-tourisme.com.
> ◖ **Location:** 69km/43mi SE of Périgueux and 12km/7.5mi S of Sarlat. The best view of La Roque-Gageac is from the west: the late-afternoon sun highlights the tall grey cliff face covered with holm oaks, while the houses, with their stone-slab (*lauzes*) or tile roofs, are reflected in the calm waters of the river below.
> ⊛ **Don't Miss:** A boat trip.

take a look at the **Manoir de Tarde**. Two pointed gabled buildings, with mullioned windows, stand next to a round tower. This charming manor house is associated with the Tarde family, whose most famous member was canon Jean Tarde, a 16C humanist, historian, cartographer, astronomer and mathematician. The impregnable **troglodytic fort** was built in the 12C and reinforced in the 17C before being dismantled in the 18C. A 140-step climb will take you within sight of what remains of the defensive system and the beautiful view will reward your efforts (⊛ *note the outline of the Château de la Malartrie on the right*).

ADDRESSES

⌂ STAY

⊖⊖⊖ **Auberge La Plume d'Oie** ℘05 53 29 57 05. www.aubergelaplumedoie.com. *Reservation required.* 4 rooms. A little village inn in an old renovated house typical of the region. The dining room is bright and cheerful with blonde wooden beams, stonework and large bay windows. A few rooms with views of the Dordogne.

Domme★★

Domme, the Acropolis of the Dordogne, is remarkably situated on a rocky crag overlooking the Dordogne Valley. This exceptional site inspired many artists including the writer Henry Miller.

A BIT OF HISTORY

A royal bastide – Domme was founded by Philip the Bold in 1283 in order to keep watch on the Dordogne valley and check the desire for expansion of the English established in Gascony. The king granted the town important privileges including that of minting coins. Domme played an important role during the Hundred Years War. In the 17C, its wine-growing and river-trading activities were thriving and its markets were renowned throughout the region.

Captain Vivans' exploit – While the struggles of the Reformation were inflaming France, Domme kept up resistance against the Huguenots who were overrunning Périgord. Finally, in 1588, the famous Protestant Captain **Geoffroi de Vivans** captured the town by cunning. One night he and 30 of his men climbed along the rocks of the cliff face known as the Barre, a place so precipitous that it had not been thought necessary to protect it, and entered the sleeping town. Vivans and his men created an

- ▶ **Population:** 1 015.
- 🕭 **Michelin Map:** 329.
- 🚻 **Info:** Pl. de la Halle, 24250 Domme. ✆ 05 53 31 71 00. www.ot-domme.com.
- ▶ **Location:** 74km/46mi SE of Périgueux and 13km/8mi S of Sarlat.
- 🅿 **Parking:** A number of car parks are available within the walls of this bastide (🕭 *see town plan*). You can also park outside the walls and catch a tourist train to the centre.
- 🕭 **Don't Miss:** The view from the Belvédère de la Barre.

infernal racket and during the ensuing confusion opened the tower doors to their waiting army. The inhabitants were too sleepy to resist, and Vivans thereupon became master of the town for the next four years. He installed a garrison, burned down both the church and the Augustine priory and established the Protestant faith.

However, noting the increasing success of the Catholics in Périgord, he sold the bastide to his rivals on 10 January 1592. The unwary purchasers found nothing but ruins.

View from Belvédère de la Barre, Domme

© Walter Bibikow / age fotostock

129

🐾 WALKING TOUR

BASTIDE★

Domme is a rare bastide in that it does not follow a perfect rectangular plan; it is more in the form of a trapezium. The surrounding fortifications have been adapted to the terrain. Inside the fortified town, the streets follow a geometric plan, as far as possible. Guided tours are available by prior arrangement with the tourist board.

▶ Start from the tourist office and follow rue Mazet (running parallel to Grand'Rue) then rue Porte Delbos.

Porte del Bos

This gateway, which has a pointed arch, was once closed with a portcullis. Walk inside the ramparts to the 13C **Porte de la Combe**.

▶ Walk towards the town along rue de la Porte-de-la-Combe.

The street is lined with fine houses. The beauty of the gold stone and the flat brown tiles is often enhanced by the addition of elegant wrought-iron balconies and brightened by climbing vines and flower-decked terraces.

▶ Rue de la Porte-des-Tours on the right leads to the Porte des Tours.

Porte des Tours

🕐🐾 *Open Feb–Dec, guided tour by prior arrangement.* €8.50.
📞 *05 53 31 71 00.*
This late-13C gateway is the most impressive and best preserved of the town's gateways. On the side of place des Armes, the wall is rectilinear but on the outside, the gateway is flanked by two massive semicircular rusticated towers, built by Philip the Fair and originally used as guard-rooms. Between 1307 and 1318, a group of Knights Templar were imprisoned there and left a mysterious message in the form of graffiti before perishing.

▶ Turn left.

Rue Eugène-le-Roy

During the period he spent in a house along this street (*plaque*), Eugène le Roy wrote two of his master-works: *L'Ennemi de la Mort* (The Enemy of Death) and *Le Moulin du Frau* (Frau Mill).

Place de la Rode

This is the place where the condemned were broken on the wheel. The *Maison du Batteur de Monnaie* (money minter's house) shows a fine Gothic style.

Grand'Rue

This shopping street is lined with shops displaying many of the culinary specialities of Périgord. Note the elegant mullioned windows of the house standing on the corner of rue Geoffroy-de-Vivans.

▶ Walk to rue des Consuls via rue Geoffroy-de-Vivans.

Rue des Consuls

The Hôtel de Ville (town hall) is located in a 13C building, which was once the Seneschal law courts.

▶ Walk along Grand'Rue to the town centre.

Place de la Halle

In this large square stands an elegant 17C covered market (*halle*). Facing it is the 15C **Maison du Gouverneur** (Governor's House) flanked by an elegant turret. It now houses the tourist office.
Destroyed during the Wars of Religion, the **church** was rebuilt in the 17C and the belfry-porch was added in the 19C.

LE PANORAMA
Belvédère de la Barre

From the promontory, the **view★★★** spans the Dordogne valley from the Montfort meander in the east to Beynac in the west. Changing with the time of day – hazy in the early morning mist, bright blue between lines of green poplars in the noonday sun, a silver ribbon in the evening light – the Dordogne winds its way through the carefully cultivated fields dotted with villages and farms.

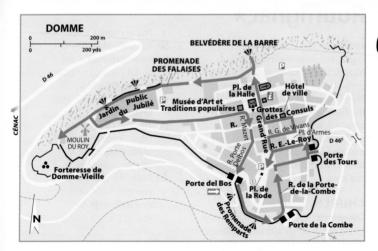

Of all the creative artists who have come here seeking inspiration, Henry Miller was perhaps the most affected, describing the area as the nearest thing to Paradise on earth. The esplanade at the end of the Grand'Rue offers the best panorama of the valley below.

▶ Follow the promenade des Falaises, a cliffside walk along the promontory.

Jardin Public du Jubilé

These attractive gardens (*viewing table*) are situated between the town and the tip of the promontory, on the site of the entrenched camp installed here in 1214 by Simon de Montfort. He had just beaten the Cathars and razed their fortress **Domme-Vieille**, leaving but a few ruins standing.

ALSO SEE

Grotte de Domme

🕐👣*Open Jul–Aug, guided tour (45min), 10am–6.40pm; Apr–May 10am–noon, 2–5.30pm; Jun–Sept, 10am–noon and 2–6pm; rest of year 11am–noon, 2.30–4.30pm.* ✆€8.50. ✆05 53 31 71 00.

The entrance is in the covered market converted into an entrance hall. The panoramic lift which brings visitors up at the end of the visit offers a magnificent view of the Dordogne valley.

These caves served as refuge for the townspeople of Domme during the Hundred Years War and the Wars of Religion. So far about 450m of galleries have been cleared for the public to visit; the chambers are generally small and are sometimes separated by low passages. The ceilings in certain chambers are embellished with slender white stalactites. There are also places where stalactites and stalagmites join to form columns or pillars. The Salle Rouge contains some fine eccentrics.

Bison and rhinoceros bones, discovered when the caves were being prepared for tourists, are displayed precisely as they were found.

Musée d'Art et Traditions populaires

🕐*Open Jul–Aug, 10.30am–7pm; Apr–Jun and Sept, 10.30am–12.30pm and 2.30–6pm.* ✆€8.50. ✆05 53 31 71 00.

In an old house on place de la Halle, this museum presents a retrospective of every day life in Domme, with displays of furnishings, clothing and farm tools. Amid the archives and photographs, note the royal missives according special privileges and exemptions to the inhabitants of Domme.

Rouffignac★

Rouffignac lies at the heart of a region rich in archaeological and historic sites, including the splendid prehistoric cave of the same name. The church is all that escaped when the Germans set about burning the village in March 1944 as a reprisal; it has since been rebuilt and is now a peaceful holiday resort and the ideal starting point for excursions in the area.

▶ **Population:** 1 557.
🚗 **Michelin Map:** 329: G-5.
🛈 **Information:** Rue du Jardin Public, 24260 Le Bugue. ☎05 53 07 20 48.
▶ **Location:** 18km/11mi N of Les Eyzies-de-Tayac.
🕐 **Timing:** Plan for 2hr, taking into account the winding access road and the waiting time.
👪 **Kids:** The cave for prehistory and Jacquou Parc for fun (👪 *see ADDRESSES*).

CHURCH

The **church** entrance is through an interesting belfry-porch with an early Renaissance door. It was built in 1530 and is decorated with Corinthian capitals. In such a holy place, it's surprising to find such profane decoration as mermaids and busts of women.

EXCURSIONS

👪 Grotte de Rouffignac★

5km/3mi S along the D 32. ♿🕐*Open Jul–Aug, 9–11.30am and 2–6pm; Apr–Jun and Sept–Oct, 10–11.30am and 2–5pm.* 🚶*Guided tour (1hr).* 👛€7 *(child 6–12, €4.60). Limited number of daily visitors.* ☎05 53 05 41 71. *www.grotteroufﬁgnac.fr.*
😊*As with all caves, bring a jumper, as the temperature inside is around 13°C/55°F.*

This dry **cave**, also known as Cro de Granville, was already well-known in the 15C. The galleries are over 8km/5mi long. An electric train carries visitors to the main galleries, making this is one of the few prehistoric sites in the area which is fully accessible to persons of limited mobility. In 1956 Professor LR Nougier brought to light a remarkable group of paintings marked with black lines and **engravings★** produced during the Middle or Upper Magdalenian Period (around 13 000 BCE). Deeper into the cave, the nickname "Cave of the Hundred Mammoths" seems appropriate. In fact, no fewer than 158 mammoth figures can be seen on the walls and ceiling. Their presence is a double mystery: they are rare elsewhere and – even more surprisingly – very few bones of the pachyderm have been found in the southwest of France. There are also engravings of horses, ibexes, rhinoceroses and bison, as well as an amazing frieze depicting two herds locked in combat. You'll also make out tectiform (roof-shaped) symbols, the likes of which can be seen in the caves of Bernifal, Combarelles and Font-de-Gaume. This suggests that the four caves were decorated by a people who shared the same culture.

Château de l'Herm

4.5km/2.7mi NW of Rouffignac on D 6. 🕐*Open Apr–Sept (except Jun) 10am–7pm.* 👛€6 *(no charge for children under 16).* ☎ 05 53 05 46 61. *www.chateaudelherm.com.*

The history of this medieval fortress, which was improved by work from 1485 to 1512, is marked by a long series of crimes. But of this dark past, only the stately ruins remain. The former castle is famous in France as the dwelling of the sinister Count of Nansac in the novel *Jacquou le Croquant* by Eugène Le Roy. Its large defence towers seem to emerge from the forest. The main building has been temporarily covered with a translucent cover to protect it from the elements. The gates have been recon-

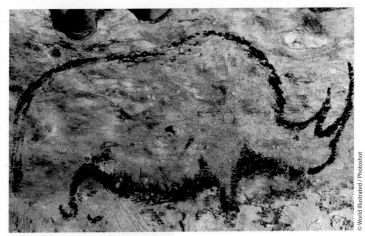

Painting of rhinoceros, Grotte de Rouffignac

© World Illustrated / Photoshot

structed on three levels. The hexagonal turret of the staircase opens onto a Flamboyant gateway showing Renaissance influences. The second arched entryway, decorated with curled cabbage leaves, rises high into the sky. This door gives access to a remarkable spiral staircase with a moulded coil in its centre. It rises in one piece, with no landing, and gives way to a star-shaped vault, crisscrossed with ribs that form a sort of stone palm tree. From the windows of this tower you can see the monumental fireplaces on each of the three levels that bear the Calvimont family coat of arms and the Barade Forest beyond.

ADDRESSES

STAY

⊜ **Chambre d'hôte Le Logis de la Mouchardie** – *La Mouchardie, 24580 Plazac. 3km/1.8mi SE of Rouffignac on D 31 and secondary road to the left.* ℘*05 53 50 45 12. www.giteperigord.com/le_logis.* 🛏. *5 rooms.* This old farm nestled in the wooded hills is as calm as you can get. The entirely renovated building includes five well-kept rooms and a charming little *gîte*. There is a pleasant terrace ideal for breakfasts in the open air and a pretty courtyard with a swimming pool.

♀/ EAT

⊜ **Le Dénicheur** – *42 av. de la Libération, 24210 Thenon.* ℘*05 53 06 37 60.* Easy to find in the middle of the village, this little Périgord-style house has been transformed into a very enjoyable restaurant. Beyond the predictable fixed menus, try the large salad platters, topped with gizzards, duck breast or foie gras. You can also enjoy your meal in the garden.

⊜⊜ **Ferme-auberge Le Puits Fleuri** – *Boujou, 2km/1.2mi SE of Rouffignac on D 31, rte de Fleurac and secondary road to the left.* ℘*05 53 05 42 95.* You'll hardly have the time to notice the sparse decoration of this *auberge*; as soon as the food arrives, it will captivate you. Quality regional dishes in copious quantities. Try the duck breast with Sarlat-style potatoes; a delight!

LEISURE ACTIVITIES

Jacquou Parc – *Mortemart, la Ménuse, 24260 Le Bugue; NW of le Bugue on D 710.* ℘*05 43 54 15 57. www.jacquouparc.com.* Located in a natural setting, this park includes three attractions in one. The animal park displays farm animals from all over the world; the water park includes water slides and a paddling pool; and the theme park offers rides for all the family to enjoy. Fast food available on site.

Saint-Léon-sur-Vézère ★

Built in a picturesque loop of the River Vézère, this charming country village possesses two castles and one of the finest Romanesque churches of the Périgord. It comes to life in August during the Festival Musical du Périgord Noir.

🐾 VILLAGE WALK

Church ★

The church was part of a Benedictine priory which was founded in the 12C. It was built on the ruins of a Gallo-Roman villa; the remains of one of the villa's walls can be seen on the riverside.

From the town square, the church's apse, perfectly smooth radiating chapels and square two-storey arcaded belltower form a harmonious whole. The church is roofed with the heavy limestone slabs (*lauzes*) of Périgord Noir.

Inside, the transept crossing is vaulted with a dome, whereas apsidal chapels are connected to the apse by narrow openings, known as *berrichon* passages, as they are particularly featured in churches in the Berry region.

The apse and south radiating chapel are decorated with the remains of **Romanesque frescoes**.

▶ Walk along the river on the left.

Château de Clérans

This elegant 15C and 16C palace, flanked with machicolated towers and turrets, stands on the banks of the river.

▶ Go into the village.

Château de la Salle

Standing on the town square, this small stone castle has a fine 14C square keep crowned with machicolations.

Chapelle du Cimetière

This small 14C chapel in the cemetery is roofed, like the church, with *lauzes*. An inscription in Occitan above the door harks back to an extraordinary event; in

▶ **Population:** 429.
🕐 **Michelin Map:** 329: H-5.
🛈 **Information:** ☎ 05 53 51 08 42.
▶ **Location:** Midway between the Grotte de Lascaux and Les Eyzies-de-Tayac.

Château de Clérans

© DEA / C SAPPA / agefotostock

1233, a servant who had let fly an arrow onto the crucifix guarding the entrance to the cemetery dropped dead on the spot, with his head turned back-to-front. In 1890, the blasphemer's grave was excavated, and a skeleton with its skull back-to-front was unearthed.

ADDRESSES

🛏 STAY

☺ **Camping Le Paradis** – *4km/2.5mi SW of St-Léon-sur-Vézère along the D 706.* ☎*05 53 50 72 64. www.le-paradis.com. Open Apr–19 Oct. Reservation recommended. 200 pitches. Restaurant.* "Paradise" is a good name for this campsite. Former farm buildings serve as facilities and the sites are attractively landscaped. Modern and comfortable. Pool, tennis court and play areas.

🍽 EAT

☺☺ **Le Petit Léon** – ☎*05 53 51 18 04. Closed Sun eve, Mon lunchtime and Sept –Jun.* This garden restaurant is a real find. White parasols shade the wooden tables under the apple trees. The dishes are inventive and tasty.

Château de Hautefort★★

The proud outline of Hautefort Castle dominates the skyline, more reminiscent of the royal palaces of the Loire valley than of the fortresses of the Périgord.

- **Michelin Map:** 329: H-4.
- **Info:** Pl. Marquis J. Francois de Hautefort, 24390 Hautefort. ✆05 53 50 40 27.
- **Location:** 41km/25.5mi E of Périgueux.
- **Don't Miss:** The superb timberwork in the NW tower of the castle.

A BIT OF HISTORY

The strategic position of the Hautefort site on a hill in the middle of an immense amphitheatre was certainly exploited very early on: in the 9C the viscounts of Limoges built a stronghold here. During the Middle Ages several castles succeeded one another, leaving some traces (the courtayrd's west corner tower). The defensive position of the castle was strengthened in the 16C (barbican flanked by two crenellated bartizans and equipped with a drawbridge) during the tumultuous years of the Wars of Religion. Complete reconstruction of the castle in the 17C led to a harmonious combination of architectural styles – Renaissance and Classical – which contributes to the building's original and elegant appearance.

In 1929, Baron Henri de Bastard and his wife bought the castle and decided to restore it; they also had the French-style gardens laid out. In 1968, fire swept through the main building but the two wings were spared. The fine interior has since been restored.

CASTLE

⏰ Open daily Jun–Aug, 9.30am–7pm, Sept 10am–6pm, Apr–May, 10am–12.30pm and 2–6pm, Oct daily 2–6pm; Mar and 1–11 Nov, weekends and public holidays 2–6pm. ⚏€8.50. ✆05 53 50 51 23.
www.chateau-hautefort.com.

The terraces of the castle are laid out as French-style gardens, planted with flowers and box trees forming geometric patterns and offering views of the 30ha/74-acre English-style park where visitors can take a pleasant stroll.

Inside the castle, the northwest tower has beautiful chestnut **timberwork★★**, the work of the Compagnons du Tour de France guild.

Château de Hautefort

© javarman /Bigstockphoto.com

Bertrand the Troubadour

The first castle of Hautefort was built by the Limousin family of Las Tours. In the 12C it passed by marriage to the house of De Born, of whom Bertrand, the very same mentioned by Dante in the *Divine Comedy*, is the best-known member. **Bertrand de Born**, the famous troubadour who was much admired in the courts of love, became a warrior-knight when it came time to defend the family castle against his brother Constantine. He succeeded in having Henry II acknowledge his rights in 1185. However, in 1186, Constantine returned to Hautefort and razed the castle. Renouncing his former life, Bertrand became a monk.

It gives access to the watch-path dismantled in the 17C. The flower-decked gallery of the main building leads to a grand staircase giving access to various rooms, including Marie de Hautefort's bedroom furnished in Louis XV style.

ANCIEN HOSPICE

The former chapel of an almshouse stands on the village square south of the castle. The edifice, shaped like a Greek cross, features a fine dome covered with slates and surmounted by a lantern. It houses the **Musée de la Médecine** (🕐 daily: Mar–May 10am–noon, 2–6pm; Jun–mid-Nov 10am–7pm. €6. 𝄞05 53 50 40 27. www.musee-hautefort. fr), which displays a reconstructed ward and presents an exhibition devoted to the progress of medicine in the 19C; another room illustrates dental care from 1870 to the present.

🚗 DRIVING TOUR

⑨ LE PAYS D'ANS★

45.9km/28.5mi round-trip. Allow 2hr30min. See route 9 on region map page 89. Leave Hautefort NE on D 72.

This little area, stretching between the Limousin and Périgord, gets its name from the largest castellan domain in the viscounty of Limoges. The landscape is a checkerboard of walnut orchards and woods, cut through by small valleys.

Boisseuilh

In the heart of this village stands a Romanesque church with a belltower featuring two arcades that was redesigned in the 17C.

▷ Leave Cherveix S (D 5).

Cherveix-Cubas

A 13C lantern of the dead stands in the cemetery. At a short distance, the church of Cherveix, which is closed to the public, houses a low-relief sculpture representing St Roch. You may access the church on Sun morning during the service or request access from the town hall (𝄞05 53 50 41 44).

▷ Leave Cherveix S (D 5).

Abbaye de Tourtoirac

🕐*Jul–Aug 10am–noon, 2–6pm; on request the rest of the year.* 𝄞*05 53 51 12 17.*

This Romanesque church has changed with the centuries. Notice the 12C doorway and the 13C mortuary recess. Behind the apse, you may explore the ruins of the 11C monastery which now stands in a public park. To the right, you'll see a barrel-vaulted Romanesque chapel with acoustic amphorae, a bread oven and the watchpath. To the left, notice the clover-shaped former abbey; its choir and transept are decorated with mural frescoes. In the cellar of the presbytery next to the church, the chapter house has been restored. It is adorned with remarkable Romanesque capitals.

Grotte de Tourtoirac

🕐 *Open Mar and Nov, weekends 2–6pm; Apr and Oct daily 2–6pm; May–Jun and Sept 10am–noon, 2–6pm; Jul–Aug 9.30am–7.30pm.* 🎫€8. 𝄆05 53 50 24 77. www.grotte-de-tourtoirac.fr.
This spectacular geologic cave has just recently opened. A light show reveals a multitude of concretions, including stalactites, stalagmites, draperies and eccentrics.

▶ Leave Tourtoirac S on D 67.

Ste-Orse

A few houses with bright golden stones encircle the Romanesque church of the village. Behind its triple-crowned doorway, the building houses a polygonal crypt that is often closed to the public.

▶ Leave Ste-Orse E and follow D 70.

Badefols-d'Ans

The Badefols seigneury was the property of Bertran de Born. The oldest part of the castle overlooking the valley is the square dungeon. The 12C church was overhauled in the 15C and 16C.

▶ Come back on D 70, then take a right on D 71 to access Hautefort through the woods; you'll get a good view of the castle from here.

ADDRESSES

🛏 STAY

☞ **Camping Village-Vacances Les Sources** – *La Génèbre, Hautefort. 4km/2.4mi S on D 704 and secondary road to the right.* 𝄆05 53 51 96 56. www.dordogne-gite.fr. . This relatively new complex of comfortable *gîtes* and chalets welcomes families to its 30ha/74-acre estate across from Hautefort Castle. Enjoy the water feature including heated swimming pools and balneotherapy baths. A tranquil, pleasant place to stay in the Périgord Noir.

☞ **Chambre d'hôte La Razoire Haute** – *Rte de Nailhac, la Razoire, Nailhac.* 𝄆05 53 51 51 74. 🅿 🔌. *5 rooms.* The owners of this bed and breakfast are retired from their farming activities, but they still enjoy receiving visitors. The rooms are simple and somewhat small but impeccably clean. You may reserve meals in the family dining room.

🍴 EAT

☞ **Les Foies Gras d'Érillac** – *Pl. Eugène-Leroy, Hautefort.* 𝄆05 53 51 61 49. Behind its wooden façade, the shop offers regional specialities such as duck and goose preserves, beverages and jams. The restaurant offers simple, well-presented cuisine, such as *bloc de foie gras* salad and roasted preserved duck.

☞☞ **Ferme-auberge Le Grand Coderc** – *Le Grand Coderc, St-Rabier.* 𝄆05 53 50 64 61. www.legrandcoderc.com. ♿🅿. *5 rooms.* Don't expect luxury or flourishes in this old, rustic house. On the other hand, you'll find all the indulgence you're looking for in the chef's delicious dishes, such as buttered cabbage with foie gras, *lièvre à la royale* and home-made ice cream. Enjoy these in the presence of the owner, whose good mood is contagious.

SHOPPING

Les Abeilles du Périgord – *24210 La Bachellerie.* 𝄆05 53 51 00 91. *Open Jul–Aug, 10am–12pm and 2.30–7pm; Mar–Dec, daily except Tue, 10am.* Visit this honey farm to learn all you've ever wanted to know about keeping bees and collecting their golden nectar. On Thursdays and Saturdays in July and August, you can even help extract the honey yourself. Honey products on sale here.

LEISURE ACTIVITIES

Étang du Coucou – 𝄆05 53 51 96 14. Located at the foot of Hautefort Castle, this lake is ideal for carp fishing; the restaurant offers "fast food". In the summertime, concert evenings are held, while in the winter, theme nights take place.

BERGERAC AND PÉRIGORD POURPRE

The Périgord Pourpre, or Purple Périgord, around Bergerac, owes its name to the wine produced here. The region is at the southwestern corner of the Dordogne and shares a border with the Lot-et-Garonne *département* in the south and the Gironde *département* in the west. The appellations associated with the region are legendary: Bergerac, Montravel, Haut-Montravel, Pécharmant and Saussignac, not to mention the famous sweet wine of Monbazillac.

Highlights

A Bit of History

The Périgord Pourpre is divided into several areas, all of which share a mild climate favourable to the cultivation of crops commonly associated with more southerly parts of the country. Tobacco, maize (corn), sunflowers and cereals all flourish in the rich alluvial deposits in the Dordogne valley, which is particularly wide here. Timber production predominates to the west of Bergerac, in an area whose slopes are covered with the vineyards of Bergerac and Monbazillac. The town of Bergerac itself is an important centre for the tobacco and wine industries.

Many people associate Bergerac and the surrounding area with Hector Savinien de Cyrano de Bergerac (1619–55) the playwright and soldier with a rather large nose. You'll find an unusual, coloured statue to the great man in Bergerac. Cyrano has become Bergerac's adopted son, although there are no connections other than his name and no indications that he ever visited the place. The Périgord Pourpre, like the rest of the Dordogne and much of Aquitaine, was part of the Guyenne region, which was dominated by the English crown during the Medieval era. Bastides and castles are reminders of the battles fought here between the English and the French. A visit to Monpazier, for example, is a picturesque trip back in time.

The Abbey of Cadouin is another exquisite reminder of this great age; its lacy sculptures have been very well preserved. The obvious affluence of this former religious community offers a striking contrast to the peaceful countryside surrounding it, where agricultre dominates the local economy.

Various religious monuments in the region often show the marks of the Saintonge style. Saintonge was the centre for the French Huguenots and is located in the Charente-Maritime region. The hallmarks of the style are barrel vaults, semicircular arches and capitals sculpted into figures that tell a story.

The influence of the English, both past and present, is an integral part of the region's flavour.

Today, visitors from the United Kingdom can often seem to be as numerous as the French locals, and a great number have homes or businesses here. They might be drawn by some mysterious force harking back to the middle ages, though the more likely reason is that these rolling hills are reminiscent of an idealised English countryside, with rambling stone houses, vineyards, orchards of plum trees, pastures and woods. In the Périgord Pourpre there always seems to be a good place to enjoy a meal, a fine bottle of the local wine, and time to relax and reflect upon the important things in life.

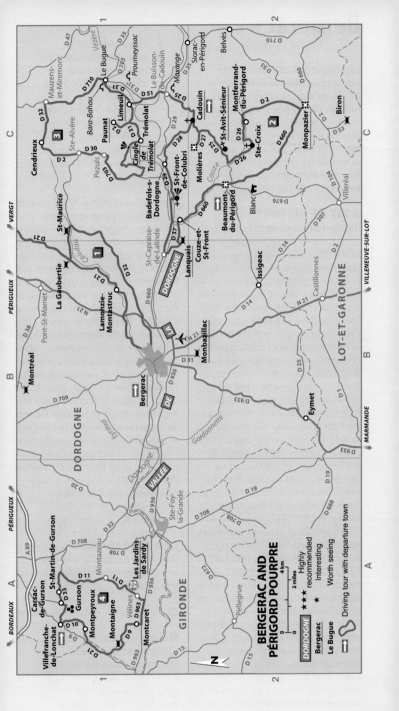

BERGERAC AND PÉRIGORD POURPRE

DORDOGNE

Bergerac

Le Bugue

Highly recommended ★★★
Interesting ★★
Worth seeing ★

Driving tour with departure town

N

0   2 miles
0   2   4km

PÉRIGUEUX

BORDEAUX

Montréal

Villefranche-de-Lonchat
Carsac-de-Gurson
St-Martin-de-Gurson
Gurson
Montpeyroux
Montaigne
Les Jardins de Sardy
Vélines
Montcaret
Montazeau

GIRONDE

Ste-Foy-la-Grande

Pont-St-Mamet
La Gaubertie
Lamonzie-Montastruc

St-Maurice

Cendrieux
Mauzens-et-Miremont
Ste-Alvère
Bara-Bahau
Paunat
Limeuil
Le Bugue
Proumeyssac
Le Buisson-de-Cadouin
Trémolat
Cingle de Trémolat
St-Front-de-Colubri
Badefols-s-Dordogne
St-Capraise-de-Lalinde
Couze-et-St-Front
Lanquais
Molières
St-Front
Couze
Beaumont-du-Périgord
Blanc

Cadouin
St-Avit-Sénieur
Ste-Croix
Montferrand-du-Périgord
Monpazier
Biron

Siorac-en-Périgord
Belvès

Villeréal

Issigeac
Castillonnès
Eymet

LOT-ET-GARONNE

Monbazillac

Gardonnette

Gironde

MARMANDE

VILLENEUVE-SUR-LOT

Pellegrue

DORDOGNE

VALLÉE DE LA DORDOGNE

139

Bergerac★
and the Vallée du Caudau

Spread out on both banks of the Dordogne where the river tends to be calmer and the valley widens to form an alluvial plain, this distinctly southern town is surrounded by prestigious vineyards and fields of tobacco, cereals and maize. A project to restore the old quarter has seen the embellishment of a number of Bergerac's 15C and 16C houses.

> ▶ **Population:** 28 691.
> ◉ **Michelin Map:** 329: D-6.
> ▯ **Info:** 97 rue Neuve-d'Argenson, 24100 Bergerac ℘05 53 57 03 11. www.ville-bergerac.com.
> ◉ **Location:** 49km/30.5mi S of Périgueux.
> ◈ **Don't Miss:** Old town; tobacco and wine museums.

A BIT OF HISTORY
Intellectual/commercial crossroads – The town's expansion began as early as the 12C. Taking advantage of the town's situation as a port and bridging point, local merchants turned a profit from trade between the Auvergne, the Limousin and Bordeaux on the coast. This flourishing city and capital of the Périgord became one of the bastions of Protestantism as its printing presses published pamphlets which were widely distributed. In August 1577 the Peace of Bergerac was signed between the king of Navarre and the representatives of King Henri III; this was a preliminary to the Edict of Nantes (1598). Despite this, in 1620, Louis XIII's army took over the town and destroyed the ramparts. After the Revocation of the Edict of Nantes (1685), the Jesuits and Recollects tried to win back their Protestant disciples. A certain number of Bergerac citizens, faithful to their Calvinist beliefs, emigrated to Holland, a country where they had maintained commercial contacts. Bergerac remained the capital of the Périgord until the Revolution, when the regional capital was transferred to Périgueux, which also became *préfecture* of the Dordogne *département*.

In the 19C, wine-growing and shipping prospered until the onslaught of phylloxera and arrival of the railway.

Bergerac today – Essentially an agricultural centre, this is the capital of tobacco in France. As a result, the Experimental Institute of Tobacco and the Tobacco Planters Centre of Advanced and Refresher Training are located here. In addition the 12 000ha/29 650 acres of vineyards surrounding the town produce wine with an *appellation d'origine contrôlée* (or controlled designation of origin) including: Bergerac, Côtes de Bergerac, Monbazillac, Montravel and Pécharmant. The Regional Wine Council, which establishes the *appellation* of the wines, is located in the Recollects' Cloisters (◉ *see Old Bergerac*). The main industrial enterprise of the town is a powder factory producing nitrocellulose for use in such industries as film-making, paint, varnish and plastics.

Famous citizens – Oddly enough, the Cyrano of Edmond Rostand's play was inspired by the 17C philosopher **Cyrano de Bergerac** whose name had nothing to do with the Périgord town. Not discouraged in the slightest, the townspeople took it upon themselves to adopt this wayward son and erect a statue in his honour in place de la Myrpe.

▰ WALK

OLD BERGERAC★★
Start in the **Ancien Port**. The *gabarres* of yesteryear moored here to drop off goods from the upper valley.

▷ Turn left at the end of quai Salvette.

Maison des Vins – Cloître des Récollets
The former Couvent des Récollets is reached via quai Salvette. ◔ ◷ *Open Jul–Aug daily 10am–7pm; May–Jun and Sept daily except Sun–Mon 10am–12.30pm, 2–7pm; rest of year daily except Sun–Mon*

Cloître des Récollets

© Christophe Boisvieux / agefotostock

10.30am–12.30pm, 2–6pm. 1st Sun of the month, 10am–1pm. ⃝*Closed Jan.* ⃝*No charge.* ⃝*05 53 63 57 55. www.vins-bergerac.fr.*

Go through the corridor into the vaulted wine cellar where the meetings of the Bergerac wine society, Conférence des Consuls de la Vinée, are held. You may watch an audio-visual presentation on the Bergerac vineyards.

The brick-and-stone cloister building was built on 12C foundations. The interior courtyard has a 16C Renaissance gallery beside an 18C gallery that houses wine exhibitions.

There is a fine view of the Monbazillac vineyards from the sumptuously decorated great hall on the first floor.

The wine-testing laboratory includes the wine-tasting room (*open to visitors*), where all the Bergerac wines are tasted annually to determine whether they are worthy of the *appellation d'origine contrôlée* – AOC – mark on the label.

The AOC system is a method of ensuring the quality of wine and here you can learn how it works. The vineyards on the banks of the Dordogne cover 12 000 ha/29653 acres, producing wine for the 13 local appellations like Bergerac and Montravel.

◗ Take a left at the end of quai Salvette.

Rue du Château

An unusual balustraded balcony overhangs a sharp bend in the street.

◗ Cross rue de l'Ancien Port; turn left.

Rue St-Clar

The walls of the corbelled half-timbered houses lining this charming street are a mixture of cob and small bricks.

◗ Turn left into rue des Rois-de-France and right into rue de l'Ancien Port.

Maison Peyrarède★

Also known as the French Kings' House, this elegant building dating from 1603 is ornamented with a corbelled turret. It houses the town's tobacco museum.

Musée du Tabac★★

Maison Peyrade, Place du Feu.
&⃝*Open Jun–Sept daily 10am–1pm, 2–6pm; Oct–May Tue–Sat 10am–noon, 2–6pm (Apr–May also Sun 2.30–6.30pm).* ⃝*Closed public holidays.* ⃝*€4.* ⃝*05 53 63 04 13. www.bergerac-tourisme.com.*

This remarkable and beautifully presented collection, which includes satirical engravings, traces the history and evolution of tobacco through the centuries. On the **second floor** works

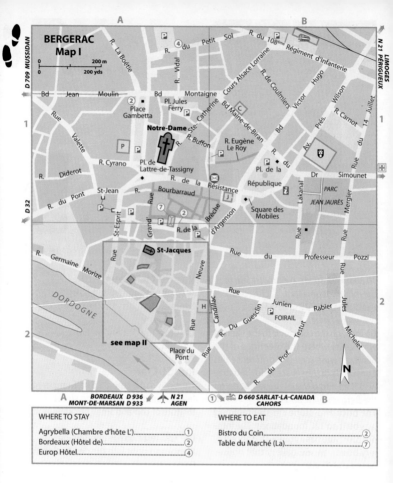

BERGERAC Map I

WHERE TO STAY		WHERE TO EAT	
Agrybella (Chambre d'hôte L')...	①	Bistro du Coin...	②
Bordeaux (Hôtel de)...	②	Table du Marché (La)...	⑦
Europ Hôtel...	④		

BERGERAC Map II

WHERE TO EAT

Côté Noix...	③
Imparfait (L')...	①

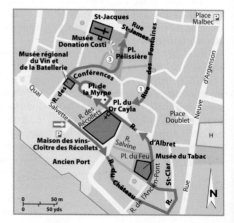

The Tobacco Industry

Until the 15C, tobacco was used only by the Native Americans, who believed it possessed medicinal properties. After the discovery of the New World, tobacco was introduced to Europe. Jean Nicot brought it into France c 1560; he sent snuff to Catherine de' Medici to cure her migraines.

The use of tobacco was controversial from the very start: Pope Urbain VIII ordered the excommunication of nicotine fiends and Louis XIII forbade its sale (before hitting on the idea of taxing it). In those days, tobacco was sold as a carrot-shaped lump which was grated into powder. The familiar diamond-shaped orange sign, Tabac, which hangs outside shops licensed to sell tobacco products, is still called a *carotte* today. At the end of the 18C snuff was sold directly as a powder. The next step in the art of smoking was the pipe. The pipe had been in use in Holland since the early 17C, but its use was considered vulgar and common. Officers of the First Empire started the fashion and were quickly followed by the Romantics, including George Sand. Finally in the mid-19C, the cigarette arrived on the scene, with accessories including elegant ivory cigarette holders.

Drying tabaco

© S. Sauvignier /Michelin

of art depicting tobacco and smokers are displayed. *Two Smokers* from the 17C Northern French School, *Three Smokers* by Meissonier and the charming *Interior of a Smoke Den* by Teniers the Younger, are among the works exhibited.

A section is devoted to the cultivation of tobacco (planting, harvesting, drying etc) with special reference to the Bergerac region.

Another room is set aside to display the techniques used to manufacture smoking accessories both in the past and throughout the world.

Rue d'Albret

At the end of this street to the right is the town hall, the former convent of the Sisters of Faith. On the left, on the corner of place du Feu, is a vast building with pointed arched doorways.

▷ Walk to place du Docteur-Cayla.

Place du Docteur-Cayla, Place de la Myrpe

The 13C chapel adjacent to the former Couvent des Récollets became a **Protestant temple** in the 18C. The charming shaded place de la Myrpe is lined with half-timbered houses. In the middle of the square stands the statue of Cyrano de Bergerac swathed in his cape.

▷ Follow the narrow street leading off the square and turn right.

Rue des Conférences

This street's name recalls the conferences held before the Peace of Bergerac. It is bordered by half-timbered houses.

Musée Régional du Vin et de la Batellerie▲

5 rue des Conférences. ◯*Open Tue–Fri 10am–noon, 2–6pm, Sat 10am–noon, 2–5pm, Sun 2.30–6.30pm.* ◯*Closed public hols, and from Oct to Apr Sat pm and Sun.* ⊕€3. ℘05 53 57 80 92. This museum is located at the end of place de la Myrpe. On the first floor, discover a display on the importance of barrel-making to the local economy. The section on wine shows the evolution of the Bergerac vineyards over the centuries and the type of houses the wine-growers lived in. On the second floor there are models of the various kinds of river boats called *gabarres*, flat-bottomed boats which sometimes have sails.

Place Pélissière

This large square was opened up after the demolition of some run-down houses. Built on several levels around a fountain, it is overlooked by **Église St-Jacques**, once a centre for pilgrims on their way to Santiago de Compostela; it now houses contemporary works of art. Underneath the **Église St-Jacques** in the Place de la Petite Mission is the **Musée Costi** (⏰*open daily Jul–Aug 2–7pm (Sun 2.30–6.30pm); ﹩€3, no charge for children under 18; ☎05 53 63 04 13)*, which contains the bronze and plaster sculptures of Constantin Papachristopoulos, also known as "Costi". From the north end of the square, you can divert from the route marked on the map and follow Grand'Rue some distance north then cross boulevard de la Résistance to reach place de Lattre-de-Tassigny and **Notre Dame**. Built in the Gothic style, this 19C church has a slender belltower. In the west chapel is an immense **Aubusson tapestry** portraying the Bergerac coat of arms.

▷ Return to St Jacques and the marked route.

Rue St-Jâmes

There are 15C, 16C and 17C half-timbered houses with mullioned windows all along this street.

▷ Turn right.

Rue des Fontaines

The Vieille Auberge at the corner of rue Gaudra has well-preserved moulded arcades, 14C capitals and pointed arched windows.

🚗 DRIVING TOUR

1 VALLÉE DU CAUDAU

60km/37mi. Allow half a day.
♿*See route 1 on region map page 139.*
Head NE out of Bergerac along the N 21 to Les Pélissous then turn right onto the D 21 E1.

Lamonzie-Montastruc

The handsome Classical building perched on a rock to the left of the road is Château de Montastruc.

▷ Continue along the D 21.

Château de la Gaubertie

Built in the 15C, this castle was completely restored in the early 20C. The large main building, its façade overlooking the Caudau valley, is flanked by a square tower on one side and a round corbelled tower on the other side. The 17C chapel is nearby.

▷ Return along the D 21.

Vergt

This large agricultural town has become one of the main strawberry centres. The sandy soil of the region is perfect for the cultivation of this fruit. *(Markets on Fri mornings.)*

▷ Rejoin the D 8 and drive towards Bergerac taking the second road on the left 1.5km/0.9mi farther on.

Lac de Neufont

This is a pleasant recreational lake with swimming beaches and pedal-boat rental. Go through **St-Amand-de-Vergt**, which has a pretty Romanesque church surmounted by a dome.

▷ Continue S.

Château de St-Maurice

The castle is partly hidden by the trees in its grounds, but its 14C and 15C buildings, pierced with Renaissance windows and crowned with machicolations, are nonetheless an attractive sight.

ADDRESSES

🛌 STAY

🛏🛏 **Europ Hôtel** – 20 r. du Petit-Sol 📞05 53 57 06 54. www.europ-hotel-bergerac.com. 22 rooms. Close to the train station, this hotel has a countryside atmosphere, especially under the trees around the pool. Rooms are ordinary but well kept.

🛏🛏🛏 **Chambre d'hôte l'Agrybella** – Pl. de l'Eglise, 24560 St Aubin de Lanquais (11km/7mi SE of Bergerac). 5 rooms. 📞05 53 58 10 76. A lovely 18C mansion, completely renovated with cosy, charming bedrooms and all mod cons. The lounge includes an open fireplace for chilly evenings. The peaceful park-gardens include a pool.

🛏🛏🛏 **Hôtel de Bordeaux** – 38 pl. Gambetta. 📞05 53 57 12 83. www.hotel-bordeaux-bergerac.com. Closed mid-Dec–early Jan. 40 rooms. 🏊 One of the oldest establishments in Bergerac. Behind its pretty Art Deco façade is a pleasant, verdant courtyard with swimming pool. The rooms are simple and colourfully decorated.

🍽 EAT

🍽 **Bistrot du Coin** – 6 r. Colonel de Chadois. 📞05 53 57 77 56. www.lebistroducoin.fr. Closed Tue and Wed. You'll recognise this restaurant by its 1950s-style corner façade. Here you'll find a low-priced fixed menu with a choice of two or three main courses. The dining room is lovely with its red walls and mosaic floor, or dine on the terrace overlooking pl. Malbec.

🍽 **Côté Noix** – Pl. Pélissière. 📞05 53 57 71 38. www.cotenoix.fr. Closed in the evening, Sun–Mon and Nov–Feb. Reservation recommended. Ideally situated on pl. Pélissière, this restaurant is located in the former Ribière mill, one of seven in the city. Examples of the daily specials are sample platters, *tourtes* and sweet and savoury tarts. Handmade ice cream and Mariage Frères teas. Sales of regional products.

🍽🍽 **La Table du Marché** – 21 pl. de la Bardonnie (pl. du Marché Couvert). 📞05 53 22 49 46. www.table-du-marche.com. Closed Wed dinner, Sun. Enjoy local and creative cuisine with fresh produce straight from the nearby covered market in this bright and modern but traditional little restaurant.

🍽🍽 **L'Imparfait** – 8 rue des Fontaines. 📞05 53 57 47 92. www.imparfait.com. Closed 20 Dec–20 Jan, Sun and Mon. Set in a medieval building in the heart of the old town, this quirkily-named restaurant serves local specialities and has an open fire for grilling meats.

CAFES

La Désirade – Rue des Conférences. 📞05 53 58 27 50. Open Jun–Sep, daily, 10am–midnight; May, 9am–7pm; Closed Oct–Apr. With a terrace in front of a fountain, this café is a cool and refreshing place to take a break. Old-fashioned ice cream and alcohol-free cocktails.

Victoria – 27 r. Bourbarraud. 📞05 53 58 48 36. Closed Sun and Mon. This charming tearoom offers an indulgent "five o'clock tea". The decoration is dominantly red and includes old paintings and Scottish tartan. On the menu, you'll find tarts and salads, homemade pastries and a choice of more than 100 teas.

SHOPPING

Markets – Market Tue morning on Gambetta square, organic market across from the town hall; Fri morning, small market in the Madeleine sector.

L'Art et le Vin – 17 Grand'Rue . 📞05 53 57 07 42. Closed Sun and Mon. The burgundy walls of this shop, located next to Les Halles, is a sign that here you are crossing into the world of wine. The selected vintages, arranged in their wooden cases, mainly come from small vineyards in the region and are featured year after year: Pécharmant, Bergerac and Monbazillac, to name a few.

La Maison des vins de Bergerac – 2 pl. Cayla, quai Salvette. 📞05 53 63 57 55. www.vins-bergerac.fr. Closed Jan, Sun and Mon. In the exceptional setting of this house built on to the Cloître des Récollets between the 12C and 17C, you'll discover a wine laboratory where each year wines are tested before receiving their AOC, as well as a shop offering the best wines in the region.

Château de Lanquais★

Nicknamed the "unfinished Louvre of the Périgord", Lanquais never rivalled the royal palace in terms of power or glory, and few people would spontaneously identify it with the Louvre. However, the same architect designed the façade of Lanquais and the Louvre's grand courtyard. There is also a parallel between the Louvre and intrigues that have taken place in these rooms and corridors.

VISIT

ⓘ *Open Jul–Aug daily 10am–7pm; Apr–Jun and Sept Wed–Mon 2.30–6.30pm.* €8 *(children 6–16 years old €6).* 𝄞*05 53 61 24 24. www.chateaude lanquais.fr.*

As you near this castle you will notice cannonball marks on the walls dating from a skirmish in 1577. Defensive elements of the fortress remain on the 14C and 15C building to the right; a Renaissance building was added on the left during the Wars of Religion. Here, bays, mouldings and window pediments decorate the **façades★** of the courtyard. The corner pavilion, based on the courtyard of the Louvre, was designed by Pierre Lescot.

The Spy and the Child

Isabeau de Limeuil, who was born at the Château de Lanquais, was one of the seductress-spies of Catherine de Médici. These infiltrators would collect information in the form of pillow talk… But beware the unfortunate spy who fell heavy with child in the course of duty! This was Isabeau's fate when she "spied" on the Duke of Condé, and the end of her "career" at the royal court.

- ⓘ **Michelin Map:** 329: E-7.
- 🛈 **Info:** 𝄞05 53 61 24 24. www.bergerac-tourisme.com.
- ◐ **Location:** The castle is located 23km/14mi E of Bergerac, 14km/8.6mi N of Beaumont-du-Périgord and 23km/14mi west of Cadouin.
- ◷ **Timing:** Allow 1hr.
- ◉ **Don't Miss:** The superb Renaissance façade.

Inside the furnished palace, you may visit the bedchambers of Madame and Monsieur; a dining room designed in the 19C featuring a ceiling painted with lily emblems and Brittany ermines; a games and music room decorated in the 18C fashion; and a blue sitting room featuring a remarkable **portico fireplace★**. You'll then venture downstairs to the recreated Renaissance kitchen featuring cobblestone flooring.

ADDRESSES

🛏 STAY

🍽 **Auberge des Marronniers** – *Le Bourg - 24150 Lanquais (13km NW of Beaumont on the D 660 and D 37).* 𝄞*05 53 24 93 78.* Pleasant traditional auberge offering an excellent range of dishes, including great classics from the Périgord region.

🍽🍽 **Chambre d'hôte Le Relais de La Vergne** – *La Vergne, Bayac (10km/6.2mi S of Lanquais on rte de Beaumont).* 𝄞*05 53 57 83 16.* 🛏 *5 rooms.* This lovely manor house artfully conjugates old-style charm and modern comfort. The pleasant upstairs rooms and ground floor suite are furnished with antiques.

🍽🍽 **Hôtel Côté-Rivage** – *Le Bourg - 24150 Badefols-sur-Dordogne (14km N of Beaumont).* 𝄞*05 53 23 65 00. www.cote rivage.com. 7 rooms.* The comfortable and tastefully decorated rooms are air-conditioned, and equipped with flat screen television, WiFi, hair dryers and direct access telephones.

Beaumont-du-Périgord

Beaumont was built as a bastide in 1272 by the Seneschal of Guyenne in the name of Edward I, king of England. Today, a few traces of its fortifications remain, such as the 13C fortified Porte de Luzier, a gateway that provides access to the town.

BASTIDE
Église St-Front
Built after 1272 in the Early Gothic style with four huge towers connected by a rampart walk, this church was the last place of refuge for the inhabitants of the town during periods of siege. The asymmetry of the towers on the main façade reflects their distinct functions: the lower was a belltower until 1789, and the higher a crenellated keep armed with machicolations. The towers frame a doorway with five archivolts, supported by clustered columns, and a **gallery★** with a beautifully decorated balustrade underneath which there is an illuminated frieze. The elegant south porch has a trefoil arcade dominated by a lancet dais. It is protected by a brattice. Major restoration work during the 19C has significantly altered the church's originally military character. Inside the church in the belltower to the left, you can see the enormous keystone (weighing 450kg) of the chancel vault. It is decorated with carved faces, including that of the church's patron, St Front. In the same side aisle towards the middle of the nave, note the chapel of St Joseph, almost certainly the remainder of a much older church.

EXCURSION
Dolmen de Blanc
3km/1.9mi S along the D 676.
According to a strange legend, a young girl lost during a storm stopped near the megaliths and prayed to be rescued. She then saw the stones move to show her the way.

▶ **Population:** 1 145.
⚲ **Michelin Map:** 329: F-7.
▤ **Info:** Office de Tourisme du Pays Beaumontais, 16 pl. Centrale, 24440 Beaumont du Périgord. ℘05 53 22 39 12. www.pays-des-bastides.com.
⊚ **Don't Miss:** The opportunity to explore this typical fortified bastide.
⊙ **Timing:** Allow a full day to visit the bastides and water mills of the area to the south of the River Dordogne.

🚗 DRIVING TOUR

② BASTIDES AND MILLS★
110km/69mi round-trip. Allow 1 day.
⚲*See route 2 on region map page 139.*

▷ Leave Beaumont travelling N along the D 660.

Château de Bannes
Perched on a rocky spur, the château was built at the end of the 15C by the bishop of Sarlat, Armand de Gontaud-Biron. What is so incongruous in this château is that the military features – machicolated towers – are tempered by the carved doorway and richly decorated dormer windows surmounted by finials and pinnacles in the Early Renaissance style.

▷ Continue along the D 660.

Couze-et-St-Front
Located at the mouth of the Couze valley, this active small town has specialised since the 16C in the manufacture of Dutch paper, which was sold as far away as Russia. It was once the most important paper-making centre in the Aquitaine, and, at its peak, 13 mills were in operation here.

Château de Lanquais

© Colin Weston / age fotostock

Out of the three remaining mills, only two, the **Moulin de la Rouzique (Eco-musée du Papier)** (🕐 🎧 *guided tour (1hr): open Jul–Aug, daily 10am–7pm; Apr–Jun and Sept–Oct, daily except Sat, 2–6pm:* 🎫 €7.50 *(children, 6–18, €5).* 🖉 *05 53 24 36 16. www.moulin-rouzique.com*) and the **Moulin de Larroque** (*workshop and craft gallery open Mon–Fri and public holidays, 9am–noon and 2–5.30pm:* 🎫 €5. 🖉 *05 53 61 01 75; www.moulindelaroque.com*) are still making filigreed paper using traditional methods.

▶ Drive W out of Couze along the D 37.

Bastides

These fortified towns (*bastidas* in Occitan) first appeared in the 13C. They were usually built to the same plan (a square or rectangle) according to a grid sytem with streets built around a main square, often arcaded, and with a covered market hall at its centre. Depending on their location, bastides were often surrounded by walls to offer increased protection.

Château de Lanquais★
🕐 *See CHÂTEAU DE LANQUAIS.*

▶ Continue along the D 37 and cross the Dordogne 1.5km/0.9mi farther on. Turn right onto the D 660 in St-Capraise-de-Lalinde.

Lalinde
Despite the fire in 1914 that largely destroyed the medieval village, the gridded plan of this 13C English bastide is still visible. You can still see the two gateways and ruins of the Roman fortifications, the Governor's mansion, the dungeon of the castle and a large number of half-timbered facades. The covered market on the centre square replaces the *halles*, which were demolished at the turn of the last century.

🎧 Tuilières Discovery Trail
Follow the banks of the river (*voie verte*) to discover various points of interest, including the Tuilières water steps, made up of six locks on either side of a reservoir; and a fish ladder permitting migrating species to pass the barrage by way of a counter-flow system through a 20m tunnel equipped with observation windows.

▶ Cross the Dordogne once again on the D 29.

St-Front-de-Colubri
Built in the 12C on top of a cliff overlooking the Dordogne, the chapel sheltered sailors venturing along the Saut de la Gratusse rapids. This passage was the most difficult of the river's middle section; specialised river-hands were needed to guide sailors through it until the mid-19C, when the Canal de Lalinde was built.
There is a marvellous **view**★ of the valley and the rapids up-river.

▶ The D 29 follows the river.

Badefols-sur-Dordogne
The village occupies a pleasant site beside the Dordogne. The country church stands close to the foot of the

castle ruins perched on the cliff. This fortress served as the hideout for local thieves and robbers who used to ransack *gabarres* as they sailed downstream.

▶ Continue along the D 29, then turn onto the D 28 4km/2.5mi farther on.

Cadouin★
See CADOUIN.

▶ Drive SE out of Cadouin along D 25. After 2km/1.2mi, turn right onto D 27.

Molières
This unfinished English bastide, founded in 1284, has a Gothic church with a façade flanked by a tall two-storey square defensive tower and the ruins of an old castle to the north.

▶ Turn back and rejoin the D 25 on the right.

St-Avit-Sénieur★
This small village is dominated by its massive **church** and monastic buildings, vestiges of a former Benedictine abbey constructed in the 11C in honour of Avitus Senior, a soldier in the service of the Visigoth king Alaric II who later became a hermit. The fortifications of the church date from the 14C. South of the church, excavations have unearthed the remains of an Augustinian settlement destroyed during the Wars of Religion, showing the bases of a primitive Romanesque church and monastic buildings.

▶ Continue along the D 25 and turn left onto the D 26, 2km/1.2mi farther on.

Ste-Croix
This village has a charming Romanesque church surrounded by the half-ruined buildings of what used to be a priory. This 12C church has a clear, uncluttered outline. The nave is covered in round tiles, in contrast to the apse and side chapel, which are covered in *lauzes* – the small limestone slabs typical of the region. A gabled belfry adorns the top of the façade.

▶ Leave Ste-Croix to the E and turn right onto the D 26.

Montferrand-du-Périgord
The main feature of this pretty terraced village above the Couze is the half-ruined château with its 12C keep.
The old houses, dovecotes and 16C covered market with its beautiful columns all add to Montferrand's charm.
🚶 In the cemetery above the village, the Romanesque chapel (accessible along a marked path starting from the foot of the castle) is decorated with a lovely collection of mural frescoes dating from between the 12C and the 15C.

▶ Return to the D 26, then turn right onto the D 2.

Monpazier★
See MONPAZIER.

▶ Drive W from Monpazier on D 660 back to Beaumont-du-Périgord.

ADDRESSES

🛏 STAY

🛏 **Camping La Grande Veyière** – *SE 2.2km/1mi on D 27, rte de Cadouin, and secondary road to the right, Molières.* ✆05 53 63 25 84. www.lagrandeveyiere.com. *Reservations recommended. 60 pitches.* Get plenty of fresh air in this hill-top campsite, laid out around a well-restored Périgord-style farm. The buildings house the food shop and bar, among other services. Large shady pitches. Swimming pool and playground.

🍴 EAT

🍴🍴 **Hostellerie de Saint-Front** – *3 r. Romieu.* ✆05 53 22 30 11. www.hostellerie-de-saint-front.com. ♿🅿. *10 rooms.* Despite the slightly decrepit appearance of the dining room, this is a worthwhile restaurant, located in the town centre. The country platters are large enough to make for a full meal. A traditional menu with a local touch and efficient service.

Monpazier★

Monpazier was one of the **bastides** built to command the roads going from the Agenais region to the banks of the Dordogne.

Its picturesque square surrounded by arcades, **carreyrous** (alleyways), old houses, churches and ruined fortifications make it the best preserved of all the Périgord bastides.

▶ **Population:** 533.

🕐 **Michelin Map:** 329: G-7.

▤ **Info:** Pl. des Cornières. ✆05 53 22 68 59. www.pays-des-bastides.com.

◖ **Location:** 46km/29mi NE of Villeneuve-sur-Lot and 50km/31mi SW of Sarlat-la-Canéda.

☺ **Don't Miss:** Pl. des Cornières.

A BIT OF HISTORY

A difficult start – The bastide of Monpazier was founded in 1284 by Edward I, king of England and duke of Aquitaine. This bastide was designed to complete the process of defence and colonisation of the Périgord begun in 1267 with the founding of Lalinde, Beaumont, Molières and Roquépine. To this end Edward I allied himself with Pierre de Gontaut, lord of Biron. But difficulties soon arose: delays in the building work; disagreements between the lord of Biron and the people of Monpazier; and renewed hostilities between the king of England and Philip the Fair.

Monpazier receives royalty – The Reformation, in which the marshal of Biron played a prominent part, marked the beginning of a violent era. In 1574, the town was betrayed and fell into the hands of the Huguenot leader, Geoffroi de Vivans, who later captured the bastide of Domme.

Buffarot the Croquant – After the Wars of Religion were over, the peasants rose again in revolt. The rebels, known as *croquants*, held a great gathering at Monpazier in 1594. The revolt flared up again in 1637. Led by a man named Buffarot, a local weaver from Capdrot, 8 000 peasants plundered castles across the countryside.

The soldiers of the duke of Épernon pursued them and, after some difficulty, captured Buffarot. He was brought back to Monpazier, tortured and broken on the wheel in the main square.

🐾 WALKING TOUR

TOWN

The town is based on a grid (400x220m) of which the main axis runs north to south. Parallel streets are laid out and four transverse roads run east to west, dividing the town into rectangular blocks. Originally all the houses had the unique characteristic of being of equal size and separated from each other by narrow spaces, *androns*, to prevent the spread of fire. Enjoy a sweeping view of the Dropt valley from the Jardin des Franciscains to the SE of the bastide.

Bastide

🕐🐾*Guided tours, Jul–Sept 10am–7.30pm; mid-Mar–Jun and Oct–mid-Nov 10am–noon, 2–6pm.* ✆€5. *Contact the tourist office.*

The general layout of the bastide is still clear, as are three of its original six fortified gateways. Several houses still retain their original appearance.

Place des Cornières★

The main square's rectangular shape echoes the bastide itself. On the south side stands a covered market housing antique weights and measures. All around, you'll see arcades, or covered galleries supported on arches; some of them are pointed and have angle irons (*cornières*). The houses overlooking the square date from the Middle Ages to the 17C.

Monpazier

© JD Dallet / age fotostock

◗ Leave the square via a cut-off corner in a wall to the left.

Église St-Dominique

The church was built in the 13C and remodelled several times: the doorway dates from the 14C. The rose window and gable were all rebuilt in the 16C. The wide nave has pointed vaulting and extends into a polygonal east end.

◗ Turn right as you come out of the church.

Chapter House

This 13C house stands near the church. It was used as a tithe barn. Paired windows light the upper floor.

Atelier des Bastides

Behind the church. ○*Open Mar–Sept, Mon–Sat 11am–1pm and 3–7pm, Sun 3–7pm.* ⊜*No charge.* ℘*05 53 22 60 38.* This centre, devoted to bastides, offers extensive information in the form of photos, models and archaeological evidence. Temporary exhibitions are organised in the summer.

ADDRESSES

🏠 STAY

⊜ **Camping Le Moulin de David** – *3km/1.8mi SW of Monpazier on the D 2.* ℘*05 53 22 65 25. www.moulindedavid.com.*

Open mid-May–early Sep. Reservation recommended. 160 pitches. Restaurant. This popular campsite is set around an old mill in a pretty valley. Friendly, quiet, comfortable, well maintained, good sports facilities and a wide range of services.

⊜⊜⊜ **Edward 1er** – *5 rue St-Pierre.* ℘*05 53 22 44 00. www.hoteledward1er.com. Closed mid-Nov–mid-Mar. 12 rooms.* The building's towers give this manor house the appearance of a small castle. Cosy, English-style interior, quiet rooms, plus a swimming pool and small garden.

🍽 EAT

⊜⊜ **Privilège du Périgord** – *58 rue Notre-Dame.* ℘*05 53 22 43 98. www. privilegeperigord.com. Closed Dec–Feb and Tue. Reservation recommended.* This 18C coaching inn covered in Virginia creeper has an attractive rustic-style dining room. In warm weather dine in the courtyard. Traditional dishes from the southwest.

SHOPPING

Markets and fairs – Traditional market on Thursday morning in place des Cornières. Wild mushroom market in October (depending on harvest) under the *halle* from 3pm.

Verrerie d'Art de Monpazier (M. Pascal Guernic) – *13 r. St-André.* ℘*05 53 74 30 82. www.artisans-d-art.com/guernic. Opening times vary. Closed 25 Dec, Jan and Mar.* This glass-blower displays an interesting collection of original works in his workshop.

Château de Biron ★

From its strategic position atop a rock, the massive bulk of the towers and walls of the Château de Biron commands this area on the borders of the Périgord and Agenais regions. The Dordogne *département* bought the castle in 1978 and initiated a restoration programme; an art centre was also established here, organising annual summer exhibitions.

⚪ **Michelin Map:** 329: G-8.
🔲 **Info:** 📞 05 53 05 65 65. www.semitour.com.
◗ **Location:** 57km/35.5m SE of Bergerac.

A BIT OF HISTORY

From the Capitol to the Tarpeian Rock – Among the many celebrated men of the Biron family, **Charles de Gontaut** met with a particularly memorable fate. A friend of Henri IV, he was appointed first Admiral and then Marshal of France. In 1598 the Barony of Biron was created for him and he eventually became Governor of Burgundy. Even these honours did not satisfy him and, in league with the Duke of Savoy, he plotted against France. Once his treason was exposed, Biron was pardoned, but he was soon involved in further intrigue. Exposed a second time, the king agreed to pardon him if he confessed. He refused and was beheaded at the Bastille on 31 July 1602. **From medieval fortress to the present building** – This castle is made up of buildings of very different styles. An 11C medieval fortress was razed by Simon de Montfort. Rebuilt in the 13C, it changed hands constantly during the Hundred Years War. In the late 15C and 16C, Pons de Gontaut-Biron decided to transform his castle into a Renaissance château. He altered the buildings east of the main courtyard and had the Renaissance chapel and colonnaded arcade built. Work was interrupted, however, and not resumed until the 18C.

CHÂTEAU

Basse cour (outer courtyard)
Surrounding the castle's living quarters on three sides, the outer courtyard includes the caretaker's lodge, chapel, receiving house and bakery. The guards' tower, now the **conciergerie**, is an elegant building in which crenellations, a watch-path and Renaissance decoration are juxtaposed. The **chapel** was built in the Renaissance style in the 16C. A pierced balustrade runs round the base of the roof.

The lower chamber once served as a parish church for the village. The upper chamber, or seigneurial chapel, features remarkable pointed vaulting. It shelters **two tombs with recumbent figures**: Armand de Gontaut-Biron, bishop of Sarlat, and his brother Pons (d 1524).

Cour d'honneur (main courtyard)
A staircase and pointed vaulted corridor give access to this courtyard. On the right, the 16C seigneurial living quarters, with Renaissance windows, lead to the large 13C polygonal keep redesigned in the 15C. On the left, the 16C–18C main building has an elegant remodelled staircase which ascends to the Great Hall of State. In the basement, the kitchen, the former garrison's refectory, is a vast room (22mx9m) with barrel vaulting.

A portico leads to the castle terraces; from there, the **view★** extends over the rolling countryside and the Birons' other fief, the bastide of Monpazier.

ADDRESSES

🏠 STAY

🛏 **Camping Le Moulinal** – 24540 Biron, 4km/2.5mi S of Biron on the Lacapelle-Biron road. 📞 05 53 40 84 60. www.lemoulinal.com. Open 1 Apr–16 Sept. Restaurant on site. Includes a lake, pool, playground and organised activities for children. Canvas bungalows and mobile homes available.

Cadouin★

The Abbey of Cadouin, founded in a narrow valley near the Forêt de Bessède in 1115 by Géraut de Sales, was occupied soon after by the Cistercians. It was extremely prosperous during the Middle Ages, particularly as a place of pilgrimage. A small village with a covered market grew around the church and cloisters, which were restored after the Revolution.

▶ **Population:** 336.
Michelin Map: 329: G-7.
Info: Pl. André-Boissière - 24480 Le Buisson-de-Cadouin. ℘05 53 22 06 09 - www.pays-des-bastides.com.
Location: 41km/25.5mi. W of Sarlat.
Don't Miss: The abbey church and cloisters.

A BIT OF HISTORY

The Holy Shroud of Cadouin – The first written mention of the Holy Shroud appeared in 1214 in an act decreed by Simon de Montfort. This linen cloth adorned with bands of embroidery had been brought from Antioch by a priest from the Périgord and was believed to be the cloth that had been wrapped around Christ's head.

The shroud became an object of deep veneration and attracted large pilgrimages, bringing great renown to Cadouin. It is said that Richard the Lionheart, St Louis and Charles V came to kneel before it in reverence. Charles VII had it brought to Paris and Louis XI to Poitiers.

Tradition versus science – In 1934, two experts attributed the Holy Shroud of Cadouin to the 11C, as the embroidered bands bore Kufic inscriptions citing an emir and a caliph who had ruled in Egypt in 1094 and 1101. The bishop of Périgueux therefore had the pilgrimage to Cadouin discontinued.

ABBEY

The **church★** building, completed in 1154, presents a massive, powerful west front divided horizontally into three sections. The middle section, opened by three round-arched windows which light the church's interior, divides upper and lower arcaded sections.

This austere architectural plan, where decoration is basically limited to the play of light, emphasises the ornamental effect brought about by the gold colour of the Molières stone. The finely proportioned building broke away from Cistercian architecture with its interior plan: a chancel with an apse between two apsidal chapels, a dome at the transept crossing capped by a pyramidal bell-tower roofed with chestnut shingles, and a more elaborate interior decoration (windows surrounded by mouldings and carved capitals). Nonetheless, the harmonious proportions and the grandeur of the construction emanate a spirituality entirely in keeping with Cistercian sanctuaries.

Thanks to the generosity of Louis XI, the **cloisters★★** (*open daily Jul–Aug 10am–7pm; mid-Apr–May and Sept–Oct 10am–1pm, 2–6pm. closed Jan and 25 Dec; €6. ℘05 53 63 36 28*) were built at the end of the 15C in the Flamboyant Gothic style. In fact, the work continued to the middle of the 16C, as the Renaissance capitals of some of the columns show. Despite the damage suffered during the Wars of Religion and the Revolution, the cloisters were saved and restored in the 19C, owing to the enthusiastic attention they were given by historians and archaeologists. Fine doors, ornate carvings and a large fresco of the Annunciation make this a spectacular visit. Four small columns cast in the form of towers are decorated with themes from the Old and New Testaments (the stories of Samson and Delilah, Job and others).

The chapter house and two other rooms have been set up as a **Musée du Suaire** (Shroud Museum), where the restored relic is on display, forming the centrepiece of an exhibition.

🚗 DRIVING TOUR

③ CADOUIN TO CENDRIEUX
68km/42mi round-trip. Allow 1 day.
🕐 See route 3 on region map page 139.

▶ Leave Cadouin travelling NE along the D 25 to Buisson-de-Cadouin, then turn N on the D 51.

Limeuil★
This old village is located on a picturesque **site★** overlooking the confluence of the Dordogne and Vézère rivers, which is marked by two bridges unusually set at right angles. You'll notice the traces of its past as a fortress as you climb up the ancient narrow streets.
The strategic position of Limeuil established its role as arsenal and watchtower quite early on. At one point the militant peasants known as Croquants gained control of the town during an uprising. Limeuil was also for many centuries a port and safe haven for heavy barges. Today it is known as a **village of traditional craftsmen** where you can see glass blowers, potters, weavers, painters and other artists at work.
From the **Jardins panoramiques** there is a fine view of the confluence of the Dordogne and Vézère (🕐open Jul–Aug, 10am–8pm; Apr–Jun and Sept daily except Sat 10am–12.30pm, 2–6pm. ⊕€7. ℘05 53 57 52 64. www.jardins-panoramiqueslimeuil.com).

▶ 2km/1.2mi, then right onto the D 2.

Paunat
This modest village has retained an imposing church, once part of a monastery under the control of the powerful abbey of St-Martial in Limoges. The austere-looking **Église St-Martial** was built in the 12C and remodelled in the 15C. The fortified belfry-porch, featuring two domed storeys, is an unusual example of Romanesque architecture in the Périgord.

▶ Turn back and take the D 31 on the right.

Trémolat
Built on a meander in the Dordogne, this charming village was made famous by the shooting of Claude Chabrol's film *The Butcher*. It has a 12C Romanesque church, a condensed version of all the religious architectural features of the Périgord region: heavy fortifications are combined with a vaulting system supporting a row of three domes and a huge defensive chamber covering the whole of the interior.

▶ Continue NW and follow the river.

Cingle de Trémolat★★
(Trémolat meander)
At the foot of a semicircle of high, bare, white cliffs highlighted by clumps of greenery, the river coils in a large loop, spanned by bridges of golden stone and reflecting lines of poplars. On the convex bank beyond this stretch of water, which is often used for water sports and rowing regattas (Trémolat Water Sports Centre), lies a vast mosaic of arable fields and meadows.

▶ Continue along the road, which offers beautiful views of the valley. Before reaching Mauzac, take a small road to the right; this will lead to D 703. At Pezuls, take D 30 towards Ste-Alvère, then head for Cendrieux on D 2.

Musée Napoléon
🕐Guided tours available (1hr): Apr–Jun, Sun and public holidays at 3pm; Jul–Aug daily except Sat 11am (from 16 Jul), 3pm and 5pm; 1–15 Sept, daily except Sat 3pm and 5pm. ⊕€7. ℘05 53 03 24 03. www.musee-napoleon.fr.
Prince Victor Napoléon, head of the imperial family and grandson of the youngest brother of Napoléon Bonaparte, took the initiative of preserving the heritage of various objects belonging to the emperor.

▶ Take D 32 towards Mauzens-et-Miremont, then D 710 to Le Bugue, in the S. Turn right on D 703, then take the D 31 back to Limeuil.

Château de Monbazillac★

As it emerges from the rolling vineyards, this château rises proudly on the edge of a limestone plateau overlooking the Dordogne valley. It is owned by the Monbazillac Wine Cooperative, which restored and refurbished it. Monbazillac, like Bergerac, actively supported the Reformation and supplied wine to Protestants who had sought refuge in the Netherlands.

CHÂTEAU

This relatively small château was built in 1550 and is surrounded by a dry moat. Its elegant silhouette is eye-catching, with an architectural style somewhere between a defensive castle and a Renaissance château. There are machicolations and a crenellated watch-path around the main building, which is flanked at each corner by a massive round tower. The façade is pierced by a double row of mullioned windows and a doorway with Renaissance-style ornamentation. Two tiers of dormer windows can be seen above the machicolations. The grey patina of the stone blends well with the brown tiled roofs of the turrets and pavilions. From the north terrace there is a good view of the vineyard and of Bergerac in the distance.

The **Great Hall**, its painted ceiling decorated with gilt foliated scrolls, has a monumental Renaissance chimneypiece, 17C furnishings and two beautiful Flemish tapestries of the same period. Several rooms are open on the first floor; note in particular the viscountess of Monbazillac's **bedchamber** furnished in Louis XIII style.

Partly hollowed out of the rock, these cellars house a small wine museum displaying harvesting and winemaking equipment used in the past, as well as a **Musée du Protestantisme et du Meuble Périgourdin** (museum of protestantism and of Périgord-style furniture). There is also a restaurant giving onto the main courtyard.

- **Michelin Map:** 329: B-7; or see Bergerac map.
- **Location:** 10km/6.25mi S of Bergerac.
- **Info:** ℘05 53 63 65 00 or ℘05 53 61 52 52 (weekends). www.chateau-monbazillac.com.
- **Don't Miss:** The tour inside the castle and a visit to the wine museum.
- **Times and Charges:** Open Jun–Sept 10am–7pm; Apr, May and Oct 10am–12.30pm and 2–6pm; Feb–Mar and Nov–Dec, 10am–12pm and 2–5pm, closed Mon. Closed in Jan. ∞€7.50.

🚗 DRIVING TOUR

Vignoble de Monbazillac
Round-trip of the wine-growing area surrounding the château (15km/9.3mi. Allow 1hr).

▶ Leave Monbazillac heading north on the D 13. Turn left onto the D 14 then left again onto the D 933 1.5km/0.9mi farther on. Drive over 2km/1.2mi along this road then turn left for the **Moulin de Malfourat**. The windmill, stripped of its sails, stands on top of a hillock. From the viewing table there is a **panorama★** of the Monbazillac vineyard and Bergerac and the Dordogne Plain to the north.

Château and vineyards at Monbazillac

© S. Sauvignier / Michelin

Issigeac

The Banège trickles through this large valley, where the multicoloured landscape is a patchwork of orchards and pastures. Issigeac has been nestled in this corner of paradise near Bergerac since medieval times. Here in this rounded village, the bishops of Sarlat would come to escape the bustle of their capital… And you'll enjoy following their example.

- ▶ **Population:** 732.
- **Michelin Map:** 329: E-7.
- **Info:** Issigeac tourist information centre, Pl. du Château. ☎05 53 58 79 62. www.issigeac.fr. Guided tours in Jul–Aug, Tue 11am.
- ▶ **Location:** Issigeac is located 18km/11.1mi SE of Bergerac on N 21 then D 14.
- **Timing:** 1hr.
- **Parking:** Car park on the church square.

OLD VILLAGE

Seen from above, the old ecclesiastical town reveals its rounded shape. The houses are grouped tightly together. In the heart of the village, a gothic church overlooks the central square; it was built by Armand de Gontaut-Biron, bishop of Sarlat. The tympanum of the portal under its bell-porch is adorned with spiral arch-mouldings.

On the other side of the square, the **Bishop's castle** was built by François de Salignac, the uncle of Fénelon, in the second half of the 17C. Fénelon, who at the time was Abbot of Carennac, would have stayed there. Only a few steps away stands the former Maison des Dîmes (House of Tithes), with its high *lauze* roof. Still, the most remarkable building remains the **Maison aux Têtes** (House of Heads), with its grimacing faces that seem to laugh at passers-by.

Eymet

Eymet is a small Périgord town known for its gourmet food such as foie gras, *galantines*, *ballottines* and other local specialities that can be seen in the windows of the many *charcuteries*.

- ▶ **Population:** 2 653.
- **Michelin Map:** 329: D-8.
- **Info:** 45 Pl. de la Bastide, 24500 Eymet. ☎05 53 23 74 95. www.eymet-perigord.fr.
- **Don't Miss:** Thur market.
- **Timing:** Allow 30min.

BASTIDE

Founded in 1256 by Alphonse de Poitiers, the bastide was ruled by several seigneurial families who were alternately in allegiance with the king of France and the king of England. Consequently, it had an eventful history during the Hundred Years War and the Wars of Religion. All that remains of the castle is the 14C **keep**. Villagers who wished to live within the fortifications were originally offered 200m²/2 000 sq ft per family for building a house, which they had to construct within two years or pay a fine. Villagers kept plots of land outside the encircling walls for agricultural production.

In town, head for **place Centrale** first, an arcaded square lined with old half-timbered or stone houses, some of which have mullioned windows. It was once accessible by three gates, two of which had towers.

Eymet has a **church**, built on the site of a former Benedictine church of Moissac Abbey. The church often played a defensive role.

The lower parts of the **mill** date from the 13C. Up until 1902 when the river traffic stopped altogether, boats were moored along the quays situated downstream.

Villefranche-de-Lonchat

Although the street layout and a few monuments are all that remains of this former English bastide, this village is the most active centre of the Gurson area, a hilly, vineyard-studded region between Libourne and Ste-Foy-la-Grande. These are no ordinary vineyards; they are at the origin of the Bergerac and Saint-Émillion vintages.

THE TOWN

The 13C fortifications of this town, which found itself in the line of fire during the wars with the English, have completely disappeared. However, the parallel streets and simple religious buildings – a church and 14C chapel – remain. Notice the Second Empire house that now accommodates the town hall and a local history museum.

🚗 DRIVING TOUR

4 LE PAYS DE GURSON
45km/27.9mi round-trip. Allow half a day. See route 4 on region map p147.

◯ Leave Villefranche-de-Lonchat travelling E along D 32.

Château de Gurson
Perched on a hillock, this castle retains a few vestiges of its fortifications. It was rebuilt in the 14C, having been given by Henry III of England, Duke of Aquitaine, to his seneschal Jean de Grailly. At the foot of the hill, a lake provides leisure activities.

◯ Return along D 32, then turn left.

Carsac-de-Gurson
The church of this village surrounded by vineyards boasts a Romanesque façade that includes all the characteristics of the Saintonge style.

◯ Leave Carsac by the NE on D 33.

- ▶ **Population:** 838.
- 🚗 **Michelin Map:** 329: B-6.
- 🅸 **Info:** ℘05 50 80 77 25. www.pays-de-bergerac.com.
- ▶ **Location:** 45km/27.9mi W of Bergerac.
- 🕐 **Timing:** 45min.
- 🎯 **Don't Miss:** Les Jardins de Sardy.

St Martin-de-Gurson
The church boasts a beautiful Saintonge-style 12C façade. The portal, which has no tympanum, opens beneath five smooth arch mouldings supported by ten columns where birds and monsters have been sculpted.

◯ Continue along D 33, then turn right on D 11. Before Vélines, take a left, then a right after the gymnasium.

Les Jardins de Sardy★
🕐Open Jul–Aug 10am–6pm; May–Jun and Sept 2–6pm. ∞€6 (no charge for under 12s). ℘05 53 27 51 45. www.jardinsdesardy.com.
The visit begins in the **scented courtyard**, where plants such as sage, lemon and camphor awaken your senses. You'll get a view of the entire garden before you stroll down the gentle slope bordered with pastel perennials to the water feature. You'll pass a statue of Saint Fiacre, patron saint of gardeners, propped up on the root of a hornbeam. Through a rose tunnel, you'll pass by a fountain of spring water before arriving in an **orchard** of apples and apricots. Bird lovers will recognise the calls of greenfinches, wrens, hedge sparrows and chaffinches.
The Château de Sardy overlooks 5 ha/12 acres of hillside vineyards. This small-scale production makes for a brilliant Bergerac. You may visit the wine cellar upon request.

◯ After Vélines, turn right on the D 936 towards Libourne. At the place called Tête Noire (3 km/1.8mi), turn right.

"…I myself am the matter of my book"

Montaigne's *Essays* have been widely read and are highly influential in the world of letters. Among his Anglophone readers were William Shakespeare, Lord Byron, Virginia Woolf and Aldous Huxley. He is recognised as the inventor of the essay form. The original title of the works, *Essais*, signifies "attempts", which reveals his penchant for exploration of the mind: *"to follow a movement so wandering… to penetrate the opaque depths of its innermost folds, to pick out and immobilise the innumerable flutterings that agitate it."* Many readers have been charmed by Montaigne's unassuming self-portrait of a doddering country gentleman, full of contradiction. In fact, he was active in public life, following a tradition begun by his grandfather, and viewed public service as a noble duty. Today's readers will find him remarkably timely in his defence of cultural relativism and tolerance, personal dignity and fidelity to nature.

Montcaret

🕐 *Open late May–late Sept 9.45am–12.30pm and 2–6.30pm; rest of year, daily except Sat, 10am–12.30pm, 2–5.30pm.*
🕐 *Closed 1 Jan, 1 May, 1 and 11 Nov, 25 Dec.* ⊕€3. ☎*05 53 58 50 18. www.monuments-nationaux.fr.*

In Gallo-Roman times, a large villa stood on the hillsides of the Dordogne where Montcaret is today. Although it was used as a necropolis from the 6C to 12C, the vestiges of this villa show that it included a peristyle, interior courtyard and **thermes** (private baths). The heating system, which worked on flue action, is as remarkable as the 4C **mosaics★**. Next to the apse, the **cruciform room** is the high point of the visit, featuring five mosaic floor coverings and a hypocaust heating system under the floor and in the walls.

Church – This church depended on the St-Florent-de-Saumur abbey. At the back of the 11C apse, four beautiful Roman and Merovingian marble capitals with acanthus decoration were put to use in the building by the Benedictine community.

▷ Leave Montcaret to the N towards St-Michel-de-Montaigne.

Château de Montaigne

🚶 *Guided tours (45mn) Jul–Aug 10am–6.30pm; May–Jun and Sept–Oct 10am–noon, 2–6.30pm; Feb–Apr and Nov–Dec 10am–noon, 2–5.30pm.*
🕐 *Closed Jan.* ⊕€8. ☎*05 53 58 63 93. www.chateau-montaigne.com.*

The essayist **Michel Eyquem de Montaigne** (1533–92) was born and died in this château. In his lifetime he served as a member of the Parliament of Bordeaux, was twice elected mayor of that city, and participated in high-level diplomatic negotiations during the Wars of Religion.

In 1571, at the age of 38, Michel de Montaigne took refuge in his family home in Périgord to reflect and write, as well as to care for his property.

The main building was rebuilt after fire ravaged it in 1885; the **library tower**, Montaigne's domain, was saved. On the top floor, his famous **library** is lined with books and decorated with Greek and Latin inscriptions.

▷ Continue along D21 to Montpeyroux.

Montpeyroux

You'll get a good **view** of the region from the hillock of Montpeyroux, where the low-lying houses give way to vineyards. In the village, the noble house of Marroux belonged to Bertrand Eyquem, the youngest brother of Michel de Montaigne. Next to the Romanesque **church**, an elegant 17C and 18C **castle** consists of a main building flanked by two square pavilions hedged in by round towers.

▷ Leave Montpeyroux on D 10 towards the N to come back to Villefranche-de-Lonchat.

Château de Montréal

Atop a rocky spur overlooking a forest, this castle is built on the foundations of a former manor house that was entirely destroyed during the Hundred Years' War. Its square shape surrounded by fortifications conceals a court built on several stories, as well as mysterious underground galleries.

- ⚓ **Michelin Map:** 329: D-5.
- **Info:** ☎ 05 53 81 11 03. www.bergerac-tourisme.com.
- ▶ **Location:** The castle is located 33km/20.5mi N of Bergerac.
- ⏱ **Timing:** 40min (guided tour).
- **Don't Miss:** The chapel; the tapestries in the sitting room; the library and the 12C staircase.

VISIT

Guided visits (40min): Jul–mid-Sept 10am–12pm, 2.30–6.30pm. €6 (children aged 8–12, €4). ☎ 05 53 81 11 03.

Surrounded by medieval fortifications that were entirely demolished, like the former castle, by the English in the 1430s, the main part of the current castle was built in the 16C. Inside, amongst the 18C and Empire furniture, notice several medallion chairs in the reception room. This room, decorated in the Louis XVI style, has retained its **Aubusson tapestries** inspired by the fables of La Fontaine.

A charming library hugs the forms of the wall of the corner tower of the building, showing off a lovely collection of bound books. In the commons, a 12C staircase vaulted with successive barrels leads to the cellar extended by a small natural cave adorned with little concretions.

A **chapel** was added in the 16C in the west part of the building to house the reliquary of a holy thorn thought to be taken from the crown of Christ. This relic was taken from the corpse of the English marshal Talbot at the Battle of Castillon, the one that put an end to the Hundred Years War.

What about the city in Quebec?

Without it being a unanimous theory, it is thought that *mons real* or "royal mount" is the origin of the name of Montréal, which was exported to the United States and Canada. **Claude de Pontbriant**, Lord of Montréal, is thought to be at the source of the name of the second-largest French-speaking city in the world after Paris. In October 1535, he was with Jacques Cartier on the banks of the St Laurent river when Cartier founded a French establishment in place of an existing Native American village, Hochelaga.

ADDRESSES

🛏 STAY

🍴🍴 **Chambre d'hôte Maison de la Forêt** – *Pas de l'Eyraud, 9km/5.5mi SW of the Château de Montréal, rte de Bergerac on D 709, Laveyssière. ☎ 05 53 82 84 50. www.aubergerac.com. 🛏 . 5 rooms.* This bed and breakfast, run by a family from the UK, has five different rooms. If you enjoy peace and quiet, opt for one that doesn't face the road.

The Périgord Blanc, or White Périgord, is the western part of the Dordogne *département*. Périgueux is its largest city and the administrative capital of the entire Dordogne. The Périgord Blanc is so called due to the frequent outcrops of chalky limestone that illuminate the open landscape as well as the houses built from local stone.

Highlights

1 Wandering around Périgeux's beautifully preserved **St-Front District** (p163)

2 Exquisite painted murals at **Vesunna** Roman site (p169)

3 **Abbaye de Chancelade**, on the Camino de Santiago pilgrimage route (p170)

4 Discover the secrets of Périgord's black gold at Sorges' **Musée de la Truffe** (p172)

5 The Botanical gardens of **Château de Neuvic** (p172)

Capital of the Périgord

Périgueux used to be two cities, one with its landmark Byzantine-style cathedral of St Front founded in the 11C and now a UNESCO World Heritage Site; and the other, older, district of the Cité to the west. The Cité was all that was left of the old Roman town of Vesunna, with the church of St-Etienne at its centre and the roman amphitheatre and Temple de Vésonne nearby. Now of course Périgueux is unified as the thriving *préfecture* of the Dordogne, with nearly 30 000 inhabitants. However, when you tour the city, you'll notice a great difference between the two districts. St-Front is in the midst of the city's day-to-day bustle, restaurants and beautiful old buildings. The Cité is the place where you will discover Périgueux's Roman past, most notably through the prestigious museum of Vesunna, whose ultra-modern architecture offers a pleasing environment in which to view the ancient ruins.

Périgord Blanc

Many visitors are drawn to the Périgord Blanc in order to visit Périgueux but, fascinating though the city may be, there is much more to the area. The abbey in Chancelade includes a museum displaying an extensive collection of religious artefacts. Sorges, the truffle capital of the Périgord, boasts a museum on the theme of its local product, and holds markets and other events with the famous fungus the centre of attention. Neuvic is home to an interesting 16C fortified castle complete with botanical gardens. The Double Forest has been a wooded area since medieval times, and like many medieval woodlands, has a reputation as a hiding-place for bandits; today it is a haven for a different, gentler kind of wildlife.

Vesunna – Musée Gallo-Romain de Périgueux

© Patrick Escudero / hemis.fr

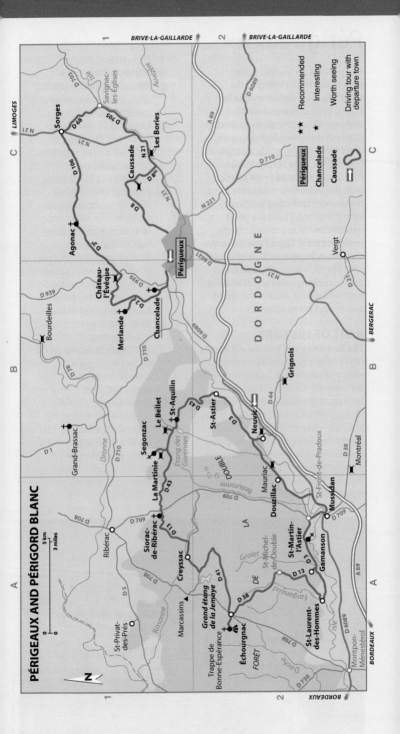

PÉRIGEAUX AND PÉRIGORD BLANC

Périgueux★★

Périgueux is an ancient town built in the fertile valley of the River Isle. Its long history can be traced in its urban architecture and two distinctive districts, each of which is marked by the domes of its sanctuary: the Cité district, overlooked by St Stephen's tiled roof, and the Puy St-Front district, with the Byzantine silhouette of the present cathedral bristling with pinnacles. There is a good overall view of the town from the bridge beyond Cours Fénelon to the southeast. Périgueux's gastronomic specialities, with truffle and foie gras occupying prize position, have become famous around the world and attract many visitors.

A BIT OF HISTORY

The Roman city of Vésone – The town of Périgueux owes its foundation to a sacred spring known as the Vésone. It was near the stream, on the Isle's south bank, that the Gaulish Petrocorii (Petrocorii, which meant the four tribes in Celtic, gave its name both to Périgueux and Périgord) built their main *oppidum* (defensive town). After siding with Vercingetorix against Caesar, the Petrocorii finally had to accept Roman domination but in fact benefited greatly

▶ **Population:** 29 573.

⚙ **Michelin Map:** 329: F-4.

🏢 **Info:** 26 pl. Francheville. ℰ05 53 53 10 63. www. tourisme-perigueux.fr.

◐ **Location:** Périgueux is located on the banks of the River Isle, 48.5km/30mi N of Bergerac and 22km/14mi S of Brantôme.

🅿 **Parking:** The town has three large underground car parks in pl. Montaigne, pl. Francheville and along espl. du Théâtre (first 35min free of charge). Free outdoor car parks can also be found along the river, along part of the allées Tourny and on pl. Mauvard.

👫 **Kids:** Ville d'Art et d'Histoire theme workshops Wed and Fri 3pm upon prior arrangement with the tourist office.

🕐 **Timing:** Once you have spent time exploring the town, allow a half-day to explore the Périgord Blanc.

☺ **Don't Miss:** St-Front district; the cathedral; Musée du Périgord.

St-Front district by the Isle

©Nicolas Thibaut/Photononstop/Tips Images

from the Pax Romana, which enabled the city to become one of the finest in all Aquitaine. Vesunna, as the town was then called, spread beyond the bend in the Isle; temples, a forum, basilicas and an arena were built and an aqueduct over 7km/4mi long was constructed to carry water to the baths. But in the 3C AD the city's prosperity was destroyed by the Alemanni, who sacked the town.

The unfortunate town – To avoid further disaster the Vesunnians shut themselves up in a narrow fortified enclosure; stones from the temples were used to build powerful ramparts and the arena was transformed into a keep.

In spite of all these precautions, the town suffered the alternate depredations of fire and pillaging by barbaric invaders such as the Visigoths, Franks and Norsemen. Such misfortune reduced Vesunna to the status of a humble village and finally even its name died; it was simply known as the city of the Petrocorii and "la Cité" eventually became the town's new name. St Front later established the town as an Episcopal seat and, in the 10C, it became the unassuming capital of the county of Périgord.

The ambition of Puy St-Front – A little sanctuary containing the tomb of St Front, Apostle of Périgord, was built not far from the Cité. Initially the object of a pilgrimage, the sanctuary became a monastic centre. The busy market town of Puy St-Front grew up round the monastery, soon eclipsing the Cité in size.

The townspeople of Puy St-Front joined the feudal alliances against the English kings, established an emancipated consular regime and then sided with Philip Augustus against King John of England. Little by little, the expanding Puy St-Front annexed the Cité's prerogatives; there were more and more squabbles between the rivals. The Cité, unable to win against its neighbour which was under the protection of the king of France, was forced to accept union. On 16 September 1240, an act of union established that the Cité and Puy St-Front, governed by a mayor and 12 consuls, would now form one community called Périgueux. Nevertheless, each town kept its distinctive characteristics; the Cité belonged to clerics and aristocrats whereas Puy St-Front belonged to merchants and artisans.

Périgueux becomes *préfecture* – In 1790, when the Dordogne *département* was created, Périgueux was chosen over Bergerac as *préfecture*. The town, which had slowly become dormant, suddenly found itself the object of a building boom. The old districts were enhanced by new avenues and squares.

WALKING TOURS

1 ST-FRONT DISTRICT★★★

The old artisans' and merchants' district has been given a facelift. A conservation programme for safeguarding this historic area was set up, and the area has been undergoing major restoration. Its Renaissance façades, medieval houses, courtyards, staircases and shops are being gradually brought back to life; the pedestrian streets have rediscovered their role as commercial thoroughfares. Place du Coderc and place de l'Hôtel-de-Ville are colourful and animated every morning with their fruit and vegetable market, whereas place de la Clautre is where the larger Wednesday and Saturday market is held. During the winter, the prestigious truffle and foie gras markets held in place St-Louis attract hordes of connoisseurs.

In summer, the restaurants, overflowing onto the pavements, serve high-quality Périgord-style cuisine in an atmosphere of days past.

▷ Start at Tour Mataguerre (tower) opposite the tourist office.

Tour Mataguerre

Part of a guided tour of the town.
This round tower (late 15C) is crowned by a machicolated parapet and pierced by arrow-slits. It is the last of the 28 towers forming the defensive system of Puy St-Front in the Middle Ages. On the side of rue de la Bride part of the ramparts can be seen.

From the top (viewing table), there is a **view★** of the old district with its tiled roofs, the towers of the noblemen's townhouses, the domes of St-Front and the neighbouring hills, one of which is the well-known Écornebœuf Hill (*écorner* means to break the horns of an animal; *bœuf* means ox). Indeed, the hill is so steep that the oxen forced to climb it would break their necks... and lose their horns.

▶ Follow rue de la Bride.

Rue des Farges

At nos 4 and 6 stands the **Maison des Dames de la Foi** (house of the women of faith). The medieval (12C) layout of its façade is still visible: pointed arches on the ground floor, rounded arches on the upper storey and a loggia beneath the eaves. A small bell-turret set in one corner brings to mind the fact that in the 17C the building was a convent.

▶ Look down passage Taillefer before turning right onto the narrow ruelle des Farges, which leads to place de Navarre. Walk up the stairs.

Rue Aubergerie

At no 16, the **Hôtel d'Abzac de Ladouze** consists of great round arch, an octagonal tower and a corbelled turret, all characteristic of 15C architecture. At nos 4 and 8 the **Hôtel de Sallegourde**, also 15C, has a polygonal tower surmounted by a machicolated watch-path.

▶ Turn left.

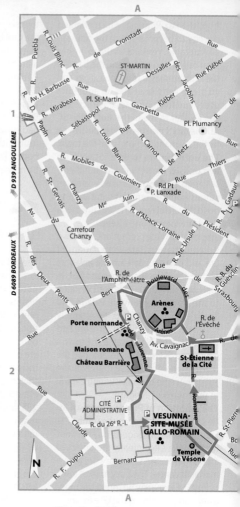

Rue St-Roch

At no 4 a small arcaded loggia is decorated with diamond-work. Farther on, on the corner of rue de Sully, note the restored half-timbered house.

▶ Bear left.

Rue du Calvaire

On their way to be executed on place de la Clautre, the condemned came up this street, their road to Calvary. At no 3 there is a door ornamented with nailheads beneath a Renaissance porch. The street leads to place de la Clautre which offers an interesting view of the imposing St-Front Cathedral.

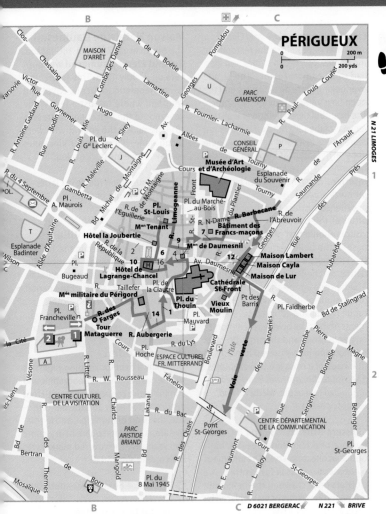

Cathédrale St-Front★★

This cathedral, now on UNESCO's World Heritage list, is one of the largest in southwest France and one of the most curious.

A chapel was first built on the site of the saint's tomb in the 6C. In 1047 a larger church was consecrated but this second building was almost completely destroyed by fire in 1120, whereupon it was decided to construct an even bigger church.

This third basilica, completed about 1173, was Byzantine in style, with a dome and a ground plan in the form of a Greek cross. This architecture, which is uncommon in France, brings to mind St Mark's in Venice and the church of the Apostles in Constantinople. This was the first domed church to be built on the Roman road, which was still used in the Middle Ages by those travelling from Rodez to Cahors and on to Saintes. In 1575, during the Wars of Religion, St Front was pillaged by the Huguenots, the treasure was scattered and the saint's tomb destroyed. Restoration was carried out with little regard for the original design. It was largely reconstructed by Abadie from 1852 onwards in the style of Second Empire pastiche. He was to use this restoration later as the inspiration for the design of the Sacré Cœur Basilica in Paris.

Exterior – *Stand in place de la Clautre for an overall view.* Before the restoration, the domes, covered in stones and tiles, had small end ornaments. The façade overlooking place de la Clautre and the open bays were part of the 11C church. The beautiful tiered belltower is all that remains of the 12C church. It is preserved more or less in its original state. Abadie drew on its lantern as inspiration for the tall pinnacles that adorn the new domes.

Interior – *Enter the cathedral by the north door.*

In order to respect the chronological order of the building's construction, visitors should first of all see, near the base of the belltower, the remains of the 11C church: two bays covered with domes perched on tall column drums. Abadie redesigned the church to the dimensions of its prestigious Romanesque model and adopted several elements from it. The boldness of its domes on pendentives and the strength of its odd-looking pillars carved in places in the shape of a cross are two examples. *A visit to the cathedral is included in the guided tour of the "Medieval and Renaissance town".*

Cloisters – The 12C, 13C and 16C cloisters are of a half-Romanesque, half-Gothic architectural style. The enormous pinecone-like mass in the centre of the cloisters once crowned the belltower; during the Revolution it was replaced by a weathercock which was later replaced by Abadie's angel.

▷ Walk to the right of the building.

Place du Thouin
The two bronze cannon with the inscription "Périgueux"1588 were excavated at place du Coderc in 1979 on the site of the armoury in the old consulate.

▷ Walk round the cathedral to place Daumesnil; then left on rue de la Clarté.

Maison Natale de Daumesnil
The house at no 7 has an 18C façade. **General Pierre Daumesnil** was born here on 27 July 1776. This soldier followed Napoleon to Arcola, Egypt and Wagram, where he lost a leg. While governor of the Vincennes fortress in 1814, he said to the enemy, who were laying siege, "I'll surrender Vincennes when you give me back my leg."

▷ Continue along rue de la Clarté, turn left then right onto rue du Serment.

Place de l'Hôtel-de-Ville
The town hall is located in the 17C and 18C **Hôtel de Lagrange-Chancel**. The 15C house at no 7 has a polygonal staircase tower characteristic of the period. Its machicolations are neo-Gothic.

▷ Walk to the left of the town hall.

Place du Coderc
Originally a field for keeping pigs, this square has become the geographic and administrative centre of the Puy St-Front district. In the early 19C the old consulate, the heart of municipal and legislative life, still had its square belfry, some 600 years old. The covered market was built on this site c 1830.

▷ Follow rue de la Sagesse opposite.

Hôtel de la Joubertie
Visits as part of a guided tour of the town. Located at no 1, this mansion contains an elegant **Renaissance staircase★**, of a square design, decorated with a coffered ceiling depicting mythological scenes including Venus putting down her weapons, which symbolises the young wife entering the household. The intertwined H and S represent the initials of the Hauteforts and Solminihacs.

Place St-Louis
This square is known locally as Foie Gras Square, as it is here that the foie gras is sold in late autumn. It features a modern fountain, decorated with a bronze sculpture by Ramon.

Maison Tenant or the **Maison du Pâtissier**, opposite, used to be the Talleyrands' townhouse; it consists of a residential part set at right angles, with an adjoining corbelled turret. The façade on rue Eguillerie has a marvellous Gothic window. **No 5 rue Lammary** has an unusual superposition of mullioned corner windows.

▷ Turn right.

Rue Limogeanne★

In the past, this street led to Limogeanne Gate (Porte Limogeanne), which opened onto the Limoges road. The street is lined with numerous stores and several elegant Renaissance townhouses.

In the courtyard of the **Hôtel de Méredieu** (no 12) there is a 15C carved doorway decorated with a 17C coat of arms.

At no 7, note the initials AC in the centre of the wrought-iron impost; these denote Antoine Courtois, the famous 18C caterer, whose partridge pâtés were the talk even of the Court of Prussia. His headquarters were in the cellars of this townhouse.

Maison Estignard (no 5) has an elegant Renaissance façade. The Regional Department of Architecture is to be found at no 3. Behind the heavy balustrade above the doorway, the inner courtyard has a lovely door decorated with grotesques on the lintel and François I salamanders on the tympanum. The huge staircase is remarkable. **Lapeyre House** (no 1), which is at the corner of place du Codern, has a corbelled corner turret.

▷ Retrace your steps and turn right onto impasse Limogeanne.

Galerie Daumesnil★

This consists of a network of courtyards and small squares linked by alleyways. The buildings, which were grafted on over the centuries, have been demolished, creating open spaces and revealing the fine 15C, 16C and 17C façades.

▷ Come out onto rue de la Miséricorde and cross rue St-Front.

On the left along rue St-Front is an unusual Masonic Lodge (Loge Maçonnique) perforated by openings like arrow-slits. The sculptures on the façade represent masonic emblems.

Rue de la Constitution

At no 3 is the **doorway of the Hôtel de Crémoux**, featuring a crocketed arch between tall pinnacles.

At no 7, the **Hôtel de Gamanson**, also called Logis St-Front, consists of two 15C wings set at right angles, linked by a staircase tower, flanked by a corbelled turret and perforated by mullioned windows. A 17C well is sheltered by a Moorish dome.

▷ Turn left onto rue du Plantier then turn right.

Rue Barbecane

The street owes its name to an old tower, now destroyed except for a wall. Before taking the stairs in rue de l'Abreuvoir, note the 19C façade of the Hôtel de Fayolle. Walk along the street then turn round to admire the 17C front of this mansion overlooking the river.

▷ Turn right.

Rue du Port-de-Graule

Just like rue Ste-Marthe which prolongs it, this street still has a medieval air about it with its large uneven paving stones, its low doors and the little staircase-alleyways that lead off it. In 1967, several scenes from the miniseries *Jacquou le Croquant*, based on local author Eugene le Roy's novel, were shot here.

▷ Walk to boulevard Georges-Saumande, on the left.

The Quays

Along the river there are several fine houses standing side by side.

Maison Lambert, on the left of Pont des Barris, is a fine Renaissance townhouse called the House with Columns because of its gallery. Next to it, **Maison Cayla**, also called the Consul's House, was built on the ramparts in the 15C. The roof is decorated with Flamboyant-style dormers. At the corner of avenue Daumesnil, the **Maison de Lur** dates from the 16C.

Continue along the quays; on the other side of avenue Daumesnil the half-timbered building, corbelled over the fortress wall, is a remainder of the **barn** attached to the cathedral, called the **Old Mill**, which once jutted out over the river.

▶ Cross Barris Bridge and immediately turn left.

Voie Verte★

This verdant path, reserved for pedestrians and non-motorised vehicles, follows the river and makes for a refreshing summer excursion. You'll pass vegetable gardens, weeping willows, lime trees, waterlilies and shady benches. You'll also enjoy what is surely the loveliest **view** over the cathedral and the mosaic of roofs of the historic district. If you have time to push south, you'll also see the 19C Moulin de St-Clair on the opposite bank.

▶ Cross back over Barris Bridge and immediately turn left.

On the riverside on the other side of avenue Daumesnil, the corbelled wooden-sided kiosk on the fortification wall is a remnant of the attic of the Vieux Moulin that used to extend over the river.

② CITÉ DISTRICT★

This district, occupying the site of ancient Vesunna, has retained numerous Gallo-Roman ruins which testify to the town's importance under Roman occupation.

▶ Leave from the tourist office, follow rue de la Cité then turn right onto rue de l'Évêché.

Arènes

A public garden occupies the space where the arena once stood. Built in the 1C, this amphitheatre, one of the largest in Gaul, had capacity for 20 000 people. Great blocks of stone still mark the stairwells, the passages between banks of seating and the vaulting, but all of the lower part of the building is still buried. Demolition of the arena began in 3C, when the amphitheatre was turned into a bastion and became part of the city ramparts. The arena was next transformed into a quarry, its stone being used to build houses in the town.

▶ On leaving the amphitheatre, take rue de Turenne on the left.

Porte Normande

This gateway formed part of the ramparts built in the 3C to protect the city from the hordes of barbarians sweeping across Europe. The story behind the name is that the gate is supposed to have played a part in the defence of the city against the Vikings, who came up the River Isle in the 9C.

Maison Romane

This rectangular 12C (Romanesque) building is neighbour to the vestiges of a tower from the Gallo-Roman defence wall, jumbled up with bits of capitals, column drums and other architectural elements. An altar on which bulls were sacrificed was discovered here; it is now on display in the Vesunna Gallo-Roman Museum (🕭 see below).

Château Barrière

This castle has a 12C keep rising above one of the towers of the ramparts. It was altered during the Renaissance period but kept the lovely main entrance door in the staircase tower. Destroyed by fire during the Wars of Religion, it was not rebuilt.

▶ Cross the bridge on the right.

👤👤 Vesunna – Musée Gallo-Romain de Périgueux★★★

🕐 Jul– Aug 10am–7pm; rest of year phone for opening hours. ◉€6.
📞 05 53 53 00 92. www.vesunna.fr.
Designed by Jean Nouvel, this museum houses the remains of an opulent Gallo-Roman residence covering 4 000sq m. Built in the centre of a garden, on one side, a mezzanine on two storeys overlooks the ancient *domus*. This section of the museum is devoted to the ancient town of Vesunna: a scale model of the town in the 2C shows how extensive it was in Roman times – the residence can easily be located near the sanctuary and the forum.

Wooden footbridges enable visitors to wander through the house. Digs have revealed the presence of a 1C building, considerably extended in the 2C. Elaborate murals can be seen on the base of the walls of the primitive house. The frieze surrounding the central pond, on the other hand, was painted when the house was extended.

Along the way, artefacts trace back the daily life of the inhabitants: their hypocaust heating system, decoration and water distribution, but also cooking, cosmetics and surgery.

Temple de Vésone

This tower, 20m high and 17m in diameter, is all that remains of the temple dedicated to the titular goddess of the city. The temple, which was built in the heart of the old Cité in the 2C AD, originally had a peristyle, and was surrounded by porticoes and framed by two basilicas. The tower is still impressive despite being damaged.

▶ Cross the bridge and turn left along rue Romaine where the remains of a Roman wall (Late Empire) can be seen.

St-Étienne-de-la-Cité★

Built in the 11C on the site of the ancient Temple of Mars, this church, the town's first Christian sanctuary, was dedicated by St Front to the martyr Stephen and was the cathedral church until 1669.

Tour de Vésone

© S. Sauvignier / Michelin

It included a row of four successive domed bays, preceded by an imposing belfry porch. When the town was occupied in 1577, the Huguenots demolished all but the two east bays. Restored in the 17C, ravaged again during the Fronde, secularised during the Revolution, St Stephen's was consecrated anew during the First Empire.

The church as it now stands is pure Périgord-Romanesque style. Inside, it is interesting to compare the architecture of the two bays built within a 50-year interval. The first (11C) is archaic, primitive, short and dark. The second bay is more slender, its dome resting on pointed arches on square pillars.

Against the south wall of the first bay is an impressive 17C **altarpiece** in oak and walnut built for the seminary.

MUSEUMS
Musée d'Art et d'Archéologie du Périgord★

🕐 Apr–Sept Mon, Wed–Fri 10.30am–5.30pm, Sat and Sun 1–6pm; Oct–Mar Mon, Wed–Fri 10am–5pm, Sat and Sun 1–6pm. 🕐 Closed Tue and public hols. ◉€4.50. 📞 05 53 06 40 70. www.perigueux-maap.fr.
Located on allées de Tourny, on the site of what was an Augustinian convent, this museum displays a large **prehistory collection**, in particular a remarkable collection of engraved objects of the Magdalenian Period (15 000–12 000 BCE), found in various

sites across the Dordogne, as well as the fossilized skeleton of the Regourdou man (Neanderthal man 70 000 BCE, *see LASCAUX*) and of the Raymonden man (*Homo sapiens*, 15 000 years old). The collection of **medieval exhibits** includes Limoges enamels, 11C capitals from the cathedral, a 13C Virgin altarpiece, 13C Rabastens diptych and 15C liturgical cupboard. The **fine arts and decorative arts department** (16C–20C), displays works by local artists next to works by French, European and Asian artists; note the portrait of Fénelon by F Bailleul (18C) and Sem by François Flameng (20C).

Musée Militaire du Périgord
◷*Open daily 2–6pm except Sun and public hols.* ⊚€4. ℘05 53 53 47 36.
Arms and weapons, standards and uniforms evoke the military history of Périgord from the Middle Ages to today.

Périgord Blanc

This calcareous land of hills topped with cereal fields and split through by the Isle valley is marked by its Gallo-Roman period. It is the transitional area between the Bordeaux region and the Limousin. Chalky patches appear over large surfaces, lending the region its nickname. However, plant life is abundant between the Auvézère and Isle valleys, while to the north, the wilderness of the Double Forest and its ponds complete the greenery.

🚗 DRIVING TOUR

① PÉRIGORD BLANC
56km/35mi round-trip. Allow half a day.
See route 1 on region map page 161.

▷ Leave Périgueux along the D 939 towards Brantôme and stop at Chancelade.

ADDRESSES

🛏 STAY
⊜⊜⊜ **Comfort Hôtel Régina** – *14 r. Denis-Papin (opposite the train station).* ℘05 53 08 40 44. *41 rooms.* Bedrooms are small, functional and colourful. Buffet breakfast. Friendly service and a good location.

🍴 EAT
⊜ **Au Bien Bon** – *15 r. des Places.* ℘05 53 09 69 91. *Closed Feb school hols and early Nov; Jul–Aug Sat, Sun, Mon eve and public hols. Rest year, closed lunch Mon–Thur, Sat eve, Fri and Sun.* Dine on seasonal local products in the rustic interior or on the summer terrace.

⊜⊜ **Au Petit Chef** – *5, Pl. du Coderc.* ℘05 53 53 16 03. Classic cheerful small bar (downstairs) and restaurant (upstairs) with few frills.

- 👓 **Michelin Map:** 329 E-F-G4.
- 🛈 **Info:** Office de Tourisme, 24420 Sorges. ℘05 53 46 71 43. www.sorges-perigord.com.
- 👁 **Don't Miss:** Musée de la Truffe (truffle museum) in Sorges.
- ◷ **Timing:** Half a day for the driving tour.

Abbaye de Chancelade★
The abbey is a peaceful haven tucked into the foot of green slopes overlooking the Beauronne: its role as a spiritual centre continues today.
Founded in the 12C by a monk who adopted the rule of St Augustine, the abbey was protected by the bishops of Périgueux and later answered directly to the Holy See. It therefore prospered and was accorded considerable privileges: asylum, safety and franchises. From the 14C the abbey's fortunes declined; the English captured it, sent the monks away

and installed a garrison. During the Wars of Religion, the abbey buildings were partly destroyed. In 1623 Alain de Solminihac, the new abbot, undertook the reformation and restoration of Chancelade. He was so successful that he was named bishop of Cahors by Louis XIII. The abbey was able to function normally until the Revolution, whereupon it became national property. The lower part of the **church** is all that remains of the original 12C church.

The Romanesque doorway features an elegant arcade, showing Saintonge influence. The conventual buildings, added in the 17C, include the abbot's lodgings and the outbuildings around the courtyard and garden, which comprise the 15C pointed barrel-vaulted laundry room, stables, workshops and a fortified mill.

A **museum** of religious art, housed in the basement of the abbot's lodgings, displays reliquaries, statues, altarpieces and paintings, including a Christ Outraged believed to be the work of Georges de la Tour.

▷ Leave Chancelade on the D 2 travelling N. The road between Chancelade and Merlande rises through a wood of chestnut and oak trees.

Prieuré de Merlande
In a deserted clearing in Feytaud Forest stand a small fortified chapel and a prior's house, as solitary reminders of the Merlande Priory founded here in the 12C by the monks of Chancelade. Both have been restored.

▷ Return to the D 2, turning left then right 2.5km/1.5mi farther on.

Château-l'Évêque
The village took its name from the Episcopal castle. The façades facing the Beauronne valley have mullioned windows, and a machicolated watch-path runs around the line of the roof.
The parish church is where St Vincent de Paul, founder of missionary organisations to help the poor, was ordained in September 1600 at the early age of 20.

▷ Leave the village travelling NE along the D 3E.

Agonac
In a pleasant setting in the wooded hills of the area known as Perigord Blanc, the **Église St-Martin** (◑open mid-Jul–mid-Aug; ⚲guided tours by prior arrangement, daily except Sat–Sun and public hols, 4–6pm; ℘05 53 06 36 71) gives this town its character.

Abbaye de Chancelade

© Patrick Escudero / hemis.fr

The square belfry and the buttresses (16C) were added to repair damage incurred during the Wars of Religion. The system of two-storey high defensive chambers encircling the 12C dome recalls the troubled times when churches were turned into fortresses.

▶ Continue E along the D 106.

Sorges

This pleasant village has a century-old reputation for producing truffles, and a museum to honour them.
The **Musée de la Truffe** (♿🕑open mid-Jun–Sept Mon–Fri 9.30am–6.30pm, Sat–Sun 9.30am–12.30pm, 2.30–6.30pm; rest of year daily except Mon 10am–noon, 2–5pm. 🕑closed 1 Jan, 1 May, 1 Nov and 25 Dec. ⊗€5. 05 53 05 90 11. www.eco-musee-truffe-sorges.com) in the tourist office is dedicated to this rare, delectable fungus and directs you to a walking tour (3km/1.9mi).

Château des Bories

At Antonne-et-Trigonant on the way back to Périgueux along the N 21. 🕑Open Jul–Aug. ⚬⚬Guided tour (45min, château and park), daily except Sun, 1–7pm. ⊗€5.50. ✆05 53 06 00 01.
A 15C–16C gem that boasts a splendid monumental staircase in the square tower, unusual vaulting over the guard-room and a fine Flemish tapestry in the long gallery.

Château de Caussade

Tucked away in a clearing of the Lanmary Forest, this noble building has all the features of a 15C fortified manor. Its polygonal fortification, surrounded by a half-filled moat, is flanked by square towers.

▶ Come back and continue along D 8 to Périgueux.

Neuvic

This peaceful village lies on the south bank of the River Isle, which flows along the edge of the Forêt de la Double, sprinkled with lakes and half-timbered clay houses.

VILLAGE
Château de Neuvic

🕑Open Jul–Aug, guided tours (1hr) daily except Mon at 3.30pm and 5pm. ⊗€5.50 (château and botanical gardens). ✆05 53 80 86 60. www.chateau-parc-neuvic.com.
Follow the rue Majoral Fournier from the centre towards the River. Take a walkway on the left lined with trees, which leads to the castle; it is currently in use as a medical training centre.
Built in 1530, the castle has retained its machicolated watch-path which is more of a decorative than a defensive feature; two main buildings surround a square keep erected at the beginning of the 16C. Inside, there are 16C and 18C frescoes.

▶ **Population:** 3 635.
✦ **Michelin Map:** 329: D-5.
🖪 **Info:** Pl. de la Mairie. ✆05 53 81 52 11. www.tourisme-isleperigord.com.
▶ **Location:** 24km/15mi SW of Périgueux via the D 1089/N 89.
👥 **Kids:** Parc Botanique; the Grand Étang de la Jemaye.
🕑 **Timing:** Take a day to explore the forest.

👥 Parc Botanique

🕑Open Jul–Aug, 10am–noon, 2–7pm; Apr–Jun and Sept–Oct, 10am–12pm, 2–6pm. 🕑Closed Mon.⊗€4 (no charge Apr–May and Sept–Oct). ✆05 53 80 86 60. www.chateau-parc-neuvic.com.
The castle grounds have been laid out as botanical gardens (6ha/15 acres) housing some 1 500 plant species (oak, dogwood, spindle tree, lilac, roses etc).

🚗 DRIVING TOUR

② FORÊT DE LA DOUBLE

🕐 *See route 2 on region map page 161. 95km/59mi round-trip. Allow 1 day.*

▶ Drive north out of Neuvic, cross the River Isle then follow the D 3 to the right for St-Astier.

Lying on the banks of the River Isle, the old town centre contains a few remaining Renaissance houses. It is overlooked by the church, supported by massive buttresses, and a magnificent 16C belltower adorned with two tiers of blind arcades. The D 43 climbs out of St-Astier on a series of steep hairpin bends to reveal beautiful views of the town before descending into the forest. The next stop is **St-Aquilin**. The church is built in a transitional Romanesque Gothic style.

From the church, drive 700m along the D 43 and turn right for **Château du Bellet**. The fine tiled roofs, massive round towers and separate dovecot of this castle, built on the side of a hill, come into view on the right. Continue on the D 43; turn right onto the D 104 3km/1.9mi farther on for **Segonzac**. As you enter the village, note the **Château de la Martinie**, a 15C building remodelled several times. The village's **Romanesque church** (11C–12C) was altered and enlarged in the 16C.

From Segonzac, return to the D 43 (right) for **Siorac-de-Ribérac**. Overlooking a small valley, the fortified Romanesque church has a single nave partly surmounted by a dome.

Drive west from Siroac; turn left to the D 13, then right to the D 44 to St-Aulaye and **Creyssac**. Surrounded by the waters of a small lake, the elegant square dovecot makes a pleasant sight. 200m farther on, turn left towards **Grand Étang de la Jemaye**. In the middle of the Forêt de Jemaye, the lake has been set up as a water-sports centre with a beach and facilities for fishing, windsurfing and a splashing good time.

Return to the road and turn right for **Échourgnac**. Not far from this village

(along the D 38) stands a **Trappist monastery** (Trappe de Bonne-Espérance). The monastery was founded in 1868 by Trappist monks from Port-du-Salut in Normandy. They set up a model cheese-making farm, collecting milk from the neighbouring farms.

Drive southeast out of Échourgnac along the D 38 to St-Michel-de-Double and turn onto the D 13 for **St-Laurent-des-Hommes**. This village boasts a few splendid traditional houses of the Double region.

Drive east on the D 3 for **Gamanson**. Set back slightly from the road, this hamlet boasts a rich collection of half-timbered and clay-walled houses

Turn back and continue along the D 3 (left) for **St-Martin-l'Astier**. The unusual outline of the Romanesque **church** is an extreme example of Double architecture. The **belltower** and **chancel** are octagonal; the latter is covered by a dome on eight engaged columns. Continue along the D 3 and cross the River Isle to see **Mussidan**. This old Huguenot city on the banks of the River Isle was besieged on several occasions during the Wars of Religion. The particularly bloody siege in 1569 inspired Montaigne's famous essays *L'Heure des Parlements Dangereuse*. Mussidan is home to the **Musée des Arts et Traditions Populaires du Périgord André-Voulgre** (🚻🕐 *open Jun–Sept 9.30am–noon, 2–6pm; Apr–May Sat, Sun and public holidays 2–6pm.* 🕐*closed Oct–Mar.* ✆€3.50. ✆05 53 81 23 55. www.museevoulgre.fr). Displayed in the lovely Périgord mansion where Doctor Voulgre lived, this collection is rich and varied; it includes furniture, objects and tools, as well as a still, a steam engine and stuffed animals collected by the doctor during his lifetime. Drive NE from Mussidan on N 89; turn left on D 3E5 3km/1.9mi farther on for **Douzillac**. Have a look at the town hall with its pepper-pot and wooden balcony. The outline of the 16C **Château de Mauriac** situated near the D 3, on the way to Mauriac, is reflected in the calm waters of the River Isle.

BRANTÔME AND PÉRIGORD VERT

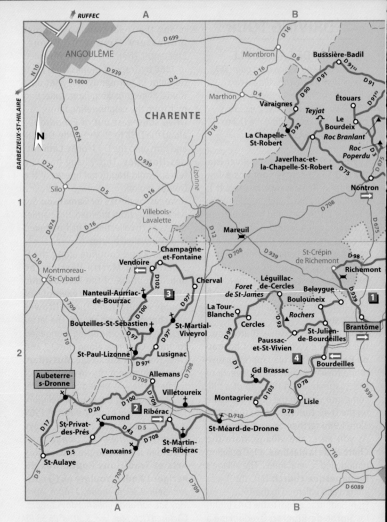

The Périgord Vert lives up to its "green" name: rolling hills, tranquil forests and leisure facilities such as the Velorail make it a great destination for green tourism. Far from the bustle of everyday life, this beautiful region is the ideal place to slow down and enjoy a stroll in sleepy, out-of-the-way villages, and the cultural heritage that has been so successfully preserved.

Highlights

1 Riverside **Brantôme** (p176)

2 The charming, steep streets of **Aubeterre-sur-Dronne** (p181)

3 Isolated **Bourdeilles** (p184)

4 Ancient **St-Jean-de-Côle** (p191)

Brantôme

The presence of the Dronne and Côle rivers in and around this cheerful village has earned it the nickname "Venice of the Périgord". Indeed, the water adds a picturesque dimension to the architectural splendour of the village. Don't miss its sights: the belltower is extraordinary, the abbey is superb and there is a real spiritual resonance throughout the net-

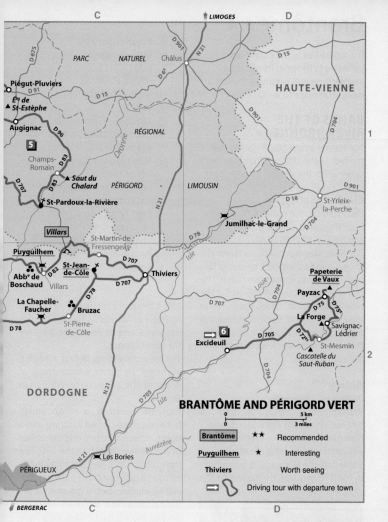

BRANTÔME AND PÉRIGORD VERT

Brantôme	★★	Recommended
Puyguilhem	★	Interesting
Thiviers		Worth seeing
⇨		Driving tour with departure town

0   5 km
0   3 miles

work of sculpted troglodyte caves. The stage set by riverside gardens comes to life in the summertime on market days, adding its convivial charm and the opportunity to bring home a little something of the Périgord, such as truffles and walnuts. There are also a few craftsmen who have set up shop along the cliffside at the end of the cave walk if you're looking for a souvenir.

Périgord Vert

The Périgord Vert is the most rural of the four Perigords with few settlements of any size. Nontron, the main town, can barely muster 3 500 souls, but this is part of the charm of this region. Green valleys with large tracts of forest and granite landscape mean that it has more in common with the neighbouring Haute-Vienne and Corrèze *départements* to the north than it does with the Dordogne. This similarity, and a desire on the part of the regional authorities to promote sustainable tourism and encourage the economic and cultural development of the area, has led to the establishment of the Parc Naturel Régional Périgord-Limousin in the northern part of the Périgord Vert and the southwest of the Haute-Vienne *département* of the Limousin.

Brantôme★★

Brantôme lies in the charming vallée de la Dronne. Its old abbey and picturesque **setting**★ make it a delightful place to visit.

BANKS OF THE RIVER DRONNE★★

The former abbey buildings, located at the foot of the cliff, overlook the island upon which the village has been built.

Clocher (Belfry)★★

Boulevard Charlemagne. &. ●●*Guided tour (1hr), 10am–6pm.* ○*Closed Jan.* ●€6.50. ♪05 53 05 80 63.

The belltower was built apart from the church upon a sharp rock towering 12m high. Vast caves spread beneath it. The tower was built in the 11C and is the oldest gabled Romanesque belltower in the Limousin style. Each of its four storeys is stepped back and slightly smaller than the one below; it is crowned with a stone pyramid.

Abbey

Boulevard Charlemagne.

Brantôme Abbey, which was founded by Charlemagne in 769 under Benedictine rule to house the relics of St Sicaire, attracted a multitude of pilgrims. Sacked by the Normans, it was rebuilt in the 11C by Abbé Guillaume. In the

▶ **Population:** 2 152.
ⓒ **Michelin Map:** 329: E-3.
ⓘ **Info:** 24310 Brantôme. ♪05 53 05 80 63. www.perigord-dronne-belle.fr.
ⓞ **Location:** 27km/17m N of Périgueux via D 939. 93km/58mi NW of Sarlat.
ⓐ **Don't Miss:** A boat trip on the river is the perfect way to discover this charming town.
⚓ **Boat Trips:** (45min) With on-board commentary, operate Apr–mid-Oct from quai du Pavillon Renaissance.

16C, it became a commandery headed by Pierre de Mareuil as abbot. Later, his nephew, Pierre de Bourdeille, became the administrator.

The present buildings were remodelled in the 18C by Bertin, administrator of Périgord and extensively restored in the 19C.

Angevin vaulting, a compromise between cross-ribbed vaulting and a dome, replaced the two original domes of the **abbey church** in the 15C. The nave is plain and elegant; a bay in the form of a cross and three depressed-arched windows below it illuminate the flat east end. Near the main doorway, go into the 16C cloistral gallery from where you'll get a glimpse of the former chapter-house.

The **convent buildings** now house the town hall and an art museum (ⓒ*see below*). A monumental staircase leads to the former monks' dormitory where temporary exhibitions are regularly held.

Musée Fernand Desmoulin

Abbaye ○*Open Apr–May , Jun and Sept 10am–12.30pm, 2–6pm; Jul–Aug 10am–7pm; Feb–Mar and Oct–Dec 10am–noon, 2–5pm.* ●€4.50. ♪05 53 05 80 63.

The museum displays a permanent exhibition of the enigmatic paintings and

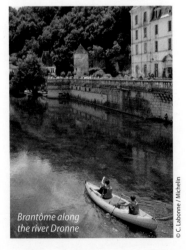

Brantôme along the river Dronne

© C. Labonne / Michelin

The Brantôme Chronicles

The literary fame of **Pierre de Bourdeille** (1538–1614), better known as
Brantôme, brought renown to the abbey of which he was commendatory abbot.
He began life as a soldier of fortune and courtier, went to Scotland with Mary
Stuart, travelled to Spain, Portugal, Italy and the British Isles and even to Africa.
Wild adventures brought him into contact with the great and famous in an era
rich in scandal. After fighting at Jarnac in 1569, he withdrew to his abbey and
began his famous chronicles. He returned to court as chamberlain to Charles IX.
In 1584 a fall from his horse crippled him, he then retreated from the restless and
impetuous Valois to the peace of his monastery to finish his chronicles. Famous
for his *Les Vies des Hommes Illustres et Grands Capitaines* (Lives of Illustrious Men
and Great Leaders), he was a witty and sometimes cynical historian.

drawings et of the artist and medium
Fernand Desmoulin (1853–1914).

Du Creusé au Construit (Troglodyte tour)

Boulevard Charlemagne (behind Abbey)
&. ©*Open 10am–6pm.* ©*Closed Jan
and 25 Dec.* ⌖€4.50. ℘05 53 05 80 63.
The fountain of this rock was originally
a place of pagan worship. The hermits
who converted it to a Christian place
of worship were succeeded by monks
who initially occupied the caves in the
rock face. Later they used the caves as
outbuildings and as refuges in the 11C,
12C, 14C and 17C when the abbey buildings came under attack. The tour shows
the monks' calefactory (heated sitting
room) and the lavacrum (bath house),
the remains of the abbey mill and the
troglodyte dovecote.

Pont Coudé

Boulevard Charlemagne.
Walk through the gardens adorned
by the Fontaine Médicis towards the
Renaissance house featuring mullioned
windows.
A 16C elbow bridge with asymmetrical
arches gives access to the **Jardins des
Moines** (Monks' Gardens).

"VENICE OF THE PERIGORD"

On leaving the Jardins des Moines, cross
the bridge to reach quai Bertin where
the old houses with their flower-covered
balconies and trellises are reflected in
the tranquil mirror of water.

Follow the numbered panels marking
the tour of the town and providing information about the different architectural
styles (*a map is available at the Tourist
Office*).

🚗 DRIVING TOUR

1 LE PÉRIGORD VERT

80km/49.7mi. Allow 1 day. &*See route 1
on region map pp174–175.*

▷ Leave Brantôme E on D 78.

Water is omnipresent in this area, filter-
ing through a dense system of streams,
replenishing lakes filled with carp and
maintaining the humidity of the woods.

Château de Lasfond à la Chapelle-Faucher

Overlooking the Côle from its cliffside,
this castle has retained its curtain wall
and postern gate. The 15C keep is
crowned with a machicolated watch-
path. The lovely stables surrounding the
courtyard were added in the 17C. An 18C
house was built adjacent to the castle.
This place has a tragic history: it was devastated by Edward, the Black Prince (the
son of Edward III) in the 14C; burned in
the 16C along with 260 Catholic villagers
by the admiral of Coligny, the Protestant leader; besieged by the royal troops
during the Fronde; and again burned in
1916 by a fire caused by lightning!

▷ Continue along D 78.

Just after St-Pierre-de-Côle you'll see the silhouettes of the two towers of the 11C and 15C **château de Bruzac** standing out against the hillside on the left side of the road. Its towers were not ruined by war, but rather neglect; they are being restored and can be visited (*contact the Tourist Office of Saint-Jean-de-Côle*).

▷ Continue along D 78 and turn left after 6 km/3.7mi.

St-Jean-de-Côle★
See ST-JEAN-DE-CÔLE.

▷ Return on D 78; turn left on D 707.

Thiviers
This busy little town is known for its markets and fairs. The **Musée du Foie Gras** (*opening times vary; €5. 05 53 55 12 50. www.tourisme-perigordgourmand.com*), is to the right of the tourist office. Thiviers is one of the main production areas.

▷ Leave Thiviers to the NE towards St-Martin-de-Fressengeas to come back to the D 707. After 3km/1.8mi, turn left on D 82. Follow this road for 3km/1.8mi, then turn left to access the Grotte de Villars 1km/0.06mi further along.

🏊 Grotte de Villars★★
16km/10mi NE; 4km/2.5mi beyond Puyguilhem. Open Apr–Jun and Sept 10am–noon, 2–7pm; Jul–Aug 10am–7.30pm; Oct–mid-Nov 2–6pm. €8. 05 53 54 82 36. www.grotte-villars.com.
The tour follows galleries linking several chambers dug out by an underground river. Among the most remarkable formations are yellow and ochre draperies (up to 6m long), two small rimstone pools, and very finely-wrought stalactites hanging from the ceiling. Halfway through the tour, a sound and light show provides a spectacular overview of the main stages which led to the formation of the cave.

▷ Return along D 82 and at Villars, turn right after the church.

Château de Puyguilhem★
Open May–Aug 10am–12.30pm, 2–6.30pm; rest of year daily except Mon–Tue. €5.50. 05 53 54 82 18.
This 16C château is typical of those built in and around the Loire valley in the days of François I. The towers, balustrades, sculpted chimneys and mullioned windows create a graceful exterior impression. Inside, the **chimney-pieces★** are particularly impressive.

▷ On the way out of the village, turn right on D 3; take the first left (D 98).

Abbaye de Boschaud
This 12C Cistercian abbey takes its name from the woody valley that surrounds it: *bosco cavo* is Occitan for "hollow wood". Devastated during the Hundred Years' War and the Wars of Religion, its ruins were given French National Heritage protection in the 1950s. The church is built in a simple style and is the only known example of a Cistercian church that had a nave vaulted in a succession of cupolas, now missing.

▷ Return along D 98 and follow this road beyond Quinsac. Turn left at St-Crépin-de-Richemont.

Château de Richemont
Guided visit (45min) mid-Jul–end Aug, 10am–noon, 2–6pm. €5. 05 53 05 72 81.
At the end of a shady lane, this building features two keeps. Built by Brantôme in the 16C, it remained in the writer's family while he himself was buried in the funeral chapel. His bedchamber on the first floor is adorned with woodwork. The D 939 leads back to Brantôme.

Ribérac

Near the *département* of Charente, Ribérac is an agricultural meeting place where farm products are exchanged all year round in large markets. This 1 000-year-old town enjoys a large number of festivals and exhibitions.

VISIT
Collégiale N.-D. de Ribérac

The former chapel of the Ribérac castle, which was destroyed during the French Revolution, the Notre-Dame collegiate church was the burying grounds for local noblemen before being seriously damaged in the Wars of Religion. The 19C renovation has brought its beauty back, and it is now used for exhibitions and concerts.

Église de Faye

2 km/1.2mi NW on D 20.
This church is dedicated to St Peter and features a sculpted wooden altar. The **tympanum**, showing Christ being worshipped by two angels, is unique in the Périgord.

🚗 DRIVING TOUR

2 LE VAL DE DRONNE

65km/40mi. Allow half a day. 🧭 *See route 2 on region map pp174–175.*

▶ Leave Ribérac SZ on D 709.

This is the last Occitan stronghold when travelling north. The countryside is wide open here and there is a concentration of domed Romanesque churches.

St-Martin-de-Ribérac

This 12C Romanesque church features two domes. Their vaults were elevated in the 19C.

▶ Leave St-Martin NE and take a right on D 710 to reach Bigoussies.

- ▶ **Population:** 4 090.
- 🚗 **Michelin Map:** 329 C-D4.
- 🗺 **Info:** Pl. du Gén.-de-Gaulle, 24600 Ribérac. ☏05 53 90 03 10. www.riberac-tourisme.com.
- ▶ **Location:** 38km/23.6mi SW of Brantôme, 17 km/10.5mi E of Aubeterre-sur-Dronne, on the western end of D 710.
- 👪 **Kids:** Paradou leisure park.
- 🕐 **Timing:** The busy Fri morning market. On other days, 1hr for the town.
- 😊 **Don't Miss:** The collegiate church; the domed roman churches; the frescoes at St-Méard.

St-Méard-de-Dronne

15C frescoes were discovered in this Romanesque church under the 19C layer of lime, and it appears that the entire interior was once painted. Take the small staircase from the balustrade to enjoy the naïve images of the devil, a burning sinner, and Adam and Eve.

👪 Moulin de la Pauze★

🕐 *Guided tour Jul–mid-Sep, 3pm.* ☞€8 (children 6–16, €5). ☏05 53 90 30 01. www.moulindelapauze.fr.
This centuries-old flour mill was recently converted into a power station. However, it remains a living museum of flour and bread. Learn about the miller's complex work and attend bread workshops. In the village near the church, an eco-museum displays farming implements.

▶ Take D 104 across the Dronne.

Villetoureix

On the banks of the Dronne, **Manoir de la Rigale** includes a Gallo-Roman tower, the centre of a former temple cella. The Romanesque church in the village is dedicated to St Martin of Tours.

▶ Continue along D 709 which cuts across D 708.

Allemans

Behind a 15C manor house, **Église St-Pierre**, a lovely Romanesque building that has been modified over the centuries, features a unique nave with two cupolas. Admire its chevet.

▶ Leave Allemans SW on the little road giving a scenic view of the Dronne valley. Cross the river at Bourg-du-Bost.

Aubeterre-sur-Dronne★★
See AUBETERRE-SUR-DRONNE.

▶ Leave Aubeterre SW on D 17.

St-Aulaye

Ste-Eulalie is the feminine version of St-Aulaye. The **Ste-Eulalie church** used to be crowned by a cupola that has been replaced by a ribbed vault.
At the **Écomusée du Cognac, du Pineau et du Vin**, discover the local beverages (○*open Jul–Aug daily except Mon, 10am–noon, 4–6pm.* €2.50 *(children under 12, €0.50).* 05 53 90 81 33).

▶ Leave St-Aulaye on D 5 towards Ribérac.

St-Privat-des-Prés

In the 12C, this beautiful Romanesque **church★** was dependent on a Benedictine priory of the Aurillac abbey, which explains the Saintonge style of its western façade. Craftsmen's workshops, an antique grocery and a turn-of-the-century school are examples of displays at the **Musée de l'Outil et de la Vie au Village**. There is also a collection of **scale models★** of French monuments (○*open Jul–Aug daily except Mon, 5–6pm.* €2.50€ *(child 1€);* 05 53 91 22 87. www.saintprivatdespres.fr).

▶ Leave St-Privat to the NE.

Cumond

In this pretty hamlet, only a few steps away from a large dovecote, you'll see a domed 12C church dedicated to St Antoine; admire its entryway, decorated with nine arch mouldings.

▶ Continue NE past a cemetery, then take a right on D 43.

Vanxains

This village boasts pretty 16C and 18C houses. Return to D 708 and right to return to Ribérac.

Aubeterre-sur-Dronne★★

Located halfway between the Charente and the Aquitaine, the village of Aubeterre overlooks the Dronne valley amid a landscape of verdant pastureland. With its picturesque, steep, narrow streets and houses adorned with wooden balconies, it is one of the prettiest villages in the area. It takes its name from the local white chalk (*alba terra* in Latin, which translates as "white land"). It is centred around place Travieux, and the bust in honour of Ludovic Travieux. This native of Aubeterre founded the League for the Defence of Human Rights.

▶ **Population:** 418.
- **Michelin Map:** 324: L-8.
- **Info:** 8 Place du Champ de Foire 16390 Aubeterre sur Dronne. 05 45 98 57 18. www.sudcharentetourisme.fr.
- **Location:** 53km/33mi W of Périgueux via D 710/D 20.
- **Parking:** Free parking in pl. du Champ de Foire.
- **Don't Miss:** Aubeterre is famous for its impressive churches.
- **Kids:** A canoe trip down the Dronne.
- **Timing:** 3hr for the village and at least 1hr for the surrounding area.

MONOLITHIC CHURCH★★

*From place Travieux go down rue
St Jean; the church is below the castle.*
🕐*Open daily, 9.30am–12.30pm, 2–6pm.
(Jun–Sept till 7pm).* 🕐*Closed 25 Dec and
1 Jan.* 👁€5. ✆*05 45 98 65 06.
www.aubeterresurdronne.com.*

This church is a rare example of a building hewn from a single block of rock. A corridor bordered with niches leads to a vast cavity cut into the rock.

A baptismal font from the 5C or 6C, sculpted in the shape of a Greek cross, testifies to the presence of a primitive church and evokes the practice of baptism by total immersion. The crypt probably hosted followers of Mithras, a god worshipped by members of a mysterious cult which was one of early Christianity's most serious rivals. The present church was probably founded in the 12C to house relics brought back from the Holy Sepulchre in Jerusalem. During the Revolution, the church was used as a saltpetre works and later as the local cemetery.

The 20m-high nave is flanked by a single aisle where a small spring venerated by early pilgrims still filters. The apse surrounds a monolithic Romanesque monument, carved from a block left in place when the church was hollowed out. In it, a shrine holds the relics of the Holy Sepulchre.

At the other end of the nave is a primitive 6C chapel, transformed into a necropolis in the 12C after work on the church was completed.

Église St-Jacques

This church, located in the upper town, features a lovely Romanesque façade sculpted with geometric patterns of Arabic inspiration. Below, there is a 16C machicolated tower.

Ancien Couvent des Minimes

This monastery was founded in 1617. You may access the chapel and charming cloister.

Vendoire

Between the Périgord and the Angoumois, the Lizonne is the natural barrier that separates what is considered the north of France from the south. On the Périgord side, Occitan is spoken with the singsong accent associated with southern speakers. On the Angoumois side, you'll hear the northern accent and the *langue d'oïl*. In the centre is the sleepy settlement of Vendoire.

SIGHTS
Village

You'll see a castle with a semicircular arch pediment built under Louis XVI. To the east, the little Romanesque church has retained its polygonal apse. The first level of the church's Saintonge-style arcatures are still visible on its western façade, although it is damaged.

▶ **Population:** 152.
◔ **Michelin Map:** 329 C3.
🛈 **Info:** Av. d'Aquitaine, 24320 Verteillac. ✆05 53 90 37 78 .
◐ **Location:** 21km/12mi N of Ribérac on D 708 then D 101.
👪 **Kids:** The ecomuseum is great for kids and includes a restaurant to refresh the weary ones.
🕐 **Timing:** 2hr 30min for the town and ecomuseum.

👪 Maison des Tourbières

3km/1.8mi W of Vendoire along the banks of the Lizonne. 🕐*Open Jul–Aug daily except Mon, 10am–6pm.* 👁€5. ✆*05 53 90 79 56.*

Peat forms through the incomplete breakdown of plant material when the soil contains too little oxygen to allow microorganisms to fully decompose organic matter. Through this slow decomposition, peat bogs can preserve fossils of extinct plants for long periods of time. During the Quaternary Period, vast peat bogs formed at the bottom of the valley on the Lizonne flood plain. 65ha/160 acres are left, of which approximately 30ha/74 acres, 4m deep, have been put to use to help you discover this unique ecosystem. You may observe the fauna and flora using the informative booklet sold on site; or enjoy a boat trip on the lake system.

The displays inside the building allow you to delve further into the subject and learn why peat was used as a fuel for thousands of years, until 1950.

🚗 DRIVING TOUR

3 LE VAL DE DRONNE

45km/27.9mi. Allow half a day. ♿See route 3 on region map pp174–175.

The craggy territroty of "Bourzac" country between Fontaine and St-Paul-Lizonne boasts rich farmlands and lovely, tranquil villages grouped around Romanesque churches, often fortified.

▷ Leave Vendoire S on D 102. On the way out of the village, turn right.

Nanteuil-Auriac-de-Bourzac

This church was built over several periods. Its Roman origins can be seen in the apse with its lovely capitals and in the domed choir. A belltower and raised apse were then added. The entryway is Renaissance.

▷ Leave Nanteuil SW on D 100. After 5 km/3mi, turn left on D 97.

Bouteilles-St-Sébastien

The church of this village is a perfect example of the wave of modifications that would alter a large number of Roman buildings in the region during the Hundred Years War. Here, the apse was raised to form a curious sort of keep with the belltower.

▷ Make a U-turn and leave the D 97 left, 2 km/1.2mi after leaving Bouteilles.

St-Paul-Lizonne

The 17C **painted ceiling★** and altarpiece in this fortified church are intact (*🕐request visit at the town hall Mon–Thu 3–6pm; ⬤no charge. ✆05 53 91 66 15*).

▷ Leave St-Paul S and go left on D 97E.

Lusignac

This village built along a crest features old houses and a 15C and 17C manor. The 15C fortified church is based on a 12C domed nave and includes a 17C sculpted wooden altarpiece.

▷ Leave Lusignac N towards Verteillac, and follow D 97E.

St-Martial-Viveyrol

The austere appearance of this Romanesque church with its two domes and belltower keep is emphasised by its narrow openings, but the defence chamber above the vaults has large openings. The four holes you can see around each of these allowed the guardians to install the props of an overhanging plank.

▷ Continue along D 97.

Cherval

This village boasts one of the prettiest **domed churches** of the region. Four successive cupolas – three on the nave and one on the choir – are supported by large arches that follow the curve of the pendentives. The choir vault is adorned with a crown sculpted into diamond tips.

▷ Leave Cherval N on D 2E, then turn left on D 100 towards Nanteuil. After 2km/1.2mi, turn right.

Champagne-et-Fontaine

Enter this fortified church with its 16C ribbed vault over a double nave through an entryway with compound arch mouldings. Notice also in the village the lovely houses and the 16C Chaumont manor.

Château de Mareuil

Moats, crenels, wide towers, a stone bridge, large openings and a Gothic chapel: a diverse collection of architecture from various periods – from medieval times to the Renaissance – is found at the defensive fortress of Mareuil. It has overlooked the comings and goings between Périgueux and Angoulême for several hundred years.

VISIT

Guided tour Jul–Aug 10.30am–noon, 2.30–6pm; rest of year 10.30am–noon, 2.30–5pm except Sun am. Closed Mar. €7. ℘05 53 60 46 18.

In the 15C, Geoffroi de Mareuil rebuilt his ancestor's castle to bring it up to date with the expectations of his time. However, a large number of defensive elements remain: the moats, fortification wall and two cylindrical towers co-exist with the Renaissance flourishes. Mareuil was the centre of one of the four baronies of the Périgord, which explains the defensive character of the fortress.

There is a flamboyant Gothic **chapel** in the left tower. Beyond the little castle that guards acces to the fortress, a central buiding is built at right angles to a former keep. When you climb the spiral staircase inside, you can visit the apartments such as the **council chamber** with its 15C cobblestone floor. In another room dedicated to the First Empire, the furnishings and documents tell the story of **Marshal Lannes**, Duke of Montebello and ancestor of the current owners.

▶ **Population:** 1 125.
Michelin Map: 329 D3.
Info: 12 r. Pierre-Degail, 24340 Mareuil. ℘05 53 05 62 41. www.mareuil-en-perigord.fr.
Location: At the intersection of the D 708 and D 939 on the Périgueux –Angoulême road, 21km/13mi from Brantôme.
Timing: Allow 1hr 15min.
Don't Miss: A full tour of the château and its council chamber.

Château de Mareuil

© Patrick Escudero / hemis.fr

What's in a name?

The name Mareuil is of Gaulish origin (Gaulish being the language spoken in this region before the Roman conquest). *Maro-* meaning "large", and *-ialo*, meaning "open space", became "Mareuil" in French.

Bourdeilles★

The impressive castle of Bourdeilles, with the village clustered below, stands imperiously above the River Dronne. It was here that the chronicler, Brantôme, was born in 1540.

▶ **Population:** 769.
🖕 **Michelin Map:** 329: E-4.
🚺 **Info:** Pl. des Tilleuls, 24310 Bourdeilles.
    𝓟05 53 03 42 96. www.bourdeilles.com.
▶ **Location:** On the River Dronne, 9.2km/5.7mi SW of Brantôme.
👁 **Don't Miss:** The village's château.
🕐 **Timing:** Allow 1hr for the château and half a day for the driving tour.

A BIT OF HISTORY

A coveted spot – In 1259 St Louis ceded Périgord and Bourdeilles, his most important barony, to the English. This incredible desertion made the country rise in revolt and divided the Bourdeille family: the elder branch supported the Plantagenets and the Maumonts, the younger branch, the Capetians. Later, after plots and lawsuits, Géraud de Maumont seized the castle of his forebears, urged on by King Philip the Fair, to whom de Maumont was Counselor. He proceeded to turn it into a fortress. Then, to show his strength in the Périgord, Philip the Fair set up a strong garrison within the fief of his enemies, the English.

The Renaissance touch – Credit for the plans for the 16C château goes to Jacquette de Montbron, wife of André de Bourdeille and sister-in-law to Pierre de Brantôme, with her active and informed interest in geometry and architecture. Building was started in haste at the promise of a visit by Catherine de Medici, but was abandoned when the visit was cancelled.

CHÂTEAU★

🕐*Open mid-Feb–Mar (school holidays) and Nov–Dec, daily except Mon 10am–12.30pm, 2–5pm; Apr–Oct 10am–1pm, 2–6pm.* 🕐*Closed Jan, Tue in Jul–Aug and 25 Dec.* ✆€8. 𝓟05 53 03 73 36. www.semitour.com.

Cross the first fortified curtain wall, pass under the watch-path to get inside the second wall and enter the outer courtyard, in which there is a fine cedar tree. The 13C **castle**, built by Géraud de Maumont, is an austere building surrounded by a quadrangular curtain wall. Inside the main building, exhibitions are held in a great hall. An early 14C high keep towers above it fom its 35m of height. From the upper platform there is a good overall view of the castle and a sweeping view of the Dronne River.

The sober, elegant 16C **château** houses remarkable **furnishings★★** collected by two patrons who donated their collection to the Dordogne *département*. Don't miss the **salon doré★★**, a sumptuously decorated room built to accommodate Catherine de Medici; or the dining hall with its 16C carved **chimneypiece★★★**. From the watch-path there is a lovely **view★** of the castle and its setting, a Gothic bridge with cutwaters and an attractive 17C seigneurial mill.

Salon doré, Château de Bourdeilles

© A.J. Cassaigne / Photononstop / Tips Images

🚗 DRIVING TOUR

④ VALLÉE DE LA DRONNE
65km/40mi. Allow half a day. ⓘSee route 4 on region map pp174–175.

▷ Leave Bourdeilles W on the D 78.

Lisle
This 14C bastide is organised around the central *halle*. The ruins of an unfinished fortress are next to the St-Martin church, fortified during the Wars of Religion.

▷ Continue along D 78, then take D 710 towards Ribérac. After 1km/0.6mi, turn right to cross the Dronne River.

Montagrier
All that remains of Église Ste-Madeleine is the 12C transept. Beneath the village lies a multitude of underground caves. A 12C water mill was converted into an electric power station between 1910 and 1930 and is now **La Maison de la Dronne et du Patrimoine Rural**, with activities and exhibitions (ⓘ*phone for opening times and tour information; boat rental; ☏05 53 90 01 33*).

▷ Continue to the village. Leave Montagrier N on D 103.

Grand-Brassac
The fortified church of St-Pierre-et-St-Paul was a refuge for the villagers in the 13C. The northern **Romanesque portal★** was reworked and sculptures were added. Above an arch, sculpted ornaments include small statues that had formerly belonged to a Magi adoration scene. Five statues (Jesus shown between St John and Mary, and lower down St Peter and St Paul) are arranged under a porch roof.

▷ Leave Grand-Brassac W on D 1. Turn right at Flayac onto D 99.

La Tour-Blanche
The former castellany of the Counts of Angoulême, this village has retained lovely old houses with Renaissance windows. To the southeast, you can see the ruins of the dungeon of a 13C castle on a built-up motte.

▷ Leave La Tour-Blanche to the E.

Cercles
All that is left of the former Roman priory is the St-Cybard church with its cruciform shape. The Gothic portal under the crenulated bell wall has retained six finely sculpted capitals.

▷ Leave Cercles to the N and take a right on D 84.

Léguillac-de-Cercles
This village is part of the Parc Naturel Régional Périgord-Limousin. Reworked and fortified, the Romanesque church features a vaulted nave with cupolas on pendentives.
To the south along the D 93 you'll notice two contrasting landscapes: to the right, the road runs along the St-James Forest, where you can ramble in search of dolmens and tumuli. To the left, the Breuil rocks dominate the landscape, surrounded by sparse vegetation.

▷ Leave Léguillac S on D 93. At Le Breuil, turn right towards Lignères. At St-Vivien, D 93 to Paussac-et-St-Vivien.

Paussac-et-St-Vivien
This village boasts several 16C houses and a 13C–15C fortified church. The church's southern façade is decorated with arcades. Inside, note the capitals decorated in low relief with naïve carvings, a large Christ in multicoloured wood and a Louis XV-style pulpit.

▷ Leave Paussac to the E.

Boulouneix
A Romanesque chapel with a domed belltower stands in a cemetery. In the chancel, 17C murals represent Mary Magdalene and St Jerome.
Just off Boulouneix, the hamlet of Belaygue includes the peaceful ruins of a little priory. The winding road to Bourdeilles passes through a verdant area near the rock called **Forge du Diable**.

Nontron

This town, known for its manufacture of knives and Hermès scarves, is committed to sustainable development and the conservation of rural heritage.

SIGHT
Atelier de Coutellerie Nontronnaise

&. *In the high town. Contact for opening hours.* &05 53 56 01 55. *www.coutellerie-nontronnaise.fr.*
Knives with wooden handles have been manufactured in Nontron since the 15C and the town is locally famous for it. Originally, the region was propitious to this industry because of the area's minerals and forges. In this workshop, large picture windows give you a view of the manufacturing process. Wall panels explain the various steps of production. Another local speciality, the miniature knife, is also made here: 12 per walnut or hazelnut, no less!

🚗 DRIVING TOUR

5 AT THE GATEWAY TO THE ANGOUMOIS

80km/49.7mi. Allow 1 day. &. *See route 5 on region map pp174–175. This tour takes place within the **Parc Naturel Régional Périgord-Limousin** and allows you to discover a part of it.*

▶ Leave Nontron E on D 707 to St-Pardoux-la-Rivière.

St-Pardoux-la-Rivière

There is a beautiful 17C and 18C church at the entrance to the village. On the former railroad that connected Nontron to Thiviers, a **greenway** has been set up. This makes for 16km/9.9mi to enjoy on foot, bike or horse, and stop over in the villages, including St-Jean-de-Côle (&. *see p191*).

▶ From St-Pardoux-la-Rivière, travel N on D 83 to Champs-Romain. Park near the cemetery.

▶ **Population:** 3 351.
&. **Michelin Map:** 329 E-F2.
🛈 **Info:** 3 av. du Gén.-Leclerc, Nontron. &05 53 56 25 50. www.nontron.fr.
▶ **Location:** At the northern tip of the Dordogne, Nontron is located along D 675, 20km/12mi north of Brantôme.
👪 **Kids:** St-Estèphe offers a pleasant ramble and swimming. The CPIE of Varaignes organises various excursions and workshops. &05 53 56 23 66. www.cpie-perigordlimousin.org.

Saut du Chalard

45min round trip on foot. A visitor's booklet is available from the St-Pardoux-la-Rivière information centre (&05 53 56 79 30). Under the pine trees, a marked trail leads to a little platform overlooking the Dronne River.

▶ Continue following D 83 (to the right). After 2.5km/1.5mi, take the D 79 to the right, then turn left on D 96 towards Abjat-sur-Bandiat. Turn left at Fargeas.

Étang de St-Estèphe

This 30ha/74-acre lake, listed as a fragile natural area, offers an exceptional diversity of fauna and flora. It is also a pleasant leisure centre, with a lifeguard on duty in Jul and Aug.

▶ Continue along the same road to the car park.

👪 Roc Branlant

To listen to the audio terminals, a pass is available at the tourist information centre in Piégut-Pluviers (&05 53 60 74 75 or www.perigordverttourisme.com). Water runs along the left bank of the stream to where this "shaking rock" is located. The flow pushes it back and forth on a north–south axis. Nature

lovers will push on to the pile of rocks called **Chapelet du Diable** (The Devil's Rosary). The nearby path leads to a reach where you can follow an ethnobotanical trail.

▷ Take D 88 left at St-Estèphe towards Nontron.

Roc Poperdu

Not far from the intersection of D 3 and D 675, this is a strange arrangement of granite blocks that is hard to see for all the plants. Make a U-turn and follow D 3.

Le Bourdeix

The church houses surprising 15C and 16C **frescoes**: white skulls on a black background, meant to stave off the plague and other maledictions. A 12C tower stands before the church.
Nearby, you can visit **Moulin Pinard**, an authentic medieval mill that still produces flour and walnut oil.

▷ Leave Le Bourdeix N on D 3.

Forges d'Étouars

🚶 1hr 30min. Private property; do not leave the path.
At the lowermost end of the hamlet, a string of ponds accompanied by interesting signposts leads to former forges. For two centuries, these produced the pig iron used in the manufacture of cannon for the royal navy in the shipyards of Rochefort (Charente-Maritime).

▷ Go back towards Bourdeix and, before the village, turn left towards Verger, then continue along the D 91E3.

Piégut-Pluviers

The high silhouette of a 23m-high round keep overlooks this village; this is all that is left of a castle destroyed in 1199 by Richard the Lionheart. The Wednesday morning **market** in this little village is one of the largest in the Périgord and has been held since 1642.

▷ Leave Piégut NW on D 91. Turn right on D 91E2 which becomes D 3.

Bussière-Badil

At the gateway to the Angoumois, this is an isolated village. Still, it's worth coming to admire the **church of Notre-Dame★**, an 11C abbey. This Romanesque building is reminiscent of the Cistercian church of Cadouin in the Périgord Noir. The rose colour of the stone brings cheer to a sober façade that opens through a portal with triple arch moulding. Influences from the Limousin are manifest in the octagonal bell wall, while the Sainteonge style is visible on the western façade. Two sentry boxes are all that remains of the 15C defence system. Inside the church, 28 capitals tell a biblical story in the triple nave.

▷ Leave Bussière-Badil W to get back on D 91.

Varaignes

Atelier-Musée des Tisserands et de la Charentaise du Haut-Périgord Limousin

🚶 Guided visits (1hr): Jul–Aug 10am–noon, 2.30–6.30pm (Sun 2.30–6.30pm); Apr–Jun and Sept–Oct 2–5pm.
☎ 05 53 56 35 76.
This museum, located in the former 13C–15C and Renaissance castle of the dukes of Cars, retraces the local history of textiles through five workshops: knitting; spinning; combing of hemp and rope; weaving and feltmaking; and slipper manufacture.
After visiting a peasant interior, discover the original decorative elements of the castle, such as fireplaces, windows and spiral staircases. Note the collection of looms.

≗ Lud'eau Vive

Discover the secrets of hydropower at this unique site on the banks of the Crochet. The wheels, gears and moving models describe the use of water energy through the centuries. An educational visit for the whole family amidst 200 plant species.

▷ Leave Varaignes to the SE. Cross D 75 and continue along D 92.

La Chapelle-St-Robert

Around 1050, Robert de Turlande, founder and first abbot of La Chaise-Dieu, sent his disciple Raoul Passeron to found a priory here. Although the monastic buildings no longer exist, the church still stands, built in chalky grey local stone. The portal is adorned with primitive capitals. Inside, note the 11C frescoes above the baptismal fonts.

▶ Leave La Chapelle-St-Robert SE to get back on D 93 (left).

Javerlhac

The 12C and 15C **church** features two asymmetric barrel-vaulted naves. In the southern wall is a funerary recess containing two worn recumbent figures. Next to the church stands a lovely 15C **castle** that belonged to Aymeric Vigier and Louis de Rochechouart.

▶ Leave Javerlhac NE on D 93.

Teyjat

Grotte de la Mairie was discovered in 1880, with its large deposit of the Upper Magdalenian Period (13 000 to 10 000 years). In 1903, D Peyrony and P Bourrinet discovered the remarkable **engravings** on large stalagmitic surfaces (note the **wild oxen★**, portrayed with vigour and precision). The mix of cold climate fauna (reindeer, horses and bison) and temperate fauna (deer) attests to the period's climate warming. This discovery was an important step in the science of prehistory: the engraved stones were found with flint and animal bones that were easy to date, proving that the works previously discovered at Font-de-Gaume and Combarelles date from the Palaeolithic Era.

▶ Come back to Javerlhac and take a left on D 75 to come back to Nontron.

Jumilhac-le-Grand

Like a fairytale castle, Jumilhac reaches to the sky with its pointy roof. This elegant exterior, adorned with finials, has braved the centuries, frost and storms, and lends an unexpected lightness to the whole structure. You'd expect to find some princess or treasure here... And you just might.

VISIT
Château

🕐 *Jun–Sept 10am–7pm.* ⊚ €7.
℘06 09 61 78 40. www.jumilhac.net.
Exterior – The medieval structure and the defensive situation of the castle are obvious. The castle's originality is in its renovation: aside from the addition of a few windows and the restructuring of a floor that was in ruins, the 13C–15C towers and watch-paths were simply crowned with steep roofs. Through this cunning innovation, Antoine Chapelle,

▶ **Population:** 1,214.
⚲ **Michelin Map:** Michelin Map 329 H-3.
🛈 **Info:** Pl. du Château, 24630 Jumilhac-le-Grand. ℘05 53 52 55 43. www.pays-jumilhac.fr.
▶ **Location:** 45km/27.9mi NE of Brantôme by way of Thiviers and 33km/20.5mi N of Hautefort.
🕐 **Timing:** Request a tour of the watch-path (if you aren't afraid of heights) and of the garden.
👁 **Don't Miss:** The view from the garden path facing the castle; the view from the garden and from D 78.

a forge master made noble by Henri IV, brought this castle up to date with his times – and with his image – at the least possible expense. He adorned the rooftops with interesting iron **finials** decorated with human and fanciful figurines according to a complex alchemic symbolism.

Interior – The two large wings that surround the courtyard were built in the 17C in the same materials as the main building. The right wing features a large staircase that leads to a few rooms that you can visit. Notice the sculpted wooden Louis XIII fireplace with allegorical statues in the immense panelled **sitting room** with parquet floors. Another interesting feature is the chamber called "de la Fileuse" (the spinner's). The naïve decorations of painted animals, angels and leaves upon its thick walls are attributed to Louise de Hautefort. The watchpath (⊘*beware of uneven surface and sharp drop to the side*) that runs under the **roofs★** gives the best view of the finials.

The French-style **hanging gardens** are landscaped around a theme of gold and alchemy. The church on the left, overlooking the castle from its octagonal bell wall, is its chapel. It contains the relic of St Eusice.

Galerie de l'Or

Pl. du Château. ◷*Phone for opening times.* ℘*05 53 52 55 43.*

Although it does not offer a recipe for the philosopher's stone, this museum recounts the efforts made to preserve the Gallo-Roman mines of Fouilloux. It recounts the history of gold prospection through the centuries, describes the steps of extraction and handling of the precious metal and presents certain uses, such as gilding, jewellery and coins.

⊘*During the season, a gold panning workshop takes place on the banks of the Isle River twice a week (*⊜€*18, child* €*15, information at the tourist office).*

Excideuil

Not far from the gorges of the Auvézère and Loue rivers, the village of Excideuil spreads below its imposing hillside fortress. The castle functioned as a watchtower over the Limousin road. As this is the tip of the Périgord Vert, the Corrèze and Périgord Noir are nearby. In this environment featuring both shale and calcareous rock, where torrential rivers meet underground waterways, you can discover the hidden vestiges of a rich industrial past while enjoying a ramble. This is a rural community which has embraced contemporary art; public areas and natural spaces around town are the canvas for various expressions of the "Excit'œil" project.

VISIT
Château

The viscounts of Limoges, aware of the strategic situation of Excideuil, transferred their court here to build

▶ **Population:** 1 226.
◔ **Michelin Map:** 329 H3-4.
🄸 **Info:** Pl. du Château, 24160 Excideuil. ℘05 53 52 29 79. www.naturellement perigord. fr. Self-guided and guided (in French) walking tours arranged.
◓ **Location:** Excideuil is 19km/12mi SE of Thiviers where the D 76 and D 705 meet.
⊘ **Don't Miss:** The fortress; the Vaux paper mill; the Savignac forge.
◕ **Timing:** Allow 1hr for the town and half a day for the surroundings.

one of the most powerful fortresses of the region. The troubadour Girault de Borneilh became the official poet of this refined world which suffered in the Hundred Years War. At the end of the 16C, it fell to the Tallayrand family,

189

who brought the furniture, fireplaces and statues to its Chalais residence and abandoned the site. The only 12C vestiges are two keeps linked by a curtain wall. The main building and smaller entry castle are 16C and 17C.

From here, go up the rue des Cendres (named for the 15C fire that ravaged the town) to place Bugeaud. On the left you will see the consulate of Excideuil, the seat of municipal magistrates, and nearby the 1913 *halle*, built from elements of the 1870 *halle*.

In the village, 19 **benches** are engraved with poems that tell of inhabitants of the village in an imitation of the troubadour style.

Église St-Thomas

This church was built on the ruins of a Benedictine priory around which the town took shape. On its western façade, notice the blind arcade, a vestige of the primitive Roman church. The building underwent 15C alterations, including the porch. Note the 17C gilded woodwork altarpiece in the Ste-Constance chapel.

🚗 DRIVING TOUR

⑥ THE AUVÉZÈRE VALLEY

55km/34mi. Allow 1 day. ⓧ*See route 6 on region map pp174–175.*

▷ Leave Excideuil NE on D 705, then take the D 4 that cuts across D 704.

Payzac

Located along the Auvézère gorges, the Payzac church, which was modified in the 17C, features a square Romanesque belltower. Inside, note the 16C Pieta.

♟️ **Papeterie de Vaux**★★ – ⓖ. *4 km/ 2.4mi away. Leave Payzac and take a right on D 80.* ⓞ*Open May–Oct daily except Mon 10am–12.30pm, 2.30–6.30pm (Sun*

2.30–6.30pm). €*5 (children aged 10–15,* €*3).* ☏*05 53 62 50 06. www.ecomusees-delauvezere.fr.* This paper mill was built in 1861 where the forges once stood along the Belles Dames stream. Up to 1968, it was still producing paper from rye hay for use in wrapping and the food industry. The original machines can be seen here, although they no longer function. You'll participate in the fabrication of paper and discover that it can be made from just about anything… even old jeans.

▷ Come back to Payzac and leave the village S on D 75E.

Forge de Savignac-Lédrier

🔊*Guided tour possible; contact the Papeterie de Vaux.*

During the reign of Louis XIV, this was one of the forges that provided pig iron to the shipyards of Rochefort for the royal marines. The castle overlooking the forge was inhabited by the forge master. The blast furnace built in 1521 forged iron until 1930; it then became a drawing plant to manufacture nails, keys and wires and closed in 1975. The eight stations of the **discovery circuit** offer opportunities to admire the organisation and architecture of the site, currently undergoing restoration.

▷ Continue along the left bank.

👁️*You'll get glimpses of the gorges along the valley to St-Mesmin.*

🔊 The GR 646 leads through the woods from St-Mesmin and offers a **view** of the river. Don't miss the **cascatelle du Saut-Ruban**.

After St-Mesmin, follow the road down (*turn right on the D 72E1 before Génis*) to the 17C Pervendoux mill and bridge.

▷ Turn left on D 4 and follow D 705 back to Excideuil.

Saint-Jean-de-Côle★

A few local businesses and a quartz mine extracting minerals of a rare purity bring this preserved medieval town to life without defacing it. The streets are lined with half-timbered houses of which many have retained their round stones; their roofs converge harmoniously. The square boasts a beautiful church, a *halle*, a castle and a few houses in golden stone that complements the brown hues of their roof tiles. The village takes its name from St John the Baptist: the church posessed the relic of one of the bones from the saint's arm, which was venerated for centuries.

▶ **Population:** 356.
  Michelin Map: 329 F-G3.
  Info: 19 R. du Château.
   ℘05 53 62 14 15.
   www.tourisme-perigord-gourmand.com.
▷ **Location:** St-Jean-de-Côle is just off D 78, located 19km/11.8mi NE of Brantôme. The River Côle crosses it.
  Timing: 1hr.
  Don't miss: Les Floralies in May.

Château de la Marthonie

© Jordi Puig / age fotostock

VISIT
Church

This chapel of the former priory was begun in the 11C. It features a bell tower with a curious shape, a square nave with one bay that is very high for its length, and **sculpted capitals★** in its right chapel and choir. Note the 17C oak woodwork in the choir and stalls. The wooden ceiling above the nave has replaced a collapsed dome, but its pendentives remain. To the right, a chapel includes a funerary recess where Geoffroy de la Marthonie, bishop of Amiens, might be the recumbent figure.

The **priory** *(private property only open for European Heritage Days)* includes a 16C cloister, the ruins of which are visible between the church and the Côle River.

Château de la Marthonie

🔊 *Guided tour (1hr 30min) as part of the village tour; information at the Tourist Office. €3. ℘05 53 62 14 15. www.ville-saint-jean-de-cole.fr.*
This 12C castle was largely destroyed, then rebuilt in the 15C and 16C; a few mullion windows remain from this period. The gallery with its lowered arcades and the interior staircase with its straight bannisters and off-centre or basket-handle arches date from the 17C.

Bridge

Covered with round stones, this bridge, featuring 15C cutwater arches, crosses the Côle and leads to the former priory mill. Follow along the river awhile to appreciate the view of the cloister.

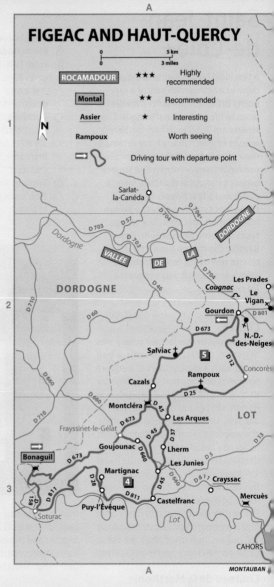

Rocamadour, La Bouriane and the Causses are located just south of the Dordogne valley, between the *départements* of the Cantal and the Dordogne. The region covers the northern Haut Quercy, the fertile Limargue in the east and the Bouriane in the west. In its centre are the limestones plateaux of the Causse de Martel and the Causse de Gramat. The former is a vast, arid, stone-covered plain, bisected by a relatively fertile zone; it is named after the medieval town of Martel. The latter is an extensive area that offers a number of natural sites, such as the Gouffre de Padirac, and the 'Black Madonna' pilgrimage site of Rocamadour, dramatically located on a cliff side.

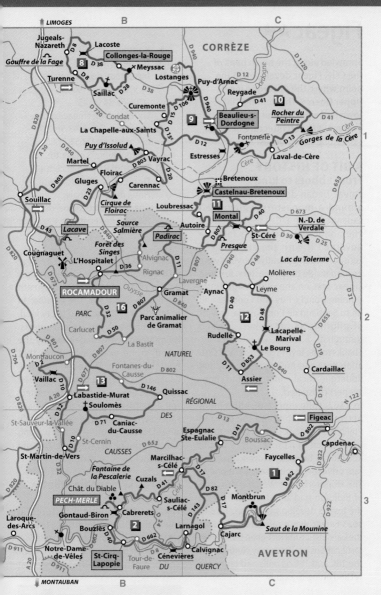

Many visitors put the medieval pilgrimage site of Rocamadour at the top of their places to visit. But the Haut-Quercy is a varied region with much to see. The Gouffre de Padirac, for example, is exceptional – a 33m chasm is descended by stairs or lift and leads to an underground river where a boat trip takes you to the Salle du Grand Dôme. The Martel Causse boasts walnut trees, truffles and lavender.

Highlights

1 Well-preserved medieval quarter of **Figeac** (p194)

2 Spectacular stalactites and stalagmites in the **Grotte de Pech-Merle** (p203)

3 Cute **Collonges-la-Rouge** (p232)

Figeac★★

Sprawled along the north bank of the Célé, Figeac developed at the point where the Auvergne meets Upper Quercy. This commercial town had a prestigious past, as is evident in the architecture of its tall sandstone townhouses.

A BIT OF HISTORY
From abbots to king

Figeac began developing in the 9C around a monastery which itself expanded in the 13C.

The abbot was the town's lord. He governed it with the aid of seven consuls. All administrative services were located inside the monastery. Because Figeac was on the pilgrimage route running from Le Puy and Conques and on to Santiago de Compostela, crowds of pilgrims and travellers flocked through it.

Thanks to the town's geographical situation between Auvergne, Quercy and Rouergue, local craftsmen and shopkeepers prospered.

In 1302, following a disagreement between the abbot and the consuls, Philip the Fair took control of the town, represented by a provost. He won the inhabitants' favour by allowing them the rare privilege of minting royal money.

The Hundred Years War and the Wars of Religion had an adverse effect on the town's development. From 1576 to 1623 Figeac was a safe stronghold for the Calvinists, until Richelieu broke their fortifications up. Prosperity continued in the 18C and 19C as mills and tanneries settled along the canal.

👣 WALKING TOUR

OLD FIGEAC★★

The old quarter, surrounded by boulevards which trace the line of the former moats, has kept its medieval town plan with its narrow, twisting alleys.

The buildings, built in elegant beige sandstone, exemplify the architecture of the 12C, 13C and 14C. Generally

- ▶ **Population:** 9 810.
- ♿ **Michelin Map:** 337: I-4.
- 🏥 **Info:** Hôtel de la Monnaie, pl. Vival, 46102 Figeac. ☎05 65 34 06 25. www.tourism-figeac.com.
- ◐ **Location:** 70km/43.5mi W of Cahors via D 653. Train station 600m S of centre.
- 🅿 **Parking:** Parking in centre.
- ☺ **Don't Miss:** The old town; Hôtel de la Monnaie; Chapelle Notre-Dame-de-Pitié; Pl. des Écritures.

the ground floor was opened by large pointed arches and the first floor had a gallery of arcaded bays. Underneath the flat tiled roof was the *soleilho*, an open attic, which was used to dry food, laundry or even hand-crafted objects. Its openings were separated by the wood, stone or brick columns that held the roof up. The buildings were flanked by corbelled towers and their doorways were elaborately decorated; spiral staircases heralded the Renaissance style. Traditional crafts are still alive in Figeac, as you can see by walking down rue de Colomb, rue Émile-Zola and rue Baduel.

Hôtel de la Monnaie (Mint)★
🏥 *Tourist Office.*

This late 13C building, restored in the early 20C, exemplifies Figeac's secular architecture with its *soleilho*, pointed arches on the ground floor and depressed arched windows that

Figeac
© bobroy20 / Fotolia.com

Jean-François Champollion

Champollion, the outstanding Orientalist whose brilliance enabled Egyptology to make such great strides, was born in Figeac in December 1790. At the beginning of the 19C, Ancient Egyptian civilisation was still a mystery, as hieroglyphics *"sacred carving"* had never before been deciphered.

By the time Champollion was 14, he had a command of Greek, Latin, Hebrew, Arabic, Chaldean and Syrian. After his studies in Paris, he began lecturing in history at Grenoble University at the youthful age of 19.

He set himself the task of deciphering a polished basalt tablet written in three different scripts: Greek, Egyptian hieroglyphics and demotic, a simplified Egyptian script that appeared around 650 BCE. The tablet had been discovered in 1799 by members of Napoleon's expedition to Egypt near Rosetta in the northwest Nile delta, from which it derives its name: the **Rosetta Stone**.

Champollion was not able to carry out his research on the stone itself, which had been seized by the English while at war with France (it is now in the British Museum in London); he had to make do with copies. Drawing on the work of a predecessor, the English physicist Thomas Young (1773–1829), who had succeeded in identifying genders and proper nouns, Champollion gradually unravelled the mystery of hieroglyphics.

In 1826, he founded the Egyptology Museum at the Louvre Palace, Paris, and became its first curator. He left for Egypt on a two-year mission and deciphered many texts while he was there. In 1831, he was appointed professor of Archaeology at the Collège de France. However, he gave only four lectures before dying a year later, worn out by his hard work.

appear either singly or in pairs or groups in the façade. It is interesting to compare the façade of this building, which was rebuilt with the elements of the former consul's house of the same period, with the other buildings' plainer façades. The octagonal stone chimney was characteristic of Figeac construction at one time, but very few examples remain.

The name *Oustal dé lo Mounédo* mistakenly refers to the Royal Mint created in Figeac by Philip the Fair. It has since been established that the stamping workshop was located in another building and that this handsome edifice was the place where money was exchanged.

It now houses the Musée du Vieux Figeac (&see Sights).

▷ Take rue Orthabadial and turn right onto rue Balène.

Rue Balène

At no 7 stands the 14C Palais Balène which houses the community hall. Its medieval fortress-like façade is lightened by an ogive doorway and chapel windows with decorated tracery.

At no 1, the 14C Hôtel de Viguier d'Auglanat, once the home of an influential family, is decorated with a lovely basket-arched doorway and castellated turret.

Rue Gambetta

This is the old town's main street. The half-timbering and decorative brickwork of the houses at nos 25 and 28 have been beautifully restored.

▷ Continue along rue Gambetta and place aux Herbes to place de la Raison.

Église St-Sauveur

This used to be an abbey-church, the oldest parts of which date from the 11C. It has kept its original cross plan: a high nave with 14C chapels off the aisles. The nave is unusual for the lack of symmetry between its north and south sides. The south side includes: in the lowest section, rounded arcades; in the middle section, a tribune with twinned bays within a larger arch; and in the upper section, 13C clerestory windows.

The chancel, surrounded by the ambulatory, was rebuilt in the 17C. Four Romanesque capitals, remnants of the earlier doorway, support the baptismal font.

Chapelle Notre-Dame-de-Pitié★

This former chapter-house became a place of worship after the departure of the Protestants in 1622.

A sumptuous carved and painted **wooden décor★** was added to it, apparently the work of the Delclaux, a family of master painters from Figeac. To the right of the altar there is a striking panel depicting the infant Jesus asleep on the cross, dreaming of his future Passion.

▷ Walk northwards along rue Tomfort then turn right.

Rue Roquefort

The house with the bartizan on a carved corbel belonged to Galiot de Genouillac, Grand Master of the Artillery of François I.

▷ Follow rue du Canal to rue Émile-Zola.

Rue Émile-Zola

This, the oldest street in the town, has retained its ogival arcades and an interesting sequence of Renaissance doorways from no 35 to 37.

▷ Turn right.

Rue Delzhens

No 3, the Provost's House (**Hôtel du Viguier du Roy**) has a square keep and a 14C watch-turret. It has been restored and converted into a hotel.

▷ Walk up the street.

Église Notre-Dame-du-Puy

The church is on a hill which gives a good view of the town and its surroundings. The Protestants used it as a

fortress, strengthening the façade with a watch-room.

This Gothic building underwent many alterations in the 17C. Its enormous late 17C sculpted walnut altarpiece frames two pictures representing the Assumption and the Coronation of the Virgin.

▷ Go back down the hill along rue St-Jacques.

Rue Malleville, Rue St-Thomas

Both these streets lead through a covered passageway painted with the coat of arms of the Hôtel de Laporte (*17C*).

Rue du Crussol

The courtyard of the 16C Hôtel de Crussol (*no 5*), now a terrace-bar, features a gallery over the courtyard stairway.

▷ Take rue Laurière then rue Bonhore.

At the far end of **rue Caviale**, opposite no 35 (**l'Hôtel d'Ay-de-Lostanges**) you'll find the street leading to the **Maison du Roi**, so called because Louis XI is supposed to have stayed there in 1463.

▷ Walk along rue Caviale.

Place Carnot

Formerly place Basse, this was headquarters to the wheat exchange which was destroyed in 1888. In the northwest corner, with a small side turret, is the **house of Pierre de Cisteron**, Louis XIV's armourer.

▷ From place Carnot, after crossing the narrow, medieval-looking rue Séguier, go through a porch to get to place des Écritures.

Place des Écritures★

Surrounded by medieval buildings, this square has an enormous (*14mx7m*) **replica of the Rosetta Stone** underfoot. This sculpture was carried out on black Zimbabwean granite by the American conceptual artist Joseph Kossuth. Unveiled in 1991, this significant con-

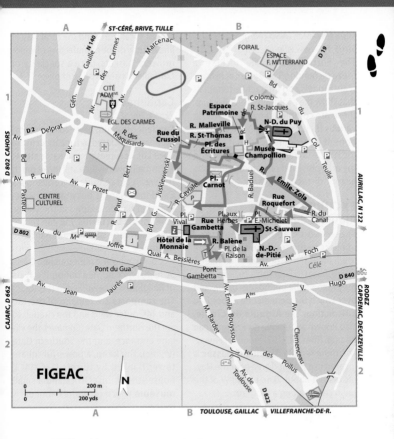

FIGEAC

0 ____ 200 m
0 ____ 200 yds

N

temporary work of art is more clearly seen from the hanging gardens overlooking the square. The French translation of the inscriptions is carved on a glass plaque kept in a small neighbouring courtyard.

Place Champollion

Two contrasting buildings overlook the square: a 14C private mansion and the town's oldest house, dating from the mid-12C, known locally as the Maison du Griffon.

▶ Continue to place Carnot then take rue Gambetta.

Hôtel Médiéval

This large group of buildings and its beautiful Gothic facade date from the mid-14C. The first building is made up of two covered towers. The second features a half-timbered structure.

▶ Return to place Vival along rue du 11-Novembre.

Musée Champollion★

Pl. Champollion. ○*Open Jul–Aug daily, 10.30am–6pm; Apr–Jun and Sept–Oct 10.30am–12.30pm, 2–6pm, Nov–Mar, 2–5.30pm.* ○*Closed Mon except during Jul–Aug; 1 Jan, 1 May, 25 Dec.* ⊛€5. ℘05 65 50 31 08.
www.musee-champollion.fr.

The museum's collections are displayed in Champollion's birthplace and in the adjacent building. An exhibition area, devoted to "signs and writing", illustrates the history of writing from its invention to the present.

Espace Patrimoine

5 r. de Colomb (not far from Musée Champollion). ○*Mid-Jul–mid-Sept 10am–12.30pm, 3–7pm; Apr–mid-Jul and mid-Sept–Oct 2–6pm.* ○*Closed*

Mon; Nov–Mar. No charge. ℘05 65 50 05 40. www.ville-figeac.fr.

The "Portrait d'une Ville" includes a frieze recounting 1 000 years of history, scale models and interactive terminals that show the evolution of architecture; these are completed by spotlights on various themes and temporary exhibitions. It is recommended that you see the keys to understanding the town and the brief presentation before visiting the historic district of Figeac.

EXCURSIONS
Aiguilles de Figeac

These two octagonal-shaped false obelisks to the south and west of the town measure respectively 14.5m and 11.5m, bases included. It is believed that they marked the boundaries of the land over which the Benedictine abbey had jurisdiction. The **Aiguille du Cingle**, also known as Aiguille du Pressoir, can be seen from the D 922, south of Figeac. The more remote **Aiguille de Lissac** is located in a wooded area near the Nayrac district about 2km/1.25mi W of the town centre along a footpath.

Cardaillac

11km/7mi N of town along the N 140 and then the D 15.

This village is the home territory of the Cardaillacs, one of the most powerful Quercy-based families. The fort stands on a rocky spur above the town. Of the triangular 12C fortification there remain two square towers: the Clock or Baron's Tower and Sagnes Tower (*only the latter is open to visitors*). A spiral staircase leads to two tall rooms with vaulted ceilings. From the platform there is a lovely view of the Drauzou Valley and the surrounding countryside.

The **Musée Éclaté** on place de la Tour (*guided tours (2–3hr) Jul–mid-Sept, daily at 3pm (from mid-Jul–Aug at 4.30pm also)*. ℘05 65 40 10 63/15 65. www. musee-eclate-cardaillac.fr) consists of several different sites scattered (*éclaté*) around the village in a determined effort to integrate evidence of the past firmly into the modern life of the village. Exhibits represent the village

school, local crafts and the rural way of life. A study of the manufacture of wine-growers' baskets, once a speciality of Cardaillac, is given pride of place.

Capdenac

7km/4.3mi SE.

Capdenac-le-Haut, perched on a promontory and enclosed by a meander in the River Lot, occupies a remarkable **site★**. This small town, which still looks much the way it did centuries ago, overlooks Capdenac-Gare, a busy railway junction that has developed in the valley. From **place Lucterius** you can follow rues Peyrolerie and la Commanderie to admire their corbelled houses with wooden panels and ribbed arches. Église St-Jean, twice burned during the Wars of Religion, was reworked in the 18C.

The **ramparts** are remains of the 13C and 14C outer walls and the citadel; so are the Northern Gate (*Comtale*), the village entrance, and the Southern Gate (*Vijane*). The **keep**, a powerful square tower flanked by turrets (13C–14C), houses the Tourist Office and a small **museum** which recounts Capdenac's history.

🚗 DRIVING TOUR

① FROM ONE VALLEY TO ANOTHER★

95km/59mi round-trip. Allow 1 day.
See route 1 on region map pp192–193.

▷ Drive W out of Figeac along the D 41 towards Cahors.

Espagnac-Ste-Eulalie

In this delightful village built in the picturesque setting of a series of cliffs, the houses with their turrets and pointed roofs are grouped round the former priory known as the **Ancien Prieuré Notre-Dame-du-Val-Paradis**, founded in the 12C. During the Hundred Years War the convent suffered considerably: the cloisters were destroyed and the church was partly demolished. It was rebuilt in the 15C, however, and the community carried on until the Revolution. The buildings are now occupied by a rural centre and holiday accommodations (*gîtes communaux*) that are managed by the local authorities.

The present Flamboyant-style **church** has replaced the 13C building (*only the walls of the nave, a doorway and ruined bays remain*). Note the unusual pentagonal east end and belfry-tower.

▶ Return to the north bank and continue along D 41.

Brengues
This small village is in a pleasant setting, perched on a ledge overlooked by a vertiginous bluff.

St-Sulpice
The houses and gardens of this old village lie within the shadow of an overhanging cliff. The approach is guarded by a 12C castle which was rebuilt in the 14C and 15C. It is still the property of the Hébrard family of St-Sulpice.

Marcilhac-sur-Célé
See *MARCILHAC-SUR-CÉLÉ*.
The D 17 runs round the Bout du Rocher cliff. The landscape is dotted with dolmens, ruins, caves and a few farms. The shaded road runs down the slopes offering fine views of the Lot valley.

Cajarc
The town was brought into the public eye when President Pompidou had a house here. Near the church, the Hébrardie Mansion with Gothic windows is all that remains standing of a 13C castle.
Inaugurated in 1989, the **Maison des Arts Georges-Pompidou** (&. ◷*Call for opening hours.* ⊕€2. ℘05 65 40 78 19) organises retrospective exhibits of contemporary European art: Hartung, Bissière and Soulages have been featured, ranking Cajarc among the foremost centres of contemporary art in the region.

▶ Drive S out of Cajarc on D 24 towards Villefranche-de-Rouergue; cross the river and turn left on D 127.

Saut de la Mounine
© Philippe Body / Hemis / Photoshot

The road follows the south bank of the Lot beginning on a ledge above the river. After Saujac it rises and winds round to overlook a wooded gorge before reaching the top of the *causse*.

Saut de la Mounine★
There is a good **view★** of the valley from the top of this cliff rising 155m above the river. The end of the spur overlooks a wide bend in the river as it encircles a mosaic of fields. To the left, on the far bank, stands Montbrun Castle.
The curious name Saut de la Mounine, "Little Monkey's Leap", comes from a rather strange legend. The lord of Montbrun decided to punish his daughter for her love of another lord's son and ordered her to be hurled from the top of the cliff; a hermit, appalled at this cruel idea, disguised a small blind monkey in women's clothes and hurled it into the air. When he saw the body falling, the father immediately regretted his brutal act; on seeing his daughter alive he was so overjoyed that he forgave her.

▶ Return to Cajarc and drive E on D 662 towards Figeac.

Montbrun
The village of Montbrun rises in tiers on a rocky promontory encircled by steep cliffs. It looks down on the Lot and faces the Saut de La Mounine (&*see above*). Towering over the village are the ruins of a fortress that belonged to one of Pope

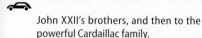

John XXII's brothers, and then to the powerful Cardaillac family.

◐ Continue along D 662.

Château de Larroque-Toirac

Guided tour (45min), Jul–Sept 10.30am–noon, 2–6pm. €6. ℘06 60 08 80 10. www.chateautoirac.com.
This 12C fortress belonged to the Cardaillac family who, during the Hundred Years War, took an active part in the region's resistance to English domination. From the church square (*parking area*), a path leads to the castle. The visit starts with a round tower built at the beginning of the Hundred Years War to withstand artillery fire, newly introduced in siege warfare. Note the charming heart-shaped opening. You'll arrive in the 15C seigneurial residence through two successive courtyards.
A spiral staircase, located in an adjacent tower, leads to the different levels. There is a Romanesque fireplace in the guardroom and a Gothic one in the great hall. The original kitchen can also be seen. To the east stands the enormous late 12C keep which was greatly reduced in height during the Revolution.

◐ Continue along the D 662.

St-Pierre-Toirac

This small village, on the north bank of the Lot, contains an interesting 11C and 14C **church**. The Romanesque apse alone belies the fortified appearance of this building which served as a defence point with its massive crenellated keep and upper floor. Recently discovered Merovingian sarcophagi have been placed behind the church.

◐ Continue along the D 662.

Faycelles

This village overlooking the Lot valley once belonged to Figeac abbey. A peaceful atmosphere pervades the old streets and the suburb of Les Carbes.

◐ The D 662 leads back to Figeac.

ADDRESSES

🛏 STAY

☺☺ **Hôtel des Bains** – *1 r. du Griffoul.* ℘05 65 34 10 89. www.hoteldesbains.fr. *19 rooms.* These renovated former public baths, dating from the end of the last century, are located near the historic centre, in a beautiful setting on the banks of the River Célé. Most rooms are air-conditioned and all have broadband connection/WiFi. Breakfast can be taken on the riverbank veranda.

☺☺ **La Bastie D'Urfé** – *Bez De Naussac, 12 Naussac. 19km (12mi) SE of Figeac.* ℘05 65 64 13 77. www.hotel-bastie-urfe-naussac. federal-hotel.com. *10 rooms.* Set in the peaceful heart of the Diege countryside, La Bastie D'Urfé combines the charm of an 18C mansion with the comfort of a contemporary-style modern home. Each room has been individually designed and equipped with *balnéothérapie* facilities.

☺☺☺ **Grand Hôtel du Pont d'Or** – *2 av. Jean-Jaurès.* ℘05 65 50 95 00. www.hotelpontdor.com. *35 rooms.* A welcoming stone house on the banks of the Célé, with some rooms offering balconies overlooking the river. A yellow and orange colour scheme, contemporary furniture and immaculate bathrooms. Fitness room and rooftop swimming pool. In summer, breakfast is served on the riverside terrace.

🍴 EAT

☺☺ **La Puce à l'Oreille** – *3 r. St-Thomas.* ℘05 65 34 33 08. This lovely medieval house is located in a little lane of the historic district, a few steps from Musée Champollion. The superb monumental fireplace warms up the elegant dining room. The cuisine is authentic and refined.

☺☺ **L'Allée des Vignes** – *32 blvd. du Tour-de-Ville, Cajarc (25km/15.5mi SW of Figeac on D 662 then D 19).* ℘06 71 80 70 74. This former presbytery has been converted in a decidedly contemporary style. The chef's gourmet, inventive style of cooking puts the spotlight on fish.

SHOPPING

Market – The town's weekly market is held on Saturdays (the largest one is the last Saturday of the month). Evening markets are held on Thursdays in July and August.

Marcilhac-sur-Célé

Marcilhac is built in the centre of an amphitheatre of cliffs in the enchanting Célé valley. Interesting old houses surround the ruins of a Benedictine abbey.

▶ **Population:** 197.
Michelin Map: 337: F-4 .
Info: Maison du Roy, 46160 Marcilhac-sur-Célé. ℘05 65 40 68 44.
Location: 47km/29.5 W of Cahors via D 653, D 17 & D 14.
Don't Miss: Abbey ruins.

A BIT OF HISTORY

An eventful past – In the 11C the modest sanctuary of Rocamadour was under the care of Marcilhac abbey, which let it fall into ruins. Noticing this negligence, monks from Tulle came to live in the sanctuary. However, in 1166, the discovery of the body of St Amadour turned the sanctuary into a rich and famous pilgrimage centre. Marcilhac recalled its rights and expelled the Tulle monks. Soon afterwards the abbot of Tulle threw out the Marcilhac monks and again occupied Rocamadour.

Lawsuits followed and the bishop of Cahors, the papal legate, the archbishop of Bourges and even the Pope himself were all called on to give judgement, but avoided reaching a decision. Finally, after 100 years of squabbling, Marcilhac accepted an indemnity of 3 000 sols and relinquished its claim to Rocamadour. Marcilhac abbey flourished until the 14C, but during the Hundred Years War it was virtually destroyed. After the Reformation, the abbey fell into the hands of the Hébrards of St-Sulpice and the monks were expelled. The abbey-church was secularised in 1764.

OLD ABBEY TOUR

Romanesque section – The west porch and the first three bays of the nave are open to the sky. They are flanked by a tall square tower, which was probably fortified in the 14C. A round-arched door on the south side is topped with sculpture forming a **tympanum** depicting the Last Judgement. Here, Christ in Majesty, surrounded by what is thought to represent the sun and moon, appears above St Peter, St Paul and two thick-set angels with open wings.

▶ Go through this doorway and enter the church to the right.

Gothic section – This part of the church, closed to the west from the fourth bay on, dates from the 15C and is built in the Flamboyant style. A Baroque stall decorated with the Hébrard family crest has a fabulous **miséricord** carved with the head of an angel. A chapel on the left of the chancel boasts 15C frescoes of Christ giving Blessing with the Twelve Apostles. Under each Apostle is his name and a characteristic phrase.

▶ Leave the church and turn right (from the second Romanesque bay) onto the path to the chapter-house.

Chapter-house – This 12C building has very delicately sculpted Romanesque capitals alternately in grey-blue limestone and rose-coloured stalagmite stone.

▶ Go towards an esplanade shaded by plane trees; a round tower marks the site of the abbot's house. By the banks of the Célé (right), the line of the rampart wall is interrupted by a postern. Return to the Romanesque ruins.

🚗 DRIVING TOUR

② CONFLUENCE OF THE ÉLÉ AND THE LOT★★

60km/37mi round-trip. Allow 1 day.
See route 2 on region map pp192–193.

▶ Drive SW out of Marcilhac along the D 41 towards Cabrerets.

Sauliac-sur-Célé

This old village clings to an awe-inspiring cliff of coloured rock. In the cliff face can be seen the openings to the fortified caves used in time of war as refuges.

⊳ As you leave Sauliac, turn right onto the D 24, which crosses the Célé.

Beyond Sauliac the valley widens out. Crops and pasture grow well on the alluvial soil of the valley bottom. The road climbs onto the *causse* and runs across it before entering the Lot valley.

⊳ From St-Martin-Labouval, follow the north bank of the Lot.

Cuzals
👥 Musée de Plein Air du Quercy

All aspects of life in the Quercy region from before the Revolution until WWII are illustrated in this park.
A 3km-/1.9mi-long discovery trail offers an insight into man's impact on the local environment.

⊳ Return to the D 41 and turn left.

Fontaine de la Pescalerie

This is one of the most attractive sights of the Célé valley; a beautiful waterfall pours out of the rock wall close to the road. It marks the surfacing of an underground river that has cut its way through the Causse de Gramat.

⊳ Continue along D 41. 1.5km/0.9mi after Liauzu, turn left onto a small road.

Cabrerets

Cabrerets, set in a rocky amphitheatre, occupies a commanding position at the confluence of the rivers Sagne and Célé. There is a good overall **view★** of Cabrerets and its setting from the left bank of the Célé, which is reached by crossing the bridge. Opposite stand the ruins of the **Château du Diable** (Devil's castle), or Castle of the English, clinging to the formidable Rochecourbe cliff.
On the far left is the impressive mass of the 14C and 15C **Château des Gontaut-**

Biron★ overlooking the valley. A big corner tower flanks the buildings that surround an inner courtyard.

⊳ On the right bank of the river, in the village, follow D 198.

Grotte de Pech-Merle★★★
👁 *See Grotte de PECH-MERLE.*

⊳ Shortly after Cabrerets the cliff road crosses the face of high stone cliffs.

Bouziès

On the bank opposite the village, the **Défilé des Anglais** (Englishmen's gorge) is the most famous of the fortified gullies built during the Hundred Years War, in cave-like openings only accessible by a rope-ladder.

St-Cirq-Lapopie★★
👁 *See ST-CIRQ-LAPOPIE.*

Beyond St-Cirq-Lapopie, the D 40, which is built into the cliff, was designed to be a tourist route. There is a good **view★** of the confluence of the Lot and the Célé from the **Belvédère du Bancourel**.

Towpath along the Lot★ (Chemin de Halage)

Take the GR 36 trail off to the right of the car park by the moorings.
After about 500m, the spectacular towpath comes into view, carved out of the rock. Here, the cliff juts out over the river. In sections such as this, the barges coming up the Lot with their cargoes of salt, dried fish, spices or plaster could not be towed by the usual teams of horses or oxen, but had to be pulled along by hand. This pathway is now a marvellous walk. At the top of the first lock there is a 15m-long bas-relief, the work of contemporary artist D Monnier, decorating the limestone wall with fish and shellfish.

⊳ Come back to D 8 and turn right. The road runs on to D 911 at Arcambal.

Château de Cénevières★

This imposing castle perches on a sheer rock face overlooking the Lot valley from a height of more than 70m.

As early as the 8C the dukes of Aquitaine had a stronghold built here. In the 13C the lords of Gourdon had the keep built. During the Renaissance, Flottard de Gourdon completely remodelled the castle. His son, Antoine de Gourdon, converted to Protestantism and participated alongside Henri IV in the Siege of Cahors in 1580. He pillaged the cathedral in Cahors and loaded the high altar and altar of the Holy Shroud onto boats returning to Cénevières Castle. The boat carrying the high altar sank in a chasm along the way. Before his death Antoine built a small Protestant church in the outer bailey. He died childless but his widow remarried and a new lineage took over Cénevières. The château was pillaged during the French Revolution. The outside of the castle has a 13C keep and 15C wings joined by a 16C Renaissance gallery. The gallery is held up by Tuscan columns and above it are dormer windows. The moat, once crossed by a drawbridge, is now filled in. Inside, the ground floor includes a vaulted salt room and kitchen. The keep has a trapdoor, giving a glimpse of the three floors of underground cellars. The adjacent chapel, still consecrated, houses the altar of the Holy Shroud.

On the first floor, the great drawing room, with a lovely Renaissance painted ceiling and recently discovered murals, contains 15C and 16C Flemish tapestries and the shrine of the Holy Shroud that was brought back from Cahors. Various objects are displayed in the next room: a Spanish helmet, a mould for cannon balls and letters from famous people.

▶ Cross the River Lot and pick up D 662 towards St-Cirq-Lapopie.

From Pont de Tour-de-Faure, admire St-Cirq-Lapopie in its remarkable setting on the river's south bank.

Calvignac

This old village, where a few traces of its fortress may still be seen, is perched on a spur on the river's south bank.

▶ Leave Calvignac W on D 8.

Larnagol

This village has retained some fine 16C and 17C façades. The castle and its buttressed keep overlook the upper part.

▶ Leave Arnagol S and cross the river.

Grotte du Pech-Merle★★★

Prehistoric tribes performed religious rites in this cave, which was only rediscovered thousands of years later in 1922. Not only is its natural decoration interesting, there are also wall paintings and carvings that are of great documentary value to prehistorians.

A BIT OF HISTORY
The underground explorers

Two boys of 15 and 16 were the heroes of the Pech-Merle Cave rediscovery. Inspired by the expeditions and dis-

- **Michelin Map:** Michelin local map 337: F-4.
- **Location:** The cave is located 7km/4.5mi N of St-Cirq-Lapopie and 32km/20mi E of Cahors.
- **Don't Miss:** A guided tour inside the cave.

coveries made throughout the region by Abbé Lemozi, the priest from Cabrerets who was also a prehistorian and speleologist, the boys explored a small fault and after several hours their efforts were rewarded by the sight of wonderful paintings.

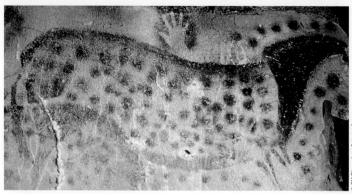

Paleolithic painting in Grotte du Pech-Merle

Abbé Lemozi, who soon afterwards explored the cave scientifically, recognised the importance of the underground sanctuary. In 1949 the discovery of a new chamber led to the finding of the original opening through which men had entered the cave about 16 000 to 20 000 years ago.

CAVE

&♿🕙 *Guided tours: Apr–mid-Nov; check website for winter openings. Access limited to 700 visitors per day (in July and August it is advisable to book 3 days in advance).* €11 *(includes visit to the museum).* ☎05 65 31 27 05. www.pechmerle.com.

The Pech-Merle Cave includes highly advanced paintings and engravings, as well as material traces of prehistoric man's sojourn there. In addition to its prehistoric interest, this cave features beautiful concretions in vast caverns with wide openings.

The upper level of the **Chapelle des Mammouths** (Chapel of Mammoths, or black frieze) is decorated with drawings of bison and mammoths outlined in black that form a frieze 7m long by 3m high.

The **Salle des Disques** is patterned with many strange concretions that look like discs. The footprints made by a prehistoric individual can be seen, petrified forever in the once-wet clay of a *gour* (natural dam).

Further on, the **Galerie des Ours** contains huge, impressive columns; eccentrics with delicate protuberances that defy the laws of gravity; and cave pearls, with colours ranging from shining white pure calcite to red-ochre (*clay and iron oxide in the limestone*).

Beyond the Salle Rouge, you'll go down a narrow passageway engraved with a bear's head to the lower level of the **prehistoric gallery**. One wall is decorated with the **silhouettes of two horses** patterned with dots like the surface around them. There are also mysterious symbols and outlined hand prints known as negative hands. These prints were made by stencilling in different pigments around the hands placed flat against the rock. The horses are depicted with distorted silhouettes similar to those at Lascaux, with huge bodies and a tiny heads. These prints and the roof of hieroglyphics once decorated a sanctuary older than that of the Chapel of Mammoths.

In the last cave to be visited, **Salle de Combel**, you'll see **bones of cave bears**.

Musée Amédée-Lémozi

&♿🕙 *Same opening times and charges as the Grotte du Pech-Merle (combined ticket).* ☎05 65 31 23 33.

This is a research and information centre on prehistory in Quercy. There is an attractive, informative display of bones, tools, weapons, utensils and works of art from 160 different prehistoric sites, dating from the Lower Paleolithic Era to the Iron Age. The visit ends with a film on Paleolithic art in Quercy.

Labastide-Murat

Labastide-Murat, which stands at one of the highest points on the Gramat Causse, was originally called Labastide-Fortunière, but changed its name to Murat in honour of the most famous of its sons.

A BIT OF HISTORY

The miraculous destiny of Joachim Murat – Murat was born in 1767, the son of an innkeeper. He was destined for the Church, but at 21 decided instead to be a soldier. The campaigns in Italy and Egypt enabled him to gain rapid promotion under Napoléon, whose brother-in-law he became by marrying the First Consul's sister, Caroline; he was promoted to marshal of the Empire, grand duke of Berg and of Cleves and king of Naples. However, his glory faded with that of his master, whom he abandoned in the dark days of the Empire. His miserable end in 1815 was in keeping with the diversity in his life: after the Bourbons had returned to Naples, he tried to reclaim his kingdom, but was taken prisoner and shot.

MUSÉE MURAT

Pl. de Tolentino. Guided visits *(30mn) by arrangement only: mid-Jul–mid-Sept, daily except Tue, 10am–noon and 3–6pm.* €3. 05 65 24 97 82. The museum is in the house where Murat was born. The 18C kitchen and the inn's saloon are on display to visitors. On the first floor you'll see mementos of the King of Naples and of his mother.

DRIVING TOUR

③ SOUTHERN CAUSSE DE GRAMAT

60km/37mi round-trip. Allow half a day. See route 3 on region map pp192–193. Drive S out of Labastide-Murat on the D 32.

St-Martin-de-Vers

In this small village the houses with brown-tiled roofs cluster round the

- ▶ **Population:** 659.
- **Michelin Map:** 337: F-4
- **Info:** 8 Grand'Rue, 46240. 05 65 21 11 39. www.tourisme-labastide-murat.fr.
- ▶ **Location:** 25km/15mi S of Rocamadour and 32km/20mi N of Cahors.
- **Timing:** Allow a full day to explore the Parc Régional des Causses du Quercy and the Causse de Gramat.
- **Don't Miss:** The Sunday morning market in July and August and the regional fair on the 2nd and 4th Monday of every month.

old priory church and its asymmetrical bell-tower.

▶ Drive E along the D 13 and turn left onto the D 10 3km/1.9mi farther on, then left again onto the D 17.

Soulomès

The Knights Templar built a commandery here in the 12C. The chancel of the church contains interesting 15C and 16C frescoes depicting episodes of Christ's life.

▶ Leave Soulomès S on D 17 and turn left onto the D 71 1km/0.6mi farther on.

Désert de la Braunhie

Here, drystone walls seem to stretch forever into the distance. The scrubby vegetation includes oaks, maples and stunted walnut trees alternated with stony heath dotted with junipers and thorn bushes.

Caniac-du-Causse

Beneath the church, the **crypt** (*light switch at the bottom of the stairs to the right*) was built by the monks of Marcilhac-sur-Célé in the 12C to house the relic of St Namphaise, an officer in the army of Charlemagne who became a hermit.

Château de Vaillac

© DeAgostini / World Illustrated / Photoshot

Espace Naturel Sensible de la Forêt de la Braunhie

Brochure available at the Maison de la Braunhie, beneath the town hall in Caniac-du-Causse and at the Tourist Office in Labastide-Murat. ℘*05 65 31 16 03.* ⚠ *7.5km/4.6mi round-trip on foot.*

◗ Follow the D 42 towards Fontanes-du-Causse.

This is the highest part of the Causse de Gramat. The trail reveals the local fauna and flora and offers an insight into the geology and history of the area.

◗ Return to Caniac-du-Causse and continue along the D 71 to Quissac.

The road runs across the most arid part of the Braunhie.

Quissac

Besides attractive farmhouses, the village of Quissac has retained its *travail à bœufs*, a farrier's sling used for shoeing oxen.

◗ Drive W along the D 146. In Fontanes-du-Causse, turn left onto the D 2 and, 4.5km/2.8mi beyond Montfaucon, turn left onto the D 17.

Château de Vaillac

The massive outline of the castle towers above the village. Built in the 15C and 16C, the stronghold comprises a large building flanked by four towers and a keep.

◗ Return to Labastide-Murat along the D 10.

ADDRESSES

⌘ EAT

☐ **Relais du Roy de Naple** – *Pl. Daniel-Roques.* ℘*05 65 30 19 56. Closed Sun out of season. 4 rooms.* Straightforward food and service for those looking for a quick, filling, pit-stop.

SHOPPING

Markets and Fairs

Labastide-Murat holds a market for local producers to sell their wares on Sunday mornings; there is also a fair the second and fourth Monday of the month.

Château de Bonaguil★★

This majestic fortress, standing on the borders of the Périgord Noir and the Quercy, is a perfect example of late 15C and 16C military architecture. One of the things that makes it unique is the fact that it appears to be a typical medieval defensive stronghold, but its design was actually adapted to the use of firearms.

- **Michelin Map:** 336: I-2.
- **Location:** 8.5km/5.3mi NE of Fumel following the D 673 and D 158.
- **Info:** Pl. Georges-Escande, Fumel. ☎05 53 71 13 70. www.tourisme-fumelois.fr.

A BIT OF HISTORY

A strange character – It was a weird quirk of character that made **Bérenger de Roquefeuil** enjoy proclaiming himself the "noble, magnificent and most powerful lord of the baronies of Roquefeuil, Blanquefort, Castelnau, Combret, Roquefère, Count of Naut." He belonged to one of the oldest families of Languedoc and was a brutal and vindictive man. The extortion and other outrages he perpetrated incited revolt.

In order to crush this, Bérenger transformed the 13C Bonaguil Castle into an impregnable fortress from which he would be able to observe and quell any signs of an uprising. It took nearly 40 years to build this anachronism while his contemporaries were building Renaissance castles along the Loire. However, his castle was never attacked and was intact until the eve of the Revolution. Although partially demolished in the late 18C, it still evokes the absolute power it once represented.

CHÂTEAU

🕐*Open Jan–Feb and Nov–Dec, school holidays 2–5pm (except 1 Jan, 25 Dec); Mar–May and Oct daily 10am–12.30pm, 2–5.30pm; Jun–Sept daily, 10am–12.30pm, 2–6pm (Jul–Aug 10am–7pm). ◎€7. ☎05 53 71 90 33. www.chateau-bonaguil.com.*

To reach the castle stronghold, you'll pass through the enormous **barbican**, which had an independent garrison, powder store, armouries and escape routes. The barbican formed part of the 350m-long first line of defence. The second line of defence consisted of five towers of which one, known as the Grosse Tour, is among the strongest round towers ever to have been built in France. The tower is 35m high and is crowned with corbels. The upper storeys served as living quarters while the lower contained weapons, such as muskets, culverins and harquebuses. The **keep** overlooked both lines of defence. It

Château de Bonaguil

© ICP / age fotostock

served not only as a watchtower but also as a command-post and was the last bastion of defence. The castle garrison of about 100 men could easily withstand a siege, with a well sunk through the rock and vaulted tunnels that enabled the troops to move about quickly.

🚗 DRIVING TOUR

4 FROM BONAGUIL TO DURVEL

80km/47.9mi round-trip. Allow 1 day.
See route 4 on region map pp192–193.

▷ Drive S out of Bonaguil on D 158.

St-Martin-le-Redon

This charming village is known for the St-Martial mineral spring, reputed to cure skin ailments.

▷ Leave St-Martin on D 673 towards Gourdon.

Montcabrier

This *bastide* was founded in 1297 by Guy de Cabrier and was granted a charter of franchises by Philip the Fair. Overlooking the square, several old houses are laid out in the regular pattern of the original plan. The church, partly rebuilt in the 14C, has a Flamboyant doorway (restored) surrounded by a fine open-bayed belltower. Inside, a plain 14C statue of St Louis, the parish's patron saint, is surrounded by ex-votos. This statue was the object of a local pilgrimage.

▷ Leave Montcabrier on the D 683 towards Gourdon.

Château de Montcléra

This late 15C castle features a fortified entry door. Behind looms the square dungeon and a main building flanked by two round towers crowned with machicolation.

▷ Leave Montcléra E to come back to the D 45 towards Les Arques.

Les Arques★ *See LES ARQUES.*

▷ Leave Les Arques W on D 45 towards Les Junies.

Les Junies

The 15C castle flanked with round towers is adorned with elegant Renaissance windows. Away from the village, the 14C Ste-Madeleine church is a sober, powerful, impressively large building. This was part of the priory attached to the Dominican Order in 1345. The priory was founded by one of the local lords, Gaucelin des Junies, cardinal of Albano.

▷ Leave Les Junies S on D 45 towards Castelfranc. The hamlet of La Masse is a stone's throw from Les Junies.

Église St-Perdulphe

The key to the church is kept under a bell in front of the house to the left of the church's entrance.
The abbot of Guéret, who was called St Pardulphe or St Pardoux and who died in 737, was known for his miraculous healing. This modest church contains well-preserved 15C frescoes, including a series of rather naïve Deadly Sins meant to warn believers, as well as a Passion of Christ.

▷ Continue along D 45.

Le Jardin des Sens de Castelfranc★

℘05 65 36 22 93.
Behind the *halle* of this peaceful *bastide*, this small ($760m^2$/2493 sq ft) sensual garden is a triumph. The Vert river brings refreshment to a variety of plants: vegetable varieties, plants used in dyeing, flowers and other plants. The concept brings the medieval garden up to date by revisiting its design and the traditional separation of uses. Here, plants are mixed according to shapes, colours and seasons, but in respect to general medieval garden architecture. The result is fresh and joyful.

▷ Leave Castelfranc W on D 811.

Puy-l'Évêque

Guided tours of the church by appointment at the church office, pl. du Rampeau, L'Abbé Charpentier, 46700 Puy-l'Évêque.

This small town, which took its current name when it came under the lordship of the bishops of Cahors, occupies one of the most picturesque sites in the valley downstream from Cahors. From the bridge into town, admire the old houses in golden stone.

The **church** was built on the northeast side of the town, at the furthest point in the defence system of which it was itself a part. In front of the church stands a massive belfry-porch flanked by a turret and buttresses. The magnificent doorway is surmounted by a pediment adorned with statues. The nave was built in the 14C and 15C and ends in a polygonal apse. In the churchyard there are many old tombs, and on the left of the church stands a wayside cross ornamented with archaic-style sculpture.

▷ Walk back towards place du Rampeau and place du Mercadiel. Beyond Grande-Rue is a maze of twisting lanes clinging to the promontory.

The 13C **keep** is all that remains of the Episcopal castle. From the **Esplanade de la Truffière**, next to the keep, admire the terraces and hillsides covered with vines and the wide alluvial valley carpeted with fields.

▷ Leave Puy-l'Évêque N on D 28.

Martignac

This small village boasts a fine rustic **church**, built of yellow stone and surmounted by a timber-framed belltower. The nave and chancel are decorated with 15C frescoes: realistic representations of the capital sins contrast with scenes depicting the Coronation of the Virgin Mary and the Arrival of the Chosen in Paradise, led by St Michael and welcomed by St Peter.

▷ Return to Puy-l'Évêque then take D 811 to Duravel.

Duravel

The 11C **church** (*keys available from the Tourist Office*) has historiated capitals decorating the chancel. There is an archaic crypt supported by columns with rough-hewn capitals. The bodies of St Hilarion, St Poémon and St Agathon lie buried at the back of the apse.

The ostension, or solemn exhibition of relics to the faithful, is held every five years.

▷ Take D 811 to Saturac then turn right to Bonaguil.

ADDRESSES

🛏 STAY

Hôtel Bellevue – *Pl. Truffière.* ℘05 65 36 06 60. www.hotelbellevue-puyleveque.com. 🛆. *11 rooms.* This hotel, built on a rocky spur overlooking the Lot, is worthy of its name ("beautiful view"). The spacious contemporary rooms are personalised. The cuisine is inventive, offering regional dishes and *brasserie*-style dining. Veranda.

🍽 EAT

Camping Moulin du Périé – *47500 Sauveterre-la-Lémance, 12km/7.5mi NW of Bonaguil on the D 440 and then the D 158.* ℘05 53 40 67 26. www.camping-moulin-perie.com. Open May 15–Sept 18. Reserv. recommended. 125 pitches. Restaurant. This campsite, laid out around a restored mill, is spacious and well-maintained. Small lake and pool, bikes and bungalows for hire, plus a restaurant serving regional cuisine.

L'Auberge – *Lavaur, 10km/6.2mi from Bonaguil (go back towards Fumel and follow the road from Villefranche-du-Perigord, then follow the Lavaur signposts).* ℘05 53 28 16 89. www.logishotels.com. *2 rooms and 3 cottages.* 🅿🔲. You'll find this *auberge* is in the middle of the countryside between fields and forest. Stop over for good regional cuisine. Two rooms with a rustic décor and family cottages are available if you'd like to stay a few days in this peaceful setting.

Les Arques★

The tranquillity of this Bouriane village is undoubtedly the reason the sculptor **Ossip Zadkine** (1890–1967) chose to live here. Russian by birth and French by adoption, he arrived in Paris in 1909, where he was first influenced by Cubism, a style that he subsequently abandoned. In 1934 he bought a house in Les Arques where he created his most important works (*Diana, Pietà, Christ*).

▶ **Population:** 207.
⏱ **Michelin Map:** 337: D-4.
ℹ **Info:** R. de la République, Cazals. ℘05 65 22 88 88.
◐ **Location:** 28km/17mi S of Gourdon and 6km/3.7mi SW of Cazals (for Tourist Office).
👪 **Kids:** Discovery circuit of the Masse valley.
◐ **Timing:** 1hr 15min for the village, museum and churches; 2 hr more for the Espace Naturel Sensible de la Vallée de la Masse.

VILLAGE
Musée Zadkine★

46250 Les Arques. ⏱*Open daily except Mon: Apr–Oct 10am–1pm, 3–7pm; Feb–Mar 2–6pm.* ⏱*Closed Jan, 1 May.* ✎€4. ℘05 65 22 83 37.
Three rooms display examples of the artist's work, including lithographs, tapestries, bronzes (*Musical Trio*, 1928) and monumental wood sculptures (*Diana*). An audio-visual presentation shows a lengthy interview with Zadkine.

Église St-Laurent★

This church in the centre of the village is all that is left of a priory-deanery founded in the 11C by the Abbaye de Marcilhac. When the nave was restored in the 20C, it was narrowed and shortened; however the apse and apsidal chapels have retained the purity of the Romanesque style. Several old features have been preserved such as the oculus in the south transept (characteristic of the Carolingian style) and the tori at the base of the columns supporting the transverse arches. The most original part of the interior is the arches. Two Zadkine works enhance the interior: the monumental **sculpture of Christ★** (*back of the façade*) and **Pietà★** (*crypt*).

Église St-André

Go down towards the River Masse, then cross D 45. ℘05 65 22 83 37.
Set in a clearing, this church displays a remarkable series of **frescoes★** from the late 15C, discovered in 1954 by Zadkine. The chancel window is framed by the Annunciation and on either side by the Apostles. They are shown with instruments representing their punishment: St Andrew with an X-shaped cross and St Matthew with a halberd; or other symbols: St Peter with his keys, St James with his pilgrim's staff and St Thomas with his architect's set-square. On the vault, spangled with red stars, is Christ in Majesty seated on a rainbow-shaped throne with one hand held up in blessing and the other holding the globe. He is surrounded by the symbols of the four Evangelists. On the pillars of the apse which support a triumphal arch, you'll see St Christopher and, on the other side, baby Jesus waiting for Christopher to help him cross the river.

Pietà by Ossip Zadkine, Église St-Laurent

© S. Sauvignier / Michelin

Gourdon★

Gourdon is the capital of the hilly green countryside of Bouriane. The town, situated on the borders of Quercy and Périgord, is stacked up the flank of a rocky hillock upon which the local lord's castle once stood. Follow the circular route of avenues that have replaced the old ramparts for pleasant views of the hills and valleys of Bouriane.

 WALKING TOUR

THE MEDIEVAL CENTRE
Rue du Majou★

The 13C fortified gateway, Porte du Majou, leads to the street of the same name. This picturesque and narrow street was once the high street; all along it reside old houses with overhanging storeys and ground floors with large pointed arches. No 17, Anglars Mansion, has pretty mullioned windows.

▶ The street leads to the esplanade, the town hall (right) and Église St-Pierre.

Hôtel de Ville (town hall)

This former 13C consulate, enlarged in the 17C, has covered arcades which are used as a covered market.

Église St-Pierre

The church (dedicated to St Peter), built in the 14C, used to be a dependency of Le Vigan abbey. The doorway is decorated with elegant archivolts and is framed by two tall asymmetrical towers. The large rose window is protected by a line of machicolations, a reminder of former fortifications. The vast nave has pointed vaulting; 17C wood panels, carved, painted and gilded, decorate the chancel and the south transept.

▶ Go round the left of the church and up the staircase leading to the esplanade where the castle once stood.

- ▶ **Population:** 4 640.
- **Michelin Map:** 337: E–3
- **Info:** 24 r. du Majou, 46300 Gourdon en Quercy. ℘05 65 27 52 50. www.tourisme-gourdon.com.
- ▶ **Location:** 26km/16mi S of Sarlat; 44km/27.5mi N of Cahors.
- **Parking:** Free parking at Quartier du Forail, Pl. Gén. de Gaulle (except Sat market) and public garden.
- **Timing:** Allow half a day to explore the Bouriane.
- **Don't Miss:** Rue de Majou; the baptismal font in the Église des Cordeliers.

Esplanade

A sweeping **view★** unfolds from the terrace (*viewing table*). Beyond the town and its roofs, which can be seen below the massive roof of the church (St-Pierre) in the foreground, you'll see the churchyard, a forest of cypress trees, and then the plateaux stretching out around the valleys of the Dordogne and the Céou.

▶ Return to place de l'Hôtel-de-Ville and go round the outside of the church starting from the right.

There are some old houses opposite the east end, including one with a lovely early-17C doorway. Opposite the south door of the church take rue Cardinal-Farinié which goes downhill and contains old houses with mullioned windows and side turrets.
Below stands the Église des Cordeliers.

Église des Cordeliers

The former church is now used for concerts and exhibits in Jul–Aug. Tours by appointment. ℘05 65 27 52 50.
This church, which used to be part of the Franciscan monastery, is worth a visit, despite being slightly marred by a massive belfry-porch which was added in the 19C. At the entrance, in the middle of the nave, stands a remarkable

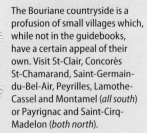

Villages of the Bouriane

The Bouriane countryside is a profusion of small villages which, while not in the guidebooks, have a certain appeal of their own. Visit St-Clair, Concorès St-Chamarand, Saint-Germain-du-Bel-Air, Peyrilles, Lamothe-Cassel and Montamel (*all south*) or Payrignac and Saint-Cirq-Madelon (*both north*).

14C **baptismal font★**. The outside is decorated with trefoiled blind arcades. The fine seven-sided apse is lit by 19C stained-glass windows.

EXCURSIONS
Grottes de Cougnac★
3km/2mi N on the D 704. 🐾 *Open Apr–early Jul and Sept 10–11.30am, 2.30–5pm; Jul–Aug 10am–6pm; Oct 2–4pm.* ⏝€7.50. ☎05 65 41 47 54. www.grottesdecougnac.com.
These caves are fascinating for two features: their natural rock formations and their Paleolithic paintings similar to those of Pech-Merle (25 000 to 18 000 BCE). The first cave consists of three small chambers with a large number of closely packed, extremely delicate stalactites. The second cave is bigger and has two remarkable chambers: the **Salle des Colonnes★** is particularly striking, and the **Salle des Peintures Préhistoriques** contains designs in ochre and black depicting ibex, mammoths and human figures.

Les Prades
7km/4.3mi NE.
Home to the **Musée Henri-Giron** (♿🕐*open by appointment.* ☎05 65 41 33 78), whose collection includes about 40 of this Belgian painter's works. His style reflects a classic heritage and Flemish influence, all the while integrating remarkably modern subjects, including some unsettling interpretations of feminine forms.

Le Vigan
5km/3mi E on the D 673.
The Gothic **church** *is* all that remains of an abbey founded in the 11C, and became a regular chapter for canons in the 14C. The spectacular east end, overlooked by a tower rising from the transept crossing, has defensive turrets tucked in between the apsidal chapels. There is fine vaulting over the nave.

Chapelle de Notre-Dame-des-Neiges
1.5km/1mi SE via rue des Nevèges from av. Gambetta. 🕐*If the chapel is closed, the key can be obtained next door. Contact the Gourdon Tourist Office for further information.*
Set in the small valley of the Bléou, this 14C chapel, a pilgrimage centre which was restored in the 17C, has a 17C altarpiece. A miraculous spring flows through the chancel.

🚗 DRIVING TOUR

⑤ LA BOURIANE
85km/53mi round-trip. Allow half a day. 🧭*See route 5 on region map pp 192–193. Drive W out of Gourdon on D 673.*

The region known as La Bouriane extends from Gourdon to the Lot valley and west of N 20. Its relatively infertile soil nevertheless accommodates chestnut, pine and walnut trees, as well as vineyards on southern-facing slopes.

▷ Leave Gourdon W on D 673.

Salviac
The Gothic church has some lovely 16C stained-glass windows depicting scenes from the life of St Eutrope.

Cazals
This *bastide*, built in 1319 on behalf of the king of England, is designed around a large central square. A castle overlooks a stretch of the River Masse offering recreation facilities.

▷ Continue along D 673.

Château de Montcléra

Behind the 15C fortified entrance gate stand a square keep and residential quarters flanked by round, machicolated towers.

▷ Continue along D 673 to Frayssinet-le-Gélat, then turn left on D 660.

Goujounac

There used to be a Romanesque priory around the church, but there are now only a few remains of this. On the south wall of the church, the Romanesque **tympanum**, depicting Christ in Glory giving the sign of God's blessing surrounded by the symbols of the four Evangelists, is the work of a Quercy artist who was probably influenced by the tympanum at Beaulieu-sur-Dordogne.

▷ Continue on D 660 and turn right on D 45.

Les Junies

The 15C castle flanked by round towers is decorated with elegant Renaissance windows. There is a massive, austere 14C church set apart from the village. This was part of a priory, which was attached to the Dominican order in 1345 and had been founded by one of the local lords, Gaucelin des Junies, Cardinal of Albano.

▷ While driving on D 45 towards Castelfranc, you can make a detour by St-Perdulphe church. in the Masse hamlet. Otherwise leave the village N on D 37.

Lherm

This little village of white-limestone houses with steeply pitched roofs covered with small brown tiles is dominated by a belltower, a turret and several dovecotes. In a small, isolated, wooded valley, the **church** (Notre-Dame-de-l'Assomption), once a priory, features a Romanesque apse and a plain barrel-vaulted nave of ashlar stone. The chancel contains a profusely decorated altarpiece of gold and carvings against a blue background, a rather grandiose, local interpretation of the Baroque style. The building was altered in the 16C to include a fine Renaissance-style door.

▷ Continue N on the D 37.

St-André
  See ST-ANDRÉ.

Les Arques★
  See LES ARQUES.

▷ Leave SE on D 150. Continue beyond Maussac and turn left on D 47. 2km/1.2mi farther on, the road leads to D 25.

Rampoux

There is an interesting red-and-white stone 12C Romanesque church here that used to be a Benedictine priory. Inside, the 15C frescoes illustrate the life of Christ in naïve style.

▷ Continue E on D 25. Turn left towards Concorès 2km/1.2mi beyond Lavercantière, then follow D 12 back to Gourdon along the River Céou and River Bléou.

Espace Naturel Sensible des Landes du Frau

Access from a car park on D 25 between Lavercantière and Degagnazes – 2.5km/1.5mi, 45min. It is strongly recommended that you obtain the information sheets of the discovery guide available at the Salviac or Gourdon Tourist Offices. ℘05 65 41 57 27 or 05 65 37 37 27 (reservations for activities).

Marshes, peat bogs, copses, wet meadows; heathers, gorses and ferns but also the housing and everyday lives of 19C woodsmen are explained all along this short but sweet circuit.

Rocamadour★★★

Rocamadour, with its slender castle keep towering above it, comprises a mass of old dwellings, oratories, towers and precipitous rocks on the rugged face of a *causse* cliff rising 150m/492ft above the Alzou canyon. This is one of the most extraordinary religious pilgrimage sites in France, both historic and steeped in beliefs and legends.

A BIT OF HISTORY

The enigmatic St Amadour – The identity of St Amadour, who gave his name to the sanctuary village, has never been firmly established. A 12C chronicler reported that in 1166 "as a local inhabitant had expressed the wish to be buried beneath the threshold of the Chapel of the Virgin, men began to dig a grave only to find the body of a man already buried there. This body was placed near the altar so that it might be venerated by the faithful and from that time onwards miracles occurred."

Who was this mysterious person whose tomb appeared to be so old? Conflicting theories have been put forward but the most widely accepted view is that the body was that of the publican Zaccheus, a disciple of Jesus and husband of St Veronica, who was obliged to flee Palestine and set up home in Limousin with his family. Following the death of Veronica, Zaccheus retired to the deserted and wild Alzou valley to preach. All this is hearsay, but one thing is certain; there was a hermit, and he often sought shelter at the rock. The

▶ **Population:** 675.
Michelin Map: 337: F-3.
Info: L'Hospitalet - 46500 Rocamadour. ℰ05 65 33 22 00. www.rocamadour.com.
Location: Northern Parc Régional du Haut-Quercy. The best way to arrive in Rocamadour is along the L'Hospitalet road. From a terrace there is a fine **view★★** of Rocamadour, with the Alzou winding its way through the bottom of a gorge, and the village clinging to the cliff face. The Cité Religieuse rises above the village, with the castle ramparts above it. There is another striking view of Rocamadour from the Couzou road (*D 32*).
Parking: There are several car parks in the valley as well as at L'Hospitalet.
Timing: Allow a full day to visit the village and Cité Religieuse and another half a day to explore the Causse de Gramat.
Don't Miss: The Cité Religieuse; the ramparts; the view from L'Hospitalet.
Kids: Rocher des Aigles; Féerie du Rail; Forêt des Singes; Parc Animalier de Gramat.

GETTING AROUND

Lift (to churches) – Open Jul–Aug 8am–8pm or 9pm, May–Jun 9am–7pm; Feb, Mar, Nov 9am–6pm. €3 round- trip, €2 single (*chidren under 8, no charge*). ℰ05 65 33 62 44.
Lift (to castle) – Open Jul–Aug 8am–10pm, May, Jun, Sept 9am–7pm; Feb, Mar, Nov, Dec 10am–12.30pm, 2–5.30pm; Apr, Oct 9am–6pm.

€4 round-trip, €2.50 single. ℰ05 65 33 62 79.

TOURS

Petit train de Nuit – Mid-May–mid-Jun and mid-Jul–mid-Aug 9.45pm, 10.15pm; mid-Jun–mid-Jul 10pm, 10.30pm; Apr–mid-May and Sept 9.30pm, 10pm. €5. ℰ05 65 33 65 99. www.lepetittrainderocamadour.com.

Rocamadour

© Christophe Boisvieux / age fotostock

Occitan expression – *roc amator* (he who likes the rock) – was adopted as the name of this village sanctuary, later becoming Rocamadour.

The fame of Rocamadour – From the time that the miracles began until the Reformation, the pilgrimage to Rocamadour was one of the most famous among Christians. Thirty thousand people would come on days of major pardon and plenary indulgence. Since the village was too small to house all the pilgrims, the Alzou valley was transformed into a vast camp. Henry Plantagenet, king of England, was miraculously cured and among the first to kneel before the Virgin; his example was followed during the Middle Ages by the most illustrious people, including St Bernard, St Louis and Blanche of Castille. Veneration of Our Lady of Rocamadour was established at Lisbon, Oporto, Seville and even in Sicily. The Rocamadour standard at the Battle of Las Navas at Tolosa routed the Muhammadans and gave the Catholic kings of Spain victory.

Pilgrimage and penitents – Ecclesiastical, and in some cases, lay tribunals used to impose the pilgrimage on sinners. On the day of their departure, penitents attended Mass and then set forth dressed wearing clothes covered with large crosses, large hats upon their heads, staffs in their hands and knapsacks on their backs. Upon reaching the end of their journey, the pilgrims stripped off their clothes and climbed the famous steps on their knees in their shirts with chains bound round their arms and neck. Before the altar to the Black Virgin they pronounced their *amende honorable*. A priest recited prayers of purification and removed the chains from the penitents, who, now forgiven, received from the priest a certificate and a kind of medal in lead bearing the image of the miraculous Virgin, called a *sportelle*.

Decline and renaissance – Rocamadour reached its zenith in the 13C. Favours not even granted to Jerusalem were granted to it; the money poured in, bringing greed with it. For 100 years, the abbeys of Marcilhac and Tulle disputed who should own the church at Rocamadour. Tulle was finally awarded the honour after arbitration. During the Middle Ages, the town was sacked several times. Henry Short Coat, in revolt against his father Henry Plantagenet, pillaged the oratory in 1183. During the Hundred Years War, bands of English and the local soldiery plundered the treasure in turn. During the Wars of Religion, the Protestant Captain Bessonies seized Rocamadour to desecrate it and lay it to waste; only the Virgin and the miraculous bell escaped. Rocamadour did not rise from its ruins. The abbey remained idle until it was dealt its final blow by the Revolution. In the 19C, the bishops

Rocamadour from a distance

© Lucio Pompeo / iStockphoto.com

of Cahors tried to revive the pilgrimage and rebuilt the churches. Though much of its splendour has vanished, Rocamadour has again found the fervour of its former pilgrims and is today a very respected pilgrimage centre.

✦✦WALKING TOUR

ECCLESIASTICAL CITY

The ecclesiastical city is a pedestrian zone. It can be accessed from the plateau ([P] car park) on foot or by lift (⊜charge), or from the Alzou valley ([P] car parks) on foot or by a small train (⊜charge) which runs to the village, and then from here to the ecclesiastical city either by the flights of stairs up the Via Sancta or by the lift.
✦✦For guided tours (groups only), contact Le Relais des Remparts.
℘05 65 33 23 23.

Go through the **Porte du Figuier** at the northern end, which was a gateway to the town as early as the 13C. Enter the main street, which is now cluttered with souvenir shops. Climb the 223 steps of the Great Stairway (Via Sancta). Pilgrims often make this ascent, kneeling at every step. Five flights of stairs lead to a terrace on which stand the former canons' quarters, now converted into shops and hotels. The terrace is called **place des Senhals** because of the pilgrims' insignia called *senhals* or *sportelles* made

there. The **Porte du Fort**, which opens under the palace perimeter wall, is an old entranceway leading to the sacred perimeter wall.

Parvis des Églises

The parvis (open space in front of the churches), which is also known as place St-Amadour, is fairly small, but it gives access to seven churches: St Saviour's Basilica opposite the stairway; St Amadour's Church below the basilica; the Chapel of Our Lady or Miraculous Chapel on the left; the three chapels of St John the Baptist, St Blaise and St Anne (✦✦*visit possible only as part of a guided tour of the Cité Religieuse*) on the right; and the Chapel of St Michael standing on a terrace to the left.

Basilique St-Sauveur

This 11C–13C Romanesque-Gothic sanctuary has three naves. One of the basilica walls is made out of the cliff's living rock, upon which the arches of the end bay are supported. The mezzanine was added in the 19C to enlarge the basilica during the great pilgrimages.
Above the altar stands a fine **16C Christ**, in polychrome wood on a cross that resembles a tree.

Eglise St-Amadour

&✦✦*Included in the guided tour of the Cité Religieuse.*
This 12C crypt lying below the basilica consists of a flat chevet and two bays with quadripartite vaulting. It used to be a place of worship: the body of St Amadour was venerated here.

Chapelle Notre-Dame

From the parvis, 25 steps lead to the Miraculous Chapel or Chapel of Our Lady, considered the Holy of Holies of Rocamadour. It is here that the hermit is believed to have hollowed out an oratory in the rock. In 1476 the chapel was crushed by falling rocks and rebuilt in the Flamboyant Gothic style. This new chapel was sacked during the Wars of Religion and the Revolution but was restored in the 19C. On the altar, in the semi-darkness of the chapel blackened by candle smoke, is the Miraculous Virgin, also called **Black Madonna★**. This rustic-style reliquary statue, carved in walnut, dates from the 12C. It is small in size (*69cm*) and was covered with silver plating of which several fragments, blackened by candle smoke and oxidation, remain. The miraculous **bell**, made of jointed iron plates and most likely dating from the 9C, hangs from the roof. It is said to have rung of its own accord to foretell miracles, for example when sailors lost at sea invoked Our Lady of Rocamadour.

On leaving the chapel, stuck in the cliff face above the doorway, one can see a great iron sword, which legend identifies as **Durandal**, Roland's famous sword. The story goes that Roland, surrounded by the Saracens and unable to break his sword to prevent it falling into enemy hands, prayed to the Archangel Michael and threw him his sword, which in a single stroke implanted itself in the rock of Rocamadour, far from the Infidels.

To the right is St Amadour's grave, believed to have been dug out of the rock on the very spot where the saint's body was found.

Chapelle St-Michel

🖐*Included in the guided tour of the Cité Religieuse.* ✆ 05 65 33 23 23.

This Romanesque chapel is sheltered by a rock overhang. The apse, which houses a small oratory, juts out towards the square. It was used for services by the monks of the priory, who had also installed a library there.

On the wall **outside** are two frescoes representing the Annunciation and the Visitation; the skill shown in this composition, the richness of colour and the grace of movement all seem to point to the works being 12C. Below them, a 14C fresco depicts an immense St Christopher.

Inside, the chancel is adorned with paintings: Christ in Majesty is surrounded by the Evangelists. Farther down, a seraph and the Archangel Michael are shown weighing souls.

PLATEAU
Stations of the Cross

A 19C shaded Stations of the Cross winds up towards the ramparts. After passing the caves (*grottes*) of the Nativity and the Holy Sepulchre, visitors will see the Cross of Jerusalem, brought from the Holy Land by the Penitential Pilgrims.

Ramparts

🕘*9am–6pm.* ⬟€2.50. ✆ 05 65 11 62 20. These are the remains of a 14C fort which was built to block off the rocky spur and protect the sanctuary. Leaning against the fortress, the residence of the chaplains of Rocamadour was built in the 19C.

Rocher des Aigles★

♿🕘*Open Apr–Sept. See website for times of displays.* ⬟€10 (children under 16, €6). ✆ 05 65 33 65 45. *www.rocherdesaigles.com.*

👥 This is a breeding centre for birds of prey. Regular demonstrations showing how they fly and hunt are popular with visitors. A running commentary helps with understanding the behaviour of these birds, some of which are endangered species.

▶ To return, go back to an esplanade on the same level as the Ecclesiastical City and take the lift to the main street near the Porte Salmon.

VILLAGE

The village is a pedestrian zone. It can be accessed from the plateau (🅿 car park) on foot or by lift (⬟charge), or from the Alzou valley (🅿 car parks) on foot or by a small train (⬟charge) which runs to the village, and then from here to the ecclesiastical city either by the flights of stairs up the Via Sancta or by lift. A tourist train offers visitors a view of the village by night.

▶ At the end of the watch-path, walk to place des Senhals and turn left.

Rue de la Mercerie

This former trading street is lined with hanging gardens. Note, on the right, the **Maison de la Pommette**, an old arcaded shop dating from the 15C and, slightly farther on to the left, a Romanesque house. The street leads to the 13C **Porte de Cabiliert**.

▶ Return to place des Senhals. Walk down the Grand Escalier and turn right.

Le Coustalou

Once you cross the 13C Porte Hugon, you'll enter a picturesque medieval quarter. The half-timbered Maison de la Louve is the best preserved of the old houses, built on the slope down to the Alzou.

▶ Return to Porte du Figuier.

Hôtel de Ville

Visits organised by tourist office, all year, 9am–noon. Closed Thu, weekends and public holidays. ℘05 65 33 63 26. www.mairierocamadour.fr. The town hall is located in a restored 15C house known as the Couronnerie or the House of the Brothers. In the council chamber there are two fine **tapestries★** by Jean Lurçat which portray the flora and fauna of the *causse*.

EXCURSION
♣♣ Espace Naturel Sensible des Vallées de l'Ouysse et de l'Alzou

4km/2.4mi W and 8km/4.9mi E. Departure from the Gouffre de Cabouy car park (along D 32 S of Cahors) and from the Moulin du Saut car park (towards Cahors, by way of Gramat then Les Aspes and Lauzou). 4.5km/2.7mi and 7.2km/4.4mi, 2hr and 3hr, yellow or red-and-white blazes. It is strongly recommended that you obtain the information sheets of the discovery guide available at the Salviac or Gourdon Tourist Offices.
The Ouysse and Alzou rivers have carved out the calcareous rock so much that Rocamadour is a perched village. The Moulin du Saut and Ouysse-et-Alzou circuits allow you to better understand this water erosion. In the first circuit, you'll also learn about mill technology, the hydrological regimes of these two rivers and the ecology of the banks and of a canyon. The second covers karst topography, groundwater emergence, erosion scarps and chasm formation.

Moulin de Cougnaguet

10km/6.2mi W along the D 673. Open Apr–mid-Oct. Tours 10am–noon and 2–6pm. €4. ℘05 65 32 63 09. www.cougnaguet.com.
The rounded arches of this fortified mill span a derivation of the Ouysse in a cool, lush and charming **setting**. The current mill was built in the 15C at the foot of a sheer cliff, on the site of an earlier example. In medieval times, grain and flour were highly sought after and needed to be defended, as illustrated here.

🚗 DRIVING TOUR

⑥ NORTHERN CAUSSE DE GRAMAT

70km/43.5mi round-trip. Allow half a day. See route 6 on region map pp192–193. Named after the market town of Gramat, the Northern Causse de Gramat lies south of the Dordogne valley.

▶ Drive N from Rocamadour on the D 32.

L'Hospitalet

The name of this village, clinging to Rocamadour's cliff face, comes from the small hospital founded in the 11C by Hélène de Castelnau to nurse the pilgrims on the road from Le Puy (Auvergne) to Santiago de Compostela. Only a few ruins of this hospital remain; the **Romanesque chapel**, which is set in the middle of the churchyard, was remodelled in the 15C. L'Hospitalet is very popular with visitors for its **viewpoint★★** which overlooks the site of Rocamadour. There is a large Tourist Information Centre (*Syndicat d'Initiative*).

Grotte des Merveilles

🕐☁🚗*Open Jul–Aug 9.30am–7pm, guided tour (45min), Apr–Jun and Sept, 10am–noon and 2–6pm; Oct–early Nov 10am–noon, 2–5pm.* ✆€7 (children 5–11: €4.50). ☎05 65 33 67 92. www.grotte-des-merveilles.com.

Discovered in 1920, this cave is only 8m/24ft deep, but has some lovely formations: stalactites, stalagmites and natural limestone dams reflecting the cave roof and its concretions.

On the walls are cave paintings dating back, most likely, to the Solutrean Period (c 20 000 BC), depicting outlined hands, black spots, a few horses, a cat and the outline of a deer.

▷ Leave L'Hospitalet E on D 36.

👥 Forêt des Singes

On the road to Figeac. ♿🕐*Open Jul–Aug, 9.30am–6.30pm; Mar–Apr and first half of Sept, 10am–noon and 1–5.30pm; May–Jun 10am–noon, 1–6pm; rest of year check website for details.* ✆€9 (children €5.50). ☎05 65 33 62 72. www.la-foret-des-singes.com.

Free to roam on 10ha/25 acres of woodland, 150 animals live in an environment similar to the upper plateaux of North Africa where they originated. You'll see Barbary apes and macaques, a species which is becoming extinct.

▷ Continue along D 36 to Rignac and turn left onto D 20.

Source Salmière

The beneficial properties of the Miers mineral water were discovered in 1624; rich in magnesium, it is used in the treatment of liver and urinary diseases and for its laxative properties.

Gouffre de Padirac★★

♿ *See Gouffre de PADIRAC.*

▷ Drive S to Padirac and turn right onto D 673, then left on D 11 2km/1.2mi farther on.

Gramat

Capital of the *causse* that bears its name, Gramat is also a busy commercial centre attracting agricultural fairs. It is the ideal starting point for visits to Padirac, Rocamadour and the area that lies between the Lot and the Dordogne. It was here that the French Centre de Formation des Maîtres-Chiens de la Gendarmerie (police dog handler training centre) was established in 1945.

▷ Take the D 677 travelling SW and turn left onto the D 14 beyond the railway line.

👥 Parc Animalier de Gramat

🕐*Open Apr–Sept, 9.30am–7pm; Oct–Mar, 2–6pm (Sun and public holidays 9.30am–6pm).* 🕐*Closed 25 Dec.* ✆€11 (children 5–14 years old, €6.50). ☎05 65 38 81 22. www.gramat-parc-animalier.com.

This nature park extends over 40ha/ 99 acres. It was acquired by the local authorities so that animals and plants could be observed in their natural environment. A botanical park is home to trees and shrubs from the *causse* (durmast oak, dogwood, ash etc).

The animal park contains mainly European species living in semi-captivity in their natural habitat. Some of these animals – wild oxen, Przewalski's horses, ibexes, bison – are species that existed during prehistoric times.

▷ Turn back and pick up D 677 on the left. In Le Bastit, turn right on D 50, then right again in Carlucet on D 32 to come back to Rocamadour.

ADDRESSES

🏨 STAY

🍽🍽🍽 **Hotel Les Esclargies** – *Route de Payrac.* ☎05 65 38 73 23. www. esclargies.com. 16 rooms. A modern hotel a short distance above Rocamadour, but from which the upper car park is easily accessible. Surrounded by oak trees amid open pastures, this is a place of calm, away from the bustle of Rocamadour, but not too far away.

Gouffre de
Padirac★★

The Padirac chasm provides access to wonderful galleries hollowed out of the limestone mass of Gramat Causse by a subterranean river. A visit to the vertiginous well and a tour of the mysterious river and the vast caves adorned with limestone concretions leave visitors with a striking impression of this fascinating underground world.

> ৬ **Michelin Map:** 337: G-2.
> ▷ **Location:** 13km/8mi E of Rocamadour.
> **Guided Tours:** (1hr 30min), Jul 9.30am–8pm; Aug 8.30am–8.30pm; Apr–Jun and Sept–mid-Nov 9.30am– 6.30pm.
> €10 (children €7).
> 05 65 33 64 56.
> www.gouffre-de-padirac.com.

A BIT OF HISTORY

From legend to scientific exploration – The Padirac Chasm was a source of superstitious terror to the local inhabitants right up to the 19C, as people believed that the origin of this great hole was connected with the devil.

Legend has it that St Martin was returning from an expedition on the *causse* where he had been looking unsuccessfully for souls to save. All at once his mule refused to go on; Satan, bearing a great sack full of souls which he was taking to hell, stood in the saint's path. Jeering at the poor saint, Satan made the following proposition: he would give St Martin the souls he had in his sack if St Martin would make his mule cross an obstacle that he, Satan, would create on the spot. Whereupon he hit the ground hard with his foot, and a gaping chasm opened up. The saint coaxed his mule forward and the beast jumped clear with such force that its hoof prints are still visible. Satan, defeated, retreated to hell by way of the hole he had created. The chasm served as a refuge for the people living on the *causse* during the Hundred Years War and the Wars of Religion, but it would appear that it was towards the end of the 19C, following a violent flooding of the river, that a passage opened between the bottom of the well and the underground galleries. The speleologist, **Édouard A Martel**, was the first to discover the passage in 1889. He then undertook nine expeditions and finally reached the Hall of the Great Dome.

Padirac was opened for the first time to tourists in 1898. Since then, numerous speleological expeditions have uncovered 22km/13.5mi of underground galleries. The 1947 expedition proved through fluorescein colouring of the water that the Padirac River reappears above ground 11km/7mi away where the Lombard rises and at St George's spring in the **Montvalent Amphitheatre** near the Dordogne.

During the expeditions of 1984 and 1985, a team of speleologists, paleontologists, prehistorians and geologists discovered a prehistoric site 9km/5.5mi

Grand Staircase, Gouffre de Padirac

© L. Nespoulous / SES Padirac

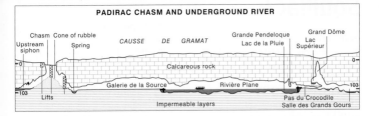

PADIRAC CHASM AND UNDERGROUND RIVER

from the mouth of the hole on an affluent of the Joly. Bones of mammoths, rhinoceroses, bison, bears, cave-dwelling lions and deer, all of which date from between 150 000 to 200 000 years ago, were excavated. Copies of some of the bones are exhibited in the entrance hall.

CHASM

Two lifts and a few staircases lead into the chasm, which is 32m in diameter, and to the pyramid of rubble, debris of the original caving-in of the roof. From the bottom of the lift (*75m*), there is a striking view of walls covered by the overflow from stalagmites and by vegetation and of a little corner of the sky at the mouth of the hole. Stairs lead down to the underground river, 103m below ground level. At the bottom, the 2km/1.25mi underground journey begins, 500m by boat and 400m on foot.

Galerie de la Source – This chamber is at the end of an underground canyon, the roof of which gets gradually higher; it is 300m long and follows the upper course of the river that hollowed it out. At the far end is the landing-stage.

Plane River – A flotilla of flat-bottomed boats offers an enchanting journey over the astonishingly translucent waters of this smooth river. The depth of the river varies from 50cm to 4m, but the water temperature remains constant at 13°C/55.4°F. The height of the roof increases progressively to reach a maximum of 78m; the different levels of erosion corresponding to the successive courses of the river can be seen from the boat. At the end of the boat trip admire the **Grande Pendeloque** (Great Pendant) of **Lac de la Pluie** (Rainfall Lake). This giant stalactite, the point of which nearly touches the water, is the

final pendant in a string of concretions 78m in height.

Pas du Crocodile – A narrow passage between high walls links the underground lake and the chambers to be visited next. Look to the left at the magnificent column known as the Grand Pilier, 40m high.

Salle des Grands Gours – A series of pools separated by *gours*, natural limestone dams, divides the river and the lake into basins; beyond them cascades a 6m waterfall. This is the end of the area open to tourists.

Lac Supérieur – This lake is fed only by water infiltrating the soil and falling from the roof; its level is 20m above that of the River Plane. *Gours* ring the lake's emerald waters.

Salle du Grand Dôme – The great height of the roof (*94m*) is most impressive in this, the largest and most beautiful of the Padirac caverns. The viewpoint, built halfway up, enables visitors to appreciate the rock formations and the flows of calcite decorating certain parts of the walls. The return trip (to the landing-stage) offers interesting views of the great pillar and the great pendant. From the end of the Galerie de la Source, four lifts lead back to the entrance.

Édouard A Martel

Édouard A Martel (*1859–1938*) is considered the father of modern speleology. His tours of the chasm were designed like Himalayan expeditions, with many local people employed to haul equipment.

Souillac★

At the confluence of the Corrèze and the Dordogne, Souillac is a bustling provincial town bisected by the N 20.

- **Population:** 3 817.
- **Michelin Map:** 337: E-2.
- **Info:** Blvd Louis Jean Malvy. 05 65 37 81 56. www.souillac.net.
- **Location:** Along the N 20, 29km/18mi E of Sarlat-la-Canéda and 39km/24mi S of Brive-la-Gaillarde.
- **Kids:** Musée de l'Automate.
- **Timing:** Spend 90min in the village and allow the rest of the day for the surroundings.

A BIT OF HISTORY

After the Benedictines settled in the plain of Souillès, (*souilh* meaning bog or marshland where wild boar wallow), they transformed the marsh into a rich estate. Souillac abbey was plundered and sacked several times by the English during the Hundred Years War and the Wars of Religion, but rose from its ruins each time thanks to the tenacity of its abbots. During the Revolution, its buildings were used for storing tobacco.

ABBEY CHURCH

Pl. de l'Abbaye. Open year-round. Summer 8am–7pm and winter 8am–6pm. 05 65 37 81 56.

Built in the 12C, this church is related to the Romanesque cathedrals of Angoulême, Périgueux and Cahors with their Byzantine inspiration, but it is more advanced in the lightness of its columns and the height of its arcades than the others. From place de l'Abbaye one can admire the attractive east end with its five pentagonal, apsidal chapels and an unusual tower on the other side of the building. **The back of the doorway★** – This composition consists of the remains of the old doorway, which was badly damaged by the Protestants and had been placed inside the nave of the new church, when it was erected in the 17C. Above the door, framed by the statues of St Peter on the right and St Benedict on the left, is a bas-relief relating episodes in the life of the monk Theophilus, deacon of Adana in Cilicia. On the right side of the door is a bas-relief of the prophet **Isaiah★★**. *The disfigured belltower, which is all that remains of the church St Martin, is now the town hall belfry.*

Musée national de l'Automate★

Enter by the parvis of the abbey-church (Abbatiale St-Pierre). Open Jul–Aug, 10am–6pm; Apr–Jun and Sept, 10am–noon, 3–6pm; Jan–Mar and Nov–Dec, Wed–Sun, 2.30–5pm; Oct Tue–Fri 10am–noon, 2.30–5.30pm, Sat–Sun 2.30–5.30pm. Closed 25 Dec and 14 Jan. €6 (children 5–12: €3). 05 65 37 07 07. www.musee-automate.fr.

The museum contains some 3 000 objects, including 1 000 automata donated by the **Roullet-Decamps** family, who for four generations were leaders in the field. In 1865 Jean Roullet created his first mechanical toy: a small gardener pushing a wheelbarrow. Note the **jazz band** (1920), a group of electric automata with black musicians performing a concert.

DRIVING TOUR

7 THE LOT AND DORDOGNE VALLEY★★★

Round-trip from Souillac – 85km/53mi. Allow 1 day. See route 7 on region map pp192–193.

Drive NE out of Souillac along the D 703.

Martel★

See MARTEL.

Continue along D 703 to Vayrac and turn N on D 20 towards Brive-la-Gaillarde. Turn left on D 119 before leaving the town.

Puy d'Issolud★

The highest point of the plateau near Vayrac is Puy d'Issolud at an altitude of 311m. The plateau is bordered by steep cliffs from which there is an extensive **view★** of the Dordogne.

Puy d'Issolud was surrounded, at the time of the Gauls, by such solid earthworks and drystone defences that it was one of the most redoubtable *oppida* of Quercy, and is said to have been the former **Uxellodunum**, site of the last Gaulish resistance to Caesar after Alésia. Some historians place Uxellodunum at Capdenac or Luzech, but archaeological research suggests that it is more likely to be Puy d'Issolud.

The battle, led by the Roman legionaries, was waged with unbelievable ferocity. After a spring had been diverted through underground caverns, causing those defending Uxellodunum to believe that their gods had deserted them by cutting off their water supply, it ended in another defeat for the Gauls.

▶ Return to Vayrac.

Vayrac

Located in place Luctérius, the **Musée Uxellodunum** (◷open Jul–Aug, daily except Mon 10.30am–12.30pm and 4–7pm; ◷closed Sept–Jun. ⊛€2. ✆05 65 32 40 26) displays prehistoric and Gallo-Roman finds discovered in and around the Puy d'Issolud *oppidum*.

▶ Continue on D 703 towards Puybrun. In Bétaille, turn right on D 20.

Carennac★

ⓘ *See CARENNAC.*

▶ Leave Carennac to the NW on D 43 which runs alongside the south bank of the river.

Beyond Carennac, the Dordogne cuts a channel between the Martel and Gramat *causses* before entering the beautiful area of the Montvalent Amphitheatre.

Floirac

A 14C keep is all that remains of the old fortifications. A lovely 15C chapel stands north of the village.

Cirque de Floirac★

There are attractive views of the valley and the *causse* cliffs from this road.

▶ Take D 140 towards Gluges then turn right on D 32 after crossing the river.

Belvédère de Copeyre★

There is a good **view★** of the Dordogne, the Floirac Amphitheatre and Puy d'Issolud from a wayside cross.

Gluges

This village lies in a beautiful **setting★** beside the river at the foot of the cliffs.

▶ Leave Gluges SW along D 43 and continue along D 23.

Creysse

The charming village of Creysse with pleasant, narrow streets, brown-tiled roofs, houses bedecked with climbing vines and flights of steps leading to their doors, lies at the foot of the rocky spur on which stands a pre-Romanesque church, the former castle chapel, with its curious twin apses. The 12C church and the remains of the 15C castle are reached by a stony alleyway, which climbs sharply to a terrace. It is from a little square shaded by plane trees, near the war memorial, that you get the best overall view of the village.

▶ Drive NW from Creysse along D 114 and, in Sozy, turn left on D 15.

Meyronne

From the bridge over the Dordogne, there is an appealing **view** of the river and the village – former home of the bishops of Tulle – with its charming Quercy houses built attractively into the cliffs.

▶ Continue SE along D 15 then turn right 1km/0.6mi farther on.

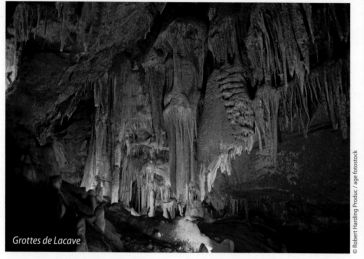

Grottes de Lacave

© Robert Harding Produc / age fotostock

Site du Moulin du Limon

The ruins of an old mill and a chasm overgrown with greenery form a charming setting.

▷ Return to Meyronne; turn left on D 23.

The road subsequently follows the course of the Dordogne through beautiful countryside of rocks and cliffs, then crosses the River Ouysse near Lacave.

Grottes de Lacave★★

🐌Visits by guided tour only (1hr 20min). ⏰Check website for opening times. ⊚€10. ℘05 65 37 87 03. www.grottes-de-lacave.com.
This series of caves was discovered in 1902 by Armand Viré, a student of the geographer and speleologist EA Martel, at the foot of the cliffs beside the river. The galleries open to visitors are 1.6km/1mi long. In the first, concretions and stalactites prevail. In the second, underground rivers run in between natural rimstone dams (*gours*) and flood out into placid lakes. In the **Salle des Merveilles**, black light first shows up the "living" part of the stalactites; then normal lighting enhances the reflection of the concretions in the lake water.

Château de Belcastel

A vertical cliff dropping down to the confluence of the Ouysse and the Dordogne is crowned by a castle standing proudly in a remarkable **setting★**. Only the eastern part of the main wing and the keep date from the Middle Ages.

▷ Turn left just before the bridge.

Château de la Treyne

⏰Open mid-Apr–mid-Nov, 10am–noon and 2–5pm. ⊚€5. ℘05 65 27 60 60. www.chateaudelatreyne.com.
The château is perched on a cliff. Burned by the Catholics during the Wars of Religion, the château was rebuilt in the 17C. The park and chapel (*where exhibitions are held*) are open to the public.

▷ D 43 leads back to Souillac. If you wish to enjoy the Dordogne a while longer, turn left at Port de Souillac and return to Souillac via Cieurac.

Martel ★

Built on the Upper Quercy causse to which it has given its name, Martel is known as the town of the seven towers. Today fine foods are part of its reputation, as it is a central market for walnuts and includes a number of cottage industries that process and preserve local produce.

A BIT OF HISTORY

The three hammers – After stopping the Saracens at Poitiers in 732, **Charles Martel** chased them into Aquitaine. Several years later he struck again and wiped them out. To commemorate this victory over the infidels and to give thanks to God, Charles Martel had a church built on the spot.

A town grew up around the church and was named Martel in memory of its founder, taking as its crest three hammers which were the favourite weapons of the saviour of Christianity.

Martel and the Viscounty of Turenne – The founding of Martel by the conqueror of the infidels is probably based more on fiction than on fact. However, it is known that the viscounts of Turenne made Martel an important urban community as early as the 12C. In 1219, Viscount Raymond IV granted a charter establishing Martel as a free town – exempt from the king's taxes, with permission to mint money. Very quickly Martel established a town council and consulate and thus became the seat of the royal bailiwick and of the seneschalship. It established a court of appeal that handled all the region's judicial matters; more than 50 magistrates, judges and lawyers were employed. It reached its peak at the end of the 13C and beginning of the 14C. Like the rest of the region, the town suffered during the Hundred Years War and during the Wars of Religion. In 1738, when the rights of Turenne were sold to the king (see TURENNE), Martel lost its privileges and became a castellany.

The rebellious son – At the end of the 12C, Martel was the scene of a tragic series of events which brought into conflict **Henry II Plantagenet**, king of

▶ **Population:** 1 650.
Michelin Map: 337: F-2 or Dordogne in the Quercy.
Info: Palais de la Raymondie, pl. des Consuls. ☎05 65 37 43 44. www.martel.fr.
▶ **Location:** 15km/9.5mi E of Souillac; 20km/12mi N of Rocamadour.
Don't Miss: Places des Consuls; Hôtel de la Raymondie.
Kids: Snakes and lizards at Reptiland; Chemin de fer touristique du Haut-Quercy "Le Truffadou" steam train, ☎05 65 37 35 81.
Timing: Half a day.

England and lord of all western France, his wife **Eleanor of Aquitaine** and their four sons. The royal household was a royal hell. Henry could no longer stand the sight of Eleanor, and shut her up in a tower. The sons thereupon took up arms against their father, and the eldest, **Henry Short Coat**, pillaged the viscounty of Turenne and Quercy. To punish him, Henry Plantagenet gave his lands to his third son, Richard the Lionheart, and stopped Henry's allowance. Henry Short Coat found himself penniless and to pay his foot-soldiers he plundered the treasure houses of the provincial abbeys. He took the shrine and the precious stones of St Amadour from Rocamadour and sold Roland's famous sword, Durandal. But as he was leaving Rocamadour after these sacrilegious acts, the bell miraculously began to toll: it was a sign from God. Henry fled to Martel and arrived there with a fever; he felt death to be upon him and was stricken with remorse. He confessed his crimes while Henry II was sent for, to come and forgive his son on his deathbed; the King was at the siege of Limoges and sent a messenger with his pardon. The messenger found Henry Short Coat lying in agony on a bed of cinders, a heavy wooden cross upon his chest. Shortly afterwards he died, a last farewell to his mother Eleanor on his lips.

WALKING TOUR

Start at the **former perimeter walls**. Wide avenues, fossé des Cordeliers and boulevard du Capitani, have been built on the site of the old ramparts (12C–13C). The machicolated **Tournemire Tower**, which used to be the prison tower, and the Souillac and Brive gateways (found at the end of Route de Souillac and rue de Brive; *not on the town plan*) hark back to the time when Martel was a fortified town, well protected by double perimeter walls. The second perimeter wall, built in the 18C, enclosed the outer town.

▷ Park in the car park along the north wall. Pass between the post office and Tournemire Tower to enter the old town.

Rue du Four-Bas

There are still some Renaissance houses along this street, which is spanned by an archway.

▷ Follow the street towards place de la Rode.

Église St-Maur

This 13C–16C Gothic church has some interesting defensive features: huge buttresses converted into defence towers, machicolations protecting the flat east end and a 40m-high belltower that looks more like a keep. Beneath the porch is a fine historiated Romanesque **tympanum** depicting the Last Judgement. The width of the nave is striking. The chancel with its stellar vaulting is lit by a large 16C **stained-glass window** showing God the Father, the four Evangelists and scenes from the Passion.

▷ Return to the centre via rue Droite.

Rue Droite

There are old townhouses all along this road, one of which, Hôtel Vergnes-de-Ferron, is adorned with a lovely Renaissance door.

▷ From place de la Bride, take rue de la Bride.

Hôtel de Mirandol

This 15C townhouse constructed by François de Mirandol features a great square tower with a spiral staircase.

▷ Rue de la Bride leads to place M.-Meteye; turn right then left.

Maison Fabri

The tower, called Court-Mantel after Henry Short Coat who died here in 1183, has windows featuring frontons decorated with balls at the intersections of their cornices on all five floors.

Place des Consuls★

In the centre of the square is the 18C **covered market** with timbering set on great stone pillars. On one side the old town measures can be seen.

Hôtel de la Raymondie★

Once the fortress of the viscounts of Turenne, built around 1280, this building was converted into a Gothic mansion in the 14C. The **façade★** overlooking rue de Senlis has remarkable apertures; a row of ogive arches on the ground floor is surmounted by seven quatrefoil rose windows.

The main entrance on place des Consuls is decorated with the town's coat of arms, a shield with three hammers. In the first-floor rooms note the two carved wooden chimney-pieces and the Renaissance bas-relief.

Musée d'Uxellodunum

🕐*Open Jul–Aug, 10am–12pm and 3–6pm. Visit by prior arrangement.* 🕐*Closed Sun, and rest of year.* ⊚€1 *(children under 10, no charge).* ℘*05 65 37 30 03.*

This museum, essentially devoted to prehistoric and Gallo-Roman archaeology, also houses medieval objects and a collection of 17C–18C chemist's jars.

Rue Tournemire

This attractive little street leads off to the left of the Hôtel de la Raymondie. The 13C **Hôtel de la Monnaie** with intersecting turrets was a coin mint (écus and deniers) for the viscounty of

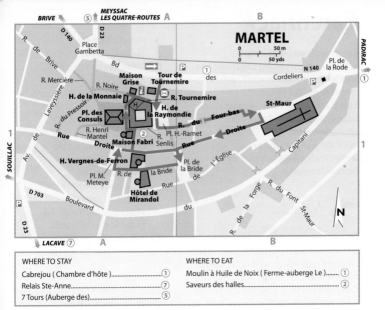

WHERE TO STAY	
Cabrejou (Chambre d'hôte)	①
Relais Ste-Anne	⑦
7 Tours (Auberge des)	⑤

WHERE TO EAT	
Moulin à Huile de Noix (Ferme-auberge Le)	①
Saveurs des halles	②

Turenne. The 16C **Maison Grise** is decorated with a carved bust and a heraldic shield with three hammers.

EXCURSION
👥 Reptiland

2km/1.2mi along the N 140 towards Figeac. 🕐 ♿ *Open Jul–Aug daily 10am–6pm; Sept–Jun daily except Mon 10am–12pm and 2–6pm.* 🕐 *Closed Dec–Feb.* €9 *(children 4–12 years, €6).* ℘*05 65 37 41 00. www.reptiland-le-renouveau.fr.*

92 species of snakes, lizards, crocodiles, tortoises and more. Explanatory panels provide information about each species. The owner, Pancho Gouygou, tries to show the peaceful disposition of his guests rather than their dangerous or spectacular side. He even claims to be able to cure anyone suffering from a morbid fear of snakes!

ADDRESSES

🛏 STAY

⊖ **Chambre d'hôte Cabrejou** – *St-Denis-lès-Martel.* ℘*05 65 37 31 89. www. ferme-cabrejou.com.* 🅿️🛏. *7 rooms.* This walnut farm has a very pretty stone farmhouse.

The rooms are simple, large and comfortable. Four of them are located in the converted barn. The pleasant garden and kitchenette are little extras that make your stay more enjoyable.

⊖⊖ **Auberge des 7 Tours** – *Av. de Turenne.* ℘*05 65 37 30 16. www.auberge 7tours.com.* 🅿️. *7 rooms.* Basic renovated rooms. A lovely dining room/veranda oriented towards the countryside. Traditional cuisine, duck dishes and a selection of local wines.

⊖⊖⊖ **Relais Ste-Anne** – *R. Pourtanel.* ℘*05 65 37 40 56. www.relais-sainte-anne.com.* ♿🅿️. *14 rooms.* This charming former girls' boarding school is surrounded by a garden. Includes an old chapel, elegant living room and personalised rooms. Just across from the hotel, a modern style of cuisine is served in a contemporary dining room with a little terrace patio.

🍴 EAT

⊖⊖ **Saveurs des Halles** – *R. Senlis.* ℘*05 65 37 35 66.* This unpretentious establishment is located in the heart of the old town, at the corner of the gorgeous place des Consuls. Locals know that the fresh products served are of the finest quality. Regional specialities are on offer alongside quite refined fare. There are a few tables on the terrace.

Carennac★

Carennac is one of the most attractive sights along the Dordogne and is classified as one of France's "Most Beautiful Villages".
This picturesque town with its tiled houses and turreted mansions clustering around the old priory was once the home of the prelate and writer François de Salignac de la Mothe-Fénélon.

 WALKING TOUR

This charming village, where some of the houses date from the 16C, has barely changed since Fénélon's day. The Île Barrade, in the Dordogne, was renamed Calypso's Island. A tower in the village is known as Telemachus' Tower. Here, it is said, Fénélon wrote his masterpiece. The deanery was suppressed by order of the Royal Council in 1788 and sold in an auction in 1791. Of the old ramparts there remains only a fortified gateway, and of the old buildings, only the castle and the priory tower.

▶ Go through the fortified gateway.

Château des Doyens

Next to the church of St-Pierre (&see below), this 16C edifice consists of a main building flanked by corner turrets and a gallery built above the church's Gothic

- ▶ **Population:** 389.
- **Michelin Map:** 329: G-2.
- **Info:** Cour du Prieuré. ℘05 65 33 22 00. www.vallee-dordogne-rocamadour.com.
- **Location:** 33km/20.5mi E of Souillac along the Dordogne, 22km/13.6mi N of Rocamadour via the *causse*.
- **Don't Miss:** The representation of Jesus being laid in the tomb at the cloister, the portal of the St-Pierre church.
- **Timing:** 2hr for the village.

chapels. The severe façade looks over the Dordogne and Calypso Island.

Espace Patrimoine

Open Jul–Sept, Mon–Fri 10am–noon, 2–6pm, Sat–Sun 2–6pm; May–Jun and Oct daily except Mon and weekends 10am–noon, 2–6pm, public holidays 2–6pm. No charge. ℘05 65 33 81 36.
The three storeys of the château are a discovery area for the Dordogne river in the *département* of the Lot. A **scale model** is enlivened by lights and sounds which create a picture of the Dordogne valley from Biards to Souillac. The other rooms also use 3D audio-visual programmes to explore various subjects:

François de Salignac de la Mothe-Fénélon

The priory-deanery at Carennac, which was founded in the 10C and attached to the famous abbey at Cluny in the following century, owes its fame to the fact that François de Salignac de la Mothe-Fénélon spent time there before he became archbishop of Cambrai. While he was still a student at Cahors, Fénélon enjoyed spending his holidays with his uncle, senior prior of Carennac. In 1681 Fénélon's uncle died and was succeeded by the young abbot, who remained at the priory for 15 years. Fénélon was greatly revered at Carennac; he enjoyed describing the ceremonies and general rejoicing that greeted his arrival by boat and his installation as commendatory prior. Tradition has it that Fénélon wrote *Télémaque* while living at Carennac. The description of the adventures of Ulysses' son was at first only a literary exercise, but was subsequently turned into a tract for the edification of the duke of Burgundy, Louis XIV's grandson, when Fénélon was appointed his tutor.

Northern entrance to Carennac

© S. Sauvignier / Michelin

flora and fauna, regional arts, the history of navigation and prehistoric times.

Musée des Alambics et Aromathèque

⏲ *Open by arrangement: Mon–Fri 5–8pm, weekends 4–7pm.*
℘ 05 65 10 91 16.
Adjacent to the park of the château, this museum is devoted to stills and aromatic plants. It offers guided tours with a demonstration of how lavender is distilled.

Église St-Pierre

In front of this Romanesque church dedicated to St Peter stands a porch with a beautiful 12C carved **doorway★**. It is well preserved and would appear to belong to the same school as the tympana of Beaulieu, Moissac, Collonges and Cahors. Inside, the interesting archaic capitals in the nave are decorated with fantastic animals, foliage and historiated scenes.

▷ On leaving the church, walk to the end of the priory courtyard.

Cloisters

⏲ ♿ *Open 10am–noon, 2–5pm.*
℘ 05 65 10 97 01. ⊛ €3.
The restored cloisters consist of a Romanesque gallery adjoining the church and three Flamboyant galleries. Stairs lead to the terrace. The chapter-house, which

opens onto the cloisters, shelters a remarkable **Entombment★** (15C). Christ lies on a shroud carried by two disciples: Joseph of Arimathea and Nicodemus.

▷ Leave the priory and walk alongside the castle overlooking the Dordogne and Calypso Island. Take the first street on the left.

A small public park gives access to a charming **Romanesque chapel**. Opposite stands a 16C house with a corner window.

▷ Turn right to walk round the former priory and return to the castle.

A bartizan still towers over the Pont de Carennac. On the other side of the bridge, another four-storey, 16C tower overlooks a small pier.

ADDRESSES

⌂ STAY

⊜⊜ **Hostellerie Fénélon** – *Le Bourg, 46110 Carennac. ℘ 05 65 10 96 46. www. hotel-fenelon.com. 18 rooms.* A large Quercy house with a family atmosphere where you may prefer the bedrooms with a view of the Dordogne. Beams, a fireplace and country ornaments give character to the dining room.

Turenne★

"Pompadour pompe. Ventadour vente. Turenne règne." This old French pun defies translation, but can be loosely construed as crediting Turenne with noble dignity, whereas the other cities mentioned are just full of hot air. Today the ruins of the proud castle, once the stronghold of the viscounts of La Tour d'Auvergne, rise above the picturesque town.

A BIT OF HISTORY

A small town with a great past – The incapability of the last Carolingians to govern the whole of their territories and the aptitude of the lords of Turenne for resisting Viking invasion seems to have been the root of the fief's emancipation from royal power. As early as the 11C, a fortress was set on the outlines of the Martel Causse. In the 15C, Turenne held sway over a third of Lower Limousin, Upper Quercy and the Sarlat area, including 1 200 villages and a number of abbeys.

The viscounty, in its heyday, enjoyed enviable privileges. Like the king of France, the viscounts ruled absolutely, ennobling subjects, creating offices and consulates, minting money and levying taxes.

WALKING TOUR

LOWER TOWN

At the foot of the hill is the Barri-bas Quarter, the old part of town.

Place du Foirail

The Hôtel Sclafer, with a loggia, was a residence for notaries in the 17C. Opposite, there is a small 15C shop with a large arcade.

▶ Follow rue du Commandant-Charolais.

- ▶ **Population:** 793.
- ⚙ **Michelin Map:** 329: K-5; or see Brive-la-Gaillarde.
- ℹ **Info:** Pl. du Belvédère. ℘05 55 24 08 80. www.turenne.fr.
- ▶ **Location:** 15km/9.5mi S of Brive-la-Gaillarde.
- ⊙ **Don't Miss:** The castle; the view from the Tour de César.

Place de la Halle

The townhouses around this square reflect the wealth of its inhabitants, especially **Maison Vachon**, the residence of the consuls of Turenne in the 16C and 17C.

Rue Droite

This narrow street, lined with old corbelled houses and small shops, climbs towards the castle.

▶ Turn right onto rue Joseph-Rouveyrol.

Rue Joseph-Rouveyrol

Note the **Maison de l'Ancien Chapitre** (old chapter-house), the tower of which is decorated with a lovely Flamboyant-Gothic-style doorway.

▶ Continue straight on along rue de l'Église.

Church

The construction of the church in the form of a Greek cross was decided upon by Charlotte de La Marck in 1593, the year Henri IV converted to Catholicism. After Charlotte's death, Elizabeth of Nassau took over the project. Just above the church, the vast Maison Tournadour was once the town's salt storehouse.

UPPER TOWN

You'll access the upper town through the **fortified gateway** of the second of the three curtain walls which protected the castle. On the right, the **Seneschal's House** boasts an elegant tower. On the left, the **Chapelle des Capucins** (*1644*) hosts various exhibitions.

Château

🕐Open daily: Jul–Aug, 10am–7pm;
Apr–Jun and Sept–Oct, 10am–noon,
2–6pm; Nov–Mar, Sun 2–5pm. ⊜€5
(children under 10, no charge).
☎05 55 85 90 66.

The castle was demolished by Louis
XV after the viscounty became crown
property. Only the Clock and Caesar's
towers, at each end of the promontory,
were spared. The site★ is remarkable.

Tour de l'Horloge

The 13C clock tower was the castle keep.
Only the guard-room with broken-barrel
vaulting is open to visitors. Above it is
the salle du trésor – the counting room,
or treasury.

Tour de César

This round tower with irregular stone
bonding appears to date from the 11C.
A staircase leads to the top, where you'll
get a sweeping view★★ of the region. In
the foreground below are the village's
slate roofs. In the distance, beyond a
green valley landscape, appear the
Monts du Cantal to the east and the Dordogne valley to the south (viewing table).
Go round the castle from the right. A
series of manor houses, roofed with
slate and flanked by squat towers, have
names which evoke their past purpose
– the Gold Foundry, for example.

🚗 DRIVING TOUR

8 SUR LES TERRES DE MON
SIEUR DE TURENNE★

50km/31mi. Allow 3hr. ⏱See route 8 on
region map pp192–193.

▶ Drive out of Turenne along the D 8
and after 3km/1.2mi, turn left towards
Lagleygeolles.

This trip crosses the central area of the
old viscounty of Turenne, which was
not united with the French crown until
1738 (⏱see above). Beyond Turenne, the
wooded hills of the Limoges region give
way to the first limestone plateaus of the
Quercy region.

Gouffre de la Fage★

🕐Open: Jul and Aug daily
9.30am–1pm, 2–7pm; Apr–Jun daily
except Wed 2–6.30pm; Sept 2–6pm
except Wed. ⊜€7.50. ☎05 55 85 80 35.
www.gouffre-de-la-fage.com.

The underground galleries in this chasm
form two separate groups that can be
visited one after the other. A staircase
leads into the chasm, which was created
by the collapse of the roof section. The
first group of chambers, to the left,
contains fine draperies in the form of
jellyfish in beautiful rich colours. In the
Organ Hall (Salle des Orgues), the concretions are played like a xylophone.
The second group bears many stalagmites and stalactites, including a forest
of needle-like stalactites hanging from
the ceiling.

▶ Return to Lagleygeolles, and
take the left turn that will bring you
to D 73.

Jugeals-Nazareth

The village of Nazareth was founded by
Raymond I of Turenne when he returned
from the first Crusade. He founded a
hospital placed under the care of the
Knights Templar. There are vestiges
of vaulted rooms equipped with wells
enclosed with gratings where lepers
were kept under the town hall.

▶ Leaving the village N on D 8, there
is a nice view on the right. At the
Montplaisir intersection, take D 38 to
the right towards Meyssac.

Château de Lacoste

This former stronghold, built of local
sandstone, has a main building flanked
by three 13C towers. It was completed
in the 15C with an elegant turret and a
polygonal staircase.

At Noailhac you enter the region of red
sandstone, which is used to build the
lovely warm-coloured villages of the
area. Soon Collonges-la-Rouge, perhaps
the best-known, can be seen against a
backdrop of greenery.

Collonges-la-Rouge★★

See COLLONGES-LA-ROUGE.

Meyssac

Meyssac is in the centre of hilly countryside where walnut and poplar trees,
vineyards and orchards prosper. Like
Collonges-la-Rouge, the town is built
of red sandstone.

The **church** is an unusual mixture of
architectural elements: a Gothic interior, a belfry-porch fortified by hoarding
and a limestone doorway in the Romanesque Limousin style. Near the church is
the **18C covered market**. The red earth,
known as Collonges clay, is used in pottery manufacture here in Meyssac.

○ Leave Meyssac S on D 14, towards
Martel. After 2km/1.2mi, turn right on
the D 28.

Saillac

The village nestles among walnut trees
and fields of maize. Inside the small
Romanesque church is a doorway, preceded by a narthex, with a remarkable
tympanum★ in polychrome stone,
relatively rare in the 12C.

The village has retained its old mill;
walnut oil is pressed here every other
year during the Walnut Festival on the
first Sunday in October.

Collonges-la-Rouge★★

**Built of red sandstone, romantic
Collonges' small manor houses and
Romanesque church are surrounded
by typical Quercy countryside of
juniper bushes, walnut plantations
and vineyards.**

A BIT OF HISTORY

The village developed in the 8C around
its church and priory, a dependency of
the powerful Charroux abbey. In the 13C,
Collonges was a part of the viscounty of
Turenne and thus received franchises
and liberties. In the 16C, Collonges was
the place chosen by prominent denizens
of the viscounty for their holidays. They
erected charming manors and mansions
flanked with towers and turrets, which
give the town its unique image.

 WALKING TOUR

○ Start near the old station
(ancienne gare); take rue de la
Barrière (left).

▶ **Population:** 470.
⌖ **Michelin Map:** 329: K-5
   or see Brive-la-Gaillarde.
▌ **Info:** Pl. de la Mairie
   - 19500 Collonges-la-
   Rouge. ℘05 55 25 47 57.
   www.ot-collonges.fr.
○ **Location:** 19km/11.9mi SE
   of Brive via D 38. For one of
   the best views of Collonges
   walk down r. de la Barrière
   into the village. Turn left
   and continue along r. de la
   Garde. You'll see the whole
   village from the west.
Ⓟ **Parking:** Motor vehicles
   are prohibited 10am–7pm
   Easter–Sept. There are
   three car parks off the main
   road above the village.
◈ **Don't Miss:** Église St-Pierre,
   Castel de Vassinhac.

Maison de la Sirène

This 16C corbelled house, with a porch
and beautiful *lauze* roof, is adorned with
a mermaid holding a comb in one hand
and a mirror in the other. The interior
is set up like the inside of a Collonges
house of yesteryear, the **Musée de la**

Sirène des Arts et Traditions Populaires. Farther along, the pointed gateway arch (Porte du Prieuré) marks the entrance of the former Benedictine priory that was destroyed during the Revolution.

Hôtel des Ramades de Friac

The *hôtel*, crowned by two turrets, was once the townhouse of the powerful Ramades de Friac family. Go past the Relais de St-Jacques-de-Compostelle and through a covered passageway. Soon afterwards, in an alley on the right, there is an old turreted house.

Château de Benge

Set against a backdrop of poplar and walnut trees is this proud towered and turreted manor house with its lovely Renaissance window. The lords of Benge owned the famous Collonges vineyards until these were decimated by phylloxera.

Porte Plate

This flat gateway, so named because it has lost its towers, was part of the town walls protecting the church, cloisters and priory buildings.

Halle

The covered market, with its massive framework supported by strong pillars, served as a central granary store and shelters the communal oven. The **Église St-Pierre★** stands opposite.

Castel de Vassinhac★

This elegant manor house was owned by Gédéon de Vassinhac, lord of Collonges, captain-governor of the viscounty of Turenne. Built in 1583, the manor house bristles with large towers and turrets with pepperpot roofs. Despite a large number of mullioned windows, its defensive role is obvious from its many loopholes and castellated turrets.

Église St-Pierre★

This 11C and 12C church was fortified during the Wars of Religion in the 16C. The great square keep was strengthened by a defence chamber communicating with the watch-path.

Tympanum★ – Carved in the white limestone of Turenne, the 12C tympanum stands out among all the red sandstone. The whole tympanum is outlined by a pointed arch ornamented with a fine border of carved animals.

Belltower★ – The 12C belltower is built in the Limousin style: two lower square levels featuring round-arched bays are surmounted by two octagonal levels flanked by gables.

Interior – In the 12C, the church had a cruciform plan around the transept crossing. The dome above the transept crosing rests on 11C pillars. Side chapels were added in the 14C and 15C, as well as a second, Flamboyant-style nave.

Chapelle des Pénitents

The 13C chapel was modified by the Maussac family during the 17C, during the Counter-Reformation.

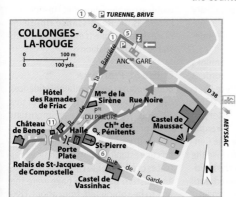

Rue Noire

This street cuts through the oldest part of Collonges, where old houses can be seen set back one from the other, ornamented with turrets and towers and adorned with climbing plants.

Castel de Maussac

This building is embellished with a turret and a porch roof above the main door. A barbican projects from the square tower, which is overlooked by a dormer window. Continue farther south along the street to enjoy a pretty **view★** of Collonges, Vassinhac Manor and the tower.

Beaulieu-sur-Dordogne★★

Built on the right bank of the Dordogne, Beaulieu is noteworthy for its fine Romanesque church, once part of a Benedictine abbey.

A BIT OF HISTORY

Foundation and growth of the abbey – Raoul, archbishop of Bourges, visited this part of the country in 855 and, enchanted by the beauty of this particular site which he christened *bellus locus – beau lieu* (beautiful place) – decided to found a community here. The monastery rose to significance despite the warlike struggles for control waged by the lords of Turenne and Castelnau. The abbots became the equals of city merchants and, as their special privileges increased, became virtually independent.

The Benedictine reform – The monks gradually came to interpret the order's rule of discipline more and more liberally. During the Wars of Religion (1562-98), they deserted their monastery. In 1663 the Abbot of La Tour d'Auvergne called on the austere Benedictine Congregation of Maurists to undertake the necessary reforms and repair the buildings. The community prospered until the Revolution drove them out again.

ADDRESSES

🛌 STAY

🍴🍴 Chambre d'hôte La Raze – *5.5km/3.5mi SW of Collonges along D 38 and D 19 (follow signs to La Raze). ☎05 55 25 48 16. 🖥. 5 rooms.* This 18C farm is a 10min walk from Collonges. The main features here are the comfortable rooms decorated with stencilled designs and an impressive English-style garden.

▸ **Population:** 1 253.
🖫 **Michelin Map:** 329: M-6.
🛈 **Info:** 6 pl. Marbot. ☎05 55 91 09 94. www.beaulieu-tourisme.com.
▶ **Location:** 46km/28.75mi SW of Brive via D 921/D 940.
👁 **Don't Miss:** The Église St-Pierre and its south doorway; the old town.
🕐 **Timing:** 1 day for the town and its surroundings.

OLD TOWN★

A maze of narrow streets and old houses is huddled around the church. Note the 16C tower with its decorative shell motif on rue Ste-Catherine. The building known as the **Renaissance House** on place de la Bridolle is embellished with statues and medallions.

Église St-Pierre★★

Both Limousin and Aquitaine influences can be seen in the architecture of this 12C abbey-church, once an important place of pilgrimage.

The sandstone building is typical of Benedictine establishments which served as places of pilgrimage. The choir, transept and eastern bay of the nave were the first to be completed, from about 1100 to 1140. In the middle of the 12C, works were continued from the southern end of the nave to the northern parallel walls. The project was finished in the 13C with the western bay of the nave and the façade.

The **south doorway★★** was carved in 1125 and is one of the great masterpieces of early Romanesque sculpture. The craftsmen who created it came from Toulouse and also worked on the carvings at Moissac, Collonges, Souillac and Carrennac.

The doorway is preceded by an open porch; the sculpture, which has been restored, is remarkable in its composition and execution. The theme on the tympanum is the Last Judgement. In the centre, Christ in Majesty dominates all by his height and extends his arm in welcome to the chosen. On either side two angels sound trumpets. Above, four angels hold the instruments of the Passion: the Cross, the Nails and the Crown of Thorns. The Apostles are grouped left and right and above them the dead rise from their graves. Monsters line the upper part of the lintel. The lower part, as at Moissac, is decorated with rosettes from which emerge chimera, serpents and monsters.

The style and proportions of the graceful **east end** of the church are highlighted by the window mouldings typical of the Limousin region as well as cornices with sculpted modillions.

As you walk around the outside of the chevet, note the vestiges of the cloisters where they once extended from the northern side of the church (sacristy).

There is no tympanum above the wide doorway of the **west front**. The tower rising up to the right was added in the 14C during the Hundred Years War. Raised higher in 1556, it served as the town belfry. Inside, the sanctuary was designed for pilgrimages and, like others built for this purpose, planned out to facilitate the movement of crowds, as evidenced in the wide aisles.

The nave has barrel vaulting. The tall, asymmetrical dome on pendentives rises above the transept from recessed

Romanesque tympanum of the south doorway, Église St-Pierre

© A. Demotes / Photononstop / Tips Images

columns. The chancel is lit by five rounded bays.

The decorative aspect is rather rustic compared to the intricate beauty of the south doorway. There are just a few sculpted capitals, at the entrance to the ambulatory and the transept chapels, featuring garlands and caryatids.

The other capitals bear geometrical designs typical of the Quercy region. In the northern arm of the transept, above the door to the stairway, there is a simple lintel carving of lions and a tree.

Trésor

Housed in the north transept, the treasury includes a remarkable 12C **Virgin and Child★** in silver-plated wood and a chased enamel shrine (chest) from the 13C.

Chapelle des Pénitents

This delightful Romanesque chapel is reflected in the waters of the Dordogne downstream from the town. Built originally in the 12C but since restored, it now hosts temporary exhibitions in summer.

EXCURSION
Château d'Estresses

3km/1.78mi S of Beaulieu. Take D 41 along the Dordogne and turn right towards Liourdes. ☎ Guided tour (1hr) May–Oct 10am–noon, 2–6pm; other

periods by prior arrangement. ☞€4
(children under 12, no charge).
☎05 55 91 10 28.

Great historic events have taken place on the Estresses plain. In 889, Eudes, the king of France, had the Normands arrested here while they were coming down the river in *drakar* boats. Later, in 1356, the Black Prince, who was devastating the region, was captured here. The Roquets, a *bourgeois* family from Beaulieu, began building the castle in the 14C and 15C. It was burned during the French Revolution and sold to three families who let it fall into disrepair. After 1918, it was sold to the grandfather of the current owners, but no archive of the castle remains. The building was lovingly restored between 1920 and 1960. It now consists of an entry porch and a 14C square tower linked together by a 16C main building. There are only a few foundations left of the horseshoe building with a dungeon at one end and of the chapel preceded by a residence that would have been perpendicular to the porch. These demolished buildings were used as a source for stones to the surrounding villages. The tour finishes in the *salle du roi Eudes*, featuring a rare basket arch and a large stone fireplace. The room has antique furniture and objects and an early 20C painting depicting Eudes' battle. The beautiful **garden** along the Dordogne is full of flowers and includes 2 000-year-old yew trees with trunks measuring more than 8m in diameter!

🚗 DRIVING TOUR

⑨ FROM PALSOU TO SOURDOIRE

24km/14.9mi. Allow 2 hr. 🕓*See route 9 on region map pp192–193.*

▷ Drive out of Beaulieu S along the D 41, turn right on D 12 and then right again on D 15E.

La Chapelle-aux-Saints
From the car park *(200m from the village)*, a path leads to the **cave** where the bones

of mankind's 45 000-year-old cousin were found. Indeed, a nearly complete Neanderthal skeleton was found in this *bouffia* (meaning "cave" in Occitan) in 1908. Also found on the burial site were everyday objects from the time. Excavations were resumed in 1999 and new cavities have been uncovered.

👫 **Le Musée de l'Homme de Neandertal** (♿🕓☞ *Guided tour (45min) in Jul–Aug 10am–noon, 2.30–6pm; Apr–Jun and early Sept–Oct daily except Thu 2.30–6pm. €5 (children 6–12, €3). ☎05 55 91 18 00. www.neandertal-musee.org)* explains the discovery of this hunter, his lifestyle and environment. The guided tour describes the scientific importance of this discovery and rectifies the image of this species, which has been mistakenly considered a thick brute for too long. The entrance to the 12C village **church** with its lovely slate roof features two columns with sculpted capitals. The birds depicted hold in their beaks a pearl-adorned crown or are shown surrounding a human figure.

Curemonte 🕓*See CUREMONTE.*
D 15 offers pretty views of Curemonte and its environment.

▷ Return to Lostanges on D 15/D 163.

Parc Botanique de Lostanges
🕓☞*Jul–Aug 10am–7pm; May–Jun and Sept, Sat and Sun and public hols 2–6pm. €5 (children aged 6–12, free). ☎05 55 25 47 78. www.jardin-de-lostanges.com.*
In a pleasant low mountain environment, this circuit allows you to discover 500 plants grouped together by geographic origin, from the faraway New Zealand to the local Corrèze varieties and even desert plants. The visit is completed by a slide show on the various regions.

▷ Go down to Puy-d'Arnac via D 940.

Puy-d'Arnac
This village is huddled around a hillock on which stands a church. From the village, a steep road gives motor access

to a platform surrounding the church (*Cafoulière site*). This area has been set up as a stopover and is the starting point for well-maintained pedestrian trails. Three orientation panels describe the sweeping **view★**. To the east and south, the Dordogne valley can be seen, with its rolling hills and fields lined with aspen trees. To the northwest, the more rugged landscapes of Mayssac and Turenne.

▷ Come back to Bealieu on D 153.

1 0 GORGES DE LA CÈRE

50km/31mi. Allow 3hr. ⓑ*See route 10 on region map pp192–193.*

▷ Exit Beaulieu S along D 940 towards St-Céré and then turn left on D 41.

The Cère river takes its source in the Cantal mountains and runs through the Quercy. Before its waters could mix with those of the Dordogne upriver of Bretenoux, at the foot of the outcropping where the famous Castelnau-Bretenoux castle now stands, the Cère had to dig its way from Laroquebrou to Laval-de-Cère, leaving jagged gorges. Once you've crossed the Dordogne, the road rises for lovely views over the valley.

Reygade

A small buiding near the cemetery houses a lat-15C masterpiece in multi-coloured stone. This is a moving **depic-**tion of Jesus being put into the **tomb★** that is possibly the work of the same artist as the one found in Carennac (in the Lot). The colours have retained almost all their vivacity, giving expression to the faces and texture to the costumes. An audio-visual presentation describes each character shown. ⓑⓄ *Jul–Aug 10am–9pm.* ⊚*€6 (machine accepting €2 coins).* ℘*05 55 28 50 19.*

▷ Come back to, and follow along, D 41. 7km/4.3mi after La Chapelle-St-Géraud, take D 13 towards Camps.

Rocher du Peintre★

A stopover verge south of Camps gives a lovely view over the wooded gorges of the Cère. Although the railroad runs from one end of the gorges to another, no other road runs along the river in the area from Laroquebrou to Laval-de-Cère.

Laval-de-Cère

Between Laval-de-Cère and Port-de-Gagnac, the twisting road rises above the valley in a hilly prairie setting overlooking the Brugale dam.

▷ 1km/0.6mi before Port-de-Gagnac, turn right on D 116E.

Before coming back to Beaulieu, enjoy the landscape one last time as you climb towards the church of **Fontmerle**.

Medieval buildings in Beaulieu-sur-Dordogne

© C. Labonne / Michelin

Curemonte★

Between the *départements* of the Corrèze and the Dordogne, this pretty little village is a real medieval treasure. The silhouette of its ramparts, dignified castles and noble houses can be seen from afar, overlooking the rolling vineyards of Branceilles. In this peaceful town, Colette wrote her *Journal à Rebours* during WWII.

VISIT

Start from the halle near the church.
Under the **halle aux grains**, set up on a pedestal, note the shaft of the sculpted cross featuring twelve 16C low-reliefs on the theme of Jesus' life.

Above the *halle* to the right, you'll see the small **Château de La Johannie**, a 14C dwelling, as well as a beautiful turreted house built a century later.

The **church** has retained its bell wall, protected by a porch roof. Inside the church you'll see a master altar featuring a painted altarpiece dating from 1672 as well as two other 17C and 18C altars. Take a right behind the church. The tower in warm colours is flanked by bastions with pepperpot roofs. These structures fortified the **Château de Plas** with its round 16C towers and the **Château St-Hilaire** with its machicolated 14C towers, which you'll successively encounter. Go up to the orientation panel where you'll discover a magnificent view over Curemonte and the wooded hills surrounding it. Go back down to the place du Château to admire several 16C and 17C turreted "noble houses". Turn left following the ramparts. This return itinerary gives lovely views over the cause of Martel and the Périgord Noir.

1.5km/0.9mi west of the village, you'll see the 11C **Chapelle de La Combe**. This chapel displays exhibitions (*⏰Jul–Aug 2.30–7pm*). To the east, the 12C **Chapelle St-Genest** houses a religious museum.

▶ **Population:** 217.
⛪ **Michelin Map:** 329: G1-2.
ℹ **Info:** Town hall tourist info centre ✆ 05 55 84 04 79. Association des Amis de Curemonte ✆05 55 25 34 76. www.curemonte.org. Info and guided tours of Curemonte, in Jul–Aug, guided tour daily 5.30pm departing under the *halle*.
▶ **Location:** 37km/22.9mi NE of Souillac, 15km/9.3mi W of Beaulieu-sur-Dordogne and 40km/24.8mi N of Rocamadour.
😊 **Don't Miss:** A walk along the ramparts; the three 14C and 16C castles; the superb view from the orientation panel.
🕐 **Timing:** 1hr.

ADDRESSES

🍽EAT

🍴 **La Barbacane** – *Pl. de la Barbacane.* ✆*05 55 25 43 29.* In the heart of this steep village, not far from Place du Château, the rustic dining room of this restaurant offers a pleasant view over the rolling hills of the Corrèze and the Dordogne. The hearty family-style cooking including pâtés, terrines, smoked ham, regional specialities and homemade pastries.

🍴🍴 **Ferme-auberge de la Grotte** – *In the village.* ✆*05 55 25 35 01. 3 rooms.* 🅿. Don't forget to reserve your table in this lovely farm. The cuisine served here deliciously represents the best that the region has to offer, such as duck breast, preserved duck, Limousin-reared Génisse beef and homemade pastries. Stay in one of three attic rooms.

Saint-Céré★

The lovely old houses of St-Céré are clustered in the cheerful Bave valley at the foot of St Laurence's Towers. St-Céré stands at the junction of roads from Limousin, Auvergne and Quercy, but is a good place to stay in its own right. It is also an excellent starting point for walks and excursions in Upper Quercy, and its renowned festival is a popular rendezvous for music lovers.

A BIT OF HISTORY

A prosperous town – In the 13C, the viscounts of Turenne, overlords of St-Céré, granted a charter with franchises and various advantages to the town. Other charters added to the wealth of the town by giving it the right to hold fairs and establish trading houses. Consuls and officials administered the town, which was protected by St Laurence's Castle and a formidable line of ramparts. Even the Hundred Years War left the town practically unscathed. With the 16C dawned a new period of prosperity.
Jean Lurçat and St-Céré – Born in 1892 in the Vosges *département*, Jean Lurçat, whose parents had planned that he would become a doctor, directed his talents instead to painting and other art forms. He soon became interested in tapestry; it is for his work on tapestry design and technique that he achieved world renown (see AUBUSSON).

- **Population:** 3 545.
- **Michelin Map:** 337: H-2.
- **Info:** Pl. de la République. ℘05 65 38 11 85. www.saint-cere.fr.
- **Timing:** Allow half a day to explore the Bave valley.
- **Don't Miss:** The Atelier-Musée Jean-Lurçat; vallée de la Bave.

After a period spent in Aubusson, he participated in the Resistance movement and thus discovered the *département* of the Lot. He settled in St-Céré in 1945. He set up his studio in St Laurence's Towers and lived here until his death in 1966. The Aubusson tapestry factory wove most of Lurçat's designs into tapestries.

WALKING TOUR

OLD TOWN
The 15–17C houses give St-Céré a picturesque character all its own.
Some houses still have half-timbered corbelled façades and brown tiled roofs.

Place de l'Église
The church of Ste-Spérie was rebuilt in the 17C and 18C in the Gothic style. **The Hôtel de Puymule** (15C), in the square near the east end, is a turreted town-

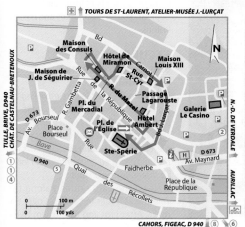

house featuring doors and windows decorated with ribbed arches.

◯ From place de l'Église, follow rue Notre-Dame and rue de la République.

Rue du Mazel

This street and surrounding area form one of the most charming districts in the old town, with old houses and fine doorways. At the corner of rue St-Cyr, note the 15C **Hôtel Ambert** with its corbelled turrets and Renaissance doorway. Farther along on the right, the narrow cobblestoned **passage Lagarouste**, with a stream down the middle, is overshadowed by tall corbelled houses.

◯ Continue along rue du Mazel.

Place du Mercadial

This was the market square where fishermen brought their catch to be displayed on the *taoulié*, a stone bench beside the 15C **Maison de Jean de Séguirier** at the corner of rue Pasteur. From this spot, there is a lovely view of the square surrounded by half-timbered houses against St Laurence's Towers. The **Maison des Consuls** has an interesting Renaissance façade overlooking rue de l'Hôtel-de-Ville.

Maison de Jean de Séguirier, Place du Mercadial

© S. Sauvignier / Michelin

◯ Follow rue des Tourelles.

Rue St-Cyr

On the corner of rue de l'Olie stands a lovely medieval house with three corbelled façades. Farther on, in rue de l'Olie on the left, the 15C Hôtel de Miramon is flanked with a corner turret.

◯ At the end of rue de l'Olie, turn right onto boulevard Carnot.

Maison Louis XIII

This mansion has an elegant façade.

◯ Return to place de l'Église.

MUSEUMS AND EXHIBITIONS
Atelier-Musée Jean-Lurçat★

◷*Open Apr–Sept daily except Mon 10.30am–12.30pm, 2.30–6.30pm.* ⬤€4. ☎05 65 38 28 21.

In the artist's studio, now a museum, the ground-floor rooms (*studio, drawing room, dining room*) exhibit Lurçat's works, including tapestries, drawings, paintings, ceramics, lithographs, gouaches and wallpaper.

Galerie d'Art le Casino

◷*Open Jul–Sept 10am–noon, 2.30–6.30pm.* ⬤*No charge.* ☎05 65 38 19 60.

In addition to temporary exhibitions, this gallery displays a large collection of **Jean Lurçat's tapestries★**. They combine a variety of forms and colours, depicting fantastic animals and cosmic visions.

EXCURSIONS
Site de Notre-Dame-de-Verdale★

9km/5.6mi E. Leave St-Céré travelling E on D 673. After 2km/1mi, turn right on D 30. 1km/0.5mi beyond Latouille-Lentillac, a narrow road branches off to the left and runs along the river. Park in the area provided and continue on foot. 🚶 *1hr round-trip on foot.*

Walk up the path running along the Tolerme as it falls in cascades over the rocks. After crossing the stream twice on primitive wooden bridges, the path climbs steeply. Shortly, the pilgrimage chapel of Our Lady of Verdale appears perched on a rocky crag. From the site, there is an extensive **view★** of the Tolerme gorges and the chestnut-covered hills.

Lac du Tolerme

23km/14.5mi E. Leave St-Céré on D 673 and continue along D 30.
The lake, at 530m, is surrounded by greenery and covers 38ha/94 acres. At the lake there is a **recreation centre** open to visitors (○*parking fee in Jul–Aug;* ☞*€5.* ✆*05 65 40 31 26).* A lakeside footpath *(4km/2.4mi)* is a pleasant place to stretch your legs.

🚗 DRIVING TOUR

1 1 VALLÉE DE LA BAVE

45km/27.9mi. Allow 3hr. 🗲*See route 11 on region map pp192–193.*

◐ *Drive W out of St-Céré.*

The towers of Montal Castle soon come into view on the left, rising above fertile fields and meadows interspersed with lines of poplars.

Château de Montal★★

🗲 *See Château de MONTAL.*

◐ *The road towards Gramat climbs above the Bave Valley, offering views of St Laurence's Towers. Join up with D 673 via St-Jean-Lespinasse.*

Grottes de Presque★

○👣*Open: Mid-Feb–Jun and Sept–mid-Nov 9.30am–noon, 2–6pm; Jul–Aug 9.30am–6.30pm.* ☞*€8.* ✆*05 65 40 32 01. www.grottesdepresque.com.*
The cave consists of a series of chambers and galleries that extend 350m into the rocks. Concretions, especially strange-shaped stalagmite piles and frozen falls along the walls, have built up in the different *salles* or chambers of the caves. Slender columns of astonishing white-

ness stand at the entrance to the **Salle des Merveilles★** (Hall of Wonders).

◐ *Continue on D 673 for Padirac then turn right on D 38.*

Cirque d'Autoire★

🅿 *Leave the car in a parking area. Take the path to the left of the road, overlooking the Autoire river and its series of waterfalls.*
Cross the little bridge and go up the steep stony path cut in the rocks. Very soon a wonderful **view★★** of the natural amphitheatre, the valley and the village of Autoire unfolds.

Autoire★

Autoire in its picturesque **setting★** is typical of the character of the Quercy region. Enchanting scenes are revealed at every street corner: a fountain at the centre of a group of half-timbered houses; old corbelled houses with brown-tiled roofs; elegant turreted manors and mansions.
From the terrace near the church, which has a fine Romanesque east end, there is a good view of the Limargue Mill and the rocky amphitheatre that lies to the southwest.

◐ *Drive N along D 135.*

Loubressac★

This old fortified town stands on a rocky spur overlooking the south bank of the River Bave. From near the church, there is a good view of the valley and of St-Céré, marked out by its towers. Walk through the enchanting narrow alleys as they wind between brown-tiled houses to the castle's postern. This 15C manor house, which was rebuilt in the 17C, stands on a remarkable **site★** at the very tip of the spur on which the village was built.

◐ *Take D 118 and then D 14 from the hamlet of La Poujade, descending towards the Bave valley. You'll enjoy fine* views★ *of the Dordogne valley dominated by the impressive outline of Castelnau-Bretenoux Castle.*

Château de Castelnau-Bretenoux★★
See CHÂTEAU DE CASTELNAU-BRETENOUX.

▷ Leave north on D 14.

Bretenoux
In its leafy riverside setting, this former bastide, founded in 1277 by a powerful lord of Castelnau, has retained its grid plan, its central square, covered arcades and parts of the ramparts.

After visiting the picturesque **place des Consuls** with its 15C turreted town-house, go through a covered alley to the old manor at the corner of the pretty rue du Manoir de Cère. Turn right and right again, returning via the charming quay along the Cère.

▷ Take D 803 and turn left at Gaubert to come back to Tauriac.

Église St-Martial
This church is made up of a Roman-esque sanctuary and an early 16C nave. Its walls and arches are entirely covered with monumental paintings of an extraordinary richness. Those along the southern side aisle depict scenes from the Creation, Adam and Eve, the Original Sin and the Sacrifice of St John the Baptist. The arches of the northern aisle show episodes from the life of the prophets, who are shown dressed in extravagant, realistic costumes.

▷ Come back to Bretenoux.
Take D 940 towards St-Céré.
After 4km/2.4mi, turn left on D 43.
5km/3.1mi after Belmont-Bretenoux, turn right on D 40.

Tours de St-Laurent
Motor vehicles are tolerated on the private road branching off to the right.
1hr on foot there and back.
Perched on a steep hill which overlooks the town, the two, tall medieval towers and curtain wall are a familiar local landmark. They were acquired by Jean Lurçat in 1945.

▷ Take a left on D 48 back to St-Céré.

ADDRESSES

🛏 STAY

Chambre d'hôte Château de Gamot – *46130 Loubressac. 5km/3.1mi W of St-Céré.* ☎*05 65 10 92 03. Closed Oct–Apr. 7 rooms.* A charming 17C family manor house in a pastoral setting. Not all en-suite, but spacious and comfortable.

Inter-Hotel Le Relais de Castelnau – *46130 Loubressac, rte De Padirac Rocamadour.* ☎*05 65 10 80 90. www.relaisdecastelnau.com. 40 rooms.* In a beautiful village setting, the hotel offers magnificent views over the Dordogne Valley and the castle; lovely swimming pool and gourmet restaurant.

Logis Villa Ric – *46400 St-Céré, rte De Leyme, 2km (1.25mi) from town.* ☎*05 65 38 04 08. www.logis-de-france.fr. 5 rooms.* Set on a hill in lush parkland with panoramic views and a beautiful outdoor swimming pool. The rooms have lots of character and the restaurant serves good regional cuisine.

🍴 EAT

Crêperie de Py – *Loubressac.* ☎*05 65 38 52 09. www.creperie-py.fr.* With its swimming pool and regular concerts, this is a popular summer spot serving crêpes and grilled meats.

Hôtel-restaurant Le France – *Av. François de Maynard.* ☎*05 65 38 02 16. www.lefrance-hotel.com.* 🅿. Comfortable, rustic-style restaurant with a shaded terrace: traditional dishes, mostly Quercy cuisine.

Le Victor Hugo – *7 av. du Maquis.* ☎*05 65 38 16 15. www.hotel-victor-hugo.fr.* Half-timbered 17C house on the banks of the River Bave. Some of the pretty little rooms have a river view and there is an outdoor terrace.

Château de Castelnau-Bretenoux★★

The scale of this castle's defence system makes it one of the finest examples of medieval military architecture. This landmark, as Pierre Loti wrote,

"...is the beacon... the thing you cannot help looking at all the time from wherever you are. It's a cock's comb of blood-red stone rising from a tangle of trees, this ruin poised like a crown on a pedestal dressed with a beautiful greenery of chestnut and oak trees."

A BIT OF HISTORY

Turenne's egg – From the 11C onwards the barons of Castelnau were the strongest in the Quercy; they paid homage only to the counts of Toulouse and proudly styled themselves the Second Barons of Christendom. In 1184 Raymond de Toulouse gave the suzerainty of Castelnau to the viscount of Turenne. The baron of Castelnau refused to accept the insult and paid homage instead to Philip Augustus, king of France. Bitter warfare broke out between Turenne and Castelnau; King Louis VIII intervened and decided in favour of Turenne. The baron was forced to accept the verdict. The fief, however, was only symbolic: Castelnau had to present his overlord with... an egg. Every year, with great pomp and ceremony, a yoke of four oxen bore a freshly laid egg to Turenne.

CHÂTEAU FORT

Open Jul–Aug 10am–7pm; May–Jun, 10am–12.30pm, 2–6.30pm; Sept and Apr 10am–12.30pm and 2–5.30pm; Oct–Mar contact for details. Closed 1 Jan, 1 May, 1 and 11 Nov, 25 Dec and Tue from Oct–Mar. €7.50. 05 65 10 98 00.

This huge fortress with its fortified curtain wall grew up during the Hundred Years War around the 13C strong keep. The castle was abandoned in the 18C

- **Michelin Map:** 337: G-2.
- **Info:** Av. de la Libération, Bretenoux. 05 65 38 59 53. www.ot-bretenoux.com.
- **Location:** 47km/29.5mi S of Tulle via D 940.
- **Don't Miss:** The view from the ramparts of the Château Fort.
- **Timing:** 2hr in the crowded high season.

and suffered depredations at the time of the Revolution. It caught fire in 1851 but was skilfully restored between 1896 and 1932.

The ground plan is that of an irregular triangle flanked by three round towers and three other towers partially projecting from each side. Three parallel curtain walls still defend the approaches, but the former ramparts have been replaced by an avenue of trees.

From along the ramparts there is a far-reaching **view★** of the Cère and Dordogne valleys to the north; of Turenne castle set against the horizon to the northwest; of the Montvalent Amphitheatre to the west; and of Loubressac castle and the Autoire valley to the south and southwest. A tall square tower and the seigneurial residence, a rectangu-

Château de Castelnau-Bretenoux

© OTVD / Cochise Ory

lar building still known as the *auditoire* (auditorium), suggest the vast scale of this fortress. The garrison included 1 500 men and 100 horses.

Inside the château, in addition to the lapidary depository featuring the Romanesque capitals of Ste-Croix-du-Mont in Gironde, there are other rooms worthy of visiting. They were decorated by the former proprietor, a singer of comic opera, Jean Moulierat, who bought the castle in 1896. The former chamber of the Quercy Estates General is lit by large windows; the pewter hall and the Grand Salon contain Aubusson and Beauvais tapestries.

▷ Leave the castle and turn left, down to the collegiate church.

Collégiale St-Louis

The church was built in 1460 by the lords of Castelnau in red-ferriferous stone, at the foot of the castle. A few canons' residences can be seen nearby.

▷ Enter the church.

The lords' chapel has lovely quadripartite vaulting, the pendant of which is emblazoned with the Castelnau coat of arms.

Château de Montal★★

This harmonious group of buildings with pepperpot roofs sits on a wooded hillside above a nine-hole golf course.

A BIT OF HISTORY
The wonder of a mother's love

In 1523 Jeanne de Balsac d'Entraygues had a country mansion built on the site of a feudal stronghold for her eldest son, Robert, who was away fighting in Italy for François I. The chatelaine had the best artists and workmen brought to Quercy, and by 1534 the masterpiece begotten of a mother's loving pride was there for all to see.

Hope is no more – Everything was ready to welcome home the proud knight. She waited day after day for her eldest son's arrival but alas, Robert's body was all that returned to the castle. The beautiful dream crumbled. Jeanne had the high window from which she had watched for her son blocked up. Beneath it, she had the despairing lament carved: Hope Is No More ("*Plus d'Espoir*"). Jeanne's second son, Dordé de Montal, a church dignitary, was absolved from his ecclesiastical duties by the Pope in order that he might continue the family

- ♿ **Michelin Map:** 337: H-2.
- ▷ **Location:** 3km/2mi W of St-Céré.
- ☞ **Visit:** Guided tour (45 min) May–Aug 10am–12.30pm, 2–6.30pm; Sept–Apr 10am–12.30pm, 2–5.30pm. Closed Mon and Tue Oct–Mar. ℘05 65 38 13 72. ⊛€7.50.
- ⊙ **Don't Miss:** A tour of the castle to admire the Renaissance staircase.

line; he subsequently married and had nine children.

Death and resurrection

Montal was declared a national asset but became uninhabitable as a result of the spoliation it suffered during the Revolution. Finally in 1879 it fell into the hands of a certain Macaire. This impecunious adventurer made a bargain with a demolition group and divided the palace into lots. 120t of carved stone were sent to Paris. The masterpieces of Montal were then auctioned and dispersed throughout the museums and private collections of Europe and the United States.

In 1908 a new and devoted owner set about finding and buying back at ransom prices all the Montal treasures until he had refurbished the castle. He donated it to the State in 1913.

CHÂTEAU

Exterior – Steeply pitched *lauze* roofs and massive round towers with loopholes give the castle its fortress-like appearance. But this forbidding exterior contrasts with the inner courtyard, designed with all the graceful charm of the Renaissance. Montal consists of two main wings set at right angles and linked at the corner by a square tower containing the staircase. The façade of the main building with all its rich decoration is one of the castle's most glorious features.

The frieze – Above the ground floor windows and doors runs a 32m-long frieze. It is a marvel of ornamental diversity: cupids, birds and dream-like figures appear beside shields and a huge human head. There are also the initials of the founder and her sons: I (Jeanne), R (Robert) and D (Dordé).

The busts – On the first floor, mullioned windows alternate with false bays featuring intricately carved pediments. These boast seven busts in high-relief, all masterpieces of realism and taste. Each statue is a likeness of a member of the Montal family; from left to right they are: Amaury with a haughty air, wearing a hat; Jeanne, his wife and the founder of the castle, appearing as a holy woman transfixed in eternal sorrow; Robert, the eldest son killed in Italy, wearing a plumed hat in the style of François I; and Dordé, the second son, as a young page.

The dormers – There are four, and their decoration brings to mind those of Chambord; the dormer gables have small supporting figures on either side and the niches contain statues.

Interior – The entrance is at the corner where the wings meet, through a door flanked by pilasters and topped with a lintel supporting several niches.

Renaissance staircase★★ – The staircase is built in fine gold-coloured stone from Carennac, beautifully proportioned and magnificently decorated. Admire the fine carving beneath the stairs: ornamented foliage, shells, imaginary birds, initials and little figures form a ceiling, with decoration which completes that of the lierne and tierceron vaulting of the vestibules.

The **guardroom**, vaulted with basket-handled arches, contains a lovely chimney-piece. The Stag Room (**Salle du Cerf**) and the other rooms house fine pieces of furniture (mainly in the Renaissance and Louis XIII styles), altarpieces, paintings and plates attributed to Bernard Palissy, as well as tapestries from Flanders and Tours, which constitute a marvellous collection.

Château de Montal

© OTVD / Cochise Ory

Assier★

Assier was the home of the *grand écuyer de France* or royal "master of stables" officer Jacques Galiot de Genouillac.

VISIT
Château

⌛ *Guided tour (30min). Jul–Aug 10am–12.30pm, 2–6.45pm; May–Jun daily except Tue 10am–12.30pm, 2–6.45pm; Jan–Apr and Sept–Dec daily except Tue 10am–12.30pm, 2–5.30pm.* €3 (visitors under 25, no charge). ℰ05 65 40 40 99. www.monum.fr.

Galiot de Genouillac built this residence between 1525 and 1535 to be as distinguished as his own title; a watercolour by Gaignières showing the castle in 1680 is proof of that. The property was sold by one of the descendants in 1766 and taken apart for its stones. Only the fortified entryway was spared, although it was simple and sober compared to the three other wings of the luxurious Renaissance dwelling. Thanks to Prosper Mérimée, the abandoned ruins were listed as a historic building in 1841.

Façades – The **exterior façade** retains traces of machicolations between the two round towers. In the centre, the monumental entryway is framed by two columns and crowned with an alcove that contained a statue of Gaillot himself, as well as a pediment where you can see the salamander representing François I. The **interior façade★** is very pure of line. It is adorned with compartmental friezes running above each storey. Various scenes from the legend of Hercules are an allusion to the omnipotence of the officer; cannons shoot flames to represent Galiot's responsibilities as artillery master.

Interior – The lower rooms with their ribbed vaults include architectural elements of the castle and a remarkable 17C recumbent figure representing Anne de Genouillac. A lovely Gothic-Renaissance staircase leads to the next floor. On the landing, a sculpted **pillar★** in pure white calcareous stone depicts Fortune on one

▶ **Population:** 684.
Ⓖ **Michelin Map:** 329: H-3.
🛈 **Info:** Pl. de l'Église.
   ℰ05 65 40 50 60
   www.otivalleecausse.com
▶ **Location:** 18km/11mi W of Figeac and 4.5km/2.7mi N of Livernon, Assier is accessible on D 653.
☺ **Don't Miss:** The frieze and tomb of the church; the castle's facade.
🕐 **Timing:** 1hr for the village and castle.

side, the trophies of Gailot on another, and on a third, Hercules battling the Nemean lion.

Church★
Key available at the Mairie.
ℰ05 65 40 57 97.

This church was built from 1540 to 1550 and remains intact. The exterior ornamentation is a long homage to the exploits and titles Galiot de Genouillac. The subject matter of the **frieze** running all around the church might be surprising, but it serves as a precious military document for historians. The **entryway** is of classic beauty.

The portico, formed by two columns topped with a triangular pediment, holds up a domed alcove. You'll also see the **tomb** of the great captain. His recumbent figure lies on a marble coffin. Above, a high-relief shows him surrounded by his military insignia and two gunners. The chapel's **vault** of 16 branches in a star shape forms a dome supported by squinches, a rare and remarkable technique.

Dovecote
Located in the north of the village, this 16C dovecote is a beautiful example of rural architecture. Its cylindrical tower (*9m in diameter*) and cone-shaped roof make this 11m structure one of the tallest in the Quercy.

🚗 DRIVING TOUR

1 2 BETWEEN CAUSSE AND LIMARGUE

40km/24.8mi. Allow 2hr. 🚶 See route 12 on region map pp192–193.

▶ Leave Assier heading NW on D 11 and turn right on D 38. At Théminettes, turn right.

Rudelle

This 13C **fortified church** is the most surprising of its kind in the Quercy. It is in fact a feudal bastion of which the oval-shaped lower level was converted in to a chapel. There is access to the defence chamber by way of the wooden staircase, the gallery, a ladder, a hatch and a stone staircase! Narrow loopholes bring a little light to this small room where the church bells now hang. You'll get a good **view** of the chevet and the entire building from the old cemetery surrounding this fortress-church *(access through a public passageway to the right of the church)*. Behind the church, the oratory is decorated with a shell, a reminder that one of the Santiago de Compostela routes came through here.

▶ Leave Rudelle NW on D 840. After 2km/1.2mi (at the place called Quatre Routes), turn right on D 40.

Château d'Aynac

℘05 65 11 08 00. www.castel-aynac.info. This 15C building in a wooded, verdant setting is now an **equestrian leisure centre**. Its towers, featuring crenellated angles and capped with domes, embrace the curious six-storey central dungeon. Notice the coat of arms of the Turenne family on the pretty entrance door.

▶ Leave Aynac E on D 39.

The road follows the **Largentié valley** and then rises towards the Leyme woods, a protected area for its hundred-year-old beech trees. Shortly after Leyme, the road *(D 48 to the right)* gives lovely **views** over the eastern Causse of Gramat. There is another sweeping view before Molières, at **Pech Mouleyret** *(follow the signposts)*.

Lacapelle-Marival

Several buildings of this old, important seigneury that belonged to the Cardaillac family from the 12C to the 18C have been preserved. The Gothic *church* and the *halle* with its chestnut carpentry, round roof tiles and stone pillars, date from the 15C. The former town gate or "arbol" was integrated into the ramparts. The town has also retained some lovely old houses.

The massive square machicolated dungeon of the castle flanked by sentry boxes on every corner dates from the 13C, while the main building, hemmed in with large round towers, was added in the 15C. Its inside features ornate 17C beams representing the castles in the Quercy belonging to the Cardaillac family, picturesque landscapes and antique figures.

▶ Leave Lacapelle S on D 940.

Le Bourg

The 12C **church** is the only remnant of a priory that was attached to the abbey of Aurillac. It includes a transept and a choir decorated with Romanesque arcatures supported by lovely capitals where birds still look down on the rare churchgoers.

▶ Leave Le Bourg SE on D 840 towards Figeac. After 1km/0.6mi, turn right on D 653 to come back to Assier.

ADDRESSES

🏨 STAY

🛏 **Chambre d'hôte Les Moynes** – *Les Moynes de St-Simon, St-Simon, 3.5km/ 2.1mi N of Assier on D11. ℘05 65 40 48 90. http://les.moynes.free.fr.* 🏊 ✉. *5rooms and 2 gîtes.* Renovated 1885 Quercy-style house tucked away on a duck farm. Cosy and attractive rooms with well-equipped bathrooms.

The Lot river cuts through the historic town of Cahors, a small city known for its strong red wine. Saint-Cirq-Lapopie is another highlight of the region, where no false note spoils this perfect chocolate-box village. However, other, more subtle charms of this countryside are to be found to the southeast of the river in the Tarn-et-Garonne as well as to the southwest in the Aveyron.

Highlights

Cahors, a Living Historic City

The picturesque vineyards of the Cahors area produce a wine so robust and deeply tannic that it is called "black" wine, a hearty red appreciated since medieval times. The history of the city itself goes back to Celtic times. Interestingly, the city's name in the ancient world was synonymous with the sin of usury, or fructifying interests on money. This reputation earned Cahors a place alongside Sodom in Dante's *Inferno*. The city boasts a large number of historic buildings in its medieval district that you'll enjoy discovering through its "Jardins Secrets de Cahors" circuit.

Scenery and Sights

If you're looking for a picture-perfect village that has inspired countless artists, Saint-Cirq-Lapopie is a must-see. Unmistakably poetic touches grace these steep romantic lanes. The view over the surrounding countryside completes the beauty of its old stones, cobbles and timber.

The churches of the area south of Cahors are a marvel for those interested in Gothic architecture. The rich religious past of this land have given rise to buildings on a monumental scale. The abbey of Beaulieu-en-Rouergue is not only awe-inspiring, but has the added interest of exhibiting contemporary art, which makes a remarkable contrast to the ancient edifice.

For a refreshing mix of geologic and prehistoric interest, stop over at the Plage au Ptérosaures de Crayssac, Les Escaliers du Temps in Bach or the Grottes de Foissac.

Forteresse de Najac

© Gwenaël Hubert / Fotolia.com

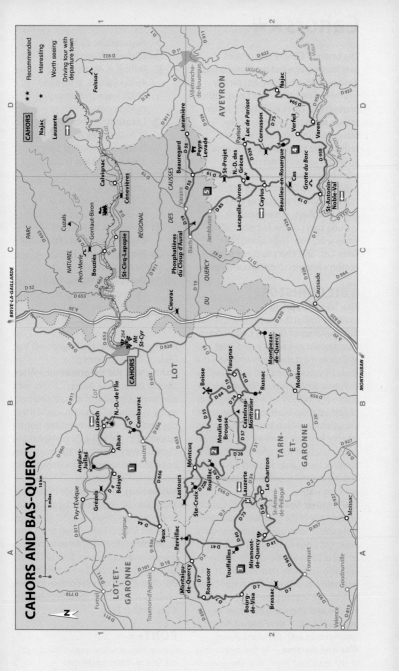

CAHORS AND BAS-QUERCY

Cahors★★

The town of Cahors still retains precious vestiges of its glorious past. **Boulevard Gambetta**, a typically southern French avenue lined with plane trees, cafés and shops, is the town's main thoroughfare. The busy, bustling atmosphere here reflects the fact that Cahors remains an important commercial and administrative centre. The former capital of the Quercy is an excellent starting point for tours of the Célé and Lot valleys, where options include tours of the famous Cahors vineyards, boat trips along the River Lot, and visits to some of the region's famous underground caves.

- ▶ **Population:** 20 194.
- ⊙ **Michelin Map:** 337: E-5.
- **Info:** Pl. F.-Mitterrand, 46004 Cahors. ☏05 65 53 20 65. www.tourisme-cahors.com.
- ◖ **Location:** 113 km/70 mi N of Toulouse by A 62, A 2 and D 820. 97km/60.5mi S of Brive by A 20 and D 820. Railway station 500m W of centre.
- **Kids:** Musée de Plein Air du Quercy, in Cuzals.
- **P Parking:** Car parks are dotted around the centre.
- ⊙ **Timing:** Allow a full day for the driving tour.
- **Don't Miss:** Pont Valentré; Cathédrale St-Étienne (north door and cloisters).

A BIT OF HISTORY

The Sacred Spring – A spring, discovered by Carthusian monks, led to the founding of Divona Cadurcorum, later known as Cadurca and later still as Cahors. First the Gauls and then the Romans worshipped the spring with a devotion which was confirmed by the discovery in 1991 of a great number of coins dating from the beginning of Christianity, which had been thrown into the fountain as offerings. The town grew rapidly in size: a forum, a theatre, temples, baths and ramparts were built. This spring still supplies the town with drinking water.

The Golden Age – In the 13C Cahors became one of the great towns of France and experienced considerable economic prosperity due in no small part to the arrival of Lombard merchants and bankers, who also operated somewhat less reputedly as usurers. Cahors became one of the leading banking cities of Europe and the word *cahorsin*, as the people of Cahors were known, became synonymous with the word usurer.

War and Decline – At the beginning of the Hundred Years War, the English seized all the towns in the Quercy. Cahors alone remained impregnable, in spite of the Black Death which killed half the population. In 1360, under the Treaty of Brétigny, Cahors was ceded to the Eng-

lish. By 1450, when the English left the Quercy, it was a ruined city.

Cahors and the Reformation – After several decades of peace, Cahors was able to regain some of its past prosperity. By 1540 the Reformation reached the city and dissension among the population led in 1560 to a Protestant massacre. Twenty years later the town was besieged and sacked by the Huguenots, led by Henri de Navarre.

Native Sons – These include Pope John XXII (1316–34), founder of the successful university in Cahors in 1332, the poet Clément Marot (1496–1544) and **Léon Gambetta** (1838–82), an outstanding lawyer and statesman. Gambetta, an ardent patriot, played an active part in the downfall of Napoleon III and in the proclamation of the Third Republic on 4 September 1870.

PONT★★

Crosses the Lot to the west of the city at the foot of President Wilson.

The Valentré bridge is a remarkable example of French medieval military architecture. The three towers, with machicolations and crenellated parapets, and the pointed cutwaters break-

Aerial view of Cahors

© Hervé Lenain / hemis.fr

ing the line of the seven pointed arches, give it a bold and proud appearance. The bridge was originally an isolated fortress commanding the river. The central tower served as an observation post while the outer towers were closed by gates and portcullises. A guardhouse and outwork on the south bank of the Lot provided additional protection. The fortress made such an impression on the English during the Hundred Years War and on Henri de Navarre at the time of the Siege of Cahors (1580) that it was never attacked.

WALKING TOUR

THE CATHEDRAL AND ITS SURROUNDINGS

The city has organised a circuit called "**Les Jardins Secrets de Cahors★**". Follow the copper nails marked with acanthus leaves hammered into the pavement. You'll see signs explaining the connection between the garden theme and the landmarks. The circuit begins at the Valentré Bridge. You can request the brochure from the Tourist Office. The allées Fénélon, running perpendicular to boulevard Gambetta, have been set up and landscaped for pedestrian use.

Cathédrale St-Étienne★
pl. Chapou.
The clergy built this church as a fortress to provide a place of safety in troubled times, as well as to bolster prestige. At the end of the 11C, Bishop Géraud of Cardaillac began to build on the site of a former 6C church. Much of his edifice remains standing to this day. The west front was built in the early 14C, and the paintings inside the domes and in the chancel were completed at the same time. The Flamboyant-style cloisters were commissioned at the beginning of the 16C by Bishop Antoine de Luzech.
Exterior – The western façade consists of three adjoining towers. The central one has a belfry above it and opens with double doors. On the first floor, the rose window is surrounded by blind arcades. In spite of windows with twin bays completing the decoration, the appearance of the façade remains austere and military.

North doorway★★ – This Romanesque door was once part of the western façade. It was transferred to the north side of the cathedral before the present façade was built. The tympanum depicts the Ascension.

Interior – Enter by the west door and cross the **narthex** which is slightly raised; the nave is roofed with two huge domes on pendentives.

There is a striking contrast between the nave, in pale-coloured stone, and the chancel, adorned with stained glass and paintings.

The frescoes of the first dome were uncovered in 1872. They show the stoning of St Stephen in the central

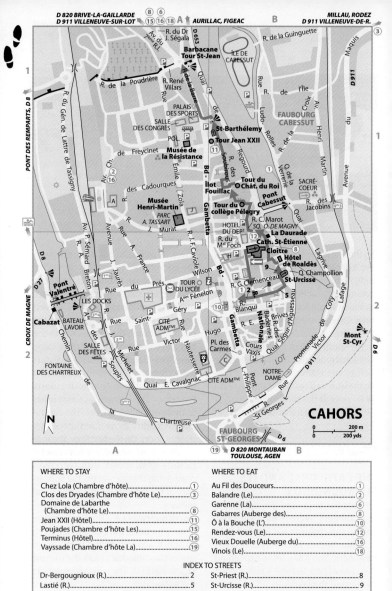

medallion with the saint's executioners surrounding the frieze and eight giant depictions of prophets in the niches.

Cloisters★ – These Renaissance cloisters were built in 1509 after those of Carennac and Cadouin, with which they share a number of stylistic similarities, Near the chancel door there is a spiral staircase, and on the northwest corner pillar there is a graceful carving of the Virgin of the Annunciation.

◉ You can access the Chapelle St-Gausbert through the cloister.

Chapelle St-Gausbert

◔*Visits by prior arrangement. Contact the tourist office.* ℘*05 65 53 20 65.*

16C Italian Rennaisance-style paintings decorate the ceiling of this former chapter-house. 15C paintings representing the Last Judgement adorn the walls. The chapel also contains the Cathedral Treasury. Enter the inner court of the former arch-deaconry of St John through the door in the northeast corner of the cloisters. Note the lovely Renaissance decoration.

▷ On leaving the cathedral, follow rue Nationale past the covered market.

Rue Nationale

This was the main thoroughfare of the active Badernes Quarter. At no 116, the panels of a lovely **17C door** are decorated with fruit and foliage. Across the way, the narrow **rue St-Priest** has retained its medieval appearance. It leads to place St-Priest which boasts a beautiful outside wooden staircase in Louis XIII style at no 18.

▷ Turn right.

Rue du Docteur-Bergounioux

At no 40, a 16C townhouse features an interesting Renaissance façade opened by windows influenced by the Italian Renaissance style.

▷ Retrace your steps and continue straight on.

Rue Lastié

Note the Rayonnant windows at no 35. At no 117, a 16C house has kept its small shop on the ground floor above which are twin bays. At the far end of the street, the pretty brick houses have been recently restored.

▷ Turn left.

Rue St-Urcisse

The late-12C church of St-Urcisse is entered through a 14C doorway. Inside, the two chancel pillars are decorated with elegant historiated capitals. Note the 13C half-timbered house (no. 68) with its *soleilho* (open attic), in which laundry was hung out to dry.

▷ Turn right.

Hotel de Roaldès

The mansion is also known as Henri IV's Mansion because it is said that the king of Navarre stayed there during the siege of Cahors in 1580.
This late 15C house was restored in 1912. In the 17C it became the property of the Roaldès, a well-known Quercy family.

▷ Turn back then right onto rue de la Chantrerie.

La Daurade

This varied set of old residences around the Olivier-de-Magny square includes the Dolive House (17C), the Heretié House (14C to 16C) and the so-called Hangman's House (Maison du Bourreau), with windows decorated with small columns (13C).

▷ Turn right, then walk down the street on the right.

Pont Cabessut

From the bridge there is a good **view★** of the upper part of the city, the Soubirous district.
The towers bristling in the distance are: Tower of the Hanged Men or St John's Tower (Tour St-Jean), the belltower of St-Bartholomew (Église St-Barthélémy), John XXII's Tower (Tour Jean XXII), Royal Castle Tower (Tour du Château du Roi) and the Pélegry College Tower (Tour du Collège Pélegry).

Tour du Collège Pélegry

The college was founded in 1368 and at first took in 13 poor university students; until the 18C, it was one of the town's most important establishments. The fine hexagonal tower above the main building was constructed in the 15C.

▷ Follow the narrow lane to the left; it runs onto rue du Château du Roi. Turn right then right again past the prison.

Tour du Château du Roi

Near Pélegry College stands what is today the prison and was once the governor's residence. Of the two towers and two main buildings erected in the 14C, the remaining tower is known as Château du Roi.

▷ Return to the prison, follow the street opposite and turn right.

Ilôt Fouillac

This area has undergone an extensive programme of redevelopment. By getting rid of the most run-down buildings, a square has been cleared. Its sides are decorated with **murals**, and it is brightened by a particularly interesting **musical fountain**.

▷ Turn right towards rue des Soubirous.

Tour Jean-XXII

This tower is all that remains of the palace of Pierre Duèze, brother of John XXII. It is 34m high and was originally covered in tiles. Twin windows pierce the walls on five storeys.

Église St-Barthélémy

This church was built in the highest part of the old town, and was known until the 13C as St-Etienne de Soubiroux, Sancti Stephani de Superioribus (St Stephen of the Upper Quarter), in contrast to the cathedral built in the lower part of the town. The church was rebuilt to its present design in several stages. The belfry, the base of which dates from the 14C, has no spire, and it is built almost entirely of brick.

The nave, with its ogive vaulting, was designed in the Languedoc style. In the chapel nearest the entrance, on the left, a marble slab and bust are reminders that John XXII was baptised in this church.

The cloisonné enamels on the cover of the modern baptismal font depict the main events in the life of this famous Cahors citizen.

▷ Walk to boulevard Gambetta and head N.

Barbican and Tour St-Jean★

The ramparts, constructed in the 14C, completely cut the isthmus formed by the meander of the River Lot off from the surrounding countryside. Remains of these fortifications can still be seen and include a massive tower at the west end, which sheltered the powder magazine, and the old gateway of St-Michel, which now serves as entrance to the cemetery. On the east side, however, where the N 20 road enters the town, the two most impressive fortified buildings remain: the barbican and St John's Tower. The barbican is an elegant guardhouse which defended the Barre Gateway; St John's Tower or the Tower of the Hanged Men (Tour des Pendus), was built on a rock overlooking the River Lot.

MUSEUMS
Musée de la Résistance, de la Déportation et de la Libération

Imp. Bessières. ⏰*Open daily 2–6pm (Oct–Mar closed Sun).* ⏰*Closed public holidays.* 🚫*No charge.*
📞*05 65 22 14 25.*
Housed in six rooms, this museum illustrates the birth of the Resistance movement in the Lot region, deportations and persecutions which followed, fighting for the liberation of France and the epic journey of the Free French from Brazzaville to Berlin. Eighteen models of war planes are also displayed and newspapers dating from that period are available to visitors.

Musée de Cahors Henri-Martin

792 r. Emile Zola. ⏰*Open daily except Tue, 11am–6pm (Sun and public hols, 2–6pm).* ⏰*Closed 1 Jan, 1 May and 25 Dec.* 🚫*No charge.* 📞*05 65 20 88 66.*
This museum is housed in the former Episcopal palace. One room is devoted to the works of the painter Henri Martin (1860–1943), a member of the pointillist movement.

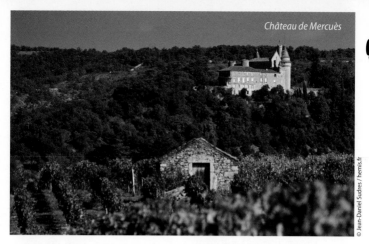

Château de Mercuès

© Jean-Daniel Sudres / hemis.fr

VIEWPOINTS
La Croix de Magne viewpoint★

5km/3mi. From the western end of the Valentré Bridge, turn right and then immediately left; take the first left after the agricultural school, and left again at the top of the rise.

Around the cross, a **view★** extends in all directions over the plateau, to the Lot River, Cahors and the Valentré Bridge.

Viewpoint to the north of the town★

5km/3mi along rue du Docteur-J-Ségala which turns right off the N 20 just beyond the Tour St-Jean.

This road offers fine views of the Lot valley and the surroundings of Cahors, including the old town built like an amphitheatre, with its pinnacles, crenellated towers and Valentré Bridge.

Mont St-Cyr viewpoint★

7km/4mi via the Louis-Philippe Bridge and the D 6 which you leave after 1.5km/1mi to reach the mount, keeping to the left.

From the top (viewing table) there is a good **view★** of Cahors. The contrast between the old and the new quarters of the town, which are separated by boulevard Gambetta, Cahors' main artery, is striking. In the background the distinctive shape of Valentré Bridge can be seen.

EXCURSIONS
Château de Mercuès

6km/3.7mi NW along the D 911.

Once the property of the count-bishops of Cahors, the château is now a hotel. It occupies a remarkable site overlooking the north bank of the Lot. In 1212 the château was a fortified castle. It was enlarged in the 14C, besieged several times and not restored completely until the 19C. There is an outstanding **view★** of the valley from the château.

West of Mercuès, the road leaves the valley for a short distance to cross a flourishing countryside of vineyards and orchards; then the road returns to follow the river.

♣ Plage aux Ptérosaures de Crayssac★

11km/6.8mi NW on D 811.
✆ 05 65 20 86 40.

Discover this former quarry where the traces of prehistoric animals, and most notably flying reptiles, were found. 150 million years ago these animals stood here on a beach, and their footprints never disappeared. Since then, the sediment and mud have turned to limestone. The fossils can best be seen at the end of the day when the sun cuts across them. New fossils are discovered frequently.

Château de Cieurac

12km/7.4mi S on D 6. Guided visit *(1hr) Jul–mid-Sept, daily except Mon 2–6.30pm; Jun and end Sept–Oct Sat–Sun 2–6.30pm. €6 (children over 10, €3).* ℰ*05 65 31 64 28.* *www.chateaudecieurac.com.*

This late 15C Renaissance castle was built on the foundations of a 13C fortress by Raymond and Jacques de Cardaillac, lords of St-Cirq-Lapopie. Under Richelieu, the second floor was demolished. Das Reich burned the castle in 1944. It has since then been entirely restored and embellished with French-style gardens. In the surrounding park, the windmill, dovecote and bread oven still stand. Today, the rooms of the castle are well-appointed with superb late **15C to 17C furnishings**★ and 16C and 17C tapestries. Note the **spiral staircase**★ featuring a different sculpture under each step like at the château de Montal. The entry door has also been worked to resemble the original.

Laroque-des-Arcs

Continue along the D 653.

This village's name is a reminder of the aqueduct which crossed the Francoulès Valley and supplied water to Cahors. A three-tiered bridge bore the 20km/12mi aqueduct from Vers to Divona (ancient Cahors).

Notre-Dame-de-Vêles

This 12C pilgrimage chapel has a lovely square belltower and a Romanesque apse.

ADDRESSES

⌂ STAY

⌂ **Chambre d'hôte Les Poujades** – *Flaynac, 46090 Pradines. 5km/3.1mi N of Cahors on D 8.* ℰ*05 65 35 33 36. 2 rooms. Cottage available.* A flower garden and shady trees surround this typical Quercy house which offers a wonderful view of the Château de Mercuès, the Cahors vineyards and the outskirts of the town. The decor is a little on the sombre side.

⌂🍴 **Chambre d'hôte Le Clos des Dryades** – *46090 Vers. 19km/11.4mi NE of Cahors on D 653.* ℰ*05 65 31 44 50. www. closdesdryades.com.* 🅿 ⚐ ≋. *5 rooms.* Nestled deep in the woods, this tiled-roof house is the perfect place to get away from it all. The rooms are comfortable and the large swimming pool is a great place to cool off on a hot summer's day. Two self-catering cottages are also available.

⌂🍴 **Chambre d'hôte Domaine de Labarthe** – *46090 Espère. 8km/5mi NW of Cahors on D 911.* ℰ*05 65 30 92 34. www. domaine-de-labarthe.com. Reservation required.* 🅿 ⚐ ≋. *3 rooms.* Guests at this manor house, complete with dovecote, are assured of the warmest of welcomes. The rooms are pretty, and fresh flowers and biscuits await you on arrival. All the rooms open onto the garden and pool.

⌂🍴 **Chambre d'hôte Chez Lola** – *76 r. Clémenceau.* ℰ*05 65 35 25 93. 3 rooms.* Set on the second floor of a restored old house in the town centre, these colourful contemporary accommodations enjoy fine views.

⌂🍴 **Jean XXII** *(previously Hôtel A l'Escargot)* – *5 blvd Gambetta.* ℰ*05 65 35 07 66. www.hotel-jeanxxii.com. Closed Feb school hols, 20 –31 Oct and Sun Oct–May. 9 rooms.* Near the Tour Jean XXI, this hotel occupies the old palace built by the pontiff's family. Functional bedrooms with colourful furnishings, plus a renovated breakfast room.

⌂🍴🍴 **Hôtel Terminus** – *5 av. Ch.- de-Freycinet.* ℰ*05 65 53 32 00. www.balandre.com.* In French, Terminus means "the end of the line", but that hardly does justice to this charming bourgeois dwelling. The large rooms are clean and quiet. The Art Deco bar will transport you back to the 1910s, the period that this house was built.

⌂🍴🍴 **Chambre d'hôte La Vayssade** – *Lalbenque, 16km/10mi S of Cahors.* ℰ*05 65 24 31 51. www.lavayssade.com.* 🅿 ≋. *5 rooms.* A rustic renovated barn set in its own grounds amid 10ha/25 acres of truffle oaks with an impressive monumental communal living room. Special truffle weekends.

Vineyards of Cahors

© A.J. Cassaigne / Photononstop / Tips Images

₹/ EAT

L'Auberge des Gabarres – *24 pl. Champollion.* ℘*05 65 53 91 47.* This inn is known for its simple tasty terroir cooking and its warm welcome. A meal on the shady terrace is a trea*t.*

La Garenne – *Saint-Henri, 7km/ 4.5mi N towards Brive.* ℘*05 65 35 40 67.* Delicious regional cuisine is served in a cosy interior that was formerly a stable .

Auberge du Vieux Douelle – *46140 Douelle. 8km/5mi W of Cahors on the D 8.* ℘*05 65 20 02 03. www.auberge malique.com.* The dining room in the vaulted cellar of this popular inn, known locally as "Chez Malique", is decked out with bright red tablecloths. Meats are grilled over a wood fire. Terrace and pool in the summer.

L'Ô à la Bouche – *134 r. Ste-Urcisse.* ℘*05 65 35 65 69. www. loalabouche-restaurant.com.* Old stone, exposed brickwork and beams and a large fireplace lend undeniable character to this restaurant, renowned for its contemporary gourmet fare. There is a small side terrace for warm weather.

Le Rendez-vous – *49 r. Clément-Marot.* ℘*05 65 22 65 10. Reservation recommended.* Near the cathedral, Le Rendez-vous has developed a reputation for its modern cuisine. The mix of colourful contemporary decor and old stonework combine well in the dining room and mezzanine extension.

Le Balandre – *5 av. Ch.-de-Freycinet.* ℘*05 65 53 32 00. www.balandre. com.* This family-run restaurant serves up a modern style of cuisine, to be enjoyed in the elegant dining room lit with stained glass. The superb selection of wines and the fixed midday menu, "La Grignotte", are little extras.

Au Fil des Douceurs – *90 quai de la Verrerie.* ℘*05 65 22 13 04.* This boat-restaurant enjoys a romantic setting with a stunning view of the Lot and old Cahors near Le Pont Cabessut. Traditional fare is served in two dining rooms, one above the other. Leave room for the excellent dessert.

Le Vinois – *Le Bourg, Caillac.* ℘*05 65 30 53 60. www.levinois.com.* In the heart of the Cahors vineyards, north of the city centre, don't miss this stunning inn that sports a minimalist contemporary style in keeping with the fashionable cuisine – expect creative twists on Quercy lamb, duck, foie gras and truffles, and of course a great choice of local wines. Jazz usually plays softly in the background. Ten designer bedrooms ().

SHOPPING

Market – *Pl. Chapou.* A traditional market is held on Wed all day and Sat mornings, where a large number of farmers sell a range of products.

EVENTS

Cahors Juin Jardins – *June* ℘*05 65 53 20 65. www.tourisme-cahors.com.*

Festival de Blues – *Mid-Jul.* ℘*05 65 35 99 99.*

Festival du Quercy Blanc – *Late-Jul to mid-Aug.* ℘*05 65 31 83 12.*

Luzech

Luzech has grown up on the narrowest part of a tongue of land almost completely encircled by a loop in the River Lot. The isthmus at this point is some 100m wide. The town is crowned by the old castle keep. To the north lies the Roman city of Impernal and to the south the Pistoule Promontory, washed by the waters of the river as it sweeps round the bend.
A reservoir has been formed by the construction of a dam upstream from the peninsula, and a water-sports centre has been set up there (*boat tours available*).

A BIT OF HISTORY
Pech de l'Impernal

A natural defensive position, this rise has been inhabited since prehistoric times. The Gauls, recognising its potential, transformed the plateau into a powerful stronghold. A citadel was constructed during the Middle Ages and Luzech became the seat of one of the four baronies of Quercy. Much coveted by the English during the Hundred Years War it nevertheless resisted all attacks and became an important central stronghold. During the Wars of Religion, it remained a faithful bastion of Catholicism under the bishops of Cahors.

▶ **Population:** 1 679.
Ⓖ **Michelin Map:** 337: D-5.
🄸 **Info:** Maison des Consuls, r. de la Ville. ℘05 65 20 17 27. www.ville-luzech.fr.
▶ **Location:** Luzech is situated 27km/17mi W of Cahors.

WALKING TOUR

▶ Start from the top of the Imperial.

Viewpoint★

From the top of the Pech de l'mpernal, the view encompasses Luzech clustered at its foot, as well as the Promontoire de la Pistoule, slicing through the wide alluvial plain like a ship's prow, and the Lot winding between rich and fertile crops.

▶ Follow the marked path (GR) down to the town.

Keep

Entrance via place des Consuls.
The entrance used to be through the small, pointed-arched doorway opening onto the first floor. From the terrace of the 12C keep there is a bird's-eye view of the brown-tiled roofs of the town,

Aerial view of Luzech

© Francis Cormon / hemis.fr

tucked amid meadows and crops with a row of hills along the horizon.

Old Town

In the old district known as the faubourg du Barry, picturesque alleyways link rue du Barry-del-Valat with the quays. Around place des Consuls, on the other side of place du Canal, several examples of medieval architecture are still to be seen: Penitents' Chapel (12C), Capsol Gateway with its brick pointed arch and Consuls' House with its elegant twinned windows.

MUSÉE ARCHÉOLOGIQUE ARMAND-VIRÉ

Maison des Consuls, r. de la Ville.
Open Jul–Aug, 10am–1pm, 2–5pm; rest of year Mon–Thu 10am–1pm, 2–5pm, Fri 10am–1pm. Guided tour (1hr). €3. 05 65 20 17 27.
Established in the fine vaulted cellar of the old Consuls' House (13C), now the tourist office, the museum retraces the history of the site of Luzech. The items displayed include the exceptional **scale model of the Column of Trajan**★, and an unusual Gallo-Roman hinged spoon made of bronze and iron.

EXCURSIONS
Notre-Dame-de-l'Île

1.2km/0.8mi S along the D 23.
The chapel, set in a calm landscape of vineyards and orchards against a backdrop of hills along the course of the Lot, stands at the furthest point of the isthmus. This Flamboyant Gothic sanctuary is a pilgrimage centre, dating from the 13C.

🚗 DRIVING TOUR

1️⃣ FROM LUZECH TO CAMBRAYRAC

55km/34mi. Allow 3 hr. See route 1 on region map p247.

▶ Drive W out of Luzech on D 8.

As the Lot flows between the tall limestone cliffs of the Quercy *causse*, its thousand curves provide a neverend-

ing variety of magnificent views. Follow the south bank for views of the valley.

Albas

From its past as the seat of the bishops of Cahors, this small town has retained ruins of the Episcopal castle and a network of narrow streets with old houses.

▶ Continue along D 8.

Anglars-Juillac

A Crucifixion adorns the church's Renaissance doorway.

▶ Continue along D 8 and turn left on D 50, 2.5km/1.5mi farther on.

Bélaye

Once the fief of the bishops of Cahors, Bélaye stands on top of a hill. An extensive **view**★ of the Lot valley unfolds from the top of the spur and from the upper square of this little village.

▶ Come back to D 8 and turn left.

Grézels

Overlooking the village is the feudal **Château de La Coste** which houses a **wine museum** (*Castle open mid-Jul–Aug, 3–6pm; guided tour of castle at 4.30pm. €4; Museum: Wed and Sun 3–6pm. No charge. 05 65 21 38 28*). The bishops of Cahors, whose fief extended over the Lot valley from Cahors to Puy-l'Évêque, built a stronghold here to mark the limits of their territory.
During the Hundred Years War, it was transformed into a fortress. Severely damaged and then restored in the 14C and 16C, it was abandoned after the Revolution. The curtain wall and corner towers are the castle's oldest parts.

▶ Continue along the D 8.

The Pont de Courbenac offers the best overall **view** of Puy-l'Évêque (*see below*).

Saux

The St-André church overlooks the village. Built in the 12C, it was reconstructed in the 15C and reworked in the 17C. It features a semicircular Romanesque chevet and a belltower pierced with four semicircular bell arches and flanked by a turret (*spiral staircase inside*). The church houses lovely Baroque furnishings including a stoup with gadroon decorations and a stone baluster gate.

Église de Cambayrac

8km/5mi S along the D 23 and D 67.
The hamlet has an odd-looking church identifiable from afar by a belfry-wall with a shape like a French policeman's hat. Inside, the Romanesque apse and the side chapels were recovered in the 17C with an unusual marble and stucco decor in the Classical style.

ADDRESSES

STAY

☞ **Chambre d'hôte Le Soleil** – *Albas, 5km/3.1mi W of Luzech on D 8.* ✆*05 65 30 91 90. www.chambredhote-lesoleil.com.* P. 3 *rooms.* This house full of character and regional touches is the perfect base from which to explore the region.

EAT

☞☞ **Auberge Imhotep** – *La Rivière Haute Albas. 4km/2.5mi W of Luzech on D 8.* ✆*05 65 30 70 91.* Imhotep is best-known as the great architect of ancient Egypt. But he also invented the method of *gavage* – force-feeding of geese to yield foie gras. This and other regional dishes are available, as well as a vegetarian menu.

☞☞ **Ô Plaisir des Sens** – *50 blvd Aristide Briand (across from the church and La Poste), Prayssac. 11km/6.8mi W of Luzech on D 9 then D 811.* ✆*05 65 22 47 12. www. restaurant-plaisir-sens.fr.* Fresh, inventive dishes that show off the flavours of the south. Reservation highly recommended.

☞☞☞ **Clau del Loup** – *Métairie Haute, Anglars-Juillac. 11km/6.8mi W of Luzech on D 9 then D 8.* ✆*05 65 36 76 20. www. claudelloup.com.* P. 3. This lovely 1818 stone dwelling is a refined universe

where delicious gourmet cuisine with a southern accent is concocted by a local chef. Terrace under the plane trees. The rooms are pleasant and prettily furnished.

SHOPPING

Markets – There is a picturesque regional market at **Prayssac** on Fri mornings, favoured by the numerous British ex-pats who have staked a claim in the surrounding area. Local farmers' market on Sun mornings in summer. The much smaller **Luzech** market takes place Wed mornings.

Cave des Côtes d'Olt, Vinvalie – *Parnac. 3.5km/2.1mi E of Luzech on D 23.* ✆*05 65 30 57 80. www.cavedecahors.fr.* This cooperative wine cellar, twinned with those of Rabastens (Tarn), Técou (Tarn) and Fronton (Haute-Garonne), gives a good overview of the variety of local production. You can't go wrong with a Château Les Bouysses or a Le Paradis.

Château Les Croisilles – *Fages, Luzech.* ✆*05 65 63 73 51.* This 30-year-old vineyard stretches over 12ha/ 29.6 acres. It is here that the Croisille family produces excellent Cahors wine. Le Divin and Le Noble Cuvée regularly win awards and make splashes in the specialised press.

Le Grenier du Voyager – *Grezels.* ✆*05 65 36 40 48.* A village bric-a-brac where collectors will find vintage objects, lovely antique wooden furnishings, mirrors and garden furniture.

LEISURE ACTIVITIES

Boat trips on the Lot – ♿ *Departures from the Base Nautique de Caix in Jul and Aug, 4.15–6.30pm.* ✆*05 65 20 18 19.* Cruises last 90min.

EVENTS

Le Bon Air est dans les Caves – *Albas, the Sat following Ascension.* ✆*05 65 20 12 21 (Albas town hall).* The cellars of the village open to celebrate Cahors wine. A very convivial atmosphere, as the name suggests.

Rencontres Internationales de Violoncelles de Bélaye – ✆*05 65 22 40 57. http://violoncelle-belaye.voila.net.* The artistic director of these musical moments, Roland Pidoux, is a renowned musician who teaches at the Conservatoire de Paris.

Le Quercy Blanc★

The region known as the Quercy Blanc, so-called because of the white colour of the chalky soil, is characterised by low, long plateaux, arranged in rows (*serres*) with narrow, fertile valleys between them. The landscape and architecture are similar to that of the neighbouring Garonne region; red-brick constructions with nearly flat roofs covered in pale-pink Roman tile. Vineyards (the noble Chasselas variety is grown in Moissac), plum trees, peach trees and melons thrive on the sunny hillsides; tobacco, sunflowers and maize grow on the valley floors.

DRIVING TOURS

2 CHURCHES AND MILLS OF LE QUERCY BLANC

60km/37mi round-trip from **Castelnau-Montratier**. *Allow 1 day. See route 2 on region map p247.*

Castelnau-Montratier

Get a town map at the tourist office.
This hilltop bastide was founded in the 13C by Ratier, lord of Castelnau. It replaced a small village, Castelnau-de-Vaux, which was destroyed by Simon de Montfort in 1214 at the time of the Albigensian Crusade. The town "**square**" is in the form of a triangle, surrounded by covered arcades and old houses. Note the **Église St-Martin** standing right at the end of the promontory. North of the promontory are three **windmills**, one of which still functions. These mills with rotating caps were once common in Quercy.

Leave Castelnau S along the D 659 and turn left 3km/1.9mi farther on.

Église de Russac

The church has an oven-vaulted Romanesque east end decorated with carved

- **Michelin Map:** 337: C/E-5/7.
- **Info:** *Office de tourisme Lauzerte:* 3 pl. des Cornières - 82110 Lauzerte. ℰ05 63 94 61 94. www.lauzerte-tourisme.fr. *Office de tourisme Montcuq:* 8 r. de la Promenade - 46800 Montcuq. ℰ05 65 22 94 04. www.tourisme-montcuq.com. *Office du tourisme de Castelnau-Montratier:* 37 pl. Gambetta, 46170 Castelnau-Montratier. ℰ05 65 21 84 39. www.castelnau-montratier.fr.
- **Location:** Between the Lot and Tarn valleys.
- **Kids:** A family programme called "Viens jouer en Quercy blanc ("Come play in the Quercy Blanc").
- **Timing:** Allow 2 full days to explore this scenic region.

€modillions; the original north doorway was walled up. Inside, note the 16C fresco in the apse, particularly the central panel depicting St George slaying the dragon.

Come back to D 659, drive 1km/0.6mi towards Castelnau and turn right onto D 26, then left onto D 214 6km/3.7mi farther on.

Flaugnac

This once-fortified village occupies a picturesque position overlooking the Lupte Valley. In the 13C, a castle stood at the end of the promontory.

Leave Flaugnac along the ridge, turn left onto D 19 then right onto D 64 6km/3.7mi farther on.

Moulin de Boisse

Demonstrations are held five times a year in this well-preserved mill (built 1669). ⊙*Open mid-Jun–mid-Sept.* ℰ05 65 21 84 39.

▶ Continue on the D 64 then the D 55.

Montcuq

This is the main town of a castellany to which Raymond VI, count of Toulouse, granted a charter of customary law in the 12C. Montcuq was the centre of many a bloody battle during the Albigensian Crusade, the Hundred Years War and the Wars of Religion. All that remains of this once fortified village is a tall castle keep (12C) on a hillock overlooking the Barguelonnette River and a few old houses between place des Consuls (near the town hall) and place de la Halle-aux-Grains.

▶ Leave Montcuq NW on D 4, then D 55.

Château de Lastours

The castle's towers on the defensive wall overlook the Séoune valley. The main building is 16C.

▶ Turn back then right onto the D 228 1km/0.6mi farther on.

Ste-Croix

This village has retained many old houses nestling round the imposing church. Note the Romanesque doorway, which once gave access to the cemetery.

▶ Continue along D 228 and turn left on D 953 to Montcuq. Drive S out of Montcuq along D 28 and turn right onto D 45 2km/1.2mi farther on.

Église de Rouillac

The 12C church was remodelled in the 15C; several chapels and a belltower were added in the 19C. In the flat east end, there are traces of Romanesque frescoes depicting the Passion.

▶ Continue on D 45. Turn left towards St-Laurent-de-Lolmie. Drive on for 2km/1.2mi, then turn left on D 28 and then left again on D 57. Follow D 104.

Moulin de Brousse

🕐 *Visits by prior arrangement.*
𝄡 *05 65 21 95 81.*
This watermill dating from the 13C has been worked by a family of millers since 1917: locally grown wheat is ground in the mill.

▶ Turn right to Castelnau-Montratier.

③ PAYS DE SERRES

70km/43.4mi round-trip from Lauzerte. Allow 1 day. See route 3 on region map p247.

Dovecote near Lauzerte

©Jean-Paul Azam / hemis.fr

Lauzerte★

This bastide was built in 1241 by the count of Toulouse and was occupied at one time by the English.

Upper Town

The pale-grey stone houses with their almost flat roofs are clustered round the church of St Bartholomew and a square, place des Cornières. This square, named after its covered arcades (*cornières*), still has one half-timbered house.

Promenade de l'Éveillé, in the once wealthy middle-class district, has retained elegant residences, some half-timbered, some Gothic in style with twin windows and some Renaissance with mullioned windows. The ground floors of several 13C and 14C houses in rue de la Garrigue and rue de la Gendarmerie were occupied by busy shops.

The Via Podiensis, which starts from Le Puy-en-Velay, runs through Lauzerte on its way to Santiago de Compostela. The landscaped **Jardin du Pèlerin** (pilgrim's garden) laid out beneath the barbican is a kind of outdoor snakes and ladders (*ask for the dice at the Tourist Office*).

▶ Leave Lauzerte travelling S along D 2; left on D 953, then right on D 81 and right again towards Ste-Amans-de-Pellagal 2km/1.2mi farther on.

Chartron

Here you'll see a fine square dovecote built on pillars. These are topped with a kind of cap (*capel*) designed to prevent various rodents from getting in. The half-timbered dovecote is covered with flat tiles and surmounted by a lantern.

▶ Turn left then immediately right 1km/0.6mi farther on and continue to Ste-Amans, then Miramont.

Miramont-de-Quercy

From the watch-path of this small village, there is a fine valley view.

▶ On leaving Miramont, turn left onto D 41 and then right onto D 953. Drive on for 8km/5mi, then turn right onto the D 7.

Château de Brassac

🕒 *Open Jul–Sept 10am–8pm; May–Jun and Sept 2–6pm.* 🕒 *Closed Mon.* ⊛ €4. 📞 *05 63 94 59 67.*

This 12C fortress towers above the Séoune valley. During the Hundred Years War, the stronghold fell successively into English and French hands. Besieged by Protestant troops during the Wars of Religion and burned down during the Revolution, Brassac was abandoned in the 19C. A fixed stone bridge, which replaced the original drawbridge, leads into the bailey (⚷ *not open to the public*).

▶ Continue on D 7 to Bourg-de-Visa.

Bourg-de-Visa

The wrought-iron structure of a covered market surrounded by arcaded houses stands in the centre of the town hall square. A few ruins are all that remains of the castle. Note the dovecote tower.

▶ Continue along the D 7 and turn left after 10km/6.2mi.

Roquecor

This village, perched on a rocky spur, towers above the Petite Séoune. Walk along rue des Coutelets, which starts opposite the town hall; the street is lined with old houses.

Continue along rue du Barry and bear left towards the **wash-house**, past the ruined ramparts of the old town, to reach a troglodytic site known as the **Roc de la Nobis**.

▶ Drive N out of Roquecor and turn right onto D 7.

Montaigu-de-Quercy

The village nestles round a promontory on which a castle once stood. Follow rue des Frères-Quémèré to place de la Mairie: note the wash-house and the 19C neo-Gothic church. Rue des Colombiers skirts the ramparts and rue des Anciens-Fours leads back to the town hall.

▶ Drive NE out of Montaigu on D 24 and turn left 2km/1.2mi farther on.

Pervillac

This hamlet boasts a Romanesque **church** remodelled in the 19C, which houses well-preserved 15C murals depicting hell, purgatory and the virtues.

▶ Turn back, then right to Montaigu and first left (D 41) to Touffailles.

Touffailles

The late-15C **Église St-Georges** overlooks the village (*on the right past the town hall*). The nave vaulting is decorated with 12 scenes depicting Christ's childhood and the Passion.

▶ Continue on D 41; left onto D 60, right onto D 73 leading back to Lauzerte.

⌂ STAY

▱▱▱▱ **Chambre d'hôte Four** – *4 r. Montmartre (in the parallel street above the Tourist Office), Montcuq.* ☏*05 65 21 23 08. www.4ruemontmartre.com. Table d'hôte*▱▱▱. At the heart of the village, in a lovely 15C house, three rooms of varying size and price feature traditional furnishings complemented by contemporary touches. The effect is discreet, delicate and elegant. In the evening, reserve a table at the restaurant.

♉ EAT

▱ **Chez Bernadette/Auberge de Miramont** – *In the village, Miramont-de-Quercy.* ☏*05 63 94 65 57.* ♿🅿. An authentic country inn where you'll appreciate the terrace full of flowers in the shade of the chestnut trees. Enjoy the delicious regional cuisine.

Montpezat-de-Quercy★

On the edge of the Limogne causse, this picturesque small Lower Quercy town, with its covered arcades and old half-timbered or stone houses, owes its fame to the 14C collegiate church of St Martin and to its artistic treasures.

A BIT OF HISTORY
The Des Prés family

Five members of this family from Montpezat became eminent prelates. Pierre Des Prés, cardinal of Préneste (now Palestrina in Italy), founded the collegiate church of St Martin, which he consecrated in 1344. His nephew, Jean Des Prés, who died in 1351, was bishop of Coïmbra in Portugal and then of Castres in France.
Three other members of the family were consecrated bishops of Montauban: Jean Des Prés (1517–39), who gave his famous Flemish tapestries to the collegiate church at Montpezat; Jean de

- ▶ **Population:** 1 480.
- ⌖ **Michelin Map:** 337: E-6.
- ▤ **Info:** Blvd des Fossés. ☏05 63 02 05 55. www.montpezat-de-quercy.com.
- ▶ **Location:** Montpezat-de-Quercy is located 29km/18mi S of Cahors and 32km/20mi N of Montauban.
- ◉ **Don't Miss:** The 16C tapestries in the Collégiale St-Martin.
- ◷ **Timing:** Allow 2hr.

Lettes (1539–56); and Jacques Des Prés (1556–89).
Des Prés was a warrior-bishop, and a committed persecutor of the Huguenots. He fought for 25 years, his diocese being one of the most ardent Protestant strongholds, and was killed in an ambush at Lalbenque, some 15km/10mi from Montpezat.

TOWN

The bastide is stacked up above the ramparts. The central place de la Résistance is surrounded by arcades and half-timbered houses. The 19C town hall replaces an older building.

To the north, the 12C cloisters of the former Couvent des Ursulines were remodelled in the 20C and now house a school.

COLLÉGIALE ST-MARTIN

This church, dedicated to St Martin of Tours, was built in 1337 by an architect from the papal court at Avignon. It is comparatively small in size and has many of the characteristics of a Languedoc building.

Nave – Unity, simplicity and harmony make a striking impression when you enter the nave. The side chapels contain several notable religious objects: a 15C Virgin of Mercy in polychrome sandstone (first chapel on the south side); three 15C–16C Nottingham alabaster altarpiece panels depicting the Nativity, the Resurrection and the Ascension (second chapel on the south side); and 15C wooden caskets with gold inlay work (fourth chapel on the north side).

Tapestries★★ – These 16C tapestries were specially made to fit the sanctuary. Woven in the north of France and consisting of five panels, each divided into three pictures, they depict the best-known historic and legendary events in the life of St Martin, including the dividing of his cloak. The excellent condition of these tapestries, the vividness and richness of their colouring and the fact that they are still hanging in the exact spot for which they were designed all contribute to their outstanding interest.

Recumbent figures★ – Although the body of Cardinal Pierre Des Prés lies beneath the paving before the chancel, his statue and tomb carved in Carrara marble were placed on the right of the chancel entrance in 1778. Opposite lies the recumbent figure of his nephew Jean Des Prés, which is a masterpiece of funerary statuary.

EXCURSIONS

Église de Saux

5km/3mi N. Leave Montpezat-de-Quercy along the D 20 towards Cahors, then turn left 2km/1.2mi farther on.

Once the centre of a large parish, this church now stands isolated in the middle of the woods. The plain interior consists of three domed bays decorated with beautiful 14C and 15C **frescoes**. The best preserved are in the chancel and show Christ in Majesty with the symbols of the four Evangelists, the Crucifixion and scenes from the Childhood of Jesus.

Molières

13km/8mi W along the D 20.

The village grew during the 13C when Alphonse de Poitiers made it into a bastide. The covered market has gone, but Molières has retained its characteristic town plan and part of its ramparts, the bulk of which was destroyed during the Revolution.

Two 19C wrought-iron footbridges linking the ramparts to some houses testify to the town's past prosperity. Note the brick-built arch with a bell hanging from it: it stands to the north, where the clock tower used to be.

ADDRESSES

🛏 STAY

🍴🍴🍴 **Chambre d'hôte Domaine Lafon** – *Domaine de Lafon, Pech de Lafon, 2km/1.2mi along the D 20 towards Molières, then turn left and continue for 2km/1.2mi towards Mirabel.* ✆*05 63 02 05 09. www.domainedelafon.com.* 🅿🍽. *3 rooms.* This 19C manor house enjoys a superb view of the surrounding countryside. The spacious rooms have been superbly decorated by the owner – a painter and former theatre-set designer.

SHOPPING

Les Vignerons de Quercy – *Montpezat-de-Quercy.* ✆*05 63 02 03 50.* Wine sales and tasting.

Caussade

Cambrai makes peppermint candy, Cherbourg makes umbrellas, Calais makes lace and Caussade makes… straw hats. In fact, two-thirds of all the straw hats manufactured in France come from this little town, which explains why you'll see references to this industry all over the place.

The town itself stands between the *causses* – limestone plateaux – of Lower Quercy (Bas Quercy) and the rich Garonne river plain. Its architecture has been damaged by various wars, but there is a relative prosperity here.

▶ **Population:** 643.
🖳 **Michelin Map:** 337 F7.
🗄 **Info:** Boulevard Didier-Rey, Caussade. ☎05 63 26 04 04. www.mairie-caussade.fr.
◖ **Location:** 50 km S of Cahors, near A 20, not far from Caylus and Montauban.
☻ **Don't Miss:** In July, "Les Estivales du Chapeau" (summertime hat festival), in Septfonds 7km/4.3mi NE of Caussade.
◷ **Timing:** 1hr for the town and its surrounding area.

VISIT

Caussade was a Protestant stronghold during the Wars of Religion. The Catholics won it back and set up a Recollets convent here in 1683. The ramparts were demolished in the 18C. In the 19C and up until the mid-20C, the city was an important manufacturer of straw hats. Fluctuations in fashion shifted its activities from old-fashioned boater's hats to beach hats.

The **church**, which was rebuilt in the late 19C by the Toulouse-born architect Gabriel Bréfeil in a Gothic style, has maintained its Toulouse-style octagonal belltower in pink brick. The three levels are surmounted by a fleche with crockets. Across from the church stands the 13C **Tour d'Arles** (Arles tower).

Nearby, the historic district includes some lovely 17C and 18C houses.

EXCURSIONS
N.-D.-des-Misères

13km/8mi SW on D 820, then D 40, in the village of Mirabel.

Overlooking the Aveyron valley, this chapel, founded in 1150, is crowned with an attractive two-storey octagonal belltower adorned with twin 16C Romanesque bays.

Puylaroque

14 km/8.6mi NW on D 17.

This lower Quercy bastide consists of a tight group of houses with very flat roofs at the top of a hillside overlooking the Candé and Lère valleys. Near the church featuring a massive square belfry attached to its main portal, the narrow streets of the village boast 13C and 14C houses with corbelling and wood panels. From the viewpoints, and especially the one close to the church, you'll discover views that sweep over the gentle hills of the countryside and the Caussade and Montauban plains.

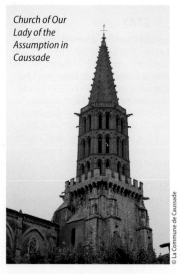

Church of Our Lady of the Assumption in Caussade

© La Commune de Caussade

Saint-Antonin-Noble-Val★

This village is organised around the former Maison des Consuls, one of the oldest civil buildings in all of France.

VISIT

In medieval times, the bridge toll (*octroi*) was an important source of revenues for the village. St-Antonin was home to rich traders of linens, furs and leathers, who built beautiful 13C–15C houses here.

WALKING TOUR

Ancien Hôtel de Ville★

Built in 1125 for a rich, ennobled *bourgeois*, Pons de Granolhet, this former town hall is one of the oldest examples of civil architecture in France. In the 14C, it was used as a Maison des Consuls. Viollet-le-Duc would restore it in the 19C and add a square belfry, crowned by a machicolated loggia in the Tuscan style. The façade is made up of two storeys: the gallery of pillars on the first floor is adorned with two pillars bearing the statues of the Emperor Justinian as well as Adam and Eve. On the ground floor, arcades open onto a museum.

Musée – Open July–Aug daily except Sun and Tue 3–6pm. 05 63 30 63 47 (tourist office). This museum displays prehistory collections, especially of the Magdelanian Period. There is also a folklore room.

Rue Guilhem-Peyre

The noble way taken by ceremonial processions begins under the former town hall's belfry. To the right are the former royal barracks called the "English barracks". In the bend in the street, there is a splendid 12C house.

◐ Go down the street towards place de Payrols, then take a right at La Perception (the tax building).

- **Population:** 1 864.
- **Michelin Map:** 337 G-7.
- **Info:** 10 r. de la Pélisserie. 05 63 30 63 47. www.tourisme-saint-antonin-noble-val.com.
- **Location:** 60km/37mi SE of Cahors, 12km/7.4mi S of Caylus and 18km/11mi E of Caussade.
- **Don't Miss:** The façade of the former town hall; the charming streets during the Sun market; the pure Romanesque style of the Varen church.
- **Parking:** The old town is surrounded by car parks: on the road from Caussade, towards Caylus, pl. des Tilleuls, or towards Le Bosc.
- **Timing:** Half a day for the town and a whole day for the surrounding area.

Rue des Grandes-Boucheries

On the corner of rue de l'Église, la Maison du Roy (King's house) features five ogee arcades on the ground floor and as many twin bays boasting capitals adorned with juvenile heads on the first floor.

◐ Go up rue de l'Église towards the town hall.

Ancien Couvent des Génovéfains

Built in 1751, this former convent now houses the town hall and tourist office. A signpost at the entrance to the gallery explains its history.

◐ Go to place de la Halle along rue St-Angel and place du Buoc.

Croix de la Halle

In front of the *halle* with its robust pillars stands a curious 15C "racket" cross sculpted on both sides. This original, rare work was a gift from the Fraternal

Society of Goldsmiths to the town. It would have originally been placed at the entrance or the centre of the cemetery, which then was located on the banks of the Aveyron where the current promenade des Moines is now.

Rue de la Pélisserie

This street is full of the 13C and 14C houses of master tanners and furriers.

▷ Turn left onto rue des Banhs.

Rue Rive-Valat

This street runs along a little canal crossed by bridges. The canal is one of the many diversions of the Bonnette river, dug in medieval times to serve as a sewage system and to supply the tanneries. The tanneries themselves had skylights in their topmost storeys, used to dry and stock skins.

▷ Rue Rive-Valat gives on to rue Droite which comes back, on the right, to place de la Halle.

Rue Droite

Two dwellings stand out on this street for the quality of their sculpted keystones: the late 15C Maison de l'Amour (house of love), depicting a kiss, and Maison du Repentir (house of repentance) where, to the contrary, two faces turn away from each other. Towards the middle of the road, you'll see a beautiful façade with double corbelling and half-timbering featuring travertine limestone and wooden cross-pieces.

▷ You'll come out on place des Capucins from the left. From here, rue du Pont-des-Vierges begins.

Rue du Pont-des-Vierges

At place du Bessarel, an old **walnut oil mill** can be seen. (*Guided tour upon request at the Tourist Office.* ☎05 63 30 63 47).

EXCURSION
La Grotte du Bosc

4km/2.4mi NW on D 75. *Guided tour (45min). Apr–May 2–5pm Sun,*

school and public holidays; Jun–Sept daily 2–5pm (Jul–Aug 10am–6pm). ⊕€7 (children aged 4–12, €5). ☎05 63 30 62 91. http://grotte.du.bosc.free.fr.

This dry underground river bed stretches for 200m under the plain between the Aveyron and Bonnette valleys. A large number of stalactites and eccentrics can be seen. The entrance hall also serves as a mineralogical and prehistoric **museum**.

🚗 DRIVING TOUR

4 VALLÉE DE LA BONNETTE TO GORGES DE L'AVEYRON

80km/49.7mi round-trip from St-Antonin. Allow 1 day. See route 4 on region map p247.

▷ Leave St-Antonin N on D 19.

Château de Cas

Guided tour (45mn). 2–6.30pm: Jun–Sept daily except Mon; Apr and Oct–Nov weekends and public holidays. ⊕€6 (children 5–14, €2). ☎05 63 67 07 40. www.chateaudecas.fr.

Built in the 12C to watch over the Bonnette valley, this castle was reworked in the 14C and 16C. It housed a lodge of the Knights Templar where Philip the Fair thought he had found the famous Templar treasure. The current castle was taken apart three times and was reconstructed and renovated from 1979 onward. You'll visit 15 pleasantly appointed rooms, as well as the chapel, garden and commons.

▷ Come back on D 19 (to the right).

Caylus ⓘSee CAYLUS.

▷ Leave Caylus E on D 926.

Parisot

In a hilly setting to the east of the village, the lac de Parisot is a pleasant lake bordered by poplar trees. Paid access to swimming, pedal boats and a campsite.

▷ Drive S on D 33.

Belfry in Saint-Antonin-Noble-Val

© Giovanni Bertolissio / hemis.fr

Château de Cornusson

This dwelling overlooking the Seye, flanked with a large number of towers, was rebuilt in the 16C.

▷ Continue along D 33.

Abbaye de Beaulieu-en-Rouergue★

See ABBAYE DE BEAULIEU-EN-ROUERGUE.
Just after the bifurcation that leads to the village of St-Igne (*don't turn, just continue on*), notice, on the right side of the road, a curious and imposing **phylloxéra cross** sculpted in 1882 following the catastrophic destruction of the vineyard. The inscription translates as "The hand of God has struck us."

▷ Follow along D 33, then turn left on D 75. At Mazerolles, continue on D 39.

Najac★ *See NAJAC.*

▷ Leave Najac W on D 594 and then take a right on D 958.

Varen

Tourist Office: Pl. de l'Église, 82330 Varen. ℘05 63 65 45 09. www.varen.fr.
Clustered around the Romanesque church protected by an impressive defence system, the village of Varen is set along the right bank of the Aveyron. Enter the historic district from the south. The **porte El-Faoure**, a former fortified door opens onto a street called "Carrera del Fabre" among other picturesque narrow streets.

The castle was built as a fortress. The "lord-prior" of Varen closed himself off in this building, defying the decisions of the bishop of Rodez, until in1553, the priory monks were replaced by more docile *chanoines*.

The late 11C **St-Pierre Church★** was designed as part of the defence system of the town. From the former portal, which was walled up in the 16C, two capitals remain, representing St Michel slaying the dragon (left) and Samson opening the lion's mouth (right). A sober square belfry stands above the flat choir between two semicircular apsidal chapels. The long nave features nine bays separated from the side aisles by square pillars. Various patterns adorn the capitals of the choir and apsidal chapels.

▷ Leavez Varen heading N.

Verfeil

Charming old dwellings awash with flowers surround a *halle* refurbished in stone. In the church you'll see a master altar in gilded wood and a 17C woodwork Christ from the Abbey of Beaulieu.

▷ Leave Verfeil SW on D 33.
After Arnac, take D 958 right back to St-Antonin along the right bank of the Aveyron.

Najac★

Najac is listed by the French Ministry of Culture and Tourism as a one of the most beautiful villages in France. It is home to a *fouace* festival (a type of unleavened bread).

THE TOWN
Bourg

The place du Faubourg was already developed in the 14C, when the south part, called l'Ardret, and the north part, l'Hinversenc, dissociated. The main street, rue du Bourguet, boasts a few 13C–16C corbelled houses. Near the town hall, the monolithic basin of the fountain bears the date of 1344 and the coat of arms of Blanche of Castille, the mother of St Louis (13C).

▶ Turn right into the rue du Bourguet, leaving the rue des Comtes-de-Toulouse on your left.

Le **Château des Gouverneurs** stands along rue Médiévale. This was the residence of various lords, as was the 13C–15C **Maison du Sénéchal** to the left and slightly higher up towards the fortress.

Forteresse★

Guided tour available (1hr) Apr–May and Sept–mid-Nov 10.30am–1pm, 3–5.30pm; Jun 10.30am–1pm, 3–6.30pm; Jul–Aug 10.30am–7pm (Wed 8pm). €5 (children €3.50). ☎05 65 29 71 65. www.tourisme-najac.com.

This masterpiece of 13C defensive architecture had an impressive garrison, and the population of the village was an amazing 2 000! Of the three primitive fortification walls, a powerful system flanked with large round towers remains. The castle itself forms a trapezoid and is built in sandstone.

The most powerful tower, to the southwest, was the dungeon. Parts of the building are ruined, essentially due to stones being taken for other uses. In one of the rooms, you'll see a scale model of the castle as it once was.

▶ **Population:** 754.

▶ **Michelin Map:** 337: H6.

▶ **Info:** Pl. du Faubourg. ☎05 65 29 72 05.

▶ **Location:** 60km/37.2mi S of Figeac and 82km/50.9mi E of Cahors.

▶ **Parking:** In season, rue Barriou and rue Bourguet in the heart of the village are restricted to pedestrians. W and N of the entrance to the village, there are three car parks.

▶ **Don't Miss:** The sweeping view from the plateau and the Fouace Festival (1st weekend after 15 August).

▶ **Timing:** 2hr for the entire site.

Once through the gates and successive fortifications, you'll arrive on the dungeon's platform to enjoy the magnificent **view★**.

▶ Go down towards rue de l'Église.

The 13C **porte de la Pique** features a murder hole and is the last gate standing of the ten that protected the village.

Église

Open 10am–noon, 2–6pm: May–Sept daily; Apr Sat–Sun.

In spite of more recent flourishes, this is an interesting Gothic building. The west façade features a rose window and the nave ends in a flat chevet. In the choir, the 14C altar is a vast block of fine sandstone. Note the Christ in the 15C Spanish School style and the 15C statues of the Virgin Mary and St John, as well as the 16C statue of St Peter in multicoloured wood. The iron cage in the nave to the left is designed to receive a large Easter candle.

▶ Come back to place du Faubourg along rue des Comtes-de-Toulouse, where medieval houses abound.

Abbaye de Beaulieu-en-Rouergue ★

Perfectly balanced between history and modernity, the 13C Cistercian church was converted into a contemporary art centre in 1970. Works by Simon Hantaï, Michaux Serpan, Dubuffet, Roger Bissière, Arpad Szenes and Maria Vieira da Silva bring a stimulating atmosphere to this secluded town of the Tarn-et-Garonne.

VISIT
Church★

This lovely example of 13C Cistercien architecture has the purest Gothic style. Its nave is vaulted with ogee arches and is lit up with lancet and rose windows with arabesque designs. A transept crossing crowned by an octagonal cupola supported by squinches leads to the seven-sided apse. Each crosspiece of the transept leads to a square chapel.

Abbey Buildings

The **chapter house**, which is the oldest part of this group of buidings, opened onto the cloister with three ogee arches which have now disappeared. The chapter house has two bays, each crowned with three ogee arch vaults supported by impressive columns. The **cellar**, on the ground floor of the lay brother building, includes ten cross-ribbed vaults resting on four columns featuring capitals adorned with leaf designs. The beauty of this room and the refinement of the sober keystones are proof of the care that the Cistercian monks brought to each building, however secondary. The dormitory was located upstairs in what is now the **exhibition hall**.

The monks' building was entirely reworked in the 17C and flanked with two turrets a century later.

Michelin Map: 337: G6.

Info: Abbey and contemporary art exhibition. Apr–Oct 10am–noon, 2–6pm. €5.50. 05 63 24 50 10. www.monum.fr.

Location: 75km/46.6mi SE of Cahors, 10km/6mi SE of Caylus and 12.5km/7.7mi NE of St-Antonin-Noble-Val on D 75.

Parking: Car park on D 33 before arriving at the buildings.

Don't Miss: The pure style of the Gothic church; the contemporary art centre in the abbey.

Timing: 2hr to fully enjoy the place.

Abbaye de Beaulieu-en-Rouergue

© Giovanni Bertolissio / hemis.fr

Caylus

Half-timbered houses, an imposing belltower and a castle in ruins perched on the hillside of the Bonnette valley: welcome to Caylus. The church of this charming village is home to an extraordinary Christ sculpted by Zadkine. This arid countryside is ideal for rambling, with its scattered megaliths and fields of lavender.

 WALKING TOUR

Covered Market

Antique cereal measures are carved into the stone of the *halle*. Its large size indicates the commercial importance of Caylus under the Ancien Régime.

Rue Droite

Strolling away from place de la Mairie, note the medieval houses along rue Droite, and especially the 13C Maison des Loups featuring wolf-shaped gargoyles.

▶ At the end of rue Droite you'll come to Église St-Jean-Baptiste.

Church

Fortified in medieval times, the church retains its heavy machicolated buttresses. The stained glass of the choir has been lovingly restored. Above the 14C nave, near the choir, a giant **Christ★** in elm wood sculpted in 1954 by **Ossip Zadkine** is poignant; the absence of a cross exacerbates the impression of suffering. The work was a gift by the artist to the community in recognition of his being taken into refuge to escape the Nazis during WW1 before he left for America.

🚗 DRIVING TOUR

⑤ LA CAUSSE DE LIMOGNE
55km/34mi round-trip from Caylus – allow half a day. See route 5 on region map p247.

- ▶ **Population:** 1 536.
- ⛪ **Michelin Map:** 337: H6.
- ℹ **Info:** R. Droite. ℰ05 63 67 00 28. www.caylus.com.
- ◗ **Location:** 60km/37mi SE of Cahors and 62km/68.5mi SW of Figeac. Access via D 19, D 52 and D 33.
- 🔭 **Don't Miss:** The sculpture of Christ by Zadkine in the church; the impressive *halle*; traces of prehistoric animal life at Escaliers du Temps.
- 👪 **Kids:** Kids will enjoy the former phosphate mine of Phosphatières du Cloup-d'Aural.
- 🕑 **Timing:** 2hr for the town, half a day for the driving tour.

▶ Leave Caylus N on D 19.

The gentle rolling hills of this countryside are relatively unspoiled. On this calcareous land, which is difficult to farm, you'll mostly see juniper and low grasses, oak woods and prairies where sheep roam. **Gariottes** (shepherds' shelters) and **caselles** (shelters for animals or tools) are scattered throughout this hilly countryside.

N.-D.-des-Grâces

This Flamboyant Gothic chapel with its *lauze* roof and lovely sculpted portal is a place of pilgrimage with a sweeping view.

▶ Continue along D 19.

Lacapelle-Livron

This *lauze*-roofed village has retained the vestiges of a Knights Templar lodge that came under the Order of Malta in 1307 and remained so until the Revolution. It is now a fortified manor with a courtyard where the original shape of the lodge is visible. To the south, the little Romanesque fortress-church is over-looked by a powerful belfry-dungeon. It faces a former mess hall that became a guard room.

▶ Continue along D 19.

Château de St-Projet
👣 Guided tour (45min). Jun–Oct, 2–7pm; Nov Sat– 2–6pm. ⚏€7 (child €5). 📞05 63 65 74 85 or 06 83 97 19 63. www.saint-projet.com.
Built in the late 13C on a Gallo-Roman tumulus, the castle housed **Queen Margaret of Valois** and her lover, pursued by the armies of Henri IV in 1595. Upon their departure, the room was walled up as it was and discovered in 1990. In 1622, Louis XIII also stayed in the castle.

▶ In Beauregard, turn right on D 55.

Prieuré de Laramière
👣 Guided tour (1hr 30min) Jul–Sept daily except Tue 2–7pm. ⚏€5 (under 15 no charge). 📞06 80 88 13 13. www.laramiere.new.fr.
This priory was founded in 1148 by the wandering Augustinian monk Bertrand de Grifeuille. The 12C and 13C buildings formed a quadrangle, but were partially demolished during the Wars of Religion. In the mid-17C, Jesuits built the Maison du Régisseur. Visit the restored buildings to discover the chapel vaults, the Romanesque pilgrimage room and the **chapter house**, which is vaulted and painted with geometric shapes. It features capitals depicting Saint Louis and Blanche of Castille. On the southern wall, funerary recesses contain the tombs of the benefactors Hugues de La Roche and his wife.
The Rausel River is absorbed by the *causse* under the priory and resurfaces at the Gouffre de Lantouy, near Cajarc.

▶ Come back towards Beauregard, 2.5km/1.5mi away.

Dolmen de la Peyre Levade
This is one of the most beautiful and heaviest megaliths among the some

800 in the Quercy, as it is estimated at 25 tonnes! A 40cm basin is carved into the raised stone.

Beauregard
This bastide was built on an existing village and retains its grid-like structure. The solid central 14C *halle* has a lovely *lauze* roof and cereal measures carved into its stone. Before the church stands a beautiful 15C cross.

▶ Continue along D 55, then turn left on D 19 towards Varaire. Turn left before Bach.

👫👤 Les Escaliers du Temps – Phosphatières du Cloup d'Aural★
👣 Guided tour (50min) with self-guided tour (30min) Jul–Aug daily 11am–6pm (1 visit per hour only); Apr–Jun and Sept–mid-Nov daiiy at 3pm and 4.30pm; Nov–Mar by arrangement. ⚏€7 (children 6–14, €4.50). 📞06 03 93 45 91. www.phosphatieres.com.
Located in an emptied cavity, this former phosphate mine is also an open book where you'll discover the "megafauna" of the Tertiary Era alongside the history of phosphate extraction. Although phosphate is used in the fertilisation industry, the two seemingly unrelated subjects are coherent, as phosphorus is derived from animal cadavers. The site is a mine of fossils of giant animals, such as felines, hyenas, rhinos and primitive horses.
The limestone plateau with its patchy plant life is cracked and very permeable to water. Infiltrations dug out cavities where the remains of animals accumulated. The fossils are therefore snapshots of various eras. To help you imagine the size of the animals, their silhouettes can be seen here and there throughout the tour.

▶ In Bach, turn left onto D 22 and follow along D 85 to come back to Caylus.

Saint-Cirq-Lapopie★★

St-Cirq-Lapopie (*Cirq* pronounced *sear*), faces a semicircle of white cliffs and is itself perched on a rocky escarpment (80m) that drops vertically to the left bank of the Lot; it is a remarkable **setting**★. The present name of the site commemorates the martyrdom of the young St Cyr, killed with his mother in Asia Minor during the reign of Diocletian. It is said his relics were brought back by St Amadour. The La Popies, local lords in the Middle Ages, gave their name to the castle built on the cliff's highest point and, by extension, to the village that grew up at its foot.

A BIT OF HISTORY

A contested stronghold – This rock commanding the valley has probably tempted would-be occupiers since Gallo-Roman times.

The history of the fortress is a long series of sieges and obscure battles until 1580. In that year, Henri de Navarre, the future

▶ **Population:** 217.
⚙ **Michelin Map:** 337: G-5.
🛈 **Info:** Place du Sombral. ✆05 65 31 31 31. www.saint-cirqlapopie.com.
◗ **Location:** 34km/21.5mi W of Cahors via D 653 and D 662. For a wonderful view of the River Lot, head to the top of La Popie Rock.
🕐 **Timing:** Allow a full day to explore the Célé and Lot valleys.

Henri IV, ordered that the walls of the valiant fortress be demolished.

The end of a craft – St-Cirq-Lapopie had a strong guild of woodturners dating back to the Middle Ages.

Until the late 19C, there were a considerable number of craftsmen still to be seen working their primitive lathes; their industry added a colourful note to the old-fashioned village alleyways.

Their shopfronts set small and large arched openings side by side. Nowadays there is only one woodworker left in St-Cirq.

St-Cirq-Lapopie rises above the Lot

Hervé Lenain / hemis.fr

VILLAGE

It is a perennial pleasure to wander along narrow, steeply sloping streets lined with houses with lovely brown-tiled roofs. The corbelled façades and exposed beams of some of the houses are further ornamented with Gothic windows, or bays with mullioned windows in the Renaissance style.

Most of the houses have been carefully restored by artists, particularly painters and craftsmen who have been attracted by the beauty of St-Cirq-Lapopie and the Lot valley. Among the most famous are the writer André Breton, who lived on place du Carol in the old sailors' inn; as well as the painters Foujita, Man Ray, Henri Martin and Pierre Daura. Daura lived in the house with carved beams (his own work) in ruelle de la Fourdonne.

La Popie – Take the path that starts on the right of the town hall (*mairie*), to reach the castle ruins and the highest part of the cliff. From the cliff top (*telescope*), on which once stood the keep of La Popie Fortress, there is a remarkable **view★★** right over the village of St-Cirq. You'll see the church clinging to the cliff face; a bend in the Lot river encircling a patchwork of arable fields and meadows delineated by poplars; and, to the north, the foothills that border the Gramat Causse.

Fortified church – *Village centre.* This 15C sanctuary stands on a rock terrace overlooking the Lot. A squat belfry-tower, flanked by a round turret, stands at the front end.

EXCURSION
Belvédère du Bancourel

To access this rocky promontory overlooking the Lot, follow D 40 towards Bouziès for 300m. At the intersection with D 8 on the left, at the start of the scenic road carved into the cliff wall, is a place where you can park and admire the scenery.

The sweeping **view★** from Bancourel takes in the Lot valley and St-Cirq where the La Popie Rock rises up.

ADDRESSES

🛏 STAY

🍽🛏🛏 **Auberge du Sombral "Aux Bonnes Choses"** – ✆05 65 31 26 08. www.lesombrai.com. *8 rooms.* A country inn in the heart of the charming medieval hill village. Take a seat in one of the two dining rooms and admire the array of decorative objects. Country cooking. A few rooms under the eaves are available.

🍽🛏🛏 **Hôtel le Saint-Cirq** – ✆05 65 30 30 30. www.hotel-lesaintcirq.com. ⚒, *25 rooms.* The hotel is made up of several buildings forming a hamlet giving on to a private park, complete with vineyards, an orchard, truffle oaks, a donkey, sheep and a swimming pool. Free shuttle to the restaurant belonging to the same owner, Le Gourmet Quercynois.

🍴 EAT

🍽🛏🛏 **Le Gourmet Quercynois** – R. de la Peyrolerie. ✆05 65 31 21 20. A nice restaurant and an interesting wine museum have been set up in this village house owned by an oenologist. Naturally, the wine list is excellent and the choices go well with the regional cuisine on the menu.

🍽🛏 **L'Oustal** – ✆05 65 31 20 17. *Reservation required.* This restaurant is small in size and big on quality. The menu features unpretentious regional dishes at reasonable prices. Afternoons, before the dinner service starts, you can enjoy a drink on the terrace.

LEISURE ACTIVITIES

Kalapca – ✆05 65 30 29 51 or 05 65 24 21 01. On the Lot and Célé rivers, recreational activities and canoe hire. Guide available.

Grottes de Foissac★

This treasure trove was discovered in 1959. The 8km/4.9mi of caves feature both concretions and traces of prehistoric man.

VISIT

Guided tour (1hr 15min) Jul–Aug 10am–6pm; Jun and Sept 10–11.30am, 2–6pm; Apr–May and Oct 2–5pm except Sat. €9 (children 3–12, €6.50). 05 65 64 60 52. www.grotte-de-foissac.fr. The caves are chilly (13°C/55°F), so wear something warm. Although the caves were discovered in 1959, the 4 000-year-old human traces were discovered only in 1965.

Note the gleaming white stalactites and the lovely rock formations in the Obelisk Chamber (**Salle de l'Obélisque**); and the reflections, stalagmites and ivory tower-like formations in the Michel Roques Gallery. In one gallery, known as the Cave-in Gallery (**Salle de l'Éboulement**), there is a roof covered with round mushroom-like formations, thus proving that the stalactites were in the gallery well before earthquakes changed the aspect of the cave. Bulbous stalactites known as onions (**oignons**) are also worth noting.

- **Michelin Map:** 337: I-4.
- **Location:** 30km/18mi W of Château de Cénevières and 15km/9mi S of Figeac, the caves are located in the village of Foissac, going S.
- **Don't Miss:** The child's footprints; the needle-like stalactites; the beautiful view from place de Montsalès (along D 87).
- **Timing:** 1hr 45min with the wait and a tour of the little prehistoric park.
- **Kids:** The park is a nice place to stroll.

These caves were inhabited during the Copper Age (2700–1900BCE), when they were used as quarries, caves and a cemetery; this last use is something of a rarity. A hearth, copper utensils and large rounded pieces of pottery were found alongside human skeletons. Some of these are accompanied by offerings, suggesting that a ritual burial took place here. A touching detail not to be missed is a child's footprint left in the clay here 4 000 years ago.

A park illustrates the daily life of Copper-Age man.

Big chamber of Grottes de Foissac

© Grottes de Foissac

LIMOGES AND HAUT-LIMOUSIN

The Limousin, with its damp, mild climate and verdant pasturelands, is ideal for breeding cattle. An essentially rural region, the Limousin is the second-least populated region in France after Corsica. However, Limoges is a large city, known the world over for its porcelain. The Le Dorat ostentations are a religious tradition in the area, when participants in costume bearing holy shrines parade through the villages. The area was marked by the various battles of Richard the Lionheart, and there is no shortage of medieval castles to be found tucked away in the countryside. However, this is also a land which was hard-hit by WW2.

Limoges

The historical capital of Limousin, Limoges is synonymous with porcelain. The kaolin mines in St-Yrieix-la-Perche and a long history of delicate crafting have made this a paradise for those seeking refined tableware. You'll learn everything there is to know about this product, its manufacture and history, as well as related crafts such as enamel, through the various museums in the area. The city also boasts a grand cathedral where work carried out during various periods has contributed to a harmonious whole.

Highlights

1 **Limoges**, porcelain capital (p280)
2 **St Léonard-de-Noblat**, a noble medieval town (p290)
3 Impressive church of **Collégiale St-Pierre du Dorat** (p296)
4 **Oradour-sur-Glane**, a poignant reminder of WWII (p298)
5 **Châlus**, where Richard the Lionheart fell (p303)

Grasslands and Woods

Limousin has given its name to a species of high-quality cows, so steak lovers should take heed. The reddish coats of the cattle make a striking contrast with the green of the hillsides. These grasslands are famous for breeding other animals as well, particularly horses. Pompadour is home to a historical stud farm which developed the Anglo-Arabian breed in France. Other related activities also flourish here: St Junien has been a prolific glove-making community since medieval times, using the high-quality kid- and lambskin on hand.

If you are a nature lover, you'll be delighted at the number of paths and trails you can follow through the woods and heathlands, as well as the natural parks, such as Arboretum de la Jonchère, featuring tree species rarely seen in Europe.

Gare des Bénédictins clock tower at night, Limoges

© Charlie Abad / Photononstop

277

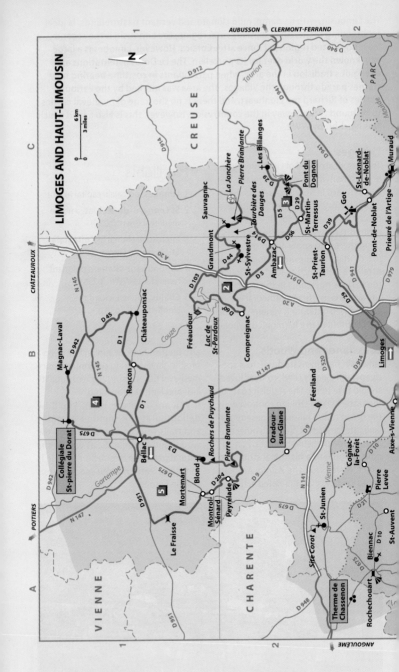

LIMOGES AND HAUT-LIMOUSIN

N

0 — 6 km
0 — 3 miles

CHÂTEAUROUX

POITIERS

ANGOULÊME

AUBUSSON ⚓ CLERMONT-FERRAND

The Ravages of War

The Limousin has been witness to brutal battles; Châlus is the place where Richard the Lionheart lost his life, but there are other villages here where he left his mark.

Much more recently, WWII ravaged this countryside. Oradour-sur-Glane is a mar-

278

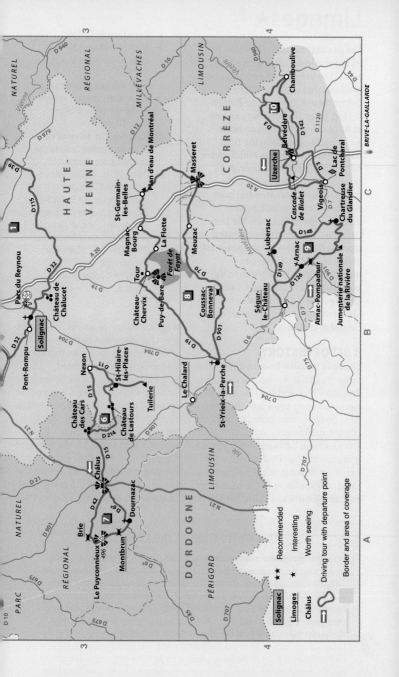

Map legend:

Solignac Recommended

Limoges Interesting

Châlus Worth seeing

Driving tour with departure point

Border and area of coverage

tyr village emblematic of the cruelty of the Nazi terror. It remains as it stood on the day of its destruction as a reminder of that terrible period. A visit there is not to be taken lightly; what occurred there is shocking. However, it can constitute an important educational visit with its first-rate memorial centre.

Limoges★

The site of Limoges was chosen for its defensive position, with a ford across the Vienne and two stepped plateaux that could be put to defensive use. In the Gallo-Roman period, when the town was known as Augustoritum, it spread out in an amphitheatre along the right bank of the river. In the Middle Ages two separate and rival townships developed: the **Cité Épiscopale**, grouped round its cathedral built on a low shelf overlooking the Vienne, and the **Château**, the busy commercial town on the opposite slope in the shadow of the powerful abbey of St-Martial. The city's industrial rise is largely due to its porcelain and enamelworks and shoe factories. Limoges also boasts a university and is the administrative capital of Limousin.

▶ **Population:** 139 150.
🕭 **Michelin Map:** 325: E-6.
🛈 **Info:** 12 blvd de Fleurus. 𝒞 05 55 34 46 87. www.limoges-tourisme.com.
◗ **Location:** Limoges extends across the N bank of the River Vienne.
🅿 **Parking:** A number of car parks are dotted around the centre (🕭 see city plan).
⊛ **Don't Miss:** Musée Adrien-Dubouché; Cathédrale St-Étienne; Église St-Michel-des-Lions; Musée de l'Émail; Jardins de l'Évêché; Cour du Temple; rue de la Boucherie; Chapelle St-Aurélien; Gare des Bénédictins.
👫 **Kids:** Parc Zoologique at Reynou.

A BIT OF HISTORY

Limoges in Gallo-Roman days – The presence of the Roman military road, Agrippa's Way, and the existence of a natural crossing point over the Vienne River certainly contributed to the birth of the Augustoritum.

This new town followed a well-ordered grid plan and quickly acquired a number of significant structures including a stone bridge, a forum, baths, aqueducts, an amphitheatre and so on. The forum was located on the site of the current town hall. Despite the many facilities offered, research has shown that Augustoritum was thinly populated.

At the end of the 4C, the barbarian invasions squeezed the town and people gathered around the St-Étienne hilltop thus forming the core of the Cité.

An enthusiastic reformer – In 1761, a young magistrate by the name of **Turgot** became general intendant of Limousin, one of the poorest regions in France. An admirer of the enlightened philosophers of his time, he seized this

The White Gold of the Limousin

In Europe, **porcelain** was imported from China until the late 17C, when the Sèvres manufacture bought the secret of hard-paste porcelain, which required 50% of kaolin, a rare white form of clay. In 1766, kaolin of remarkable purity was discovered in various parts of Limousin and, after encouraging experiments had been carried out at the Royal Factory at Sèvres, Turgot, who was then general intendant of Limousin, set up a porcelain works in 1771. This was under the patronage of the count of Artois and marked the beginning, for Limousin ceramics, of an era of prosperity which was hardly interrupted even by the troubled years of the Revolution. After 1815 the industry concentrated round Limoges which, because of its position on the Vienne, could land the wood for the kilns from lumber rafts floated down river. Nowadays, more than 50% of all the porcelain made in France comes from Limoges, a world-famous manufacturing centre.

Cathédrale St-Étienne and the medieval bridge over the Vienne

© Christian Guy / hemis.fr

opportunity to put his theories into practice and modernise the region. He built a network of modern roads, developed new industries (including the porcelain industry following the discovery of kaolin deposits), replaced Limoges' fortifications with wide boulevards and built a college and a hospital.

Famous citizens of Limoges – Many Limoges natives have become famous. Among the artists are **Léonard Limosin** (1505–76) enameller and painter in ordinary to the king's royal chamber. By his skill in engraving, painting and decoration he became one of the leaders of the great school of enamel artists of the 16C whose fame lasted until the 18C. The painter Auguste Renoir (1841–1919) worked here early in his career as a painter of porcelain.

Famous statesmen include Pierre Vergniaud (1753–93), the orator of the Girondin Group, and Sadi Carnot (1837–1894) who became president of the Republic.

LA CITÉ

Situated on a height overlooking the River Vienne, the Cité is Limoge's historic district. Built in 1210 to provide access to the Cité, the humpback **Pont St-Étienne** is made up of eight pointed arches. There is a good view from the bridge.

Cathédrale St-Étienne★

The cathedral was successor to a Romanesque church of which only a part of the crypt and the lower storeys of the belfry remain. The Gothic cathedral was begun in 1273; the chancel and transepts were completed during the 14C. Jean de Langeac undertook the completion of the cathedral in 1537, but died just three years later. It was left to Monsignor Dusquesnay to complete the cathedral between 1876 and 1888.

The **St John doorway★** is really the cathedral's main entrance. Made of very fine-grained granite, it was built in 1516–30 when the Flamboyant style was at its peak. The square **belfry** is 62m/204ft high. The lower three storeys are Romanesque and the upper four storeys are Gothic. The top three are octagonal, a design often found in Limousin architecture. The belfry stood apart from the nave until last century when a modern narthex and three bays were added. The **nave** achieves a unity of style despite taking 600 years to build. The boldness and elegance of line of the roof vaulting are wonderful. The triforium acts as a base for the clerestory windows.

The **rood screen★** (*end of the nave under the organ-loft*), built for Jean de Langeac by Touraine artists in 1533, once separated the chancel from the nave.

Manufacture Bernardaud

A Guide to Limoges Porcelain

True porcelain (hard-paste): Resonant when struck, this porcelaine is translucent and made from ground feldspathic rock and the special white clay known as kaolin. Porcelain is also what we call china, because that is where it was first made.

Artificial porcelain (soft-paste): Made using clay and ground glass, this material has a softer body and can be cut with a file, whereas true porcelain cannot. Dirt accumulated on an unglazed base is difficult to remove; on true porcelain it comes off easily.

Bone china: Developed by Josiah Spode the Second, bone china contains calcined bones in a hard-paste formula, making it chip-resistant. It is especially popular in England and the United States.

Earthenware: Opaque and porous, earthenware, the most common type of pottery, is made from clay baked at low temperatures.

Stoneware: Fired at high temperatures until it is vitrified (glasslike and non-porous), stoneware does not require a glaze; lead, salt and feldspathic glazes are used for decorative effects. Stoneware came from China to Europe in the 17C. By the early 19C its popularity had been superseded by porcelain.

Faience: Tin-glazed earthenware made in France, Germany, Spain or Scandinavia. In Italy, this material is called Faenza majolica (the town of Faenza, the origin of the name, was a major Renaissance production centre). In the Netherlands or England, it is referred to as Delft, after the Dutch city famous for its production.

Creamware: This fine white English lead-glazed earthenware (also produced for a brief period in France) is more durable and less expensive to produce than faience. Wedgwood and Leeds are the best-known manufacturers.

The three **tombs**★ round the chancel are of considerable decorative interest:

♦ the tomb of Raynaud de la Porte (14C), bishop of Limoges;

♦ the tomb of Bernard Brun in the pure 14C French style, adorned with four low-relief panels; and

♦ the **tomb of Jean de Langeac**, built in 1544, an example of the Renaissance style at its most delicate.

Musée des Beaux-Arts De Limoges★

1 pl. de l'Évêché ⏱*Open daily except Tue: Apr–Sep, 10am–6pm; Oct–Mar, 10am–noon, 2–5pm (Sun 2–5pm). Closed 1 Jan, 1 May, 1 and 11 Nov, 25 Dec.* ⬤*No charge.* ✆*05 55 45 98 10. www.museebal.fr.*

The museum is housed in the elegant 18C former archbishop's palace.

The museum displays 500 **Limousin enamels**★ dating from the 12C to the 21C. The Middle Ages was an especially rich period for this type of art and it is well represented in the display cases.

Cloisonné enamels use an early technique where thin strips of metal are soldered to a metal base to outline the design. Although this process works well for gold, it is less effective for copper and was soon replaced by **champlevé**, where the lines of the design were cut away from the surface and enamel was applied to the recesses.

The third technique is that of **painted enamels**; the design is painted on the enamel covering the copper plate.

In the series of painted enamels are two plaques by Monvaerni (*late 15C*), and a **Nativity triptych** (*1515-20*). Limoges is still an international centre of enamel art and hosts the Biennale International de l'Art de l'Émail.

Egyptology – The two rooms in the Egyptology section present a particularly rich collection of terracotta figurines and bronze statuettes.

Lapidary Museum – The fine vaulted cellars which were formerly the bishop's palace kitchens make a good setting for the ancient and medieval exhibits of the Lapidary Museum. These include Iron Age funerary items, stone lions, gravestones and statues characteristic of local Gallo-Roman works in granite. The Middle Ages are represented by a collection of sarcophagi, a 9C mosaic from the tomb of St Martial, and low-relief sculptures.

Ancient Limoges – Scale models illustrate the evolution of the city from its founding up to medieval times. A rare **fresco** (*early 2C*), discovered on the site of a villa, hints at the luxury of the residence.

French painting – This collection includes 17C–18C works (*Bataille de Constantin* by Charles Le Brun), landscapes of Limoges and the area by Courtot, and canvasses by Renoir (*Portrait de Mademoiselle Laporte*), Guillaumin, Pascin and Suzanne Valadon.

Jardin Botanique de l'Évêché★

These pleasant bishop's palace gardens rise in terraces above the Vienne and provide a good view of the cathedral and the palace. They include a themed garden and a "wild" garden featuring five natural environments typical of the region.

Cité des Métiers et des Arts

5 r. de la Règle ○*Open May–mid-Jun and last 2 weeks in Sept Wed, Sat–Sun and public holidays, 3–7pm; mid-Jun–mid-Sept daily 3–7.30pm.* ⊚€4. ℘*05 55 32 57 84. www.cma-limoges.com.*
This centre, located in the Bishop's Palace gardens, presents the work of the **Compagnons du Tour de France** and of France's finest workers in the building trade. The different stages a young *compagnon* has to go through to master his trade are illustrated on the mezzanine.

Musée de la Résistance

7 r. Neuve-St-Étienne. ♿○*Open mid-Jun–mid-Sept 10am–6pm; rest of year 9.30am–5pm (Sun 1.30–5pm).*
⊚*No charge.* ℘*05 55 45 84 44.*
www.resistance-massif-central.fr.
During WW2, the Limoges area was hard-hit by the numerous deportations and massacres (⚑*see ORADOUR-sur-GLANE and TULLE*). In the series of rooms which make up the museum, posters, maps, documents and photos are displayed, evoking the dark days of the war. Courageous men and women of the Haute Vienne, led by Georges Guingouin, were some of the first in France to band together in the Resistance movement.

☙ WALKING TOUR

Château District walk

The neighbourhood known as Le Château rose up long ago around the abbey of St-Martial and the château. Today it serves as Limoges' downtown, busy with shops and activity.

Église St-Pierre-du-Queyroix

The flamboyant façade dates from 1534. The well proportioned 13C bell-tower served as a model for two nearby churches, St-Michel and St-Étienne.

▶ Walk west on rue St-Martial.

St-Martial Abbey remains

Once located outside the city walls, place de la République stands over the site of a Gallo-Roman necropolis where St Martial was buried. His tomb was highly venerated and a chapel was built above it in the 6C. The chapel's keepers adopted the Benedictine rule in 848, and the abbey grew, becoming affiliated with Cluny in 1063. During the Middle Ages, it was the site of intensive religious, cultural and artistic activity. Later the abbey declined and its buildings were destroyed during the Revolution.

Crypte St-Martial

◔ ⌁ *Open 10am–6pm. For information on guided tours (1hr), contact the Tourist Office.*
☏ *05 55 34 46 87.*
The current stairway was added in the 13C to improve the flow of pilgrims. Martial and his two companions (Alpinien and Austriclinien) were laid to rest in the two big tombs measuring more than 2.80m long, still on view. In the 9C, Martial's remains were exhumed and placed in a golden reliquary on the main altar in the new basilica. The second room or sanctuary contains the enormous granite 4C tomb known by the name of Tève-le-Duc. Beyond and below, there is a large room that shores up the churches of St-Pierre and St-Benoît, installed on the Gallo-Roman ruins and on the site of an early Christian cemetery.

▶ Cross rue Jean-Jaurès and follow rue du Clocher; turn right on rue Gaignolle.

Place du Présidial

Note, at the corner of rue Haute-de-la-Comédie, the former **Hôtel Maledent** built in 1639. Admire the pretty **place Fontaine-des-Barres** (*16C*) below.
The north doorway of the church of **St-Michel-des-Lions** opens onto this square where the 17C–18C royal administrative buildings remain standing.

Église St-Michel-des-Lions★

Construction began in 1364 and continued until the 16C when a west bay was added. Outside near the belfry door on the south side you'll see the two granite lions that have given the church its name. Behind the high altar, a monumental altar of carved stone supports a 19C gilded wooden reliquary shrine containing relics of St Martial, including the saint's skull.

▶ Go down rue Ferrerie then rue du Temple.

Cour du Temple★

Rue du Consulat, with its 18C buildings, is linked to rue du Temple by a narrow passage (*at no 22*), which opens onto 16C half-timbered houses and arcaded galleries, known as the temple courtyard.

▶ Continue along rue du Consulat then rue des Halles.

Les Halles

Built at the end of the 19C, the covered market stands on **place de la Motte**, probably named for the *motte*, or hillock, where the viscounts' castle stood.

Rue de la Boucherie★

This picturesque street is lined with half-timbered houses, some of which still have the accoutrements of the 80 butchers' shops which once operated there. On the last Sunday in October, a regional festival known as the Frairie des Petits Ventres brings back the memory of bygone activities.

Maison Traditionelle de la Boucherie
🕐*See Abbaye St-Martial.*
The butcher's stall at no 36 is now devoted to preserving the heritage of the meat trade in Limoges. In the kitchen, which is also a shop, visitors can admire the butcher's block and its accessories, a 19C icebox and a hearth where tripe was prepared. Upstairs are the furnished rooms where about 25 people lived.

Place de la Barreyrrette
The name of this square comes from the fence (*barrière*) around the holding pen for animals awaiting slaughter.
The pens disappeared when the municipal slaughterhouse was opened in 1832.

Chapelle St-Aurélien★
A 14C monolithic cross marks the entrance to this unusual little building dating from 1475. Founded to hold the relics of St Aurélien, the chapel was sold at an auction in 1795 and secretly purchased by the butchers' guild, which still maintains it today.

▷ Walk across place des Bancs to rue Haute-Vienne.

Aquarium du Limousin
👥♿🕐*Open daily 10.30am–6pm (Jul–Aug 10am–7pm).* 🕐*Closed 25 Dec, 1 Jan.* ⊗€8.50 (children, 3–12, €5). ✆05 55 33 42 11. www.aquariumdulimousin.com.
Set up beneath place Haute-Vienne on the site of an old reservoir, the aquarium has made use of the vaulted architecture to welcome European freshwater fish, tropical species, piranhas and more.

Boulevard Louis-Blanc
Take a stroll along this "porcelain" avenue. Even the square in front of the town hall is adorned with a porcelain fountain.

▷ Place Wilson; left on rue du Collège.

Pavillon du Verdurier
👄*During exhibits or included in the guided tours organised by the Tourist Office.*

Built after WW1 to store meat, this edifice has a rather unusual appearance with its mosaics and floral friezes on a ceramic background.

▷ Return to your starting point via place St-Pierre on the right.

ADDITIONAL SIGHTS
Musée National de la Porcelaine Adrien-Dubouché★★
♿🕐*Open daily except Tue, 10am–12.30pm, 2–5.45pm.* 🕐*Closed 1 Jan, 1 May and 25 Dec.* ⊗€4.50, no charge 1st Sun of the month. ✆05 55 33 08 50. www.musee-adriendubouche.fr.
The museum, founded in 1845, became a national museum in 1881. It is named after the director Adrien Dubouché, who provided it with the foundation of its collections. Today the collection, which includes items dating from the pottery of ancient times to porcelain from factories in production at Limoges today, shows the evolution of ceramics and glassware in France and throughout the world.

Ground floor – To the left of the vestibule and its 1898 bronze statue of Adrien Dubouché, eight display cases are given over to fine earthenware, popular in the 19C, and to clay pieces formed from slip (*Vase aux Musiciennes* by Aube). A collection of pieces by **Théodore Deck** (1823–91) recalls his important role in ceramic arts in the 19C. One room provides explanations of the manufacturing techniques of the four major families of ceramics (pottery, earthenware, stoneware and porcelain). The right-hand wing displays 19C porcelain. Over 1 000 pieces of Limoges porcelain amply demonstrate the reason for the worldwide renown of porcelain manufactured here since 1771.

Salon d'honneur – This room houses precious items from the Far East: Tang earthenware, Song porcelain, Yuan blue-and-white ware and much more.

First floor – The history of ceramic manufacture, from its origins in the Middle East to medieval times, is traced in the **right wing**. The **left wing** contains the

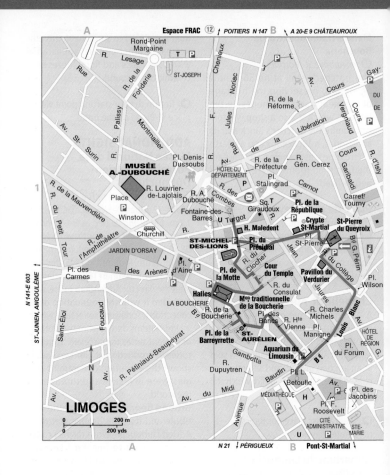

LIMOGES

18C porcelain collection. The **soft-paste porcelain** technique (without kaolin), was perfected in the 17C. First produced in Rouen, major manufacturing began in Saint-Cloud in 1677. Several centres around Paris became famous for their wares: Chantilly, Mennecy, Vincennes and **Sèvres**.

The first **hard-paste** porcelains manufactured in Europe were made in the **Meissen** factory in Saxony in 1710. Kaolin was found near Limoges in 1768, enabling the development of hard-paste production in Sèvres, Paris, Lille, Bordeaux, Orléans and Valenciennes.

Le FRAC Limousin

From pl. Denis-Dussoubs, follow r. François-Chenieux then turn left onto av. G.-et-V.-Lemoine and left

again onto impasse des Charentes. ☆①*Open daily except Sun, Mon and public hols, 2–6pm.* ☞€1.50. ✆05 55 77 08 98. www.fraclimousin.fr.

The Fonds Régional d'Art Contemporain (Regional Collection of Contemporary Art), created in 1982, is located in a former grocery warehouse.

Gare des Bénédictins★

This is one of the landmarks of Limoges. Built from 1923 to 1929, it stands as a symbol of the town's prosperity and expansion between the two World Wars.

EXCURSION
Aixe-sur-Vienne

This town is a gateway to the Parc Naturel Régional Périgord-Limousin. Every seven years, during the *ostensions*

N 21 PÉRIGUEUX, BORDEAUX

🚗 DRIVING TOUR

1 VIENNE TO BRIANCE★
90km/54mi. Allow 2hrs 30mins.
See route 1 on region map pp278–279.

▷ Leave Limoges on the N 21 towards Périgueux.

This picturesque road winds its way through meadows along the Briance valley. At **Pont-Rompu** hamlet, there is a view on the right of a picturesque old bridge with pointed cutwaters. This was part of the ancient Roman road from Limoges to Bordeaux.

ÉGLISE ABBATIALE DE SOLIGNAC★★

An interesting Romanesque church is all that remains of the once-famous abbey founded in 632 by St Eligius near the green valley of the River Briance.

Abbey-Church

🕐✎Guided tours available.
For information, contact the tourist office, ℘05 55 00 42 31.
The present church dates from the first half of the 12C and is strongly influenced by the Périgord style of architecture.

Exterior – The big belltower built at the same time as the abbey was replaced in the 19C by a belfry-wall. As you walk around the northern side of the church, admire the harmony of the construction. Large buttresses and recessed columns reach up to the ledge around the roof; on the lower part, groups of four arches fall alternately on plain pilasters and bases embellished with scrolling designs. A bas-relief of Christ in Majesty rises above the north-transept doorway.
Interior – *Go in through the door in the porch.* The main body of the church is covered over with vast semicircular domes. The stalls, on each side of the nave, mostly date from the 15C. The carved misericords and armrests depict foliage, animals and grimacing faces.

(✎*see Introduction*), 20 reliquaries are carried in a procession to Notre-Dame-d'Arliquet by representatives of different trades.

Maison de la Porcelaine

🕐Open Jul–Aug daily 10am–7pm
(Sun and public holidays 10am–1pm,
3–7pm); Apr–Jun Sept and Dec
10am–1pm, 2–7pm (Sun and public
holidays 10am–1pm, 3–7pm); rest
of year daily except Sun 10am–1pm,
2–7pm. ✎Guided visits: Jul–Aug
10am, 11am, 3pm, 4pm; rest of year
Mon–Fri, 3pm. 🕐Closed 1 Jan, 1 May,
1 Nov and 25 Dec. ✎No charge.
℘05 55 70 14 68.
www.maisonporcelaine.com.
A visit to this workshop provides an insight into porcelain making.

The transept is asymmetrical. Its southern arm is roofed with barrel-vaulting. Note the 18C polychrome woodwork Virgin. In the north transept a glass case contains works of art including the 12C reliquary-bust of St Théau in gilded copper and silver.

The chancel is punctuated by seven arcades and three chapels. Two 17C frescoes represent the Temptation of Christ and the Olive Garden. On the right pillar, note the restored distemper painting of St Christopher.

Monastery buildings – The buildings, which were ravaged during the Revolution, are occupied by student missionaries. The courtyard faces the south side of the church, which was connected to the cloisters by an archway leading from the second bay. The pointed arch, under which you pass as you go around towards the front of the buildings, may have been another entrance to the cloisters.

▷ Follow D 32 to Le Vigen then turn left onto D 704. A short distance beyond the railway bridge, turn right onto D 65 towards Boisseuil.

👥👤 Parc Zoologique et Paysager du Reynou

Le Vigen. ⏰*Open Apr–Oct daily 10am–7.30pm; Nov Wed, Sat, Sun, public and school holidays 10am–5.30pm; rest of year, call for details.* 🎫*€14 (children, 3–12, €10).* ✆*05 55 00 40 00. www.parczooreynou.com.*

Laid out in 1870 for the porcelain manufacturer Haviland, this landscaped park is planted with 150 different species of trees surrounding a castle.

In a nearby **zoo**, 120 species of animals from the five continents roam around in relative freedom.

▷ Return and continue along the D 32.

Château de Chalusset

⚠*Access to the ruins is strictly forbidden for safety reasons; however, a footpath enables visitors to walk right*

round. It is also possible to visit the medieval village of Le Bas-Chalusset and the Tour Jeannette. ⏰*Jul–Aug 10.30am–6.30p; Apr–Jun and Sept–Oct 10.30am–12.30pm, 1.30–6.30pm.* 🎫*No charge;* 🗣*possibility of guided tours by appointment.* 🎫*€5.* ✆*05 55 00 96 55.*

The impressive ruins of Chalusset Castle are a perfect example of medieval military architecture. The castle was built in the 12C. In 1577 it fell into the hands of the Huguenots who used it as a base for their battles against Limoges. The troops of Limoges took the notorious castle by force and dismantled it (1593). In Le Chatenet, the picturesque D 39 on the left (towards St-Léonard-de-Noblat), crosses the River Vienne. Turn left on reaching the confluence of the Vienne and the Maulde, overlooked by the **Château de Muraud** perched on a promontory.

Vallée de la Maulde

The road runs up the Maulde valley through a rocky, wooded gorge. The river has been transformed by the French electric company into a giant, watery staircase, with remote-controlled dams.

The **Barrage de l'Artige**, the last dam of the series, regulates the flow of water coming from the others upstream. The road overlooks the dam and affords a fine view of the valley and the ruins of the priory of Artige.

Ancien Prieuré de l'Artige

A narrow road opposite the dam to the left leads to the entrance of the Priory. Founded in the 12C and secularised shortly before the Revolution, part of this priory was subsequently left to fall to ruin. From the road you can see the vast buildings with their round tiled roofs, the arcades between the chapterhouse and the cloisters, and the remains of emblazoned doors.

▷ D 39 follows the Vienne, framed by overhanging rocks, then rises above the river.

St-Léonard-de-Noblat★

⏱ See ST-LÉONARD-DE-NOBLAT.

Pont-de-Noblat

In the Vienne valley, on the outskirts of town, this area has developed on both sides of the river. A 13C bridge spans the water; old houses line the time-worn path known as the *pavé*.

Promenade du Chêne de Clovis

🚶 Between the bridge and the church, a steep path leads to a plateau where a castle once stood.

▶ N 141 crosses the Vienne and follows the river valley before it rises up to a plateau. At St-Antoine, take D 124 for a panoramic view of the Ambazac hills, then turn left on D 39, a lovely country road.

St-Priest-Taurion

This town rests peacefully at the fork of the River Taurion and River Vienne, in a green valley cut across with dams.

▶ After Le Palais, take D 29 along the valley back to Limoges.

ADDRESSES

🛏 STAY

⌂ **Chambre d'hôte M. et Mme Brulat** – *Imp. du Vieux Crezin, Feytiat. 5km/3mi E of Limoges. Take the A 20, exit 35, and head towards Feytiat; in Crézin follow signs to Le Vieux Crézin.* ℘05 55 06 34 41. *3 rooms.* Peace and quiet reign supreme in this large stone house in the countryside just 10min from the centre of Limoges. Offers comfortable bedrooms, a relaxing lounge, and a games room with billiards and darts.

⌂🍴 **Hôtel Familia Nos Rêves** – *16 r. Gén.- Bessol.* ℘05 55 77 41 43. *www.hotelhf.com.* 🅿. *12 rooms. WiFi.* This hotel is near the train station, but that is not its only advantage: its attractive contemporary style and family atmosphere will make you feel right at home.

⌂🍴🛌 **Hôtel Richelieu** – *40 av. Baudin.* ℘05 55 34 22 82. *www.hotel-richelieu.com. 41 rooms.* This hotel near the town hall brings together comfort and 1930s décor. There are also contemporary rooms in the extension.

🍴 EAT

⌂ **Chez François** – *Halles Centrales.* ℘05 55 32 32 79. Housed in the *Halles de Limoges*, a listed historical monument, this friendly bistro bases its menu on produce from the market. From the dining room, decorated with a fresco of sculpted wood, you can see the chef at work.

⌂ **La Bibliothèque** – *7, r. Turgot.* ℘05 55 11 00 47. This attractive bar-pub-restaurant occupies what was the old library, serving carefully prepared and beautifully presented traditional local fare.

⌂ **Le Bistrot du Boucher** – *29 bis, blvd Louis Blanc.* ℘05 55 10 20 00. *www.bistrotduboucher87.com.* This bright, cheery, modern chain restaurant specialises in top-quality meat but also uses seasonal and local produce.

⌂ **Chez Alphonse** – *5 pl. de la Motte.* ℘05 55 34 34 14. Tucked away behind the *halles,* this bistro is a popular local haunt. Tables are decorated with chequered tablecloths and a menu which is written up on the blackboard.

⌂🍴 **Le Pont St-Étienne** – *8 pl. de Compostelle.* ℘05 55 30 52 54. *www.lepont sainteetienne.fr.* Attractive bay windows with views of the old stone bridge and the river. The menu features a number of imaginatively named dishes. Summer terrace.

⌂🍴 **Le Versailles** – *20 pl. Aine.* 05 55 34 13 39. *www.brasserie-le-versailles-limoges. com.* Old French movie memorabilia fills the walls of this pleasant brasserie.

⌂🍴 **Les Petits Ventres** – *20 r. de la Boucherie.* ℘05 55 34 22 90. *www.les-petits -ventres.com.* Classic French cuisine is served in these two typical 15C houses run by two young and enthusiastic owners. The cuisine is high on quality with traditional dishes based on liver, tongue, pigs' trotters, tripe and so on.

⌂🍴🛌 **Le Bœuf à la Mode** – *60 r. François-Chenieux.* ℘05 55 77 73 95. *www.leboeufalamode.fr.* Excellent meaty cuisine served in a friendly and traditional ambience.

St-Léonard-de-Noblat★

The belltower of the old church in St-Léonard-de-Noblat is a remarkable example of Limousin-style Romanesque architecture. The main industry in town is the manufacture of porcelain.
The valley is famous for the distinctive, ruddy brown cattle known as *vaches Limousines*, of which St-Léonard is an active export and breeding centre.
For visitors with a sweet tooth, St-Léonard is memorable for its *massepain*, a speciality found in local pastry shops, made with sweet almond paste.

A BIT OF HISTORY
A hermit
Long before the Roman conquest, the road from Bourges to Bordeaux was used by pilgrims on their way to Compostela.
The town was named after the hermit **Léonard**, the godson of Clovis, who early in the 6C chose the area as his place of retreat. His piety and the many miracles he performed made him one of the most popular saints in the Limousin. A village was built alongside the retreat and took the name Noblat (derived from *nobiliacum*, meaning noble site). Léonard's help was invoked in protecting horses and seeking the release of prisoners. Because he was the patron saint of prisoners, it is the tradition in St-Léonard to celebrate the Quintaine in November: a small wooden prison or *quintaine* is trampled down by riders on horseback armed with clubs.

A great scholar
Joseph-Louis **Gay-Lussac** (1778–1850) was born in St-Léonard. This physicist and chemist discovered the law of expansion of gases and made ascents in a balloon to examine whether the Earth's magnetic attraction decreased as the altitude increased. In addition to his scientific achievements and

- **Population:** 4 640.
- **Michelin Map:** 325: F-5; or see Limoges map.
- **Info:** Pl. du Champ de Mars. ☎05 55 56 25 06. www.tourisme-noblat.fr.
- **Location:** 21km/13mi E of Limoges.
- **Don't Miss:** The collegiate church and belfry.
- **Kids:** Historail.

awards, Gay-Lussac represented the Haute-Vienne in the French *Chambre des Députés*.

MEDIEVAL TOWN
Two names are mentioned for every street: the present name in blue and the medieval name in red.
It is easy to imagine the layout of the medieval town: the ring of boulevards follows the path of the old defensive wall, whose vestiges can be seen on boulevard Carnot (*south*) and rue Jean-Jaurès (*northwest*).
Start from **place Gay-Lussac** (*commemorative monument and birthplace of the scientist*). This was the centre of activities during the Middle Ages: the town's butchers had their stand here. Note the corner house dating from the 13C featuring a large bay surmounted by two storeys with twin windows.
Follow rue Gay-Lussac to **place de la République**: no 18, known as the Maison de la Tour Ronde (*16C*), has a picturesque corbelled turret. On the corner of **rue de la Halle**, another 16C building, known as the Maison de la Tour Carrée, features a square bartizan. As you walk towards **place Noblat**, note the 13C house with its shop entrance surmounted by twinned windows.

SIGHTS
Ancienne Collégiale★
Call the Tourist Office for information.
This 12C former collegiate church has been restored and remains a fine specimen of Romanesque architecture. It is said that Richard the Lionheart contrib-

uted to the construction of the church on his release from prison in Austria.

Exterior – The **belfry★★**, built above a porch which is open on two sides and embellished with remarkable capitals, adjoins the third bay of the nave. The belltower consists of four storeys built square, surmounted by two recessed storeys which are octagonal in shape. Each level is adorned with beautiful blind arcades. The final touch of elegance is given by the stone spire which was constructed in the 12C.

Situated between the belfry and the transept, the **Rotonde du Sépulcre**, now restored to its original appearance, was probably built by a knight returning from the Holy Land.

The church's **west front**, built in the 13C, has a wide doorway flanked by small columns decorated with finely carved, crocketed capitals supporting the covings. The **east end** rises harmoniously in tiers and the chapels are roofed with rounded tiles.

Interior – The church went through several building stages (*scale model at the entrance*), which are apparent in the disunity of style within. The powerful **nave** has groined, barrel and broken-barrel vaulting; the **crossing** is roofed with a high dome on pendentives placed atop a drum pierced by eight windows. Smaller, less ornate domes rise above the end of each transept arm.

In the 17C, a new vault, higher than the cupola in the transept, was added on and the church had to be shored up.

The 15C oak-wood stalls (1) are sculpted with satirical motifs. On the gilded main altar (2), dating from the 18C, the relics of St Léonard are in a case below his statue. In the south transept, a wall niche holds the saint's tomb (3) and a revered lock bolt; the bolt is symbolic of St Léonard's power to intervene on prisoners' behalf (tradition also holds that it is effective in curing cases of sterility).

Belltower, St-Léonard-de-Noblat

© OT Noblat

Musée Gay-Lussac

R. Jean Giraudoux. ♿ ◷Open Jul–Aug, Mon–Sat 10am–1pm, 3–6pm, Sun 3–6pm; mid-Aor–Jun and Sept–mid-Oct daily except Sun 10am–1pm, 3–6pm; rest of year call for information. ⊜No charge. ℘05 55 56 35 88.

The museum devoted to this great man of science is located in a former convent. His memory and accomplishments are recalled in documents, objects (*a hot air balloon basket; the re-creation of a 19C chemistry laboratory*) and instruments (*barometer, oven and more*).

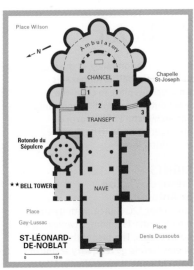

Moulin du Got

© Philippe Roy / hemis.fr

EXCURSION
👤👤 HistoRail
On the D 39 S of town. 🕐*Open Jul–Aug, daily except Sat–Sun and public holidays, 10am–noon, 2–6pm.* ⮑€5 *(children, 8–16, €3.50).* 🗪05 55 56 11 12. www.historail.com.

This museum explores the history of the iron horse. Genuine train parts, working models on six different scales, re-creations and simulations bring the heyday of the railways back to life.

👤👤 Moulin du Got
At Le Pénitent, 1.5km/0.9mi W. Follow the signposts. ♿🗪Guided tour *(1hr 30min) Jul–Aug 10.30am and 2.15–5.15pm, Sat 2.15–5.15pm; mid-*

May–Jun Wen and Sat 3pm; rest of year call for information. ⮑€7.50 (children under 12, €3.50). 🗪05 55 57 18 74. www.moulindugot.com.

This early 16C mill on the Tard, a tributary of the Vienne, invites you to discover its workshops and the importance of paper manufacture in the Limousin in the 18C. The museum is original because it includes both a **paper mill** and **printing shop** to show you the entire process of fabrication of the printed page.

First you'll go down to the **machine shop**, which contains a pool where straw macerates in lime milk before being crushed under the grindstones; a hollander, used to refine the straw paste; a vat for handmade paper; paper machine for mechanically produced paper; a hydraulic press that compacts the paper and rids it of most of its water; and a drying station. Once you've seen this, you'll move along to the **printing workshop**. This includes a type case (with movable type used in letterpress printing); a linotype machine (for typesetting line by line); various printing presses; and various presses for graphic effects such as a lithographic press.

As you leave the mill, a lane on the right takes you down to see the bucket wheel, restored in 2002 to its original condition.

Ambazac

Near the Taurion valley, at the foot of Mount Gerbasou, Ambazac is a marvellous place to enjoy the great outdoors, rambling or fishing. The architecture of the town is also interesting, with its church as the centrepiece.

SIGHTS
Trésor de l'Église St-Antoine ★★
This sober 12C church, with its choir rebuilt in the 15C, houses two exceptional pieces. The first of these is the impressively large **reliquary shrine of Saint Étienne**. It was crafted in 1189 in

▶ **Population:** 5 542.
🖤 **Michelin Map:** 325: F5.
ℹ **Info:** 3 av. du Gén.-de-Gaulle. 🗪05 55 56 70 70. www.tourisme-ambazac.fr.
👁 **Don't Miss:** Trésor de l'Église d'Ambazac; Lac de St-Pardoux.
▶ **Location:** 20km/12.4mi NE of Limoges between the Marche and the Limousin.
🕐 **Timing:** 2hr to explore Le Val du Taurion, and a half-day to discover the mounts of Ambazac.

embossed, chiselled copper adorned with *champlevé* enamel, precious stones and intaglios (engraved gems). The shrine's two levels are crowned with a bird which might represent the soul of the saint or the dove of the Holy Spirit. The second piece is the **dalmatic** said to have belonged to Saint Étienne de Muret. This religious garment is made of a dull red silk embroidered with brilliant gold patterns and decorated with a two-headed Byzantine eagle.

These ornaments show a marked Moorish influence. According to the folklore, the garment was given to St Étienne in 1121 by the Empress Matilda, but analyses of the fabric lead scientists to believe that it actually dates from the second part of the 13C. It was probably brought back from Spain by a pilgrim of Compostela.

👥 Musée de Minéralogie et de Pétrographie

5 av. de la Libération. 🏍 🕐*Open Jul–Aug 10am–noon, 2–6pm (Sat–Sun 3–6pm); rest of year 2–5pm.* 🕐*Closed Mon and public holidays.* 🎫€5 *(children under 15, €3).* ☎05 55 56 59 14. http://musee.ambazac.free.fr.*

On the three levels of this museum, more than 500 stones and 3 000 minerals from all over the world are on display. The lower ground floor is dedicated to petrology and contains large stones such as volcanic bombs, fossilised limestone, pegmatites and more.

Amongst the marvellous specimens on the upper ground floor, note the rose quartz of Madagascar, halite from Saudi Arabia and orbicular granite from the Guéret Mountains.

The first floor is reserved for minerals and metallic minerals. You'll be surprised by the rich collection of silver, nickel, cobalt, chrome, iron, aluminium and gold. Brightly coloured **uranium** and uraniferous rocks, which were exploited in the Limousin for 50 years, are shown in a separate exhibition.

🚗 DRIVING TOUR

2 LES MONTS D'AMBAZAC★

60km/37.2mi. Allow half a day. See route 2 on region map pp278–279.

▷ Drive NW out of Ambazac towards A 20.

Compreignac

This village grew up on the road from Limoges to Châteauponsac, where religious structures were built. **Eglise St-Martin** was fortified in the 15C and 16C and is crowned with a machicolated gallery. Its portal is elegant with a frieze of soberly sculpted capitals.

▷ Leave Compreignac N on D 60 A.

Lac de St-Pardoux★

🏊 This lake, which has recently been cleaned, stretches over 330ha/815acres in this pleasant setting perfect for nature lovers and leisure seekers. The equipment is based in **Chabannes** (*beach, sailing boat base, walking trail departure points*) and **Santrop** (*water centre*) in the south, as well as in **Fréaudour** (*motorboat base and beach*) in the north.

▷ Leave St-Pardoux E on D 103. After Razès, cross A 20 and follow D 44.

St-Sylvestre

The church here contains a remarkable reliquary **bust★** of Saint Étienne de Muret from the abbey of Grandmont.

▷ Leave St-Sylvestre N on D 78.

Grandmont

The foundations and a few cut stones are all that are left of the abbey of Grandmont. The edifice was built in the 12C and was expanded in the 14C and 15C. The abbey was restored in the 18C after having been damaged during the Wars of Religion and the Hundred Years War, but was demolished just before the revolution when the Order was disbanded. You can see the plans of the abbey near the **Chapelle de**

Pèlerinage, which contains copies of the reliquary shrine of Ambazac and of the reliquary cross of Gorre.

▶ Before entering St-Léger, turn right on D 28A.

Sauvagnac

This miniscule village has its origins as a priory of the abbey of Grandmont.
Chapelle – A place of pilgrimage to the Virgin Mary whose richly dressed statue crowns the master altar. To the right of the choir is a 15C Pietà.
Pierre Branlante – 🐾 *1hr round-trip from the chapel.* This "shaking stone" is found in a disarray of granite blocks, but the real attraction is the extraordinary **view**★★ over Ambazac, with Limoges to the southwest; Mount Gargan and the Monédières mountains to the southeast; and Puy de Dôme and Puy de Sancy to the east.

▶ Leaving the village, turn right and then follow the road to the left.

🐾 *1hr round-trip.* A lovely walk leads to **La Tourbière des Dauges** (*peat bogs*).

▶ Continue along D 28A, then take D 914 left.

👥 Arboretum de la Jonchère★

These superb woodlands were created in 1884 to produce trees to reforest the Ambazac mountains and the Plateau de Millevaches; today they are managed by the National Forestry Commission. Along the blazed trail, you'll discover some 60 botanic species and especially trees from the American Northwest such as sequoias, western red cedars, Douglas firs and white firs, as well as rare species such as the Verzy beech with its curious spiral trunk.

▶ D 914 will bring you back to Ambazac.

③ LE VAL DE TAURION★

30km/18.6mi. Allow 2hr. See route 3 on region map pp278–279.

▶ Drive SE out of Ambazac on D 5 and, after the railway bridge, turn right on D 56.

St-Martin-Terressus

The village overlooks the reservoir of the Barrage de St-Marc.
D 29 and D 5 give various opportunities to view the dam and the **reservoir**.

Pont du Dognon★

This bridge spans the Taurion in a remarkable environment of wooded cliffs dotted with boulders.

▶ Leave D 5 and turn right on D 29.

Église des Billanges

This 12C–15C fortified church contains a 13C enamelled shrine.

▶ Follow D 5 which leads to Ambazac.

ADDRESSES

🛏 STAY

😊😊 **Chambre d'hôte Le Château de St-Antoine** – *22 av. de Maison-Rouge, Bonnac-la-Côte. 10km/6.2mi W via D 920 and D 220. ☎05 55 36 61 71. www.chateau-de-st-antoine.com.* ♿🅿️🚭. *5rooms.* This pretty castle is furnished with antiques and offers five very different rooms. Some are spacious, others small; the same goes for the bathrooms. A small kitchen is available for your use. An unpretentious establishment.

🍴 EAT

😊😊 **Ferme Auberge de la Besse** – *La Besse, Les Billanges. 15km/9.3mi E via D 5 and D 29. ☎05 55 56 57 76. www.fermedelabesse.fr.* ♿🅿️🚭. *3 rooms.* This simple ivy-covered farm offers authentic farm products and a warm welcome. Poultry, sheep, rabbits, cattle and pigs are raised here, and vegetables – sometimes rare ones – are grown in the garden.

Bellac

Bellac rises up on a spur overlooking the valley of the Vincou, which flows into the Gartempe. This hilly green setting is situated between the Limousin plateaux and the plains of the Poitou. The town is associated with the novelist and playwright Jean Giraudoux.

THE TOWN

Once you have enjoyed a view of the town, start your tour at no 29 rue Thiers, where a plaque commemorates La Fontaine's stay in the local inn. He is said to have written one of his fables here.

Église Notre-Dame

Pl. de l'Église

The church, built on a terrace overlooking the Vincou, is built in a mix of Romanesque and Gothic styles. A huge square belfry surmounts the two naves, one 12C and Romanesque, the other 14C and Gothic. The two naves lead to the chancel, which ends in a flat east end. The southern doorway is adorned with small, serpentine capitals.

To the left of the entrance, in a chest set in the wall, there is a beautiful 12C **shrine★** (*the oldest in Limousin*), embellished with *cabochons* and medallions of *champlevé* enamel. Among the figurative decorations on the sacred receptacle are the symbols of the four Evangelists around the figure of Christ.

Giraudoux's childhood home (Maison Natale)

4 r. Jean Jaurès. ◐*Open Jul–Aug 2.30–5pm.* ◉€4. ℘*05 55 68 10 61.*

Châteauroux may claim the glory of having educated **Jean Giraudoux** (1882–1944) at its *lycée*, but he was born in Bellac. The author's birthplace is now home to an exhibition of letters, photographs, set models and posters for his plays. In his room, the library includes a priceless collection of his books and manuscripts. In 1951, a **monument** commemorating the author, by the sculptor Chauvenet, was erected beneath the magnificent trees of the town hall garden.

▶ **Population:** 4 317.
⚕ **Michelin Map:** 325: D-4.
🛈 **Info:** R. des Doctrinaires. ℘05 55 68 12 79.
◐ **Location:** 45km/28mi NW of Limoges via N 147. For a good view of the village head for the terrace 100m up r. Lafayette.
🅿 **Parking:** Park on pl. de la République near the 16C town hall.
◐ **Timing:** Allow half a day to visit the sights and villages of the Basse-Marche area.

Author of five novels, numerous short stories and influential political and literary essays, Giraudoux is best-known for his 15 plays. He created a new type of drama for the theatre, combining irony, poetry and magic. His style is sparkling, full of twists and innovations.

The Bellac he knew as a child is depicted in an early work of poetic fiction, *Suzanne et le Pacifique*: "a countryside of streams and hills, a patchwork of fields and chestnut woods; for it was a land with a long history, it was the region of Limousin".

Every year in July, a festival (*theatre, music, dance*) commemorates this talented native son.

🚗 DRIVING TOURS

4️⃣ THE BASSE-MARCHE★

55km/34mi. Allow 2hr 30min. See route 4 on region map pp278–279.

◐ Drive E out of Bellac along the D 1 towards Châteauponsac.

Rancon

The 12C lantern of the dead is surmounted by a cross with five foils (cusps).

The 13C **church**, built in the transitional Romanesque-Gothic style and fortified in the 14C, was formerly part of the town's defensive perimeter. Note the machicolations on the chevet and the openings for the archers; the 16C belfry, a square tower, ends in an onion-shaped dome covered with shingles. In the chancel is a fine 13C wooden Christ.

Châteauponsac

The oldest part of this small town is huddled around the **church**, dating largely from the 12C, though the pointed vaulting was added in the narrow nave and aisles in the 15C. The tall transept is crowned with a dome on pendentives. The chancel has fine round columns with carved capitals. Also of interest are the stone pulpit dating from 1642, a great 18C lectern and 16C–17C painted wooded statues.

Go around the church and walk to the promontory for a **view of the Gartempe**. From there the valley can be seen sloping steeply on the left bank. The Sous-le-Moutier quarter is in the foreground, with its busy pattern of old houses and terrace gardens.

Musée René-Baubérot

○*Open daily Jun–Sept and school hols, 2–6pm; rest of year Wed, Sat, Sun and public hols, 2–6pm.* ○*Closed 25 Dec –1 Jan.* ☞*€6 (children €2.50).* ☎*05 87 59 51 18. www.museechateauponsac.fr.*
Housed in a former Benedictine priory (*1318*), this museum recreates a dozen scenes of daily life, including a Limousin home, a young girls' bedroom, various workshops and a forge.
The impressive archaeological collections (*prehistory, Gallo-Roman and medieval periods*) include a quartz **polishing tool** used in the making of flint axes, Gallo-Roman chests, funerary urns, pottery and other items, most of which have been discovered in the local area. The Maison du Terroir organises a number of annual exhibitions.

▷ Follow D 45, which wends its way through pleasant farmland.

Magnac-Laval

This town is famous for a procession to St Maximus which travels more than 50km/32mi on Whit Monday (Pentecost). The pilgrims, wearing garlands of flowers around their necks, leave after midnight mass and return the following day after sunset.
The 12C **church** has a flat east end and a hexagonal belfry. It contains the relics of St Maximus.

Collégiale St-Pierre du Dorat★★

⚹*See COLLÉGIALE ST-PIERRE DU DORAT.*

5 LES MONTS DE BLOND

60km/37.2mi. Allow 2hr 30min.
See route 5 on region map pp278–279.

▷ Drive S out of Bellac along the D 3.

The Blond Mountains are the first summits that you would see if you were to approach from the Atlantic. They appear as a series of hills that culminate at Rochers de Puychaud (*515m*).
This mysterious land steeped in legends offers megaliths, stone crosses and isolated chapels in a verdant countryside sprinkled with lakes.

Blond

The late 12C **fortified church** appears massive from the outside. Its vast nave features six lateral chapels adorned with wooden statues. Above the portal framed by large buttresses and crowned with a bell, you'll see the remains of machicolations.

▷ From place de l'Église, follow the signposts marked "Rochers de Puychaud". The road goes into the heart of the Blond Mountains.

Rochers de Puychaud

To the left of the road, you'll see curious piles of granite, where some believe there are sacrificial stones. The plaque commemorating the Occitan poet Frédéric Mistral is a reminder that this is the edge of Occitan country.

▷ Just after Boscartus, take the signposted road left.

Pierre Branlante

This unstable disarray of stones is lost in the woods.

▶ Come back to D 204.

Peyrelade

At the entrance to the hamlet, a road to the left leads to a rocky platform with a good **view** over the mounts of the Limousin as well as the Nontron area.

👥 Montrol-Sénard★

🗣 *Guided tour available by prior arrangement.* 📞*05 55 68 12 79.*

The inhabitants of Montrol-Sénard open certain buildings to the public that perfectly illustrate turn-of-the-century life through everyday objects.

With the theme map "Nostalgie rurale", begin your tour at the charming school (*across from the church*) which functioned from 1877 to 1952. You'll then come to the **Chabatz d'Entrar** house, a one-room farm labourer's residence. Next to this is the stable-cellar and, above, the attic where you'll discover old-fashioned occupations such as hemp and linen work, weaving and sewing, as well as village traditions.

At the baking room and bread oven, illustrated panels explain bread making. The visit also includes an old-fashioned butcher's, pigsty, chicken coop, drinking trough, farrier's shop and boot repair shop. Pass through the Café d'Angèle before going to the barn-stable.

On your way back, you'll see the washhouse where women caught up on the latest news. The little 12C–13C Romanesque church features an interesting granite cross. Don't forget to have a look at the blacksmith's before going to the cemetery to see the lantern of the dead and the hosanna cross, a feature of western France's mortuary traditions. Crafts and regional products are on sale in the village during the summer.

▶ Follow D 5 A towards Bellac.

Mortemart★

🏛*Château des Ducs , Mortemart. Call for hours.* 📞*05 55 68 98 98.*

This charming village is the hometown of the Mortemart family, including the Marquise de Montespan, who was Louis XIV's mistress. A private Augustinian convent stands next to the church. On the other side of the road, the imposing Carmes convent has been converted into a bed and breakfast. As you stroll through the village, you'll see the remains of the castle that has been largely remodelled, lovely stone houses and the wooden *halle*.

The church, like the Augustinian convent, dates from the 14C and was built by Cardinal Gauvain. It is crowned with an unusual bulbous belltower with a slate roof. Its choir is separated from the nave by a wooden barrier. The 15C choir stalls are particularly beautiful: various occupations are sculpted into the backrests and armrests, while animals and demons decorate the reverse side of the seats, called *miséricordes*. The monumental altar is made up of a Baroque altarpiece in 17C gilded wood featuring a depiction of the Virgin Mary's Assumption (*1651*). Two reliquary busts of a duke and duchess, a Pietà and two paintings complete the scene. In the choir, you'll also see a 17C gilded wooden lectern, a 14C multi-coloured stone statue of Mary and coats of arms along the floor.

▶ Leave Mortemart NW on D 4.

Château du Fraisse

🕐*Open May–Sept 2–6pm.* ✎€8 (*children, 8–18, €5*). 📞 *05 55 68 32 68. www.chateau-du-fraisse.com.*

This 13C building was entirely rebuilt in the 15C and 16C to the plans of an Italian architect. You can visit this elegant Rennaisance castle and its lovely commons as well as its large park by prior arrangement. You can also stay in the charming bed and breakfast.

▶ Continue along D 4 until you reach Mézières-sur-Issoire and come back to Bellac on D 951.

Collégiale St-Pierre du Dorat★★

Every seven years the Le Dorat ostensions give rise to unique ceremonies involving sappers and drummers in the uniforms of the First Empire (1804–14).

COLLEGIATE CHURCH

A collegiate church is a church other than a cathedral that has a chapter of canons, or a church under the pastorate of more than one minister.

Construction of this impressively massive church (*77m long, 39m wide at the transept*) began in about 1100 on the site of a 10C monastery. After 50 years of work, it became as we see it today.

Exterior

The building, which is built in fine grey granite, is striking in size and proportion. The west front opens with a wide, **multi-foil doorway** showing a Mozarabic influence which might have been inspired by the pilgrims who had journeyed to Santiago de Compostela. An elegant **octagonal belfry** on three tiers of unequal height surmounted by a soaring spire topped with a 13C copper-gilt angel, rises above the transept.

Collégiale
St-Pierre
du Dorat

© Paul M R Maeyaert / agefotostock

- **Michelin Map:** 325: D-3.
- **Location:** 56km/35mi NW of Limoges via N 147 and D 675 from Bellac.
- **Info:** 17 pl. de la Collégiale, 87210 Le Dorat. ℘05 55 60 76 81. http://ot-ledorat. boonzai.com.

From below place de l'Église, there is a good overall view of the **chevet**, apse, apsidal chapels and stone belfries. The central apsidal chapel supports a semicircular tower which formed part of the 15C town's defence system. Two rectangular abutments shore up each apsidiole; each of the bays has a single Limousin-style arch. At the entrance there is a pre-Romanesque granite baptismal font.

Interior

From the first domed bay, which is 12 steps above the level of the rest of the nave, the majesty of the building is striking. The four following bays are broken barrel vaults on joists. Narrow aisles provide support for the central arching.

Crypt

🕐 *Guided tours Jun–Sept daily except Sun 10am–noon.* €1. ℘05 55 60 76 81.
This 11C crypt is reached from the south transept. It extends the length of the chancel and resembles it in plan and proportion.

Sacristy

This small religious museum exhibits a multi-coloured statue of St Anne, a Pietà dating from the 15C and a 13C reliquary cross with two cross-pieces which belonged to the treasure of the collegiate church.

Oradour-sur-Glane★★

Ruined, fire-scarred walls and a cemetery stand in memory of the 642 victims of a brutal attack by a detachment of SS troops, one of the cruellest events of WW2. An oddly peaceful impression seizes the visitor to this commemorative site, despite the fact that part of the horror of the massacre was that Oradour had been chosen for its very innocence and insignificance, the better to terrorise the French. The atrocity took place just four days after the announcement of the Allied landings in Normandy.

A BIT OF HISTORY

10 June 1944 – The people of Oradour, a large Limousin village, were going about their daily affairs on a busy Saturday morning. There were visitors from the city out for a day in the country, and visitors from the outlying farms had come to town for the day; a party of teenage cyclists was passing through. At 2pm, as a cordon of German soldiers closed all the exits, a column of lorries and armoured cars entered the village. Curiosity soon gave way to fear. On Nazi orders everyone gathered on the fairground: men, women and 247 schoolchildren brought there by their teachers. The women and children were locked in the church, the men in the barns and garages. Grenade explosions and machine-gun bursts killed a great many; fire and dynamite completed the massacre. One woman managed to get out of the burning church through a window in the east end; a young boy and a few men were the only others to escape death.

VISIT
Centre de la Mémoire★
Access to the ruins of the martyred village. ⏱*Open daily: Feb and Nov–mid-Dec 9am–5pm; Mar–mid-May and mid-Sept–Oct 9am–6pm; mid-May–mid-Sept 9am–7pm.* ⊕€8. ✆05 55 43 04 30. www.oradour.org.

▸ **Population:** 2 246.
⚗ **Michelin Map:** 325: D-5.
▮ **Info:** Pl. du Champ-de-Foire. ✆05 55 03 13 73. www.oradour-sur-glane.fr.
▸ **Location:** 24km/15mi NW of Limoges.

Ruins stand to commemorate WW2 victims

© Clément Philippe / agefotostock

This centre, located at the entrance to the ruins, houses a permanent exhibition about the rise of Nazism and 10 June 1944.

The ruins
Entrance via the Centre de la Mémoire.
Go through the outer walls and along the streets of the ruined village. For a guide, refer to the old church, where 500 women and children died. The Maison du Souvenir (*with objects that survived the flames*), and to the cemetery (*resting place of the victims*), are touching.

The new Oradour
Nearby, a new Oradour has been built. The modern church with its luminous stained-glass windows and square belfry may surprise at first, but it has been designed to blend harmoniously with the surroundings.

Saint-Junien

Saint-Junien is a busy town
known for its paper mills, taweries
(leather dressing works) and glove
factories. The collegiate church is
Romanesque-Limousin in style.

A BIT OF HISTORY

St Junien, the miracle worker – For
some 40 years in the 6C, a hermit named
Junien lived in this place, using waters
from a sacred spring to cure those who
came, often from afar, to see him. His
reputation was so great that when he
died in 540, the bishop of Limoges
personally presided over his funeral
ceremonies and ordered the construction of a sanctuary above his tomb. A
monastery grew up and soon a settlement formed around it.

The development of glove-making –
St-Junien lies in the centre of a livestock
rearing region where kid and lambskin
abound. In addition, the waters of the
Vienne possess exceptional properties
for tanning.

Glove-making began here in the Middle
Ages and by the 15C had made the town
famous. It is even said that Louis XI was
received in great style at St-Junien and
accepted pairs of gloves from the master
glove makers.

Today, 300 workers in seven workshops
produce over 480 000 pairs of gloves
each year, representing 45% of all French
production.

Collégiale St-Junien★

The nave and transept of this remarkable
Romanesque-Limousin building are late
11C. The main part of the building was
completed when the façade was added
at the end of the 12C. The plain, square
chevet is 13C. The central belltower was
rebuilt after crumbling in 1922.

Inside, the **nave** and the **chancel** are of
equal length. The transept is punctuated
by bays, one of which is quite narrow and
extends into the side aisle. The chapels
have primitive pointed arches. The
crossing is surmounted by an octagonal cupola with flat pendants, pierced by
four Limousin-style bays and a multi-foil

> ▶ **Population:** 11 455.
> ⚲ **Michelin Map:** 325: C-5.
> 🚩 **Info:** Place du Champ de
> Foire. ✆ 05 55 02 17 93.
> www.saint-junien-
> tourisme.fr.
> ◗ **Location:** 12km/8mi
> NE of Rochechouart and
> 27km/17mi W of Limoges.

occulus. There are traces of 12C and 13C
frescoes in several places, in particular
on the vaulting of the second bay of the
nave. The third bay on the north side
houses an enamelled 13C reliquary.

Behind the main altar is **St Junien's
tomb★**, a masterpiece of 12C Limousin sculpture. Two-thirds of the tomb
is made of sculpted limestone; the
remainder is just a plaster covering
added in the 20C when the high altar
was moved. On the east side, Christ
is shown in glory surrounded by the
symbols of the Evangelists; medallions
depict the theological and moral virtues.
On the north face the Virgin, within a
glory, holds the infant Jesus; seated on
one side are the figures of the twelve Old
Men of the Apocalypse. On the opposite side the other twelve Old Men are
portrayed together with a medallion of
the Holy Lamb.

In the second bay on the northern side of
the chancel is the **Chapelle St-Martial**.
Of Gothic design, it once harboured the
relics of the saint, whose life is depicted
in the partly-visible 13C frescoes.

Chapelle Notre-Dame du Pont

Quai des Mégisseries. ◷*Open Jul–Aug,
2–6pm.* ✆*05 55 43 06 90.*

Standing on the right bank of the River
Vienne beside a 13C bridge equipped
with cutwaters is the elegant Chapel of
Our Lady of the Bridge.

There is a legend that the statue of the
Virgin which now stands in the apse was
originally found alongside the bridge on
the river bank; the statue was immediately taken in solemn procession to the
collegiate church, but the next day was
found, once more, on the river bank. The

people of St-Junien erected a chapel to the Virgin on the spot where the statue was found. The present church was built in the 15C on the site of the earlier sanctuary.

EXCURSIONS
Site Corot
2km/1.2mi NW along N 141. 15min round-trip on foot. As you leave town, take a sharp right turn at the bend in the road, then turn left immediately on a small road. Follow this road as far as the porcelain factory and park at the entrance of the lane.

Walk for a few minutes beside the river to reach the setting of the stream, flowing past rocks and trees, which inspired Corot and many other painters.

👤👶 Féeriland
17km/10.4mi E on N 141. Exit at Barre, then take D 28 and follow the signposts. L'Ebourliat, Veyrac. ♿🕐*Jul–Aug*

10.30am–7pm; Apr–Jun 2–6pm; other periods call for hours. 🎟€8 *(children under 12,* €5.50*).* ✆*05 55 03 16 71. www.feeriland.com.*

This unusual mix of dioramas and **automated replicas** transports you to a Gallic village, a Feudal motte, a superb fortress, the castle of Azay-le-Rideau, a Far West village, a Carnival scene, and "Fourmiville", where giant ants prevail. A small exhibition of Asian insects and serpents completes the fantastic voyage.

Église de St-Victurnien
9km/5.5mi E on D 32.

The church houses an altarpiece decorated with 14C paintings of the Passion and the Ressurection, a 13C *champlevé* enamel shrine and a Virgin with Child in 14C multi-coloured stone. In the cemetery (*towards Oradour-sur-Glane*), you'll see a lantern of the dead with openings allowing the insertion of one's head to ask the saint for healing.

Rochechouart

On the last day of the ostensions (⚓*see Introduction*), held once every seven years, a unique procession takes place in Rochechouart, with participants wearing special costumes and carrying precious shrines.

A BIT OF HISTORY
A distinguished family tree – The Rochechouart family can be traced back beyond the year 1000: their first castle rose up near the monastic settlement governed by the Charroux abbey. One of the sons of the viscount of Limoges became the lord upon his marriage to Ève d'Angoulême, whose dowry was the Rochechouart title and property. Around 1205, Viscount Aymeric de Rochechouart married the beautiful Alix de Mortemart. When the lovestruck castle steward failed to seduce her, he took revenge by telling his master that the viscountess had solicited him. The jeal-

> ▶ **Population:** 3 796.
> 🎣 **Michelin Map:** 325: B-6.
> 🏢 **Info:** 6 r. Victor Hugo. ✆05 55 03 72 73. www.tourisme-meteorite.com.
> ◖ **Location:** 42km/26.25mi W of Limoges via N i41/D 941.
> 😎 **Don't Miss:** The frescoes in the castle.

ous and impulsive Aymeric had his wife thrown to a lion in the east tower. Two days later, he found the lion crouched docilely at his wife's feet. The guiltless woman was returned to favour, and the steward was thrown to the lion, whose appetite had returned.

In the struggle facing off Capetians and Plantagenets, the Rochechouart family sided with the king. One family member died at the Battle of Poitiers protecting the king.

Château, Rochechouart

The Mortemart line (☝see *Château de MEILLANT*) is also replete with historical figures. The château was buffeted by wars and often threatened with ruin, but always saved, often with the help of Rochechouart wives who brought hefty dowries into their alliances. In 1836, the State acquired the buildings.

TOWN
Church
This is the former priory-church, consecrated in 1067; only the western doorway, the northern wall and part of the transept and chancel have survived.

Rue Jean-Parvy
Note the 15C **Maison des Consuls**, and, farther on, a corner tower which stood within the medieval city wall.

Château★
The castle stands in a remarkable **setting★** above the confluence of the Graine and the Vayres and is mostly late 15C. The 12C keep which flanks the entrance fort was razed level with the rooftops in the 16C.
The second tower on the left end of the façade bears a lion carved in granite, perhaps in homage to the beautiful Alix, or more likely the crusading viscounts of Limoges. A drawbridge leads to the fort's entrance.

Cour d'Honneur
The buildings lining the court on three sides were restored in the 18C and now house a museum.

Promenade des Allées
Leaving the château, a promenade on the left features a shady terrace fragrant with age-old lime trees. From the site of the cross standing at the end of the walk, there is a good **view★** of the Graine and Vayres valleys and of the castle.

SIGHTS
Musée Départemental d'Art Contemporain★
Pl. du Château. ◷*Open Mar–Sept 10am–12.30pm, 1.30–6pm; Oct–mid-Dec 10am–12.30pm, 2–5pm.* ◷*Closed Tue and mid-Dec–Mar.* ◷€5. ℘05 55 03 77 77. www.musee-rochechouart.com.
The Haute-Vienne General Council began building up this collection in 1985; it has become a significant centre for contemporary art. Raoul Hausmann, a major exponent of Dadaism, is particularly well represented.
Frescoes★ – Besides the main focus on contemporary art, the museum has reserved two rooms to a remarkable group of 16C frescoes. The **salle d'Hercule** is decorated with rare murals painted in *grisaille*. Nearby, the **salle des chasses** has older frescoes, depicting scenes of a royal hunt.

👤👤 Espace Météorite

16 r. Jean Parvy. ♿ ⏰*Open Jul–Aug 10am–noon, 1.30–6pm (weekends and public holidays 2–6pm); Apr–Jun and Sept daily except Sat 10am–noon, 2–6pm (Sun and public holidays 2–6pm); rest of year Mon–Fri 10am–noon, 2–5pm.* ⏰*Closed mid-Dec–mid-Jan.* ◉€4. 📞05 55 03 02 70. www.espacemeteorite.com.*

Rochechouart was built over a 20km/ 12mi-wide crater caused by a large meteorite that crashed in the area some 200 million years ago.

EXCURSIONS
Église des Salles-Lavauguyon

16km/9.9mi SW on D 10 then D 34. ⏰*Jul–Aug 2.30–6.30pm; May–Jun and Sept 2.30–5pm.* 👥*Guided tours available (45min) by appointment.* ◉€2.50. 📞05 55 00 30 68.

Largely built in the 11C and 12C, the Église St-Eutrope, named for its Eastern orientation, features a nave that rises in stages towards the choir. The latter dates from the 13C with its flat chevet.

Restoration work has uncovered beautiful 12C **frescoes★** that had been hidden under a thick layer of mould. Their vivid colours, especially the blues and greens, are astonishing. From top to bottom, you'll recognise the Annunciation to the Virgin Mary, the Creation of Adam and Eve, the Vices and the lives of various saints, as well as a series of other characters.

Dolmen de la Pierre Levée

12.5km/7.7mi E. Take D 10 towards Aixe-s-Vienne. Just before the intersection with D 21, you'll pass Chez-Moutaud. The site is located 500m after this village along a small road on the left.

👥This peaceful raised monolith is located in a clearing.

Cognac-la-Forêt

17km/10.5mi E on D 10.

To the west of the village (*200m on D 209*), the cemetery features a 12C **lantern of the dead**. Notice the epitaphs etched on porcelain plaques.

Châlus★

The old city of Châlus, overlooked by its keep, recalls the memory of **Richard the Lionheart's** tragic death. On every side are the densely wooded, solid granite masses of the Châlus hills, the last buttresses of the Massif Central.

CHÂTEAU DU HAUT-CHÂLUS★★

The remains, known as Châlus-Chabrol, are privately owned and stand on rising ground in the upper part of the village.

Donjon – This cylindrical keep (*25m high and 10m in diameter*), an excellent illustration of feudal military architecture, dates from the 11C. Originally, it had four levels, but the highest one, crowned by machicolations, fell in 1870. The keep's thick, smooth gneiss walls were a good protection against attack by battering ram, axe and fire.

▶ **Population:** 1 628.
🖎 **Michelin Map:** 325: C-7.
🛈 **Info:** 28 av. François Mitterand. 📞09 60 07 30 07. www.tourismemonts dechalus.fr.
▶ **Location:** 35km/21.9mi SW of Limoges via N 21.
◉ **Don't Miss:** Castles in the land of Richard the Lionheart.

A short distance from the keep are remains of the **chapel** where King Richard's remains were brought. At the time, the chapel was Romanesque; in the 15C a side chapel was added. One arch of it still stands.

Main building – Perhaps the most spectacular part of the tour is the exhibit on the discovery of 11C and 13C architectural remains. The main building opens onto a 13C room which contains

A Fatal Siege

Legend has it that in 1199 a serf belonging to Adhemar V, viscount of Limoges, discovered a treasure trove of "ninepins and large balls, all in solid gold" (these items now figure in the arms of Châlus along with a longbow). The viscount of Limoges hid the treasure in his castle at Châlus. The news reached Richard the Lionheart, king of England and lord of Western France. He demanded his share of the booty as overlord, but his vassal refused to give it up. This provided Richard with a pretext for punishing his vassal, who had once sided with the king of France. But while laying siege to Châlus, Richard was struck on the shoulder by an arrow from a prototype of a new crossbow. He refused to dress the wound, which turned black; the poison went to his heart and so he died, at age 42. All the castle defenders were hanged except the sharp-eyed archer; he was flayed alive in spite of the fact that he was pardoned by the king on his death bed.

a Romanesque column squeezed into a wall erected at a later date. In the next room, you can see the other side of it, as well as two Romanesque windows. The walls are hung with the coats of arms of the castle's different owners. A little corridor leads to the oldest section, dating from the 11C. Beyond an escape shaft tucked into a nook in the fortifications, a six-sided room forms the base of a corner tower; note the vaulted ceiling and loopholes. Beside this tower room, a smaller room dissimulates another shaft, 16m high, and the walled-off entrance to the watch-path. The lower level, once open to the air, was the ground floor.

The 17C wing features two drawing rooms furnished in 17C–18C style and an 18C oak staircase leading to a large exhibition hall where a collection of fancy dress for the Venice Carnival is displayed. The barn houses a small museum devoted to regional crafts.

Gardens – A medieval herb garden surrounding a central closed fountain has been laid out on the esplanade, in front of the castle, whereas the French-style garden with its rosemary maize, rose trees and hornbeams, is laid out at the foot of the 17C building.

Boutique des Monts de Châlus

Along the N 21, next to the Tourist Office. ♿🕐*Open mid-Jun to mid-Sept, 10am–12 pm and 2–6.30pm (except Mon mid-Jun–mid-July and mid-Aug–mid-Sept); rest of the year, daily except*

Sat–Sun, 10am–noon and 2–5pm. ∞€4. ☎05 55 78 51 13.

This exhibition centre, devoted to chestnut trees and their various uses, offers visitors interactive terminals and video presentations as well as a reconstructed hoop-wood maker's hut.

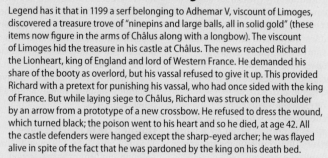

🚗DRIVING TOURS

⑥ SUR LA ROUTE RICHARD CŒUR DE LION

45km/27.9mi. Allow 2hr. See route 6 on region map pp278–279.

▶ Leave Châlus NE on D 15.

Château des Cars

🎧*Guided tours possible by arrangement (1hr).* ∞€3 (children under 12, no charge). ☎09 60 07 30 07. www.lescars87.com.

This 13C fortress, a former dwelling of the Limousin governors, was retouched in the 15C and 16C. It was occupied by the English during the Hundred Years War and taken back by **Bertrand Du Guesclin**. Its 13C tower and two large 15C towers subsist.

A lapidary room shows the artefacts (*engraved stones, coins, pottery and more*) found on site, while the permanent exhibition "Autour du Château des Cars" recounts the history of the place and its occupants.

Across from the castle, the magnificent mansard **stables** were built by one of the lords of Cars before the Revolution.

🚗 Leave Cars SE on D 214. The road separates the forest of Cars (to the right) from that of Lastours (to the left). Turn left on D 59 A when you come out of the woods.

Château de Lastours
Ruins of a 12C keep and restored 13C–16C buildings (*private property*).

🚗 Continue along D 59 A.

Église de St-Hilaire
This little 12C Romanesque church has a pretty octagonal belfry with rounded arch windows.

🚗 Take D 15 A towards St-Hilaire-les-Places. Continue on D 15A towards Ladignac-le-Long for 4.5km/2.7mi.

🚶🚶 Tuilerie de Puycheny – Atelier-musée de la Terre★
♿🕐Guided tour (2hr). Jul–Aug Mon and Wed 2–6pm; May–Jun Wed 2–6pm. ◉€4. ☎05 55 58 35 19.
Discover the manufacturing process of tiles in detail in this living workshop-museum, located in buildings where tiles were made up until 1955. There were no less than 120 such manufacturers in the *département* at the turn of the century. Clay modelling workshops are available all year round.

🚗 Come back to St-Hilaire-les-Places, then take D 11 towards Nexon.

Nexon
This peaceful village is one of the birthplaces of the famous Anglo-Arabian horse breed and is today resolutely oriented towards the circus.
Jardin des Sens – *Near the post office and La Résidence du Parc.* 🕐*Guided tour available by arrangement (1hr 30min).* ◉€2.50 (under 12, no charge). ☎05 55 58 28 44. www.tourisme-pays-de-nexon.com. 🚶🚶Nexon's **Parc du Château** is home to a "Citizen's garden" created by volunteers and schoolchildren. Located near a nursing home, the garden is a colourful bridge between generations. Themes include a bamboo labyrinth, ephemeral landscape, orchard, vineyard, medicinal garden, wash-house, scented bridge, bird feeder garden and flower cutting garden.

🚶 The nearby forest is part of the castle grounds. You can access it from the garden along a pleasant wooded path.
Château – *The castle only opens for European Heritage Days.* Built in the 15C and 17C, then damaged during the Revolution, this castle was entirely restored last century and houses the town hall. The tourist office is located in the former stables. The grounds are open to the public. You can see the rehearsals of the **École du Cirque Fratellini** in the circus tent permanently set up in the park.
Église St-Jean-Baptiste – This composite building includes a Romanesque sanctuary, transept and belfry, as well as a 15C nave with a ribbed vault. There are interesting pieces inside: a 13C enamelled copper shrine, the 14C main **shrine** of St Ferréol crafted by the Limousin native goldsmith Aymeric Chrétien, and wooden statues of St Catherine (*15C*) and St Roch (*16C*).

🚗 Come back to Châlus along D 15.

7 MONTS DE CHÂLUS
20km/12.4mi. Allow 2hr. See route 7 on region map pp278–279.

🚗 Leave Châlus SW on D 6 bis towards Nontron.

Dournazac
The 12C **Église St-Sulpice**, reworked in the 14C, has retained its apsidal chapels and interesting sculpted capitals under the cupola of the transept crossing.

🚶🚶 Châtaigneraie Conservatoire
🕐Apr–Oct. Call for tour information. ☎05 55 78 43 08.
This chestnut discovery circuit is accessible to all ages (*45min, wear comfortable shoes*). Eight well-illustrated panels explain the history of "bread trees", as they were called; as well as their varieties, cultivation and use in French cookery.

▶ Leave Dournazac NW on D 64.

Château de Montbrun★

🕙 *Guided tour (2hr) Jun–Aug 2–6pm.* 👓 *€10 (children under 12, €5).* 📞 *05 55 05 01 44.*

This imposing castle stands deep in a valley, where it reflects in the waters of a pond surrounded by lawns and trees. Constructed in the late 12C, it once defended the borders of the ducal realm of Aquitaine, and still boasts a moat, high walls and an impregnable square keep surmounted by machicolations.

▶ Continue along D 213. The road passes by Puyconnieux (alt. 496m). Just afterwards, turn right on D 100.

Château de Brie★

🕙 *Guided tour (40min) Apr–Sept Sat–Sun and public holidays 2–7pm.* 👓 *€6 (children under 12, €4) for combined ticket with Le Petit Monde des Automates.* 📞 *05 55 78 17 52. www.chateaudebrie.fr.*

Château de Montbrun

© J.-C.&D. Pratt / Photononstop

This fortified house was built around 1500. It boasts 16C–18C furnishings and a Gothic granite stairway.

👥 In the commons, 70 automated characters of **Le Petit Monde des Automates** take you on a journey through Turkey, Africa, London and Paris.

▶ At the intersection, take D 42 towards Châlus.

St-Yrieix-la-Perche

Bordering the Périgord Vert region, St-Yrieix (pronounced St-Irieh) stands at the centre of a rich stock rearing region and has a thriving cattle market. Nearby kaolin deposits are the origin of Limoges porcelain.

▶ **Population:** 6 910.
🚲 **Michelin Map:** 325: E-7.
ℹ **Location:** 58 blvd Hôtel de Ville. 📞 05 55 08 20 72. www.tourisme-saint-yrieix.com.
👁 **Don't Miss:** Collégiale du Moustier; Musée de la Porcelaine.
🕐 **Timing:** Allow a full day.

A BIT OF HISTORY

The origins – A Gallo-Roman settlement called Attanum was probably the first on the site. Around 530, Aredius founded a monastery there. A hamlet grew up next to it and took the name St-Yrieix, a transformation of Aredius, to which La Perche was added in the 15C.

Darnet and kaolin – Limoges owes its porcelain to St-Yrieix. Searches for kaolin were being made all over south-west France in the 18C, when, quite by chance, a local surgeon by the name of Darnet met a chemist and showed him his wife's mixture for making her laundry snow-white. Analysis revealed the pure kaolin content. In 1771 Darnet was charged by the king to supervise kaolin mining. Since 1774, a porcelain factory has been operating in Seynie, 1km/0.5mi from St-Yrieix.

The last gold mine – Gold mining in France and in particular in the St-Yrieix area goes back to Roman times. However, it was only rediscovered in 1866 when an engineer revealed that ancient fortifications were in fact disused Gallo-Roman gold mines.

Le Bourneix near St-Yrieix-la-Perche was the last working gold mine in the European Union. The mine yielded around 2t of gold every year until it closed down in 2001.

TOWN
Collégiale du Moustier★

Pl. Attane. The church stands on the site of the abbey founded by Aredius. It is a curious mix of Romanesque and Gothic styles. All that remains of the Romanesque church is the belfry-porch with its two narrow aisles. The nave has ogive vaulting and is very wide but the length is limited to two bays.

Treasury – In a niche in the chancel rests the 15C reliquary head of St-Yrieix, made of wood plated with chased silver; the facial hair is picked out in gold. A niche in the nave contains a small ornate 13C reliquary of enamelled gilt copper.

Tour du Plô – Near the collegiate church stands this 13C keep with twin windows; it once formed part of the monastery's fortified precincts.

EXCURSIONS
Le Chalard★

8km/4.9mi NW on D 901.
This village and priory were founded by St Geoffroi (*c. 1060–1125*). Upstream, the **gorges de l'Isle** conceal rocks and rapids.

Church – Fortified by the English during the Hundred Years War, this Romanesque church has a massive square belfry. In the polygonal choir are lovely Limousin arcatures and granite capitals sculpted with grimacing faces. In the right side of the transept, a large 15C **bahut** is sculpted with flamboyant patterns. In the nearby wall, a recess contains the 13C enamelled shrine containing the skull of St Geoffroi.

Cimetière des Moines – The monk's cemetery includes a unique gathering of some 40 12C tombs, of which most are shaped like ornate little churches.

Musée de la Porcelaine

Head towards Limoges. After 2km/1mi, turn left towards the lake.
🕐*Open daily Jul–Aug 10am–noon, 2–6pm; Sept–Jun, daily except Sat–Sun and public hols 9am–noon, 2–6pm.*
👓€2.50. ℘05 55 75 10 38.
This rich collection dates from the 18C to the present day. Next to the soft-paste porcelain from Vincennes, Arras and Strasbourg are fine specimens in soft and hard paste from the count of Artois' factory. Germany and England are represented, as are 19C French works, essentially from Limoges.

🚗DRIVING TOUR

8️⃣ FORESTS AND LAKES
45km/27.9mi. Allow 2hr. See route 8 on region map pp278–279.

▶ Leave St-Yrieix E on D 901.

Coussac-Bonneval★
🚩 *11 pl. aux Foires, Coussac-Bonneval.*
℘*05 55 75 28 46.*

Château de Bonneval
🕐🚶 *Guided tour (45min) Jul–Aug 2.30–7pm; May and weekends of Apr and mid-end Jun and mid-end Sept 2.30–6pm. Call for other periods.*
👓*€10 (children under 12, €5).*
℘*05 55 75 29 09 or 05 55 08 45 81.*
www.chateaudebonneval.fr.
This square castle with an interior courtyard, which belonged to **Claude Alexandre de Bonneval**, stands on a hill overlooking the village of Coussac. The outer galleries feature stained-glass windows. The corner towers are crowned with machicolations and pepperpot roofs; the dungeon and Tour du Diable are joined to a tower. The interior of the 14C **château** was reworked in the 18C and 19C.

It contains a collection of period furniture from the Renaissance to the Directoire period (*at the end of the Revolution*).

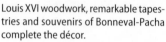

Louis XVI woodwork, remarkable tapestries and souvenirs of Bonneval-Pacha complete the décor.

The small 12C **church** retains some traces of its frescoes, a 16C low-relief in multi-coloured wood, a Pièta and a 17C Lebrun painting, *Dieu le Père*.

A large 12C lantern of the dead, which was restored in the 14C, used to stand at the entrance to the cemetery.

▷ Leaving Coussac, take a left on D 70.

The road runs along **Étang de la Marche** (*picnic area*), a water reservoir created for fishing.

▷ 2km/1.2mi after Gabie-de-la-Poule, turn right (and follow the road to the left at the bifurcation). Just after Rouffardie, cross D 215 towards Meuzac. Leave Meuzac E on D 244.

Masseret

In the centre of this village stands a modern tower with a viewing table at its top (*104 steps*) offering a beautiful 360-degree **view★**: to the north you'll see the Ambazac hills; to the east the Millevaches plateau and the Monédières massif; and on a clear day the Auvergne mountains.

The Romanesque **church**, largely restored in the 16C, has a shrine dedicated to St Valérie dating from the 13C (*key available from the chemist's opposite the church*).

▷ Leave Masseret to the N. Follow D 20E8 and take D 216 at La Porcherie.

Église de St-Germain-les-Belles

This is a 14C fortified church. Inside, to the right of the chancel, a spiral staircase gives access to the lookout points high above the tall pointed vaulting as well as the watch-path (*guided tours, apply to the Tourist Office*).

Magnac-Bourg

The church in this village boasts beautiful late 15C **stained-glass windows**.

Sentier d'Interprétation – *In Magnac-Bourg, take D 215, then C 1 towards Condamines and Le Cluzeau and then follow the signposts for "Lande du Cluzeau et de La Flotte". The path begins at the former tile factory of Le Cluzeau. You can park there.* 🚶4km/2.5mi. This pleasant circuit, sprinkled with panels on the local fauna, flora and geology, allows you to discover 120ha/296 acres of **ophite heathland**. Amongst the lovely wild heather and fescue grass, you might see a Dartford warbler, a hen harrier, or any number of other species.

▷ Leave Magnac-Bourg SE on D 215 towards Chavagnac. After 3km/1.8mi, turn right towards Château-Chervix.

La Flotte

Here you are in the serpentine heathlands. Serpentine is a metamorphic stone of a dark green colour that is protected by special regulations.

🚶 Walk towards the Roches du Loup. You'll get a good view of the Monédières and Mount Gargan.

▷ Come back to the chapel at the exit to the village and turn right towards Fayat.

Forêt de Fayat★

🚶 This 700ha/1729-acre space is planted with hardwoods and resinous plants, and crisscrossed with a large number of blazed trails.

▷ At the end of the road, take a right.

Château-Chervix

Climb up to the village square. This 32m-high dungeon is the only remnant of the 12C castle.

▷ Leave Château-Chervix NW on D 31, then turn left on D 19 to come back to St-Yrieix-la-Perche.

The road offers lovely points of view of the **Puy de Barre** (*alt. 533m*).

Arnac-Pompadour★

These two villages in the Corrèze, just 2km/1.2mi apart, today form a single administrative area (*commune*). The château and title of Pompadour were given by King Louis XV to his favourite in 1745. In 1761, the king established a famous stud farm here which, in the 19C, saw the development of the Anglo-Arabian breed in France. A number of important horse races and other competitive events are held here regularly in summer.

▶ **Population:** 1 227.
⌚ **Michelin Map:** 329: J-3.
Info: 1 pl. de la Poste, 19230 Arnac-Pompadour. ℰ05 55 98 55 47. www.pompadour.net.
Don't Miss: National Stud Farm (Haras National) and Château de Pompadour.

CHÂTEAU

⌚ *Open 10am–noon, 2–6pm: Apr–Sept daily; rest of year daily except Sun–Mon.* ⊛€7. ℰ05 55 98 51 10. www.les3tours-pompadour.com.
This imposing 15C castle with its magnificent façade stands in a delightfully verdant setting. The château is home to the stud farm's administrative offices.

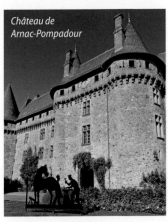

Château de Arnac-Pompadour

© Christian Guy / imagebr / age fotostock

HARAS NATIONAL (NATIONAL STUD FARM)

BP5 19230 Arnac-Pompadour.
⌚ *Guided tours (1h) Apr–Oct 10am–noon, 2–6pm.* ⊛€5. ℰ05 55 98 51 10. www.les3tours-pompadour.com.
The Puy-Marmont stallion farm, in a park opposite the château, is home to forty or so thoroughbreds, including pure-bred English, Arabian and Anglo-Arabian stal-

lions. A number of other horses (*draught horses from the French regions of the Ardennes, Brittany and Franche-Comté, Percherons etc*) are also stabled here.

🚗 DRIVING TOUR

9 UPPER AUVÉZÈRE VALLEY

35km/21.7mi. Allow 2hr. See route 9 on region map pp278–279.

▷ Leave Arnac-Pompadour on the D 126.

Église d'Arnac

This 12C church, with its severe appearance and imposing dimensions, is an unusual mix of the Romanesque and Gothic styles. The doorway, characteristic of the Limousin style, is decorated with capitals, medallions and pointed, hanging ornaments at the apexes of the vaults. Three statues are set into the façade above: from left to right, St Martial, the Virgin and St Pardoux, the two saints being patrons of the Limousin region. Inside the nave, the keystones bear the arms of Pompadour, and the transept has preserved its Romanesque appearance. Interesting historiated capitals adorn the columns in the nave, including scenes of the Annunciation and Daniel in the Lion's Den.

▷ Continue on D 126; left on D 127.

Ségur-le-Château★

This charming village is a maze of old houses crowning two steep hills. On top of one of these hills stand the ruins of a 12C–13C castle with its double curtain walls. It is possible that Ségur's origins go back as far as Gallo-Roman times; it certainly played an important role in the Middle Ages and under the Ancien Régime. Cradle of the first viscounts of Limoges, when feudalism was at its peak, this prosperous settlement was the birthplace, in 1470, of Jean d'Albret, first king of Navarre and grandfather of Jeanne d'Albret, the mother of Henri IV. However, Ségur's main claim to fame derives from the time (15C to mid-18C) when it served as the seat of the high court of appeal for hundreds of feudal jurisdictions in the Limousin and the Périgord. Ségur's charm lies in its beautiful residences built by the many court officials who lived here. These include the **Maison Febrer** (*15C*), with its Renaissance chimneys and turrets and **Maison Henri IV**, named in honour of the d'Albret family. Today the long robes and powdered wigs of magistrates are long gone, replaced by artists who depict the village's half-timbered houses embellished with turrets, crowned with characteristic pointed brown-tiled roofs, and fronted by Gothic doorways opening onto narrow, winding lanes.

▷ Head NE out of Ségur along D 149.

Lubersac

In the **Église St-Étienne** (*if the church is closed, contact the Tourist Office*) note the remarkable **historiated capitals★** decorating the chancel and the delicately carved capitals adorning the north and south apsidal chapels. The village also boasts a fine arcaded house with Renaissance windows known as the **Maison des Archiprêtres**.

▷ Leave Lubersac to the SE along D 148. In St-Pardoux-Corbier, take D 54E1 to Fargeas, and then D 148 to Troche.

Chartreuse de Glandier

For information, call ☏ 05 55 98 55 47.
A **Carthusian monastery** (*chartreuse*) was established in the heart of the Loire valley in the 13C. Destroyed during the Revolution, the order repurchased it in 1860 and rebuilt it over a period of 10 years. Nowadays the buildings serve as a medical centre, with an exhibition area devoted to its history, including a scale model of the site. One of the **monk's pavilions** has been reconstructed; its two floors show a workshop on the ground floor, with a bedroom and library on the floor above.

Jumenterie Nat. de la Rivière

♿*For information, call ☏ 05 55 98 55 47.*
Domaine de la Rivière, covering an area of 88ha/217 acres, was created in the 18C on the site of a ruined 15C castle, of which only the towers and a Gothic chapel remain. It became a national centre for breeding mares in the 19C. Today, some 40 mares are permanently based here. In the months of May and June, proud mothers can be seen gambolling in the fields with their colts. The riding centre also owns a dozen stallions.

▷ Take D 7E3, then D 7 to come back to Pompadour.

ADDRESSES

🛏 STAY

🛏 **Chambre d'hôte Ferme de la Petite Brunie** – *2km/1.2mi NE of Pompadour along the D 54E1 towards St-Pardoux-Corbier.* ☏*05 55 73 34 17. www.la-petite-brunie.com. 5 rooms.* 🍽. This bed and breakfast used to be the farm's pigsty! The bright, modern rooms overlook a secluded garden and meadows. The hearty breakfast includes cold meats, pastries and homemade jam. Dinner here is traditional family cooking.

🛏 **Chambres d'hôte à la Ferme du Domaine de la Roche** – *St-Julien-le-Vendomois. 7km/4.2mi NW of Arnac along the D 126.* ☏*05 55 98 72 87. 4 rooms, reservation required.* 🍽🍷. Enjoy the peacefulness of this charming farm in the heart of the countryside. The simple attic bedrooms are housed in a separate 18C building. Homemade and regional products, including foie gras, confit and jams are also on sale here.

Uzerche★★

Uzerche, a charming small Limousin town, stands on a promontory encircled by a bend in the River Vézère. On this picturesque site, a surprising number of buildings are crowned with bell-turrets, watchtowers and pepperpot roofs. It is said that "he who has a house in Uzerche has a castle in Limousin".

A BIT OF HISTORY

In 732, the Saracens, after being beaten at Poitiers, attacked Uzerche. The town was protected by solid walls with 18 fortified towers; it held out for seven years. Surrender seemed near until the besieged hit on a trick: they presented the emir with their last fatted calf and their last ration of corn.

Amazed at such abundance, the Saracens raised the siege. The Uzerche arms – two bulls – recall this trick. The old town was never taken by force during any of the many sieges of the Middle Ages. When Charles V authorised the town to add three gold lilies to its arms, he also gave it the appellation "Uzerche the Virgin", and its crest *non*

> ▶ **Population:** 3 126.
> **Michelin Map:** 329: K-3.
> **Info:** Pl. de la Libération, 19140. ✆ 05 55 73 15 71. www.pays-uzerche.fr.
> **Location:** 30km/18.5mi NW of Tulle and 38km/24mi N of Brive-la-Gaillarde.
> **Timing:** A full day for the Upper Vézère valley and the Gorges de la Vézère.
> **Don't Miss:** Eglise St-Pierre; the view of the town from the Ste-Eulalie district.

polluta (never sullied) confirms the glorious epithet.

UPPER TOWN WALK

▶ Leave from place Marie-Colein.

Rue Gaby-Furnestin

On the left, you will see the 16C timbered house in which Alexis Boyer, surgeon to Napoleon I, was born. In this street which extends onto rue Jean-Gentet, note a group of renovated old houses with fine carved doorways.

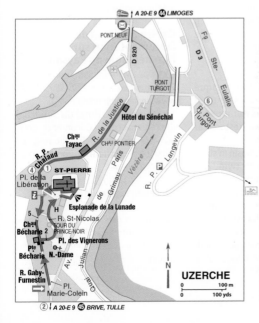

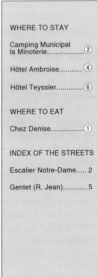

WHERE TO STAY

Camping Municipal la Minoterie.................②

Hôtel Ambroise...........④

Hôtel Teyssier.............⑥

WHERE TO EAT

Chez Denise................①

Porte Bécharie

This fortified gateway is the only one of the old city gates that is still intact. Adjoining the gateway is a building known as the Château Bécharie, which is flanked by a square tower and a pendant turret; in the left wall is a great stone emblazoned with the Uzerche arms.

▶ Take Escalier-Notre-Dame on the right immediately beyond the Bécharie Gateway.

Place des Vignerons

This little square, the wine-grower's square, was formerly the fruit market. It is surrounded by old houses and the chapel of Notre-Dame, the oldest church in Uzerche. The covered La Perception passageway leads to a small terrace which affords a bird's-eye view of the Vézère and of part of the town.

Leave the **Tour du Prince Noir** (Black Prince's tower) on your left and walk along rue St-Nicolas. This will bring you out onto place de la Libération. The square is dominated by the impressive mass of the church of St-Pierre.

Esplanade de La Lunade

From this esplanade there is a **view** immediately below of the La Pomme district which rises in terraces along N 20; of the Vézère meander; and of the hills beyond encircling the town.

Église St-Pierre★

This is an interesting Romanesque church, built in several phases. Fortified during the Hundred Years War, repaired in the 17C, the church was restored at the beginning of the 20C.

The 12C **belltower** is Limousin in style. Three square levels with twin windows and gables are surmounted by a fourth, octagonal level; this, in turn, is topped with a shallow roof covered in shingles. To the southwest stands a massive **round tower**, erected as the defence point for the main door, built of rough-hewn stone with loopholes.

Since restoration work on the church was undertaken in the 20C, this tower is all that remains of the ancient defence system. The perimeter wall included 18 towers and five fortified gateways. Beneath the chancel, the 11C **crypt** is believed to be the oldest in the region. The **nave** has broken-barrel vaulting and is flanked by narrow aisles. An octagonal dome rises above the transept crossing.

Rue Pierre-Chalaud

This street is lined with old houses adorned with Gothic and Renaissance doors and timbered houses. At the end of it the **Château Tayac** (12C–14C) is a fine house with turrets and a door surmounted by a shield.

Hôtel du Sénéchal

This 17C hotel was the property of the seneschal of Chavailles, who was royal officer of justice. Louis XIII visited him and his family here in 1632. The buildings, arranged in a U shape, are visible from the road below. Three towers – polygonal, round and square – punctuate the façade. On the side facing rue de la Justice, the little turret with a sentry box is topped by a pepperpot roof. The *hôtel* now houses an archaeology centre.

Centre Régional de Documentation sur l'Archéologie du Paysage

🕐🦽 *Open Mon–Fri 9am–noon, 2–5pm.* 🚫 *No charge.* 📞 *05 55 73 26 07. www.archeologie-paysage.org.*

Set up in the 17C **Hôtel du Sénéchal**, the regional centre documents recent archaeological research in the area, covering the period from the Iron Age to the late Middle Ages.

▶ Return to place de la Libération.

Walk along rue Jean-Gentet, where you will notice carved doorways, to the Bécharie Gateway and place Marie-Colein.

🚗 **DRIVING TOUR**

1 0 VALLÉE DE LA VÉZÈRE
55km/34mi. Allow 3hr. See route 10 on region map pp278–279.

▶ Drive NE out of Uzerche on D 3 towards Eymoutiers.

Belvédère
Travel 800m from the bridge and before a turning on the left you'll get a good overall **view★★** of Uzerche perched on top of a rock and the Vézère running below.

▶ Continue along D 3 and turn right onto D 26 shortly after Eyburie.

Chamboulive
The countryside is a pleasant mixture of volcanic *puys*, hills and meadows. The **church**, a Romanesque edifice renovated in the 15C, has a raised, deep belfry-porch.

▶ Take D 142 towards Uzerche and turn left onto D 920 just before reaching Uzerche.

Vigeois
An abbey was founded here in the 6C. The present **church** dates only from the 12C, although it has been much restored. A street leads down to the **old bridge**, also 12C, which runs a quiet course here. Nearby is **Pontcharal Lake**; the recreation centre is spacious and welcoming.

▶ Drive N out of Vigeois along D 7 towards Arnac-Pompadour then turn right beyond Jargassou Bridge. Follow C 7 then V 1.

Cascades de Bialet
🚶 *Picnic area.* A footpath starts at the wooden bridge across the stream; other wooden bridges crisscross the water. (*take care that children do not fall in*).

▶ Continue on the minor road, which goes steeply down to Uzerche.

Uzerche

© G. Labriet / Photononstop

ADDRESSES

🛏 STAY

🛏 **Camping Municipal la Minoterie** – *Left bank of the Vézère via quai Julian-Grimau.* ☎05 55 73 12 75. *50 pitches.* Here, the gentle lapping of the Vézère will lull you to sleep at night. The pitches are set up around an old mill. Wide range of activities.

🛏🛏 **Hôtel-Restaurant Jean Teyssier** – *R. du Pont Turgot.* ☎05 55 73 10 05. *www.hotel-teyssier.com. 14 rooms.* The small, leafy terrace of this hotel near the town centre looks out over the Vézère.

🍽 EAT

🍽🍽 **Chez Denise** – *8 r. Porte-Barachaude.* ☎05 55 73 22 12. Cross the threshold of this modest house near the periphery of the old city and get a table on the balcony. You'll enjoy both the food and the view.

ACTIVITIES

Base de Loisirs de la Minoterie – ☎05 55 73 02 84. *www.vezerepassion.com.* This recreation area on the banks of the Vézère offers canoeing, kayaking, rafting, climbing, mountain-biking and other outdoor activities.

Bas-Limousin is crisscrossed by the Corrèze, Vézère and Dordogne rivers and their many tributaries, wild gorges and waterfalls. A large number of dams have been built and their reservoirs are perfect for water sports, as are the area's many lakes. Diverse mineral wealth, especially slate, but also red sandstone and white limestone, give texture to the landscape and houses. This is a place where you can enjoy the great outdoors, as well as a few historic sites that have been well adapted to educational visits.

Highlights

1 The spectacular waterfalls of **Gimel-les-Cascades** (p318)

2 **Les Pans de Travassac**, breathtaking sheets of slate (p320)

3 The picturesque Corrèzian village of **Saint-Robert** (p322)

4 The impressive **Tours de Merle** citadel (p335)

5 Driving Tour along the **Dordogne** past dams and reservoir lakes (p338)

Water, Water, Everywhere

The powerful waterfalls of Gimel-les-Cascades are a perfect example of the type of rugged beauty that this area has to offer. Don't forget your walking boots, as you'll have to wander out among the craggy gorges for the best views.

You'll never be far from impressive volumes of water, whether it is crashing down a dizzying cliffside or lying still and tranquil in a wooded lake.

The series of dams along the Dordogne and its tributaries are interesting both for their technical characteristics and for the possibilities they offer for boating or just enjoying the view. Don't miss Barrage de l'Aigle in Aynes, which handles colossal volumes of water. Another spectacular dam is in Bort-les-Orgues, where you can join a boat ride to sightsee from the water or enjoy a guided tour on land. Views of the pillar-like cliff sides above the village make it unique.

Minerals and Folkloric Wealth

The geology of the region combines several types of rock, creating a mosaic of colours and adding a striking dimension to the landscape and its buildings. The most characteristic rock is the slate that you'll see on the roofs of almost all the houses and churches. This was a slate-mining area for hundreds of years. It's hard not to be amazed by the dizzying sheer slate walls of Les Pans de Travassac in Donzenac.

Tours de Merle

© Colin Weston / age fotostock

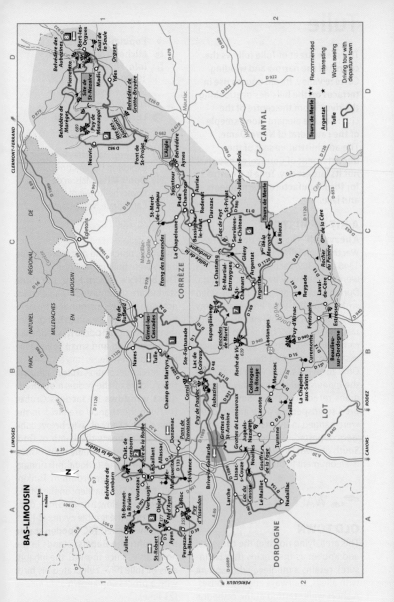

The inhabitants of the area are nostalgic for the past, and where popular traditions can be enhanced, no effort has been spared to do so. This is well illustrated in the village of St-Junien-aux-Bois, with the reproduction of medieval farms and a village called Les Fermes du Moyen Age en Xaintrie. Continue this trip through time with Les Tours de Merle: here, the ruins of a medieval citadel include no less than seven castles, as well as replica of a medieval farm, gardens and the remains of a toll bridge. There are also a few picturesque villages in Bas-Limousin which have stood the test of time, such as Saint-Robert and Argentat. The centres of Tulle, the administrative capital, and Brive-la-Gaillarde, the most populated and culturally active city in the region, are charming.

Tulle

The main street of Tulle follows the course of the narrow and winding Corrèze valley. Its old houses rise in terraces on the hillsides overlooking the river. From the centre of the city rises the elegant stone steeple of the cathedral of Notre-Dame. The administrative seat of the *département* of Corrèze, although not its largest city, Tulle is a centre for the manufacture of armaments and lace.

▶ **Population:** 14 923.
🕐 **Michelin Map:** 329: L-4.
ℹ **Info**: Pl. Jean-Tavé, 19000 Tulle. ℘05 55 26 59 61. www.tulle-coeur-correze.com.
▶ **Location**: 27km/17mi northeast of Brive-la-Gaillarde.
🕐 **Timing**: Half a day for exploring Upper Corrèze.
☺ **Don't Miss**: Maison de Loyac; belltower of the Cathédrale Notre-Dame.

A BIT OF HISTORY

A heavy toll – During the Hundred Years War the town fell twice to the English, in 1346 and 1369. Each time, the invaders were driven away by the local militia. During the Wars of Religion, Tulle sided with the papists. The Protestant army under the viscount of Turenne failed to take the city in 1577 but in 1585 Turenne came back and, with bloody vengeance, assaulted and sacked the city.

On 8 June 1944 Tulle was liberated by the *maquis*, but the next day the Germans retook the town. Several hundred townspeople were arrested: 99 were hanged in the streets, the others were deported. 101 never came back. South of town (*N 89, the road to Brive*), is a monument to the victims of Nazism.

🐾 WALKING TOUR

OLD TOWN

This area, lying north of the cathedral and known as the Enclos (the Enclosure), retains a medieval atmosphere with alleys, stairways and old houses. A short walk starting at the cathedral (*15min round-trip*) offers a view of the edifice.

Cathédrale Notre-Dame

In 1103, Abbot Guillaume wanted his abbey, which was then very prosperous, to have a setting worthy of such abundance. He undertook the reconstruction of the church and the cloistral buildings.

The nave, porch and first storey of the belfry were built in the 12C.

The **belfry★** is 73m high; the three storeys are surmounted by an elegant octagonal spire surrounded by bell-turrets. The ogive-vaulted **porch** contains a tiers-point doorway, adorned with moulding and small columns in the Limousin style.

The interior decoration is plain, although the colours of the modern **stained-glass windows** by Jacques Gruber (1979) in the chancel are vivid: in the centre is Our Lady of Tulle; below, John the Baptist bears the Lamb of God. The border shows, on the right, Bishop Dumoulin-Borie (a local missionary who suffered martyrdom in Tonkin) and, below, St Sebastien; on the left, St Jacques and, below, a hanged man, commemorating the terrible events of 1944. A much-venerated **16C wooden statue of St John the Baptist** stands in the north aisle. Since the 14C, the inhabitants of Tulle have celebrated his birth with a procession known as *la lunade* (23 June).

Cloisters – Built in the early 13C, the building has been greatly damaged over time. However, the the west gallery and two bays in the north and east galleries are still standing. The south gallery was destroyed in the 19C for the purposes of a municipal theatre project. Many vestiges are displayed along the galleries: a collection of 16C–18C fire-

Maison de Loyac facade

© Jean-Paul Garcin / Photononstop

backs, statues, copies of recumbent figures representing popes from the Limousin, and various stone fragments.

Maison de Loyac★

This is the most outstanding secular building in Tulle. Built in the early 16C it has an attractive façade: the windows and door are framed by small columns and are topped by accolades adorned with sculptured foliage, roses and animals.

▷ Take rue de la Tour-de-Maïsse, to the left of the building.

Rue de la Tour-de-Maïsse

This street is a narrow stairway, where the roofs of corbelled houses almost meet above the alley.

▷ Bear left again onto rue de la Baylie and yet again onto the sloping rue des Portes-Chanac.

Rue des Portes-Chanac

Along this steep street, you will notice, among a group of old houses on the left (at no 9), a sculptured doorway belonging to a late Renaissance mansion.

Rue Riche

Note the carved façade at no 13.

▷ Rue Riche returns to the cathedral.

MUSEUM
Musée du Cloître de Tulle

🕑*Open Mon, Wed-Sat and 1st and 3rd Sun of the month: Nov–Apr 1–6pm; May–Oct 10am–1pm, 2–6.30pm.*
🕑*Closed Tue and 1 Jan, 1 May, 1 Nov and 25 Dec.* ⊛*No charge.*
✆*05 55 26 91 05.*

This museum is adjacent to the west gallery of the cloisters. The ground floor is used for **temporary exhibitions**. The spiral staircase dates from the Middle Ages; it leads to the **first-floor** rooms, which display a collection illustrating the history and **popular arts and traditions** of Tulle and its region. One of the rooms devotes pride of place to the **accordion**, whose manufacture Corrèze was once famed for. Those on display date from 1832 to 1950, and include the work of a local craftsman still in business. The second floor houses a collection of **swords** and **firearms**, regional **ceramics** and **religious art**.

🚗 DRIVING TOUR

① UPPER CORRÈZE VALLEY
140km/87mi. Allow half a day.
See route 1 on region map p315.

▷ Drive SW out of Tulle on D 89 towards Brive-la-Gaillarde.

Surging forth to the west of Meymac, at an altitude of nearly 900m, the River Corrèze crosses the Monédières range and digs a deep valley in the granite. It is the main artery of the *départe-ment* which bears its name, and passes through Tulle and Brive before joining forces with the Vézère.

The road follows the west bank of the Corrèze and almost immediately runs by the **Champ des Martyrs**, a monument to the massacre of 99 young men in Tulle on 8 and 9 June 1944.

▶ Continue on N 89 towards Brive.

Cornil

A four-storey square tower above the village, all that remains of the castle, rises next to the Romanesque church. There is a scenic overlook of the bend in the river.

▶ In the village, take D 48E.

Parc du Coiroux

This park has been developed around a large lake with swimming beaches and sailing, golf and tennis facilities.

▶ Turn left on D 48 outside Coiroux.

Ste-Fortunade

Near a much-restored 15C **castle** stands a small Romanesque church. On the left at the entrance to the south chapel is the **reliquary-head★** of St Fortunade. This is a delightful 15C work in bronze.

▶ Follow D 940 for 1km/0.5mi, turn left onto D 1 and follow D 10 to Marc-la-Tour. Take D 125E to St-Bonnet-Avalouze, continue along D 61E to St-Martial-de-Gimel, then drive along D 53.

Gimel-les-Cascades★★

🛈*Le Bourg, Gimel-les-Cascades.*
🕑*Open Apr–Sept Mon–Fri 10am–noon, 2–5pm, Sat until 6pm, Sun 2–6pm (Jul–Aug 9.30am–12.30pm, 2–6.30pm).*
☎*05 55 21 44 32.*

The Montane, also called the Gimelle, flows from a height of 143m through wild gorges. **Gaston Vuillier** (1845–1915) brought attention to this little town through watercolours where he lovingly depicted this natural beauty; you can see his works at the Musée du Cloître in Tulle. He also had a blazed trail set up along the gorges at the turn of the century. Thanks to his efforts, the waterfalls of Gimel would become the first protected natural site in France.

Cascades★★ – 🚶*1hr round-trip on foot. A tiring walk.* Access through the Vuillier park (*signposted trails:* 🕑*open Jul–Aug 10am–7pm, Apr–Jun and Sept–Oct 10am–6pm.* ⊗€6. ☎*05 55 21 26 49*).

La Queue de Cheval, Gimel-les-Cascades

© Christian Guy / hemis.fr

The best views over the waterfalls can only be seen by crossing through the parks. The first one, **La Grande Cascade** or Grand Saut ("Big jump"), leaps from a height of 45m. Just afterwards, the second, **La Redole**, takes a 27m plunge. From here you can see both of these waterfalls. The third, called **La Queue de Cheval** ("the Ponytail"), comes suddenly into view on a rocky promontory as it crashes into the **Gouffre de l'Inferno** ("Hell's abyss").

◖ Take the D 53 towards Touzac.

The road runs alongside the southern shore of the ▲▲ **Étang de Ruffaud**. This lovely stretch of water with bathing beaches lies in a romantic setting. The **Étang de Brach**, 3.5km/2mi farther on, has boating facilities.

◖ Continue E on D 53.

The village of **Bar** sits on a promontory overlooking the valleys of the River Vimbelle and the River Corrèze.

Naves

The 15C church, flanked by a fortified turret, contains a huge **reredos★** in sculpted wood. The vertical imagery is centred around Christ; horizontally, the carvings detail the founding of the church (St Peter in chains).

◖ Follow D58; turn right on N120 just before turning left to return to D58.

The road winds down to the river and follows its course to Tulle.

ADDRESSES

🏠 STAY

🛏 **Camping du Lac de Bournazel –** *Seilhac, 15km/9.3mi NW of Tulle on D 1120 then D 44.* ✆*05 55 27 05 65. www.camping-lac-bournazel.com. Chalets for 4 to 6 people each.* In this pleasant natural environment along a lake, enjoy this well-equipped campsite and its various activities.

🍴 EAT

🛏🛏 **La Ferme du Léondou –** *19700 St-Salvadour. 12km/7.2mi N of Naves. Take the N 120, the D 53 towards Corrèze, then the D 173.* ✆*05 55 21 60 04. www. leondou.com.* Leave the beaten path to discover this old barn with its handsome wood troughs and grand fireplace. Local traditions are taken seriously in this kitchen: you'll get a chance to taste *flognarde*, guinea fowl with veal sweetbreads, *la poux*, blood pudding with chestnuts, and more.

🛏🛏 **La Toque Blanche –** *Pl. M.-Brigouleix.* ✆*05 55 26 75 41. www. latoqueblanchetulle.com.* This downtown restaurant gives diners a choice between the rustic dining room and the veranda. The white chef's cap – *la toque blanche* – rides atop the head of the family son, who concocts a tasty cuisine. Good value for the price. A few rooms upstairs if you'd like to stay.

🛏🛏 **Le Central –** *12 r. de la Barrière.* ✆*05 55 26 24 46.* This impressive house near the Corrèze is home to this first-floor restaurant featuring an attractive dining room with exposed beams, stonework and lace tablecloths. Le Central enjoys an excellent local reputation for the quality of its traditional local cuisine.

BARS / CAFÉS

La Taverne du Sommelier – *8 quai de la République.* ✆*05 55 26 57 63. www.taverne-du-sommelier.fr. Open daily 8.45am–1am.* This traditional *brassserie* has a wide range of wines by the glass.

SHOPPING

Maugein Accordéon – *Rte de Brive, Zone Industrielle de Mulatet.* ✆*05 55 20 08 89. Tours by arrangement.* This brand of accordions was established in 1919. The manufacturer, who has been in business longer than any other French accordion maker still in activity, was the first to introduce the MIDI-system accordion nationally in September 1984.

Le Point de Tulle – *2 r. des Portes-Chanac.* ✆*05 55 26 71 75/06 85 18 16 25.* Cathy Vedrenne is an experienced lacemaker who demonstrates a rare needle technique. She invites you to discover this traditional lace shop.

Donzenac

Built on the side of a hill on the brink of the Brive basin, this old slate quarry village is located in a strategic position that made it very desirable in the past, and particularly during the Hundred Years War. Its old houses, its church featuring a 14C belfry and the elegant Renaissance façade of its *Chapelle des Pénitents* bring the village charm. Coming from Donzenac, don't miss the beautiful Vézère gorges and their natural treasures.

VISIT
Pans de Travassac★

Guided tours (1hr 30): Jul–Aug 10.30–11.30am, 2.30–5.30pm; May–Jun and Sept–Oct Sun and public holidays 2.30–5.30pm. €8. 05 55 85 66 33. www.lespansdetravassac.com.

Before WWI, the slate quarries of Donzenac and Allassac were thriving. During this period, the thatched roofs in the area were massively replaced with slate roofs. However, for various reasons, the last quarries closed in 1982.

Veins and sheets – As soon as you arrive in the car park overlooking the Saut de la Girale (140m), you'll get a taste of the vertiginous allure of this site, entirely dug out by man for more than three centuries. Over footbridges and platforms, discover the various shapes cut into this fascinating metamorphic rock and experience the thrills familiar to slate workers!

Slate workshop – The tools and techniques used by slate workers are immutable. A working quarry has been recreated to show you the extraordinary dexterity that is necessary to cut, split and trim slate. Only 20% of the stone removed can be used. Incredibly, a trimmer on the site could shape 2 000 to 5 000 slates per month.

- **Population:** 2 545.
- **Michelin Map:** 329: K4.
- **Info:** 2 r. des Pénitents. 05 55 24 08 80. www.brive-tourisme.com.
- **Location:** 10km/6.2mi north of Brive-la-Gaillarde.
- **Kids:** An educational booklet is available from the Tourist Office to help kids discover the town.
- **Timing:** A full day to visit Donzenac and the gorges.

DRIVING TOUR

2 UPPER CORRÈZE VALLEY★
45km/27.9mi. Allow 3hr. See route 2 on region map p315.

▷ Drive W out of Donzenac on D 25.

Downstream from Uzerche, the Vézère goes through deep gorges. There are some fine **views** from the Site de la Roche and from villages on both sides of the gorges.

Allassac
The distinctive houses of this town are built in black schist and roofed with slate; some have red-sandstone corner pieces (*rue L. Boucharel*).
The **church**, commemorating the beheading of John the Baptist, is also built of black schist, except for the lovely **southern door★**, where various colours of sandstone are set in contrast. The nearby **Caesar's Tower** (30m) is all that remains of the old medieval fortifications.

▷ Leave N on D 9.

Site de la Roche★
A pretty little road leads to the edge of a precipice overlooking the Vézère gorges. To the right, a rocky trail leads to a **viewing table** (391m).
The view extends over the wooded **gorges du Saillant.**

To the left, a path leads to an overlook, where there is another spectacular **view** over the gorges.

▷ Return to D 9 and, just before Le Pilou, turn left onto D 9E3.

Belvédère de Comborn
The belvedere overlooks a meander of the Vézère and affords a view of the ruined **Château de Comborn**.

▷ Continue along D 9E3 until you reach the château.

Château de Combron
⤵ Guided tour available by prior arrangement. ☏ 05 55 73 77 23.
This castle was the property of the powerful and cruel Comborn family. The vestiges of the 11C dungeon overlooking the Vézère are enclosed in later architectural additions. The new owner has begun to excavate the ramparts and has begun restoration of the interior of the 18C addition (⊶ no public access). Three vast cellars of the same period have been well preserved.

▷ Come back to D 3 and turn left.

Vertougit
This charming village is beautifully located, just across from the Site de la Roche, overlooking the **gorges de la Vézère**. There is a good view from the viewing table.

▷ Return to D 134 and turn right to Voutezac.

Voutezac
Built into the hillside, this agreeable village has a fortified church with a 15C square tower.

▷ Drive along D 134 towards Allassac.

Le Saillant
This hamlet is on a pleasant site at the mouth of the gorges. From the **old bridge** spanning the river, admire the Lasteyrie du Saillant manor, where the revolutionary orator Mirabeau

(brother of the Marquis du Saillant) regularly came to visit. Do not miss the **six stained-glass windows★** by Marc Chagall in the former castle chapel.

▷ Cross the Vézère and take D 148 S for 2.5km/1.5. Cross back over the river.

Chapelle Ste-Marguerite
This graceful Roman-style monument in red sandstone stands on a ledge, giving a lovely view of the Vézère valley.

▷ Go back towards the river but turn right onto D 9. After 3km/1.8mi, turn left onto D 9E2 which shortly crosses the Vézère.

St-Viance
This attractive red sandstone village is located along the Vézère river. Inside the church, tucked away in a choir alcove, is one of the most beautiful pieces of enamelwork in the entire Limousin region, a 13C *champlevé* enamel shrine.

▷ Leave St-Viance E on D 133. D 25 will take you back to Donzenac.

ADDRESSES

🏠 STAY
⊖⊜⊜ **Auberge sur Vézère** – *Le Bourg, St-Viance.* ☏05 55 84 28 23. www.auberge survezere.com. 🅿. *10 rooms.* This little inn at the entryway to the village is run by a Franco-British couple. The rooms are efficient and well-equipped. Modern dishes are served in a family atmosphere in the bright dining room or on shady terrace under the trees.

🍴 EAT
⊖⊜ **Le Périgord** – *9 av. de Paris, Donzenac.* ☏05 55 85 72 34. The front of this restaurant is covered with Virginia creeper. Inside, enjoy regional traditional cuisine amongst an exhibition of local art.

Saint-Robert★

In this wooded area on the site of a Merovingian city, many bloody battles were fought during the Wars of Religion. Today the village of Saint-Robert and its typically Corrèzian landscape makes it a perfect place to ramble.

Its Grand-Place, its sturdy white stone houses roofed in slate and its church have been the set of a French mini-series called *Des Grives aux Loups*, based on the novel by local author Claude Michelet.

▶ **Population:** 342.
⌾ **Michelin Map:** 329-I4.
▤ **Info:** Pl. de la Prévôté - 19310 St-Robert. ✆ 05 55 24 08 80. www.brive-tourisme.com.
⊘ **Don't Miss:** The peaceful valleys of the Yssandonnais; the Gallo-Roman ruins of Le Puy d'Yssandon and the rotunda-shaped church of St-Bonnet-la-Rivière.
▶ **Location:** 25km/15.5mi NW of Brive-la-Gaillarde, on the border between the *départements* of the Corrèze and Dordogne, St-Robert is located on a hillock.
◷ **Timing:** Half a day for the area.

SIGHTS
Church

The only remains of the 12C church are the transept, of which the crossing holds up an octagonal belfry; and the large choir. The choir is lit up by high windows and is separated from the ambulatory by six columns featuring interesting historiated capitals showing scenes from the Bible. Those adjacent to the wall of the ambulatory are more archaic (notice the two old men pulling on each other's beards). In the nave, there is a 13C life-sized woodwork Christ in the style of the Spanish School.

▚ DRIVING TOUR

③ L'YSSANDONNAIS
60km/37mi. Allow half a day. See route 3 on region map p315.

▷ Drive E out of St-Robert on D 5.

The Yssandonnais is the western part of the Brive basin. Its territory was a *pagus* (a native Latin word from the root *pāg-*, loosely translating as a "boundary staked into the ground", which later became the smallest administrative district of a province) during the High Middle Ages with Yssandon as its capital.

The varied geologic environment, including black shale and hillocks of red sandstone as well as light-coloured limestone mounds called *puys*, explains the attractive contrasts of materials used to build the local villages.

The hilly landscape includes grasslands and lines of poplar trees in the dales, tobacco and corn fields, orchards of walnut and other fruits in the well-exposed areas, and oak forests along the *puys*.

Ayen

The former castellany of the viscounty of Limoges, Ayen is known for the 12C funerary recesses on the outside of its church walls.

To the east of the village, **Mont d'Ayen★** (*377m*) is a lookout point over the vineyards where a picnic area is set up. An orientation panel identifies the points of interest (*St-Robert, Les Monts Dore, Allassac*).

▷ Leave Ayen SE on D 2. At La Contie, turn left on D 140E.

Perpezac-le-Blanc

This pleasant village with its golden limestone houses is overlooked by an elegant castle (*not open to visitors*).

▷ Leave Perpezac S on D 39. Just before Brignac-la-Plaine, turn left on D 3.

View of Brive Basin from Puy d'Yssandon

© Christian Guy / hemis.fr

Puy d'Yssandon★

This site has been occupied for an extremely long time. A Gallic *oppidum* and Gallo-Roman vestiges have been found here. The **tower** is the only remaining part of the medieval fortress, which was the property of the powerful Pompadour and Noailles families.
All alone at the end of the road, the 12C **church** overlooks the Brive basin; you'll find a little orientation panel behind the cemetery. The view sweeps over the Limousin elevations, the hills of the Périgord and the plain of Brignac.

▷ Come back to D 151 and take a right. At La Prodelie, turn left. This little road will soon join D 5. Take a left towards Ayen.

Le Roc

This rustic hamlet overlooks the Manou Valley. Above stands the Château de St-Aulaire, built entirely in red sandstone.

▷ Come back to D 5 via St-Aulaire. Just afterwards, take a right on D 3.

Objat

Pl. Charles-de-Gaulle, Objat. ℘*05 55 24 08 80. www.objat.fr.*
The economic centre of this rural area is the village of Objat, where apples and

free-raised veal are the main products. This type of veal, which is raised on its mother's milk, unlike many other varieties, is very sought-after and guaranteed high quality. The town is known for its large cattle markets.

▷ Leave Objat NE on D 901.

St-Bonnet-la-Rivière

This village features a picturesque Romanesque **church** in red limestone. The building has a rotunda shape and a belfry porch. Legend has it that the knight of Cars, Lord of St-Bonnet-la-Rivière, made a wish during his captivity in the Holy Land to build a church in the image of St-Sépulcre on his fief.

▷ Continue along D 901.

Juillac

Ascend to Châtenet (*345m*), where, amongst the orchards, you will discover a pretty **view** (*orientation panel*).

▷ Leave Juillac S on D 39, then take D 71 back to St-Robert.

Brive-la-Gaillarde

Brive owes its suffix "La Gaillarde" (the bold) to the courage displayed by its citizens during sieges in centuries past. This busy town stands in the alluvial plain of the River Corrèze: as a result of its fertile soil, the surrounding area is an important centre for market gardening and fruit growing. Located at the crossroads of the Bas-Limousin (Lower Limousin), the Périgord and the limestone plateaux of the Quercy, the town is an important railway junction with a thriving economy. Since 1982, an important annual book fair (the Foire du Livre) has been held in the town. No mention of Brive can be made without reference to its rugby union team, one of the most respected in France.

A BIT OF HISTORY

A brilliant career – Guillaume Dubois (1656–1723), the son of an apothecary from Brive, took the Orders and became tutor to Philip of Orléans. He became prime minister when Philip was

> ▶ **Population:** 48 949.
> 🚗 **Michelin Map:** 329: K-5.
> 🛈 **Information:** Pl. du 14 Juillet, Brive-la-Gaillarde. ℘05 55 24 08 80. www.brive-tourisme.com.
> ◗ **Location:** 94km/58.75mi S of Limoges via the A 20.
> 👥 **Kids:** Lac de Causse, in the Vallée de la Couze.
> ⊙ **Don't Miss:** Hôtel de Labenche; Lower Corrèze Valley; the Corrèze Causse; Gouffre de la Fage.

appointed regent during the minority of Louis XV. Offices and honours were heaped upon him; he became archbishop of Cambrai and then a cardinal. He made an alliance with England which ensured a long period of peace in France.

A glorious soldier – Guillaume-Marie-Anne Brune (1763–1815) enlisted in the army in 1791 and rose to become a general commanding the army in Italy in 1798. Following victories in Holland and Italy, he was appointed ambassador to Constantinople. Elected *maréchal de France* in 1804, he was ban-

Aerial view of Brive-la-Gaillarde

©Gérard Labriet/Photononstop

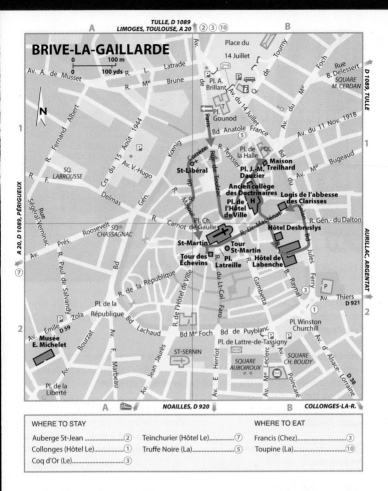

WHERE TO STAY		WHERE TO EAT	
Auberge St-Jean ....②	Teinchurier (Hôtel Le)................⑦	Francis (Chez)................................③
Collonges (Hôtel Le)...................①	Truffe Noire (La)...........................⑤	Toupine (La)..................................⑩
Coq d'Or (Le)............................③			

ished by Napoleon soon afterwards for his republican attitude. He became the symbol of the Revolution and died, a victim of a Royalist mob, in 1815 at Avignon.

☙ WALKING TOUR

OLD TOWN
The old town located in the heart of the city, bounded by a first ring of boulevards, has been successfully restored. The buildings, old and new, create a harmonious ensemble of warm beige sandstone and bluish-tinted rooftops.

▶ Start from the Tourist Office (pl. du 14-Juillet). Follow avenue de Paris then rue de Toulzac across boulevard

Anatole-France and turn immediately right onto rue de Corrèze.

Chapelle St-Libéral
This Gothic chapel holds temporary exhibitions throughout the year.

▶ Continue along rue de Corrèze then follow rue Majour.

Collégiale St-Martin
In this church, only the Romanesque transept, apse and a few of the capitals remain of a 12C monastic community. Inside, over the transept crossing, is an octagonal dome on flat pendentives, characteristic of the Limousin style. The nave and side aisles are 14C. The chancel was faithfully rebuilt by Cardinal

Old town, towards Collégiale St-Martin

Dubois in the 18C. Note the 12C baptismal font decorated with the symbols of the Evangelists.

Archaeological crypt
Vestiges of previous churches have been uncovered beneath the chancel, including the primitive construction dating from the 5C over the tomb of St Martin the Spaniard.

▷ Coming out of the church, take rue des Échevins on the left.

Tour des Échevins
In the narrow rue des Échevins stands a townhouse with a fine corbelled Renaissance tower featuring mullioned windows.

▷ Retrace your steps and turn right.

Place Latreille
This square was once the spiritual and commercial heart of the city and is still surrounded by old houses. The house known as **Tours St-Martin** dates from the 15C and 16C.

▷ Continue straight on along rue du Docteur-Massénat then turn right onto rue Raynal.

Positioned at the corner of rue Raynal and rue du Salan is the 18C Hôtel Desbruslys.

▷ Walk along rue Raynal and enter the Hôtel de Labenche through the small door on the left.

Hôtel de Labenche★
From the inner courtyard, the view encompasses the two buildings standing at right angles that support the arcaded gallery. Built in 1540 by Jean II de Calvimont, lord of Labenche and the king's keeper of the seals for the Bas-Limousin, this mansion is a magnificent example of Renaissance architecture in Toulouse style and is the most remarkable secular building in town.

Musée d'Art et d'Histoire de Labenche★
&🕐*Open daily except Tue: Apr–Oct, 10am–6.30pm; Nov–Mar, 1.30–6pm.* 🕐*Closed 1 Jan, 1 May, 1 Nov and 25 Dec.* ⬜€5. *No charge for temporary exhibitions.* 🖉*05 55 18 17 70.*
The Roman-style **main staircase** of the Hôtel de Labenche exudes the same exuberance as the outside. Among the 17 rooms, pay particular attention to the Counts of Cosnac room decorated with a marvellous set of **tapestries**, known as the Mortlake tapestries, made in the

17C using the widely renowned techniques of English high-warp tapestry. In the Cardinal Dubois room, there is a wonderful 11C silver and bronze **eucharistic dove** hanging above the altar. One of the main attributes of this museum is the successful reconstruction of the various series of excavations.

▷ Continue along boulevard Jules-Ferry and turn left onto rue du Dr-Massénat.

Logis de l'Abbesse des Clarisses

"Residence of the Mother Superior of the Order of St Clare". This Louis XIII building is distinguished by its dormer windows with semicircular pediments decorated with keel-shaped spheres.

▷ Turn right onto rue Teyssier.

Ancien Collège des Doctrinaires

This college was maintained by the Brothers of Christian Doctrine, who were open-minded humanists as much as they were men of faith, and its prosperity increased up until the Revolution. Today these 17C buildings house the town hall.

▷ Turn right.

Place Jean-Marie-Dauzier

On this large square, modern buildings (*Crédit Agricole bank*) and old turreted mansions form a harmonious architectural unit. The 16C **Maison Treilhard** consists of two main buildings joined by a round tower and decorated by a turret.

▷ Retrace your steps. Walk back to the collegiate church across place de l'Hôtel-de-Ville, then turn right onto rue de Toulzac.

ADDITIONAL SIGHT
Musée Edmond-Michelet

◔*Open daily exc Sun, 10am–noon and 2–6pm.* ◔*Closed public hols.* ✆*No charge.* ✆*05 55 74 06 08.* *http://museemichelet.brive.fr.*

The museum traces the history of the Resistance movement and deportation through paintings, photographs, posters and original documents relating to the camps, especially Dachau, where Edmond Michelet, former minister under General de Gaulle, was interned.

🚗 DRIVING TOURS

4 BASSE VALLÉE DE LA CORRÈZE ★
Round-trip of 45km/27.9mi. Allow 3hr. See route 4 on region map p315.

▷ Take the N 89 out of Brive-la-Gaillard NE towards Tulle.

Aubazine★ &*See AUBAZINE.*

▷ Drive E along D 48.

Puy de Pauliac★
30min round-trip. Alt. 520m.
🚶 The footpath makes its way through heather and chestnut trees, leading upwards to reveal a splendid **view★**. A **viewing table** helps to identify the Roche de Vic to the southeast and the Monédières range to the north.
The **Parc du Coiroux** is set around a large lake with swimming beaches and sailing, golf and tennis facilities.

▷ Return to Aubazine. Drive SE along D 130 and D 175 to Lanteuil, then drive back to Brive along picturesque D 921.

5 LA CAUSSE CORRÈZIEN★
Round-trip of 45km/29mi. Allow 3hr. See route 5 on region map p315.

▷ Leave Brive on the D 920S towards Cahors.

The road rises above the Brive basin.

Grottes de St-Antoine

These caves, hollowed out of sandstone, were used as a retreat by St Antony of Padua. Follow the Stations of the Cross to the top of a hill for a view of Brive.

▶ Take the small signposted road to the left.

Grottes de Lamouroux

This group of caves on five levels was used as a refuge in times of danger.

Noailles

Noailles is overlooked by its hilltop church and Renaissance **château**, seat of the De Noailles family.

The **church**, topped with a Limousin-style bell-gable, has a Romanesque apse and chancel. There is a painting by Watteau's teacher Claude Gillot (*Instruments of the Crucifixion*).

▶ Leave Noailles on D 158 heading W.

The road climbs towards the lake and Corrèze Causse, an area of white limestone.

Lissac-sur-Couze

Set back from the lake, this elegant manor, flanked by battlemented turrets, was a military tower in the 13C and 14C.

👥 Lac du Causse★

Also known as the Lac de Chasteaux, this superb stretch of water (90ha/222 acres), set in lush green countryside in the lovely Couze valley, is a recreation centre.

▶ Leave Lissac SW on D 59.

Lac du Causse

© Tim Mannakee / Sime / Photononstop

The itinerary runs along the lake shore, revealing its extent and beauty.

▶ Turn right off D 19 onto D 154 towards Chartrier-Ferrière.

Le Maillet

The limestone walls of the houses in this hamlet are constructed in a traditional way using house-martin mortar, lumps of clay pressed between the stones.

▶ Continue along D 154.

Nadaillac

This charming country village is famous for its high-quality truffles. Some of the medieval houses have typical *lauze* roofs.

▶ Leave Nadaillac on D 63.

Farther on, scenic road D 60 weaves in and out of the edges of the *départements* of the Dordogne and Corrèze.

▶ In Larche, take N 89 back to Brive.

ADDRESSES

🛏 STAY

🍽 **Auberge St-Jean** – ☎05 55 22 87 55. www.auberge-saint-jean.fr. *27 rooms.* A welcoming village set against a backdrop of hills and valleys. Purpose-built rooms. The restaurant has a rustic charm with its stones, beams, fireplace and gleaming copper. The terrace gives a view of the surrounding countryside.

🍽🍽 **Collonges** – 3 pl. Winston Churchill. ☎05 55 74 09 58. www.hotel-collonges.com. *WiFi. 24 rooms.* A family-run hotel set back slightly from the main boulevard encircling the centre of town. Cosy lounge-bar and modern bedrooms.

🍽🍽 **Hôtel Le Coq d'Or** – 16 blvd J-Ferry. ☎05 55 17 12 92. www.hotel-coqdor.com. *WiFi. 8 rooms.* Just off the centre of town, this renovated hotel offers rooms decorated with period furniture and Toile de Jouy fabrics.

🍴🍽 **Le Teinchurier** – *Av. du Teinchurier. 3km/1.8mi W of the centre on the Périgueux road.* ☎*05 55 86 45 00. www.hotel-brive-la-gaillarde.com. WiFi. 40 rooms.* On the outskirts of town with easy access from Clermont, Cahors and Bordeaux. Pastel shades decorate the contemporary dining room, where the focus is on simple local cuisine. Spacious, functional bedrooms with good soundproofing.

🍴🍽🍽🍽 **La Truffe Noire** – *22 blvd Anatole-France.* ☎*05 55 92 45 00. www.la-truffe-noire.com. WiFi. 27 rooms.* The Black Truffle occupies a 19C regional-style house on the edge of the old town. A welcoming lounge with an imposing fireplace and attractive guestrooms furnished with a contemporary feel. The pleasant dining room and shaded terrace are the setting for Corrèze specialities, including the trademark truffle.

㎡/ EAT

🍽 **La Toupine** – *11 r. Jean-Labrunie.* ☎*05 55 23 71 58. Reservation required.* A popular local haunt in the old town serving value-for-money cuisine.

🍽🍽 **Chez Francis** – *61 av. de Paris.* ☎*05 55 74 41 72. Reservation required.* An authentic Parisian bistro in the centre of town. Simple but tasty traditional cuisine.

MARKETS

Marché Brassens – *Pl. du 14-Juillet. Open Tue & Sat, 8am–12.30pm.* This wonderful covered market, named after George Brassens, who mentioned it in a well-

known song, sells a huge range of local products.

Duck and goose fairs – These typical markets are held four times a year between Dec and Feb.

SHOPPING

Distillerie Denoix – *9 bd du Mar.-Lyautey.* ☎*05 55 74 34 27. www.denoix.com.* Founded in 1839, this distillery produces and markets Le Suprême de Noix walnut liqueur and Le Quinquinoix, an aperitif also made of walnuts. Violette de Brive mustard is also sold here.

La Boutique CA Brive – Corrèze – *21 r. Toulzac.* ☎*05 55 17 15 32. www.cabrive-boutique.com.* The official shop for CA Brive, the well-known rugby club who won the European Championship in 1997 and were finalists for the European Cup in 1998. The graphic black-and-white logo is a Brive classic.

Domaine de Lintillac – *1 Lintillac, Ussac.* ☎*05 55 87 65 24.* This small-scale cannery offers typically southwestern products from its on-site farm: foie gras, rillettes, preserved duck, cassoulet and other delights. The owner also runs a chain of restaurants in Paris, Lille and Brussels.

Poterie des Grès Rouges – *Av. du Quercy, Meyssac.* ☎*05 55 84 07 57. www.poterie-meyssac.com.* The last guardian of a thousand-year-old tradition, this craftsman offers a visit to his workshop. Tableware and useful or decorative objects are manufactured with the local red clay. The shop offers a large selection of objects crafted here.

Aubazine★

The village of Aubazine and its Cistercian abbey, formerly known as Obazine, are pleasantly situated between the River Corrèze and River Coiroux, on a promontory set back from the main road.

A BIT OF HISTORY

At the beginning of the 12C, a group of men and women united by a common desire to lead a life of fasting and prayer, gathered together in the forest of Aubazine to join the hermit St Ste-

▶ **Population:** 874.
⚲ **Michelin Map:** 329: L-4.
🇮 **Info:** Le Bourg, Aubazine. ☎05 55 25 79 93. www.pays-aubazine-beynat.fr/en.
▶ **Location:** 17km/11.25mi SW of Tulle via D 1089/D 130.
◈ **Don't Miss:** The 12C Abbaye d'Aubazine, a superb example of a Cistercian abbey.
◷ **Timing:** 1hr.

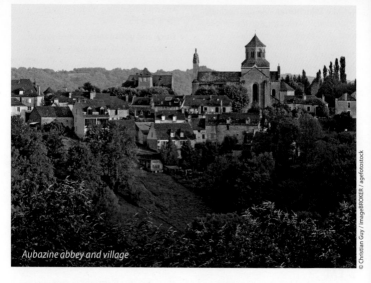
Aubazine abbey and village

© Christian Guy / imageBROKER / agefotostock

phen. Having adopted the rule of St Benedict, this small community built a monastery at Aubazine, and then a convent, just 600m away in the Coiroux valley. In 1147, both communities were admitted into the Cistercian Order and this dual monastery was preserved until the Revolution. The founder had decreed that the women take vows of complete enclosure, so they were totally dependent, both spiritually and materially, on the monastery. This no doubt gave rise to the local joke that anyone with a daughter at Coiroux gained a son-in-law at Aubazine.

ABBEY★

The abbey was built in the second half of the 12C and dedicated to the Blessed Virgin. In the 18C it was truncated, losing six of its nine bays, so it is easy to imagine how large the original was.

Belltower★ – The belltower crowning the transept crossing is of a very original design; the transition from a square shape to an octagonal one is a technical achievement unique to that time.

Interior – The central nave has a barrel vault and the huge square of the transept is crowned with an elegant dome. The stained-glass windows in grisaille are the only ones to have been permitted in a Cistercian church.

Furnishings★ – In the south arm of the transept you'll find the remarkable limestone **tomb of St Stephen★★** made between 1250 and 1260. The face of the recumbent figure was disfigured by the faithful flock, who believed that the dust they obtained by scraping at the stone held miraculous powers. The 12C liturgical cupboard was made from oak beams; its sides are decorated with blind arcades. The **Coiroux Entombment** is a piece of polychrome stonework rediscovered in 1895.

Convent Buildings

Contact the tourist office for hours.
℘05 55 25 9 93.
Once part of the men's monastery, the convent buildings are home to a community of Catholic nuns. The visit includes the large fish-breeding pond. The water of the pond is sourced via the impressive 12C **Canal des Moines** (monks' canal).

Convent

600m from Aubazine along the road to Palazinges.
The church walls are all that remain of the convent, which was abandoned in 1791. However, recent excavation work has unearthed the irrigation system for drinking water and the arched doorway

by which the monks and nuns communicated. This is designed like a lock chamber; one of the communities had the key to the outside door and the other the key to the inside door.

EXCURSIONS
Le Calvaire
1km/0.6mi E via D 48 towards Le Chastang. At Le Saut-de-la-Bergère, take a left, park and continue on foot.
Go up to the cross topped by a statue of St Étienne for a remarkable view, especially when the sun is setting over the village.

Puy de Pauliat
3km/1.86mi E on D 48 towards Le Chastang. At Puy de Pauliat, park and continue on foot following the signposts.
From here you can access the **orientation panel** (alt. 520m); the **cromlech**, a curious Neolithic alignment of stones around a central block; and the **Ermitage**, from where you'll get a good view of the area and of the three pillars of the **dolmen** in pink gneiss.

ADDRESSES

🏨 STAY
🛏 **Campéole Le Coirous** – *Parc Touristique du Coiroux, 5km/3.10mi E via D 48, rte du Chastang, along a lake, within a leisure park.* ℘05 55 27 21 96. *www.camping-coiroux.com.* ♿. *166 pitches.* This campsite is sure to please, with its large, verdant pitches and its tranquillity. The entire campsite is well-kept and includes various equipment and activities for the whole family, including a new heated swimming pool.

🛏 **Village Vacances Révéa Les Hameaux du Perrier** – *Le Perrier, Beynat.* ℘05 55 84 34 48. *www.chalets-en-france.com.* 🏠. With a whopping 98 brand new chalets, this new holiday village was built on a large scale. Each cottage includes a covered terrace, a shower room, two bedrooms and a fully-equipped kitchen. On-site, you'll find two swimming pools, including one that is covered and heated, as well as two large games rooms.

🛏🛏 **La Tour** – *Place de l'Église, 19190 Aubazine.* ℘05 55 25 71 17. *19 rooms.* This hotel, standing opposite the abbey, consists of two attractive houses. The oldest is flanked by a tower. Its traditional bedrooms are decorated with colourful wallpaper. The restaurant specialises in regional cuisine served in rustic-style rooms adorned with copper and pewter pots. The hotel bar is popular with locals.

🛏🛏 **Chambres d'hôte La Lupronne** – *Le Mons, D 1, Cornil. 8km/4.9mi NE on D 1089 and D 1.* ℘05 55 27 26 47. *http://lalupronne.free.fr.* 🅿 🏠. *5 rooms.* This Napoleonic house was designed to be self-sufficient. It has retained its well, chestnut drying shed and all its annexes. Thoughtful renovation has restored the original beauty to the space. The wood fire is occasionally used for rustic *table d'hôte* meals.

🍴 EAT
🛏🛏 **Hôtel-Restaurant St-Étienne** – *Pl. de l'Église.* ℘05 55 25 71 01. *www.les aintetienne.com. 52 rooms.* You can't miss this pretty stone building with its tower overlooking the village square. The large dining room is furnished with antiques and two imposing fireplaces, offering a choice place to enjoy your meal, unless you prefer the terrace. Standard, clean, comfortable rooms.

LEISURE ACTIVITIES
Parc du Coiroux – *4km/2.5mi E of Aubazine along the D 48.* ℘05 55 27 25 66. *www.golf-coiroux.com.* This 180ha/445-acre park offers a broad range of activities, including swimming in the lake, archery, tennis, volleyball, horse-riding and golf. The park also features a campsite and restaurant.

Argentat★

The name of the town has evolved from the Celtic *argentoratum*, meaning "the passage of the river". In the 17C and 18C, Argentat enjoyed great prosperity as a result of the transport of wood along the Dordogne by traditional, flat-bottomed *"gabarres"* to Bergerac, where it was used in the barrel-making industry. Many of the elegant buildings in the centre of town and along the river bank, with their turrets and pepperpot towers, date from this period.

▶ **Population:** 3 042.
Michelin Map: 329: M-5.
Info: Place de Maïa. ☏05 55 28 16 05. www.tourisme-argentat.com.
▷ **Location:** 44km/27.5mi E of Brive via the D 941. If possible, try to approach Argentat on N 120 from the south for a great view of the town.
Don't Miss: The view of the town from the bridge carrying D 1120 over the river.
🕐 **Timing:** Allow at least 1hr to explore the town.
Kids: Older children will enjoy canoeing on the river and all ages will appreciate a trip on a *gabarre* boat.

☙ WALKING TOUR

Built in 1844, the riverside embankment of **quai Lestourgie** along the Dordogne is lined with fine houses crowned with turrets, gables and pepperpot towers. In olden days, it was here that the typical *gabares* were moored to load up their precious cargo. Walk onto the **bridge** for a pleasant view of the town, with its impressive houses fronted by wooden balconies jutting out over the river. Argentat's busy main street divides the town into two distinct districts. Note the unusual mix of **lauze** (roughly hewn slabs of limestone) and slate roofs. Beyond the bridge, continue along the riverside promenade as far as **rue des Contamines**, passing typical narrow streets along the way. Continue towards the centre via **place Delmas**, surrounded by old houses such as the Manoir de l'Eyrial and the Maison Filliol. From the church of **St-Pierre**, head down the steps towards **rue Ste-Claire.** Cross rue Henri IV to **rue des Goudous**, where the construction date on several impressive houses has been chiselled

Argentat

© Mick Rock / Cephas / Photononstop

into the lintels. Beyond the **Chapelle Jeanne d'Arc**, rue Ledamp returns to the car park.

👥🧍 **Maison du Patrimoine** – *Av. Gilbert-Dillange.* 🕐*Open Jul–Aug 10am–noon, 3–6pm (Tue 3–6pm); Jun and Sept daily except Tue 10am–noon, 3–6pm.* 📞*05 55 28 06 16. www.argentat.fr.* This little exhibition is a good introduction to the town of Argentat, presenting its history and local archaeological sites (Gallo-Roman villa of Longour, Gallic village of Le Puy-du-Tour).

Artefacts, a scale model of the Puy-du-Tour *oppidum* and well-illustrated panels explain the evolution of the site: its strategic position during Antiquity, its fortified nature during the Middle Ages, the end of its independence when the viscounty was purchased by Louis XV, its religious conflicts and more. A documentary explores the history of the flat-bottomed *gabares* and their crews, called *courpets* in Argentat.

🚗 DRIVING TOURS

6 LA XAINTRIE★ AND THE DORDOGNE VALLEY
Round trip of 55km/34mi. Allow half a day. See route 6 on region map p315.

The name **Xaintrie** is a corruption of Saint-Trie. It consists of a granite plateau deeply cut by the gorges of the Dordogne, the Maronne and the Cère, where moorland and scrubland alternate with pine and silver birch woods. There is a marked contrast between the White Xaintrie in the north (St-Privat) and the Black Xaintrie in the south (Mercœur).

▷ Leave Argentat S towards St-Privat then turn left onto D 129.

Barrage d'Argentat
This is one of five dams with a hydroelectric power station on the Upper Dordogne. It was built 2km/1.2mi upstream from Argentat to maximise the use of the waters from the Le Chastang reservoir. It rises to a maximum height of 35m, with a crest spanning 190m. Four sluices can empty 4 000m^3/880 000 gallons per second. This power station has five hollow piles, three of which are equipped with hydroelectric generators.

🚶 Near the church of **St-Martial-Entraygues** on the west bank of the Dordogne, a trail leads to the promontory of the **Roc Castel**, with its viewpoint over the river and dam.

Chapelle de Glény
The chapel, all that remains of the former church, has an attractive chevet and a bell-gable (a high wall pierced with openings).

Barrage du Chastang★
🚶 Less than 1.6km/1mi beyond the dam, a narrow winding path is signposted off to the right of the D 29. It leads to a belvedere on the left bank of the Dordogne, from where there is an impressive view of the dam and reservoir. The power station at this dam is the largest producer of electricity in the whole valley.

Servières-le-Château
This former stronghold, owned in turn by the Turenne and Noailles families, enjoys a picturesque **setting★** overlooking the deep gorges of the Glane. The stone *lauze* roofs of the village are encircled by jagged rocks and pine trees.

▷ Head north out of Servières along D 75.

👥🧍 Lac de Feyt
Stop on the north side of the Barrage de la Glane to admire the splendid view of this 65ha/161-acre lake, a popular outdoor leisure and sailing centre.

▷ Continue along D 75 towards Darazac.

Darazac
A pretty village of stone houses.

▷ Continue along the D 13 towards Bassignac-le-Haut.

Bassignac-le-Haut

Near the church stands a 16C limestone wayside cross; the four sides of the shaft are carved with scenes from Jesus' life. From the **belvedere★** situated to the north of the village (D 13), you can appreciate a meander of the Dordogne. The road to Chapeloune offers other fine views.

Pont de Chambon

This is the ideal place for a break, particularly for anglers; boat trips aboard a traditional *gabarre* are available.

▷ Continue along D 13 on the opposite bank of the river.

La Chapeloune

Two walks offering fine views start nearby. On a 30min round-trip heading south from D 13, there is a **viewing table**. A forest road leads down to a clearing affording a splendid view of the Chastang reservoir and the Cantal mountain range.

Grotte des Maquisards

🚶 *1hr 30min round-trip heading N from the parking area (D 13).*
Enjoy this typical scrubland and the fine view. ⊘*Beware, the last 200m to the cave are only suitable for experienced walkers.*

St-Merd-de-Lapleau

Note the shape of the belfry-porch of the church with its row of four bays, each fitted with a bell.

▷ Continue along the road running alongside the church.

Étang des Ramandes★

🚶 The ideal place for relaxing or for a walk (*2hr*) through the 260ha/642-acre pine and spruce forest.

▷ Return to Bassignac-le-Haut. Take the D 72 towards Auriac.

Auriac

The church of this charming village contains a 17C carved-wood crozier.

▷ Leave Auriac E on D 65 towards Spontour. At the intersection, turn right on D 678 towards Barrage de l'Aigle. You are entering the Cantal.

Aynes

The granite houses with their slate roofs are grouped round the chapel.
The road, which is now laid out as a corniche road, provides views from different angles of the L'Aigle Dam.

Barrage de l'Aigle★★

The dam is impressively large and its design is bold. Two ski-jump flood control gates can let 4 000m³/880 000gal through per second.

Belvédère

Park opposite Barrage de L'Aigle and continue on foot up D 16 to the overlook built below the dam (the path lies between two road tunnels).
From the overlook there is a good **view★** of the entire dam and the valley below it.

▷ Retrace your steps and drive past Aynes. Turn right on D 678 towards Pleaux and Spontour, then turn left on D 166 towards Auriac. Once you arrive in Auriac, follow D 65 towards St Privat and then take D 111.

🏠👥 St-Julien-aux-Bois

Le Puy-d'Arrel. 🕐*Jul–Aug 10am–7pm; Easter to Sept daily except Sat 2–6pm.* 🗣*Guided tours by arrangement.* ⊜€5.50 (children under 12, €3). 📞05 55 28 31 30.
This unique village, hidden away in the forest, invites you to discover the life of 13C–14C peasants. Les **Fermes du Moyen Âge en Xaintrie** is a reproduction of old-fashioned *boria* (farms) and a *mas* (village) with thatch-roofed or chestnut-shingled houses surrounded by gardens. Follow along the little stone walls and enter the houses to read the panels which explain the hard life and habitat of these people, who were bound to their lords. In the gardens, you'll see the types of plants they cultivated (grapes, hemp, medicinal herbs,

broad beans, and more) and the types of farm animals they raised (black pigs, sheep, goats, cows and poultry). An excellent illustration of medieval times in France.

▷ Follow D 980 W.

St-Privat
The 13C and 16C church is crowned by an imposing square tower.

▷ Leave St-Privat S on D 13.

Tours de Merle★★
🕓 Jul–Aug 10am–7pm; Apr–Jun 2–6pm; call for other periods. ✎€6 (children under 6, €3.50).
✆05 55 28 22 31.
A narrow, stony path offers access to the **citadel** on its northern side. The citadel is a string of seven castles placed north to south, forming more or less dismantled sets of 12–14C dungeons, towers and central buildings along various levels. A ghostly atmosphere hangs over the impressive façades, fireplaces suspended in mid-air and staircases leading nowhere (some buildings are off-limits for security reasons). As you discover these ruins, note the vestiges of the 13C **seigneurial chapel** dedicated to St Léger, the ruins of the 14C castle of Hugues de Merle, and the 13C **dungeon** that belonged to his brother Fulcon, which includes a cellar, kitchen, bedchamber, spiral staircase and dovecote. To the south are two interesting 13C and 14C **square towers** which belonged to the lords of Carbonnières and Pesteils. As you climb the ever-narrowing staircase in the second tower, which features a lovely barrel-vaulted room, enjoy the superb **view★** over the Upper Auvergne to the east and the Limousin to the northwest.
👥 Take time to discover the **park**, a pleasant 10ha/25-acre area around the fortress crossed by the Maronne. You'll see the **archaeological farm**, a reconstruction of a typical 14C peasant's habitat with a thatched roof stable. Farther down, along the river, you'll see the pretty **medieval gardens**, including

fruits, vegetables, medicinal plants and plants used for dyeing. You'll also see the vestiges of a **medieval toll bridge**, rebuilt in 1735 and washed away in a flood five years later. Higher up the river, you'll find the ruins of a 14C mill.

▷ Leave D 13 and drive towards St-Bonnet-les-Tours.

Vallée de la Maronne
The D 136 climbs through a wooded landscape to a plateau with fine views of the Tours de Merle. The road passes through St-Bonnet-les-Tours, before skirting the foot of the **Château du Rieux** (13C and 16C).

▷ Beyond Sexcles, N 120 follows the east bank of the Maronne to Argentat.

⑦ VALLÉE DE LA SOUVIGNE★
Round-trip of 45km/28mi. Allow 3hr. See route 7 on region map p315.

A varied drive along the Souvigne valley where you'll see a church, a calvary and a pretty view before returning to Argentat.

▷ Head NW out of Argentat along the N 120 towards Tulle.

The road climbs through the wooded hills of the Souvigne valley.

Église de St-Chamant
The doorway of this church, fronted by a belfry-porch and wooden gallery, is particularly interesting. Note the doorway capitals and the tympanum.

▷ Drive N out of St-Chamant along D 11 to St-Bonnet-Elvert, then turn left towards Forgès.

Calvaire d'Espargilière
🚶 *15min round-trip on foot.*
The view from the calvary extends over meadows to the wooded hillsides of the surrounding valleys.

🚗

● Cross N 120 to reach the west bank of the Souvigne. In Grandchamp, turn onto D 113E.

Cascades de Murel★

🚶 Walk along the banks of the crystal-clear Valeine to reach this waterfall, situated in a delightful setting of greenery and rocks.

● Return to Grandchamp. Turn left onto D 113, which flanks the hillside and provides fine views of the Souvigne valley. Continue to Albussac along D 87 before turning right on D 176 towards Sirieix.

Roche de Vic★

🚶 15min walk. Alt. 636m.
This bare-flanked hill of granite blocks is crowned by a small chapel and a statue of the Virgin Mary. The **view★** from here encompasses the Lower Limousin (viewing table). The hills roll northward as far as the Massif des Monédières, and south to the Causse de Quercy.

● Follow D 940 as far as La Grafouillère, then turn left onto D 169 leading back to Argentat.

ADDRESSES

🏠 STAY

⊝ **Camping Le Gibanel** – 4.5/2.8mi NE of Argentat on D 18 towards Égletons. ☎05 55 28 10 11. www.camping-gibanel.com. 250 pitches and mobile homes; restaurant and pizzeria. One of the most pleasant campsites in France, located along the banks of the Dordogne and shaded by large trees on the grounds of the Château de Gibanel. Excellent facilities, including two swimming pools, sports activities, evening entertainment and more.

⊝⊝ **Hôtel Fouillade** – 11 pl. Gambetta. ☎05 55 28 10 17. www.fouillade.com. 15 rooms. This peaceful hotel invites you to relax in its purpose-built, modern rooms featuring comfortable beds. Traditional dishes with a regional accent are served under the beams of the rustic dining room or on the front terrace.

⊝⊝ **Hôtel Le Sablier du Temps** – 13 r. J-Vachal. ☎05 55 28 94 90. www.sablier-du-temps.com. ▣. 24 rooms. A tree-lined garden with a swimming pool surrounds this hotel near the centre of town. The modern rooms are personalised and very well-kept. The local cuisine is served in a large dining room-veranda opening onto a terrace.

🍴/EAT

⊝⊝ **St-Jacques** – ☎05 55 28 89 87. The chef here prepares tasty, contemporary dishes while his charming spouse serves you. The dining room is comfortable and refined, with a veranda and a shady terrace.

⊝⊝ **Auberge des Gabarriers** – 15 quai Lestourgie. ☎05 55 28 05 87. This inn is located in a pretty 16C house along the banks of the Dordogne. The dining room is as rustic as you please; meats are grilled on a spit. A lime tree shades the riverside terrace. The charming rooms also look out over the river.

⊝⊝ **La Vieille Auberge** – 5km/3.1mi NW of Les Tours de Merle via D 111. ☎05 55 28 20 60. ▣. A few miles from the medieval site, this charming turn-of-the-century country inn is an enjoyable place to stay, with its greenery and swimming pool. Simple décor and regional cooking, where local dishes such as cabécou, duck breast, and preserved duck meet Auvergne-based specialities such as pounti.

⊝⊝ **Les Voyageurs** – St-Martin-la-Méanne. ☎05 55 29 11 53. A charming stone inn where time stops to give you time to appreciate the local flavours served in this rustic interior or, in the summer, in the garden alongside a lake (fishing).

Bort-les-Orgues

The town of Bort, on a lovely site in the Dordogne valley, is known for its huge dam *(barrage)* and for the cliffs rising above it.

The cliffs are known as *les orgues* because the rock formation, seen from below, resembles the pipes of a massive organ.

TOWN
Church
Boulevard de la Nation.

Dating from the 12C–15C, the plain architecture provides a frame for a 15C statue of St Anne, modern stained-glass windows and a bronze Christ sculpted by Chavignier. Next door, the former priory was built in the 17C.

Cascade du Saut de la Saule
2.5km/1.5mi SE, then 30min round-trip on foot. Take the road that climbs towards the Institut Médico-pédagogique, continue along the alleyway crossing the Rhue then turn left and follow the river.

The path reaches a small gorge and then continues to some rocks towering above the Saut de la Saule where the River Rhue flows over a 5–6m rocky shelf.

- **Population:** 2 988.
- **Michelin Map:** 329: Q-3.
- **Info:** Pl. Marmontel, Bort-les-Orgues. ℘05 55 96 02 49. www.bort-artense.com.
- **Location:** 120km/75mi E of Brive via A 20/A 89/D 879.
- **Don't Miss:** The dam or the cliffs *(orgues)*.
- **Timing:** Allow 2hr to visit Les Orgues de Bort and 1 day to explore this part of the Dordogne valley.
- **Kids:** The Insects of the World exhibition in Ydes.

Barrage de Bort (Bort Dam)★
Boat trips Jul–Aug 11.15am, 2pm, 2.30pm, 3.15pm, 4pm, 5pm; May, Jun and Sept 2.30pm, 3pm, 4pm; Apr and Oct by prior arrangement. Minimum 15 people per boat. €9 (children aged 5–14, €6; children 3 and 4, €4.50). ℘05 55 46 21 67. www.vedettespanoramiques.fr There are car parks on either side of the dam, on the D 979 and D 922.

From the road across the top of the dam (390m long), the upstream view encompasses the vast reservoir, criss-crossed by the wakes of **pleasure cruisers**. The reservoir has a capacity of 477m^3/16 845 cubic ft and is 21km/13.1mi long.

Cliffs, Bort-les-Orgues

© A. Demotes / Photononstop / Tips Images

🚗 DRIVING TOURS

8 LES ORGUES DE BORT★

Round-trip of 15km/9mi. Allow 2hr.
See route 8 on region map p315.

This tour takes in the cliffs at close quarters and also affords sweeping views of the Dordogne valley and the mountains of Cantal.

▶ Leave Bort along D 127 S near the cemetery.

The view to the left encompasses the Rhue valley.

▶ Just beyond the last houses in Chantery, take a stairway to the right leading directly to the stone columns. Follow the signs to the Grottes des Orgues and the Site d'Escalade des Orgues.

The 80–100m high organ pipes, spread over a distance of 2km/1.2mi, are composed primarily of phonolite rock, known also as clinkstone or soundstone.

▶ Go back to the D 127, continue for 2km/1mi until the right turn-off marked Point de Vue des Orgues, and drive a short distance to the car park and picnic area on the plateau (alt. 769m). From the parking area, there is a 15min round-trip walk to the scenic overlook.

🚶 From here you'll get a wide **panoramic view★★** over the Dordogne valley, the Cantal region and the Mont Dore range. To the southwest, Lake Madic lies on the former course of the Dordogne.

▶ Retrace your steps and drive along the D 127 for 500m. A path on the left climbs to a rocky outcrop (15min round-trip on foot).

The view includes the Puy de Sancy, the Cantal mountains, the Dordogne river and its tributaries, the Monédières range and the Plateau de Mille Vaches.

From the D 979, as you travel towards Bort, keep an eye out for the pretty **Pierefitte Château** on the right, as well as more views of the lake and dam.

🚴 ALONG THE DORDOGNE

Round-trip of 95km/59mi. Allow 1 day.
See route 9 on region map p315.

Here the Dordogne used to flow through narrow gorges. The dams and reservoir lakes now succeed one another down the valley, forming a gigantic water stairway 100km/60mi long. They have altered the appearance of the countryside, but often fit remarkably well into the beautiful valley settings.

This tour offers a view of the dam and lake and also the Dordogne and Diège gorges from the calvary at St. Nazaire. It includes a visit to the resort of Neuvic.

▶ Leave Bort-les-Orgues on D 922 heading N then turn left onto D 979.

Belvédère des Aubazines

This viewpoint on the right side of D 979 (*picnic area*) offers a view of the dam and its 1 400ha/3 460-acre lake.

▶ Continue along D 979 and turn left onto D 127 2km/1.2mi farther on.

St-Nazaire Site★★

30min round-trip on foot.
🚶 After parking the car, bear right along the ridge on the slope and later follow a path to the Calvary, lined with the Stations of the Cross. You'll pass a statue of St Nazarius on your way to the tip of the promontory from where there is a fine view of the Dordogne and Diège gorges.

▶ Drive to St-Julien-près-Bort and continue along D 127.

The road crosses the Diège, climbs wooded slopes and provides views of the river as far as Roche-les-Peyroux.

▶ After Liginiac take D 42E on your left.

View of the Dordogne from St-Nazaire Site

©Christian Guy/hemis.fr

Belvédère de Marèges
The road drops down to the **Marèges Dam** in a series of hairpin bends. 500m farther on, a belvedere affords a view of the dam and its lake hemmed in by steep banks forming a picturesque wild setting.

▶ The D 42 leads to D 20. 2km/1.2mi farther on, turn right onto D 183 towards Plage de Liginiac.

Two beaches line the shores of Triouzoune lake. The Neuvic d'Ussel dam to the south contains this impressive reservoir covering 410ha/1 013 acres, ideal for water sports enthusiasts.

Puy de Manzagol
Alt. 698m.
From the summit (*viewing table*) there is a vast panorama of the Triouzoune lake and the Massif Central.

▶ D 183 and then D 982 on the left skirt the beautiful lake.

Neuvic
This attractive resort built on the hillside has a beach with a sailing school and a centre for water skiing. Its old narrow streets feature granite houses, fortified gate and a church with a characteristic belfry-porch.

Musée de la Résistance Henri-Queuille
🕐 *Open 10am–noon, 2–5.30pm: Jul–Aug daily; rest of year Mon–Fri.* ✎*No charge.* 📞*05 55 46 30 60. www.musee-henriqueuille.com.*
This museum is dedicated to the Resistance movement in Corrèze where, in 1944, fierce fighting prepared the way for the liberation of the region.

Maison de l'Eau et de la Pêche
Next to the church. 🕐*Open Jun–Sept by prior arrangement. Call for times.* 📞*05 55 95 06 76.*
This information centre presents an exhibition devoted to fishing methods, water treatment and fish species that are commonly found in the local rivers. Excursions are organised on the themes of fishing and nature.

▶ Drive S out of Neuvic along D 982 towards Mauriac.

Pont de St-Projet
This suspension bridge provides a good view of the reservoir.

▶ Turn back and follow D 168.

Route des Ajustants★
The Ajustants tourist road follows the Dordogne valley with its rock-strewn

The Dordogne from Belvédère de Gratte-Bruyère

wooded slopes, providing beautiful views of the L'Aigle reservoir.

Belvédère de Gratte-Bruyère★

This is a magnificent viewpoint (*picnic area*) from which to see the Sumène flowing into the Dordogne.

▶ Shortly before Sérandon, turn right onto D 20E1.

Ydes

This small village lies on the banks of the Sumène, in an area dotted with basalt peaks. The 12C church is typical of the Upper Auvergne Romanesque style; the east end is decorated with carved modillions representing lively young faces.

Insects of the World exhibition

Entrance behind the town hall. ᰔ. ⏲*Open Jul–Aug, daily 2–7pm.* ⚭€3. ℘*04 71 40 82 51. www.ydes.fr.* ᰁᰁ This exhibition is mainly devoted to butterflies and moths. The sizes and colours of some of the specimens on display are remarkable.

▶ Return to D 15 then bear left onto D 130.

Madic

This attractive village is the starting point of a pleasant walk round the lake of the same name.

▶ D 30 and D 922 lead back to Bort-les-Orgues.

ADDRESSES

🛌 STAY

⚭⚭ **La Siauve** – *R. du Camping, Lanobre. 3km/1.8mi SW on D 922, Bort-les-Orgues road and than a small road to the right, 200m from the lake (direct access).* ℘*04 71 40 31 85.* ᰔ. *220 pitches.* This lakeside campsite offers you a natural camping experience in a beautiful setting. Enjoy the lakeshore and fishing, rambling and biking to discover the area. Chalets and huts for hire.

⚭⚭ **Central Hôtel** – *65 av. de la Gare.* ℘*05 55 96 81 05. www.centralhotelbort.com.* ᰔᐃ. *21 rooms.* The rooms of this hotel in the centre of town are mostly renovated and feature mod cons and good soundproofing. You'll enjoy the rooms in the annex that look out over the Dordogne. Serving an excellent selection of local dishes at affordable prices.

ACTIVITIES

Site d'Initation à l'Escalade –

℘*05 55 96 02 49.* A large number of exterior and interior climbing walls are set up along the Bort-les-Orgues plateau. You can even climb impressive phonolite columns that are 80–100m high. Information at the tourist office of Bort-les-Orgues.

Beaches – *Neuvic.* There are two

beaches on the shores of Lac de Triouzoune: Liginiac in the east and Neuvic in the west. In the south, the Barrage de Neuvic-d'Ussel is a dam offering a vast 410ha/1013-acre reservoir ideal for boating.

From the contemporary art and landscape centre on the island on the Lac de Vassivière to the "largest tapestry in the world" made in Felletin and hanging in Coventry cathedral, what stands out in this rural area is the community passion for arts and crafts. Its status as a natural regional park also indicates that wildlife here is protected and ecology encouraged to thrive alongside more artistic growth. Local heritage preservation is also a priority, and there are interesting remains from the past to be visited, such as the Gallo-Roman remains scattered in a lush valley near Cars.

A Passion for Arts and Crafts

Ussel, the largest town in this rural area, features a museum that explores old-fashioned crafts. In Meymac, a contemporary art centre has been set up in the unusual abbey-church. Work by figurative artist Paul Rebeyrolle is on show in the village of Eymoutiers. Felletin, the village that claims to have made the largest tapestry in the world, offers various ways to discover its local handicraft, as well as diamond cutting. But perhaps the most prestigious of all is the contemporary art and landscape centre located on the island of Lac Vassivière, which is completed by a beautiful sculpture garden.

Natural Discovery

This natural regional park offers environments such as the peat bogs of Longéroux and the arboretum of St-Setiers for your leisurely exploration. Kids will enjoy the Espace Minéralogique in Eymoutiers, the Cité des Insectes in Chaud and the Maison de l'Arbre in Chambaret.

Highlights

1 Charming **Meymac** old town and abbey (p345)
2 Rare flora and fauna at the **Tourbière du Longéroux** (p346)
3 Remote, evocative **Gallo-Roman remains at Cars** (p347)
4 **Lac de Vassivière**, where art meets nature (p354)
5 Tapestry tours in **Felletin** (p356)

The Ruins of the Past

In addition to the exploration of history through craftsmanship, you can also visit a few historic sites such as the Gallo-Roman remains at Cars, the ruins of Ventadour or the fascinating village of Clédat, a village typical of the Plateau de Millevaches, which is undergoing restoration. There are also several medieval sites in the area around Felletin.

Parc Naturel Régional du Plateau du Millevaches outside Meymac

© Christian Guy / hemis.fr

Map content:

A   B

D 7

Lac de la
Vaud Gelade

St-Marc-à-Loubaud

D 50

1

Mont-Larron
△ 624

D 16

Mont-Larron

Pont de Sénouei

Fleix

D 5

Route circumlacustre

D 16

Martineix

D 233

Lac de
Vassivière

Mᵒⁿ des chevalier de Pallie

Peyrat-le-Château

D 13

Gentioux-Pigerolles

D 8

Bujaleuf

Maulde

Taurion

D 14

D 940

Centre international d'art et du paysage

Le Rat

Vienne

D 43

D 979

Eymoutiers

Négarioux

D 992

Plateau

HAUTE-

D 940

D 814

Chaud

Tarnac

D 160

VIENNE

D 160

2

PARC   NATUREL

D 97

RÉGIONA

7

Mont Gargan
731

D 12

D 979

D 164

D 78

Vestiges gallo-romains des Ca

Chamberet

Lac de Viam

Bugeat

D 16

Lac des
Bariousses

Monceaux-la-Virole

Rocher des Folles

Treignac

EN   LIMOUSIN

CORRÈZE

D 16

Puy
Pantout
△ 770

†Lestards

D 940

Puy Messou
△ 907

Clédat

Vézère

Les Monédières

824

Col des Géants

Corrèze

Col du Bos
809

D 128

908

Suc-au-May

Chaumeil

12

Cirque de Freysselines

La croix-sous-l'Arbre

Puy de Sarran
† 820

Le Tourondel

Sarran

D 26

D 142

Égleto

3

N

Corrèze

† N.-D. du
Pont du Salut

D 1098

Suc-au-May ★★ Recommended

Meymac ★ Interesting

Ussel Worth seeing

⬅ Driving tour with departure point

Border and area of coverage

TULLE, BRIVE-LA-GAILLARDE

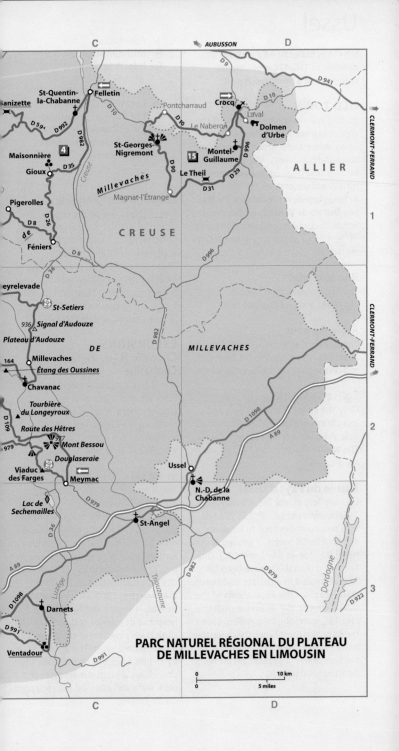

AUBUSSON

St-Quentin-la-Chabanne
Felletin
Pontcharraud
Le Naberon
Crocq
Laval
Dolmen d'Urbe

St-Georges-Nigremont
Montel-Guillaume
Le Theil

ALLIER

Maisonnière
Gioux
Millevaches
Magnat-l'Étrange

Pigerolles
de
Féniers

CREUSE

eyrelevade

St-Setiers

936 Signal d'Audouze
Plateau d'Audouze

DE

MILLEVACHES

164 Millevaches
Étang des Oussines
Chavanac

Tourbière du Longeyroux
Route des Hêtres
977 Mont Bessou
Douglaseraie
Viaduc des Farges
Meymac

Ussel
N.-D. de la Chabanne

Lac de Sechemailles

St-Angel

Darnets

Ventadour

CLERMONT-FERRAND

CLERMONT-FERRAND

PARC NATUREL RÉGIONAL DU PLATEAU DE MILLEVACHES EN LIMOUSIN

0   10 km
0   5 miles

Ussel

Ussel has maintained a certain
number of 15C–17C monuments,
souvenirs of a prosperous past.

OLD TOWN

Follow rue de la Liberté behind the
church to place Joffre, where a fountain
flows, and wander around the narrow
surrounding streets. Many of the old
houses have been restored; admire the
turrets and decorative doorways.

Behind place de la République, the **Maison Ducale de Ventadour** is an elegant
Renaissance residence built by the dukes
of Ventadour at the end of the 16C to
replace the austere feudal castle.

Rue Michelet

The 17C building at no 18 houses printing works and an exhibition hall.

Aigle Romain

The Roman Eagle monument, carved
in granite, was discovered in the Peuch
mill on the banks of the River Sarsonne.

Église St-Martin

Only the chancel and flat east end of
this church are late 12C. The nave and
side aisles were rebuilt in Gothic style.
The western facade and 19C belltower
are modern.

Musée du Pays d'Ussel

⊙*Open daily except Tue mid-May–Sept
2–6pm.* ⊛*No charge.* ✆*05 55 27 54 69.*
This museum, devoted to local crafts
and traditional trades, is housed in the
Hôtel Bonnot de Bay (*early 18C*). Old-
fashioned workshops have been faithfully recreated to illustrate traditional
crafts. Explore the implements of the
village smithy; the weaver, including a
rare 18C loom; the clog-maker, called
the *galochier*; the milliner; the caner; the
basket-weaver; and the woodworker. On
the floor above, a display case presents
selected local writers.

> ▶ **Population:** 10 245.
> ⚙ **Michelin Map:** 329: O-2.
> 🛈 **Info:** Pl. Voltaire.
> ✆05 55 72 11 50.
> www.ot-ussel.fr.
> ◗ **Location:** 17km/10.5mi
> E of Meymac; 31km/19mi
> NW of Bort-les-Orgues.
> 👪 **Kids:** A discovery booklet
> is available.

Chapelle des Pénitents

The religious life of the region, from
historical context to local processions,
popular devotions and brotherhoods,
is addressed in this exhibition.

There are some remarkable pieces of
local art here: a gilded wooden altar
screen made in 1711; a 1664 painting
by the Cibille brothers, *Pentecoste*; and
several painted wooden statues.

EXCURSIONS

Chapelle N.-D.-de-la-Chabanne

1km/0.6mi S, access by r. Pasteur.
From the esplanade near this pilgrims'
chapel, there is an extensive **view**,
reaching the Plateau des Millevaches
(*northwest*), the Monts Dore (*east*), and
the hills of Cantal (*southeast*).

St-Angel

*9km/5.5mi SW on D 1089. Information
at the Ussel Tourist Office.*
The neatly grouped buildings of this
village on a rocky spur overlooking the
right bank of the Triouzoune include a
fortified church, to which a few buildings of the former priory of St-Michel-des-Anges are attached. The façade of
the **church★**, supported by thick buttresses, is severe and forbidding. The
height of its interior is surprising. The
choir is very elegant in cut stone with
a star-shaped vault. The apse is lit up
by arched windows. Underneath, little
chapels are arranged in recesses of the
thick walls and adorned with sculpted
cul-de-lampes.

Meymac★
and Plateau de Millevaches

Perched on the edge of the Millevaches plateau, Meymac is one of the prettiest villages in Corrèze, with its streets and old houses clustered around the old abbey of St-André. In bygone days, the mountain folk came to town to trade their wool, cheese and chestnuts for products manufactured on the plains. Today, forestry is at the forefront of the local economy: the technical school here trains future foresters. Meymac is also an attractive rustic tourist site.

> ▶ **Population:** 2 526.
> 🕐 **Michelin Map:** 329: N-2.
> 🏠 **Info:** Pl. de l'Hôtel de Ville. 𝄞05 55 95 18 43. www.tourismemeymac.fr.
> ▶ **Location:** 49km/30.5mi NE of Tulle via the D 1089.
> 🕐 **Timing:** Allow half a day for Meymac and a full day to explore Plateau de Millevaches.
> 🖇 **Don't Miss:** The contemporary art centre.

OLD TOWN

The *vielle ville* is a charming place for a stroll. To the left of the church, an early-19C **covered market**, its framework resting on granite pillars, is set in a square formed by the buildings of the Hôtel-Dieu, erected in 1681.

Follow the street up towards the **clock tower**, which once guarded the castle gate, and discover the 15C–16C sculpted doorways and stair towers with pepperpot roofs amongst the granite houses with steeply sloping slate roofs. Past the clock tower, a fountain embellishes a pretty little square.

Abbey-church

In 1085, Archambaud III founded a Benedictine abbey on the site of a church his forefathers had built. The church was under construction in the 12C, and was finished in the 13C after modifications to the initial plans were made. There are some unusual aspects to the plans, such as a deviation of the transept arms and an irregular alignment of the apse and its chapels.

The belfry-porch has a multifoil doorway in the Limousin style with an arch on either side. The porch is adorned with Romanesque capitals carved in the archaic style.

The nave has ogive vaulting and continues into a chancel which is equally wide. Note a 12C **Black Virgin★** on the pillar to the left of the chancel. With the exception of the turban on her head, the statue is typical of Auvergne style in the posture and position of the long, protective hands.

Fondation Marius-Vazeilles

🕐*Open Jul–Aug daily 10am–12pm, 2.30–6.30pm; Apr–Jun and Sept–Oct, daily except Thu, 2.30–6pm.* ✇€4. 𝄞05 55 95 17 05. *www.mariusvazeilles.fr.*

Established in a building beside the abbey, the foundation owns interesting archaeological collections illustrating human settlements and life on the Millevaches Plateau from prehistoric times (stone tools) and the Gallo-Roman period (funerary items, vestiges from habitations) to the Middle Ages.

Centre d'Art Contemporain

🕐*Open Jul–Aug, 10am–1pm, 2–7pm; Sept–Jun, 2–6pm.* 🕐*Closed Mon.* ✇€5. 𝄞05 55 95 23 30. *www.centre-art-contemporain-meymac.com.*

In the southern wing of the old cloisters of the abbey of St-André, this art museum presents spotlights on young artists as well as retrospectives (François Bouillon, 1990, Jesus Rafaël Soto, 1992, Gérard Garouste, 1996) and thematic exhibitions on trends in contemporary art. The monumental sculpture in front of the centre is by Robert Jakobsen.

🚗 DRIVING TOUR

1 PLATEAU DE MILLEVACHES★

98km/61mi round-trip. Allow 1 day.
See route 1 on region map pp342–343
and map opposite.

The "plateau of a thousand cows" or, as some say, a thousand springs, is now the Parc Naturel Regional de Millevaches en Limousin and forms a kind of stepping stone into the Massif Central.

▶ Leave Meymac travelling N along D 36.

Mont Bessou

Along with the Puy Pendu just across the way, this is the highest point on the plateau (977m). These 67ha/165 acres are now a municipal park. An artificial lake offers a shady resting area. A road goes all the way round the mount.

▶ Continue to D 979 and turn towards Bugeat. 3km/1.9mi farther on, turn right onto D 109 towards Celle.

Tourbière du Longéroux★

🚶 The source of the Vézère is located in this 255ha/630-acre conservation area. At Le Longéroux, the average thickness of the peat is 2m. The study of fossilised pollen shows that the bog is 8 000 years old. The heath is home to a well-adapted fauna (lizards, vipers, meadow pipits) and is the favourite hunting ground of the short-toed eagle. The discreet presence of otters is a sure sign of the quality of the area's freshwater supply. Three marked paths offer nature lovers the opportunity of exploring this wild area: *200m round-trip, 5km/3mi round-trip (yellow markings), 20km/12mi round-trip (blue markings).*

▶ Continue to St-Merd-les-Oussines and turn right onto D 164 towards Millevaches.

Étang des Oussines★

🚶 This site is home to otters. A path runs round the 15ha/37-acre lake filled with water from the Vézère River.

▶ Go back to D 164 and turn right 1.5km/0.9mi further on.

Église de Chavanac

The small 13C–14C church houses a stone polychrome statue, known as **la Dansarelle**, said to represent Salomé, the bewitching biblical figure who charmed Herod into bringing her John the Baptist's head on a platter.

▶ Continue along D 36 towards Felletin.

Millevaches

This little village (alt. 912m) sits in the middle of the plateau of the same name, and is indeed characteristic of the region.

▶ Continue along D 36 for 3km/1.9mi.

Plateau d'Audouze

The streams that run down from the western and northern slopes of the Audouze plateau provide the waters for the Vienne river. The streams from the eastern and southern slopes contribute to those for the Diège, a tributary of the Dordogne. The Ardouze Beacon (*Signal d'Ardouze*), which is off-limits because of its military nature, towers over the plateau.

▶ Continue along D 36 then turn right onto D 174.

Arboretum de Saint-Setiers

&🕐 *Open daily Jul–Aug 10am–12pm and 2.30pm–6pm; rest of year by prior arrangement.* ⊗€6 *(children, 6–12, €3).* 📞 *05 55 95 61 75.*
www.parc-arboretum.com.
The owner of a tree nursery has opened his park to the public. Stroll along alleyways lined with a variety of trees to discover more than 100 species, including a Douglas pine planted in 1895 and now more than 50m high. A former greenhouse contains an exhibition on the economical use of wood and offers a detailed study of 24 tree species.

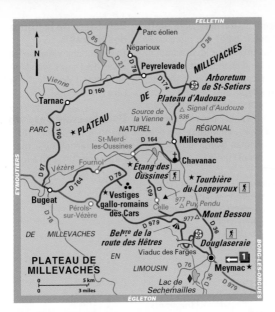

Before leaving, make a detour via the D 174E3: the road starts climbing behind the town hall to a spot above the village which affords a magnificent **panorama★★** of the Massif Central (*picnic area*).

◗ Turn back, then follow D 174E1.

Peyrelevade

This attractive town with its slate-roofed houses welcomes tourists. The church and the Templar's Cross date from the 13C. If you like peat bogs, make a detour (*3km/1.9mi N along D 78*) to Négarioux.

◗ Continue along D 21 for 2km/1.2mi then bear left onto D 160.

Tarnac

The **church** in this village is partly Romanesque and partly Gothic. The northern doorway is adorned with sculptures: St George appears on the right, St Gilles on the left.
In the village, note the two ancient oaks and the lovely Fontaine St Georges.

◗ Continue along D 160.

Bugeat

Near the source of the river, this sizeable town sits between the Millevaches Plateau and the Monédières hills. Gallo-Roman vestiges reveal that this land has been occupied since ancient times despite the rugged climate. Today, the proximity of the forest and rivers make Bugeat a centre for sports and recreation.

◗ Leave Bugeat towards Meymac then turn left onto D 164. In Fournol, turn right onto a minor road which joins D 78 via Les Fargettes.

Gallo-Roman remains at Cars★

In the middle of the wilderness, **Gallo-Roman remains** emerge from the greenery. The ashlar stone blocks now in a pile were once part of a temple and mausoleum.
The **temple** was rectangular, with a semicircular apse; visitors can still see the foundations, the podium and the monumental staircase.
The **mausoleum** was certainly very large, with a funeral urn in its centre.
The impressive **tank** above (weighing about 8t) was a reservoir which supplied water to the building.

The so-called **thermes** were probably not public baths, but more likely a luxurious private residence built in the mid-2C and abandoned at the end of the 3C. Elements found on the site, including a hypocaust heating system (hot air circulated through brick pipes), a mosaic, marble panelling and fragments of painted walls, demonstrate the penetration of Roman civilisation into this hidden corner of France.

▶ Continue on D 78. Shortly before Pérols-sur-Vézère, turn left onto D 979 towards Meymac, drive for 8km/5mi; turn right onto D 979E.

Treignac
and Les Monédières

From the D 16 to the north, there is a fine view of Treignac and its picturesque setting.

LOWER TOWN
The old Gothic **bridge** spanning the fast-flowing Vézère affords a view of the castle ruins towering above the river, the old slate-roofed houses and the church. This slate-roofed square **church** features a hexagonal belltower; inside, note the pointed vaulting on massive pillars and granite dolmen-shaped altar.

UPPER TOWN
This district stretches between place de la République and place du Collège and includes a 15C granite covered market. Note the numerous scallop shells reminding visitors that Treignac was once a stopover for pilgrims on their way to Compostela.

Musée des Arts et Traditions Populaires de la haute et moyenne-Vézère
◷*Open Jul–Aug daily except Tue 2.30–6.30pm.* ⊛€1.50.
✆*05 55 98 15 04.*
Located in the house of Marc Sangnier, founder of the Auberges de Jeunesse

Belvédère de la Route des Hêtres
This panoramic **view★** extends over the vallée des Farges, with Mont Bessou to the east and Meymac and Sechemailles Lake to the south.

Douglaseraie des Farges
🚶*3km/1.9mi NW via D 109.*
A path starting near the Viaduc des Farges runs through a forest (20ha/49 acres) of conifers rising to a height of 40m!

> ▶ **Population:** 1 376.
> ⚕ **Michelin Map:** 329: L-2.
> ℹ **Info:** 1 Pl. de la République.
> ✆05 55 98 15 04.
> www.vezeremonedieres-tourisme.com.
> ▶ **Location:** 37km/23mi NE of Uzerche.
> 👥 **Kids:** Maison de l'Arbre.
> 🙂 **Don't Miss:** Massif des Monédières; Suc-au-May.
> 🕐 **Timing:** 1hr for a leisurely stroll around the village and to the Rocher des Folles.

(youth hostels), this museum contains ethnographic collections.

EXCURSIONS
Rocher des Folles
45min round-trip on foot; the path starts at the SW end of the village.
🚶 A pleasant blazed trail up to the Rocher des Folles – crazy women's rock – affording fine views of Treignac, the gorge and wooded hills of the Vézère.

Lac des Bariousses
4km/2.5mi N along D 940.
The road follows the shoreline of this lake and makes for a picturesque drive. There is a recreation centre amongst the chestnuts, oaks and evergreens.

Chamberet

10km/6.2mi NW along D 16.

On the outskirts of this village along the road to Eymoutiers there is an **arboretum** (*no charge*). Located in the municipal park, it consists of some 100 species of trees surrounding a pond with a playground and picnic area. Next to the arboretum is the **Maison de l'Arbre et de la nature** (*open Jul–Aug 10am–noon, 2–6pm; Jun daily except Tue and Thu 2–6pm; rest of year by prior arrangement. €3.50 (children under 15, €2). 05 55 97 92 14*). This "tree centre" provides comprehensive information about trees, but also about other species and the ecosystems they live in. There are attractive interactive panels for children as well as guided discovery trails and workshops (*for children over 3*).

Barrage de Monceaux-la-Virole

17km/11mi NE along D 940 and D 160.

The first of the dams on the Vézère straddles Lake Viam.

🚗 DRIVING TOUR

② LES MONÉDIÈRES TO ÉGLETONS★

105km/65.2mi round-trip. Allow 1 day. See route 2 on region map pp342–343 and map above.

▶ Leave Treignac travelling SE along D 16 towards Égletons.

Église de Lestards

Note the unusual thatched roof of the Romanesque church.

▶ On leaving the village, turn right onto D 32.

Col des Géants

You'll get glimpses of the **Puy Messou** (907m) to the right and the Suc-au-May to the left.

▶ Turn left onto D 128E.

The road soon emerges from the conifer forest, affording a wide view across the heath of the **Col du Bos**.

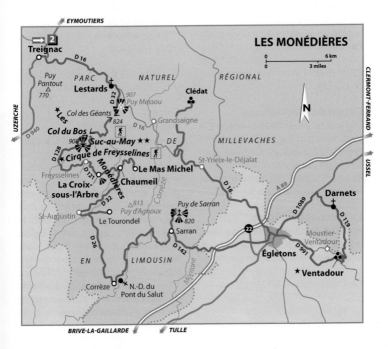

View from Suc-au-May

©Christian Guy/hemis.fr

Suc-au-May★★

▶ Park in the area provided. 15min round-trip on foot. Alt. 908m.

From the viewing table, there is a **view** of the Limousin countryside and the Millevaches Plateau to the northeast. You'll see the Monédières Massif in the foreground and, on a clear day, the mountain ranges of the Auvergne.

▶ Return to Col de Bos and turn left on D 128.

Note to the right the long ridge of the **Puy Pantout** (*770m*).

▶ At the end of the road, turn left onto D 121.

Cirque de Freysselines

This natural amphitheatre surrounds a small hamlet of the same name. Drive east through the village (*D 121*) for a better view of the *cirque*.

▶ A path (*12km/7.5mi round-trip*) runs round the *cirque* towards Suc-au-May.

La Croix-sous-l'Arbre

In a bend, to the right of the road, there is a fine view of Chaumeil (the main village in the area) and Puy de Sarran.

▶ Continue along D 121.

Chaumeil

This attractive village, capital of the Monédières, with its sturdy granite houses roofed with slates or stones, is clustered round the 15C **church** adorned with a fine 16C porch.
Maison des Monédières includes a shop where you can buy local products.

▶ Continue along D 121 and turn right on D 32. Turn left towards Barbazanges.

Le Tourondel

The **bread oven** within its carefully restored shelter with a thatched roof is worth a detour.

▶ Come back to St-Augustin and take D 26 S towards the village of Corrèze.

Corrèze

When you enter Corrèze, you'll see the 17C **chapelle des Pénitents-Blancs** on the right. The vestiges of the fortifications of this medieval village remain, including the **porte Margot**, a gate giving access to a little square surrounded by lovely granite houses with Renaissance facades and slate roofs. In the centre of this square, the 15C **Église St-Martial** features an English-style belltower and, inside, an attractive 18C altarpiece. In a particularly pleasant **site★**, the **chapelle N.-D.-du-Pont-du-Salut** (*600m from the church along rue Talin*) is nestled between the rocks and the Corrèze.

Sarran

♁♁ Musée du président Jacques Chirac – &③*Open Feb–Dec 10am–12.30pm and 1.30–6pm.* ③*Closed 1 Jan and 24–25 Dec.* ⊗€4.50 *(under 23, €3).* ☏*05 55 21 77 77. www.museepresidentjchirac.fr.*
Traditional local building materials (oak, chestnut, granite and slate) are subtly combined with glass and metal in this contemporary museum designed by **Jean-Michel Wilmotte**. Based on a donation of formal gifts received by **Jacques Chirac** during his two terms as president, the collection shows a splendid variety through its 5 000 pieces over 5 000m²/16 400sq ft of space.

Puy de Sarran

A rough, narrow road snakes through this pine forest and climbs to 820m over 1.5km/0.9mi. From there you can take in a beautiful **view★**.

▷ Leave Sarran via D 142.

Égletons

Centre de Découverte du Moyen Âge – ③*Open Jun–mid-Sept daily exc Tue, 10am–noon, 2–6pm; rest of year call for details.* ③*Closed mid-Nov–mid-Feb.* ⊗€3 *(children under 12, €1.50).* ☏*05 55 93 29 66.* The tour begins with a short video about Bernard de Ventadour, 12C troubadour, and continues with an exhibition on life in medieval times. In the summer, enjoy various workshops: illuminations, stained glass and forging.

▷ Follow D 991 SE.

Ruines de Ventadour★

Access by a trail, 30min round-trip on foot. ③*OpenJul–Aug 10am–noon, 2–6pm; mid–end Jun and 1–15 Sept Thu–Sun 10am–noon, 2–6pm.* €3 *(child €2.50).* ☏*05 55 93 04 34. http://chateau-ventadour.com.*
This **medieval fortress** stands proudly on a wind-beaten escarpment with a dizzying **view**. Ventadour seems impenetrable… But it was won by treason and remained in English hands for 13 years of the Hundred Years War. During the

Heather and Bilberries

In late summer the slopes are covered with a carpet of pink heather. Slowly but gradually bilberries (known as blueberries in North America) are replacing the heather above 700m, creating a new source of income and activity, especially at harvest time. Picked with an adroit movement of the hand, the fragile berries are dispatched to markets, canning factories and pharmaceutical laboratories.

Renaissance, the viscounts found it too austere and abandoned it, favouring elegant houses in Ussel.
Le Tour des Fossés – *7km/4.3mi circuit from the castle, keeping to the right.* Continue the access trail to a narrow paved road and plunge into a 15-degree hairpin turn taking you into the "trenches". Halfway down, you'll pass the ruins, then arrive at D 991 to enjoy gorgeous **views★** over the ruins and the meanders of the Luzège.

▷ Take D 119 towards Prailloux and Darnets.

Darnets

The Romanesque and Gothic church St-Martin-St-Maurice includes the vestiges of mural paintings, including the coats of arms of Sedeilles.

▷ Come back to Égletons on D 119 and D 1089, then take D 16 towards Treignac. After approximately 18km/11.1mi, turn right towards Grandsaigne and then Vialle.

Clédat

Within a pine forest, you'll find the ruins of a typical village that was built among enormous round rocks. Abandoned in 1963, this site is being restored, beginning with the Romanesque chapel dedicated to St Madeleine.

▷ Come back to Treignac on D 16.

Eymoutiers
and Vallée de la Maulde

The only part of the Monastère d'Eymoutiers still standing is the collegiate church built from the 11C to the 15C.

VILLAGE
Église
Pl. du Chapitre.
The largest part of the nave and the belfry-porch are Romanesque. The elegant chancel is lit by 15 remarkable stained-glass windows dating from the 15C. The church also contains a fine 13C reliquary **cross★**.

Espace Paul Rebeyrolle
Rte de Nedde. &♿🕒*Open Jun–Aug 10am–7pm; rest of year 10am–6pm (5pm in Dec).* 🕒*Closed Christmas hols, Jan and 1 May.* ⊛€5. 𝄽*05 55 69 58 88. www.espace-rebeyrolle.com.*
This building exhibits 43 works by Paul Rebeyrolle, a figurative artist born in 1926. His pastoral compositions are inspired by local landscapes but the man himself was obsessed by suffering.

Espace Minéralogique
Opposite the Espace Paul Rebeyrolle. &♿🕒*Open Jul–Aug 10am–noon, 2.30–7pm; Jun and Sept 10am–noon, 2.30–6pm.* ⊛€3. 𝄽*05 55 69 27 74.*

▶ **Population:** 2 041.
&♿ **Michelin Map:** 325: H-6.
🏢 **Info:** 17 av. de la Paix, 87120 Eymoutiers. 𝄽05 55 69 27 81. www.tourisme-eymoutiers.fr.
◗ **Location:** 45km/28.1mi W of Limoges via D 879.
🧒 **Kids:** Cité des Insectes.
🕒 **Timing:** Half a day to enjoy the village, its art exhibit and natural observatories; half a day for the driving circuit and attractions at lac de Vassivière.

Learn all about the properties and uses of various minerals, as well as the discovery of dinosaurs' eggs.

EXCURSIONS
Chaud
13km/8mi SE along D 992. In Nedde, turn right onto D 81 then, after crossing the river, right onto D 81A.
Located on the edge of the Millevaches plateau, this village houses a centre devoted to the natural environment of the Limousin region.
A typical Auvergne barn houses the themed exhibitions of the **Cité des Insectes** (🧒🕒*open 10.30am–7pm.*

Espace Paul Rebeyrolle

©Espace Paul Rebeyrolle

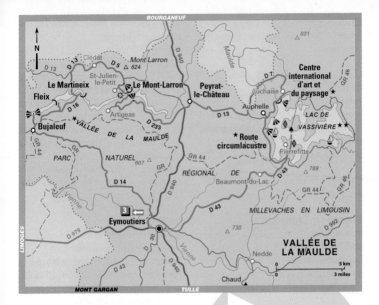

€8 (children, 4–15, €5.50). ℘05 55 04
02 55. www.lacitedesinsectes.com). The
garden, which contains aromatic and
melliferous plants, enables visitors to
watch insects in their natural environment.

Mont Gargan

23km/14mi SW along the D 30.
The road climbs steeply at first, leading to the summit, which is crowned by
the ruins of a chapel. As you go round
the chapel, you'll enjoy a vast **view★★**,
southeast over the Monédières Massif,
north over the hills of Marche and west
over the Limousin mountains.
In July 1944, the mountain was the
site of a bloody battle between German troops and the Resistance led by
Georges Guingouin.

L'Escale

*7km/4.5mi E of Peyrat-le-Château along
the D 13 and D 222. Rte Circumlacustre,
Lieu-dit Auphelle, Peyrat-le-Château.
℘05 55 69 41 35.*
The owners of this bar-restaurant organise regular boat excursions on Lac de
Vassivière that include lunch on board.
If you prefer to stay on dry land, enjoy
a leisurely drink on the terrace.

🚗 DRIVING TOUR

③ VALLÉE DE LA MAULDE

*70km/44mi round-trip. Allow half a
day. See route 3 on region map pp342–
343 and map above.*

▷ Drive NW out of Eymoutiers
along D 14.

Bujaleuf

Bear left to reach the bridge spanning
the reservoir from which you can enjoy
a good **view★** of the two shores of the
lake forming the recreation centre.
Beyond Bujaleuf, the D 16 descends
into the valley, affording lovely views.
Barrage de Fleix is a simply built dam,
50m long and 16m high, supported by
vertical buttresses and surrounded by
lovely woods.

Barrage du Martineix

A construction similar to the previous
one, this dam stands in a wild but beautiful site.

▷ Drive along D 13 towards Peyrat.

Shortly after Clédat, D 5 skirts Mont
Larron.

▷ Turn right onto D 5A1 towards St-Julien-le-Petit then left just beyond the cemetery.

Usine et Barrage du Mont-Larron

This stark-looking building is the control centre for a series of dams. To the right of it, a path leads to the foot of the massive dam. A path to the right climbs to the crest of the dam.

▷ Turn left onto D 233 just before Artigeas.

Peyrat-le-Château

In this rolling landscape where broom and heather alternate with pine and beech, the remains of a castle stand by a lake. The square keep of this fortress was once the home of the Lusignan family.

Musée de la Résistance

Avenue de la Tour, Peyrat le Château. ○*Open Jul–Aug 10am–12.30pm, 3–5.30pm; Jun daily except public holidays 10am–noon, 3–5.30pm; May and Sept daily except public holidays 3–5.30pm.* ○*Closed Tue and Oct–Apr.* ⊛*€3 (children under 12, no charge).* ℘*05 55 69 76 70.*
This small museum is devoted to the local resistance movement, named "Maquis Guingouin" after its leader.

Maison des Moulins

Maison de l'Eau. ♿♂♿☞*Guided tours Jul–Aug Tue–Thu 2.30pm and 3.45pm; rest of the year by prior arrangement.* ○*Closed Nov–Mar.* ⊛*€6.50 (children under 5, no charge).* ℘*05 55 69 26 05.*
A flour mill operated on the site until 1900. It was replaced by a paper mill that closed down in 1934. The museum features 13 working scale models (*1:10*).

▷ Leave Peyrat E on D 13, then turn left onto D 7 towards Royère. 5km/3mi farther on, turn right towards the Vassivière Dam.

A short distance beyond Auchaise, the **route circumlacustre**★, which skirts the west shore of Vassivière lake via **Auphelle**, offers pleasant views of the lake and its islands.

Lac de Vassivière★★

You'll find this lake in a protected site among dark green hills. This 1 000ha/ 2 471-acre reservoir is created by the Vassivière dam on the Maulde.
Every year, large nautical events take place here. One of the islands features a contemporary art centre and a sculpture park. *You can reach the island from the hamlets of Broussas and Auphelle.* ℘*05 55 69 41 35.*

Île de Vassivière

Take the road around the lake south towards Beaumont-du-Lac. Turn right on the road that leads north to Pierrefitte. Park in the car park. ℘*05 55 69 65 95. www.lelacdevassiviere.com.*
In the western part of the lake, Île de Vassivière brings together the natural beauty of the site and works of art in a spectacular layout arranged in 1991. Whether you come on foot or by tourist train, you'll get far-reaching **views**★ over the lake and its surroundings. A neoclassical castle and park featuring granite sculptures is located across from an animal enclosure. Continue the road to the Centre International d'Art et du Paysage, where a path leads off to the new sculpture garden.

Centre International d'Art et du Paysage★ (CIAP)

℘*05 55 69 65 95.*
www.lelacdevassiviere.com.
The Milanese architect Aldo Rossi and his French counterpart Xavier Fabre designed these buildings, including the gallery and the lighthouse, to be closely in communion with the natural environment. Four temporary exhibitions per year are held in these brick-and-granite structures. The artists are oriented towards experimentation, exchange and the visual arts. The link between art and landscape is central to the centre.
The **gallery** resembles a church nave with its compressed barrel arch in wood. French and foreign artists are regularly invited here to exhibit, such as Ilia and

Emilia Kabakov, Michelangelo Pistoletto, Andy Goldsworthy, Michael Sailstorfer and others.

The **lighthouse** also houses a few works. Inside, a spiral staircase gives access to the base of the lamp and offers a view over the lake.

Parc des Sculptures

🕙 *Open Jul–Aug 11am–7pm; rest of year daily except Mon 11am–1pm, 2–6pm.* ✆ *€3 (under-18s, €1.50).* 🔊 *Guided tours available.* 📞 *05 55 69 27 27. www.ciapiledevassiviere.com.*
This is the essential complement to the art centre. Along the circuit you'll discover permanent installations in the woods including works by some 30 artists: David Nash, Kimio Tsuchiya, Dominique Bailly and Jean-Pierre Uhlen, among others, of whom some also exhibit works in the gallery. Independently of the sculpture garden, the trails throughout the island offer various points of view.

🔆 The **Librairie** is a bookshop offering a selection of nearly 12 000 books on contemporary art, architecture, landscaping and gardens. The **Relais Artothèque** is a permanent collection of photographs, drawings and prints, and the **Vidéothèque** contains some hundred films.

The **café** on the ground floor opens onto the lake and prairie with an immense plate-glass window.

▶ Drive to Beaumont-du-Lac via D 43 which leads back to Eymoutiers.

ADDRESSES

🛏 STAY

🛌 **Chambre d'hôte Ferme Équestre des Villards** – *Peyrat-le-Château. 2 km/1.2mi from Peyrat-le-Château towards Lac de Vassivière then Villards.* 📞 *06 83 55 55 59 . www.fermequestrevillards.com.* 🍴 *. 4 rooms.*
The smallish – but comfortable – rooms are located in a former farmhouse near Vassivière Lake, featuring a living room with fireplace and a billiards table. The

Lac de Vassivière

© Jimjag / Fotolia.com

owners also offer horse or pony rides (for children), all-terrain bike hire and rambling circuits up to several days long.

🍽🍽 **Le Relais du Haut-Limousin** – *2 blvd Karl-Marx.* 📞 *05 55 69 40 31. WiFi. 9 rooms.* This family hotel has been entirely renovated and offers attractive rooms. Traditional cuisine on the first floor in the restaurant or on the ground floor in the bistro.

GUIDED TOURS

Eymoutiers – During July and August the tourist office in Eymoutiers organises walking tours (1hr 30min) of the town's main sights, providing a fascinating insight into the town's history and architecture.

Pays Monts et Barrages – In July and August, you can enjoy a guided tour of this area of mountains (*monts*) and dams (*barrages*) covering some 30 villages between Limoges and Vassivière in the company of a qualified local guide. The summer programme for this area includes themed walks, evenings with storytellers and days when the public help restore local buildings.

For further information, contact the Syndicat Intercommunal Monts et Barrages in Bujaleuf, 📞 *05 55 69 57 60. www.ville-saint-leonard.fr.*

MARKET

According to locals, the weekly Thursday market has taken place in Eymoutiers since 1270.

Felletin
and La Montagne Limousine

This small industrial town claims to have woven the largest tapestry ever made (22mx12m), which hangs in Coventry cathedral.

A BIT OF HISTORY
The birthplace of tapestry – Felletin owes its long-standing tradition to a group of Flemish weavers who settled there. In 1689 Felletin became a royal manufacturer, entering into fierce competition with the nearby town of Aubusson.

Today, the former rivals have joined forces and contribute to the renewal of tapestry weaving undertaken by Jean Lurçat. A new generation of talented cartoon designers soon followed Lurçat including artists such as Prassinos, Tourlière and Wagensky.

TOWN
Filature Terrade
R. de la Papeterie. Guided tours by prior arrangement Jul–Aug, Tue and Thu 3.30pm. €4.50 (children under 10, no charge). 05 55 66 54 60.
A guided tour of the tapestry workshops and of a wool mill gives an insight into the various stages of tapestry making.

Ateliers de Tapisserie Pinton
Guided tour (1hr 20min) by prior arrangement. Jul–Aug: Tue and Thu 10.30; school hols (during other periods): Tue 10.30am. €4.50 (children under 16, no charge). 05 55 66 54 60. www.ateliers-pinton.com.
This factory created the largest tapestry in the world! Visit the workshops to discover the various steps of manufacture, from design to carding to weaving.

Église du Moûtier
The three-tiered square belltower, dating from the 15C, dominates the whole town. The 15C frescoes decorating the nave are particularly noteworthy; there are also traces of medieval murals in the transept.

- **Population:** 1 867.
- **Michelin Map:** 325: K-5.
- **Info:** Place Quinault, 23500 Felletin. 05 55 66 54 60. www.felletin-tourisme.com.
- **Location:** 97km/60.6mi E of Limoges and 10km/6mi S of Aubusson.
- **Timing:** Allow a full day to explore the Montagne Limousine region.
- **Don't Miss:** Felletin's tapestry workshops.

Église Notre-Dame-du-Château
Rue du Château. Themed exhibitions on tapestries; May–Oct: call for opening hours. 05 55 66 54 60.
This Gothic church dates from the late 15C. Its typical Languedoc style is unusual in the Limousin region.

Diamanterie
On the edge of the River Creuse. Guided tours by prior arrangement Jul–Aug, Wed and Fri (except public holidays) 3.30pm. €3. 05 55 66 54 60.
These works belonged to a cooperative of diamond cutters until 1982.

Château Arfeuille
4km/2.5mi towards Crocq. Open Jul–Aug, 2.30–6.30pm, guided tour at 3.30pm and 5pm or in the morning by prior arrangement. €3. 05 55 66 40 40.
This is one of five castles in France to have remained in the same family since the 12C. Originally a 12C fortress, the current building is 15C with an 18C wing under renovation. The castle holds various summertime exhibitions.

Pont de Sénoueix

© S. Sauvignier / Michelin

🚗 DRIVING TOUR

④ LA MONTAGNE LIMOUSIN★
75km/47mi round-trip. Allow 1 day.
See route 4 on region map pp342–343.

▷ Leave Felletin SW on D 992.

The road winds pleasantly along the Gourbillon valley.

St-Quentin-la-Chabane
This hamlet takes its name from one of the surrounding hills, the Puy de Cabanne. Its 13C **church** features a Limousin-style door and bell-gable. Beneath the chancel, an 11C crypt harbours a Black Virgin.

▷ Continue along D 992 for 5km/3mi, then take D 59A to the right towards La Nouaille.

Domaine de Banizette★
🎫Guided tour (1hr 15min) Jul–Aug at 3pm, 4.15pm and 5.30pm; May–Sept Sat, Sun and public hols. ఆ€7.
℘05 55 83 28 55. www.banizette.com.
This 17C lordly manor, which has been partially transformed into a museum of rural life, shows what a life on a large farm was like at the beginning of the 20C. The flower garden featuring a central fountain and the three blazed forest trails are also interesting.

▷ Leave the manor and turn right on D 59. At St-Marc-à-Loubaud, turn left and take D 16 towards Gentioux.

Site du Pont de Sénoueix★
This ancient Roman bridge over the Taurion has only one original arch left. The carefully mounted stones defy time, while the trickle of water at the river's source seems to mark it.

Gentioux
As of the 11C, Gentioux attracted stone-masons from around the Creuse. The 13C **church**, rebuilt in the 15C by the Knights of Malta, is adorned with curious 16C sculptures. The town's monument to the victims of WWI is unique and moving in its pacifist expression.

▷ Leave Gentioux on D 8 towards Pigerolles. After 3km/1.8m, turn left on D 35.

Maison des Chevaliers de Pallier
🕐🎫Open mid-Mar to mid-Nov, 10am–6pm; guided tours available in Jul–Aug. ఆ€6. ℘05 55 67 91 73.
This chapel was built in the 12C by the Knights Templar. Its doorway is flanked by two buttresses and crowned with a

357

pointed arch and 14C sculpted tympanum. Inside, several displays relate the history of the Templars in the *département* of the Creuse.

The **medieval garden★** is particularly interesting, illustrating the symbolic meaning of medieval gardens.

▷ 1km/0.6mi before the town of Le Rat, take a small lane on the right marked Chapelle. Park just beyond the turn-off and continue on foot.

Site du Rat★

🚶 *1.2km/0.7mi on foot there and back (follow the path that climbs on the left).* The short walk leads to one of the loveliest **sites** on the plateau. A magnificent row of ancient trees shades the path to the 17C granite **Chapelle St-Roch**.

▷ Continue along the same road and turn left in Malsagnes.

Pigerolles

When snow is plentiful, this village is an ideal cross-country ski resort.

▷ Take D 8 towards La Courtine.

Féniers

Note yet another fine belfry-porch. Follow the D 26 along the Gioune gorge and admire the lovely views of the Auvergne mountain range.

Gioux

Note the granite table in the village and the Gallo-Roman site (1C and 3C) in Maisonnière, 1.5km/0.9mi to the north.

▷ Take D 35, then D 982 back to Felletin.

Crocq

This little medieval stronghold retains its cobbled streets, although its fortifications have long since fallen. It is located on a high point, surrounded by woodlands, meadows and lakes.

A BIT OF HISTORY

Formerly under the feudal wing of Auvergne, Crocq made up one side of a defensive triangle, with Auzanac to the northeast and Herment to the southeast. Facing the stronghold of St-Georges-Nigremont (🐾*see below*) on high ground, Crocq was the leading line of defence against attacks from the Limousin region. The town gave its name to the famous peasant-rebels known as *croquants*.

TOWN
Chapelle Notre-Dame-de-la-Visitation
Rue de l'Église.
Founded at the end of the 12C, this small Romanesque edifice was thoroughly remodelled in the 15C and 16C

- ▸ **Population:** 442.
- 💧 **Michelin Map:** 325: L-5.
- 🗋 **Info:** 4 pl. Georges Hubert. 📞05 55 67 49 02.
- ▷ **Location:** 159km/99.4mi E of Limoges. Climb the towers of the castle for an impressive view of the surrounding area.
- 👀 **Don't Miss:** The triptych in the Chapelle Notre-Dame-de-la-Visitation.
- 🕐 **Timing:** Half a day for the village and driving tour.

and restored in the 19C. It is surmounted by a belfry-gable and a lantern of the dead, removed to the top of the building. Inside, there is a remarkable **triptych★** painted on wood, installed on the northern wall in 1995. This work, designed around 1530, relates the life of St Eligius in seven panels. An interesting feature on the representation of the Last Supper is the fork that is portrayed, as this utensil was not in common use before the 17C!

Castle Towers
Rue de l'Église.

Connected by a curtain wall, these towers are the only vestiges of the defensive 12C castle that fell under assault by the troops of Edward the Black Prince in 1356. Recently restored, the towers have been fitted with stairs making it possible to reach the orientation table in the eastern tower.

The table indicates the sites in the vast **panorama★**: the Combraille to the north; the Dôme range and the Puy de Dôme to the east; the Dore range and the Sancy peak to the southeast; and the Millevaches Plateau to the southwest.

View of the town of Crocq

© S. Sauvignier / Michelin

🚗 DRIVING TOUR

5 LE PAYS DE FRANC-ALLEU★
Round-trip of 45km/27mi. Allow 3hr.
See route 5 on region map pp342–343.

The name of this region recalls the Hundred Years War, which devastated it; in 1426, as compensation, an exemption from duties (*alleu*) was granted.

▶ Leave Crocq on D 996. Drive past the stadium, then turn left towards Dimpoux and park at Laval.

🚶 A pleasant lane bordered by beech and pine leads to a heath carpeted in fern. After 1km/0.5mi, in a little copse, stands the **Urbe Dolmen**.

You can return to Laval by continuing down the lane, which shortly leads back to the road.

There is a good view of Crocq as you head back to D 996.

▶ At the crossroads, turn left on D 996.

After 2km/1.2mi through the heart of the Urbe Forest, look for a little road on the right leading to the **church of Montel-Guillaume**, with its curious polychrome statues (*information at the town hall: ☎05 55 67 40 32*).

▶ Return to D 996 and turn right (1km/0.6mi) on D 29.

At St-Agnant-près-Crocq, follow the D 31 as it winds around ponds and lakes (Étang de la Motte is especially inviting). Nearby, the 15C **Château du Theil** (☛ *not open to the public*) is well sheltered behind its wall.

▶ At Magnat-l'Étrange, turn N on D 90.

St-Georges-Nigremont

Where the Limousin hills meet the Millevaches Plateau, St-Georges-Nigremont stands on a hill (referred to as Nigers Mons in Latin texts) facing a former Gallic *oppidum*. This hillside fort served as an important religious and administrative centre under the Merovingian and Carolingian dynasties.

From the terrace near the church, a wide **panorama** (*orientation table*) extends northeast to Crocq and beyond to the Combraille hills; to the southeast, you'll see the hills of Auvergne.

▶ Continue along D 90 then turn right on D 10. At Pontcharraud, take D 21 SE for 7km/4.2mi, then turn left on D 28. The road leads back to Crocq by way of the hamlet of Naberon, once home to a Knights of Malta lodge.

The Creuse has a wooded landscape and secluded atmosphere that lends itself well to legends, as well as to the howls of wolves. The local history of the area gave rise to various castles and churches, including some founded by the Order of Hospitaliers, and others from the distant Gallo-Roman Era. Vestiges of the past can be found everywhere, especially in Aubusson, world-famous for its tapestries.

Highlights

1 Precious artefacts at Guéret's **Musée d'Art et d'Archéologie de la Sénatorerie** (p360)

2 Immaculately restored **Château de Boussac** (p368)

3 Dazzling tapestries at **Musée Départemental de la Tapisserie** (p371)

4 **Château de Villemonteix,** elegant inside and out (p372)

5 **Moutier-d'Ahun** church (p373)

Guéret

In Guéret, the largest town of the area and capital of the *département*, you can visit the Musée d'Art et d'Archéologie, where the most interesting finds from local digs are displayed alongside diverse artefacts, often from faraway countries. The collection is varied and some objects are quite precious. For a change of pace, enjoy a walk through the Chabrières Forest or visit the wolves that live in the nearby park.

Aubusson, Tapestry Capital

If you enjoyed Felletin (see p356), you will love Aubusson. The undisputed centre of tapestry is home to the Musée Départemental de la Tapisserie, a must-see for tapestry lovers. Various historic buildings of the town make beautiful settings for these fine works of art. The variety of styles ranges from the 14C to the resolutely contemporary movement inspired by Jean Lurçat. You can even visit the former royal factory that still operates in this prestigious town.

Legends and Literature

The monoliths found in the area are shrouded in mystery. These stones and their spooky nature inspired local legends. Their eeriness resonated with author Georges Sand, who mentioned them in her work. If you have read some of her novels, don't miss the Château de Boussac, where the writer penned *Journal d'un Voyageur Pendant la Guerre*. The castle also welcomed other interesting characters, including a companion of Joan of Arc and the Prince Cem, who was also kept prisoner in the Zizim Tower in Bourganeuf in the 15C.

Château de Boussac

© Joel Damase / Photononstop

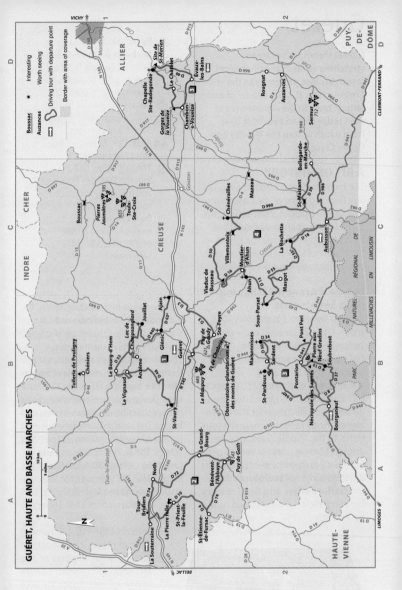

Among the other castles in this area, Château de Villemonteix stands out for its exceptional collection of period furniture and tapestries, even if its outward appearance is unconventional.

Finally, there is no shortage of churches to be admired, and those of Moutier-d'Ahun and Chambon-sur-Voueize are particularly interesting.

Healing Waters

This area of the Limousin also features a *station thermale*, or hydrotherapy centre, built around several mineral springs with medicinal properties that were already known to the Romans: Évaux-les-Bains. As in the surrounding region, Gallo-Roman deposits in the area reveal, among other finds, the ingenious heating and plumbing systems used in ancient times.

Guéret

Guéret stands on a plateau stretching as far as the Chabrières forest, in close proximity to the Creuse valley. It is the capital of and largest town in the *département* of the Creuse and an excellent base from which to tour the Marche and Upper Creuse.

A BIT OF HISTORY

The town developed around a monastery founded in the 8C by a count from Limoges, in a place known as Garactus, at the foot of a hill called Grandcher. In 1514, Guéret became the capital of the county of La Marche and has been an administrative centre ever since.

▶ **Population:** 13 573.
Michelin Map: 325: I 3-4.
Info: 1 r. Eugène France, Guéret. ℘05 55 52 14 29. www.gueret-tourisme.fr.
▶ **Location:** 66km/41mi W of Montluçon and 93km/ 58mi NE of Limoges.
Kids: Parc Animalier des Monts de Guéret.
Timing: Allow half a day to tour the Pays des Trois Lacs and half a day for Haute Vallée du Taurion.
Don't Miss: The enamelwork in Musée d'Art et d'Archéologie de la Sénatorerie.

Musée d'Art et d'Archéologie de la Sénatorerie

Av. de la Sénatorie. ◔*Open May–Oct 10am–12pm, 2–6pm; rest of the year, 1st Sun of each month, 2–6pm.* ◔*Closed Tue and public hols.* €3.50. ℘05 55 52 37 98.

The museum is in a fine 18C Classical building surrounded by a large flower garden. The collection of local **archaeological finds** ranges from prehistoric times to the Middle Ages. One room displays Chinese works of various periods as well as Japanese prints and *objets d'art*. Monumental **sculptures** depicting **Gallic deities** and Gallo-Roman funerary stelae are exhibited in the basement.

Other works from the Middle Ages to the 20C, including *Eve* by Rodin and a *Bust of Rodin* by Camille Claudel, are displayed in various parts of the museum.

The museum houses a magnificent collection of Limousin **champlevé enamelwork★** from the 12C to the 15C. Note in particular a processional cross, pyxes and a collection of shrines (chests and boxes). The vivid colours of the enamels harmonise with the gilding and polished stones. The works include an early 13C Crucifixion; a late 13C Adoration of the Magi; a late 12C Stoning of St Stephen, also known as the Malval Shrine; and a late 12C Martyrdom of St Thomas à Becket.

Several of the 15C–18C painted enamel pieces can be attributed to great masters of the art, namely Limosin, Laudin and Nouailher. There are also displays of glazed earthenware from Nevers, Moustiers, Rouen, Strasbourg and Delft, as well as Italian majolica earthenware and glassware.

The painting section displays works by 17C French, Flemish and Dutch artists as well as more recent works by Guillaumin, Suzanne Valadon and Marinto, among others.

© Musée d'Art et d'Archéologie de Guéret

Malval shrine

Hôtel des Moneyroux

Château des Comtes de la Marche.

This Late Gothic-style building, contemporary with the Palais Jacques Cœur in Bourges (ⓒ *see BOURGES*), consists of two buildings joined by a corner turret. The right wing was built after 1447 by Antoine Alard, lord of Moneyroux; his successor, Pierre Billon, had the other wing built at the beginning of the 16C. The façade is pierced by a large number of mullion windows and is topped by dormer windows ornamented with finials and pinnacles.

EXCURSIONS

Forêt de Chabrières

Take D 940 S dir. Eymoutiers, 2km/1.25mi.

🚶 The forest is dense with pine, oak, beech and birch trees; bracken forms a thick carpet underfoot.

There are many marked footpaths and mountain-bike tracks offering various possibilities. One of them starts from the animal park and runs past legendary stones (*10km/6.2mi, itinerary no 24, explanatory panels and brochure available at the Tourist Office*).

Stonemasonry works established along the road leading to Le Maupuy testify to the importance of this activity in the past.

Les Loups de Chabrières, Parc Animalier des Monts de Guéret

On the road to Bourganeuf. 🕐*Open daily: Feb–Dec 1.30–6pm (May–Aug 10am–8pm).* ⌨€10 *(children aged 4–12, €7).* 🖉05 55 81 23 23. *www.loups-chabrieres.com*

👥 Located in the heart of the forest, this animal park offers a fine panoramic view of the Puy de Dôme and Massif du Sancy, as well as a glimpse of the wolves in the pen below, from its wooden watch-path. Farther on, a trail offers visitors the possibility of observing the wolves more closely.

A tour of the museum provides information on popular beliefs, on myths connected with wolves and on their future. If you are keen to get to know them better, don't miss their feeding time at 4pm. The park is also home to an **observatory** (🕐*open 10 Aug only at 9pm;* ⌨*no charge.* 🖉*05 55 81 23 23).*

Le Maupuy

Take D 914 W towards La Brionne 2km/1.25mi.

The summit of this 685m-high rocky plateau, along with its neighbour the Puy de Gaudy (621m), forms a natural barrier protecting Guéret. The view from the top provides surprising contrasts in landscapes.

Landscape around Guéret

© Authors Images / Photoshot

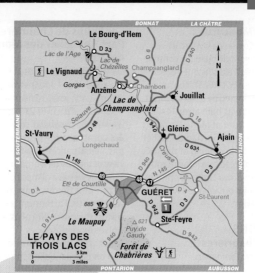

🚗 DRIVING TOUR

1 PAYS DES TROIS LACS★

*75km/47mi round-trip. Allow half a day.
See route 1 on region map p359 and
map above.*

◗ Drive W out of Guéret along N 145
towards La Souterraine.

Église de St-Vaury

Behind the altar in this church you'll see
a limestone bas-relief depicting scenes
from the Passion. There are also two
small 13C enamelled reliquaries.

◗ Continue NE along the D 48.
The road veers to the left 3km/1.9mi
beyond Longechaud.

Le Vignaud

🚶 *1hr 30min round-trip on foot from a
place known as Courtille.*
A marked path leads to the Jupille
meander where you might see per-
egrines wheeling over the rocks in
search of prey.

◗ Continue along D 48.

Le Bourg-d'Hem

This village is picturesquely situated on a
hill overlooking the Creuse Valley; there

is a fine **view** from the square behind
the church.
Two nearby lakes, Lac de l'Age and Lac
de Chézelles, offer swimming, fishing
and hiking.

◗ Drive E along D 33.

Anzême

This pleasant little village boasts a fine
belltower clad with chestnut-wood
shingles. From the square in front of
the church, there is a fine view over the
gorge of the River Creuse and the **Pont
du Diable**.

◗ Turn back then right after
the bridge.

Lac de Champsanglard

This is the largest of the three reservoirs
along the River Creuse at 55ha/136 acres.
Water sports are available near the dam
at Chambon.

◗ Drive on to Champsanglard, then
follow D 14 which runs on to D 6 and
turn left 1km/0.6mi farther on.

Jouillat

The local **church** (12C–13C) has a single
nave which ends in an apse with five
arcades. Note the sculpted capitals.

A 13C **fresco** representing Christ decorates the chancel vaulting. Outside, on the southern side, a Carolingian tomb is embellished by a pattern of squares and rosettes, as well as a granite lion. The **château** is an attractive 15C square building flanked by corner towers.

▷ Take D 940 towards Guéret.

Église de Glénic

Perched on a promontory above the Creuse, the Romanesque **church** was fortified during the Hundred Years War. The east end is protected by towers. The other corners have corbelled turrets. The fourth bay and the chancel are elevated. In the 15C, the nave was lengthened and diagonal ribbed vaulting was added. Beyond the 12C doorway, surmounted by a niche with a Romanesque statue of the Virgin, a 14C fresco faces the entrance, illustrating the fall of Adam and Eve.

▷ Drive E along D 63A.

Église d'Ajain

The **church** (13C) was fortified with a watch-path atop the battlements, and buttressed watchtowers. In the nave with its diagonal rib vaulting, a cornice runs the length of the walls above expressive grimacing faces (mascarons).

▷ Leave Ajain travelling S along D 3.

Ste-Feyre

⚷ Not open to the public.

The town is overlooked by its 18C **château**. The **church**, built in the 13C and fortified in the 14C, has an elegant Limousin-style doorway on the west front. The single nave has four bays; the last of these forms the chancel. It is flanked with an aisle on the 16C south side and has three chapels on the 15C north side. In one of these chapels, note the polychrome stone statuary also dating from the 15C of St Anne and the Virgin and Child.

▷ D 942 takes you back to Guéret.

La Souterraine

Located in a verdant basin of the Monts de la Marche, La Souterraine was built atop the vestiges of a Gallo-Roman villa, "villa Sosterranea" or "underground villa". It has managed to retain some medieval features. This is a stopover on one of the main roads of the Compostela pilgrimages.

◣◣WALKING TOUR

Porte St-Jean

Also called "Porte de Breith" or "Porte Notre-Dame", this 13C–15C gateway is located near the Église Notre-Dame. You'll recognise it by its two corbelled turrets and its crenellations and machicolations.

▶ **Population:** 5 522.
🜂 **Michelin Map:** 325: F3.
🛈 **Info:** Pl. de la Gare.
 ☏ 05 55 63 10 06.
 www.lasouterraine.fr.
▷ **Location:** 30km/18.6mi W of Guéret on N 145. 10km/6.2km E of exit 23 on A 20.
👥 **Kids:** Le Cirque Valdi and Scénovision.
🕓 **Timing:** Half a day for the village and its surroundings.

Église Notre-Dame★

This 12C–13C church was built in granite, lending it a severe appearance. Its façade, featuring a portal with multi-lobed arches flanked by two dome lights, shows the Mozarabic influence brought by pilgrims from Compostela. The tympanum of the south lateral door is adorned with a typically Limousin

Romanesque depiction of the Virgin Mary; the robust buttresses supporting the transept are also built in this style. In the 19C, a belfry was added to the 13C bell wall. The building is an invitation to follow the changing architecture from the Romanesque period, with the second, barrel-vaulted bay; to the Gothic period, with the transept and choir, through to the groin vaults of the side aisles. The harmonious nave features interesting capitals. The double transept is the most original part of the building. An oval cupola on pendentives was built in a trapezoid shape over the crossing of the first bay. In the Gothic choir, notice the 12C stone altar table.

Crypt – ⊙*Jul–Aug 3–6pm, except public holidays.* ⊘*No charge.* ℘*05 55 63 10 06.* This crypt was built by the monks of the Abbey of St-Martial of Limoges c 1020. It housed the remains of the donor Géraud de Crozant, founder of that abbey. The columns and inscriptions of a Gallo-Roman sanctuary are visible here.

EXCURSION
Chéniers
40km/25mi NE on D 951 (towards Aigurande), then right on D 46.

Ecomusée Tuilerie de Pouligny★
⊙*Open mid-Apr–Jun and Sept–Oct 2–6pm; Jul–Aug daily 10am–noon, 2–7pm.* ⊘€8 (children, 6–12, €4). ℘05 55 62 19 61. www.tuilerie-pouligny.com.

This tile factory was opened in 1830 by Jean Monsieur and enjoyed a prosperous period until the beginning of the 20C. From hand moulding to mechanical manufacture, the factory continued operating until 1962. In 1995, the village bought it to restore it for visitors. Today it houses an ecomuseum of crafts and trades relating to the elements of earth and fire.

You'll visit the **pottery workshop**, where various types of tiles are described through various media, including a model of the original site. Nearby, you'll see the area where clay was worked, the machines and tools used in the manufacturing process, and the drying area.

Next, you'll visit the **great kiln** containing pieces waiting to be fired. Along the *sentier des tuiliers*, or "tile trail", you'll see the extraction furrows and wash-house. You'll also see the **halle des fours**, a gallery exhibiting kilns from around the world and describing diverse firing techniques. The tour finishes with the forge and wagon-maker's workshop, but if you'd like to go further, you can participate in one of the many pottery and enamel workshops available. Pottery exhibitions are also regularly held.

🚗 DRIVING TOUR

② BETWEEN HAUTE MARCHE AND BASSE MARCHE
50km/31mi round-trip. Allow 3hr. See route 2 on region map p359.

Tour des Bridiers
➤*Guided tour available from the tourist office of La Souterraine.* ⊘*No charge.*

This imposing dungeon is the last vestige of a 13C fortress. Below, a pretty medieval garden includes a vegetable patch, medicinal and dyeing plants and culinary herbs.

▷ Join the D 74.

Noth
This charming 13C church was fortified in the 15C.

▷ Leave Noth S and cross N 145. After Lizières, turn left on D 72.

Le Grand-Bourg
In the year 776, a church dedicated to St Léobon stood here, but it was replaced between 1150 and 1200 by a new chapel, dedicated to the same saint. This was adjoined to a church dedicated to the Virgin Mary, which is all that remains today.

St Léobon is depicted on the keystone. The stained-glass windows date from the 19C. In the choir, a 12C granite statue of Mary with Child is reminiscent of the Auvergnat style.

▶ Leave Le Grand-Bourg S on D912A.

Bénévent-l'Abbaye

In addition to its interesting church and charming old houses, this village offers an original sight called Scénovision that depicts life here at the turn of the century.

Eglise – The church was originally founded in the 11C on the Compostela road to contain the relics of St Barthélémy. The present church was entirely built in the 12C in a Romanesque transition style. Inside you'll see sculpted capitals on the 38 enormous pillars. In the southern crossing of the Chapel of St Barthélémy you'll see a reliquary bust and a wooden statue. In the northern crossing, there is a tombstone, a recumbent figure and an engraved slab.

Scénovision – ⏱*Open Jul–Aug daily 9.45am–7.15pm (Sun 1.45–7.15pm); Jun and Sept daily 1.45–7.15pm; mid-Feb–May school holidays daily 1.45–6.45pm (outside school holidays weekends and public holidays only); Oct–Dec school holidays daily 1.45–6.45pm (outside school holidays weekends and public holidays only).* ⊜€10 (children 6–11, €6, 12–17, €8.50). ℘05 55 62 31 43. www.benevent-scenovision.fr. Using the techniques of theatre and cinema, including stage sets and 3-D films, you'll be transported into six authentic and entertaining scenes to discover the Creuse as it was 100 years ago.

▶ From the church of Bénévent, follow the signs towards Marsac, then turn left in the rue Auguste-Faure (Gendarmerie).

Puy de Goth★

Park at the intersection of the three paths and follow the one to the left. 🚶 *30min round-trip on foot.*
Enjoy the beautiful **view** from the top (543m) over the Monts de la Marche and Monts du Milousin in the southwest and the Monts d'Auverge in the southeast, including the Puy-de-Dôme and the Puy de Sancy on a clear day.

▶ Leave Bénévent SW on D 10. After 1km/0.6mi, turn left on D 10 towards St-Priest-la-Feuille.

St-Priest-la-Feuille

Access via D 74. 🚶*15min round-trip on foot.*
A picturesque walk takes you by the Dolmen de la Pierre Folle, or "foolish rock dolmen", where, according to legend, it is better not to venture once night falls. If strange dancers appear and try to kiss you… run away!

▶ Follow D 10 back to La Souterraine.

ADDRESSES

🛏 STAY

⊜⊜⊜ **Hôtel Sas à La Porte St-Jean** – *2 r. des Bains, La Souterraine. ℘05 55 63 90 00. WiFi. www.hotel-restaurant-alaportesaintjean.com. ♿. 37 rooms.* With its back turned to the Porte St-Jean, this hotel-restaurant offers purpose-built rooms that are always being improved upon. Some feature balneo baths; others are newly decorated to reveal stone walls. In the annex, there are a few family suites. The cuisine is classic and traditional.

🍴 EAT

⊜ **Nougiers** – *2 pl. de l'Église, St-Étienne-de-Fursac. ℘05 55 63 60 56. www.hotel nougier.fr. 12 rooms.* For three generations, the art of receiving has been cultivated in this village inn. The cuisine is delicious and well presented. The rooms are pleasant. Swimming pool.

Château de Boussac ★

If you love old stones, literature and lonely landscapes of heath and rocks, Boussac is for you. Between the Champagne Berrichonne and the Marche, this old fortified town is spread over a promontory above the Petite Creuse. This is where George Sand wrote her 1870 *Journal d'un Voyageur Pendant la Guerre.*

▶ **Population:** 1 602.
⊙ **Michelin Map:** 325: K2.
▯ **Info:** Pl. de l'Hôtel-de-Ville, Boussac. ℘09 77 85 75 92. www.tourismeboussac.fr.
◑ **Location:** 40km/24.8mi NE of Guéret.
☺ **Don't Miss:** The view over the castle from the bridge over Petite Creuse; the exceptional panorama for the observation tower of Toulx-Ste-Croix.
▣ **Parking:** There are various car parks in the centre of town, but it is better to park outside the old town.
◷ **Timing:** 2hr for the castle and surrounding area. In the summertime, Aubusson tapestries are exhibited in the castle.

VISIT

Guided tours Easter–Sept 9am–noon, 2–5.30pm. €12. ℘05 55 65 07 62.

Built in the 12C and partially destroyed during the Hundred Years War, Boussac Castle shows an austere front on its side facing the Petite Creuse, with its brown stones and rectangular shape weighed down by massive towers. The lord of Boussac, Royal Marshal and a companion of Joan of Arc, Jean I de Brosse, whose coat of arms appears above the entryway, had the castle rebuilt in the 15C and the mullion windows and turrets adorned with blazons and crests to ornament the main building.

Along the tour, you'll discover the **Salle des Gardes** featuring fireplaces engraved with coats of arms. From 1660 to 1882, this room housed the famous series of tapestries de *La Dame et la Licorne* (The Lady and the Unicorn) that are now exhibited at the National Museum of the Middle Ages in Paris. In the 19C, these major works of medieval art made in Flanders in the 15C were sold to a rich collector. The proceeds from the sale were used to pave the village fairground and to build the statue of Pierre Leroux (1797–1871) in the square that bears his name.

This philosopher and Saint-Simonianist humanitarian was a friend of George Sand and founder of *La Revue Sociale*. On the first floor of the castle, you can visit **George Sand's bedchamber** (her first countryside novel, *Jeanne*, is set in this castle) and, on the second floor, the salon du prince Zizim ("Prince Cem" in English, *see Bourganeuf p375*).

EXCURSIONS
Pierres Jaumâtres

6km/3.7mi S of Boussac. Take D 917, and after 2km/1.12mi, turn right towards St-Silvain-Bas-le-Roc. *30min round-trip on foot.*

At the top of Mount Barlot, surrounded by a heathland covered with heather, a curious pile of granite blocks stands at 595m of altitude. In her novel *Jeanne*, George Sand described these as "monstrous tables… terrifying altars". From here, enjoy the **view★** to the north over the Berry and the Bourbon area and to the south over the Monts de la Marche and the Monts du Limousin.

Toulx-Ste-Croix

11km/6.8mi S of Boussac. Take D 917 and, after 2km/1.2mi, turn right towards St-Silvain-Bas-le-Roc. At Le Pradeau, continue along D 67.

This village is located on the former Gallic *oppidum* which was surrounded by a triple fortification. The Gallo-Roman city that followed, Tullum, left behind a few traces that are currently being excavated around the cemetery.

Church– This curious 11C and 12C granite Romanesque building was originally attached to its belltower by three bays which are no longer standing. In the tower, which has been largely modified, there are a few tombs, as well as early Christian funerary urns. A Gallo-Roman low-relief engraving can be seen in the south wall. Stone lions guard the exterior of the church. They were probably used long ago to mark the limits of a territory or a cemetery.

Observation tower – *200m for the church.* From the top platform of this observation tower (*74 steps*), you'll enjoy a sweeping **panorama★★**. The view takes in the Berry and the Bourbon region to the north; the Monts de la Marche and the Monts du Limousin to the west; and the Mounts of Madeleine, le Forez, Dôme and Dore to the south and southeast.

ADDRESSES

♈ EAT

⌂ **La Bonne Auberge** – *1 r. des Lilas, Nouzerines.* ℘*05 55 82 01 18. www.la-bonne-auberge.net.* &. *6 rooms.*
A traditional inn that you'll recognise by its green shutters. The main dining room is bright and cheerful, and the cuisine is regional. You can also enjoy the garden terrace.

Évaux-les-Bains

Thermal baths and the charms of hydrotherapy are rare in the Limousin! The waters of Évaux have radioactive properties that were already used by the Romans, as the vestiges of their thermal baths attest. But even if you aren't here for therapeutic reasons, you'll enjoy the fresh air and pleasant environment.

▶ **Population:** 1 457.
⏣ **Michelin Map:** X325: L3.
🛈 **Info:** Place Serge-Cléret. ℘05 55 65 50 90. www.ot-evauxlesbains.com.
▷ **Location:** Just off D 993.
👥 **Kids:** Kids aged 5–9 will enjoy the *Guide Lud'eau* available at the Tourist Office.
🕔 **Timing:** 3hr for the town and its surroundings.

THE TOWN
Station Thermale
The lightly mineralised waters of Évaux contain sodium sulphate and possess radioactive properties.
Three springs (*sources*) are currently in use: that of **Ste-Marie**, that of **Le Rocher** and that of **César** (61°C/141.8°F). They are used to treat rheumatic conditions – which is the speciality of the hydrotherapy station – but also venous and gynaecological problems.

Église St-Pierre-et-St-Paul
This lovely Romanesque building has retained its interesting belfry-porch, of which the last, octagonal level, built in the 13C, supports a high fleche covered with shingles. The church burned in the 16C and was rebuilt in the Gothic style. However, the three arches at the entrance to the choir are the originals. Having been damaged in 1942, the church has since been restored. The simplicity of its architecture enhances the beauty of its stone with its ruddy ochre tones.

Inside, you'll see the shrine of St Marien. At one time, Évaux-les-Bains and Chambon-sur-Voueize were engaged in a long-term dispute over the shrine. To settle the quarrel, the relics were placed on an ox-driven cart with no driver. The treasure was promised to the village where the team of oxen stopped!

From the adjoining little square, you'll get a good view of the chevet, the terracing of the nave and side aisles, and the belfry-porch.

🚗 DRIVING TOUR

③ GORGES AND VALLEY
30km/18.6mi round-trip. Allow 2hr 30min. See route 3 on region map p359.

▶ Leave Évaux-les-Bains NW on D 915 towards Marcillat. After 1km/0.6mi, turn left on D 40, then take a small road left towards Entraigues.

Site de St-Marien★
🚶20min round-trip on foot.
A pleasant wooded path takes you down to a promontory crowned by a sort of chapel overlooking the confluence of the Tardes and the Cher.

Chapelle Ste-Radegonde
🚶300m from the road; take the path going up.
A suspended bridge gives access to the left bank of the Tardes and the little 13C chapel.

▶ Turn left on D 996 towards Évaux-les-Bains on your way out of Budelière. 1km/0.6mi after the railway crossing, take D41A towards Lépaud. At the intersection, turn left onto D 917.

Gorges de la Voueize★
The overhanging road overlooks the river winding through the rocks covered with trees, ferns and heather.

Chambon-sur-Voueize★
The large church, medieval bridge and spectacular gorges are three reasons to visit this village at the confluence of the Voueize and the Tardes.

L'Église Ste-Valérie★ is one of the largest and most interesting of all those built in the Limousin Romanesque style. Founded by the Abbey of St-Martial of Limoges to house the relics of Ste Valérie, the church was built in the 11C or early 12C. Pillaged and mistreated in the 15C and 16C, it was reworked c 1850.

The building is immense, measuring 87m long and 38m wide at the transept crossing.

Above the porch stands the 13C bell-tower called **tour des Bourgeois**. The corner tower was used to store the monastery's manuscripts, which is why it is called **tour du Chartrier**. Inside the church, you'll be surprised by the harmony of the proportions. The choir is the most interesting part, with its triumphal arch featuring sculpted capitals. The woodwork is finely achieved: notice the 17C altarpiece dedicated to Ste Valérie. To the right of the choir, through the second apsidal chapel of the south crossing where you'll see an early 16C Pieta, you'll access the **salle du trésor**, or treasure room, where a reliquary bust and precious works of art are kept.

From the church, bear left to follow the **Grande Rue du Puy**. This is the place where you'll get the best view of the brown tiles of the roofs grouped around the church and its two towers. From there, rue Cueille goes down to the Voueize. At the corner of rue Lépaud, rue des Forts gives a lovely perspective on the tour des Bourgeois. Across from no 3 rue de a Brèche, cross through a bell-gate to see a part of the former ramparts.

Don't miss the 14C **bridge★** and its cutwaters.

ADDRESSES

🍴 EAT

🍽🍴 **Le Coq d'Or** – *7 pl. du Champ-de-Foire, 23130 Chénérailles.* 📞*05 55 62 30 83. www.restaurant-coqdor-23.com. Closed late Jun–early Jul, Sun eve, Wed eve, Mon.* The many cockerels that decorate the colourful interior of this restaurant have been brought from all over the world by customers. Tasty food available *à la carte* or from set menus at a variety of prices. Warm welcome.

Auzances

During medieval times, this was part of the Auvergne region. Auzances, one of five castellanies of Combraille, formed the line of defence against the Limousin border along with Crocq. Only bits of walls and towers in the Cendres district, which was burnt during the Wars of Religion, attest to the former importance of this fortified city occupied by the English in 1357. The ruins of the castle were demolished in 1830.

SIGHTS
Église St-Jacques
This Romanesque building, reworked in the 15C, houses the work *Descente de Croix* by Daniel de Volterra, given by Pope Innocent X to Canon Brousse in 1640. Behind the altar you'll see a lovely multicoloured 16C Pieta. Note also the surprising Byzantine-style frescoes, painted in 1965 by the Russian **Nicolas Greschny** (1912–85). Outside, the Gothic capitals of the northern doorway feature mysterious faces.

Chapelle Ste-Marguerite
In this 17C chapel, you'll find Gallo-Roman vestiges found in Coux d'Auzances, Cujasseix (*see below*) and Les Vergnes. In an exhibition space adjoining the chapel, you'll see fragments of the aqueduct and funerary boxes as well as medieval tombs.

EXCURSIONS
Rougnat
3km/1.8mi N on D 996.
The **Gallo-Roman villa** of Cujasseix was discovered in 1972 in the north of the village. The villa was made up of residential buildings arranged around a 40m by 35m courtyard as well as farm buildings. The archaeological digs uncovered rooms heated by hypocaust, private baths and the remains of

- **Population:** 1 336.
- **Michelin Map:** 325: M4.
- **Info:** 6 r. de la Mairie. ℰ05 55 67 17 13.
- **Location:** 30km/18.6mi NE of Aubusson on D 988 on the road from Crocq to Montluçon.
- **Don't Miss:** L'Eglise St-Jacques; the mural paintings of the Gallo-Roman villa of Cujasseix; gorgeous views from the Sermur tower.
- **Timing:** 2hr for the town and its surroundings.

a refined painted décor, including a lion with a woman's head, deer, birds, cats and flowers. Examples of these are on display at the Ste-Marguerite chapel. The 12C and 13C **Église St-Laurent** features lovely Louis XV-style woodwork and a series of 21 depictions of scenes from the life of Christ attributed to the Italian **Giovanni Lombardi** (1682–1752). Approximately 2km/1.2mi from Rougnat in the village of Courtioux, a 15C fortress along the Cher is easily recognisable with its machicolations. **Château Bodeau** *(private property)*, was the set of Alain Corneau's film, *Tous les Matins du Monde* (1991).

Sermur
10km/6mi SW on D 996, then D 25.
This charming village overlooks the verdant hills of Combraille.
From the church, you can follow a path that crosses through woods and then climbs steeply to the ruins of a **square tower**, the only remaining part of a feudal fortress destroyed at the beginning of the Hundred Years War. From there (alt. 712m), you'll get a fantastic **view★★** over the Millevaches plateau and the Auvergne volcanoes.

Aubusson★

and the Upper Creuse valley

Aubusson, situated in the upper valley of the Creuse, still manufactures the tapestries and carpets that have been world-famous for the past five centuries. A College of Decorative Arts, opened in 1884, offers courses aimed at keeping up this tradition. The Centre Culturel et Artistique Jean Lurçat was established to promote this exceptional craft.

A BIT OF HISTORY

Tapestry-making – It would appear that tapestry weaving was imported from Flanders in the 14C by Marie de Hainault, who was to become Countess of Marche, although it was only in the 15C that the tapestry weavers of Aubusson started to receive wider acclaim. The Lady and the Unicorn, a 15C masterpiece now in the Cluny Museum in Paris, is believed to have been woven by the craftsmen of Aubusson. Their fame peaked in the 16C and 17C with verdures (flower and foliage designs in shades of green) as well as sacred, mythological and historical themes. Colbert granted them the title of royal tapestry-makers in the 17C.

With the departure abroad of many of the weavers, following the Revocation of the Edict of Nantes in 1685, the industry faced ruin. It recovered only at

▶ **Population:** 3 844.
🚗 **Michelin Map:** 325: K-5.
ℹ **Info:** R. Vieille. ☎05 55 66 32 12. www.tourisme-aubusson.com.
◐ **Location:** 87km/60.6mi E of Limoges via the N 141. Start from the tourist office in the old town.
🅿 **Parking:** See town plan.
👁 **Don't Miss:** The Musée Départemental de la Tapisserie; the Château de Villemonteix.
🕐 **Timing:** Allow half a day for the Upper Creuse valley, a day for Aubusson.

the beginning of the 18C, thanks to the work of certain painters of that time, such as Watteau, Lancret and Boucher. The 19C was a period of decline, due in part to the aftermath of the Revolution but also to the development of a new source of competition: wallpaper. During the 1930s fresh impetus came when the artist Jean Lurçat played a decisive role in the rebirth of the art of tapestry-weaving. A new generation of cartoon designers soon emerged including artists such as Prassinos, Tourlière, Picart-le-Doux and Wagensky.

Nowadays the town takes pride in maintaining its old weaving methods and tools. The great speciality of Aubusson

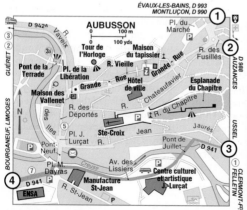

WHERE TO STAY

Chambre d'hôte
  M. et Mme Dumontant........①
Chambre d'hôte
  Ourdeaux.............................③
Hôtel de France...................⑤
Hôtel Villa Adonis...............⑦

WHERE TO EAT

Le Viaduc..............................②

is *basse-lisse* (low-warp) tapestry using horizontal looms; the same technique is used in Beauvais and Gobelins.

OLD TOWN

Aubusson's old town straddles both sides of Grande-Rue, running east to west through the town from place de la Liberation to place du Marché, behind which lies the **rue Vieille** to the north. This cobbled pedestrianised street is lined with old houses which have been completely renovated and converted into art galleries and craft and antique shops. Above the rue Vielle is the round medieval stone structure of the **tour de l'horloge**, with its open belfry which, due to its strategic location, was once used as a watchtower.

Below the tour de l'horloge is the **Pont de la Terrade**, the first bridge to be constructed at Aubusson. From this old bridge, an interesting 16C construction with pointed cutwaters, there is a pleasant view of the houses rising in terraces on the left bank of the Creuse.

Returning to the **place de la Libération** at the foot of the Grande-Rue, there is a 16C turreted house known as the **Maison des Vallenet** and a fountain dating from 1718 which are the main attractions in this square. Take the rue Barabant leading south from the Grande-Rue to the rue Châteafavier which leads to the **Église Ste-Croix**. This sturdy church with its centrally placed spire was built in the 13C and largely remodelled in the 19C. From the terrace near the church, a steep path climbs to the summit of the hill and the **wsplanade du Chapitre**, where the 11C–13C ruins of the castle of the counts of Aubusson still stand.

MUSEUMS AND EXHIBITS

A combined ticket for the Musée Départemental de la Tapisserie, Exposition Collection Fougerol and Eglise du Château in Felletin is available from the tourist office of Aubusson. ⊚€9. ℘05 55 66 32 12.

Musée Départemental de la Tapisserie★

Av. des Lissiers. ♿🕐*Open Jul–Aug, daily 10am–6pm (Tue 2–6pm); Sep–Jun, daily (except Tue) 9.30am–noon, 2–6pm.* 📷*Guided tour (included) at 11am, 2pm and 6pm.* 🕐 *Closed 25 Dec and 1 Jan.* ⊚€5. ℘05 55 66 33 06. www.cite-tapisserie.fr.

The collection includes all types of tapestries and carpets from the 17C, 18C and 19C. The 20C is illustrated with various works by contemporary artists including Lurçat, Gromaire, Saint-Saëns, Picart le Doux, Tourlière and Julien. The modern works demonstrate the brilliance of the period of renewal inspired by Lurçat. A tour of the museum concludes with an exhibition on the history and technique of this art.

Manufacture de Tapis et de Tapisseries St-Jean

3 Av. des Lissiers. 📷*Guided tours (1hr 30mn) 9am–noon, 2–5pm (weekends and public holidays 3–5pm).* ⊚€12. ℘05 55 66 10 08. www.manufacture-saint-jean.fr.

This former royal factory works only by commission. Carpets made by specialised weavers on high-warp looms are produced in the **savonnerie** workshop. Other carpets (**ras**), with a rougher-finished feel, are woven on a low-warp loom, with a cotton warp.

The restoration workshop handles carpets which have been damaged over time. After finding the right colours and materials, the tapestry workers rebuild the warp and weft.

Exposition Collection Fougerol

56 r. Jules Sandeau. 🕐*Call for opening times.* ⊚€4 (children under 15, no charge). ℘05 55 66 32 12.

This exhibit presents scenes from life in the 16C–19C.

L'Exposition – Tapisseries d'Aubusson, Felletin

Grande-Rue. ⏱*Mid-Jun to mid-Sept. Call for times.* ⊘*No charge.* ☎*05 55 66 32 12.*
The summertime exhibit in the Hôtel de Ville comprises tapestries and carpets worked to traditional and modern designs.

Maison du Tapissier

R. Vieille. ⏱*Open daily Jul–Aug 9.30am–6.30pm (Sun and public holidays 10am–noon, 2–5pm); rest of the year daily except Sun 10am–noon, 2–5pm.* ⊘*€5 (children under 16, no charge).* ☎*05 55 66 32 12.*
In this lovely 16C house, local furniture and other objects evoke life in Aubusson in bygone days. On the upper floor, an old-fashioned workshop displays a low-warp loom, reels, wheels for preparing shuttles and bobbin stands, as well as several tapestries, cartoons and embroidered pieces.

EXCURSION
Château de Mazeau

10.5km/6.2mi E. From Villemonteix, go to Chénérailles. Then take D 4 to Peyrat-la-Nonière and follow the "Château de Mazeau" signposts. ⏱*Guided tours mid-Jul–mid-Aug 2–8pm.* ☎*06 45 00 10 33.*
This unconventional castle, slightly lost in the undergrowth, is currently being restored. Built on a Gallo-Roman site, the castle was given over for defence by the Cistercian monks of Bonlieu. Later it was sold and remained within the same family until the Revolution, when it became a simple farm building.
It features a 14C tower within a stone shell, which is to be removed. The tower adjoins the early 16C castle. An "Italian gallery" can be distinguished by its terra cotta tiles. Inside, vast fireplaces still bear their original grey paint. The castle also retains its cellar and two jail cells, two spiral staircases and living rooms with 18C woodwork.
Across from the castle, an annex houses the former kitchen. The building that hems in the courtyard was the soldiers' quarters.

One of the owners of this property participated in the Crusades, as is recounted in an engraving on one of the fireplaces.

🚗 DRIVING TOUR

④ HAUTE VALLÉE DE LA CREUSE
Round-trip of 90km/ 54mi. Allow half a day. See route 4 on region map p359.

▷ From Aubusson, drive NE along the D 998 towards Auzances.

Bellegarde-en-Marche
The main street of this village features some lovely 17C buildings, including a clock tower surmounted with a bell and covered with chestnut shingles. You'll also see some lovely houses, including a few with turrets.

▷ Come back towards Aubusson on D 39, which passes through La Chassade.

St-Maixant
A charming church and a late 14C castle stand on the village square.

▷ Return to D 990.

Église de Chénérailles
Built in the 13C, this church contains a handsome **haut-relief★** in memory of Barthélemy de la Place, the church's founder.

▷ Follow the D 55 towards Ahun then turn right.

Château de Villemonteix★
⏱*Guided tours Easter to Oct 2–7pm (Jul–Aug 10am–noon, 2–7pm).* ⊘*€7.* ☎*05 55 62 33 92. www.chateau-villemonteix.cla.fr.*
The entrance yard to this 15C feudal stronghold is preceded by two corner towers. It was formerly protected by a moat and drawbridge.
The watch-path, supported by corbels and two gargoyles, has a watchtower

at each end. On the western side, two more towers fill out the defensive structure, safeguarding the rear of the central building.

This tastefully restored castle contains a fine collection of **period furniture★★** and Aubusson, Felletin and Flemish **tapestries★★** dating from the 16C to the 18C.

▷ Leaving the château, turn left and go back to D 53. Beyond Cressat, follow D 50.

Viaduc de Busseau

This 300m viaduct spanning the Creuse blends into the landscape.

▷ Cross the viaduct; left on D 16.

Moutier-d'Ahun★

An old bridge with cutwaters that spans the Creuse and a village grouped around its church against a charming backdrop of green hills and prairies: welcome to Moutier-d'Ahun.

Church – In its present state, the church is comprised of a Romanesque part, including the transept, belltower and choir; and a Gothic part, the 15C western entranceway. You'll enter the building through a beautiful granite **portal** built in the 15C Flamboyant style. Under its high gable, it is adorned with six arch mouldings decorated with images of prophets, angels, jugglers, musicians and dancers. The nave no longer exists; two rows of lime trees mark the spot where the bays stood. The transept arms have also been destroyed.

The crossing is surmounted by a large square Romanesque belltower, pierced through on each side with three twin openings on small columns with smooth capitals.

A Gallo-Roman funerary stele decorated with figures and an inscription is built into the façade. As you pass beneath the large squinch-supported cupola of the transept, you'll access the choir through a triumphal arch made up of three juxtaposed arcades. The choir with its flat chevet and the two chapels were crowned with ogive vaults in the 15C.

Outside, a chevet has retained the traces of the 14C fortifications.

The **woodwork★★** and stalls embellish the walls of the apse and of the choir. All these sculptures were carried out from 1673 to 1681 by Simon Baüer, a master sculptor living in the Auvergne, upon request by the monks of Moutier-d'Ahun.

On both sides of the master altar, the two parts of a vast altarpiece are made up of very finely worked spiral columns supporting an arched pediment. The part of the choir along the altarpiece is adorned with panels that form a monumental door, giving access to a 15C chapel. Patterns of fauna and flora and fantastical creatures ornament the 26 stalls. The sculptor seems to have played on opposing symbols of good and evil through his choice of animals and caryatids. The grate of the gate to the choir is surmounted with a two-sided Christ sculpted in oak. Various objects from the former monastery are assembled in the sacristy, including 12C polychrome granite statues representing St Benoît and St Antoine the hermit, 15C and 17C shrines and a 17C Christ sculpted in boxwood.

Pont de Moutier – This 11C bridge is formed by eight arches in a picturesque structure spanning 100m/328ft across the Creuse River below the village. So why is this medieval bridge, listed as a historic building since 1920, often mistakenly called the "Roman bridge"? Probably because a ford already existed in its place in Gallo-Roman times, Moutier-d'Ahun having then been an important intersection.

▷ Take D 13.

Ahun

This small town on the banks of the Creuse was once the brilliant *Acitodunum*, a major city on the map of the Roman Empire, and probably one of the first places to be evangelised by St Martial. It is home to the **Église St-Sylvain**. On the outside, between the arched bays of the chevet, the capitals crowning the columns of this church are carved with animals and palmettos. Inside, the remarkable **woodwork★** panels and columns date from the late 17C.

▶ Take D 13 towards Pontarion.

Église de Sous-Parsat

The small church features surprising **frescoes★**, the work of Gabriel Chabrat. Light filters through the windows, also designed by Chabrat, accentuating the unique ambience of the church.

▶ Drive to Le Sec via D 45, and then on to Chamberaud. Turn right onto D 16 towards St-Sulpice.

Masgot

🕐 �& *Guided tour (45min), Jul–Aug 10am–noon, 2.30–7pm; mid-Apr–Jun and Sept daily except Mon 2.30–6pm; rest of the year daily except Mon and weekends 2–5pm.* 🕐 *Closed mid-Dec– mid Jan.* ᴂ€3. ℘05 55 66 98 88. www.masgot.fr.

The main attractions in Masgot are the **stone sculptures** by the artist François Michaud (1810–90). Using local granite, Michaud brought a new dimension to this traditional local craft. His home has become a **museum**.

▶ At the end of the path leading to the village, go back to Chamberaud and turn right onto D 55 to reach La Rochette via Ars.

Chapelle de la Rochette

Built in 1569 in Romanesque style and since restored, the chapel has a belfry topped with wooden shingles.

▶ Drive to Aubusson along D 18.

ADDRESSES

🏠 STAY

◒◒ **Hôtel Villa Adonis** – *14 av. de la République.* ℘05 55 66 46 00. The stone exterior of this house conceals a cosy, well-kept contemporary interior. The rooms are comfortable, and on the garden side, you'll get a view of a superb sequoia that grows along the river.

◒◒ **Hôtel Le France** – *6 r. des Déportés.* ℘05 55 66 10 22. www.aubussonle france.com. 21 rooms. Near Ste-Croix church, this pretty 18C dwelling offers comfortable, tasteful rooms with antique furnishings and luxurious fabrics. In the elegant dining room or on the terrace along the interior courtyard, you'll be served smart traditional cuisine.

◒◒ **Chambres d'hôte M. et Mme Dumontant** – *Les Vergnes, St-Pardoux-le-Neuf. 7km/4.3mi E of Aubusson on D 941.* ℘05 55 66 23 74. www.lesvergnes.fr. 🅿 ⊠. 6 rooms. If you're looking for peace and tranquillity, you'll find it in this 18C estate located in the midst of the countryside. The spacious rooms have been renovated. Features a fishing pond and two swimming pools, including one covered pool. Three *gîtes* are available for longer stays.

🍽 EAT

◒ **Le Relais des Forêts** – *41 rte d'Aubusson.* ℘05 55 66 15 10. www.relais-des-forets.fr. ᴐ 🅿. If you'd like to try the local specialities, they are waiting for you at Le Relais. Treat yourself to a potato pâté, a bolete mushroom omelette, a Creuse-style fondue or meat fresh from the Limousin.

◒ **Le Viaduc** – *9 Busseau-Gare, Busseau-sur-Creuse.* ℘05 55 62 57 20. www.restaurant-leviaduc.com. 5 rooms. This inn enjoys a favourable situation: its rustic dining room and terrace overlook the 1863 viaduct that crosses the Creuse. Traditional cuisine brought up to date and prepared with quality ingredients. Upstairs you can stay in one of the well-kept rooms.

◒◒ **Le Lion d'Or** – *11 pl. du Gén.-d'Espagne.* ℘05 55 66 65 71. http://liondor-aubusson.com. 🅿. In a ravishing setting, delicious innovative and traditional cooking is served at a very affordable price.

◒◒◒ **Les Mille Sources** – *Le Bourg, St-Marc-à-Loubaud.* ℘05 55 66 03 69. 🅿. The jovial host of this charming old farm will greet you like an old friend. Challans ducks and leg of lamb roasted in the period fireplace of the rustic dining room.

Bourganeuf

Bourganeuf is built on a rocky spur overlooking the Taurion valley among wooded hills. Nothing seems to faze this town in the heart of the Limousin, and in fact, it has always been ahead of its time. With the arrival of Prince Cem, the town had already discovered the refined pleasures of the Orient in medieval times. Then, four centuries later, Bourganeuf became the first town in Europe to be lit by electricity.

THE TOWN

From the Latin *Burgum novum*, the town of Bourganeuf developed around a house built by the Knights of the Order of Saint John (or the Order of Hospitallers) to accommodate religious pilgrims.

Tour Zizim

Pl. du Mail. You may visit the ground floor, but the rest is closed for work.
Guided tour (45mn) by prior arrangement in mid-Jul–mid-Sept daily except Tue 11am–12.30pm.
€4 (children under 12, no charge).
05 55 64 12 20.

This tower is part of the castle, where the great priory of Auvergne of the Order of Saint John of Jerusalem was based. Prince Cem was held in captivity here. The tower is topped by a superb **framework★** and contains objects gathered from the local Gallo-Roman excavations (these are not always on display during the work). From the top floor of the tower, enjoy pretty **views** over the town and surrounding countryside.

Hôtel de Ville

Open only during exhibitions daily except weekends and public holidays 9am–noon, 2–5pm. No charge.
05 55 64 07 61.

In the Salle du Conseil, there is a magnificent 18C **Aubusson tapestry★**. Note the symbols of the *Ancien Régime*, a sceptre and the hand of Justice; and those of Liberty, *fasces lictoriae* and the scales of Justice. Two symbols surround

- **Population:** 2 910.
- **Michelin Map:** 325: H5.
- **Info:** Pl. du Champ-de-Foire. ℘05 55 64 12 20. www.ot-bourganeuf.com.
- **Don't Miss:** Tour Zizim, Eglise St-Jean and Musée de l'Électrification.
- **Location:** Bourganeuf is located at the intersection of D 941 from Aubusson (40km/24.8mi), to Limoges (50km/31mi) and D 940 from Guéret (33km/20.5mi) to Eymoutiers (30km/18.6mi) at the foot of the plateau de Millevaches.
- **Kids:** Enjoy a walk in the woods of the Taurion valley and visit the Espace Pêche et Nature de Pontarion, a nature observatory that also offers an interesting discovery circuit.
- **Timing:** Take time to wander through the Taurion valley in the morning and come back to Bourganeuf to visit the town at midday.

the curious central motif of an eye in the centre of an oak leaf crown.

Church

Built by the Order of Hospitallers next to their castle, this church was entirely reworked in the 15C, as is evidenced by the ogee arches and lateral chapels. An octagonal cupola on pendentives supports the belltower.

In the choir, there is a pretty keystone adorned with a Christ in Majesty and a 15C silver reliquary hand. The organ, built in the 1820s, is the work of the Alsacian organ builder Joseph Callinet.

Musée de l'Électrification

La Grand'Eau. Open Jul–Aug daily 2–7pm (Wed and Sat 10am–noon, 2–7pm). €4 (children under 11, €3).
05 55 64 26 26.

In 1886, 60 light bulbs lit up the night in the village of Bourganeuf. But soon, the current in the Verger stream that provided energy to the dynamo through a bucket wheel would prove too weak to support them. You'll learn what happened next through written and audiovisual media in this museum.

🚗 DRIVING TOUR

5 HAUTE VALLÉE DU TAURION
Round-trip of 50km/31mi. Allow 3hr. See route 5 on region map p359.

▶ Leave Bourganeuf NE on D 940A towards La Chapelle-Taillefert, then turn right on D 50.

Sardent
The Chapel of St-Pardoux, 2km/1mi outside of the village, rises up on the right. This lovely site is popular with pilgrims who come for the virtues attributed to the water.

▶ Drive E along D 50 to Maisonnisses.

Maisonnisses
Near the source of the River Gartemps, the village was once a headquarters for the Knights Templar. Only the church has survived; it contains a **recumbent figure★** discovered in 1830 and replaced in its wall-niche tomb in 1955. It probably represents a 13C knight.

▶ Leave the village on D 34, travelling S to St-Hilaire-le-Château.

Pont Peri
🚶 A footpath leads to this Roman bridge spanning the Gosne. In the picturesque setting, admire the vaulting arch formed by massive hewn stones.

▶ Return to St-Hilaire-le-Château, then take N 141 towards Bourganeuf.

Pontarion
Settled along the banks of the Taurion, the salient feature of the hamlet is the 15C **château** with its corner towers and battlements. The south façade faces

the river and can be admired from the water's edge. Nature lovers will enjoy the arboretum, belvedere, garden and nature trail at the foot of the castle.
The **church** (13C) has a characteristic Limousin doorway decorated with a frieze. Inside, the tombstones honour stonemasons.

▶ After crossing the River Taurion, turn left on D 13.

Nécropole des Sagnes
🚶 *A path leads through the woods (800m) to this Gallo-Roman site used for funeral ceremonies.*
The burial grounds contained incinerated remains in 300 tombs, some in the form of funerary urns. Since then, nature has taken the site back, and it is a good place for a countryside stroll.

▶ Continue along D 13.

Pierre aux Neuf Gradins
🚶 Walk under oak trees along a steep path to this mysterious and lovely site; or follow the signs from the north for easier access.

▶ Continue on D 13 to Soubrebost.

Soubrebost
This is the native village of **Martin Nadaud** (1815–98). He was an exceptional character with progressive, revolutionary ideas. The nickname of this Creuse-based mason who became a politician could be translated as "the blue-collar MP". His life is described through an interesting, interactive **museum circuit (La Martinèche)** set up in his former home. ⏱🚶 *Mid-Jun–mid-Sept 2.30–6.30pm; rest of the year Sun and public holidays 2.30–6pm.* ⊛€6 *(children under 16, €4).* 📞*05 55 64 25 15. www.martinadaud-martineche.com.*

▶ Continue on D 13. Turn right on D 37, then right again on the D 8 to come back to Bourganeuf.

SANCERROIS *and Sologne Berrichone*

Beyond Bourges with its incredible cathedral, historic district and numerous museums, there are numeous cultural aspects of this region that shouldn't be overlooked. The music festival Printemps de Bourges, which each year brings together a striking number and variety of eminent and lesser-known musicians, is not to be missed. The wine of the Sancerre region, among its other products, is just as famous. And if you're interested in witchcraft, this is a region rich in legends that will fascinate you!

Printemps de Bourges

This music festival was created in April 1977 and has grown ever since. Shows take place in a dozen different venues and the street attractions are as interesting as the music. Over the decades, artists who have played at the festival include the French performers Téléphone, Charles Trenet, Claude Nougaro, Patricia Kass, Johnny Hallyday, Véronique Sanson, Juliette Gréco and Abd al-Malik, but also international artists such as Joe Cocker, Murray Head, Touré Kunda, Miles Davis, Nina Simone, The Cure, U2 and Frank Zappa. Now in its 34th year, the festival remains fresh and exciting.

Sancerre Wine

"...This land," wrote Balzac in 1844 in *La Muse du Département*, "produces many generous vintages of rich bouquet, so similar to those of Burgundy that an untrained Parisian palate cannot taste the difference." Vineyards are planted on every sunny hill of this region. The Sancerre label only applies to white Sauvignon wines and to red and rosé wines made from the Pinot grape.

Highlights

1 Magnificent early Gothic **Cathédrale St-Etienne** (p383)

2 **Palais Jacques-Cœur**, a sumptuous Gothic mansion (p386)

3 The world-renowned wine and cheese of **Sancerre** (p394)

4 **Aubigny-sur-Nère**, city of the Stuarts (p399)

5 **Mehun-sur-Yèvre** porcelain manufacturing (p402)

Witchcraft in the Berry

The flat landscape, often swathed in mist, and solitary trees, burnt by lightning or twisted by the wind, create dark and menacing silhouettes in the lonely countryside of the Berry. The Compagnons de Vin de Bué, a local winegrowers' association, give this advice: it is best to seek out spirits in the small hours, as in the daylight you can see right through them.

Timbered home and church, Aubigny-sur-Nère

© Gérard Labriet / Photononstop

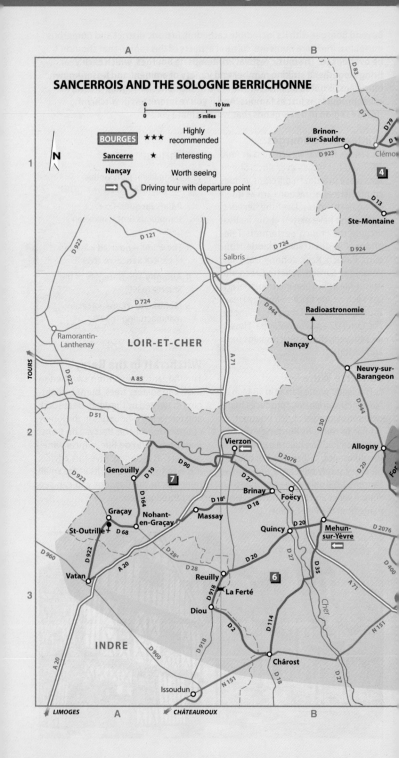

SANCERROIS AND THE SOLOGNE BERRICHONNE

0   10 km
0   5 miles

BOURGES	★★★	Highly recommended
<u>Sancerre</u>	★	Interesting
Nançay		Worth seeing
	Driving tour with departure point	

N

Brinon-sur-Sauldre

Clémor

D 83   D 7   D 79

4

D 923

Ste-Montaine

D 13

D 922   D 121   Salbris   D 724   D 924

LOIR-ET-CHER

Radioastronomie

D 944

Nançay

D 724

Ramorantin-Lanthenay

TOURS

D 922

A 85

Neuvy-sur-Barangeon

D 944

D 51

D 922

A 71

Vierzon

D 90

D 2076

Allogny

For

Genouilly

D 19

7

D 27

Brinay

Foëcy

D 164

Nohant-en-Graçay

D 18⁶

D 18

Massay

D 20

Mehun-sur-Yèvre

D 2076

Graçay

St-Outrille

D 68

Quincy

D 20

D 35

D 400

D 960

D 922

A 20

D 28⁶

D 28

D 20

D 27

6

A 71

Vatan

Reuilly

La Ferté

Cher

N 151

D 918

Diou

D 114

INDRE

D 2

D 918

D 960

Chârost

D 18

D 27

A 20

N 151

Issoudun

LIMOGES

CHÂTEAUROUX

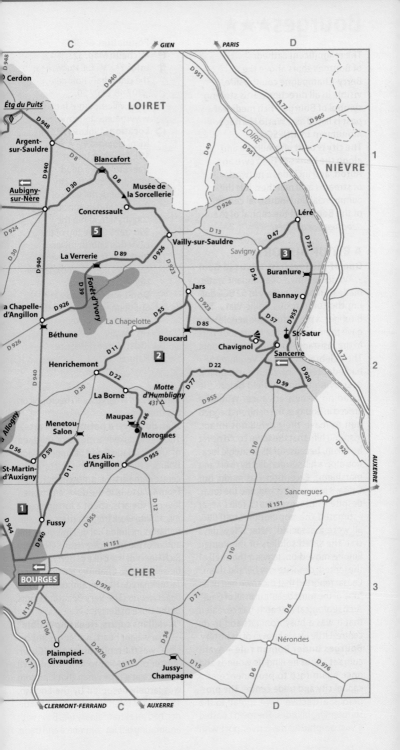

C   *GIEN*   *PARIS*   D

D 948

Cerdon

Étg du Puits

D 940

D 951

A 77

LOIRE

D 965

LOIRET

D 948

Argent-
sur-Sauldre

D 8

D 49

D 951

NIÈVRE   1

Blancafort

D 8

D 30

Musée de
la Sorcellerie

D 926

Léré

Aubigny-
sur-Nère

Concressault

5

D 13

D 47

D 751

D 924

Vailly-sur-Sauldre

Savigny

3

D 926

La Verrerie

D 89

D 926

D 923

D 54

Buranlure

D 940

D 30

Forêt d'Ivory

D 39

Jars

Bannay

D 57

D 955

St-Satur

a Chapelle-
d'Angillon

D 926

La Chapelotte

D 55

D 923

D 85

Sancerre

Béthune

D 926

Boucard

Chavignol

D 22

D 11

2

D 22

D 59

D 920   2

Henrichemont

D 940

D 22

D 77

D 955

A 77

D 20

La Borne

Motte
d'Humbligny
431

Maupas

D 46

D 955

D 10

D 920

Menetou-
Salon

Morogues

Les Aix-
d'Angillon

D 955

a Allogny

D 56

D 59

AUXERRE

St-Martin-
d'Auxigny

D 11

Sancergues

1

D 12

N 151

D 955

Fussy

D 944

D 940

N 151

D 10

3

BOURGES

CHER

D 976

D 71

D 6

N 142

D 106

D 976

D 2076

Nérondes

A 71

D 119

D 36

Plaimpied-
Givaudins

D 15

D 6

Jussy-
Champagne

CLERMONT-FERRAND   C   *AUXERRE*   D

Bourges★★★

The magnificent cathedral of Bourges soars above the Berry-Champagne countryside, visible in all directions. This striking symbol of Bourges' rich medieval past is listed as a World Heritage Monument by UNESCO.

The city is built on a hillside and along the banks of the Yèvre and Auron, and includes a network of streams and marshes. It is the commercial and industrial centre of the Berry and the capital of the *département* of Cher.

A BIT OF HISTORY

One of the loveliest towns in Gaul

– Avaricum, town of abundant water, made its mark in history in 52 BCE during the tumultuous Gallic Wars. The Bituriges, a powerful Celtic people who gave their name to the town, took part in the resistance to Roman occupation. The celebrated warrior Vercingétorix had adopted a scorched-earth policy, destroying town and field before the invading army's advance. When he arrived in Bourges, the denizens begged him to leave their dwellings intact, assuring him that the town could never be taken, because of its strategic location atop a hill surrounded by rivers and marshland. Exception was made, but Caesar's legions attacked, and the town, despite its bravest efforts, fell. Caesar estimated the population at 40 000: all were massacred. After a few days rest, the sated soldiers of the Roman Empire moved on, leaving the shell of the looted, desolate city behind them. Caesar reported that the town had been "one of the most beautiful in all of Gaul". Archaeological research has revealed that it was a busy ironcraft and trade centre. Little else is known of its history.

Bourges under Roman rule

– Avaricum set about healing its wounds and once again rose to prominence as a capital city and trade centre. The prosperous, attractive town spread to the surrounding hillsides. The town boasted a vast amphitheatre, a river port with

> ▶ **Population:** 66 381.
> ⚙ **Michelin Map:** 323: K-4.
> ▤ **Info:** 21 r. Victor-Hugo (near the cathedral), Bourges. ℘02 48 23 02 60. www.ville-bourges.fr or www.bourgestourisme.com.
> ◖ **Location:** 196km/122.5mi NE of Limoges via A 20/N 151. The city's tourist train provides a good introduction to the city. For a wonderful view of Bourges and its surrounding countryside, climb the 396 steps to the top of the cathedral's north tower.
> Ⓟ **Parking:** There are several car parks dotted around the city (⚙see city plan).
> ⊛ **Don't Miss:** Cathédrale St-Étienne; Palais Jacques-Cœur; Hôtel Estève; Les Marais.
> ⚑ **Kids:** Musée d'Histoire Naturelle.

harbour and wharves, and necropoli on the outskirts.

Jean de Berry: a patron of the arts

– The young duke Jean de Berry, third son of King John the Good of France, made Bourges the capital of his duchy and a centre of the arts of utmost importance. From 1360 to 1416 the duke, an inspired lover of the arts, spent a fortune commissioning work from painters. The illuminators included Pol de Limbourg, the author of the *Très Riches Heures* (The Very Rich Hours of the Duke of Berry), now to be seen in the Chantilly Museum; and Jacquemart de Hesdin, author of the *Très Belles Heures* (The Very Beautiful Hours of the Duke of Berry).

"A vaillans cœurs, riens impossible"

– "To a valiant heart, nothing is impossible" was the motto of **Jacques Cœur**, Master of the Mint to King Charles VII of France at a time when that kingdom was largely occupied by the English. This man of humble origin, son of a furrier, had an extraordinary life. Born with an amazing gift for commerce and trade, he soon made a colossal fortune. Given charge of the finances of Bourges, he became, in 1442, counsellor to Charles VII and principal emissary for the kingdom's expansion of trade. He built a magnificent palace at Bourges, though he was to see little of it. He was hated by many courtiers who were jealous of his political and diplomatic offices, the king's favour and honours that he had been granted. He thus fell into disgrace, a victim of his own advancement. He was arrested in 1451 and condemned to perpetual banishment, confiscation of all his property and a heavy fine.

But this was not the end for Jacques Cœur: he escaped from prison, sought refuge in Rome and was given command of a fleet of ships by the Pope. In 1456 while he was on the Ninth Crusade in Chios, he died.

The University, a cradle of new ideas – Charles de Berry, Louis XI's brother, founded the university of Bourges in 1463. Its influence spread far beyond the duchy for over a century. The law school attracted many students, including some from abroad. German students brought with them the new doctrines of Luther: Calvin, a student at Bourges, was influenced by these views which informed his *Institutes of the Christian Religion*. In spite of persecution, his ideas soon gained support in Bourges and throughout Berry.

The duchy was thus divided and became a battlefield during the period of the Wars of Religion. The prosperity of the city, much reduced by a terrible fire in 1487, came to an end during the war.

Decline and expansion – By the mid-17C, Berry had entered a sort of stupor which lasted two more centuries. As it was located off the main routes, it was bypassed while cities like Tours and Orleans, on the River Loire, underwent economic expansion. The *bourgeoisie* were not drawn into industry and trade here as they were elsewhere. Their lives were circumscribed by regional politics and religion.

The construction of the Berry canal (1819–42), the railway and the establishment of the armaments industry in Bourges under the Second Empire breathed new economic life into the region.

Since the end of WWII, Bourges has expanded rapidly. Various industries have arrived here, creating thousands of jobs. The development of the A 71 motorway has also contributed to the lively dynamics of the town today.

A city of music – The cultural influence of Bourges is far greater than its small size might suggest. As well as the Maison de la Culture. Bourges also hosts the renowned musical festival, **le Printemps de Bourges**, a yearly event drawing crowds of young fans of popular music.

CATHÉDRALE ST-ÉTIENNE★★★

Force of architecture, harmony of proportion and richness of decoration make this cathedral a marvel.

Construction took place in two stages. During the first stage, from 1195 to 1215, the chevet and the chancel were built outside the fortifications that protected the city at the time, due to lack of space. During the second stage, from 1225 to 1260, the nave, west front and final embellishments were added. The cathedral was consecrated on 13 May 1324.

Additions and restorations – The southern tower was consolidated during the 14C by a reinforced arcade. Once the west front had been remodelled, it was possible to install the great window above the central door.

Misfortune struck when, at the end of 1506, the north tower collapsed. It was rebuilt, but in 1562, a Protestant army pillaged the cathedral and destroyed the statues adorning the west front.

Some restoration was undertaken in the 19C in the form of additional balustrades, belltowers and pinnacles.

Since the 20C, a preservation campaign has been undertaken to prevent further deterioration of the stone carvings by pollution.

Cathédrale Saint-Étienne

© Brigitte Merz / Look / Photononstop

Outside

West front – Five **doorways** beneath individual gables stand in a line beneath the great stained-glass window, known as the *grand housteau* – the great western gable. The theme of the **central doorway** is the Last Judgement. Great vitality and realism make the doorway one of the masterpieces of 13C Gothic sculpture.

The tympanum of **St Stephen's doorway** is devoted to episodes in the life and the martyrdom of St Stephen, patron of the cathedral.

The story of St Ursinus, the first bishop of Bourges, and of St Justus is depicted on the tympanum of **St Ursinus' doorway**. The **Virgin's doorway** and **St Guillaume's doorway** had to be partly rebuilt after the collapse of the north tower in the 16C.

Two **towers** of unequal height frame the five doorways. On the right, the so-called *Tour Sourde* (or "deaf tower'", because it had no bell) was never completed. Its plain style contrasts with the flamboyantly decorated *Tour de Beurre* ("butter tower") on the left.

◗ Go round to the north side of the cathedral.

North side – The north side is embellished by a 12C **doorway**, which was incorporated in the present cathedral. On the tympanum are scenes from the Vigin's life.

East end – Note the little turrets above the chevets' radial chapels.

South side – The south side is adorned with a 13C **doorway**. Christ appears in majesty on the tympanum, surrounded by the symbols of the Evangelists.

◗ Enter the cathedral by the south.

Inside

Nave – St-Étienne Cathedral is one of the largest Gothic cathedrals in France at 124m long, 41m wide and 37m high to the top of the inner vaulting. There are no transepts and this gives the nave with its four side aisles a feeling of greater majesty; the five aisles correspond to the five doorways. The columns of the nave rise in a single thrust to a height of 17m. They are surrounded by groups of smaller columns, some of which reach the vaulting. To extend the perspective the architect slightly increased the distance between the pillars in the chancel.

An original feature of the building is the differing heights of its double side aisles with windows on two levels. The five bands of light and shade created within the cathedral considerably enhance the architectural effect (◖*see cross-section*). A double ambulatory continues the line of the twin aisles. Five small semicircular radial chapels open onto the apse.

◗ Turn right and enter the chancel via the second south aisle.

Chapelle St-Jean-Baptiste – This chapel contains two beautiful frescoes dating from the late 1460s depicting the Crucifixion and the Resurrection.

Chapelle Tullier – The chapel is lit by Lescuyer's fine Renaissance windows. Although these **stained-glass windows**★★★ have incurred some damage over the years, they are among the most remarkable in France, dating from the 12C to the 17C.

The five apsidal chapels and the windows between them are adorned with windows shaped to fit the architecture and medallion windows. Most of these were made between 1215 and 1225.

The artist who created the **Last Judgement and the New Alliance** employed an exuberant, majestic style in his depictions of people and their clothing.

The master who accomplished **the Good Samaritan** master is also probably the artist responsible for the intermediate windows representing the Passion and the Apocalypse, the windows of St Mary the Egyptian, St Nicholas and the martyrdom of St Stephen in the radial chapels.

The master responsible for the **St Stephen reliquaries** illustrates some of the typical traits of Gothic representational art: elongated bodies on spindly legs, disproportionately large heads and faces seeming to express displeasure; and yet these windows are lively and evocative.

Crypt★★ – ○ ⌖ Guided tours (1hr). Jul–Aug at 9.45am, 11am, 12,15pm, 2.15pm, 3.15pm, 3.45pm, 4.45pm and 5.45pm; rest of year daily except Sun am 10am, 11.15am, 2.30pm, 4pm, 5.30pm. ⌖ €7.50 combined ticket with ascent of north tower. A long sloping gallery leads down to the vast late-12C crypt. Twelve large windows light the sanctuary. Six massive pillars (2.10min diameter)

support the vaulted ceiling on diagonal ribs which, in turn, support the cathedral above.

In the crypt, note the **recumbent white marble figure** of the Duke of Berry, the only vestige of a grandiose mausoleum (*1422*).

Ascent of the north tower – ○*Open Jul–Aug 9.30am–6pm; rest of year daily except Sun am 9.30–11.30am, 2–5.30pm.* ⌖*Guided tours: Apr–Sept 9.45–11.45am, 2–5.30pm, Sun and public holidays 2–5.30pm; rest of year 9.30–11.30am, 2–4.45pm, Sun and public holidays 2–4.45pm.* ○*Closed 1 Jan, 1 May, 1 and 11 Nov and 25 Dec.* ⌖*€7.50 combined ticket with the crypt (visitors under 26, no charge).* ✆*02 48 65 49 44.*

An attempt to complete the northern tower at the end of the 15C resulted in its collapse in 1506. Reconstruction lasted until 1540, carried out under the direction of architect Guillaume de Pelvoysin, who introduced new decorative

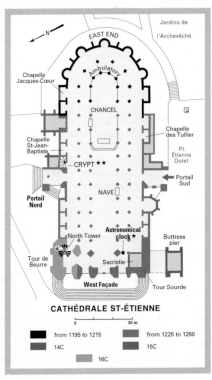

CATHÉDRALE ST-ÉTIENNE

■ from 1195 to 1215	■ from 1225 to 1260
■ 14C	■ 15C
■ 16C	

elements in the Renaissance style. A spiral staircase (*396 steps*) leads to the top (*65m*), where a **view★★** rewards those who climb it.

Organ – The organ case dates from 1663. The old pipes are still in place but the mechanism has been changed many times.

Astronomical clock★ – Designed by mathematician and astronomer Jean Fusoris in 1424, this magnificent clock (6.2m high) is set in a square frame, surmounted by a concave roof and a bell. The decorative elements were designed by Jean Grangier.

PALAIS JACQUES-CŒUR★★

Guided tour (1hr). Open Apr–Sept 10am–noon, 2–6pm; rest of year 9.30am –noon, 2–5pm. Closed 1 Jan, 1 May, 1 and 11 Nov, and 25 Dec. €7.50 (visitors under 26, no charge).
02 48 24 79 41.

Architectural elegance, richness and variety of decoration make this one of the most beautiful and sumptuous secular buildings of the Gothic age.

This splendid mansion was commissioned in 1443 for Charles VII's famous Master of the Mint, and was undoubtedly intended as the place to which he would retire.

Jacques Cœur fell into disgrace in 1451 and so never enjoyed his palace. In 1457 it was restored to his heirs and from then on knew many changes of fortune. In 1679 it belonged to Colbert (1619–83); soon afterwards it was acquired by the city of Bourges. It was bought by the State in 1925 and has since been completely restored.

Exterior

Jacques Cœur's Palace consists of four main buildings round a central court. Whereas the west face looks like the exterior of a fortress with massive towers and bare walls, the **east face** draws attention through the delicacy and richness of its decoration. This appears, in one instance, as a motif of hearts and shells – emblems from Jacques Cœur's coat of arms – adorning the mullioned windows of the top floor and the balustrade at the base of the eaves. On either side of a balcony, note the amusing figures of a man and a woman. To the left of this wing, at the base of the octagonal staircase tower, Jacques Cœur's motto may be seen inscribed: *A vaillans cœurs, riens impossible* (To a valiant heart, nothing is impossible).

As you enter the **central court** you'll notice a striking difference between the sober appearance of the galleries and the rich decoration of the main living quarters which include banquet and ceremonial halls as well as private apartments.

Interior

A tour of the palace will give you an idea of the luxury to which a wealthy burgher with good taste and practical sense could aspire.

On the ground floor, the taste for luxury is evident in the magnificence of the **dining hall** with its monumental chimney-piece (restored in the 19C) and a loggia to accommodate musicians. The practical sense comes out in the installation of running water, a **boiler room** and **bathroom** and the planning of staircases and corridors so that those wishing to take a bath could do so without going outside to adjoining buildings.

Of particular interest on the first floor are the **Salle des Échevins** decorated with 17C murals depicting rural and hunting scenes; the **treasury**, which has a heavy iron door closed with a secret lock; the **attic** with its wooden vaulting in the shape of an inverted boat keel; the **council chamber**, which houses a model of the original palace; the **galleries** where Jacques Cœur used to receive the town's merchants; and the chapel.

WALKING TOUR

OLD TOWN

The whole town centre is part of a preservation and renovation scheme which aims at restoring the **half-timbered houses★**, of which many date from the 15C and 16C, to their former glory. The old district lying north of the cathedral offers a particularly pleasant stroll.

Jardins de l'Archevêché★

Designed in the 17C and extended in the 18C, these gardens feature splendid flower beds, fine shaded alleyways, ornamental ponds, bronze vases and a bandstand. From the garden's beautiful flower beds and shaded alleys, you'll get a good view of St Stephen's Cathedral.

Place Étienne-Dolet

As you walk across the square, note on your left the façade of the former **archbishop's residence** which now houses the Musée des Meilleurs Ouvriers de France (◐ *see below*). Walk the length of the **cathedral★★★** and admire the successive doorways.

Grange aux Dîmes

Opposite the cathedral's north doorway at the corner of rue Molière, this massive tithe barn with its buttresses and stairway designed as a half-timbered balcony was used to store the dues paid to the church.

◐ Short walk down rue des Trois-Maillets then turn left through a porch.

Promenade des Remparts★

The ramparts are visible in several places and especially along the **Promenade des Remparts** behind and below the cathedral. Ingeniously integrated into the fabric of the contemporary town, the dressed stone wall dates back to the 3C, when it was erected for protection against barbarian invasions.

◐ Take the George Sand stairs on the left.

This passageway, known as *casse-cou* (breakneck) – one understands why on rainy days – runs through the ramparts and leads to place George-Sand. Cross **rue Porte-Jaune** and admire the massive cathedral towers on your left. Next, rue St-Michel-de-Bourges leads into the town centre's high street; note **Louis

XI's statue** near the neo-Gothic post office dating from 1926.

◐ Follow rue Moyenne and turn right onto rue Mayet-Genetry.

The lovely **Fontaine Bourdaloue** adorns place de la Préfecture.

◐ Walk along rue des Armuriers.

Jacques Cœur's "Birthplace"

A half-timbered, corbelled house, standing at the corner of rue d'Auron and rue des Armuriers, bears an inscription describing it as the house in which Jacques Cœur was born (c 1395–1456). In fact it was built early in the 16C on the site of a house that came to Jacques Cœur through his marriage.

◐ Follow rue d'Auron and turn right onto rue des Arènes.

Église St-Pierre-le-Guillard

According to legend, funds for building the church were provided by a Jewish man, Zacharie Guillard, whose mule knelt before the Holy Sacrament as it was being carried by St Antony of Padua through Bourges in about 1225.
A massive belfry-porch leads to the nave flanked by side aisles to which chapels were added in the 15C.

◐ Continue along rue des Arènes then turn right.

Rue des Linières

A steep, attractively cobbled street.

Place des Quatre-Piliers

Three splendid 17C and 18C mansions, Hôtel Témoin (the former library), Hôtel Bengy and Hôtel Méloizes, overshadow the fountain decorating the square.

◐ Follow rue Jacques-Cœur.

Palais Jacques-Cœur★★

◐*See p386*. Walk to place Jacques-Cœur to admire his statue and the remarkable façade of his mansion, which was restored in 1998.

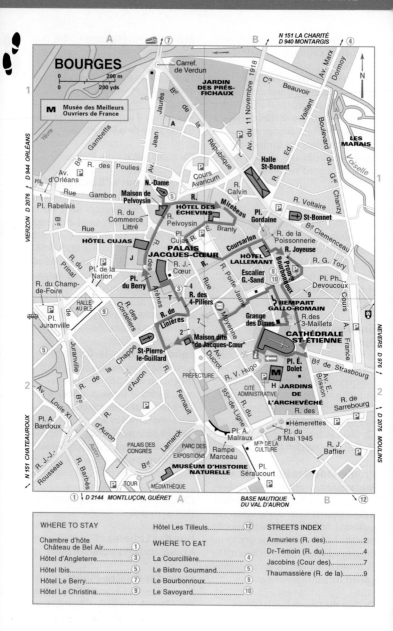

BOURGES

M	Musée des Meilleurs Ouvriers de France

WHERE TO STAY		
Chambre d'hôte Château de Bel Air	①
Hôtel d'Angleterre	③
Hôtel Ibis	⑤
Hôtel Le Berry	⑦
Hôtel Le Christina	⑨

Hôtel Les Tilleuls	⑫

WHERE TO EAT	
La Courcillière	④
Le Bistro Gourmand	⑤
Le Bourbonnoux	⑧
Le Savoyard	⑩

STREETS INDEX	
Armuriers (R. des)	2
Dr-Témoin (R. du)	4
Jacobins (Cour des)	7
Thaumassière (R. de la)	9

▶ Retrace your steps and go down the stairs on your right, leading to the lower part of town.

Place du Berry

Facing you is the west front of Palais Jacques-Cœur built on the remains of the Gallo-Roman ramparts.
From here it looks like a fortress flanked with massive towers, in contrast to the earlier view.

▶ Walk along rue des Arènes.

Hôtel Cujas★

This elegant building was designed in about 1515 by Guillaume Pelvoysin for Durando Salvi, a rich Florentine merchant who had settled in Bourges.

Musée du Berry★

4 rue des Arènes. ⏱*Open daily except Tue 10am–noon, 2–6pm.* ⏱*Closed 1 Jan, 1 May, 1 and 11 Nov and 25 Dec.* ⊛*No charge.* ℘*02 48 70 41 92.*
This quiet, unpretentious museum, housed in the Hôtel Cujas, contains **archaeological collections★** (dating from prehistory to the end of the Gallo-Roman period), sculpture, furniture and pottery as well as a fine collection of **statues★** including *The Prophets* (1382) by Jean de Cambrai and André Beauneveu and *The Weepers* from the Duke of Berry's tomb by Jean de Cambrai.

▶ Cross place Planchat to rue Pelvoysin.

Maison de Pelvoysin

An interesting group of old, half-timbered houses stand at the corner of rue Pelvoysin and rue Cambournac. Next to these you'll see the house of Pelvoysin, the cathedral architect.
This stone building now houses the savings bank. The street was so narrow when it was being built that the architect designed the front to stand at an angle to the street, giving the house an appearance of greater width and dignity. The courtyard is best viewed from rue Cambournac.

Église Notre-Dame

The church was gutted by the fire of 1487. Various modifications were made to the original plan as it was rebuilt, including the addition of side aisles and the square tower which rises at the north end of the west front. In the south aisle, opposite the door, a **white-marble baptismal font** adorned with fleurs-de-lis bears an inscription from the *Romance of the Rose*, the French medieval poem which inspired Chaucer.

▶ Walk across place de la Barre.

Rue Mirebeau

This pleasant pedestrianised street is lined with timber-framed houses whose ground floors are often occupied by shops. Opposite yet another passage called *casse-cou*, you'll see the doorway of the former Augustine convent. Enter the courtyard to admire the trapezium-shaped cloisters.

▶ Walk up the steep, dark passage casse-cou (Mirebeau stairs); once at the top, turn right onto rue Branly.

Hôtel des Échevins★

This former town hall now houses the Musée Estève. (♿*see Sights*). There is a striking difference in architectural style between the two parts of the building. The living quarters at the far end of the courtyard were built in 1489 in the Flamboyant Gothic style.
A fine **octagonal tower★★** juts out from the façade. Inside, a spiral rises up its three storeys.

Musée Estève★★

Hôtel des Echevins, 13 rue Eduard Branly. ♿⏱*Same hours as Musée du Berry.* ⊛*No charge.* ℘*02 48 24 75 38.*
Since 1987, this museum has been home to a unique collection of 130 works by the artist **Maurice Estève**.
Born in Culan in 1904, Estève had no formal training as an artist. His work reveals a stunning evolution in technique, while themes from his native Berry are repeated over time: the home (curtains,

a window, a table, other household objects), his grandmother (*Paysanne Endormie aux Rideaux Verts*, 1924) and the natural environment (*Châtaigneraie*, 1927).

During his stay in Paris, Estève was influenced by the Surrealists and, later, Cézanne. Up to 1947, his work shifted between the figurative (*La Toilette Verte*, 1934) and the abstract (*Embarquement pour Cythère*, 1929), before settling on the latter. Most of his paintings are a subtle combination or a juxtaposition of masses of colour.

▶ Continue along rue Branly to place Cujas then turn onto rue des Beaux-Arts.

Rue Coursalon

There is a fine view of place Gordaine along this lively pedestrianised street. Turn right onto a narrow street with a 15C house on the corner.

▶ Return to rue Coursalon.

Place Gordaine

This flower-decked square situated at the intersection of the pedestrianised streets is popular with visitors. Note the stone on which Calvin used to stand to advocate the reformation.

▶ Turn right onto rue Bourbonnoux.

Hôtel Lallemant★

Altered in the 17C this mansion has retained the name of Jean Lallemant, the rich cloth merchant who had it built. The site straddles the town's Roman wall and certain parts of the house are on different levels.

It now houses the **Musée des Arts Décoratifs** (*5 r. de l'Hôtel-Lallemant;* ○*Open daily except Mon 10am–noon, 2–6pm.* ○*Closed 1 Jan, 1 May, 1 and 11 Nov and 25 Dec.* ⊗*No charge.* ☏*02 48 70 23 57*).

A sloping ramp, covered with barrel vaulting and used to lead horses in and out of the building, goes through to the **main courtyard** which is on two levels. The large main building shows the styles of different architectural periods: the

mullioned windows and arcades are 15C, the doors to the corridors and the window-frames of the bays above the passageway are 16C and the entablature and round frontons bearing the arms of the Dorsannes who once owned the mansion are 17C. An Italian-style loggia features 17C frescoes of hunting scenes and a polychrome bas-relief dedicated to St Christopher.

On the top floor, one room houses a notable **collection of miniatures★**, master craft pieces all perfectly executed, which provide an unusual and thorough summary of the history of furniture from Louis XV to Art Nouveau.

▶ Return to the main building and take the spiral staircase opposite the information desk.

Enamels, porcelains and ivories, as well as Renaissance and 17C French and Flemish tapestries are displayed in the elegant rooms.

▶ Walk up the street opposite Hôtel Lallemant that curves around to the right.

Rue Joyeuse

Note the carved-wood pillar on the street corner supporting the Maison des Trois-Flûtes (*now a bakery*). Walk up this peaceful street lined with private mansions.

▶ Return to rue Bourbonnoux via place Louis-Lacombe.

If you like cobblestones, walk along rue Moncenoux, then turn right onto rue de la Thaumassière.

Rue Bourbonnoux

There are a large number of craftsmen's workshops along this former high street among the timber-framed houses. Farther along the street reaches the east end of the cathedral.

Musée des Meilleurs Ouvriers de France

Place Etienne Dolet. ♿ ⏰ *Open daily except Mon 10am–noon, 2–6pm.*
⏰ *Closed 1 Jan, 1 May, 1 and 11 Nov and 25 Dec.* 🎫 *No charge.* ☎ *02 48 57 82 45*
Housed in the former archbishop's residence, this unusual museum contains exceptionally fine objects made by gifted craftsmen.

LES MARAIS

Before you take a stroll through the town's unusual wetlands, go into Église St-Bonnet, which links the historic part of the city and the rural district known as the Marais.

Église St-Bonnet

This 1510 church was remodelled in the 20C, when two bays and a neo-Flamboyant facade were added.
Inside, the most remarkable features are the **stained-glass windows** by Jean Lescuyer and a work by the 17C local painter Jean Boucher.

▶ From place St-Bonnet, walk along rue Voltaire towards the Marais, then cross boulevard du Général-Chanzy.

Les Marais★

A pleasant walkway wanders through the wetlands and canals formed by the River Voiselle, winding among the many garden plots held by the residents of Bourges. A gate marks the border between the town and the Marais.

▶ Go through the gate and walk along the narrow road on the left. At the end of the road, walk across the footbridge on your left, then bear right. A path skirting the *Voiselle* and the Marais de Mariens leads to the River Yèvre.

Digue de l'Yèvre

Flat-bottomed boats are moored beneath a willow tree.

▶ Retrace your steps and take the first path on the right.

Rue de Babylone

There is a fine view of the cathedral to your left. On the right beyond the Marais Hauts, the horizon is barred by the town's northern suburb and the convent of the Sisters of Charity.

▶ Follow avenue Marx Dormoy on the left, then turn right beyond the bridge onto cours Beauvoir.

Jardin des Prés-Fichaux★

A beautiful garden has been laid out on marshland between the river and the close of St-Ambroise abbey where Protestants would gather in the 16C to sing.

▶ Return to place St-Bonnet along boulevard de la République. Note the lively covered market on your left just before the square.

ADDITIONAL SIGHT
Musée d'Histoire Naturelle a

Les Rives d'Auron. 👥♿⏰*Open daily 2–6pm (school holidays 10am–noon and 2–6pm).* ⏰*Closed 1 Jan, 1 May, 1 Nov and 25 Dec.* 🎫*€5 (child €2.50).* ☎*02 48 65 37 34. www.museum-bourges.net.*
The Natural History Museum was created in 1927 and renovated in 1989. It is interactive, entertaining and educational, with an emphasis on the regional environment as well as the work of local naturalists and scientists.

EXCURSIONS
Plaimpied-Givaudins

12.6km/7.8mi S on D 2076, then D 46.
Along the Auron and the old Berry canal, the **abbey-church of St-Martin** is all that remains of the large abbey founded by Richard II, Archbishop of Bourges. The building work, which lasted a century, began at the end of the 11C. Although the façade and the side elevation are very plain, the chevet is unexpectedly rich in ornamentation. The interior of the church owes its originality to its **capitals**.
The oldest of these is located in the choir. Its depictions of monsters and demons show an Oriental influence.

The pillar to the right separating the nave from the transept features the most remarkable of all the capitals: the Temptation of Christ.
Left of the choir, a staircase descends into the lovely crypt. Its trefoil plan features vaults supported by four monolithic columns.

▶ Continue along D 106 and take a left on D 71. At Crosses, turn right on D 15.

Château de Jussy-Champagne

25km/15.5mi E on D 2076. Guided tour (40min) Jul–Aug 2–7pm. €6 (children under 10, €3). ℘02 48 25 00 61.

In a verdant setting among centuries-old trees, this elegant early 17C castle is built in a harmonious mix of brick and stone. You will enter through the courtyard framed by two arched galleries designed by the architect Jean Lejuge. A beautiful Louis XIV-style dining room with a finely sculpted, marble-encrusted 17C stone fireplace awaits you. The various reception rooms feature Louis XIII, Louis XIV and Regency furniture, as well as tapestries and antique paintings. Note the work *Le Magicien* by Michel Gobain, a student of Georges de La Tour; and four paintings over the doors inspired by *Les Beaux-Arts* by Carle van Loo.

▶ Leave Jussy S on D 36.

🚗 DRIVING TOUR

1 FORÊTS ET VIGNOBLE

62km/38.5mi. Allow half a day.
See route 1 on region map pp380-381.

▶ Leave Bourges NW on D 944.

Forêt d'Allogny

D 56 offers views of these dark, mysterious woods. The close-growing trees are mainly oaks, with patches of red firs, birches and beeches.

Vergers de St-Martin-d'Auxigny

Enjoy the view as you descend into the Moulon valley, and notice the contrast with the landscape you've just been through. Here, vineyards and apple trees mark the outskirts of this apple-growing area. If it's harvest time, you can always stop off at one of the large warehouses you'll see along the road for a taste of the wares, which especially include golden apples.

▶ Leave St-Martin-d'Auxigny NE on D 59.

Menetou-Salon

🏠 *23 rue de la Mairie.* ℘02 48 64 87 57.
The vineyards stretching from Menetou to Morogues, 10km/6.2mi east of here, used to be among the finest in France. The Menetou AOC is especially appreciated for its Sauvignon whites with citrus and floral notes and spicy, even minty undertones. There are also a few rosé wines with white fruit and nutty notes, but especially fine Pinot Noir reds with ripe cherry and plum flavours that are to be kept for five to seven years.
The village features a **castle** which was once the property of Jacques Cœur and now features a **collection of antique cars** (call for hours; ℘02 48 64 80 54; www.chateau-menetou-salon.com) set in a magnificent forest that might give you an urge to wander *(access to walking trails on route d'Henrichemont).*

▶ Leave Menetou-Salon S on D 11 towards Bourges.

Fussy

In June of 1940, the frontier of the Occupation cut the Cher in two.
Musée de la Résistance – *Pl. Paul Novara.* ℘02 48 69 44 36. Call for hours. A large collection of documents, including photos and posters, and objects such as arms, flags and uniforms tell the story of the Berrichone resistance movement.

▶ D 940 will take you back to Bourges.

ADDRESSES

🛏 STAY

😊🛏 **Hotel Ibis Bourges** – *R. Vladimir Jankelevitch, Quartier du Prado.* ℘*02 48 65 89 99. www.accorhotels.com. 86 rooms.* A comfortable, smart chain hotel in the centre of town.

😊😊 **Chambre d'hôte Château de Bel Air** – *Lieu-dit le Grand-Chemin, Arcay. 16km/10mi S of Bourges on the D 73.* ℘*02 48 25 36 72. ◺. 6 rooms.* Surrounded by spacious grounds, this 19C château is calm and comfortable. The vast entrance hall leads to the dining room with its massive fireplace. Large bedrooms on the upper floor.

😊🛏 **Hôtel Christina** – *5 r. Halle.* ℘*02 48 70 56 50. www.le-christina.com. WiFi. 64 rooms.* Two categories of well-maintained bedrooms are available in this city-centre hotel: cosy and chic (😊🛏🛏) or smaller and functional (😊🛏).

😊🛏 **Hôtel Les Tilleuls** – *7 pl. Pyrotechnie.* ℘*02 48 20 49 04. www.les-tilleuls.com. WiFi. 39 rooms.* Situated in a quiet part of town, this hotel offers guests accommodation in the main building. In the annex, the rooms are less spacious and more basic but they are air-conditioned.

😊🛏🛏 **Le Berry** – *3 pl. du Général Leclerc. WiFi.* ℘*02 48 65 99 30. www.le-berry.com.* This modern five-storey hotel close to the historic centre offers attractive, colourful, spacious bedrooms and a pleasant restaurant, all of which belie its plain exterior.

😊😊🛏 **Best Western Hôtel d'Angleterre** – *1 pl. des Quatre-Piliers* ℘*02 48 24 68 51. www.bestwestern-angleterre-bourges.com. 31 rooms.* The city's former court of justice is located close to the Palais Jacques-Cœur. All the mod cons in the bedrooms, including air-conditioning for most; their décor is sober yet modern. Buffet breakfast. Friendly staff.

🍽 EAT

😊😊 **Le Bourbonnoux** – *44 r. Bourbonnoux.* ℘*02 48 24 14 76.* You'll find this restaurant among craft shops, along a street just a few steps away from St-Étienne Cathedral. A warm welcome and a dining room pleasantly decorated with bright colours and exposed beams. Popular with locals.

😊😊 **Le Bistro Gourmand** – *5 pl. de la Barre.* ℘*02 48 70 63 37. Reservation recommended.* A delightful bistro specialising in regional and Lyonnais cuisine. The sober décor here is enhanced by gentle candlelight. The terrace looks onto the Église Notre-Dame.

😊😊 **Le Savoyard** – *40 r. Bourbonnoux.* ℘*02 48 02 57 27.* As the name suggests, the focus here is on the cuisine of Savoy, with a menu that includes cheese fondues, raclettes, tartiflettes etc. Wooden skis, clogs, cowbells and other typically Savoyard objects adorn the cool stone vaults of this former coal cellar.

😊😊 **La Courcillière** – *R. de Babylone.* ℘*02 48 24 41 91. www.lacourcilliere.com.* Located in the the Marais district just a stone's throw from the city centre, this pleasant, rustic restaurant has a terrace by the water facing the gardens. Down-to-earth, reasonably priced cuisine.

😊😊 **Le Jardin Gourmand** – *15 bis av. E.-Renan.* ℘*02 48 21 35 91.* This pleasant bistro is slightly off the lively centre of town. The setting is rather plain but the servers are friendly. You'll enjoy specialities from the Berry and Lyon regions with seasonal products.

😊😊🛏 **Le d'Antan Sancerrois** – *50 r. Bourbonnoux.* ℘*02 48 65 96 26. www.dantansancerrois.fr.* Enjoy the elegant setting among the old stones and modern furniture with greyish-blue hues. The chef will delight your tastebuds with original cuisine.

Sancerre★

High above the banks of the River Loire, Sancerre towers above St-Satur and St-Thibault. From this vantage point, a wide view sweeps over the river and Nivernais to the east and Berry to the west. This little city enjoys neat vineyards that yield flinty white wines and goatherds that produce delicious cheese. The two products are renowned in France, especially the cheese from Chavignol. This creamy and savoury goat's cheese is so well-loved that no one is put off in the slightest by its amusing name, Crottin (roughly translated as something you'd rather not step in). The steep streets of the town are enticing with their tempting food shops, restaurants and wine merchants.

OLD TOWN

You'll enjoy strolling around the old neighbourhoods, where the interesting houses and vestiges are marked with informative panels. A brochure called "Fil d'Ariane", available from the tourist office, explains these 28 points of interest in English.

Around the renovated Nouvelle Place, shops sell local crafts and pottery.

▶ **Population:** 1 607.
Michelin Map: 323: M, N-3.
Info: Espl. Porte-César.
&02 48 54 08 21. www.tourisme-sancerre.com.
▶ **Location:** 46km/29mi NE of Bourges via D 955. For a wonderful view of the surrounding area, head for the Esplanade de la Porte César.
Timing: Allow a full day to explore the Sancerrois region.
Don't Miss: The village's renowned vineyards.

Esplanade de la Porte César★★

NE edge of town. See map.

From this terrace, there is a great **view★★** over the vineyards, St-Satur and the viaduct, St-Thibault and the Val de Loire, and even farther afield to the Puisaye region of woods and lakes, between the Loire and the Loing, northeast of Sancerre.

Tour des Fiefs

Open Apr–mid-Nov 2–6pm, Sat–Sun 10am–noon. No charge.
&02 48 78 51 52.

A Strategic Location

Sancerre, already well-known in Roman times as the site of an *oppidum*, has long stood watch over the Loire. It may have been the 9C residence of Robert le Fort, an early member of the Capetian dynasty. Later, the city played an important role in the Hundred Years War, as the gateway to Berry, placed between the Burgundians and the English. Charles VII, the so-called king of Bourges, assembled 20 000 warriors there and personally commanded them for a time.

Sancerre became a stronghold of Protestantism, withstanding the assault of royal forces. The Treaty of St-Germain (1570) and the St Bartholomew's Day Massacre (1572) had no effect on those who held to their reformed views of religion and refused to give in. On 3 January 1573, the Maréchal de La Châtre, accompanied by 7 000 men, laid siege to Sancerre.

After an intense artillery preparation, an assault took place on three fronts, but the local resistance was strong. Capitulation came after seven long months of struggle. The population's surrender was accepted with honour, and they were granted the freedom of their religion.

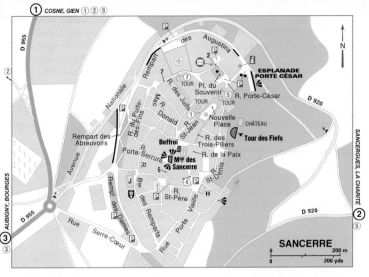

This 14C cylindrical keep is the only vestige of the château of the counts of Sancerre, a Huguenot citadel bitterly defended during the 1573 siege.

From the top, there is a wide **scenic view★** of the Loire valley and the hills of Sancerre.

Belfry

This 1509 belfry serves the church of Notre-Dame de Sancerre.

Maison des Sancerre

3 r. du Méridien, 18100 Sancerre.
⏱*Open Jun–Sept 10am–7pm; Mar–May and Oct–Nov 10am–6pm.* 📞*02 48 54 11 35. www.maison-des-sancerre.com*
Near the church, the restored Maison Farnault (14C) houses the **Maison des Sancerre**, a wonderful place to get information about wines in general and particularly the Sancerre region. Enjoy interactive presentations, videos and a relief model. The interviews with wine professionals are particularly interesting, showing the human side of the wine industry.

This is also a good spot to pick up information about the various cellars and estates in the region. The visit concludes with a tasting.

🚗 DRIVING TOURS

② LE SANCERROIS★

77km/48mi round-trip. Allow 6 hr.
See route 2 on region map pp380–381.

▶ Drive SW out of Sancerre on the D 955 towards Bourges. Then turn right on the D 923.

At the intersection with D 7, there is a splendid **view★★** over Sancerre high atop its bluff, the vineyards, St-Satur and, beyond, the Loire valley.

Chavignol

This lovely little wine-growers' village is nestled in a hollow with vineyards all around.

The name is synonymous with one of France's tastiest and most popular cheeses, **Crottin de Chavignol**.

▷ Just outside the village, take a little road on the right which leads to the hamlet of Amigny.

On the Sens-Beaujeu road, near the intersection with the D 85, there is a nice **view★** of the village of Bué and the rolling countryside.

Château de Boucard

Guided tours Jul–Aug 2–6pm daily except Mon and Tue. €7.
02 48 58 72 81.
Built between the 14C and the 16C, this castle is surrounded by a moat and well-kept outbuildings. The furnished interior has several impressive chimneys and a chapel which was specially redesigned to allow the Princesse de la Trémoille to attend Mass without leaving her bedroom.

▷ Continue along D 74.

Jars

This charming town includes a manor house with round towers, a 15C–16C church in pink and white stone and a mill.

▷ Return to Le Noyer and drive SW along D 55.

Henrichemont

In the early 17C, Sully, minister to Henri IV, decided to create a refuge for his fellow Protestants. As he already owned a château in Chapelle-d'Angillon, he decided to build a town nearby, in a sandy, deserted place, which he called Henrichemont in honour of the king. Although the building was never completed as planned, the design included eight streets like the spokes of a wheel converging on a central square. A few 17C houses with arched doorways and the old well with decorative mouldings are intact (*see La Borne, below*).

The rich clay soil of the Berry makes it perfect for potters. The abundant timber was another important factor of pottery production in the past, when wood-burning kilns were the rule. Gallo-Roman earthenware household objects are on display in the Berry Museum (*see BOURGES*).

For a resolutely modern view of pottery, don't miss the **Centre Céramique Contemporaine** (*open Apr–Sept 11am–7pm; rest of year 2–6pm. closed Jan. 02 48 26 96 21. www.laborne.org*), where the exhibition is completed with a shop selling pottery and related books.

▷ Leave Henrichemont E on D 22.

La Borne

Here in La Borne, you'll see more contemporary pottery in the **Musée de la Poterie** (*open Jul–Aug 3–7pm; rest of year weekend and public holidays 3–7pm. €4. 02 48 26 73 76*), established in an old chapel.

Musée Vassil Ivanoff

Open Jul–Aug daily except Mon–Tue 2–7pm; rest of year weekends 2–7pm. Closed Oct–Apr. €2.50. 02 48 26 96 24.
www.musee-ivanoff.fr.
The Bulgarian ceramic artist Vassil Ivanoff discovered the book *Art of Pottery* in Paris in 1922. He became interested in learning new techniques and came to live in La Borne in a small house which doubled as his workshop. He built his own kiln and set to work, producing some 3 000 pieces before his death in 1973.

The museum houses a generous collection of the artist's work: vases, pots, cups, engraved plaques and pieces with tubular structures. Some of the work can be defined as figurative or abstract sculptures. The red enamels known as bull's blood are especially eye-catching. His workshop can be seen on request.

▷ Leave La Borne SE on D 46.

Église de Moroges

This 13C Romanesque church, fronted by an octagonal belfry-porch in reddish stone, has a wonderful wooden dais inside, which was originally in the Sainte-Chapelle in Bourges.

▷ Leave Moroges W on D 59.

Château de Maupas

Guided tours (30min) Jul–Aug 2–7pm; May–Jun and Sept daily except Mon 3–7pm. €8. ℘*02 48 64 41 71. www.chateaudemaupas.fr.*
Set in a forest on the edge of a lake, this castle partly dates from the 13C. It was rebuilt in the 15C, then was transformed in the 17C and 18C, when it fell into the hands of the Maupas family.
The furnishings are attractive and pride of place is given to the **collection of plates**★ (880 pieces) dating from the 17C–19C.

▷ Return to Moroges; take D 185 NE.

Les Aix-d'Angillon

This village is located at the edge of the vast plain of the area known as the Champagne Berrichonne, at the foot of the Sancerre hills. It features a historic quarter with an old gate and a **Romanesque church** with a high transept crossing framed with "Berrichon passageways" (narrow openings linking the transept arms to the nave) and crowned with a cupola on squinches.

▷ Follow D 955, then D 44 to the Motte d'Humbligny (431m/1414ft), the highest point in the Sancerre area.

A picturesque road takes you along the Grande Sauldre valley to Neuilly-en-Sancerre. Turn right on D 49 and follow it to Neuvy-Deux-Clochers.

▷ Leave Humbligny NE on D 74.

Tour de Vesvre (*Guided tours Jul–Aug 2.30–5.30pm.* ℘*02 48 79 03 13. www.latourdevesvre.fr*) At the bottom of a valley, this partially restored tower

listed as a historic building was a 12C lordly manor built in the place of a 9C aristocratic dwelling. The site includes a 10C motte and a 16C barnyard.

③ ALONG THE LATERAL CANAL EAST OF PAYS FORT

60km/36mi round-trip. Allow half a day. See route 3 on region map pp380–381. Drive SW out of Sancerre on the D 955 then turn left towards Baugy.

Cross the vintners' village of Vinon and go on to St-Bouize to reach the road which runs alongside the **Loire lateral canal**. The canal, which is parallel to the river, has many locks; since 1836 it has been navigable from Roanne to Briare.

St-Satur

This village was once called Château-Gordon, until the relics of the African martyr Satyrus were brought here and it was renamed St-Satur. The village is home to the **Église St-Guinefort**. The first church went up in the 12C but was later completely destroyed by the English. A new abbey-church was begun in 1362, but only the chancel and apse were finished.

St-Thibault

This river port was bustling with activity until the mid-19C.

▷ Continue on D 955.

Saint-Thibault quays along the Loire

© M. Guillot / Michelin

Bannay

Tucked between the northern edge of the Charnes wood and the canal, this village in the vineyards has a curious church with two pepperpot roofs.

○ Continue along D 955.

Facing the road which leads to Cosne-sur-Loire, the 15C Château de Buranlure has a lovely natural setting; the road then follows the canal for about 5km/3mi as far as the lock in the Houards.

Léré

This hamlet on the border of the region known as the Pays Fort and the Val de Loire was once fortified, but all that remains of the fortifications are the round towers and curving rue des Remparts.

Collégiale St-Martin

This building, though heavily restored after the 16C, has kept its Romanesque apse, adjoining a 15C chancel. Above the Gothic doorway, note the tympanum where a few sculpted figures remain intact. Despite the damage, one can still recognise St Martin sharing his cloak.

○ Leave Léré SW on D 47.

Following the Judelle valley as far as Savigny, the road goes through eastern **Pays Fort**, a verdant landscape of meadows and hedgerows. The D 54 takes you back to the vineyard south of the typical village of Ste-Gemme.

○ Return to Sancerre on D 86 (towards Sury-en-Vaux) and D 57.

ADDRESSES

🛏 STAY

⊝ **Chambre d'hote Le Floroine** – Le Floroine, Ménétéol-sous-Sancerre. ℘02 48 54 02 74. www.le-floroine.com. 5 rooms. Simply but cheerfully furnished, comfortable rooms in an attractive and friendly family-run restaurant-bar-hotel at the water's edge.

⊝⊜ **Chambre d'hote Le Moulin du Grand Senais** – Crézancy-en-Sancerre. 7km/4.2mi SW of Sancerre via D 955 and D 22. ℘02 48 79 06 64. 🍴. 4 rooms. In a small park in the heart of the vineyards, this pretty inn is set in an enchanting spot. Traditional cuisine. Enjoy a games room and, in the lovely garden, a small swimming pool.

⊝⊜⊞ **Hôtel de la Loire** – 2 quai de la Loire, 18300 St-Satur. ℘02 48 78 22 22. www.hotel-de-la-loire.com. This pretty three-star hotel is located by the banks of the Loire 2km/1mi from Sancerre. The spacious, comfortable bedrooms are decorated with various themes: African, Indian and Colonial, to name a few. The George Simenon bedroom is where the renowned author stayed for a year while writing.

🍷 EAT

⊝ **Auberge Ferme des Pellets** – Les Pellets, Moroques. 5km/3mi N of the Château de Maupas on D 46 towards La Borne. ℘02 48 26 90 68. 🅿 🍴. This is the perfect place to try the Crottin de Chavignol goat's cheese, served several ways in a rustic dining room.

⊝⊜ **Auberge Joseph Mellot** – 16 Nouvelle Place. ℘02 48 54 20 53. www.josephmellot.com. This authentic country inn is run by a venerable family of wine-growers. Enjoy generous portions of local specialities.

⊝⊜⊞ **Le Laurier** – 29 r. du Commerce, St-Satur. 3km/1.8mi NE of Sancerre on the D 955. ℘02 48 54 17 20. www.lelaurier18.com. This former coaching inn has a splendid exterior and a charming interior. Simple bedrooms. Traditional cuisine.

⊝⊜⊞ **La Pomme d'Or** – Pl. de la Mairie. ℘02 48 54 13 30. Reservation required. This little neighbourhood restaurant has a bistro atmosphere.

⊝⊜⊞ **La Tour** – 31 Nouvelle-Place. ℘02 48 54 00 81. www.la-tour-sancerre.fr. The eponymous14C tower of this restaurant presides over the village square. There are two dining rooms: one, with a fireplace, is situated in the old section. The other, upstairs, offers a sweeping view.

Aubigny-sur-Nère★

Situated on the borders of the Berry and the Sologne, Aubigny is a small, bustling town on the banks of the Nère river, which flows partly underground here.

A BIT OF HISTORY

City of the Stuarts – In 1423 **Charles VII** gave Aubigny to a Scotsman, John Stuart, his ally against the English. He was succeeded by Béraud Stuart and then by Robert Stuart, known as the Marshal of Aubigny, who fought in Italy under François I.

Craftsmen from Scotland settled here, either working as weavers – using white wool from the Sologne – or as glass-makers.

TOWN
Ramparts

The line of the old town wall, built originally by Philippe-Auguste, is marked by the streets encircling the town centre and two round towers overlooking the mall.

Old Houses★

A number of early 16C half-timbered houses are still standing along rue du Prieuré and its continuation, rue des Dames, two charming streets hung with shop signs from the town hall to the church. No 10 rue du Pont-Aux-Foulons is the only house to have survived the fire of 1512. In rue du Bourg-Coutant stands the **Maison du Bailli★** with its carved beams, and almost opposite, at the corner of rue de l'Église, the pretty Maison François I.

Ancien Château des Stuarts

Rue du Château.

This 16C building was erected by Robert Stuart and modified by Louise de Kerouaille, duchess of Portsmouth; it now serves as Aubigny's town hall. In the charming irregular courtyard, note the mullioned windows and round or polygonal turreted staircases.

▶ **Population:** 5 769.
 Michelin Map: 323: K-2.
 Info: 1, rue de l'Église, Aubigny-sur-Nère. *𝒞*02 48 58 40 20. www.tourisme-saudre-sologne.com.
 Location: 46km/28.75mi N of Bourges via D 940.
 Don't Miss: A unique way of discovering the area is by cycle-rail (*cyclodraisines*) along the old railway tracks.

🚗 DRIVING TOUR

4 INCURSION EN SOLOGNE
50km/31mi round-trip. Allow 3 hr. See route 4 on region map pp380–381.

▷ Drive W out of Aubigny on the D 13 towards Pierrefitte-sur-Sauldre.

Ste-Montaine

This village is built on the legend of St Montaine who intervened to allow a servant to carry water in a basket.

▷ Follow D 13 for 4km/2.4mi, and then, after crossing a small bridge, turn right on C 1.

Brinon-sur-Sauldre

A villager of Brinon-sur-Sauldre inspired the character Raboliot in the novel of the same name written by **Maurice Genevoix** in 1925.

Here you'll find a lovely example of a **caquetoire** church (with an exterior gallery supported by the south façade of the building). You'll get a nice view of the Sauldre and of an old wash house.

▷ Leave Brinon E on D 923.

Cerdon

You'll get a lovely **view** over this well-kept village from the bridge over the Grande Sauldre (*picnic area*).

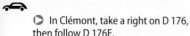

▶ In Clémont, take a right on D 176, then follow D 176E.

Étang du Puits★

This large, sunny pond is full of carp, bream and pike, of which some specimen attain the respectable weight of 7kg/15lb. A pleasant walk along the **Sauldre canal**. Climb the embankment. The road that runs around Etang du Puits gives good views.

▶ At the end of the road (D 765), turn right on D 948.

Argent-sur-Sauldre

The castle now houses a museum.
Musée des Métiers – Open Easter–Sept 1–6pm. €5.50. 02 48 73 33 10. www.argentsursauldre.com. Scenes from daily rural life in the 18C and 19C are conjured through this rich collection of some 3 000 tools and 2 000 miscellaneous objects displayed on three floors.
Église St-André – The former castle chapel features a sturdy 16C belfry-porch topped by a fleche that was reworked in the 17C. The baptismal font chapel houses a surprising 16C depiction of the Trinity.

▶ Follow D 940 to come back to Aubigny.

5 IN THE FOOTSTEPS OF LE GRAND MEAULNES

55km/34mi round-trip. Allow 3 hr.
See route 5 on region map pp380–381.

▶ Drive NE out of Aubigny on the D 30.

Château de Blancafort★

9km/5.6mi NE along the D 30.
Guided tours (45min): Jun–Sept 10am–7pm; Apr–May and first 2 wks in Oct daily except Tue 10am–noon, 2–6.30pm. €9.50. 02 48 58 60 11. www.chateaublancafort.com.
This 15C red-brick château features a library with Regency panelling.

▶ From Blancafort, take the D 8 towards Vailly-sur-Sauldre.

Musée de la Sorcellerie

Open Apr–Jun and Sept–mid-Nov 10am–6pm; Jul–Aug 10am–7pm. €8.50 (children, 4–13, €5.50). 02 48 73 86 11. www.musee-sorcellerie.fr.
Some 20 scenes delve into the world of witchcraft, sorcery and superstition.

▶ D 8, which climbs towards Barlieu, gives a lovely view over the Grande Sauldre Valley.

Vailly-sur-Sauldre

Note the **pyramidal barn** (*on D 11, just before the edge of the village*), a rural building typical of **Pays Fort**.

▶ Leave Vailly W on D 926 towards La Chapelle-d'Angillon. Approx. 1km/0.6mi after Villegenon, turn right on D 89.

Château de la Verrerie★

11km/7mi SE along the D 89.
Guided tour (45min): 11am–5pm (hourly except 1pm); Jul–Aug daily; Apr–Jun and Sept–Oct daily except Mon–Tue. €10. 02 48 81 51 60. www.chateaudelaverrerie.com.
The graceful **Renaissance gallery★** of this castle was erected by Robert Stuart in 1525. In the 19C wing note the four remarkable 15C alabaster **weeping figures★** from the tomb of Jean de Berry.

La Chapelle-d'Angillon

R. de la Fontaine-St-Jacques. 02 48 73 43 41.
This little village is the birthplace of writer Alain-Fournier. **Château de La Chapelle-d'Angillon** (guided tours (1hr) 9am–noon, 2–6pm (Sun 2–6pm). €8 (children under 7, no charge). 02 48 73 41 10. www.chateau-angillon.com).
This castle, first built in the 11C, features an elegant Renaissance gallery.
The **Musée Alain-Fournier** traces the life of the author through various objects and even holograms.
The **Fondation Royale Albanaise** is a conservatory of Albanian objects from the 18C and 19C and features two beautiful 17C tapestries from Felletin.

Nançay

This village is home to many artists' studios, as well as one of Europe's most modern astronomical observatories.

VILLAGE
Grenier de Villâtre

R. des Faubourgs. Ⓞ*Open mid-Mar to Nov, Sat 10am–12.30pm and 2.30–7pm.* ᴖ€*5. (children under 18, €3).* ☏*02 48 51 80 22. www.capazza-galerie.com.*
Established in the nicely restored stables of the château, the Galerie Capazza exhibits sculptures, pottery, drawing and other works by 65 different artists. One of the rooms, the **Musée Imaginaire du Grand Meaulnes**, features the family memorabilia of Alain Fournier.

EXCURSION
The following attractions are handled by Pole des Etoiles. Combined tickets for various combinations of the three sites are available. Ⓞ*Open Feb–Dec daily 9.30am–12.30pm, 1.30–5.30pm (Jul–Aug 9.30–6.30pm).* ᴖ€*6–12.* ☏*02 48 51 18 16. http://poledesetoiles.fr.*

Station de Radioastronomie
2km/1.2mi N along the D 29 towards Souesmes. ☛*Guided tour (1hr 15min) 1.5km/0.9mi round-trip, Jul–Aug at 11am and 4pm.*
Created in 1953 by the École Normale Supérieure, the station came under the authority of the Paris Observatory in 1956. The main field of study involves radio waves from around the universe which provide useful information on the solar system and distant galaxies.

👪 Ciel Ouvert en Sologne
Route de Souesmes (D29). ♿*Permanent and temporary astronomy exhibitions.*

👪 Planetarium★
Route de Souesmes (D29).
♿Ⓞ*3 different shows at 10am, 2pm and 3pm.* Go on a spectacular trip with Michel Boujenah to discover the main stars and constellations in the sky in a way that is both poetic and scientific.

▶ **Population:** 882.
⏱ **Michelin Map:** 323: J-2.
🛈 **Info:** 5 r. du Château.
  ☏02 48 58 40 20.
◖ **Location:** 15km/9.5mi NE of Vierzon.
👪 **Kids:** Planetarium; Ciel Ouvert en Sologne.

Radio telescope
© S. Sauvignier / Michelin

ALMA, La quête de nos origines cosmiques ("ALMA, In search of our cosmic origins") describes a machine in the Chilean desert that can explore the depths of the cosmos. Learn all about the new European radio-telescope ALMA.
Les Mystères du Ciel Austral ("The Mysteries of the Southern Sky") takes place in the Atacama Desert. You'll learn all about the VLT (Very Large Telescope), but also about the constellations in the southern hemisphere.
Poussière de Lune ('Moondust') explores how Earth, the moon and sun were created, and how important it is to keep dreaming.

Mehun-sur-Yèvre★

This charming old town on the banks of the River Yèvre and the Berry Canal is a centre of porcelain manufacture. Jean de Berry's castle, where Joan of Arc met the King of France, towers above the river.

> ▶ **Population:** 6 820.
> ✆ **Michelin Map:** 323: J-4.
> 🛈 **Info:** Pl. du 14 Juillet. ℘02 48 57 35 51. www.ville-mehun-sur-yevre.fr.
> ▶ **Location:** 13km/8mi NW of Bourges; 17km/10.5mi SE of Vierzon.
> 🕐 **Timing:** Allow an hour or two to explore the Fôret d'Allogny and half a day to tour the Reuilly-Quincy vineyards.

A BIT OF HISTORY

The third son of King John the Good, **Duke Jean de Berry** (1340–1416), was a lavish patron of the arts and admirer of the art of manuscript illumination. He rebuilt Mehun Castle in 1386. Here, amid a brilliant court, he welcomed writers such as Froissart and miniaturists like the Limbourg brothers and André Beauneveu. Beauneveu, who was also a sculptor and architect, worked for a lengthy period at the castle. The Duke left the castle to his grand-nephew Charles VII, who received Joan of Arc here in the winter of 1429 and 1430.

TOWN
Porte de l'Horloge
R. Jeanne-d'Arc.
A 14C gateway standing at the top of the street.

Rue Jeanne-d'Arc
This street leads down to Yèvre. No 87, the house where Joan of Arc stayed, has elegant bays with trilobed arches; to the left is the esplanade to the castle.

Jardin du Duc-Jean-de-Berry
Pl. Jean-Manceau.
Enjoy fine views of the public washing boards and 12C watermill. A shaded promenade alongside the Berry canal has views of the castle and church.

Pôle de la Porcelaine
R. des Grands Moulins. ♿ 🕐*Open Jul–Aug, daily 2.30–6.30pm; Mar–Apr and Oct Sat–Sun and public holidays 2.30–6pm; May–Jun and Sept Tue–Sun 2.30–6pm.* 🕐*Closed Nov–Feb.* ∞€5 *(children under 12, no charge).* ℘02 48 57 06 19.

This glass building near the castle displays fine porcelain items, including rare and unusual tableware, a 1900 fountain, a pedestal table and more. A 10min sound and light show illustrates the transformation of kaolin into porcelain.

Musée Charles VII
place Jean-Manceau. 🕐 ☞⚊ *Guided tours. Same opening times and charges as the Pôle de la Porcelaine.*
This marvellous fairy-tale castle has been admired by the sculptor Claus Sluter and the painter Holbein. Only two round towers remain; the one named after Charles VII has been extensively restored. The original plan of the castle is still visible. Note the position of the bastion jutting out like a spur towards the river. The Limbourg brothers' miniature of the *Très Riches Heures* ("The Very Rich Hours of the Duke of Berry"), of which the original is now displayed in the Condé Museum of Chantilly north of Paris, shows the castle as it existed in the 15C.
The castle was dismantled in the 17C and slowly fell into ruins. Excavations have revealed that over 10 castles were built here between the 10C and the 15C.

Collégiale Notre-Dame
R. des Grands Moulins.
In the 11C, this Romanesque church started with the horseshoe-shaped chancel. A chapel was added in the 15C. At the entrance to the nave, on the left beside the baptismal font, is a 15C relics

cupboard. It was fitted in the 17C with a carved wooden door representing the Education of the Virgin. In the northern part of the nave, there is a Crucifixion painted by Jean Boucher from Bourges, the master of Mignard.

EXCURSION
Foëcy
6km/3.7mi NE on D 60.
During the 19C and 20C, several porcelain factories were set up in Couleuvres, Noirlac, Mehun, Vierzon and Foëcy. Along the banks of the Cher and Yèvre, this village features a museum created by the Deshoulières family, porcelain and ceramic artisans for more than two centuries.

Musée de la Porcelaine – *R. Louis-Grandjean.* ⏰*Open Mon–Sat 9.30am–5pm.* ☎*02 48 53 04 55.* ⬤*€5 (children under 12, no charge).* 👤👤 In this charming museum set up on the site of a former factory, the history of porcelain and tableware is told through giant comic strips. Some twenty machines, some of which feature moving parts, illustrate the evolution of manufacturing and porcelain firing techniques. Don't miss the **museum collection**★ and its superb stoneware and porcelain pieces by Louis Lourioux, designed between 1895 and 1930; the plasters of the famous 19C Parisian porcelain maker Samson; and models by Philippe Deshoulières and other designers. A decoration workshop, including serigraph machines and temporary theme exhibitions, completes the tour. Before leaving, have a look into the shop (500sq m/1640sq ft) adjoining the museum, which offers a selection of articles at factory prices.

🚗 DRIVING TOUR

6 REUILLY-QUINCY VINEYARDS
62km/39mi round-trip. Allow half a day. See route 6 on region map pp380–381.

◗ Leave Aubigny W on D 13 towards Pierrefitte-sur-Sauldre.

◗ Leave Mehun S on D 35 to Ste-Thorette. Turn right onto D 23 then left onto D 114 towards Plou.

Chârost
The origins of this hamlet go back to the Bronze Age. In Antiquity and the Middle Ages, Chârost enjoyed prosperity, as witnessed in the remains of the feudal castle, the defensive wall (*northern gateway to the city*) and especially the church. The **Église St-Michel** is a vast 12C Romanesque building. Its wide nave with 19C timber framework leads to a hemispherical sanctuary.
Go round the building and into the **cemetery**. From there, observe the apse and the wealth of carved ornamentation. Among the admirable capitals, look for the harpy, a creature half woman, half bird, bearing a wheel.

◗ Leave Chârost W on D 2.

Diou
Near the pretty 13C church of St-Clément, a lawn rolls down to the water's edge, where a mill straddles the river alongside a dovecote.

◗ Leave Diou travelling N on D 918 towards Mehun.

Château de la Ferté
⊶ *Not open to visitors.*
This is a lovely classical 1659 manor with four corner towers.

Reuilly
This village is known for its AOC wines, mainly white wines from Sauvignon grapes.

◗ Drive E on D 20 towards Mehun.

Quincy
The vineyards of Quincy and Brinay spread over 180ha/445 acres on the west bank of the River Cher. They produce one of the most distinctive white wines of the Loire region. Very dry and crisp without being sharp, with a fairly high alcohol content, this wine is at its best during the first two years.

Vierzon

Vierzon came about in 1937 when four local administrative districts, Vierzon-Ville, Village, Bourneuf and Forges, were joined. This is the gateway between the Champagne Berrichonne region and Sologne; the Sologne forests begin just northwest of town.

A BIT OF HISTORY

Industrial heritage – The Comte d'Artois, brother of Louis XVI, opened a forge in Vierzon in 1779. In no time a number of industries began work, particularly in ceramics and, later, mechanical construction. The first porcelain factory went into operation in 1816.

At the turn of the 20C, there were a dozen such enterprises in town, making it second only to Limoges.

In the mid-19C the Société Française de Matériel Agricole was established here. It manufactured the first threshing machine in France, among other farm equipment. The iron architecture of the Grand Magasin de la Société Française and the presence of the canal, created in 1835 to link Vierzon to Montluçon, are reminders of this period. Today, the canal is closed to traffic, but you can enjoy a walk along its banks beneath the poplars.

OLD TOWN

This pedestrian area has been artfully developed around the winding streets and old, half-timbered houses up against a slope watched over by a Gothic **belfry**, formerly the gate to the city.

Église Notre-Dame

This church, built in the 12C, enlarged and renovated in the 15C, is fronted by a belfry-porch and a basket-handled arch above the doorway.

Inside, admire the restored barrel-vaulting and the Renaissance windows representing the Crucifixion (*south wall of the chapel of Ste-Perpétue*). In the transept, a painting by Jean Boucher depicts John the Baptist.

> ▶ **Population:** 26 946
> ⌚ **Michelin Map:** 323: I-3.
> 🛈 **Info:** 11 r. de la Société Française. ℘02 48 53 06 14. www.officedetourismede vierzon.com.
> ◉ **Location:** 39km/24mi NW of Bourges and 58km/36mi NE of Châteauroux.
> 👪 **Kids:** The Maison de l'Eau and Hameau des Automates in Neuvy-sur-Barangeon.
> 🕐 **Timing:** Allow half a day to explore the Champagne-Berrichonne.

Square Lucien-Beaufrère★

This garden, designed in 1929 in the Art Deco style, replaced an abbey whose remaining buildings now house the town hall offices. At the entrance, the 1935 **Auditorium Wash-house** by Eugène Karcher is decorated with enamelled tiles. The monument to fallen heroes ting from the same period is embellished with low-relief sculptures representing the trades practised in Vierzon. From the banks of the Yèvre there is a pretty view over the old town.

👪 Musée Laumônier de la Locomotive à Vapeur

15 r. de la Société-Française. ♿🕐*Open May–Sept Tue–Sun 2–6pm, Sat 10am–noon; Oct–Apr Tue–Fri 2–5.30pm; Sat 10am–noon.* ☜*No charge.* ℘*02 48 71 10 94. www.ville-vierzon.fr.*

This steam-train museum is the work of a former depot master in Vierzon, which has been an important railroad junction since 1847. It traces more than 150 years of railroad history through a rich collection that includes scale models. Eugénie is one of the most remarkable of these, a superb prototype of a locomotive and its machinery built in 1840 by a student of the school of petty officers of the marine ports of Rochefort. Another gem is the 1/11 model of the Micado 141 R. 1208, powered by coal and steam. Discover also the model of an **estacade**, or coal charging station, as well as that of an

Vierzon

© Office de Tourisme de Vierzon et son pays

engine shed. You'll also be treated to a 15min documentary made in 1940 by the SNCF showing life aboard a Pacific 231.

EXCURSION
Neuvy-sur-Barangeon
19km/11.8mi NW along D 926.

Maison de l'Eau
🕒*Open Apr–Jun and Oct 10am–1pm, 2–5pm Wed, Sat and public holidays; Jul–Sept daily except Mon 10am–1pm, 2–6pm.* ⊛€4 *(children 5–14 years old, €2.50).* 𝒫*02 48 51 66 65.* *www.lamaisondeleau.org.*
👫 This 16C watermill at the edge of a lake features animated scenes and audio guides that depict the role of water through the seasons, from spring rain falling on the Auvergne to frozen waterfalls in the Alps. There is also a section devoted to Neuvy and local millers and another one to the fauna and flora of the Sologne lakes.

Musée d'Histoire Militaire, Historimage
Along the road to Bourges, within the Fédération Maginot complex.
🕒*Open daily except Mon–Tue 2–6pm.* ⊛€2. 𝒫*02 48 52 64 00.*
This museum, which illustrates the uniforms and equipment of French and foreign soldiers from WWI to the present,

stages an amazing show entitled "Le Carrousel de la Paix" involving automata and special effects.

Le Hameau des Automates★
Opposite Historimage, along the D 944.
🕒*Call for opening times and prices.* 𝒫*02 48 51 63 00.*
👫Two separate shows present the technical and artistic aspects of automata and the poetic charm of doves and pigeons. There are also reconstructions of Renaissance scenes and a video presentation illustrating the making of automata.

🚗 DRIVING TOUR

⑦ CHAMPAGNE BERRICHONNE
75km/46.5mi. Allow 2hr. See route 7 on region map pp380–381.

▷ Drive SE out of Vierzon on the D 27 towards Quincy.

Brinay
This tranquil village on the banks of the Cher upstream from Vierzon features a Romanesque church worth visiting for its 12C **frescoes★**.

▷ Take D 18E towards Méreau.

Massay
The **church**, rebuilt between the 14C and the 16C, was once part of a Benedictine abbey founded in the 8C.
The remains of the abbey include the chapter-house, 13C parts of the dormitory, 12C cellars, and tithe barns. The 12C abbot's chapel (also known as St-Loup) is well preserved. It stood in the centre of the cloisters. The abbot's lodging dates from the 17C.

▷ Leave SW towards Châteauroux.

Vatan
Église St-Laurian
This restored church still features its 16C chancel and stained-glass windows recounting the life of St Laurian. There

are some interesting 8C paintings and sculpted door leaves dated 1498.

Musée du Cirque
⚘ ⏱ *Open daily except Mon and public holidays, 10am–noon, 2–6pm (Tue, 2–6pm).* ✆€4 (child €2). ☎02 54 49 77 78. www.musee-du-cirque.com. This museum displays an interesting collection of posters, accessories, models and costumes connected with the circus.

▷ Take the D 922, N of town.

St-Outrille
This village has an interesting **collegiate church**. Romanesque and Gothic styles are both present: the nave is 15C while the chancel, side chapels (except one) and the transept date from the 12C. The east end is surmounted by a curious twisted belltower covered with shingles. The western doorway dates from the 14C.

Graçay
This medieval town, separated from St-Outrille by the River Fouzon, still has its ramparts and a few old houses. The interesting **Musée de la Photo** retraces the history of photography. ⏱*Open Jul–Aug Wed–Sun 10am–noon, 2–7pm; Apr–Jun and Sept–Nov Wed–Sat 9am–noon, 2–6pm (Sun 10am–noon, 2–6pm).* ✆€5. ☎02 48 51 41 80. www.museephoto.com.

▷ Leave the village E on D 68.

Nohant-en-Graçay
Inside the charming **Église St-Martin** *(contact the town hall, ☎02 48 51 40 65),* the columns supporting the vaulting of the central tower bear remarkable 12C capitals. The unusual belltower with its spiral spire is similar to the one in St-Outrille.

▷ Leave Nohant N on D 164.

Genouilly
At the far end of town stands the 12C **Église St-Symphorien**. Its stained-glass windows date from 1536.
The chancel is covered by a 13C vault, exceptional in Berry because it is built in a style typical of the region of Anjou. In the southern chapel, the mausoleum of the La Châtre family dates from the turn of the 16C and 17C.

▷ Return to Vierzon on D 19 and D 90.

ADDRESSES

🏠 STAY
⊖⊖ **Hôtel Le Chalet de la Forêt** – *143 av. Édouard-Vaillant.* ☎02 48 75 35 84. www.lechaletdelaforet.com. 10 rooms. This hotel at the northern gate of Vierzon is a pleasant stopover. The pool's terrace is a fine place to relax; the rooms are comfortable. Meals are concocted from fresh ingredients bought from local growers. Friendly reception.

⊖⊖ **Arche Hôtel** – *13 r. du 11 Nov 1918.* ☎02 48 71 93 10. www.arche-hotel.fr. 41 rooms. The modern glass façade of this hotel just a minute from the arches of the old bridge across the Yèvre playfully catches the sun. Practical, soundproofed rooms. Straightforward meals with an accent on salads and grilled fare served in a contemporary dining room.

🍽 EAT
⊖⊖ **Victor-Hugo** – *5 r. Victor-Hugo.* ☎02 48 75 43 34. Closed Sun. This restaurant in the centre of town owes its reputation to the irreproachable quality of the food. Both dining rooms have a subdued ambience. In fine weather, enjoy the courtyard.

⊖⊖⊖ **Le Relais de Vouzeron** – *2 pl. de l'Église, Vouzeron. 15km/9mi NE of Vierzon via the D 926 and D 104.* ☎02 48 51 61 38. Situated in a tranquil village in the heart of the forest, this old post house is quite charming. The flowery façade gives you an idea of the intimate parlour, inviting dining room and lovely bedrooms within. Serving distinctive cuisine.

This area of the Cher is bordered by the *départements* of Indre-et-Loire to the east, Vienne to the southeast and Loir-et-Cher to the northeast. Its long history continues to be revealed in ongoing archaeological excavations and is manifest through its many castles. The area also includes the Parc Naturel Regional de Brenne, land of a thousand lakes and naturalist's paradise.

A Long History

The ancient civilisation of Argentoma-gus excavated at Saint-Marcel dates back to the 1C. If you're interested in protohistory, by all means visit the on-site museum, where you'll see some of the objects found there.

The Hundred Years War made its mark on this countryside. The ruins of the Crozant fortress and various churches are examples of the numerous fortified places that are still part of this landscape. A Renaissance gem, the Château de Valençay is an extravagant leisure palace worthy of the Loire valley. Various other castles, such as Bouges, are lovely in their own right. Add the literature of George Sand, who was based in the artist's village of Gargilesse-Dampierre, and the evolution of men's fashion to be discovered at Argenton-sur-Creuse, and you'll see that there is something for everyone in this area's rich history.

Natural Beauty

In the "Land of a thousand lakes", fish breeding and fishing are matters of tradition. In fact there are some 1 500 lakes and ponds in the area. This environment has given rise to an incredibly rich biodiversity. The Reserve Naturelle de Chérine, with its wildlife observatories, is just one example of how visitors can fully enjoy and appreciate this ecosystem. The area is also home to France's largest zoological reserve, where you can go on a safari to discover various animals and learn about what's being done to save endangered species. Needless to say, this is the perfect area for leisurely walks among lakes and woods, as well as a must-visit for any birdwatcher.

Highlights

1 **Château de Valençay**, a Loire-style castle in the Berry (p410)

2 Beautifully furnished **Château de Bouges** (p413)

3 **La Brenne**, land of a thousand lakes (p416)

4 Leafy **Gargilesse-Dampierre**, the culturally vibrant village of George Sand (p425)

5 Massive ruined fortress at **Crozant** (p427)

Parc Naturel Regional de Brenne

© Bertrand Rieger / hemis.fr

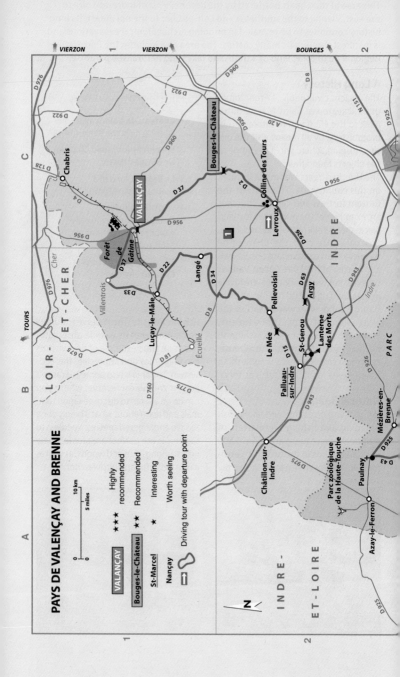

PAYS DE VALENÇAY AND BRENNE

VALENÇAY	★★★	Highly recommended
Bouges-le-Château	★★	Recommended
St-Marcel	★	Interesting
Nançay		Worth seeing
		Driving tour with departure point

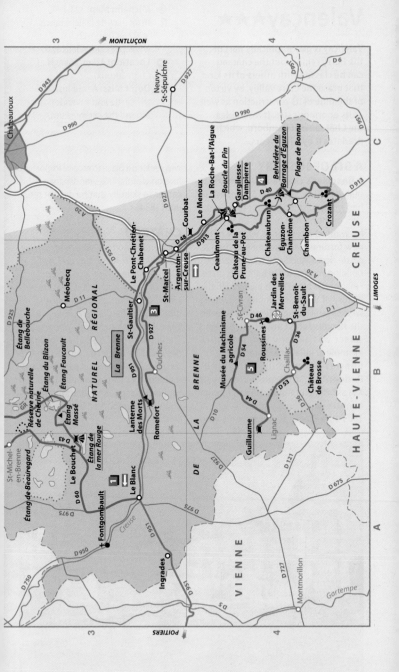

Château de Valençay★★★

Valençay is geographically part of the Berry region, but the château can be classed with others of its kind that grace the Loire valley, by virtue of the time of its construction as well as its enormous size. It resembles the Château de Chambord, which predates it by a few years.

- **Michelin Map:** 323: F-4.
- **Info:** 2 av. de la Résistance. ℘02 54 00 04 42. www.pays-de-valencay.fr.
- **Location:** 42km/26km N of Châteauroux.
- **Don't Miss:** A tour inside the castle and a wander around the car museum.

A BIT OF HISTORY

A financier's château – Valençay was built c 1540 by Jacques d'Estampes. He had married the daughter of a financier, granting him a large dowry, and he wanted a residence worthy of his new fortune. He therefore had the 12C castle demolished and the sumptuous building you see today built in its place. Finance has often been involved in the history of Valençay; among its owners were several Farmers-General and even the famous **John Law**, whose banking career was an early and instructive example of inflationary practices.

Charles-Maurice de Talleyrand-Périgord began his career under Louis XVI as bishop of Autun. He was foreign minister when he bought Valençay in 1803 at the request of Napoleon, who was seeking a place to receive important foreign visitors. Talleyrand managed his career so skilfully that he did not retire until 1834.

CHÂTEAU

Open Jul–Aug 9.30am–7pm; Jun 9.30am–6.30pm; May and Sept 10am–6pm; mid-Mar–Apr 10.30am–6pm; Oct–mid-Nov 10.30am–5.30pm. €12 for admission to château and grounds (children, under 9, €4). ℘02 54 00 10 66. www.chateau-valencay.fr.
The entrance pavilion is a huge building, designed like a keep only for decorative purposes, with various windows, turrets and fancy machicolations. The steep roof is pierced with high dormer windows and surmounted by monumental chimneys.

Château de Valençay

© A. Chicurel / hemis.fr

Such architecture is also found in the Renaissance châteaux of the Loire Valley, but here we see the first signs of the Classical style, as in the superimposed pilasters with Doric, Ionic and Corinthian capitals. The Classical style is even more evident in the huge corner towers: domes replace the pepperpot roofs which were the rule in the Loire valley in the 16C.

West Wing – The west wing was added in the 17C and altered in the 18C. At roof level the mansard windows alternate with bulls' eyes (round apertures). The tour of the ground floor includes the great Louis XVI vestibule; the gallery devoted to the Talleyrand-Périgord family; and the Grand Salon and Blue Salon which contain numerous works of art and pieces of Empire furniture, including the so-called Congress of Vienna table. On the first floor, the bedroom of Prince Talleyrand is followed by the room occupied by Ferdinand, the future king of Spain; the apartments of the duke of Dino and those of Madame de Bénévent; the great gallery and great staircase. Something of the spirit of the festivities organised by Talleyrand and his master chef, Marie-Antoine de Carême, still lingers in the great dining room and the kitchens.

Park – Black swans, ducks and peacocks strut freely through the formal gardens near the château. Under the great trees in the park, deer, llamas, camels and kangaroos roam in vast enclosures.

▲▲ Musée de l'Automobile★

&. ⏲ *Open Jul–Aug 10am–12.30pm, 1.30–7pm; Jun 10am–12.30pm, 2–6.30pm; rest of year 10.30am–12.30pm, 2–6pm.* ⏲ *Closed mid-Nov–Mar.* ☞€5.50 *(Children under 17, €3.50).* ✆ *02 54 00 07 03. www.musee-auto-valencay.fr.*

This car museum features the Guignard brothers' collection. Their grandfather was a coachbuilder from Vatan (*Indre*). You'll admire over 60 vintage cars dating from 1898, perfectly maintained in working order, including the 1908 Renault limousine used by Presidents Poincaré and Millerand; there are also

road documents from the early days of motoring and old Michelin maps and guides from before 1914.

EXCURSION
Chabris

14km/8.6mi NE on D 4.
Chabris, of Roman origin, produces quality wines and goat's cheese along the left bank of the Cher.

Church – *Restoration underway.* This church is dedicated to St Phalier, a 5C saint who blessed women with fertility. Pilgrimages take place every 3rd Sunday in September and have done for a very long time. As you go round the chevet, you'll notice curious primitive sculptures as well as pieces of an older church. The current church dates from the 15C. The 11C crypt is built in a "confession" shape, with passages and openings to venerate the saint's relics.

ADDRESSES

⋔/EAT

🍴 **Le Lion d'Or** – *14 pl. de la Halle.* ✆*02 54 00 00 87.* This former coaching inn is delightfully old-fashioned and ideally located across from the covered market. The dining room, decorated with woodwork in the style of the 1930s, is charming. In the summer the shaded terrace is a refreshing place to eat.

🍴🍴 **Auberge St-Fiacre** – *36600 Veuil. 6km/3.6mi S of Valencay. Take the D 15, then a side road.* ✆*02 54 40 32 78.* This low 17C building in the middle of a flowery village has set up its terrace by a stream beneath several horse chestnut trees. In chilly weather, the warmth of the country-style hearth and the dining room with its imposing beams is most hospitable.

ACTIVITIES

Sound and Light Show – This nightly show, based around the theme of *Capitaine Fracasse*, a swashbuckling novel by Théophile Gautier, takes place throughout August at 10pm. ☞€15. *Call for times and to reserve at the Tourist Office,* ✆*02 54 00 04 42.*

Levroux

Set between the wooded landscape of the Boischaut and the rich farmlands of the area known as Champagne Berrichonne, Levroux is the heartland of tradition. As well as producing savoury goat's cheeses, it is also home to tawing (a form of leather processing using alum and salt) and parchment industries.

▶ **Population:** 2 834.
- **Michelin Map:** 323: F-5.
- **Info:** Maison de Bois, pl E Nivet. ☎ 02 54 35 63 39.
- **Location:** 20km/12mi N of Châteauroux; 55km/34mi SW of Vierzon.
- **Don't Miss:** The stalls and organ case of St-Sylvain.

A BIT OF HISTORY

A land steeped in history – The area has been inhabited since prehistoric times. The settlement of Levroux appeared at the end of the Celtic period. It was probably one of the *oppida* burned to the ground by the Gaulish leader Vercingétorix as Caesar's armies approached in 52 BCE. Once the *Pax Romana* was established, Levroux grew quickly, spreading from the towers on the hill to the area where the city now stands.

The historical interest of this sector is such that the district of Levroux has become one vast archaeological site. Besides the Gallo-Roman theatre, several villas have been discovered and are now being carefully unearthed.

In the Middle Ages, the town grew around the feudal château of the princes of Châteauroux and the church of Saint-Sylvain, where pilgrimages took place. There are several well-preserved 15C and 16C buildings in Levroux.

TOWN
Collégiale Saint-Sylvain★
Pl. de l'Hôtel de Ville.
In the early 11C, Eudes de Déols founded a collegiate church in Levroux and made a special land grant to the canons.
Part of the town thus took on a separate status and became a place of refuge.
The church was built in two stages beginning in the late 12C. The crypt, the apse and the large belltower came before the vaulting in the nave and the construction of the porch, undertaken around 1263.
The east end of the church is a heptagonal apse flanked by a square belltower. The main doorway bears a much-damaged tympanum; the sculpted imagery represents the Resurrection of the Dead and the Last Judgement. Inside, the nave and side aisles are impressive for their soaring height. The chancel was built in transitional Romanesque-Gothic style; note the keystone in the sanctuary, showing Christ bestowing blessings. The restored late-15C **organ case★** is one of the three Gothic organ cases left in France.

Maison de Bois (Maison St-Jacques)
Pl. Victor-Hugo.
This wooden house was built between 1536 and 1547. Located in a street which leads to the façade of Saint-Sylvain, it is decorated with angelic carvings and the blazons of François I and Henri de Valois (later to become Henri II), as well

"Wild man" on the Maison de Bois

© S. Sauvignier / Michelin

as curious figures in the angles (note the **"wild man"** covered with leaves). The house was once used as a hospice for pilgrims on their way to Santiago de Compostela.

Porte de Champagne
R. de Champagne.
Close to the church, this former town gate (1435–1506) was turned into a prison at the beginning of the 19C. It is framed by round towers and roofed with dark brown tiles.

Musée du Cuir et du Parchemin
31 r. Gambetta. &&Open May– Dec, Mon and Sat 10am–12.30pm, 3–6pm,Thur and Fri 3–6pm. &&€3. &02 54 35 48 90.
www.valencay-tourisme.fr.
This small temporary museum in the Tourist Office is devoted to techniques of dressing hides by "tawing" and to the manufacture of parchment.

EXCURSIONS
Colline des Tours
1km/0.6mi N on D 956 (intersection with D 2); access by a road that goes up the hill.
A large number of archaeological remains were found on this *oppidum*, including a Gallic rampart or *murus gallicus*. In this type of wall, uncut stones are reinforced with a chain of crossed beams. The ruins of the castle built in the 14C by Bertrand de La Tour d'Auvergne stand alone. An entryway framed by two large round towers and a main building with a Gothic door overlook this site, from where you will enjoy a lovely **view** over Levroux.

Châtillon-sur-Indre
42km/26mi E of Levroux on D 926 and D 943.
This picturesque village comes to life with its Friday market.
Église Notre-Dame★ The former collegiate church of St-Outrille was founded in the 11C by Guy, Lord of Châtillon, to house the relics of the saint, who had been archbishop of Bourges in the 7C.

The building took place over two centuries, but the oldest elements – the choir and transept – date from the end of the 11C.
Château (&*Interior closed to the public.*) This castle, built by Pierre de La Brosse, and its chapel date from the 13C.
Tour de César – In the centre of the village, you'll notice a large 12C dungeon and its fortification wall. It was converted into a water tower in 1927. From the top, enjoy a sweeping view over the entire Indre valley.

🚗 DRIVING TOUR

1 CASTLES OF BOISCHAUT AND THE CHAMPAGNE BERRICHONNE AREA
100km/62mi round-trip. Allow 6hr. See route 1 on region map pp408–409.

▷ Leave Levroux NE on D 2.

Château de Bouges★★
9.5km/6mi NE. &*Château de BOUGES.*

▷ Leave Bouges N on D 37.

Château de Valençay★★★
22km/13.7mi N. &*Château de VALENÇAY.*

▷ Leave Valençay NE on D 37. At Villentrois, go S on D 33.

Luçau-le-Mâle
This village had excellent flint resources. A museum on site explains the history, extraction, cutting and commercialisation of the stone (**Musée de la Pierre à Fusil**; &*02 54 40 51 11.)*

▷ Leave Luçay SE on D 22; you'll pass through Langé. After the church of Entraigues, turn right on D 34, then follow D 33C.

Palluau-sur-Indre★
25km/15.5mi W on D 28 and D 15.
The 12C keep of the **castle** is known as the Tour de Philippe Auguste in memory of his visit in 1188.

The former **St Laurence Priory** contains remarkable Romanesque frescoes. Note, in particular, a magnificent **Virgin in Glory★** decorating the oven vaulted apse and a Christ in glory in the chancel.

▷ Leave St-Genou S on D 63B to the hamlet of Estrées.

Ancienne Abbaye de St-Genou
3km/2mi SE of Palluau.

This church was once part of a Benedictine abbey founded in 828. The relics of St Genou, who was sent to evangelise Gaul by Pope Sixtus II, gave the church its name. Begun in 994 and consecrated in 1066, the abbey went into decline in the early 16C, gradually falling into ruin. It was completely restored soon after being registered as a historic building (1882). Only the transept and the choir, in the Berry Romanesque style, give a clue to the church's past. Beyond the triumphal arc, the vast choir has an oven-shaped vault. The monumental columns feature remarkable **capitals** with fantastic animal figures and episodes from the life of St Genou.

▷ Leave St-Genou S on D 63B to the hamlet of Estrées.

Lanterne des Morts
From this 12C monument there is a good view over the valley.

▷ Come back to St-Genou, than head NE on D 63.

Château d'Argy★
16km/10mi SW along D 926 and D 63.
🕐*Open Jul–Aug 10am–noon, 2–6pm; Apr–Jun and Sept–Oct daily except some Wed 10am–noon, 2–6pm.* €5. *Guided tours available (45min.* €6). ℘02 54 84 21 55. *www.chateaudargy.fr.*

This impressive château, fortified in the 12C, features a square 15C keep. This is an excellent example of military architecture with its trefoil machicolations and guard towers.

In the courtyard, the carefully restored **Louis XII-style gallery★** contrasts with the severity of the outer walls. Nearby, a mill and a building housing a museum devoted to rural traditions (*traditions paysannes*) date from the 19C.

▷ Leave Argy E on D 63, then take D 926 back to Levroux.

Château d'Argy
© Werner Otto / age fotostock

Le Blanc

This busy village is the commercial centre of the area, attracting fairs and markets and drawing inhabitants to its shops and cinemas. The upper town is a picturesque labyrinth of old houses, whereas the lower town gathers around the church of St-Génitour.

ÉCOMUSÉE DE LA BRENNE

Château Naillac. ⏱*Open Jul–Aug 10am–12.30pm, 2–6pm; Apr–Jun and Sept daily except Mon 2–6pm; rest of year daily except Mon 2–5.30pm.* ⏱*Closed Jan–Mar, 11 Nov and 25 Dec.* 🎫*€4 (children under 16, €2).* 📞*02 54 37 25 20.*

This ethnographic museum, housed in Château Naillac, illustrates the history of the Brenne region and its population, but also its bird life, myriad lakes, local agriculture and architecture.

EXCURSIONS
Abbaye de Fontgombault★

8.5km/5.2mi NW on D 950.

On the right bank of the Creuse, northwest of the village of the same name, this elegant abbey is perfectly suited to the Berry countryside. The only remaining vestige of the monastery whose abbots contributed to the development of fish breeding in the Brenne, today it serves the congregation of Solesmes, who bring Benedictine tradition to life. It is not rare, for example, to hear Gregorian chants as you approach.

Ingrandes

9km/5.5mi SW on D 951.

This village, at the meeting points of the Berry, Limousin and Poitou, was the last home of **Henry de Monfreid** (1879–1974), author of *Secrets de la Mer Rouge* and many other novels.

Musée Henry-de-Monfreid – ♿⏱*Open Apr–Sept Mon–Fri 3–6.30pm, Sat, Sun and public hols 3–7pm.* ⏱*Closed Tue.* 🎫*€3 (children under 12, no charge.* 🚶*Guided tours available (1hr).* 📞*02 54 28 67 98. www.henrydemonfreid.com).* This museum presents written docu-

- ▶ **Population:** 6 968.
- 🎯 **Michelin Map:** 323 C7.
- 🛈 **Info:** Pl. de la Libération, Le Blanc. 📞02 54 37 05 13. www.tourisme-leblanc.fr.
- ◔ **Location:** Le Blanc is located on the banks of the Creuse. The D 951 passes through, linking Argenton-sur-Creuse (40km/24.8mi) to Poitiers (60km/37.2mi).
- 👁 **Don't miss:** Ecomusée de la Brenne.
- ◔ **Timing:** Le Blanc is a stopover for enjoying the natural environment of La Brenne.

Abbaye de Fontgombault

© Nicolas Thibaut / Photononstop

ments, arms, paintings and photographs of this intrepid traveller who found himself lost at sea in the Indian Ocean for a dozen days at the age of 79.

ADDRESSES

🍴 EAT

La Brenne★★

The northern limit of La Brenne is marked by the River Claise and the eastern limit by the Fôret de Lancosme. The Creuse valley borders La Brenne to the west and south. The region's main feature is its 7 500ha/18 533 acres of lakes. At the end of 1989, the Parc Naturel Régional de la Brenne was created, covering 1 660km²/640sq mi and involving 47 different local governments and 32 000 inhabitants. For information on tourist and cultural activities here, visit the Maison du Parc. The natural environment is a haven for wildlife, in particular some 100 species of birds. The Réserve Naturelle de Chérine is a good observation point.

- **Michelin Map:** 323: C/E-6/7.
- **Info:** Maison du Parc, Le Bouchet, Rosnay. ☎02 54 28 12 13. www.parc-naturel-brenne.fr.
- **Location:** 102km/63.7mi N of Limoges via A 20/D 927/ D 134 to St-Gaultier on the edge of the park.
- **Don't Miss:** Étang de la Mer Rouge.
- **Timing:** Allow at least half a day to explore this fascinating area.

A BIT OF HISTORY

Land of a thousand lakes – La Brenne is a land of legends. Its elves, fairies and sorcerers have inspired painters and

Wildfowl of the Brenne

Black-tailed Godwit

Purple Heron

Reed bunting

Short-toed eagle

© R. Corbel / Michelin

poets. The name conjures Geoffroy de Brenne, lord of Mézières in the 13C. These once-neglected woodlands and moors were cleared out by monks who engineered the ponds for the purposes of cultivating fish to enjoy on meatless fast days.

Later, in the 19C, the region was further improved to reduce the risk of malaria. Roads were laid and swampy lands drained, opening the land to agriculture. Today the area is a patchwork of mixed uses.

The ponds and lakes mark the landscape and symbolise the close link between man and nature in addition to providing a rich ecosystem and a lovely setting. The waters are also a major factor in the local economy. Over 1 000t of fish (carp, roach, tench, pike, bass and eel) are drawn out annually. There are approximately 1400 lakes in the park, which makes it one of the largest wetland areas in France. The lakes are interconnected and every year a sluice gate is opened to drain the waters.

🚗 DRIVING TOUR

② LAND OF A THOUSAND LAKES

80km/49.7mi round-trip. Allow half a day. See route 2 on region map pp408–409.

▷ Drive N out of Le Blanc on D 975. Cross the railway line and turn right.

Étang de la Mer Rouge

🔲 The Red Sea Lake is believed to have been given its name by a former owner, Aimery Sénébaud, on his return from the Holy Land, where he had been imprisoned beside the Red Sea. It is the biggest lake in La Brenne, with a surface area of 180ha/445 acres. It provides a natural refuge for migrating waterfowl. The church of Notre-Dame-de-la-Mer-Rouge, rebuilt in 1854, stands on a headland to the south and is the site of a yearly pilgrimage.

Château du Bouchet

🚗 *Guided tours (45min) Jul–Aug 10.30am–noon, 2–7pm (Sun 2–6.15pm). €5 (guided tour). €2 (exterior only). ℘06 72 01 62 15.*

This impressive medieval fortress, occupied by the English during the Hundred Years War, was restored in both the 15C and 17C. For 300 years it belonged to the Rochechouart-Mortemart family and served for some time as the residence of the Marquise de Montespan. Born a Rochechouart-Mortemart, she was the daughter and sister of the lords of Le Bouchet; her portrait hangs inside the castle. From the keep and the terrace you'll enjoy a view of the Brenne countryside and the Red Sea Lake.

▷ Drive past the Maison du Parc. Turn left at the intersection with D 44 then right onto D 17A at Le Maupas. There is a parking area a little farther on.

Étang Massé

Le Blizon, Rosnay. ◷ 🚶Guided tours. Call for hours and prices. ℘02 54 28 12 13. www.parc-naturel-brenne.fr.

In the early morning or late evening, the observation post overlooking the lake is the perfect spot to watch one of the richest natural spectacles in La Brenne, featuring wading birds such as bitterns as well as European pond turtles.

▷ Slightly farther on, the Blizon discovery trail branches off to the left.

Sentier Découverte de l'Étang du Blizon

1.5km/0.9mi, allow 30min.

🔲 Informative panels on the theme of dragonflies and frogs line this discovery trail which skirts the edge of the Blizon lake.

▷ Turn left at the end of D 17A. Leave the car in the Étangs Foucault parking area on the right.

Réserve Naturelle de Chérine

© Nicolas Thibaut / Photononstop

Étangs Foucault

A lookout post, located at the end of the marked path, offers good views of ducks, ospreys, herons, egrets and other local species.

▶ Turn back and follow D 15 to Mézières-en-Brenne.

Mézières-en-Brenne

This, the largest town in Brenne, is built on the poplar-lined banks of the Claise. The **church** belfry, flanked by two stone turrets, has a sculpted porch. The nave features wooden vaulting with painted uprights and crossbeams. Note the beautiful stained glass of the Renaissance chapel to the right of the chancel.

Maison de la Pisciculture de Brenne

Open mid-Mar–Oct, daily except Sun and Tue, 3–6pm (last entrance 30min before closing); Nov–mid-Mar by prior arrangement with the tourist office. *Closed 1 Jan, 1 May and 25 Dec.* *€2.50 (children aged 2–12, €1.20).* *02 54 38 12 99.*

Established in one of the last vestiges of the 11C stronghold, this nature museum is one of the branches of the Écomusée de la Brenne. Fish and fishing in the region, past and present, are depicted in the exhibition, which includes aquariums.

Église de Paulnay

This 12C–13C **church** has an interesting Romanesque **doorway★**. Three rows of finely sculptured covings are supported on elegant capitals.

▶ Drive S along D 43 to St-Michel-en-Brenne then turn onto D 44.

Réserve Naturelle de Chérine

Saint Michel en Brenne. Apr–Sept 10am–12.30pm, 2–6pm; Feb–Mar and Oct Sat 2–5, Sun 10am–12.30pm, 2–6pm; rest of year Sun 10am–12.30pm, 2–5pm. Closed Tue. Guided tour (3hr) available Easter–Sept. €7. 02 54 28 11 02. www.reserve-cherine.fr.

From the edge of a 26ha/64-acre lake, observe at your leisure the amazing diversity of this unspoilt ecosystem, the home of colourful birds such as purple herons and wild ducks.

Maison de la Nature et de la Réserve *3km/1.86mi from St-Michel-en-Brenne along the D 6A. Call for times. €3. 02 54 28 11 00.* Located along the **Étang de Cistude**, the exhibitions of this little centre will help you discover the natural environment of the area. In the centre, a path leads to a **nature observatory**. You can request a pair of binoculars to better enjoy the wildlife form this discreet wooden structure.

Sentier de Découverte de l'Étang de Beauregarde ✦ *4km/2.4mi round-trip on foot.* Enjoy this walk on the theme of the tortoise and the hare. Information panels describe the various species that you may encounter.

▶ Return to Le Blanc along D 17.

EXCURSIONS
Azay-le-Ferron

12km/7.4mi NW of Mézières-en-Brenne on D 925. ◷ *Apr–Jun and Sept daily 10am–6pm; Jul–Aug, daily 10am–6.30pm; Oct–mid-Nov 10am–5.30pm.* ◉ *€8 (children 6–18, €4.50).* ✆ *02 54 39 20 06. www.chateau-azay-le-ferron.com.* Between the Touraine and Berry, Azay-le-Ferron is overlooked by the four buildings of its 15C–17C **château★**. The centre building is the **Pavillon François I**. Inside, you'll see furniture, artwork and tapestries c 1519. Outside, enjoy the landscaped park, French-style garden and yew topiaries.

Parc Zoologique de la Haute-Touche

5km/3.1mi N of Azay-le-Ferron on D 14. ♿ ◷ *mid-Apr–mid-Nov 10am–6pm.* ✦ *Guided tour available (1hr).* ◉ *€10 (children under 16, €8).* ✆ *02 54 02 20 40. http://haute-touche.mnhn.fr.* 👥 The Forest of Preuilly is the ideal setting for this reserve, part of the National Museum of Natural History and the largest zoological reserve in France. A thousand animals from over a hundred different species live here in semi-liberty in vast wooded enclosures. You can **drive** along to discover European fauna such as wolves, ibex and deer along a 4km/2.4mi-long safari. **On foot** or **by bike**, you can follow the blazed trails *(all-terrain bike hire available).* The white trail takes you on a discovery of animals from the five continents: felines, canines, primates, lemurs, birds and more. The red trail features an animal husbandry zone, where research is carried out in an attempt to save endangered species such as the European lynx and the Sumatran tiger.

☞The high-tech laboratory of the park helps reintroduce animals into their natural habitat through its research in such diverse fields as assisted reproduction and the study of maternal behaviour of animals in the wilderness.

Étang de Bellebouche

10km/6.2mi E of Mézières-en-Brenne on D 925. ◉ *Paid parking on Sat–Sun and in Jul–Aug, €4.50. Dogs not allowed on site.* ✆ *02 54 38 32 36.* 👥 Enjoy the fine sandy beach stretching over 900m along the 120ha/296 acres of this leisure lake *(no lifeguard on duty).* Five footpaths around the lake, which you can also enjoy on an all-terrain bike or on horseback, include a fitness

Château d'Azay-le-Ferron

© Cyrille Gibot / agefotostock

trail and discovery trail (7.5km/4.6mi, 3hr). There are three little nature observatories; you'll get the best view from the one located in the southwest. Pedal boats and kayaks are available for hire on the lake.

Méobecq

20km/12.4mi SE of Mézières-en-Brenne on D 21 and D 11.

When you come out of the Lancosme forest, you'll happen upon this village, which bears the vestiges of an 11C abbey. In the **church**, the open nave was only enclosed with a classic façade in 1658. One of the bays of the nave, the transept and the chevet have stood the test of time in spite of heavy alterations. Note the capitals featuring leaves and animals. In the **frescoes** near the windows, the names of various characters are still legible. The white night (*left of the left-hand window*) and Jesus Resuscitated are particularly interesting.

ADDRESSES

🛏 STAY

🍽🛏 **Chambre d'hôte Le Château de Boisrobert** – *Boisrobert. Neuillay-les-Bois. 3km/2mi E of Neuillay-les-Bois on D 21.* ℘*02 54 39 46 18. www.chateaudeboisrobert.com* 🅿 🚭. *5 rooms.* This beautiful late 19C dwelling opens onto an immense park that appears to be a verdant Garden of Eden with its tree-lined pond. Enjoy the luxurious living room, bar area and fireplace, as well as the four large bedrooms decorated on various themes. There is also a 19C-style five-person family suite. Meals are made from fresh produce.

🍽🛏 **Chambre d'hôte La Presle** – *Rte de Châteauroux. 36290 Mézières-en-Brenne. Turn left after leaving the village.* ℘*02 54 38 12 36. 3 rooms.* This attractive little 17C farmhouse offers guests a choice of three comfortable bedrooms with Louis XV furniture, delicate English wallpaper and views over the garden or surrounding fields. Communal breakfast around a large table.

🍽 EAT

🍽 **Le Bellebouche** – *Base de Loisirs de Bellebouche, Mézières-en-Brenne. 9km/5.5mi E of Mézières towards Châteauroux on D 925.* ℘*02 54 38 30 77. www.lebellebouche.com.* This outdoor recreation centre includes an on-site restaurant. Located in a natural setting on the edge of the lake, its terrace is a pleasant place to relax, unwind and enjoy views of the neighbouring pine forest. Contemporary, reasonably priced cuisine.

🍽 **Espace Dégustation de la Maison du Parc** – *Hameau du Bouchet, Rosnay.* ℘*02 54 28 53 02.* This renovated farmhouse, part of the old château, serves an interesting choice of copious, inexpensive local specialities such as fried fish, cheeses, bread, rillettes and more. Terrace with views of the lake.

🍽🍽 **Auberge de la Gabrière** – *2 La Gabrière, Lingé. 9km/5.5mi S of Mézières. Head towards Le Blanc, then La Gabrière along D 15 and D 17.* ℘*02 54 37 80 97.* This spacious country restaurant is well situated opposite the Étang de la Gabrière. The menu features a good choice of freshwater fish and seasonal game. Very popular at weekends. Basic rooms.

SPORT AND LEISURE

Base de Loisirs de Bellebouche – *10km/6mi E of Mézières-en-Brenne along D 925.* A natural sandy beach. Three nature trails for walkers, mountain bikes and horses, including a fitness trail. Discovery trail (*7.5km/4.5mi, 3hr*) around the lake, with three observation areas.

Centre Équestre Poney-Club de la Virevolte – *Le Fresne, Douadic. 9km/5.4mi E of Rosnay and 11km/6.5mi N of Le Blanc on D 17. Open Jul–Aug Mon–Sat. Other periods daily exc Tue and school hols; during school hols, Mon–Sun. Closed first two weeks in Sept, 1 Jan and 25 Dec.* ℘*02 54 37 10 28.* Offering incursions into the heart of the Land of a Thousand Lakes and riding lessons for children.

Domaine Ste-Marie – Éric Aphatie – *Mézières-en-Brenne. Open Mar–Nov, daily by prior arrangement.* ℘*02 54 38 01 18.* Take a horse-drawn carriage ride and hear all about the history of La Brenne and its local customs. Your host will also point out the many species of birds that can be seen here.

Saint-Marcel★

The medieval hamlet of St-Marcel stands on a hill overlooking the right bank of the Creuse, on the site of the Gallo-Roman town of Argentomagus. An archaeological dig on-site and in the surrounding area revealed traces of ancient monuments. A large number of items were excavated of which some are now exhibited in the local museum.

▶ **Population:** 1 638.
◔ **Michelin Map:** 323: F-7.
▤ **Info:** 13 pl. de la République, Argenton sur Creuse. ℘02 54 24 05 30.
⊙ **Location:** Northern outskirts of the town of Argenton-sur-Creuse.
⊛ **Don't Miss:** Théâtre du Virou; Musée Archéologique d'Argentomagus.

A BIT OF HISTORY

Archaeological excavations – The development of trade, abundant game and rich resources of water and wood explain why this land was occupied so long ago, giving rise to a diversity of archaeological discoveries. Magdalenian reindeer hunters dwelled in caves here (14000–8000 BCE) and their Gallo-Roman successors built an *oppidum*, or fortified city, here.

Following the Roman conquest (*50 BCE*), **Argentomagus** underwent spectacular demographic and economic growth, as trade, crafts and especially metalworking developed. The site figures on a 15C reproduction of the road network of the lower Roman Empire known as the **Peutinger Table**, and is mentioned in a 4C text as the leading Gallic arms factory. For two centuries the site expanded beyond the bounds of the original *oppidum*, although it never become a major city.

ARCHAEOLOGICAL SITE

✆*No charge.* ℘*02 54 24 47 31.*
In addition to the sections known as Mersans and Virou, other areas have been explored, including a necropolis called Champ de l'Image (*200m NW of the museum*).

Les Mersans

This plateau (*27ha/67 acres*), protected by cliffs and a moat, was the first urban core here. The so-called Sergius Macrinus house was discovered here, as well as a religious enclave made up of two **temples** and a square edifice. Along with most of the rest of the town, these temples were destroyed during a Barbarian invasion in 276.

To the east of the temple area, the forum and other ancient monuments are still to be unearthed. In 1967, a **monumental fountain**, the largest of its kind from the period, was discovered. Its exact purpose is uncertain, but it probably had a cultural role before it being filled in by metalworkers some time after 276.

Théâtre du Virou★

Return down the hill towards Argenton; turn right just before the railway bridge. Continue for about 200m, then take a steep path on the right which goes up to the theatre.

Until 1966, only a part of the outside wall was visible. Now the building has been entirely uncovered, revealing the two successive stages of construction: the first, rustic period, from the early 1C, and a second part dating from the 2C. These improvements brought the theatre in line with Roman design: the circular seating (*84m in diameter*) could accommodate up to 6 000 spectators.

Musée Archéologique d'Argentomagus★

♿⊙*Open daily Jul–Aug, 9.30am–noon, 2–6pm; Sept–Jun, daily except Tue, 9.30am–noon, 2–6pm.* ⊙*Closed 1 Jan 1 May, 25 Dec.* ✆*€4.50 (combined ticket with Musée de la Chemiserie, €7). No charge 1st Sun of the month.* ℘*02 54 24 47 31. www.argentomagus.fr.*

Musée Archéologique d'Argentomagus

© Philippe Renault / hemis.fr

Enjoy this museum of ancient cultures which includes **prehistory and Gallo-Roman collections**.

Finish the visit with a walk through the **crypte archéologique★★**, 150m along the remains of the north moat where a rare domestic altar has been left in place (🔍*see photograph*).

MEDIEVAL VILLAGE

At the town hall and in the museum, a map is available for a self-guided tour.

Church★

R. de l'Ormeau.

To the left of the nave, the **massive 14C belltower** was used as a keep. At the end of the nave, to the left above the door, a 15C **Fresco of Our Lady** (Notre-Dame-de-Pitié) depicts St Louis in a fur coat presenting a priest to the Virgin holding the infant Jesus. The **treasure** contains several processional crosses (13C), a 15C sculpted shrine representing the martyrdom of St Marcel and St Anastase, a gilded copper shrine from the 13C adorned with Limoges enamel, the arm of St Marcel and a 14C reliquary. The **medieval streets** include remains of the 15C fortifications, various entranceways surmounted by lintels and sometimes tympana bearing family coats of arms.

ADDRESSES

ⵖ/ EAT

⊖ **Auberge de Thenay** – *Base de Loisirs de Bellebouche, Mézières-en-Brenne. 9km/5.5mi E of Mézières towards Châteauroux on D 925.* ℘*02 54 38 30 77. www.auberge-de-thenay.fr.* This outdoor recreation centre includes an on-site restaurant. Located in a natural setting on the edge of the lake, its terrace is a pleasant place to relax, unwind and enjoy views of the neighbouring pine forest. Contemporary, reasonably priced cuisine.

⊖⊖ **Le Boisseau** – *Boisrobert. Neuillay-les-Bois. 3km/2mi E of Neuillay-les-Bois on D 21.* ℘*02 54 39 46 18. www.chateau deboisrobert.fr.* 🅿 🍽️. *4 rooms.* This beautiful late 19C dwelling opens onto an immense, verdant park with a tree-lined pond.

⊖⊖⊖ **Auberge des Saveurs** – *Rte de Châteauroux. 36290 Mézières-en-Brenne. Turn left after leaving the village.* ℘*02 54 38 12 36. www.auberge-des-saveurs.fr.* This attractive little 17C farmhouse offers guests a choice of three comfortable bedrooms with Louis XV furniture, delicate English wallpaper and views over the garden or surrounding fields. Communal breakfast around a large table.

Argenton-sur-Creuse★

Argenton is a pleasant provincial town with picturesque old houses lining the banks of the River Creuse. In the 19C, the town was a centre for the garment industry and still specialises in high-quality men's shirts.

A BIT OF HISTORY
The town of Argenton-sur-Creuse replaced the Gallo-Roman settlement of Argentomagnus which straddled a hill, the Colline de St-Marcel, 2km/1.2mi north of the town.

 WALKING TOUR

Église St-Sauveur
The foundations of the church probably date from the settlement of the lower town in the 13C. The neo-Gothic belfry-porch in front of the church is crowned by a pierced stone spire (*50m*). The nave, rebuilt in the 19C, features groin vaulting with emblazoned keystones.

▶ Head out of the church and turn left onto rue Grande.

Impasse de Villers
Note the Hôtel de Scévole, a fine 17C–18C manor.

▶ Turn right at the end of rue Grande.

Vieux Pont
This bridge was originally built in the 17C and rebuilt in the 19C. It provides a good **view★** of the River Creuse, the old quarter and the upper part of town. To the left you can admire a fine stretch of the Creuse and its twin overflows that provide water for mills; as well as houses with balconies, balustrades, wooden galleries and slate roofs, either overlooking the river or built into the now-overgrown cliff. To the right, you'll see the stone spire of St-Sauveur, and in the far distance the belfry of the Église

▶ **Population:** 5 120.
⏱ **Michelin Map:** 323: F-7.
ℹ **Info:** 13 pl. de la République, Argenton-sur-Creuse. ℘02 54 24 05 30. www.ot-argenton-sur-creuse.fr
▷ **Location:** 92km/57.5mi N of Limoges via the A 20. The Vieux Pont spanning the Creuse provides a perfect vantage point from which to admire the river, Argenton's old quarter and the upper part of the town.
🅿 **Parking:** Adequate parking in the east of the town (see map).
😊 **Don't Miss:** The Musée de la Chemiserie, highlighting the history of the town's garment-making industry.

St-Marcel. The imposing gilded statue of Notre-Dame of Argenton dominates the Chapelle Notre-Dame-des-Bancs. Beyond the bridge, note the old house with a small Renaissance door.

Rue Raspail
On the right, the **ancien collège**, now home to a regional archaeological restoration centre, was built in the late 15C Renaissance style. It is crowned with a bell-turret and adorned with a sculpted doorway. The building is also known locally as the old prison, for it served that purpose in 1782.

Chapelle St-Benoît
This former Gothic collegiate chapel (15C–16C) was restored and re-consecrated in 1873. The belfry was added in 1965. Outside, admire the fine doorway with wreathed columns; on the left is a 1485 statue of the Virgin and Child.

▶ Cross rue Victor-Hugo.

Rue de la Coursière
This picturesque street opposite the chapel leads uphill, providing a good view of the town.

Chapelle Notre-Dame des Bancs

This pilgrimage chapel is all that remains of a fortress dismantled in 1632. It was built in the 15C on the site of the ruins of a 2C sanctuary. Its interior is dominated by an enormous gilded statue of the Virgin Mary unveiled in 1899, weighing around 3t and measuring 6.5m in height. The small statue that stands above the high altar is venerated under the name of the Good Lady of Argenton (*Bonne Dame d'Argenton*); it is said that she protected the town from the plague in 1632. The sanctuary was completely restored in the late 19C.

From the **terrace**, the extensive **view★** takes in the picturesque riverside quays, houses adorned with gables, turrets, and slate or brown-tile roofs; the belfries of the Église St-Sauveur and Chapelle St-Benoît; and the valley of the Creuse that encircles the town.

▶ Retrace your steps and turn left along rue Victor-Hugo.

Pont-Neuf

Situated farther downstream, this bridge provides a panorama of the town.

Rue Charles-Brillaud

At the end of the street is the first machine-made garment workshop here, founded in 1860 by Charles Brillaud. It now houses the Musée de la Chemiserie.

Musée de la Chemiserie et de l'Élégance masculine

&.◷Open Jul–Aug, daily, 10am–12.30pm, 2–6.30pm (Mon, 2–6.30pm); Sept–Jun, daily except Mon, 9.30am–noon 2–6pm. ◷Closed 23 Dec to mid-Feb. ⊜€4.50 (children under 18, €2.50) –combined ticket with the Musée Archéologique d'Argentomus, €7. ℘02 54 24 34 69.

This attractive museum, spread out on several levels, provides an insight into the shirt (*chemise*) industry in Argenton and the local area. A production workshop exhibits several machines and accessories. Diagrams and plans explain the various stages of manufacture.

The museum also displays shirts worn by stars such as Richard Burton, Charlie Chaplin and Frank Sinatra, and includes a simulation cabin with a virtual overview of men's fashion over the ages.

🚗 DRIVING TOUR

③ HILLS AND CASTLES

50km/31mi round-trip. Allow 3hr.
See route 3 on region map pp408–409.

St-Marcel★

◔See ST-MARCEL.

▶ Take D 927 across the A 20 motorway.

Le Pont-Chrétien-Chabenet

The 15C Château du Broutet now serves as the town hall. Château de Chabenet, restored in the 19C, is visible above the limestone cliffs. The covered wooden bridge (1847) was built when the Paris–Toulouse railway opened.

▶ Continue along D 927.

St-Gaultier

This village is nestled amid white chalky hills dotted with wooded groves. The **priory** dates from the 12C. After admiring the Romanesque capitals inside, follow the steep path that leads down to the river, where you will be rewarded with a fine view of the River Creuse.

▶ Continue along N 151.

Lanterne des Morts de Ciron

This 12C funerary lantern is crowned with a conical roof.

▶ Cross the River Creuse via D 44.

Château de Romefort

Although the château is not open to visitors, it is worth stopping to admire its superb position perched above the river. The main building dates from the 14C;

the square keep to one side from the 12C. It was once surrounded by three protective walls punctuated with towers that now form rows of jagged ruins.

◗ Follow D 3 to Oulches, then continue along D 927.

Between Rivarennes and Thenay, enjoy scenic views of St-Gaultier, built on several levels above the river, which is spanned here by an attractive stone bridge.

◗ D 48 leads back to Argenton.

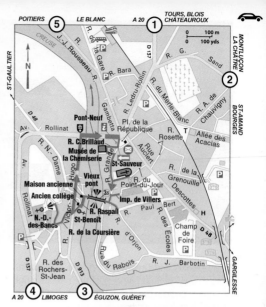

④ VALLÉE DE LA CREUSE★
Round-trip of 80km/50mi. Allow half a day. See route 4 on region map pp408–409.

◗ Leave Argenton SE on D 48 towards Gargilesse.

Château du Courbat
This graceful manor is surrounded by a moat. The tower dates from the 13C, the building itself from the 17C. Restored in 1989, it now serves as the town hall.

◗ Continue along D 48.

Le Menoux
This village overlooking the river (🅟for the best views head for the Colline de Balicave) was once famous for its wines, as can be seen in the wine-growers' houses and cellar entrances.
The 19C church has been decorated by the Bolivian painter Jorge Carrasco. His house, just a few doors away, is open to the public.

◗ Return to D 48.

Barrage de la Roche-Bat-l'Aigue
Follow the road as it winds uphill and bear right onto a narrow road that runs close to the fast-flowing waters of the Creuse. A small dam (*barrage*), a spillway and a leisure area are enclosed between rocks and high wooded slopes.

◗ Return to Badecon-le-Pin, then take D 40.

La Boucle du Pin★
As you come out of Les Chocats, you'll get a good **view★** of the **Le Pin meander** (*boucle*), a wide bend made by the Creuse in a cirque of rocks and hills.
On the opposite side of the river above a high promontory stands the Romanesque church of Ceaulmont.

Gargilesse-Dampierre★
This is one of the most attractive villages in the valley, with its pleasant leafy setting, picturesque streets, old houses and church.
The village itself has an interesting literary history as **George Sand** (🅖*see NOHANT*) lived here and chose it as the background for several of her novels and accounts of rural legends and life.

Gargilesse-Dampierre

© Davidmartyn / Dreamstime.com

Claude Monet and Théodore Rousseau were among several painters of their time who stayed in Gargilesse, attracted by the village's natural beauty.

The **castle**, once the home of the former lords of Gargilesse, now houses art exhibitions.

Church★

The 11C–12C Romanesque church stands within the walls of a medieval castle rebuilt in the 18C. The old keep and a door flanked by two towers are still standing. The church is well proportioned and has interesting historiated capitals portraying the 24 Old Men of the Apocalypse.

A 12C Virgin and Child stands in the main chapel. The crypt is enormous and decorated with 12–15C **frescoes** depicting the Instruments of the Passion, St Gregory Celebrating Mass, the Apparition of Christ, Crucifixion, the Assumption, the Resurrection of the Dead, the Visitation and the Three Kings.

Maison de George Sand

Guided tours, Apr–Sept, call for hours. €5 (no charge for children). 02 54 47 84 14.

Mementos of the novelist, her son Maurice and her granddaughter Aurore are all on display in this small house.

▷ Continue along D 40. Beyond Cuzion, turn right onto D 45 towards

Éguzon. 2km/1.2mi farther on, turn right towards the Moulin de Châteaubrun.

Châteaubrun

The massive towers of Châteaubrun, a 12C fortress built in a picturesque setting overlooking the valley by Hugues de Lusignan, inspired George Sand to describe this wild country in two of her novels, *Le Péché de Monsieur Antoine* and *Les Maupras*.

▷ Turn right onto D 45E just before Pont-des-Piles.

Belvédère du Barrage d'Éguzon★

This belvedere above the dam provides a superb view of the reservoir (Lac de Chambon) blending into a landscape of hills and rocks and, downstream, the valley of the River Creuse.

▷ Head to D 40, then turn right onto D 40A.

Plage de Bonnu

Before heading down to the Lac de Chambon, take a moment to admire, to the right, an elegant castle surrounded by a moat.

Ruines de Crozant★

See Ruines de CROZANT.

▶ A narrow road skirting the foot of the ruins runs down to the lake.

👥 Chambon

This resort, set in beautiful surroundings, makes use of the stretch of water contained by the Barrage d'Éguzon dam to offer a full range of water sports. In season there is a regular boat service to the **Plage de Fougères**.

Éguzon

Éguzon was formerly a fortified town. On rue Athanase-Bassinet, the daily life and traditional crafts of the region are brought to life in the **Musée de la Vallée de la Creuse** (&.📷guided tours (45min), mid-Mar–mid-Nov 10am–noon, 2–6pm (weekends and public holidays 2–6pm). ⊙€3 (children under 18, €1.50). ℘02 54 47 47 75).

▶ Continue on D 45 to Pont-de-Piles. Turn left onto D 72, then follow D 913.

Ruins of the Château de la Prune-au-Pot

⊙ᴇThe ruins of the castle are closed to visitors.
It was here that Henri IV stayed during the siege of Argenton in 1589.

Ceaulmont

The name of this town derives from its dominant position. In a meadow to the right of the road, note the charming little Romanesque church on the edge of a spur. Skirt it to the south side to enjoy a fine **view★** of a loop in the Creuse, with the plateaux of the Marche and Combraille in the background.

▶ Return to D 913 which leads back to Argenton-sur-Creuse.

Ruines de Crozant★

The massive Crozant fortress, known as the "Key to the Limousin", rises from a rocky promontory commanding the confluence of the Creuse and the Sédelle. Although it is in ruins, it is still an impressive castle.

A BIT OF HISTORY

In the 13C, the Comte de la Marche, Hughes X de Lusignan, reinforced an existing wooden structure and the building began to take on the appearance of a fortress. Strong in his position, Hughes X revolted against Blanche de Castille and then St Louis. Crozant eventually fell to the royal troops.
The Count and his father-in-law and ally Henry III of England were defeated at Saintes in 1242.
Several thousand men could be garrisoned in the citadel which, a century later, would resist the attacks of Edward the Black Prince.

- 🕭 **Michelin Map:** Michelin local map 325: G-2.
- 🅸 **Info:** Mairie, 23160 Crozant. ℘05 55 89 80 12.
- ▶ **Location:** 85km/53mi NE of Limoges. The most spectacular view of Crozant, the castle ruins and the Creuse valley, with the river cutting its way through the ravines, appears as you approach from the E along the D 30.
- 🚫 **Don't Miss:** A tour of the fortress; a boat trip on Eguzon lake with l'Hôtel du Lac (℘05 55 89 81 96).

After several changes of hand, the Wars of Religion and an earthquake brought calamity and, by 1640, ruin.

VISIT

🕐Open Jul–Aug, daily 10am–noon, 2–7pm, Sun and public hols 10am–7pm; Jun 2–7pm weekends and public

holidays; Apr–May and Sept daily
2–6pm (Sat–Sun and public hols
10am–noon, 2–6pm); Oct–mid-Nov
Sat–Sun 2–6pm. ⊜€5.
℘05 55 89 09 05.

Medieval visitors passed through the
Charles VII gate to enter the first courtyard. The **square keep**, in the second
courtyard, was the 12C castle. A steep
ramp leads to the third courtyard, the
twin-walled section built by Hughes X.
The base of the massive tower built by
Isabelle d'Angoulême in the 13C stands
on a rise 5m/16ft high.
The line of towers continued to where
the ground floor of the Tour Colin
remains intact.

EXCURSIONS
Fresselines
*8km/5mi SE along the minor road
skirting the cemetery.*
The poet **Maurice Rollinat**, George
Sand's godson, worked and died here
in this village still favoured by artists.
🚶 A rocky path leads from the church
to the **confluence of the two Creuse
rivers★** (*1hr round-trip on foot*), in picturesque surroundings. Claude Monet
loved to set up his easel here.

Les Jardins Clos du Préfons
*5km/3.1mi S along D 913 towards
Dun-le-Palestel; turn right in Maisons.*
🕐*Open Jul–Aug daily except Mon and
Tue 2.30–5pm; Jun and Sept–Oct by prior
arrangement.* ⊜€5. ℘05 55 89 82 59.
Seven small enclosed gardens are
planted here around traditional Creuse
houses.

Saint-Benoît-du-Sault

St-Benoît-du-Sault has taken the
place of the former city Salis, the
domain of the Lords of Brosse. Stroll
around the narrow streets of the
village to discover the old houses
and ramparts dating from medieval
times when the village was a large,
fortified city. It took its current name
from a Benedictine priory founded
here at the end of the 10C.

VISIT
Old town
The oldest part of the town, Le Fort,
adjacent to the church, is surrounded
by solid ramparts and enclosed by a
fortified gateway near a belfry.
Beyond Le Fort, the mercantile city
developed in the 15C. This district was
enclosed by a second, lower fortification. Its walls, a watch-path and the
Grimard tower are still standing.

▶ **Population:** 652.
⌚ **Michelin Map:** 323 E8.
🛈 **Info:** 2 pl. du Champ-de-
    Foire, St-Benoît-du-Sault.
    ℘02 54 47 67 95.
▶ **Location:** On a rocky
    spur overlooking the
    Portefeuille valley,
    20km/12.4mi SE of
    Argenton-sur-Creuse.
😊 **Don't miss:** The frescoes
    in the church.
👥 **Kids:** Jardin des Merveilles
    with 4 000 plant species.
🕐 **Timing:** A full day for the
    town and its region.

▶ Leave pl. des Augustins and follow
the path skirting the SE part of town.

This path overlooks the banks of the
Portefeuille. Take in the **views** over the
valley and the Château de Montgarnaud.

After the quartier du Portugal, walk along the watch-path that leads to the church.

Église

Building on this church began in the 11C; it is partially Romanesque. Its nave features a lovely framework. The 14C bell-tower houses a granite baptismal basin.

Terrace of the former priory

Enjoy the **view** over the Portefeuille Valley and the dam. On the right, notice the stacked terraces and tile-roofed houses. Take rue Sous-le-Mur, rue de la Demi-Lune and the covered lane called Four-Banal to come back up to the gate.

Place de la République

This square is surrounded by houses with uneven rooftops.

Rue de la Roche

Note the group of old houses, including the 15C **Maison de l'Argentier** adorned with a studded door below a sculpted lintel.

🚗 DRIVING TOUR

5 AUTOUR DE L'ANGLIN

55km/34mi round-trip. Allow 2hr 30min. See route 5 on region map pp408–409.

Leave St-Benoît N on D 10, then take D 46 towards St-Civan.

Église de Roussines

This church features a series of **15C frescoes**. In the choir bay, one painting represents Christ surrounded by evangelists and angels playing various instruments. In the third bay, admire the representation of the seven deadly sins: pride, greed, lust, gluttony, wrath, sloth and envy.

Continue along D 46 to St-Civan. Take a left at the church on D 54.

Musée du Machinisme Agricole

Open Jul–Aug daily 2–7pm; rest of the year Wed and Sat 2–6pm. Closed Nov–Mar and public holidays. €4 (children under 15, €1.50).
A collection of more than 500 pieces of farm machinery, some of which are antiques.

Turn right on D 55 which runs along the Roche-Chevreux pond a little further on. At Lignac, turn right on D 53.

Château-Guillaume★

Open Jun–Oct 2.30–6pm. €6 (children aged 6–16, €3).
Visit this impressive Romanesque dungeon crowned with machicolations and surrounded by four towers and ramparts. This was a defensive building during the 11C when it belonged to **Guillaume X**. In the 15C building, you'll see the **Salle des Gardes**, where various souvenirs are displayed.

Come back to Lignac and follow D 53 to Chaillac. Leave the village E on D 36 and turn right at the La Barytine factory road.

Château de Brosse

This fortress was burned by the English during the Hundred Years War. If you walk down along the surrounding walls and go round to the right, you'll get a good view of the fortifications clinging to the rocks above a little tributary of the Anglin.

Come back towards Chaillac. D 36 leads back to St-Benoît-du-Sault.

The many castles of the Champagne Berrichonne, such as Ainay-le-Vieil and its gardens, are delightful for a romantic excursion. In fact, if you love gardens and well-landscaped medieval villages, you'll be in your element in this pretty corner of France. And don't miss the various religious monuments, of which the Abbaye de Noirlac is perhaps the most remarkable.

Highlights

1 **Château de Nohant**, dedicated to the memory of author George Sand (p442)

2 **Château d'Ainay le Vieil**, "The Little Carcassonne" (p445)

3 Flamboyant Gothic and early Renaissance elegance of **Château de Meillant** (p450)

4 **Abbaye de Noirlac**, medieval monastery *par excellence* (p451)

5 Extraordinary riverside garden of **Apremont-sur-Allier** (p452)

less spectacular, the Château de Nohant and the museum set up in George Sand's former house are essentials for readers of her works.

These fertile lands have given rise to extraordinary gardens, and many of the monuments you'll visit take pride in their landscaping. From the city garden of Châteauroux to the mystic gardens of the Priory of Notre-Dame d'Orsan, every terrace is a little celebration of nature's abundance. The Parc Floral of Apremont-sur-Allier is a garden on the scale of a valley set against the backdrop of one of the most beautiful villages of France and a must-see for garden lovers.

Castles and Gardens

The stunning castles of this area with their pointed roofs remind us that the Loire valley is not far away. Among the marvels you'll want to visit here are the Château de Meillant, a magnificent castle with a Flamboyant tower; the remarkable Château d'Ainay le Vieil, dubbed "The Little Carcassonne" because of its resemblance to its namesake, featuring English-style gardens that seem an extension of the reverie it inspires; while

Religious Monuments

Various medieval monasteries shaped the destiny of this rural area, giving rise to religious buildings such as the Abbaye de Noirlac. Its ornate cloisters contrast with the minimalism of its sanctuary, but the impeccable monument as a whole exudes a sense of peace and order. As you drive through the countryside, don't hesitate to try the doors of small churches. They have much to tell about this area's rich history.

Abbaye de Noirlac

© Patrick Keirsebilck / agefotostock

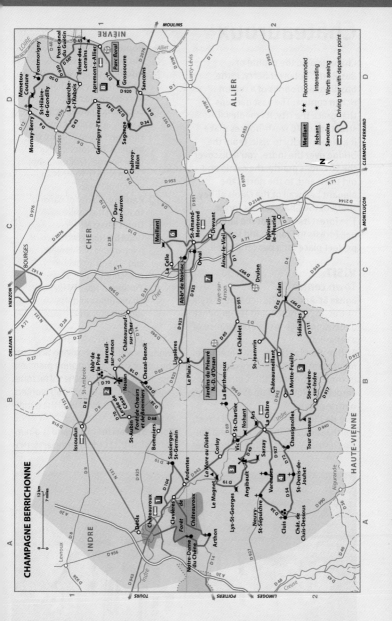

Agriculture and Metallurgy

The main feature of this area's landscape is farmland, as rich fertilisers have transformed the light, sandy soil into fertile fields. Among these are the pastures of white Charolais cattle, raised for their excellent beef. They are at the heart of one of the foremost livestock markets in Europe which takes place in Sancoins.

In the past, the natural resources of the area, which included wood and minerals, made this a metallurgic centre. Though little is left to see of the blast furnaces that once created a prosperous local economy – except for a few ruins at La Guerche-sur-l'Aubois – you can learn all about the evolution of the metal industry at the Halle de Grossouvre.

Châteauroux

Châteauroux, the capital of Bas-Berry, or Lower Berry, is the bustling metropolis of a region rich in culture. The vast gardens that grace the city, its medieval streets and old wash-houses make it a pleasant city to visit. From the bridge over the Indre, you'll discover the St-Gildas prairie, the castle and old town and, to the north, the elegant bell wall of the Déols abbey, south of the Châteauroux forest. The forest itself one of the largest oak forests in France, and the perfect place for a peaceful stroll.

VISIT
Town centre

Eglise St-André – The neo-Gothic style of this 1876 church and its immense dimensions give it the appearance of a cathedral.

Eglise St-Martial – This medieval monument is the only very old church in the city besides the Couvent des Cordeliers. Note the late 15C 35m-high **belfry-porch**.

Rue de l'Indre – Along this old street, which used to be the weaving and tanning district, you can still admire dormer

- ▶ **Population:** 46 386.
- ♿ **Michelin Map:** 323: G6.
- 🅘 **Info:** 1 pl. de la Gare. ℘02 54 34 10 74. www.chateau roux-tourisme.com.
- ◖ **Location:** Châteauroux is easily accessible from Limoges (120km/74.5mi N on the A 20 motorway) or from Bourges (70km/43.4mi SW on N 151). There is an airport in Déols.
- 🅿 **Parking:** Plenty of parking spaces in the centre.
- ◈ **Don't Miss:** Musée-Hôtel Bertrand with its mementoes of Napoléon and art and archaeology collections.
- 🕑 **Timing:** A full day for Châteauroux and its surrounding area.

windows with pulleys giving access to the upper storeys for storing merchandise. In the mid-16C, 120 wool factories employed no less than 3 000 workers, and the activity thrived until the middle of the 19C.

Porte St-Martin – This gate is a remnant of the 12C–15C ramparts that

Château Raoul, Châteauroux

© Office de Tourisme Châteauroux Sud Berry - Sébastien Roy

guarded Château Raoul. Enjoy the **view** of the city from here.

Château Raoul – Built in the 15C by Guillaume III de Chavigny on the site of a 12C–13C fortress, this castle looks more like a lordly estate than a fortress. It was renovated beginning in 1880.

Eglise Notre-Dame – This neo-Romanesque church was completed in 1882. The belltower rises to a height of 50m/164ft and the dome is topped with a copper statue of the Virgin Mary.

Ancien Couvent des Cordeliers

4 r. Alain-Fournier.   *Open daily except Mon: Jun–Aug 10am–noon, 2–6pm, Sat–Sun 10am–12.30pm, 2–6pm; Sept 10am–noon, 2–6pm; rest of year 2–6pm.* *No charge.* *02 54 61 12 30.*

This monastery was built in 1214 by Guillaume I de Chavigny and his brother Jean upon their return from the Crusades. Its rectangular plan is very minimalist, characteristic of churches which depended upon charity for their livelihood. Since 1979, this church has become a cultural centre and makes a beautiful backdrop for large works of art. The **Biennale de Céramique Contemporaine** is held here.

Musée-Hôtel Bertrand

Open daily except Mon: Jun–Aug 10am–noon, 2–6pm, Sat–Sun 10am–12.30pm, 2–6pm; Sept 10am–noon, 2–6pm; rest of year 2–6pm. *No charge (audioguide €4).* *02 54 61 12 30.*

This building was built in 1769 by Martin Boucher, royal engineer and the grandfather of Maréchal Bertrand. The latter, who is the subject of the statue by Marochetti that stands in the courtyard, died here in 1844.

The ground floor exhibits a large collection of items having belonged to General Bertrand, **Napoléon Bonaparte** and their entourage. The emperor's **aviary** decorates the building's rotunda. You'll see a dining room ready for service, a Chinese room full of silk and heady incense, and objects from the famous expedition to Egypt.

Le Couvent des Cordeliers, Châteauroux

© Photo Club Belle-Isle / Jean Zucchet

Rural life in the Berry is depicted through the reconstruction of an old-fashioned kitchen.

The museum features **15C–19C paintings** by Flemish, Dutch and French artists, as well as **sculptures and decorative arts** from various periods, including a bust of Paul Claudel as a child by his sister Camille. The numerous **20C works of art** include paintings by Boutet, Detroy, Caillaud and Maurice Estève, as well as sculptures by Hans Hartung and J Carrasco.

The **archaeology** section explores the Gallo-Roman and Roman civilisations.

EXCURSION
Déols

N of Châteauroux on D 920. *Guided tour (1hr 30min) of the abbey, old town, crypts of the St-Etienne church and belltower (optional) with a guide or audio guide. By request at the Tourist Office.* *€3.50 (children under 12, €1.50).* *02 54 07 58 87.* *www.deols-tourisme.fr.*

Although today Déols seems like a suburb of Châteauroux, in fact it is much older. The Gallo-Roman city was one of the first Christian areas of the Berry in the 4C. Lord Léocade, protector of the Bourges church, was the dominating character. He and his son Ludre became canon priests, and their tombs highly venerated.

Abbaye Notre-Dame – In the 9C and 10C, a powerful feudal dynasty emerged. One of the princes of Déols, **Ebbes le Noble**, founded a Benedictine abbey in the year 917 affiliated with the order of Cluny. His wealth was such that he was nicknamed "la mamelle de St-Pierre" ("St Peter's nipple"). The construction of the abbey continued until the 13C and flourished from its location along the Compostela road. The Hundred Years War and the Wars of Religion progressively drove it to ruin. It became public property in 1626 and was even used as a source of building stone. In the Tourist Office you can see a scale model of the abbey in its heyday. Today, little is left of this group of buildings that stretched over 2ha/4.9 acres. All that is remains of the church is a magnificent **belltower★**, which escaped ruin because it was used as a landmark on the road from Issoudun to Déols. At the base of the tower, note the historiated capitals, including a remarkable depiction of Daniel in the Lions' Den. The ruins of the monastery buildings include the Gothic arcades of the cloister, a turret that served as a monk's prison, and vaulted rooms. Work is in progress to reveal the 12C crypt and its seven radiating chapels, to restore the northern part of the building and create a museum display of the stones recovered.

Gates to the city – As the first fortifications had been destroyed by the lord of Châteauroux, the villagers obtained the right to build the ramparts anew in 1453. Two of those three gates are still standing.

Porte de l'Horloge, or "clock gate", welcomed pilgrims on the road to Compostela. Until recently, the towers were used as a prison.

Porte du Pont-Perrin, or "Perrin Bridge gate", has lost its defensive elements. It originally included four towers, of which only the covered passage remains. This gate opened onto the bridge it was named after, which collapsed in 1640 and was replaced in 1750.

North of the rue de l'Horloge, the 12C **Église St-Etienne de Déols** is one of the oldest Christian places of worship in the Berry. It is built on the site of a pre-Roman basilica that included crypts containing the relics of St Léocade and St Ludre, which were the objects of large pilgrimages.

You can see their tombs to the left and right of the choir. The tomb of Léocade was reconstructed in limestone in the 19C. That of Ludre is the oldest, in white marble. When you come out of the church, note, in the first chapel to the right, four 17C panels illustrating the **Miracle of Déols**.

🚗 DRIVING TOUR

1 CHÂTEAUROUX FOREST
60km/37.2mi round-trip. Allow 3 hr. See route 1 on region map p431.

▷ Leave Châteauroux S on the D 990 and, at the Poinçonnet exit, head S on D 67.

This remarkable oak forest marks the boundary between the cereal fields of Champagne and the copse of Boischaut.

▷ Take the forest road of Orangeons. At the crossroads called Carrefour des Druides, follow Beauregard.

At the Orangeons intersection, a dead-end forest road gives access to the botanic trail, fitness trail and picnic area of **Carrefour Bertrand**.

Chapelle Notre-Dame-du-Chêne
In a clearing, this very old chapel, which was rebuilt in 1862, still receives pilgrimages on Whit Monday and holds other unusual ceremonies.

▷ Follow Beauregard. At the Pin roundabout, follow D 40. Turn left on D 14.

Église d'Arthon

The walls of this 12C church dedicated to St Martin are decorated with frescoes painted c 1945 by the artist Malespine.

◯ Follow D 45 to the intersection of Riau-de-la-Motte. Turn right on the Artois road. At the Picard crossroads, take the Clavières road NE.

🐾This road gives access to the **Étang des Berthommiers** (*Carrefour Chandaire*), a lake encircled by a short walking trail (*1km/0.6mi*).

◯ After crossing the Indre, turn right onto a small road.

Clavières

These forges, which were renamed in the 16C, ceased their activity in 1875. If you follow the right bank of the Indre, you'll discover a pretty castle at the end of a pleasant walk.

◯ Come back to D 943 and follow it towards La Châtre.

Ardentes

The **St-Martin church** dates from 1117, when its possession was confirmed by the abbey of Déols. The 12C **St-Vincent church** was reworked in the 15C. Its belfry-porch was added in the 19C.

◯ Leave Ardentes NE on D 19.

Église de Sassierges-St-Germain

This Romanesque church with its 12C single nave features a 13C polygonal apse and a square belltower with a wooden shingle roof. The four sculpted capitals of the main entryway in the west are similar to those of Déols abbey.

◯ Follow D 104 until you reach Etrechet, then follow D 943 to Châteauroux.

ADDRESSES

🛏 STAY

⊖ **Chambres d'hôte Claudine Daguet-Rault** – *Villecourte, rte de la Champenoise, Coings.* ✆*02 54 22 12 56. http://villecourtelocation.fr.* 🅿 📺. *2 rooms.* Perfectly restored former 19C farm, the barn and stables now pleasant, well-equipped and air-conditioned studios. They all give onto the perfectly kept garden and lawn.

⊖⊖ **Hôtel Boischaut** – *135 av. de La Châtre.* ✆*02 54 22 22 34. www.hotel-chateauroux.com.* 🅿. *WiFi. 27 rooms.* Only a few minutes from the centre of town, choose from rooms with practical, rustic or wrought-iron furniture.

⊖⊖⊖ **Hôtel Colbert** – *3 av. de La Châtre.* ✆*02 54 35 70 00. www.hotel-colbert.fr. WiFi.* ♿. *74 rooms.* This former tobacco factory has been converted into a hotel with designer touches.

🍽EAT

⊖ **Côté Cour** – *78 r. Grande.* ✆*02 54 27 21 81. www.restaurant-nullepartailleurs.com.* Grilled meat or **steak tartare**, fish, homemade chips… When it's nice outside, a partially covered courtyard is a favourite spot for the regulars.

⊖ **Le Bistrot Gourmand** – *10 r. du Marché.* ✆*02 54 07 86 98.* This little bistro-style restaurant is completed by a patio-terrace bursting with flowers in the summertime.

⊖⊖ **Le Lavoir de la Fonds Charles** – *26 r. Château-Raoul.* ✆*02 54 27 11 16.* This former house includes a pleasant terrace and a veranda overlooking the Indre and its verdant surroundings.

SHOPPING

Le Croquet de Charost – *36100 Neuvy-Pailloux.* ✆*02 54 49 58 75.* Crunchy, sweet croquets de Charost are a regional speciality that you can buy here directly from the factory store.

Issoudun

Issoudun dates back to Gallic times: Uxellodunum comes from a Celtic term meaning a high – and thus fortified – site. Later, during the Middle Ages, Issoudun was the stake in many a battle, the most famous being that between Philip Augustus and Richard the Lionheart.

A BIT OF HISTORY

Honoré de Balzac (1799–1850) stayed at Frapesle Castle near Issoudun, where he wrote most of César Birotteau and researched material for *La Rabouilleuse* (*The Black Sheep*). Issoudun still has the peculiar street names which appear in Balzac's works: rue du Boucher-Gris (drunken butcher street), rue à Chercher (hard-to-find street).

 WALKING TOUR

▶ Start from place St-Cyr.

Église St-Cyr

There is a very fine 14C–15C **stained-glass window** in the church. It is divided into five vertical sections and, in addition to depicting the Crucifixion, features medallions illustrating scenes from the lives of St Cyran and St Juliet.

▶ Walk up to place du 10 Juin.

Beffroi

The belfry, flanked by two round towers of unequal size, served as a gateway through the castle wall to the town in the 12C. Dismantled during the Wars of Religion, it was restored in the Renaissance style and used as a prison until 1914.

Place des Miroirs

The façade of the **Hôtel de Ville**, or town hall, dates from 1731. It is attached to a modern building and fronted by a courtyard designed by Marin Kasimir. This work, known as Place des Miroirs, is made of eight glassed-in spaces surrounded by steps and waterworks.

▶ **Population:** 13 090.
◉ **Michelin Map:** 323: H-5.
🛈 **Info:** Pl. St Cyr. ✆02 54 21 74 02. www.issoudun.fr.
▶ **Location:** 35km/22mi S of Vierzon; 37km/23mi W of Bourges.
🅿 **Parking:** Car parks are dotted around the centre (*see town plan*).
🕐 **Timing:** Half day to explore the Chœurs and Bommiers forests.
◈ **Don't Miss:** Musée de l'Hospice St-Roch.

Tour Blanche

◷*Open Jul–Aug, daily 2–6pm; Jun and Sept, Tue–Sun, 2–6pm; Apr–May, Sat–Sun, public holidays 2–6pm. ⊛€3. ✆02 54 21 74 02.*

This tower, standing in the middle of the town hall gardens, was built at the end of the 12C by Richard the Lionheart. The inside is octagonal, the outside nearly circular; it is 28m high and the walls are 3.5m thick.

The four floors in the tower are open to the public. First you'll see the 8m-high former cellars accompanied by an audio-visual presentation about Richard the Lionheart and Philip-Augustus. You'll move on to a lofty vaulted hall where the original entrance was located and see a presentation of King Arthur's legends. Finally you'll visit a room devoted to the Hundred Years War and an exhibition area displaying a model of the town as it was in the 17C.

From the top platform there is a view over the countryside between the valleys of the Indre and the Cher.

👥 Parc François-Mitterrand

Access via the panoramic lift built within the fortifications.

This pleasant park is easily reached from all parts of town. It stretches across both sides of the river and is an ideal place for a family picnic.

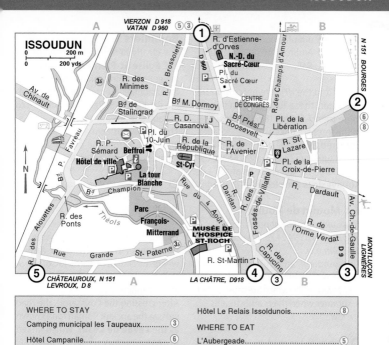

Musée de l'Hospice St-Roch★

&. ○Open May–Sept, Mon–Tue, 2–7pm, Wed–Sun and public holidays 10am–noon, 2–7pm; Oct–Apr, daily except Mon and Tue, 2–6pm, Sat–Sun and public holidays, 10am–noon, 2–6pm. ○Closed Jan, 1 May, 1 Nov, 24–26 Dec. ⊶No charge. ℘02 54 21 01 76. This museum is housed in the former hospital (Hôtel-Dieu) which is built on piles over the River Théols in a picturesque setting. St Roch is legendary for healing victims of the plague in the 14C. Legend has it that he himself was stricken with the plague, but was saved by a dog. He is often pictured with one in paintings and statuary.

Sculpture – This sculpture collection gives an insight into past local monuments: capitals, statues of the Virgin Mary and columns dating from the 8C to the 15C. The **salle des hommes** (men's ward) gives access to the **chapel** built around 1500. The most outstanding items are two 15C carvings of the **Tree of Jesse★★** showing the genealogy of Christ.

Ancient medicine – The last wing, the **salle des femmes** (women's ward), displays a collection of instruments used by surgeons, dentists and gynaecologists. The **apothicarie★** (pharmacy), facing a garden where medicinal herbs are cultivated, houses a valuable pharmaceutical collection.

Basilique Notre-Dame-du-Sacré-Cœur

This late-19C neo-Gothic basilica is a popular place of pilgrimage, as the numerous ex-votos testify. The stained-glass windows are particularly interesting: abstract designs in various hues of blue along the aisle contrast with more classical designs in the nave and chancel.

🚗 DRIVING TOUR

② FORET DE CHŒURS ET DE BOMMIERS

60km/37.2mi round-trip. Allow 3 hr.
See route 2 on region map p431.

Drive E out of Issoudon on the D 8 towards St-Ambroix. At St-Hilaire, turn on to the D 84E.

Located in the *départements* of Indre and Cher, these lovely forests cover more than 7 500ha/18 525 acres. 75% of the trees are oaks.
Bordered by woods, the route follows the picturesque Arnon valley. Above the river bank rise the remains of the 12C **Abbaye de la Prée** (*concerts in season*).

👤👤 Moulin de Nouan

Guided tour by appointment.
€2. ℘06 85 94 24 76. www.moulin denouan.fr.cr.
This windmill, an unusual site in the region, was mainly used to back up the many watermills, which are often stilled in summer when rivers and streams are low.

Return to the road and turn right on D 9.

Mareuil-sur-Arnon

This village, nestled among the copses, was one of the metallurgical centres of the upper Arnon valley. All that remains of the old forge is a tall brick chimney alongside the lake. Southwest of the town of Mareuil, this 3ha/7.5-acre lake now serves as a recreation centre.

Outside of Mareuil, turn right on D 18.

Abbaye de Chezal-Benoît

Founded in 1093 by the monk André de Vallombreuse, this former Benedictine monastery has kept the 12C nave of the church and the community buildings. It is now a psychiatric hospital.

Leave Chezal SW on D 65E.

Travel along the southern edge of the **Forêt de Chœurs**, where many forest roads and trails lead to the central point known as La Croix Blanche.

At Pruniers, turn right on D 925.

Bommiers

The clearly Benedictine design of the 12C **Église St-Pierre** is typical of the lower Berry. The capitals, also 12C, create an admirable ensemble: Christ Handing the Keys to St Peter and the Law to St Paul.
The 48 magnificent 1511–15 **stalls★** were taken from the chapel and the Minimes convent in Bommiers.

Take D 925 towards Lignières. 1km/0.5mi before Pruniers, turn left on D 68.

The road back to Issoudun crosses the **Bommiers Forest** as far as **St-Aubin**, where the church houses a 15C group of sculptures depicting St Anne, the Virgin and the infant Jesus.
After crossing the Cousseron, the road crosses the ancient Roman road known as the **Levée de César**, which linked Argentonmagus (see St-MARCEL) to Bourges.

ADDRESSES

🛏 STAY

Hôtel Le Relais Issoudun – *88 rte de Bourges. NE on N 151. ℘02 54 03 04 05. 16 rooms.* Simple accommodation in a large historic building.

Hôtel Campanile – *Route 151 (Bourges). ℘02 54 21 06 40. www.campanile.fr.* Chain hotel with well-equipped rooms.

🍽 EAT

L'Aubergeade – *321, rte d'Issoudun, Diou. ℘02 54 49 22 28.* This lively restaurant boasts a garden terrace where traditional local dishes are served.

La Cognette – *Blvd Stalingrad. ℘02 54 03 59 59. www.la-cognette.com. Closed Jan, Sun eve, Tue lunchtime and Mon (Oct–May).* Classical, refined cuisine served in a pleasant orangerie with a Victorian canopy.

La Châtre

La Châtre is built on a hill overlooking the Indre valley in the centre of the area known locally as the Vallée Noire (Black Valley) beloved by George Sand. Only the old castle keep recalls the fact that the town had a military origin and was a Roman encampment, or *castrum*, which came to be called Châtre over time.

OLD TOWN

Around the church and towards the river, the **old town** will tempt you to a stroll. Start from place George-Sand and walk past the town hall, the former Carmelite abbey-church with its 14C carved doorway and the fine Villaines mansion, now the municipal library.

Admire the **Maison Rouge**, a fine 16C timber-framed residence (*place Laisnel-de-la-Salle*) and private mansions in the Classical style farther on along rue de **Bellefond**. A fine Gothic **statue** of the Virgin Mary stands on place Notre-Dame. From place de l'Abbaye overlooking the River Indre, walk down the stairs lined with flower beds. They lead to the **Pont aux Laies**, an old humpback bridge offering a charming view of the picturesque surroundings. At the river's edge, former tanneries with their typical sheltered porches are now quiet, and the water runs clear beneath them.

Donjon
rue Venôse.

From 1743 to 1934, the prison at La Châtre, an old feudal fortress in the control of provincial lords, was "nothing more than a huge square tower, blackened by the centuries and standing straight upon the rock on the side of a narrow ravine where the River Indre flows amid luxuriant green" (George Sand, *Mauprat*). Built in the 15C by Guillaume III de Chauvigny, it now houses a museum.

- **Population:** 4 482.
- **Michelin Map:** 323: H-7.
- **Info:** 134 r. Nationale. ℘02 54 48 22 64. www.pays-george-sand.com.
- **Location:** 37km/23.1mi SE of Châteauroux via D 943.
- **Timing:** Allow a full day to explore the rural backwaters of the Berry as described in the works of George Sand.
- **Don't Miss:** Musée George Sand et de la Vallée Noire.

Musée George Sand et de la Vallée Noire

71 r. Venôse. Open Jul–Aug daily 10am–noon, 2–6.30pm (Sun 2–6.30pm); May–Jun and Sept 10am–noon, 2–6.30pm (Sun 2–6.30pm); Apr and Oct 2–6.30pm; rest of year 2–5pm. Closed Tue (except Jul–Aug); Jan and 25-26 Dec. €3. ℘02 54 48 36 79. The upper floor of this museum is devoted to George Sand and her guests at Nohant. Exhibits on the other floors evoke the folklore and art of the Black Valley.

Église St-Germain
Pl. de l'Église.

The porch and tower crumbled in 1896, carrying the 12C nave with them. Inside, the pillars and Romanesque capitals have been reconstructed.

EXCURSIONS
Église de la Berthenoux
12km/7.5mi NE via D 940 and D 68.

This vast 12C church is surmounted by a powerful belfry crowning a fine dome resting on squinches. Note the sculpted capitals in the transept.

🚗 DRIVING TOURS

③ GEORGE SAND TOUR
60km/37mi round-trip. Allow 1 day. See route 3 on region map p431 and map overleaf.

This tour wanders through the country-side that served as backdrop for Sand's novels set in rural Berry.

▶ Leave La Châtre travelling NE on D 940 towards Bourges. Drive along the car-racing track and turn left.

Château d'Ars
Surrounded by a large park, this 16C castle was chosen by George Sand as the setting for her novel *Les Beaux Messieurs de Bois-Doré*. It now houses the George Sand and Romanticism International Centre and its exhibitions.

▶ Drive to D 943 and turn towards Châteauroux.

Château de Nohant★
See NOHANT.

▶ Turn back; continue on D 943.

Fresques de Vic★
Built along the Roman road, this village (which in Latin, *vicus*, simply means village), features a small Romanesque church, **Église St-Martin**, decorated with interesting **frescoes** brought to light in 1849. Though the faces lack expression, the composition is so skill-fully assembled, the movement is so realistic and the detail is so accurate that the technique was later copied in the pictorial and sculptural art of Limousin and the southwest.

▶ Cross D 943 (minor road opposite rue de l'Église).

St-Chartier
Admire this interesting little church and château (⚬ not open to the public), restored in the 19C, as you stroll through the **park**.

▶ Come back to D 943 via D 69.

Corlay
These landscapes inspired the one described in *Fanchon the Cricket*. A rest area overlooks the green Indre valley (*for a closer look, drive down the D 69*).

▶ Turn left on D38 5km/3mi farther on.

La Mare au Diable
🚶 A forest clearing off the D 38 was probably the site of the marsh known as the haunted pool (*La Mare au Diable*), the title of one of Sand's novels.

Château du Magnet
This 15C castle stands in a pastoral land-scape surrounded by greenery.

▶ D 19 on the left runs through charming countryside crisscrossed by hedges.

Château de Lys-St-George
This castle features towers that rise straight up out of the moat. From the terrace you will see the 15C façade and the Gourdon valley.

▶ Continue along D 19 and turn left 3km/1.9mi beyond Tranzault.

Château de Sarzay
🕐 *Open 10am–noon, 2–6pm.* ⬤€6.
📞*02 54 31 32 25. www.sarzay.net.*
Blanchemont Castle in George Sand's novel *The Angibault Miller* is based on Sarzay, a proud feudal domain with tile-roofed, tall round towers.

▶ Drive N along D 41.

Moulin d'Angibault
Stop by the mill which stands on the Vauvre, a tributary of the Indre.

▶ Take D 49 back to La Châtre.

④ SOUTHWEST BOISCHAUT
50km/31mi round-trip. Allow 4 hr.
See route 5 on region map p431 and map above.

▶ Leave SW on D 73 towards Le Magny.

Église de Chassignolles
The **church** is crowned by a large belfry-tower. A small Renaissance door with an emblazoned pediment opens into the north transept.

◗ Turn back and continue along D 72.

St-Denis-de-Jouhet
The Gothic church has a shingle-covered steeple as well as 12C and 13C stained-glass windows.

◗ Leave the village via D 54.

Cluis
The chancel of the 13C **church** ends with two apses bearing noteworthy capitals. One of the side chapels has a splendid 14C white-marble **Virgin and Child★**.

◗ Drive NE along D 38.

Cluis-Dessous
Among the medieval castle ruins you'll see part of a curtain wall, a gate with two towers and a central building.

◗ Continue on D 38 towards Mouhers.

Neuvy-St-Sépulchre
This small town gets its name from the **basilica** modelled on the Holy Sepulchre in Jerusalem. It consists of a rectangular structure completed in 1049 joined to a vast **rotunda★** 22m across; the upper part was restored by Violet-le-Duc in the 19C.

◗ Leave Neuvy E on D 927.

Abbaye de Varennes
◷*Open Jul–Aug 1–7pm.* ⊚*No charge.* ℘*02 54 31 30 59.*
George Sand wrote of this 1148 abbey in her novel *Les Beaux Messieurs de Bois-Doré* (1857).

◗ Come back to D 927 which leads back to La Châtre.

Château de Nohant★

George Sand grew up in the manor here, near the Indre valley in this quaint Berry village clustered round a little square, where centuries-old elms shade the village church and its rustic porch.

A BIT OF HISTORY
The passionate life of George Sand (1804–76)

Amandine-Aurore-Lucile Dupin was born into scandal. Her mother, Sophie, married the girl's father, an army officer, just before she was born. The accidental death of her father did nothing to calm the stormy family atmosphere. Her wealthy grandmother agreed to raise her, on the condition that Sophie stay out of sight. Thus, in her early childhood, Aurore developed a sense of rebellion and a sensitivity to injustice and social charade, but also a deep attachment to nature and the Berry countryside. Both would later mark her work. She was married at 18 to Baron Casimir Dudevant and had two children, Solange and Maurice. She left this profoundly unhappy marriage, established herself in Paris with Jules Sandeau in 1831, and began writing for the satirical review *Figaro*. Her first independently written novel, *Indiana* (1832), was an immediate popular success. She thereafter kept up a prolific pace of literary production to support her family.

Her encounter with the poetic author Alfred de Musset and their trip to Venice fuelled her romantic works, most notably, *Lélia*, which amazed readers with its frank discussion of women's sensual feelings and a passionate call for the right to emotional satisfaction.

Sand's reputation for iconoclasm sprang from such themes and also from exaggerated reports of her unconventional behaviour: she smoked regularly and in public, occasionally dressed like a man and carried on love affairs with Musset, Prosper Mérimée and Frédéric Chopin.

Yet she remained an idealist, convinced of the virtues of marriage between equals, and enraged at the prevalent social system which made such marriages impossible.

An uncommon woman

France's leading woman author produced what are sometimes called socialist novels, including the *Consuelo* cycle. Dedicated to the advance of democracy, she put her pen to political pamphlets, created a local newspaper, and rejoiced when the French monarchy fell and the Second Republic was established. The return of Napoléon III so disappointed Sand that she withdrew to the estate at Nohant.

She continued to write successful plays and the ever-popular pastoral, or rustic, novels with their tender descriptions of the Berry countryside: *The Haunted Pool*, *The Country Waif*, and *Fanchon the Cricket*. In her final years, she undertook charitable works which earned her the affectionate title *la bonne dame de Nohant* (the good lady of Nohant).

MAISON DE GEORGE SAND★

🔊 *Guided tours (1hr): May–Aug 9.30am–12.30pm, 2–6.30pm; Apr and Sept 10am–12.30pm, 2–6pm; rest of year 10am–12.30pm, 2–5pm.* 🕐 *Closed 1 Jan, 1 May, 1 and 11 Nov and 25 Dec.* 💶 *€7.50.* 📞 *02 54 31 06 04.*

This country estate was built around 1760 on the site of an old château. Now a museum, it is devoted to the memory of George Sand and her many guests. The old-fashioned charm of Sand's home has remained unchanged since the 19C, and the visitor almost expects to find the author herself sitting at her desk.

⚙ **Michelin Map:**
323: H-7; or see La Châtre.
▶ **Location**: 6km/4mi N of La Châtre.
⊙ **Don't Miss**: The Maison de George Sand.

Châteaumeillant

The land where Châteaumeillant stands was often disputed as are, its neighbouring vineyards, which produce outstanding "grey wines". During medieval times, coins were minted in this village. Today, it has managed to maintain lovely monuments from its past, such as the Chapître church, now the town hall; the castle; and especially the St-Genès church.

VILLAGE
Église St-Genès
This church, built in grey and pink stone from the quarries of Saulzais-le-Potier (*25km/15.5mi E on D 62*), owes its name to **St Genès**, evangelist and martyr in the 3C. The building's Berry-style entry façade is very harmonious; its small columns feature interesting sculpted capitals. Inside, note the height of the Romanesque nave, where a wooden vault has replaced a barrel vault.

In front of the cul-de-four chevet, the **choir**★ is surrounded by six apsidial chapels. Four of these are connected to it by twin semicircular arches. Have a look at the **historiated capitals**: you'll see the Creation of Adam, the Temptation, the Casting Out of Paradise, Cain killing Abel, and other depictions.

Musée Archéologique Émile-Chénon
Closed for renovation.
This museum, established in the 14C–16C Hôtel de Marcillac, exhibits a large Gallo-Roman and medieval collection gathered from excavations in the area, including knapped flints, potteries, ampohorae and coins.

🚗 DRIVING TOUR

5 SOUTH OF CHÂTEAUMEILLANT
75km/46.6mi round-trip. Allow 4hr. See route 5 on region map p431.

▶ **Population:** 2 015.
🖐 **Michelin Map:** 323: J7.
🛈 **Info:** 68 r. de la Libération. 02 48 61 39 89. www.chateaumeillant-tourisme.fr.
◉ **Location:** In the valley of the River Sinaise, this village is located 17km/10.5mi E of La Châtre and 64km/40mi S of Bourges .
👪 **Kids:** Sidailles lake and its fully equipped beach is an invitation for the whole family to enjoy water-sports together.
🕐 **Timing:** 1 day to visit Châteaumeillant and its surroundings.
◉ **Don't Miss:** The view of Culan castle from D 943, where the bridge crosses the Arno river; the excellent "grey wine" produced in the area.

▶ Leave Châteaumeillant W on D 943 towards La Châtre. At Champillet, turn left onto D 36.

La Motte-Feuilly
The 15C **castle** of this village is described in Georges Sand's novel *Les Beaux Messieurs de Bois-Doré*.

▶ Continue along D 36. At Pouligny-St-Martin, turn left on D 54B.

St-Sévère-sur-Indre
This village includes a **market square** with a 15C fortified gate, a 16C stone cross and a 17C **halle**. In 1947, Jacques Tati shot his legendary film *Jour de Fête* here. The **park** offers a pleasant stroll around an 18C castle. From the terrace, enjoy the view over the Indre.

Maison de Jour de Fête
🕐 *Open Jul–Aug 10am–7pm (last showing 6.15pm); Apr–Jun and Sept 10am–noon, 2–6pm (last showing 5.15pm); other periods, Sat–Sun and*

Château de Culan

© Office de Tourisme de Pays catégorie III de Châteaumeillant

public hols 2–6pm (last showing 5.15pm). 🕐*Closed mid-Nov–Mar.* ⊛€8 (children 12–17, €7; 6–11, €5). ✆02 54 30 21 78. www.maisondejourdefete.com.

Visit a 1940s post office where, if you pick up one of the many antique telephones, you'll hear extracts from the cult film. In the "open-air cinema", you'll experience the greatest moments of its production through a sound and light show. You'll then visit the sets of the bistro and butcher's shop.

▷ Leave Ste-Severe SE on D 917 towards Boussac. At Le Genet, turn left on D 17. Then, at Pérassay, take D 71D towards Culan.

👥 Lac de Sidailles

This 90ha/222-acre water reservoir was created in 1976 in the Arnon valley to provide drinking water for the south of the Cher. A water-sports base and beach have been set up at Pointe de Carroir, where the pleasant environment is ideal for a hike.

▷ Leave Sidailles N on D 997.

👥 Château de Culan★

🔊*Guided tour of the château (1hr).* Jul–Aug 10.30am–12.30pm, 2–7pm; Easter–Jun and Sept 2–6pm. ⊛Gardens and château €10 (children under 15, €5). Gardens and museum only, €7.50. ✆02 48 56 66 66. www.culan.fr.

The powerful medieval fortress of Culan stands four-square with its massive round towers looking straight down into the gorges of the River Arnon. Captured by Philip Augustus in 1188, it was rebuilt in the 13C and considerably altered during the 15C. Joan of Arc and Louis XI were guests here. In the 17C, the castle passed into the hands of Michel Le Tellier, father of Minister Louvois.

▷ Leave Culan NW on D 65 towards Le Châtelet. At St-Maur, take the road towards Privet.

St-Jeanvrin

Here you'll find the little restored 12C **Église St-Georges**. If the door is open, have a look inside at the pretty **16C frescoes**.

▷ Across from the church, a small road leads to Châteaumeillant via Sept-Fronds.

Château d'Ainay le-Vieil ★

Memories of Napoléon Bonaparte's Egypt campaign and the perfume of roses drift through this castle, the former property of Jacques Cœur. Here, medieval times meet the Renaissance for a beautiful architectural harmony. It is nicknamed "Le Petit Carcassonne" or "Little Carcassonne" because of the resemblance between the two castles, notably in the postern gate and ramparts. This fortress, like its cousin in the southwest, seems impenetrable.

- **Michelin Map:** 323-L6.
- **Info:** ℘02 48 63 50 03. www.chateau-ainay levieil.fr.
- **Don't Miss:** The scenes from Christ's childhood and the Lescuyer stained glass in the coffered vault oratory; the delicious perfumes of the rose garden and other themed gardens on the castle grounds.
- **Location:** Located on the historic **Jacques-Cœur road**, which crosses the *départements* of Cher and Loire, the Château d'Ainay-le-Vieil is located in the Cher valley at the edges of the Berry and Bourbon regions, 11km/6.8mi SW of St-Amand-Montrond.
- **Timing:** At least 1hr 30min for the castle and its rose garden, which is at its best in June.

VISIT
Château

Guided tour (1hr): Jul–Aug 10am–7pm; Mar–Jun and Sept–mid-Nov daily except Tue 10am–noon, 2–6pm. Closed mid-Nov–Feb. €8.50 (children aged 5–15, €4). ℘02 48 63 50 03. www.chateau-ainaylevieil.fr.

The octagonal 12C–14C castle, surrounded by nine towers, stands in a charming landscape. Once through the postern gate, you'll be surprised by the contrast between the gracious Flamboyant Gothic building, with its warm ochre tones, and the fortified building. The early 16C hexagonal tower adorned with spiral columns is reminiscent of the Meillant style. From the entry building, you'll access the watch-path, which offers a lovely **view** over the moat filled with waterlilies and the crenellated ramparts. Inside, the castle is surprisingly well decorated. Admire the beamed ceiling and sculpted fireplace of the dining room and the large fireplace of the great room, decorated with the coats of arms of Louis XII and Anne of Brittany. In the oratory, with its superb Renaissance coffered vault, you'll especially note the 16C Lescuyer stained-glass windows and the walls decorated with scenes from the childhood of Christ, to which the famous painter François Boucher contributed. The king's bed-

chamber displays various souvenirs of the Colbert and Villefranche families, having to do with the captivity of Marie-Antoinette and Napoléon Bonaparte's Egyptian campaign.

Jardins ★

Outdoors, delight in the **English garden** (*7ha/17.2 acres*) with magnificent centuries-old trees. The **rose garden**, inaugurated in 1987, includes 180 varieties of botanical roses (those that exist in the wild) and old roses (hybrids created from the 15C onwards using botanical roses). Enjoy the heady aromas, dainty colours and grand names, such as the Colbert rose.

You'll access the Isle and its surrounding canals by crossing a stone bridge. You'll discover the **Isle garden** in place of the former vegetable garden. The **Chartreuses** date from the 17C. Located on a terrace overlooking the canals, they include five areas enclosed by high walls. Through their themes, they represent the evolution of French gardens.

The **bouquet garden** along the canal includes perennial plants that flower as the seasons pass. In the **sculpted orchard**, fruit trees are trimmed and trained onto trellises or allowed to grow freely into their natural shapes. The **meditation garden** is a serene area where water, the symbol of life, trickles gently in a fountain.

A yew cabin, boxwood hedges and a fresco of St Francis of Assisi speaking with birds, by the artist Giotto, invite you to a calm, reflective moment. The **medicinal cloister garden** contains medicinal plants, but also plants used for dyeing and culinary herbs.

The final garden, the **embroidered beds**, is reminiscent of French gardens prized by André Le Nôtre, royal gardener in the 17C. Boxwood borders are cleverly used to form lily and scroll shapes.

Église St-Martin

This 13C church features a massive belfry-porch.

EXCURSION
Épineuil-le-Fleuriel
19.5km/12mi E.

Épineuil was the childhood home of author **Alain Fournier** from 1891 to 1898. Readers of his most famous work *Le Grand Meaulnes* will recognise the fictional Sainte-Agathe, where the story was set.

L'École du Grand Meaulnes

Open Apr–Jun and Sept–Oct daily except Tue 10am–noon, 2–6pm; Jul–Aug 10am–12.30pm, 2–6pm. €6. 02 48 63 04 82. www.grandmeaulnes.eu.

The universe of the author, and of the young heroes of *Le Grand Meaulnes,* is re-created here in the schoolhouse.

St-Amand-Montrond

The original village developed around a monastery founded in the 7C by St Amand, a disciple of St Colomban. Later a castle rose above it, on the hill known as Mont-Rond, and served to protect the growing town. It was destroyed in the 17C. St-Amand-Montrond is capital of the region known as Val de Germigny, where the fields are dotted with white Charolais cattle. A park on the hilltop offers a fine view of the town and its surroundings.

> ▸ **Population:** 10 761.
> ◔ **Michelin Map:** 323: L-6.
> ▣ **Info:** Pl. de la République. 02 48 96 16 86. www.st-amand-tourisme.com.
> ▶ **Location:** 44km/27.5mi S of Bourges.
> ◉ **Don't Miss:** Château de Meillant; Abbaye de Noiriac.

SIGHTS
Église St-Amand

This 12C Romanesque church with a Benedictine floor-plan opens with a beautiful round-arched doorway framed by two multifoiled bays. The nave is rather dark with its barrel-vaulting. The transept crossing features pointed arches which probably replace an earlier cupola. In the 15C, side chapels were added. The Romanesque designs of the capitals in the nave are interesting: birds with long, twining necks; monstrous faces; and acanthus leaves.

Musée St-Vic

Cours Manuel. Open Apr–Sept 10am–noon, 2–6pm (Sun and public holidays 2–6pm); rest of year 10am–noon, 2–5pm (weekends and public holidays 2–5pm). Closed Mon–Tue, 1 Jan, 1 May, 25 Dec. No charge. 02 48 96 55 20.

The 16C St-Vic mansion, set amid a pleasant garden, was the town residence of the commendatory abbots of

Noirlac (&see NOIRLAC). The exhibit area presents a wide panorama of this region, rich in history and vestiges.

There are rooms devoted to materials related to the old castle; local ethnography (*furnishings, pottery, headdresses*); the ceramic work of the potters of La Borne; the work of the clog-maker Louis Touzet; as well as landscapes by Brielman, Cals, Delavaux, Detroy and Osterlind.

Cité de l'Or - Pyramide des Métiers d'art

145 r. de la Cannetille. & ⓘOpen Apr–Sept 10am–7pm; Oct–Mar 10am–noon, 2–5pm. ⓘClosed Tue, 1 Jan and 25 Dec. €6. 02 48 82 11 33. www.cite-or.com.

This vast complex testifies to the importance of gold and jewellery in the town's economic development.

EXCURSIONS
Chalivoy-Milon

24km/14.9mi NE on D 6.

The beautiful early 12C **Église St-Éloi★** features interesting **frescoes** that were discovered in the choir in 1868. Note the sculpted capitals of the columns at the entrance of the choir, the stained-glass windows and, in the nave, the lovely 16C framework that resembles the inverted hull of a ship.

Outside, admire the cornice with sculpted brackets that embrace the choir and the ante-choir.

▷ Come back to Dun-sur-Auron, then take D 14 W.

Châteauneuf-sur-Cher

22km/13.6mi NE on D 2144, then D 35.

This town is located on the right bank of the Cher River at the base of the **château**, a powerful 11C fortress rebuilt in 1581 and reworked in the 17C and 18C. The **Basilique Notre-Dame**, dating from the end of the 19C, was built with funds gathered in an original way. In 1865, the abbot Ducros requested that all the believers in France send him "two cents" in exchange for a prayer addressed to the Virgin Mary. Two thou-

sand marble *ex-voto* (votive offerings in fulfilment of a vow) decorate the walls of the white basilica.

🚗 DRIVING TOURS

6 GRAND BOIS DE MEILLANT
25km/15mi round-trip. Allow 3hr.
See route 6 on region map p431 and map below.

▷ Leave St-Amand along D 10 towards Dun-sur-Auron. The road goes through the forest, Grand Bois de Meillant.

Château de Meillant★★
& See Château de MEILLANT.

▷ Leave Meillant SW on D 92.

La Celle

The 12C **Church of St-Blaise**, originally a dependency of Déols abbey, has an impressive square belfry and an east end adorned with modillions and Romanesque capitals. The west front is adorned with unusual carvings. Inside, the apsidal chapels are separated from the chancel by massive columns featuring interesting capitals. The church contains the tomb of St Silvanus, the legendary apostle of Berry, whose relics were moved from Levroux to La Celle in the 15C.

Bruère-Allichamps

A Gallo-Roman milestone was found in the town in 1757. It was erected in its present site at the junction of the N 144 and the D 92 in 1799. Since 1865, this point has been popularly held to mark the geographical centre of France. D 35 follows the course of the picturesque Cher valley, rich in meadowland.

Abbaye de Noirlac★★
&See Abbaye de NOIRLAC.

▷ The N 144 follows the north bank of the Cher to St-Amand-Montrond.

7 LE BOISCHAUT

Round-trip of 75km/47mi. Allow 4hr.
See route 7 on region map p431 and
map opposite.

▷ Leave St-Amand S on D 97.

Drevant

This quiet village is infused with a
feeling of timelessness. The ruins of a
theatre and traces of a **forum**, **baths**
and **temple** are the remnants of a Gallo-
Roman rural sanctuary. The Berry canal
runs through a park by the ruins.

▷ Continue S, cross the River Cher
and turn left in La Groutte.

Ainay-le-Vieil★
Chateau: *See p445.*

▷ Drive W along D 1, then turn left
onto D 997 at the Fosse Nouvelle
crossroads.

Jardins Artistiques de Drulon

Open mid-Apr–Oct 10am–7.30pm
(Oct, Sat–Sun only). €9. 02 48 56
65 96. www.drulon.com.
This extraordinary 15ha/37-acre landscaped park surrounding a former
15C–17C hunting lodge offers a variety
of settings for some 100 sculptures by
contemporary European artists. Enjoy
the flower garden, the marsh skirted by
footpaths and natural labyrinths, and
the secret garden with its fishponds.

▷ Come back to D 997 on the left
and drive to Loye-sur-Arnon to pick up
D 951 on the left.

Le Châtelet, Abbatiale de Puy-Ferrand

The former abbey church of Puy-
Ferrand, south of Le Châtelet, is a fine
Romanesque building. The façade is
ornamented with bays, finely carved
capitals and geometrical designs.

▷ Leave Le Châtelet NW on D 951,
then turn right onto D 65.

Jardins du Prieuré Notre-Dame d'Orsan★

Open Apr–Sept 10am–7pm.
Closed Oct–Mar. €10 (children
under 8, €5). 02 48 56 27 50.
www.prieuredorsan.com.
In the Our Lady of Orsan priory, the
design of this "mystic garden" serves the
monastic community's earthly needs,
through the vegetable garden and
orchard; as well as its spiritual needs,
through greenery and meditation areas.
The gardens are organised around the
Charmilles cloister, the symbolic centre of the monastery. Four lanes, representing the four rivers of Paradise,
cross at a fountain surrounded by grape
vines. Indeed, grape vines, wheat and
olive trees are indispensable elements
of sustenance throughout the grounds,
symbolising wine, bread and holy oil.
The numerous adjoining gardens
include a medicinal garden; aromatic
herb and vegetable garden; Mary's
garden, with roses, lilies and violets; a
pergola surrounded by olive gardens;
and a **labyrinth**, symbol of the difficult
path to salvation. Don't miss the wheat
square, which includes cabbages, broad
beans, leeks and radishes, according to
season; the three orchards enclosure;
the apple orchard; and the berry alley,
which includes raspberries, mulberries
and blackcurrants. Oak tiles and chestnut gates add charm to the garden.
In addition to the enclosed gardens,
the Orsan estate stretches over approximately 14ha/34.5 acres. A pleasant
promenade (3km/1.8mi) along the **pré
fleuri**, or "flowering meadow", takes you
on a discovery of the copses of southern
Boischaut.

▷ Follow D 65 towards Lignières.

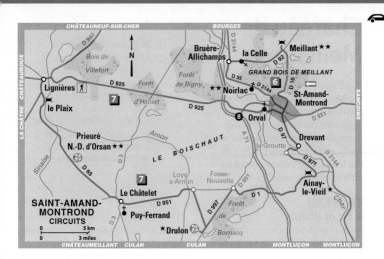

Château du Plaix

Guided tours: mid-Jun–mid-Sept daily except Mon and Tue 2–7pm; May–Jun and mid-Sept–Oct weekends and public holidays 2–7pm. €6. ℘*02 48 60 22 14.*

This small castle, surrounded by a moat, houses the **Musée des Arts et Traditions Populaires**, where temporary exhibitions on various themes are organised every three years. Nearby stands a typical Berry house with its 1850 interior.

Lignières★

In the heart of a landscape of well-kept family farms and meadows neatly bordered by hedgerows, this small town was a centre of Calvinism when the famous protestant reformer was a student in Bourges. The Classical **château** (*closed to the public*) was designed by François Le Vau, brother of the more famous Louis. Near the banks of the Arnon, there is a pretty 12C church.

▶ Continue E along D 925.

Église d'Orval

The church features a 13C reliquary cross in gold-plated silver with cross-pieces embellished with enamel.

ADDRESSES

🛏 STAY

⊜⊜ **Chambre d'hôte La Trolière** – *Orval. 4km/2.4mi W of St-Amand-Montrond towards Châteauroux then 500m/550yd after the last roundabout on the right.* ℘*02 48 96 47 45. 4 rooms.* This large bourgeois family home offers comfortable rooms in pastel tones decorated with etchings and porcelain pieces. You'll appreciate the pervasive quietude and charm of the site.

⊜⊜⊜ **Chambre d'hôte Domaine de la Vilotte** – *Lieu-dit la Vilotte, Le Châtelet. 6km/3.6mi SE of Châtelet on the D 951 and a secondary road.* ℘*02 48 96 04 96. www. domainedevilotte.com. 5 rooms.* The rooms of this elegant 19C manor house are warm and welcoming, furnished with attractive antiques. The grounds boast a lovely rose garden and a lake with a boat for guests.

Château de Meillant★★

The trees in this castle's park reveal the beauty of its architecture only a little at a time. The plain front enhances the elegance and rich decoration of the east façade, which features all the beauty of line of the late Gothic period graced by an Italian influence.

> ⚓ **Michelin Map:** 323: L-6.
> ▷ **Location:** 7.5km/4.5mi N of St-Amand-Montrond and 39km/24mi S of Bourges.
> ⏱ **Timing:** ☞⌐Guided tours Jul–Aug 10am–6.30pm; Apr–Jun and Sept–mid-Nov 10am–noon, 2–6pm; Mar 2–6pm. ✐€8. ✆02 48 63 32 05. www.chateau-de-meillant.com.

CHÂTEAU
A Bit of History

Pierre of **Amboise** obtained the Meillant lands by his marriage in 1453. His son, Charles I, decided to modernise the castle. Following his death, it was left to his grandson, Charles II, to finish the work. Charles II was to become grand-master, marshal and admiral of France. He enjoyed such prosperity as governor of Milan that he was able to complete the work planned for Meillant and also that for Chaumont in the Loire valley. The château was restored in 1842.

Exterior

The feudal character of the château can now only be seen in the southern facade.

Château de Meillant

© Wysocki-Frances / hemis.fr

The east façade is very different and approaches the Loire style in the richness of its decoration.

The pierced balustrade running at the base of the eaves, carved dormer windows and chimneys ornamented with flamboyant balustrades are all overshadowed by the incredibly intricate decoration of the Lion's Tower by Giocondo, one of Michelangelo's assistants. This tower owes its name to the lead lion on its topmost lantern turret. A pretty 16C well and an elegant chapel of the same period, with buttresses topped by pinnacles, complete this harmonious group of buildings.

Interior

Note the remarkable furnishings in the main dining hall and the great salon. Beyond the library, replete with rare books and overlooking the chapel, is the so-called **Cardinal d'Amboise Bed Chamber**, perhaps the loveliest room in the château.

Note the wooden **statue** from Germany dated 1568. The Protestant origins of the statue recall the visit of Calvin in 1529.

EXCURSION
Dun-sur-Auron

14km/8.6mi N on D 10. 🅸 *Pl. Gustave-Vinadelle, Dun-sur-Auron.* ✆*02 48 59 85 26. www.tourisme-dunsurauron.com.* The fortified town of Dun has lost its military character. A lovely 16C belfry, the ruins of ramparts and old houses are reminders of its rich past.

Abbaye de Noirlac★★

Between the Cher river and the Meillant forest, this 12C–14C abbey, one of the best-preserved monasteries in France, is well worth a visit.

- ⚅ **Michelin Map:** 323.
- **Info:** ☎02 48 62 01 01. www.abbayedenoirlac.fr.
- ▶ **Location:** S of Bourges.
- **Don't Miss:** Les Traversées–Rencontres Musicales in mid-June and July.
- ⏱ **Timing:** Apr–Sept 10am–6.30pm; rest of year 2–5pm. ⏱Closed 24 Dec–Jan. ⌨€7.

A BIT OF HISTORY

The foundation – This abbey on the right bank of the Cher was founded around 1130 by Robert of Clairvaux, St Bernard's cousin. It later came to be known as Noirlac. The first years were difficult: in 1149, Bernard himself went begging for a royal grant of wheat. The situation improved when Ebbes V of Charenton made a significant gift that ensured the continuity of the community. The hard-working monks went to work on the land, clearing and building, and by its fiftieth year, the abbey boasted a vast domain.

From destruction to restoration – After the surge of recruits in the 12C and 13C, fewer monks inhabited Noirlac in the 14C, and commercial activities there slowly came to a halt. From 1510, the abbot was appointed by the king to manage the place in absentia. The Wars of Religion brought about further destruction; only six monks were still living on the site when the French Revolution occured. The abbey was declared national property and sold. By 1820 it had become a porcelain factory. Prosper Mérimée discovered it in 1838, but not until 1909 did the Cher *département* acquire it. The buildings were still in use for humanitarian purposes until 1949, but by 1950, a vast restoration programme was undertaken.

ABBEY

The abbey buildings are set up in a typical Cistercian pattern.

Church – Work on the church started in 1150 and lasted for 100 years, thus illustrating the passage from Romanesque to Gothic style. The sanctuary was built first, followed by the nave and the side aisles. The simplicity of line and the lovely pale stone add to the beauty of the architecture and to the sense of peace. The rule of the order forbade sculpted ornamentation, so the capitals are plain and the windows uniformly grey in tone.

Abbey buildings – The other buildings date from various times: late 12C for the east wing and lay brothers' building; early 13C for the refectory; late 13C and early 14C for the cloister galleries. The staircase with wrought-iron banister and dormitory rooms date from the 18C.

Cloisters and adjacent buildings – The eastern and southern galleries have the most ornate carvings. All feature fine ogive vaulting and rich ornamentation which contrasts with the simplicity of the church.

Only a portion of the **lay brothers' building** still stands. It was the economic centre of the monastery. On the upper floor, the lay brothers had their dormitory which today serves as an exhibition area.

ADDRESSES

☕ EAT

⊜⊜ **Auberge de l'Abbaye de Noirlac** – *Noirlac.* ☎02 48 96 22 58. *http://auberge abbayenoirlac.free.fr.* Enjoy a relaxing lunch in this small bar-restaurant. The attractive dining room is embellished with wooden beams and a tiled floor.

Apremont-sur-Allier★

Apremont is listed as "one of the most beautiful villages in France", and is definitely worth a look. Eugène Schneider, who was forgemaster in 1830, is responsible for the restoration of the village. The castle and floral park, listed as a "Remarkable Garden", are located on a hillock overlooking the Allier. At the base of the hillock, the village features lovely stone houses with well-trimmed hedges along the riverbanks.

SIGHTS
The village

This chocolate box village includes houses that have been carefully restored or rebuilt under the auspices of French industrialist Eugène Schneider. Along the main street, the half-timbered houses are of a pink ochre tone and are topped by slate and tile roofs. At every turn, walls covered with vines, structured hedges and charming terraces abundant with flowers add to the charm inherent in these old stones by the riverside.

As you stroll along, note the well planted with flowers near the church, the Brasserie du Lavoir, Conciergerie and 15C **Maison des Mariniers** across from the old loading port of Apremont.

🚶👤 Parc Floral★★

🚹🕐 *Open Apr–Sept 10.30am–12.30pm, 2–6.30pm.* ☜€8.50 *(children aged 7–12, €5.50) – combined ticket with Musée des Calèches, €9.50.* ☎02 48 77 55 06. www.apremont-sur-allier.com.

To create this marvellous garden stretching over 5ha/12.3 acres, an entire valley had to be landscaped. Ponds were created, a former stone quarry was transformed into a waterfall, prairies were turned into lawns and tree plantations, and bulldozers were called in to hoist trees and bushes… but the result is simply breathtaking.

▶ **Population:** 73.
🅖 **Michelin Map:** 323: O-5.
🅖 **Don't Miss:**
An unforgettable walk between the ponds full of white waterliies of the Parc Floral, amongst flowering hedges and trees. Admire the earthenware frescoes by Nevers on the neo-Classical Russian pavilion.
▶ **Location:** 60km/37mi E of Bourges.
🚹👤 **Kids:** After the Musée des Calèches, which will fill their heads with fairy tales, let them play in the Parc Floral.
🕐 **Timing:** 1 day to visit the Parc Floral, Musée des Calèches and the village itself. When the sun begins to go down, you'll see the houses of the village taking on their prettiest colours.

Designed in an 18C English-garden style, with exotic touches here and there, the Parc Floral d'Apremont is a tranquil environment for all its plants: conifers (*weeping cedars, golden arborvitae, Japanese cryptomeria, and others*); deciduous trees (*purple beeches, magnolias, gingkoes, ornamental apple trees, to name a few*); flowering bushes (*rhododendrons, azaleas, lilacs, rose bushes, and more*); and all sorts of perennials (*especially white and silver flowers inspired by the Sissinghurst castle grounds' "White Garden" in the Weald of Kent*). This gorgeous collection stands before a delightful group of medieval houses.

While you stroll through the park, you'll enjoy the **pergola**, heaped with clusters of flowers; the **water garden**, which reveals creeping conifers and rockery plants among the waterfall's rocks; a bright red Chinese bridge built in 1985 to cross one of the park's ponds; the **Turkish pavilion** built on piles in 1994, decorated with scenes representing the four seasons and the various stages of life; and the **belvedere**, a neo-Classical Russian pavilion featuring a superb series of earthenware frescoes by Nevers depicting imaginary travels around the world.

Château

In the 14C, the Apremont castle was a forbidding fortress that was used as a State prison by the dukes of Bourgogne, then allies of the English. During the 16C and 17C, it changed hands several times. In 1722, the Roffignac family would sell it to Louis de Béthune. In 1894, the daughter of the owner was wedded to Eugène Schneider, forge-master in Le Creusot. He would become obsessed with embellishing this magnificent dwelling. His descendants carried on his work. The castle may no longer be visited, but you can climb onto the ramparts to get a particularly lovely **view** over the village and the Allier Valley. When the weather is clear, you'll be able to make out the buttresses of Le Morvan.

≗≗ Musée des Calèches

Open Apr–Sept, 10.30am–12.30pm, 2–6.30pm. ∞€9 (children under 13, €7) – combined ticket with the Parc Floral, €9. ✆02 48 77 55 06. www.apremont-sur-allier.com.
This museum, located in the former stables of the castle, presents a collection of 19C carriages. The late 19C stables were built on the grounds of a glass factory. The wooden stalls still bear the names of horses. The carriages are surprisingly well preserved, including a town car, a two-seater pony cart, a hunting station-wagon, a benched chariot, a saloon car that was used to transport the earnings of the workers in Le Creusot, an English handcart, a master's omnibus, two bicycles and a buggy for two children, among others. You'll even see the carriage of the imperial prince, son of Napoleon III, and Empress Eugénie. The museum also includes a replica of the statue of Eugène Schneider that stands at Le Creusot. On your way out, you'll cross the room where the horses' meals were prepared. Among the harnesses, notice the Amazon saddle. The stalls and gardens adjoining the stables feature temporary exhibitions.

🚗 DRIVING TOUR

8 VALLÉE DE L'ALLIER ET DE L'AUBOIs

108km/67.1mi round-trip. 4hr.
See route 8 on region map p431.

▷ Leave Apremont N on D 45 towards Cuffy.

Écluse des Lorrains

This curious round lock on the Allier provides water for the reach of the bridge-canal of Le Guétin.

Part of Parc Floral, Apremont-sur-Allier

▶ Follow D 45, then turn right on D 976.

Pont-canal du Guétin

This 1838 construction allows the lateral canal of the Loire to cross the Allier on a watery bridge of 343m (18 arches) with a system of chamber locks.

▶ Turn back, then turn right on D 45. At Cuffy, turn left on D 50E towards Torteron. After Malnoue, turn left on D 920.

La Guerche-sur-l'Aubois

A blast furnace and other vestiges of forges are a reminder of this town's industrial past (✎ *guided tours available*). Enjoy a relaxing stroll at **Étang de Robinson** (*a lake offering swimming and other leisure activities*).

▶ Leave La Guerche N on D 920, then turn left on D 50. At Torteron, take D 26 and then turn right on D 189.

Abbaye de Fontmorigny

🕐 *Open Jul–Aug Tue–Sun 2–8pm; May–Oct Sat–Sun and public hols 2–8pm.* ✎€5 *(visitors under 18, no charge).* ✆*02 48 76 12 33. www.abbayedefontmorigny.com.*
This remote Cistercian abbey grew abundantly in medieval times before succumbing to history's transformations. It rose again in the 18C before being sold during the French Revolution. It was then converted into a farm and living quarters for metalworkers until

the beginning of the 20C, when it fell in to ruin. The current owners have been restoring and resuscitating this monument for the past few years. The grounds include a 12C church, large fishpond, lay brothers' buildings and a 17C-style garden. Piano, baroque and historical music concerts are regularly held.

▶ Take up D 189 on the left, then take D12 towards Menetou-Couture.

Château de Menetou-Couture

✎*Guided tour (45 min) Jul–Aug Tue–Fri and Sun 2–6.30pm; Sept Sat–Sun 2–6pm.* ✎€5 *(children under 12, no charge).* ✆*02 48 80 25 08.*
This castle is especially remarkable for its 15C dungeon dwelling measuring 30m.

▶ Continue along D 12.

Église de St-Hilaire-de-Gondilly

This beautiful church is probably Romanesque, although its origins are not clearly known. It is a charming sight on a grassy area full of tall trees, and well-lit at night.

Mornay-Berry

This rare 13C military design features a polygonal wall with 17 facets – but no towers – and a defensive ditch that is still full of water. **Château la Grand'Cour** was the property of the Mornay family. Three little gardens of medieval inspiration surround the castle. These include an enclosed **garden** with old roses, a

A Life's Work

In 1894, **Eugène Schneider** (1868–1942), forge-master at Le Creusot, married Antoinette de Raféllis Saint-Sauveur, whose family had owned the Château d'Apremont since 1722. Stunned by the estate's beauty, Schneider bought it from his wife's family. With the help of an architect, **M. de Galéa**, he undertook a meticulous restoration work of the castle and hamlet. He even demolished and rebuilt the local houses that did not correspond with the medieval Berry style so that they would fit in. Many years later, in 1970, **Gilles de Brissac** took up the work left off by Eugène Schneider when he began the first work on the floral park. The park opened in 1976 to bring a touch of perfection to this beautiful village.

labyrinth of hornbeams and a large pond with a pretty view of the castle. (*guided visits Jul–Aug 3–8pm; rest of the year by arrangement. €6 (children under 12, no charge). 02 48 80 24 45. www.lagrandcour.fr.)

▶ At Mornay-Berry, take D 6 to Nérondes, then take D 43.

Germigny-l'Exempt

In this land of Charolais cattle, notice the lovely belltower of the Romanesque church and the charming wash-house with 12 pillars inviting you to wander around.

▶ As you leave Germigny, follow D 43. Just after Vereaux, turn right on D 76.

Château de Sagonne

Open Jun–Sept 10am–noon, 2–6pm; mid-Apr– and Oct Sun and public holidays 2–6pm. €8 (children under 14, €4). 02 48 80 01 27. www.chateausagonne.com.

This imposing 12C and 14C fortress, which has retained a part of its defensive features, was the property of the architect Jules Hardouin-Mansart, who became count of Sagonne. The large dungeon conceals a chapel decorated with *trompe l'œil* and a chamber featuring painted decorations. Portraits, documents, arms and period furniture are souvenirs of Gabrielle d'Estrées and Mansart.

▶ Come back to D 34 at Givardon. 2km/1.2mi after Nérondes, turn left on D 41 which leads back to Sancoins along the dungeon of Jouy.

Sancoins

Sancoins is at the heart of Charolais cattle farming. The town quickly became a European centre for **livestock markets**. Every **Wednesday**, this market takes place, starting at 5.30am. Small-scale breeders, cooperatives and merchants come together to form one of the largest markets of its kind in France, representing 10% of all French livestock exports.

The market place occupies a triangular plot of land spanning 17ha/42 acres located 1.5km/0.9mi from Sancoins. Sancoins is also the perfect base from which to visit the many surrounding castles and gardens, and to enjoy the Allier and Aubois valleys.

Halle de Grossouvre

Open Jul–Aug 10am–6.30pm; rest of year daily except Mon 9.30am–12.30pm, 2–5.30pm. Closed Jan–mid-Feb, 25 Dec. €8. 02 48 77 06 38. www.espacemetal.com.

Listed as a historic building, this 1844 hall is now the only remnant of what were the great metalworks of Grossouvre. It is now a welcome centre dedicated to the history of metalworking in the Cher. Learn all there is to know about iron, cast iron and steel, from mineral extraction to transformation to the evolution of ironwork and its uses.

▶ Turn right (across from the castle) on D 76.

ADDRESSES

STAY

Chambre d'hôte Manoir Le Plaix – *Lurcy-Lévis, Pouzy-Mésangy. 1.5km/0.9mi N of Pouzy-Mésangy on D 234.* 04 70 66 24 06. http://manoirleplaix.blogspot.com. . *3rooms.* This 16C fortified manor has been lovingly restored. The original staircase leads to the rustic bedrooms.

EAT

Auberge du Pont-canal – *37 r. des Écluses, Le Guétin.* 02 48 80 40 76. This family inn is located just next to the bridge over the Allier. The main room has been renovated and the veranda opens onto the countryside. Traditional cuisine.

INDEX

INDEX

458

INDEX

INDEX

K

L

INDEX

INDEX

INDEX

🛏 STAY

🍷/EAT

MAPS AND PLANS

THEMATIC MAPS

MAPS AND PLANS

Sarlat and Périgord Noir

Bergerac and Périgord Pourpre

Périgueux and Périgord Blanc

Brantôme and Périgord Vert

Figeac and Haut-Quercy

Cahors and Bas-Quercy

Limoges and Haut-Limousin

Bas-Limousin

Parc Naturel Régional du Plateau du Millevaches en Limousin

Guéret, Haute and Basse Marches

Sancerrois and Sologne Berrichone

Pays de Valençay and Brenne

Champagne Berrichonne

MAP LEGEND

	Sight	Seaside resort	Winter sports resort	Spa
Highly recommended ★★★		🛁🛁🛁	❄❄❄	✚✚✚
Recommended ★★		🛁🛁	❄❄	✚✚
Interesting ★		🛁	❄	✚

Additional symbols

🛈	Tourist information
══ ══	Motorway or other primary route
❶ ❶	Junction: complete, limited
⊐══⊏ ══	Pedestrian street
ɪ══ɪ	Unsuitable for traffic, street subject to restrictions
▭▭▭▭ ----	Steps – Footpath
🚂 🚉	Train station – Auto-train station
🚌 S.N.C.F.	Coach (bus) station
———	Tram
⊙	Metro, underground
🅿	Park-and-Ride
♿	Access for the disabled
✉	Post office
☎	Telephone
✉	Covered market
⁝✕⁝	Barracks
△	Drawbridge
⊌	Quarry
✕	Mine
B F	Car ferry (river or lake)
�019Boat	Ferry service: cars and passengers
⟳	Foot passengers only
③	Access route number common to Michelin maps and town plans
Bert (R.)...	Main shopping street
AZ B	Map co-ordinates

Selected monuments and sights

◉ ➡	Tour - Departure point
⛪ ♱	Catholic church
⛪ ♱	Protestant church, other temple
✡ ▢ ☪	Synagogue - Mosque
▭	Building
■	Statue, small building
♱	Calvary, wayside cross
◎	Fountain
●——•■	Rampart - Tower - Gate
⋊	Château, castle, historic house
∴	Ruins
⌣	Dam
✿	Factory, power plant
☆	Fort
∩	Cave
▭	Troglodyte dwelling
🚩	Prehistoric site
▾	Viewing table
Ⱳ	Viewpoint
▲	Other place of interest

Special symbol

⠿	Fortified town (bastide): in southwest France, a new town built in the 13-14C and typified by a geometrical layout.

Abbreviations

A	Agricultural office (Chambre d'agriculture)
C	Chamber of Commerce (Chambre de commerce)
H	Town hall (Hôtel de ville)
J	Law courts (Palais de justice)
M	Museum (Musée)
P	Local authority offices (Préfecture, sous-préfecture)
POL.	Police station (Police)
🛡	Police station (Gendarmerie)
T	Theatre (Théâtre)
U	University (Université)

Sports and recreation

🐎	Racecourse
⛸	Skating rink
〰 🏊	Outdoor, indoor swimming pool
🎥	Multiplex Cinema
⛵	Marina, sailing centre
⛰	Trail refuge hut
▭-■-■-■-▭	Cable cars, gondolas
▭+++++▭	Funicular, rack railway
🚂	Tourist train
◆	Recreation area, park
🎢	Theme, amusement park
🦌	Wildlife park, zoo
🌐	Gardens, park, arboretum
🕊	Bird sanctuary, aviary
🚶	Walking tour, footpath
🙂	Of special interest to children

COMPANION PUBLICATIONS

REGIONAL AND LOCAL MAPS

To make the most of your journey, travel with Michelin maps at a scale Regional maps nos 521, 525, 526, 519 and 522 and the new local maps, which are illustrated on the map of France below.

MAPS OF FRANCE

And remember to travel with the latest edition of the map of France no 721, which gives an overall view of the Dordogne-Berry-Limousin region, and the main access roads which connect it to the rest of France. The entire country is mapped at a 1:1 000 000 scale and clearly shows the main road network. Convenient Atlas formats (spiral, hard cover and mini) are also available.

INTERNET

Michelin is pleased to offer a route-planning service on the Internet:
www.viamichelin.com
www.travel.viamichelin.com
Choose the shortest route, a route without tolls, or the Michelin recommended route to your destination; you can also access information about hotels and restaurants from *The Michelin Guide*, and tourists sights from *The Green Guide*. There are a number of useful maps and plans in the guide, listed opposite.

The Michelin Adventure

It all started with rubber balls! This was the product made by a small company based in Clermont-Ferrand that André and Edouard Michelin inherited, back in 1880. The brothers quickly saw the potential for a new means of transport and their first success was the invention of detachable pneumatic tires for bicycles. However, the automobile was to provide the greatest scope for their creative talents. Throughout the 20th century, Michelin never ceased developing and creating ever more reliable and high-performance tires, not only for vehicles ranging from trucks to F1 but also for underground transit systems and airplanes.

From early on, Michelin provided its customers with tools and services to facilitate mobility and make traveling a more pleasurable and more frequent experience. As early as 1900, the Michelin Guide supplied motorists with a host of useful information related to vehicle maintenance, accommodation and restaurants, and was to become a benchmark for good food. At the same time, the Travel Information Bureau offered travelers personalised tips and itineraries.

The publication of the first collection of roadmaps, in 1910, was an instant hit! In 1926, the first regional guide to France was published, devoted to the principal sites of Brittany, and before long each region of France had its own Green Guide. The collection was later extended to more far-flung destinations, including New York in 1968 and Taiwan in 2011.

In the 21st century, with the growth of digital technology, the challenge for Michelin maps and guides is to continue to develop alongside the company's tire activities. Now, as before, Michelin is committed to improving the mobility of travelers.

MICHELIN TODAY

WORLD NUMBER ONE TIRE MANUFACTURER

- 70 production sites in 18 countries
- 111,000 employees from all cultures and on every continent
- 6,000 people employed in research and development

Moving
for a world

Moving forward means developing tires with better road grip and shorter braking distances, whatever the state of the road.

CORRECT TIRE PRESSURE

RIGHT PRESSURE

- Safety
- Longevity
- Optimum fuel consumption

-0,5 bar

- Durability reduced by 20% (- 8,000 km)

-1 bar

- Risk of blowouts
- Increased fuel consumption
- Longer braking distances on wet surfaces

forward together
where mobility is safer

It also involves helping motorists take care of their safety and their tires. To do so, Michelin organises "Fill Up With Air" campaigns all over the world to remind us that correct tire pressure is vital.

WEAR

DETECTING TIRE WEAR

The legal minimum depth of tire tread is 1.6mm. Tire manufacturers equip their tires with tread wear indicators, which are small blocks of rubber moulded into the base of the main grooves at a depth of 1.6mm.

Tires are the only point of contact between the vehicle and road.

The photo below shows the actual contact zone.

If the tread depth is less than 1.6mm, tires are considered to be worn and dangerous on wet surfaces.

NEW TIRE

WORN TIRE
(1,6 mm tread)

Moving forward
means sustainable mobility

INNOVATION AND THE ENVIRONMENT

By 2050, Michelin aims to cut the quantity of raw materials used in its tire manufacturing process by half and to have developed renewable energy in its facilities. The design of MICHELIN tires has already saved billions of litres of fuel and, by extension, billions of tons of CO2.

Similarly, Michelin prints its maps and guides on paper produced from sustainably managed forests and is diversifying its publishing media by offering digital solutions to make traveling easier, more fuel efficient and more enjoyable!

The group's whole-hearted commitment to eco-design on a daily basis is demonstrated by ISO 14001 certification.

Like you, Michelin is committed to preserving our planet.

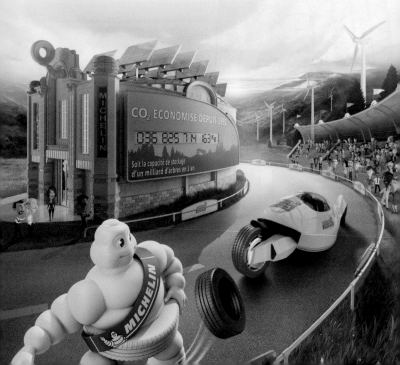

Chat with Bibendum

Go to
www.michelin.com/corporate/en
Find out more about
Michelin's history and the
latest news.

QUIZ

Michelin develops tires for all types of vehicles.
See if you can match the right tire with the right vehicle...

Solution : A-6 / B-4 / C-2 / D-1 / E-3 / F-7 / G-5

Michelin Travel Partner

Société par actions simplifiées au capital de 11 288 880 EUR
27 cours de l'Île Seguin - 92100 Boulogne Billancourt (France)
R.C.S. Nanterre 433 677 721

© Michelin Travel Partner
ISBN 978-2-067204-18-8
Printed: April 2015
Printed and bound in France : Imprimerie CHIRAT, 42540 Saint-Just-la-Pendue - N° 201504.0159